Land Rover
Owners Workshop Manual

J H Haynes Member of the Guild of Motoring Writers
and John S Mead & M S Daniels

(314-12AG7/529-2AA7/5568-256)

Models covered

Land Rover Series II, IIA & III models (inc. County) with 88 & 109 inch wheelbase
Petrol: 2¼ litre (2286cc) 4-cylinder
Diesel: 2¼ litre (2286cc) 4-cylinder

*Does NOT cover models with 6-cyl or V8 petrol engines, 2.5 litre diesel engine,
24v electrical systems or forward control models*
Does NOT cover 90 or 110 Series

ABCDE
FGHIJ
KLMNO
PQRST

© Haynes Publishing 2013

A book in the **Haynes Owners Workshop Manual Series**

ISBN 978 0 85733 568 5

British Library Cataloguing in Publication Data

A catalogue record for this book is available from the British Library.
Printed in the USA

Haynes Publishing
Sparkford, Yeovil, Somerset BA22 7JJ, England

Haynes North America, Inc
861 Lawrence Drive, Newbury Park, California 91320, USA

Haynes Publishing Nordiska AB
Box 1504, 751 45 UPPSALA, Sverige

Contents

LIVING WITH YOUR LAND ROVER

Roadside repairs

Routine Maintenance

Contents

REPAIRS & OVERHAUL

Engine and Associated Systems

Transmission

Brakes

Electrical

Suspension

Body Equipment

Additional information

REFERENCE

Index

Introduction to the Land Rover

First introduced in 1948 at the Amsterdam motor show, the Land Rover was primarily designed for use by farmers as a combined tractor/pick-up truck and only a limited production volume was anticipated. However, the vehicle was a phenomenal success and by 1951 it was outselling the Rover saloon cars.

The Land Rover's great strength lay in the short, rigid box-section chassis and simple rugged construction, the problem of corrosion and weight was overcome by the use of aluminium for the bodywork. The original model was fitted with the existing Rover P3 1.6 litre engine and gearbox. A new transfer box obviously then had to be designed and built, and such was the success of this unit that the basic design has remained virtually unchanged to the present day.

In 1952 the 1.6 litre engine, which featured the overhead inlet side exhaust valve layout designed by Rover, was bored out to a 2 litres capacity. In 1958 the Series II model was introduced with a new 2,286 cc overhead valve engine which is still fitted on current models. The waistline body panels were rounded off and the wheelbase had been standardised to 88 inches for the short wheelbase model and 109 inches for the long wheelbase model.

The Series III model was produced in 1971 and incorporated an all-synchromesh gearbox and a full-width instrument panel. The front grille was also modified.

One of the greatest moments in the Land Rover success story came in 1976 when the one millionth vehicle was delivered.

The long wheel base Land Rover used as a project vehicle for this manual

SWB Land Rover – a project vehicle used for this manual

Acknowledgements

Thanks are due to Land Rover Limited for the provision of technical information and certain illustrations. The petrol Land Rover used as the project vehicle for the compilation of this manual was kindly loaned by Mr Gordon Knott; the diesel-engined model was loaned by Mr R Herniman. Thanks are also due to Draper Tools Limited, who provided many of the workshop tool, and all those at Sparkford who assisted in the production of this manual.

We take great pride in the accuracy of information given in this manual, but vehicle manufacturers make alterations and design changes during the production run of a particular vehicle of which they do not inform us. No liability can be accepted by the authors or publishers for loss, damage or injury caused by any errors in, or omissions from, the information given.

Working on your car can be dangerous. This page shows just some of the potential risks and hazards, with the aim of creating a safety-conscious attitude.

General hazards

Scalding

• Don't remove the radiator or expansion tank cap while the engine is hot.
• Engine oil, transmission fluid or power steering fluid may also be dangerously hot if the engine has recently been running.

Burning

• Beware of burns from the exhaust system and from any part of the engine. Brake discs and drums can also be extremely hot immediately after use.

Crushing

• When working under or near a raised vehicle, always supplement the jack with axle stands, or use drive-on ramps. *Never venture under a car which is only supported by a jack.*
• Take care if loosening or tightening high-torque nuts when the vehicle is on stands. Initial loosening and final tightening should be done with the wheels on the ground.

Fire

• Fuel is highly flammable; fuel vapour is explosive.
• Don't let fuel spill onto a hot engine.
• Do not smoke or allow naked lights (including pilot lights) anywhere near a vehicle being worked on. Also beware of creating sparks (electrically or by use of tools).
• Fuel vapour is heavier than air, so don't work on the fuel system with the vehicle over an inspection pit.
• Another cause of fire is an electrical overload or short-circuit. Take care when repairing or modifying the vehicle wiring.
• Keep a fire extinguisher handy, of a type suitable for use on fuel and electrical fires.

Electric shock

• Ignition HT and Xenon headlight voltages can be dangerous, especially to people with heart problems or a pacemaker. Don't work on or near these systems with the engine running or the ignition switched on.

• Mains voltage is also dangerous. Make sure that any mains-operated equipment is correctly earthed. Mains power points should be protected by a residual current device (RCD) circuit breaker.

Fume or gas intoxication

• Exhaust fumes are poisonous; they can contain carbon monoxide, which is rapidly fatal if inhaled. Never run the engine in a confined space such as a garage with the doors shut.
• Fuel vapour is also poisonous, as are the vapours from some cleaning solvents and paint thinners.

Poisonous or irritant substances

• Avoid skin contact with battery acid and with any fuel, fluid or lubricant, especially antifreeze, brake hydraulic fluid and Diesel fuel. Don't syphon them by mouth. If such a substance is swallowed or gets into the eyes, seek medical advice.
• Prolonged contact with used engine oil can cause skin cancer. Wear gloves or use a barrier cream if necessary. Change out of oil-soaked clothes and do not keep oily rags in your pocket.
• Air conditioning refrigerant forms a poisonous gas if exposed to a naked flame (including a cigarette). It can also cause skin burns on contact.

Asbestos

• Asbestos dust can cause cancer if inhaled or swallowed. Asbestos may be found in gaskets and in brake and clutch linings. When dealing with such components it is safest to assume that they contain asbestos.

Special hazards

Hydrofluoric acid

• This extremely corrosive acid is formed when certain types of synthetic rubber, found in some O-rings, oil seals, fuel hoses etc, are exposed to temperatures above 4000C. The rubber changes into a charred or sticky substance containing the acid. *Once formed, the acid remains dangerous for years. If it gets onto the skin, it may be necessary to amputate the limb concerned.*
• When dealing with a vehicle which has suffered a fire, or with components salvaged from such a vehicle, wear protective gloves and discard them after use.

The battery

• Batteries contain sulphuric acid, which attacks clothing, eyes and skin. Take care when topping-up or carrying the battery.
• The hydrogen gas given off by the battery is highly explosive. Never cause a spark or allow a naked light nearby. Be careful when connecting and disconnecting battery chargers or jump leads.

Air bags

• Air bags can cause injury if they go off accidentally. Take care when removing the steering wheel and trim panels. Special storage instructions may apply.

Diesel injection equipment

• Diesel injection pumps supply fuel at very high pressure. Take care when working on the fuel injectors and fuel pipes.

 Warning: Never expose the hands, face or any other part of the body to injector spray; the fuel can penetrate the skin with potentially fatal results.

Remember...

DO

• Do use eye protection when using power tools, and when working under the vehicle.

• Do wear gloves or use barrier cream to protect your hands when necessary.

• Do get someone to check periodically that all is well when working alone on the vehicle.

• Do keep loose clothing and long hair well out of the way of moving mechanical parts.

• Do remove rings, wristwatch etc, before working on the vehicle – especially the electrical system.

• Do ensure that any lifting or jacking equipment has a safe working load rating adequate for the job.

DON'T

• Don't attempt to lift a heavy component which may be beyond your capability – get assistance.

• Don't rush to finish a job, or take unverified short cuts.

• Don't use ill-fitting tools which may slip and cause injury.

• Don't leave tools or parts lying around where someone can trip over them. Mop up oil and fuel spills at once.

• Don't allow children or pets to play in or near a vehicle being worked on.

Dimensions

Overall length
    88" basic and Station Wagon .... 142.56 in (3.62 m)
    109" basic and Station Wagon .... 175.0 in (4.44 m)
Overall width
    All Series II models .... 64.0 in (1.63 m)
    All Series IIA and III models .... 66.0 in (1.68 m)
Overall height (with hood up)
    88" basic .... 77.5 in (1.97 m)
    109" basic .... 81.0 in (2.03 m)
Overall height (with cab or hard top)
    888 basic .... 76.875 in (1.95 m)
    88" Station Wagon .... 77.875 in (1.98 m)
    109" basic .... 81.0 in (2.06 m)
    109" Station Wagon .... 81.375 in (2.07 m)
Wheelbase
    88" models .... 88.0 in (2.23 m)
    109" models .... 109.0 in (2.77 m)
Track
    All models except 109" Series III .... 51.5 in (1.31 m)
    109" Series III .... 52.5 in (1.33 m)

Weights

Kerb weight (with 5 gals/22.5 litres of fuel)
    88" basic .... 3097 lb (1405 kg)
    88" Station Wagon (Series II) .... 3423 lb (1553 kg)
    88" Station Wagon (Series IIA) .... 3435 lb (1557 kg)
    88" Station Wagon (Series III) .... 3425 lb (1554 kg)
    109" basic .... 3471 lb (1574 kg)
    109" Station Wagon .... 3922 lb (1779 kg)
Maximum payload (road)
    88" basic (with driver and two passengers) .... 1000 lb (454 kg)
    88" Station Wagon (with driver and six passengers) .... 100 lb (45 kg)
    109" basic (with driver and two passengers) .... 2000 lb (908 kg)
    109" Station Wagon (with driver and nine passengers) .... 400 lb (181 kg)
Maximum payload (cross country)
    88" basic (with driver and two passengers) .... 800 lb (363 kg)
    88" Station Wagon (with driver and five passengers) .... 50 lb (23 kg)
    109" basic (with driver and two passengers) .... 1800 lb (816 kg)
    109" Station Wagon (with driver and nine passengers) .... 200 lb (91 kg)
Maximum roof rack load
    All models .... 112 lb (50 kg)
Maximum laden trailer weights
    Cross country .... 1 ton (1020 kg)
    Road (unbraked) .... 0.5 ton (500 kg)
    Road (overrun brakes) .... 2 tons (2040 kg)
    Four wheel trailer with power brakes .... 3 tons (3060 kg)
Towbar nose weight
    Minimum .... 50 lb (25 kg)
    Maximum .... 112 lb (55 kg)

Capacities

Engine .... 11.0 Imp pt: 13.0 US pt: 6.0 litres
Engine oil filter .... 1.5 Imp pt: 1.8 US pt: 0.85 litre
Main gearbox .... 2.5 Imp pt; 3.0 US pt: 1.5 litres
Transfer box .... 4.5 Imp pt; 5.5 US pt: 2.5 litres
Differentials
    Standard (front and rear) .... 3.0 Imp pt; 3.5 US pt; 1.75 litres
    ENV (front and rear) .... 2.5 Imp pt; 3.5 US pt; 1.4 litres
    Salisbury (rear) .... 4.5 Imp pt; 5.5 US pt; 2.5 litres
Swivel pin housing .... 1.0 Imp pt; 1.2 US pt; 0.5 litre
Fuel tank
    88" models .... 10.0 Imp gall; 12.0 US 45.0 litres
    109" models .... 15.0 Imp gall; 18.0 US gall; 68.0 litres
Cooling system
    Series II, IIA .... 17.5 Imp pt; 21.1 US pt; 10.0 litres
    Series III .... 13.75 Imp pt; 16.5 US pt; 7.8

Puddles on the garage floor or drive, or obvious wetness under the bonnet or underneath the car, suggest a leak that needs investigating. It can sometimes be difficult to decide where the leak is coming from, especially if an engine undershield is fitted. Leaking oil or fluid can also be blown rearwards by the passage of air under the car, giving a false impression of where the problem lies.

 Warning: Most automotive oils and fluids are poisonous. Wash them off skin, and change out of contaminated clothing, without delay.

Identifying leaks

 The smell of a fluid leaking from the car may provide a clue to what's leaking. Some fluids are distinctively coloured. It may help to remove the engine undershield, clean the car carefully and to park it over some clean paper overnight as an aid to locating the source of the leak.
Remember that some leaks may only occur while the engine is running.

Sump oil

Engine oil may leak from the drain plug...

Oil from filter

...or from the base of the oil filter.

Gearbox oil

Gearbox oil can leak from the seals at the inboard ends of the driveshafts.

Antifreeze

Leaking antifreeze often leaves a crystalline deposit like this.

Brake fluid

A leak occurring at a wheel is almost certainly brake fluid.

Power steering fluid

Power steering fluid may leak from the pipe connectors on the steering rack.

Jacking, towing and wheel changing

Jacking

Note: *To raise the vehicle, a hydraulic jack with a minimum load capacity of 1500 kg must be used.* **Never** *work under a vehicle supported solely by a hydraulic jack - always supplement the jack with axle stands.*

1 The jack supplied with the vehicle tool kit should only be used for changing the roadwheels - see "*Wheel changing*" later in this Section. When carrying out any other kind of work, raise the vehicle using a hydraulic jack, and always supplement the jack with axle stands positioned under the axles **(see illustration)**. **Do not** jack the vehicle, or position axle stands under any of the following components.

a) *Body structure.*
b) *Bumpers.*
c) *Underbody pipes and hoses.*
d) *Suspension components.*
e) *Gearbox/transmission/transfer gearbox housings.*
f) *Engine sump.*
g) *Fuel tank.*

2 Position axle stands under the appropriate axle tubes, as required. **Never** *work under, around, or near a raised vehicle, unless it is adequately supported in at least two places.*

Towing

When towing a trailer or another vehicle, the specified maximum weights must not be exceeded and the towbar nose weight must be within the specified limits. It is recommended that if the total trailed weight exceeds 2 tons (2040 kg), the trailer should have a separate braking system controlled from the driver's cab.

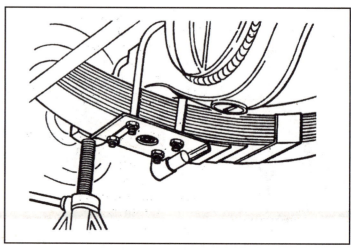

Correct position of axle stand

Wheel changing

When changing a roadwheel, place the jack supplied with the vehicle beneath the axle tube by the wheel to be removed. Apply the handbrake and engage four-wheel drive, then loosen the wheel nuts, raise the jack, and remove the wheel. Always supplement the jack with axle-stands or blocks before working under the vehicle. Remember to engage two-wheel drive after changing a roadwheel.

Jump starting

Jump starting will get you out of trouble, but you must correct whatever made the battery go flat in the first place. There are three possibilities:

1 *The battery has been drained by repeated attempts to start, or by leaving the lights on.*

2 *The charging system is not working properly (generator drivebelt slack or broken, generator wiring fault or generator itself faulty).*

3 *The battery itself is at fault (electrolyte low, or battery worn out).*

When jump-starting a car using a booster battery, observe the following precautions:

A) Before connecting the booster battery, make sure that the ignition is switched off.

B) Ensure that all electrical equipment (lights, heater, wipers, etc) is switched off.

C) Make sure that the booster battery is the same voltage as the discharged one in the vehicle.

D) If the battery is being jump-started from the battery in another vehicle, the two vehcles MUST NOT TOUCH each other.

E) Make sure that the transmission is in neutral (or PARK, in the case of automatic transmission).

This procedure is for negative earth vehicles

1 Connect one end of the red jump lead to the positive (+) terminal of the flat battery

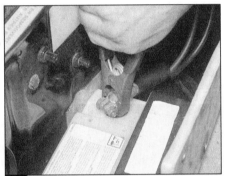

2 Connect the other end of the red lead to the positive (+) terminal of the booster battery.

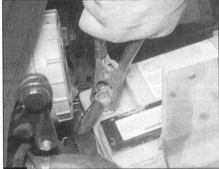

3 Connect one end of the black jump lead to the negative (-) terminal of the booster battery

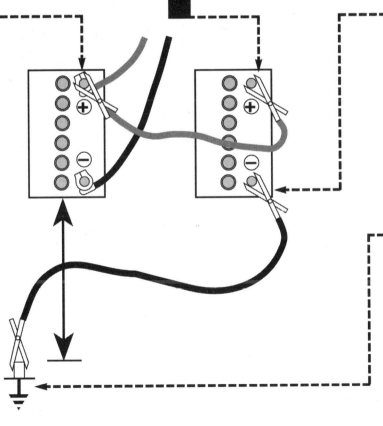

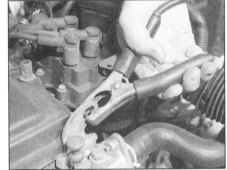

4 Connect the other end of the black jump lead to a bolt or bracket on the engine block, well away from the battery, on the vehicle to be started.

5 Make sure that the jump leads will not come into contact with the fan, drive-belts or other moving parts of the engine.

6 Start the engine using the booster battery, then with the engine running at idle speed, disconnect the jump leads in the reverse order of connection.

The maintenance schedules listed in this Section are based on those recommended by Leyland and apply to a Land Rover that is being used in the conventional manner, ie; normal roadwork, trailer towing and light cross-country duties.

If the vehicle is used in rough terrain and is constantly working in mud and dust, the oil should be changed more frequently and the aircleaner should be cleaned daily. In exceptionally harsh conditions or if the vehicle is used for deep wading, the engine oil should also be changed daily.

The gearbox, transfer box, differential and swivel pin oils should also be changed more frequently if the vehicle is being used in the conditions described in the previous paragraph. In particular the propeller shaft sliding joints should be lubricated frequently if driving through sand.

If the vehicle is driven constantly with the low transfer ratio engaged or as a stationary power source then obviously the mileage reading cannot be used for deciding the frequency of service intervals. When used in these conditions the engine and transmission service periods must be based on hours running time or fuel consumption and for this purpose a conversion chart is given at the end of this Section.

Maintenance intervals - later models

From 1981 the maker's recommended maintenance interval for all Series III petrol models is increased from 4,000 to 6,000 miles (6,000 to 10,000 kms), or the equivalent in hours of running time or fuel consumed.

Weekly (or daily if operating under severe conditions)

- [ ] Check the tyre pressures, including the spare wheel.
- [ ] Examine tyres for wear or damage.
- [ ] Check brake fluid reservoir level.
- [ ] Check braking efficiency. Try an emergency stop. Is adjustment necessary?
- [ ] Check all the bulbs.
- [ ] Check wipers, wiper blades and horn.
- [ ] Check windscreen washer level.
- [ ] Check the sump oil level and top-up if required.
- [ ] Check the radiator coolant level and top-up if required.
- [ ] Check the battery electrolyte level and top-up to the level of the plates with distilled water as needed.

Every 4000 miles (6000 km)

In addition to all the items listed above, carry out the following:

- [ ] Change the engine oil and renew the oil filter element.
- [ ] On vehicles fitted with the oil bath type air cleaner, empty out the oil, clean out the casing and refill.
- [ ] Check the carburettor slow running speed and adjust if necessary (petrol models).
- [ ] Clean and adjust the spark plugs (petrol models).
- [ ] Check the contact breaker points and adjust if necessary (petrol models).
- [ ] Lubricate the contact breaker cam and centrifugal advance mechanism (petrol models).
- [ ] Drain the water from the fuel filter and sedimenter (diesel models).
- [ ] Check the fan belt tension and adjust if necessary.
- [ ] Check the gearbox and transfer box oil levels and top up if necessary
- [ ] If a drain plug has been fitted in the flywheel housing, remove it and allow any oil present to drain out.
- [ ] Check the fluid level in the clutch reservoir and top-up if necessary.
- [ ] Check the oil levels in the front and rear differentials and top up if necessary.
- [ ] Check the oil levels in the front swivel pin housings and top-up if necessary.
- [ ] Examine the front wheel hubs for any sign of oil leakage.
- [ ] Check the steering box and steering damper oil levels, topping-up if necessary.
- [ ] Examine the rubber boots on all steering joints and renew them if torn.
- [ ] Have the front wheel alignment checked.
- [ ] Check and adjust the brake shoes (do not forget the handbrake shoes) .
- [ ] Lubricate the propeller shaft sleeves and, if grease nipples are fitted, lubricate the universal joints.
- [ ] Road test vehicle and rectify any faults that are found.

Every 8000 miles (12 000 km)
Carry out the checks listed under the heading 4,000 miles (6,000 km), plus the following:
- [ ] Remove the engine breather filters and wash them out in petrol.
- [ ] Fit a new set of spark plugs
- [ ] Check the tappet clearances and adjust if necessary.
- [ ] Clean the battery terminals and coat them with petroleum jelly.
- [ ] Take the vehicle to the local garage and have them check the headlamp beam alignment.
- [ ] Check all lights and instruments for correct operation.
- [ ] Lightly oil the door locks, hinges, handbrake and throttle linkages.

Every 12 000 miles (18 000 km)
Carry out the checks listed under the heading 4,000 miles (6,000 km), plus the following:
- [ ] Remove the injectors, check and if necessary adjust (diesel models).
- [ ] Renew the fuel filter element(s) (diesel models).
- [ ] Clean the sedimenter (diesel models).
- [ ] Clean out the fuel sediment bowl adjacent to the fuel pump.
- [ ] Lubricate the dynamo rear bearing.
- [ ] Drain and refill the gearbox and transfer box.
- [ ] Drain and refill the front and rear differentials.
- [ ] Drain and refill the front axle swivel pin housings.

Note: *the above last three checks replace the oil level checks listed in the 4,000 miles (6,000 kms) service.*

- [ ] Check all body bolts for tightness.
- [ ] Check the tightness of the road spring 'U' bolts and spring clips.
- [ ] Check all the propeller shaft bolts for tightness and the universal joints for wear.

Every 20 000 miles (30 000 km)
Carry out the checks listed under the heading 4,000 miles (6,000 km), plus the following:
- [ ] Clean the emission control flame-trap, if fitted.

Every 24 000 miles (36 000 km)
Carry out the checks listed under the headings 4,000 miles (6,000 km), 8,000 miles (12,000 km) and 12,000 miles (18,000 km), plus the following:
- [ ] Lubricate the propeller shaft sliding joints.

General
- [ ] **IMPORTANT:** The brake fluid should be renewed every eighteen months, and if the vehicle is going to be used for touring in mountainous terrain it must be renewed within a period of nine months prior to the tour.
- [ ] All the rubber seals in the braking system should be renewed every three years or 40,000 miles (64,000 km), whichever occurs first.

Conversion chart
The following chart can be used to convert hours running time or fuel consumption into an equivalent mileage.

Fuel consumption – diesel models

kms	Miles	Litres	Gallons	Hours' running time
6,000	4,000	610	135	160
12,000	8,000	1,220	270	320
18,000	12,000	1,830	405	480
24,000	16,000	2,440	530	640
30,000	20,000	3,050	665	800
36,000	24,000	3,660	800	960

Fuel consumption – petrol models

kms	Miles	Litres	Gallons	Hours' running time
6,000	4,000	900	200	160
12,000	8,000	1,800	400	320
18,000	12,000	2,700	600	480
24,000	16,000	3,600	800	640
30,000	20,000	4,500	1,000	800
36,000	24,000	5,400	1,200	960

Checking the tyre pressures

Topping-up the brake fluid reservoir

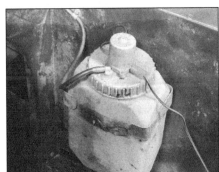

Windscreen washer reservoir

Location of the engine oil dipstick

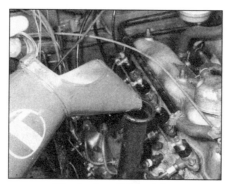

The engine oil filler tube

Topping-up the battery

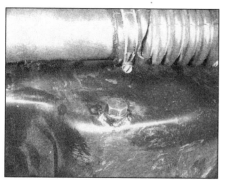

Engine sump drain plug

Refilling the oil-bath air cleaner

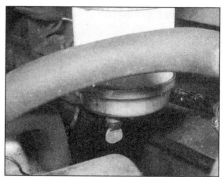

The fuel filter water drain tap

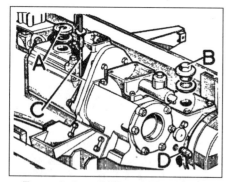

**Transmission oil filler and level plugs
(earlier models)**

A *Filler cap, main gearbox section*
B *Filler plug, transfer box section*
C *Oil level dipstick, main gearbox*
D *Oil level plug, transfer box*

Main gearbox oil filler/level and drain plugs

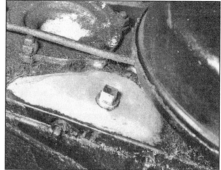

Transfer gearbox oil filler/level plug

Flywheel housing drain hole and plug

Topping-up the clutch fluid reservoir

Front axle oil drain and filler plugs

Rear axle oil filler plug

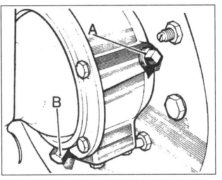

Swivel pin housing oil level and drain plugs

A *Filler/level plug*
B *Drain plug*

Steering box oil filler plug

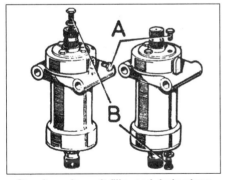

Steering relay unit filler and drain plugs

A *Ail filler hole and plug*
B *Breather hole and plug on early type, drain plug on later type*

Transfer gearbox oil drain plug

Rear axle oil drain plug

Tyre condition and pressure

It is very important that tyres are in good condition, and at the correct pressure - having a tyre failure at any speed is highly dangerous. Tyre wear is influenced by driving style - harsh braking and acceleration, or fast cornering, will all produce more rapid tyre wear. As a general rule, the front tyres wear out faster than the rears. Interchanging the tyres from front to rear ("rotating" the tyres) may result in more even wear. However, if this is completely effective, you may have the expense of replacing all four tyres at once! Remove any nails or stones embedded in the tread before they penetrate the tyre to cause deflation. If removal of a nail does reveal that the tyre has been punctured, refit the nail so that its point of penetration is marked. Then immediately change the wheel, and have the tyre repaired by a tyre dealer.

Regularly check the tyres for damage in the form of cuts or bulges, especially in the sidewalls. Periodically remove the wheels, and clean any dirt or mud from the inside and outside surfaces. Examine the wheel rims for signs of rusting, corrosion or other damage. Light alloy wheels are easily damaged by "kerbing" whilst parking; steel wheels may also become dented or buckled. A new wheel is very often the only way to overcome severe damage.

New tyres should be balanced when they are fitted, but it may become necessary to re-balance them as they wear, or if the balance weights fitted to the wheel rim should fall off. Unbalanced tyres will wear more quickly, as will the steering and suspension components. Wheel imbalance is normally signified by vibration, particularly at a certain speed (typically around 50 mph). If this vibration is felt only through the steering, then it is likely that just the front wheels need balancing. If, however, the vibration is felt through the whole car, the rear wheels could be out of balance. Wheel balancing should be carried out by a tyre dealer or garage.

1 Tread Depth - visual check
The original tyres have tread wear safety bands (B), which will appear when the tread depth reaches approximately 1.6 mm. The band positions are indicated by a triangular mark on the tyre sidewall (A).

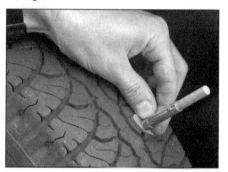

2 Tread Depth - manual check
Alternatively, tread wear can be monitored with a simple, inexpensive device known as a tread depth indicator gauge.

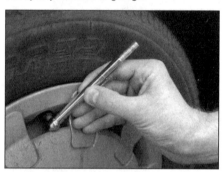

3 Tyre Pressure Check
Check the tyre pressures regularly with the tyres cold. Do not adjust the tyre pressures immediately after the vehicle has been used, or an inaccurate setting will result.

Tyre tread wear patterns

Shoulder Wear

Underinflation (wear on both sides)
Under-inflation will cause overheating of the tyre, because the tyre will flex too much, and the tread will not sit correctly on the road surface. This will cause a loss of grip and excessive wear, not to mention the danger of sudden tyre failure due to heat build-up.
Check and adjust pressures
Incorrect wheel camber (wear on one side)
Repair or renew suspension parts
Hard cornering
Reduce speed!

Centre Wear

Overinflation
Over-inflation will cause rapid wear of the centre part of the tyre tread, coupled with reduced grip, harsher ride, and the danger of shock damage occurring in the tyre casing.
Check and adjust pressures

If you sometimes have to inflate your car's tyres to the higher pressures specified for maximum load or sustained high speed, don't forget to reduce the pressures to normal afterwards.

Uneven Wear

Front tyres may wear unevenly as a result of wheel misalignment. Most tyre dealers and garages can check and adjust the wheel alignment (or "tracking") for a modest charge.
Incorrect camber or castor
Repair or renew suspension parts
Malfunctioning suspension
Repair or renew suspension parts
Unbalanced wheel
Balance tyres
Incorrect toe setting
Adjust front wheel alignment
Note: *The feathered edge of the tread which typifies toe wear is best checked by feel.*

Buying spare parts

Spare parts are available from many sources, for example: Leyland garages, other garages and accessory shops, and motor factors. Our advice regarding spare part sources is as follows:

Officially appointed Leyland garages - This is the best source of parts which are peculiar to your vehicle and are otherwise not generally available (eg; complete cylinder heads, internal gearbox components, badges, interior trim etc). It is also the only place at which you should buy parts if your vehicle is still under warranty - non-Leyland components may invalidate the warranty. To be sure of obtaining the correct parts it will always be necessary to give the storeman your vehicle's engine and chassis number, and if possible, to take the old part along for positive identification, Remember that many parts are available on a factory exchange scheme - any parts returned should always be clean! It obviously makes good sense to go straight to the specialists on your vehicle for this type of part, for they are best equipped to supply you.

Other garages and accessory shops - These are often very good places to buy materials and components needed for the maintenance of your vehicle (eg; oil filters, spark plugs, bulbs, fan belts, oils and greases, touch-up paint, filler paste etc) . They also sell general accessories, usually have convenient opening hours, charge lower prices and can often be found not far from home,

Motor factors - Good factors will stock all of the more important components which wear out relatively quickly (eg; clutch components, pistons, valves, exhaust systems, brake cylinders/pipes/hoses/seals/shoes and pads etc). Motor factors will often provide new or reconditioned components on a part exchange basis - this can save a considerable amount of money.

Vehicle identification numbers

The chassis number will be found on a plate attached to the dash-panel. The plate also displays information on the vehicle's maximum laden weight and the maximum front and rear axle loads.

The engine number is stamped on the front left-hand side of the engine block.

The transmission number will be found on the rear, right-hand side of the gearbox (see photo)

For modifications, and information applicable to later models, see Supplement at end of manual

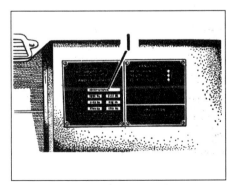

Vehicle identification plate

1 Chassis number

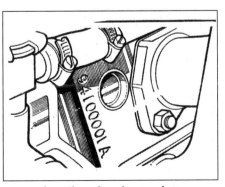

Location of engine number

Transmission number

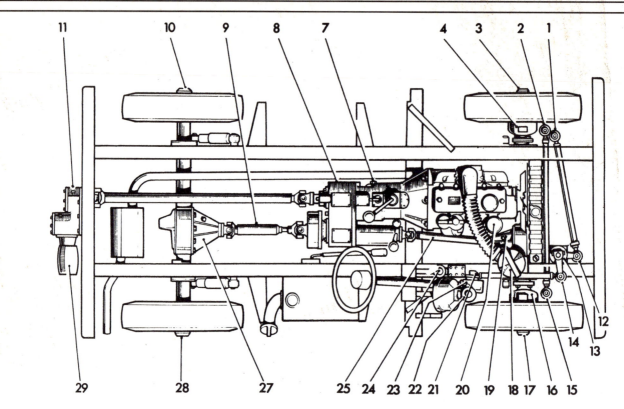

These recommendations apply to temperate climates where operation temperatures are above −10°C (14°F). Information on recommended lubricants for use under extreme winter conditions can be obtained from Land Rover Ltd, Technical Service Department, or a Land Rover distributor or dealer.

Component or system	Lubricant type or specification
18 Air cleaner	Multigrade engine oil, vicsosity range SAE 10W/40 to 20W/50, to API SE or SF
20 Engine	
4 Swivel housing, LH	Hypoid gear oil to SAE 90EP, to API GL4
7 Main gearbox	
8 Transfer box	
11 Rear power take-off	
13 Steering relay	
16 Swivel housing, RH	
19 Front differential	
23 Steering box	
27 Rear differential	
29 Pulley unit	
1 Drag link balljoint, LH	Multi-purpose lithium-based grease to NLGI-2
2 Trackrod balljoint, LH	
3 Front hub, LH	
9 Rear propeller shaft	
10 Rear hub, LH	
12 Drag link balljoint, RH	
14 Longitudinal arm balljoint, front	
15 Trackrod balljoint, RH	
17 Front hub, RH	
21 Longitudinal arm balljoint, rear	
25 Front propeller shaft	
28 Rear hub, RH	
22 Brake fluid reservoir	Hydraulic fluid to FMVSS 116 DOT 3
24 Clutch fluid reservoir	

Chapter 1A
Petrol engine

For modifications, and information applicable to later models, see Supplement at end of manual

Contents

Degrees of difficulty

| **Easy,** suitable for novice with little experience | ![spanner icon] | **Fairly easy,** suitable for beginner with some experience | ![spanner icon] | **Fairly difficult,** suitable for competent DIY mechanic | ![spanner icon] | **Difficult,** suitable for experienced DIY mechanic | ![spanner icon] | **Very difficult,** suitable for expert DIY or professional | ![spanner icon] |

Specifications

Engine, general

Capacity (piston displacement) . . . . 2286 cc (140 cu in)
Number of cylinders 4
Bore . . . . 3.562 in (90.47 mm)
Stroke . . . . 3.5 in (88.8 mm)
Compression ratio . . . . 7 : 1 or 8 : 1
BHP at 4,250 rpm. . . . . 77 (7 : 1) 81 (8 : 1)
BMEP . . . . 7 : 1 134 lb/in^2 (9.4 kg/cm^2) at 2,500 rpm
                                                                                 8 : 1 137 lb/in^2 (9.6 kg/cm^2) at 2,500 rpm
Maximum torque . . . . 7 : 1 124 lb/ft (17 mkg) at 2,500 rpm
Firing order. . . . . 1 - 3 - 4 - 2
Piston speed at 4,280 rpm . . . . 2,500 ft/min (12.6 m/sec)
Compression pressure (at starter motor cranking speed, with engine hot) 7 : 1 145 lb/in^2 (10.2 kg/cm^2)
                                                                                 8 : 1 160-170 lb/in^2 (11.2-11.9 kg/cm^2)

Camshaft

Journal diameter . . . . 1.842 in − 0.001 (26.70 mm − 0.025)
Clearance in bearing . . . . 0.001 to 0.002 in (0.02 to 0.05 mm)
Endfloat . . . . 0.0025 to 0.0055 in (0.06 to 0.14 mm)
Cam lift - inlet . . . . 0.257 in (6.53 mm)
Cam lift - exhaust. . . . . 0.257 in (6.53 mm)

Camshaft bearings

Type . . . . Split, steel backed, white metal lined
Internal diameter (line-reamed in position) . . . . 1.843 in + 0.0005 (46.8 mm + 0.012)

Connecting rods

Bearing fit on crankpin	0.001 to 0.0025 in (0.025 to 0.063 mm)
Bearing nip	0.002 to 0.004 in (0.05 to 0.10 mm)
Endfloat at big-end	0.007 to 0.011 in (0.20 to 0.30 mm)
Gudgeon pin bush, fit in small-end	0.001 to 0.003 in (0.02 to 0.76 mm) interference
Gudgeon pin bush internal diameter - reamed in position	1.000 in + 0.0003 (25.4 mm + 0.008)
Fit of gudgeon pin in bush	0.0003 to 0.0005 in (0.007 to 0.012 mm) clearance

Crankshaft

Journal diameter	2.5 in − 0.0005 (63.5 mm − 0.012)
Crankpin diameter:	
Early models	2.126 in − 0.001 (53.9 mm − 0.025)
Late models	2.312 in (58.7 mm)
Endfloat (controlled by thrust washers at centre bearings)	0.002 to 0.006 in (0.05 to 0.15 mm)
Regrind sizes:	

Undersize	Journal dia.	Crankpin dia.
0.010 in	2.490 in	2.302 in
-(0.25 mm)	-(63.24 mm)	-(58.47 mm)
0.020 in	2.480 in	2.292 in
-(0.50 mm)	-(62.99 mm)	-(58.22 mm)
0.030 in	2.470 in	2.282 in
-(0.76 mm)	-(62.73 mm)	-(57.96 mm)
0.040 in	2.460 in	2.272 in
-(1.01 mm)	-(62.48 mm)	-(57.70 mm)

Flywheel

Number of teeth	97
Thickness at pressure face	1.250 to 1.226 in (31.75 to 31.14 mm)
Maximum permissible run-out on flywheel face	0.002 in (0.05 mm)
Primary pinion bush - fit in flywheel	0.001 to 0.003 in (0.02 to 0.07 mm)
Internal diameter - reamed in position	0.878 in +0.0005 (22.3 + 0.013 mm)
Fit of shaft in bush	0.001 to 0.003 in (0.025 to 0.076 mm)
Maximum refacing depth	0.030 in (0.76 mm)
Minimum overall thickness after grinding	1.485 in (37.7 mm)

Engine timing markings

Early engines	Timing marks and pointer at flywheel
Later engines	Valve timing marks at timing chain wheels
	Ignition timing mark on crankshaft pulley, timing pointer at engine front cover
TDC (74-76 octane fuel)	When opposite pointer, No. 1 piston is at top dead centre (TDC)
3° BTDC (80-85 octane fuel); 6° BTDC (90-95 octane fuel)	When opposite pointer, indicates firing point of No.1 cylinder when both valves are closed

Gudgeon pin

Fit in piston	Zero to 0.0002 in (0.005 mm) interference
Fit in connecting rod bush	0.0003 to 0.0005 in (0.007 to 0.012 mm) clearance

Main bearings

Clearance on crankshaft journal	0.001 to 0.0025 in (0.02 to 0.06 mm)
Bearing nip	0.004 to 0.008 in (0.10 to 0.15 mm)

Cylinder bores

Nominal diameter (new)	3.562 in (90.47 mm)
Rebore sizes	+0.020 and 0.040 in (0.50 and 1.01 mm)

Pistons

Type	Light alloy, tin plated, flat top
Clearance in bore, measured at bottom of skirt at right angles to gudgeon pin	0.0019 to 0.0023 in (0.048 to 0.058 mm)
Clearance in bore, measured at top of skirt at right angles to gudgeon pin	0.003 to 0.004 in (0.08 to 0.10 mm)
Fit of gudgeon pin in piston	Zero to 0.0002 in (0.005 mm) interference
Gudgeon pin bore	0.9998 in + 0.0002 (25.37 mm + 0.005 mm)

Piston rings

Compression (2):	
Type	Taper periphery
Gap in bore	0.015 to 0.020 in (0.38 to 0.50 mm)
Clearance in groove	0.0018 to 0.0038 in (0.046 to 0.097 mm)
Scraper:	
Type	Slotted, square friction edge
Gap in bore	0.015 to 0.020 in (0.38 to 0.50 mm)
Clearance in groove	0.0015 to 0.0035 in (0.038 to 0.089 mm)

Rocker gear

Bush internal diameter, reamed in position . . . . 0.53 in + 0.001 (13.4 mm + 0.12 mm)
Shaft clearance in rocker bush. . . . . 0.0005 to 0.0015 in (0.013 to 0.038 mm)

Tappet clearance . . . . 0.010 in (0.25 mm) hot or cold

Timing chain tensioner

Fit of bush in cylinder. . . . . 0.003 to 0.005 in (0.07 to 0.12 mm) interference
Fit of bush in idler wheel . . . . 0.001 to 0.003 in (0.02 to 0.07 mm) interference
Fit of idler wheel on steel shaft. . . . . 0.001 to 0.003 in (0.02 to 0.07 mm) clearance
Fit of piston in cylinder bush . . . . 0.0003 to 0.0013 in (0.008 to 0.033 mm) clearance

Thrust bearings, crankshaft

Type . . . . Semi-circular, steel back, tin plated on friction surface
Standard size, total thickness . . . . 0.093 in – 0.002 (2.362 mm – 0.05)
Oversizes . . . . 0.0025 in (0.06 mm); 0.005 in (0.12 mm);
0.0075 in (0.18 mm); 0.010 in (0.25 mm)

Valves

Inlet valve:
    Diameter (stem) . . . . 0.3112 in – 0.0005 (7.9 mm – 0.013 mm)
    Face angle . . . . 30° – 1/4
Exhaust valve:
    Diameter (stem) . . . . 0.3415 – 0.0005 in (8.67 mm – 0.013)
    Face angle . . . . 45° – 1/4
Fit of inlet valves in guide. . . . . 0.001 to 0.003 in (0.02 to 0.07 mm)
Fit of exhaust valves in guide. . . . . 0.0023 to 0.0038 in (0.058 to 0.096 mm)

Valve seat

Seat angle - inlet . . . . 30°
Seat angle - exhaust . . . . 45°

Valve guides

Inlet guide bore size, after fitting . . . . 0.3125 in + 0.0015 (7.93 mm + 0.04)
Exhaust guide bore size, after fitting . . . . 0.3435 in + 0.0015 (8.73 mm + 0.04)

Valve springs

Early type:
    Inner:
        Length - free. . . . . 1.61 in (40.89 mm)
        Length under 17.5 lb (7.9 kg) load . . . . 1.38 in (35.1 mm)
    Outer:
        Length - free. . . . . 1.76 in (44.9 mm)
        Length under 46 lb (21 kg) load . . . . 1.50 in (38.3 mm)
Later type:
    Inner:
        Length - free. . . . . 1.680 in (42.67 mm)
        Length under 17.7 lb (8 kg) load. . . . . 1.462 in (37.13 mm)
    Outer:
        Length - free. . . . . 1.822 in (46.28 mm)
        Length under 46 lb (21 kg) load . . . . 1.587 in (40.3 mm)

Valve timing

Inlet opens . . . . 6° BTDC
Inlet closes . . . . 52° ABDC
Inlet peak . . . . 113°
Exhaust opens . . . . 34° BBDC
Exhaust closes . . . . 24° ATDC
Exhaust peak . . . . 95°

Vertical driveshaft gear

Backlash . . . . 0.006 to 0.010 in (0.15 to 0.25 mm)
Internal diameter of bush. . . . . 1.063 in + 0.001 (27.0 mm + 0.02)
Fit of gear in bush. . . . . 0.001 to 0.003 in (0.02 to 0.07 mm) clearance

Lubrication

Lubricant type/specification. . . . . Multigrade engine oil, viscosity range SAE 10W/40 to 20W/50, to
API SE or SF
Oil capacity (with new filter) . . . . 11.5 Imp pints (6.5 litres)

Oil pump, early type

Type	Spur gear
Drive	Splined shaft from camshaft skew gear
Endfloat of gears	0.002 to 0.005 in (0.05 to 0.12 mm)
Radial clearance of gears	0.002 to 0.005 in (0.05 to 0.12 mm)
Backlash of gears	0.004 to 0.008 in (0.10 to 0.20 mm)

Oil pump, late type

Type	Skew gear
Drive	Splined shaft from camshaft skew gear
Endfloat of gears:	
Steel gear	0.002 in (0.05 mm) to 0.005 in (0.12 mm)
Aluminium gear	0.003 in (0.07 mm) to 0.006 in (0.15 mm)
Radial clearance of gears	0.001 to 0.004 in (0.02 to 0.102 mm)
Backlash of gears	0.006 to 0.012 in (0.14 to 0.28 mm)

Oil pressure, engine warm

2,000 rpm	45 to 65 lb/in² (3.16 to 4.57 kg/cm²)

Oil pressure relief valve

Type	Non-adjustable
Relief valve spring:	
Free length	2.670 in (67.82 mm)
Compressed length at 5.7 lb (2.58 kg) load	2.45 in (61.23 mm)

Torque wrench settings

	lbf ft	kgf m
Connecting rod cap nuts	*25	3.5
Main bearing cap bolts	85	11.5
Cylinder head bolts	65	8.9
Rocker shaft bolts:		
1/2 in UNF bolts	65	8.9
5/16 in UNF bolts	18	2.4
Flywheel bolts	60-65	8.5-9
Starter dog (crankshaft pulley)	150	20.5
Clutch housing bolts	40	5.5
Camshaft sprocket bolt	30	4.15

35 lbf ft (4.9 kgf m) if the bolts have machined threads, (ie. threaded portion is same diameter as bolt shank).

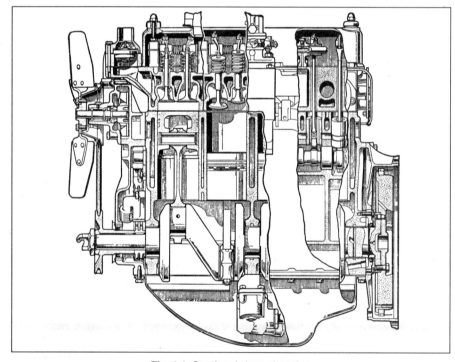

Fig. 1.1. Sectional view of engine

1 General description

The Land Rover engine covered in this manual is the 2 1/4 litre, four cylinder overhead valve type. Optional compression ratios of 7 : 1 or 8 : 1 are available.

The crankshaft is supported by three shell-type replaceable bearings. The crankshaft endfloat is limited by the centre bearing.

The camshaft runs in four bearings and is chain driven from the crankshaft sprocket. Chain tension is controlled by an idler sprocket operated by the engine oil pressure.

The roller-type cam followers act directly on bronze slides which operate the valves via pushrods and rocker arms. The valves operate in guides which are an interference fit in the cylinder head.

On earlier models the crankcase ventilation is achieved by washable filters in the oil filler cap and engine breather filter. Later models have a crankcase emission control system which ensures that the engine fumes are drawn back into the combustion chamber via the air-intake.

A pump located inside the crankcase sump provides a pressurised oil feed to all the important engine bearing components and an external full flow oil filter is fitted. The oil pump, which is shaft driven from the camshaft incorporates a pressure relief valve.

2 Major operations possible with the engine in the vehicle

The following components can be removed from the engine for inspection or overhaul without having to lift the engine out of the vehicle:
1 The cylinder head.
2 Oil sump.
3 Oil pump (after removing sump).
4 Timing cover and oil seal.
5 Timing sprockets, tensioner and chain.
6 Pistons and connecting rods (through top of cylinder bores after removing sump and cylinder head).
7 Camshaft and followers.
8 Crankshaft rear oil seal (necessitates the removal of gearbox).

3 Major operations only possible after removal of the engine from the vehicle

The Land Rover engine is very accessible; however, removal of the crankshaft, replacing the camshaft bearings, or re-boring the cylinder block requires the removal of the engine from the vehicle.

4 Method of engine removal

Before the engine can be removed it

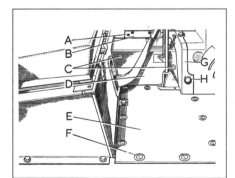

Fig. 1.2. Floor and transmission panels

A Screws (9 off), left-hand floor board
B Floor board, left hand
C Screws (4 off), tunnel cover
D Gearbox tunnel cover
E Floor board, right-hand
F Screws (12 off), right-hand floor board
G Front panel for gearbox tunnel cover
H Bolts (4 off), front panel

is necessary to detach it from the clutch housing. It is not possible to remove the engine complete with transmission.

5 Engine removal

1 To remove the engine, it is first necessary to remove the floor panels to enable the clutch housing to be detached from the rear of the engine.
2 Remove the knob and locknut from the transfer lever and remove the screws from the dust cover at the base of the lever.
3 Remove the knob and locknut from the four-wheel drive selector lever and lift off the spring and sleeve.
4 Referring to Fig. 1.2, remove the securing screws from the two front floor panels and remove the panels from the vehicle.
5 Remove the screws from the transmission tunnel cover and lift off the cover.
6 Remove the bolts from the transmission front cover and lift away the cover.
7 Open the bonnet and disconnect the bonnet support rod.
8 Remove the split-pins from the bonnet hinges, and with the help of a friend, raise the bonnet and slide it off the hinges.
9 Remove the three nuts securing the exhaust pipe to the manifold.
10 Remove the complete air cleaner assembly, (refer to Chapter 3 if necessary).
11 Disconnect the battery leads, remove the battery clamp and lift out the battery.
12 Drain the coolant into a suitable container and then, referring to Chapter 2, remove the radiator grille and the radiator and cowl assembly .
13 Disconnect the heater hoses from the rear of the engine (photo).
14 Remove the choke and throttle cables from the carburettor.
15 Disconnect the ignition HT lead from the coil and the LT wire from the distributor.
16 Remove the engine earthing strap from the right-hand side chassis member.
17 Disconnect the fuel inlet pipe from the fuel pump.
18 Remove the clips retaining the battery lead cable, speedometer cable and electrical

5.13 Heater hoses at rear of engine

harness from the right-hand side of the engine block.
19 Remove the starter motor lead from the switch on the rear bulkhead (photo).
20 Detach the electrical leads from the rear of the dynamo or alternator (refer to Chapter 10 if necessary).
21 Using a suitable hoist, attach lifting slings or chains to the engine and raise the hoist until the weight of the engine is just being supported.
22 Remove the bottom retaining nut from the left hand side engine mounting (Fig, 1,3).
23 Remove the two nuts securing the right-hand side engine mounting bracket to the chassis.
24 Slowly raise the engine until there is just enough room to remove the left-hand side engine mounting and the right-hand side mounting and bracket. Now lower the engine back to its original position.
25 Place a jack or block beneath the front of the gearbox to support its weight.
26 Remove all the bolts securing the clutch housing to the rear of the engine (see Fig. 1.4).
27 Pull the engine forward on the hoist just sufficiently to disengage the gearbox input shaft from the engine and clutch assembly
28 Check carefully that all cables, pipes and wires have been detached, then slowly lift the engine out of the vehicle (photo).

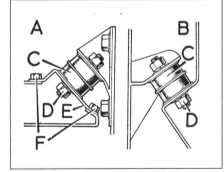

Fig. 1.3. Engine mountings

A RH side mounting
B LH side mounting
C Suspension rubbers
D Lower centre bolt
E Support bracket at RH
F Support bracket bolts

5.19 Starter motor cable attachment point

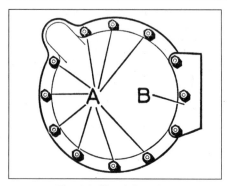

Fig. 1.4. Clutch housing

A Clutch housing to engine bolts
B Clutch slave cylinder mounting bolts

6 Engine - dismantling general

1 It is best to mount the engine on a dismantling stand but if one is not available, then stand the engine on a strong bench so it is at a comfortable working height. Failing this, the engine can be stripped down on the floor.

2 During the dismantling process the greatest care should be taken to keep the exposed parts free from dirt. As an aid to achieving this, it is sound advice to thoroughly clean down the outside of the engine, removing all traces of oil and congealed dirt.

3 Use paraffin or a good grease solvent. The latter will make the job much easier, as, after the solvent has been applied and allowed to stand for a time, a vigorous jet of water will wash off the solvent and all the grease and filth. If the dirt is thick and deeply embedded, work the solvent into it with a wire brush.

4 Finally wipe down the exterior of the engine with a rag and only then, when it is quite clean should the dismantling process begin. As the engine is stripped, clean each part in a bath of paraffin or petrol.

5 Never immerse parts with oilways in paraffin, ie: the crankshaft, but to clean, wipe down carefully with a petrol dampened rag.

 TOOL TiP *Oilways can be cleaned out with wire. If an air line is present all parts can be blown dry and the oilways blown through as an added precaution.*

6 Re-use of old engine gaskets is false economy and can give rise to oil and water leaks, if nothing worse. To avoid the possibility of trouble after the engine has been reassembled **always** use new gaskets throughout.

7 Do not throw old gaskets away as it sometimes happens that an immediate replacement cannot be found and the old gasket is then very useful as a template. Hang up the old gaskets as they are removed on a suitable hook or nail.

8 To strip the engine it is best to work from

5.28 Hoisting out the engine

the top down. The sump provides a firm base on which the engine can be supported in an upright position. When the stage is reached where the sump must be removed, the engine can be turned on its side and all other work carried out with it in this position.

9 Wherever possible, replace nuts, bolts and washers fingertight from wherever they were removed. This helps avoid later loss and muddle. If they cannot be replaced then lay them out in such a fashion that it is clear from where they came.

7 Ancillary components - removal

1 With the engine removed from the car and separated from the gearbox, the externally mounted ancillary components should now be removed before dismantling begins.

2 The following is a suggested sequence of removal, detailed descriptions are to be found in the relevant Chapter of this manual.

Dynamo or alternator (Chapter 10)
Clutch assembly (Chapter 5)
Manifolds and carburettor (Chapter 3)
Flywheel (eight bolts) (Section 15, Chapter 1)
Engine mounting brackets (Section 5, Chapter 1)
Oil filter (Section 11, Chapter 1)
Distributor and spark plugs (Chapter 4)
Fuel pump (Chapter 3)
Fan assembly (Chapter 2)
Water pump/thermostat assembly (Chapter 2)
Starter motor (Chapter 10)

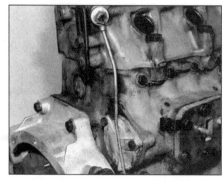

8.1(h) Oil feed pipe to cylinder head

8 Cylinder head - removal

1 If the head is to be removed with the engine still in the vehicle, first carry out the following operations:
a) *Remove the bonnet.*
b) *Remove the air cleaner.*
c) *Disconnect both battery leads .*
d) *Drain the cooling system.*
e) *Disconnect the throttle and choke controls and fuel inlet pipe from the carburettor.*
f) *Remove the hoses from the thermostat housing.*
g) *Disconnect the exhaust pipe from the manifold.*
h) *Remove the oil feed pipe at rear right-hand side of the engine (photo).*
I) *Disconnect the HT leads from the spark plugs.*

2 Remove the three rocker cover securing nuts and lift off the cover.

3 Undo the large and small bolts retaining the rocker shaft brackets to the cylinder head, but do not attempt to remove the rocker shaft at this stage.

4 As the rocker shaft will tend to spring apart while being removed, great care must be taken to note the assembly order of the rocker springs and spacers on the shaft (see Fig. 1.8). **Note:** *A good method of removal is to turn the rocker cover upside down and secure it to the three rocker shaft studs using the cover nuts. The complete rocker shaft assembly can then be lifted off without any risk of it coming apart.*

5 Lift out the pushrods and keep them in the correct order to ensure that each pushrod is replaced in its original position. Punch eight holes in a piece of cardboard, number them one to eight and place the pushrods in order through the card.

6 Unscrew each of the cylinder head bolts a half turn at a time in the reverse order to that shown in Fig. 1.5.

7 With ail the bolts removed, lift the cylinder head from the block. If it is stuck, tap it upwards using a block of wood and a hammer. On no account insert any lever into the gasket joint.

8 Remove the cylinder head gasket.

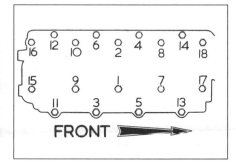

Fig. 1.5. Tightening sequence for cylinder head bolts

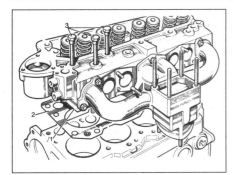

Fig. 1.6. Cylinder head and gasket

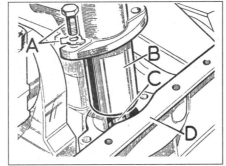

Fig. 1.7. Removing the oil pump

A Securing bolts   C Driveshaft
B Pump   D Crankcase

9 Cylinder head - dismantling

1 The valves can be removed from the cylinder head by the following method. Compress each spring in turn with a valve spring compressor until the two halves of the collets can be removed. Release the compressor and remove the spring and spring retainer.

2 If, when the valve spring compressor is screwed down, the valve spring retaining cap refuses to free, to expose the split collet, do not continue to screw down on the compressor as there is a likelihood of damaging it.

3 Gently tap the top of the tool directly over the cap with a soft-faced mallet. This will free the cap. To avoid the compressor jumping off the valve spring retaining cap when it is tapped, hold the compressor firmly in position with one hand.

4 Slide the rubber oil control seal off the top of each valve guide and valve and then drop out each valve through the combustion chamber.

5 It is essential that the valves are kept in their correct sequence unless they are so badly worn that they are to be renewed. Numbering from the front of the engine, exhaust valves are 1-4-5-8 and inlet valves 2-3-6-7.

10 Sump - removal

1 The sump can be removed quite easily with the engine still in the vehicle.

2 First drain the engine oil into a suitable container.

3 The Land Rover has considerable ground clearance and it is possible to remove the sump without raising the vehicle. However, if it is decided to jack the vehicle up, ensure that it is securely supported on heavy duty axle stands before working beneath it.

4 Unscrew and remove all the sump bolts, releasing them only one half turn at a time in a diagonal sequence to avoid distortion.

5 If the sump is stuck tight, run a blunt knife round the gasket to release it.

11 Oil pump and oil filter - removal

1 If the oil pump is to be removed with the engine still in the vehicle, first remove the sump as described in the previous Section.

2 Remove the two securing bolts and withdraw the pump complete with drive shaft.

3 The oil filter is simply removed by unscrewing the centre bolt. As the oil filter body is withdrawn, a loss of oil trapped within it will occur so have a suitable container at the ready to drop the oil into.

4 Discard the internal filter element. The new element will be supplied complete with new sealing rings.

5 To remove the oil filter housing, first detach the oil pressure switch lead and then remove the two retaining bolts and prise the housing away from the cylinder block (photo).

6 When refitting the housing, a new gasket must be used.

12 Timing cover, gears and chain - removal

If the timing cover, gears and chain are being removed with the engine in the car, then the following operations must first be carried out:

Drain the cooling system.
Remove the radiator and fanbelt.
Remove the water pump pulley and fan.

11.5 Removing the oil filter housing

Remove the dynamo adjusting arm.
Separate the by-pass hose from the thermostat housing.

1 Unscrew and remove the crankshaft starter dog. If the sump has been removed, place a block of wood between a crankshaft web and the internal wall of the crankcase to prevent the crankshaft rotating as the bolt is unscrewed. If the engine is in the car or the sump has not yet been removed, withdraw the starter motor and jam the flywheel starter ring gear with a large screwdriver or cold chisel. The crankshaft starter dog can then be unscrewed.

2 Withdraw the crankshaft pulley. If this is tight, use two levers placed behind the pulley at opposite points to extract it.

3 Unscrew and remove all the nuts and bolts securing the timing cover and water pump to the cylinder block, including the front sump bolts and lift off the cover and pump assembly.

4 Before the chain or tensioner is removed, the following method should be used to ensure correct engine timing during reassembly.

5 On earlier engines, remove the inspection plate from the flywheel housing and rotate the engine until the TDC mark is in line with the pointer (see Fig. 1.8).

6 Using a scriber and steel rule, scratch an alignment mark on the camshaft and camshaft sprocket and a matching mark on the cylinder block timing casing (photo).

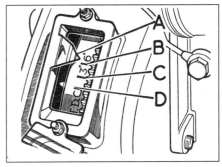

Fig. 1.8. Timing marks on the flywheel (earlier engine)

A *Timing pointer*
B *6° mark, align when using 90-96 octane fuel*
C *3° mark, align when using 80-85 octane fuel*
D *TDC mark, align when using 74-76 octane fuel*

12.6 Timing marks scribed across the camshaft sprocket and front face of cylinder block

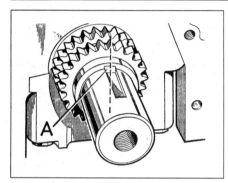

Fig. 1.9. Crankshaft positioned for engine timing (the keyway 'A' must be vertical as shown)

7 As an additional precaution make a similar mark on the crankshaft sprocket and cylinder block.

8 On later engines with the timing pointer on the front of the timing case, rotate the crankshaft until the keyway in the crankshaft is in the position shown in Fig. 1.9 (vertical position) and then check that the 'P' marks on the camshaft sprocket are aligned as shown in Fig. 1.10. **Note:** If the camshaft timing marks do not line up, rotate the crankshaft 360°. The marks should then be aligned.

9 Remove the nut and two bolts and withdraw the complete chain tensioner assembly.

10 Remove the camshaft securing bolt and washer and using a gear puller tool, remove the camshaft sprocket complete with chain.

13 Camshaft and tappets - removal

1 It is possible to remove the camshaft with the engine still in the vehicle, but first the cylinder head, timing cover and chain must be removed as described in the previous Sections.

2 Remove the distributor and adaptor plate from the cylinder block (Fig. 1.11).

3 Lift out the distributor drive shaft (earlier engines), or the drive shaft coupling (later engines).

4 Unscrew the grubscrew from oil filter

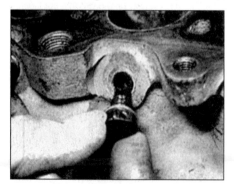

13.7 Removing a tappet guide securing bolt

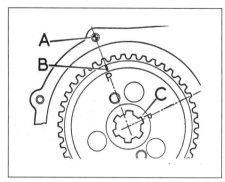

Fig. 1.10. Timing marks on camshaft sprocket (later engines)

A Bolt hole on top, front of engine
B Mark on sprocket perimeter
C Mark on sprocket that must line up with master spline on camshaft

housing face (Fig. 1.12) and lift out the distributor and oil pump drive assembly using a pair of thin-nose pliers.

5 Using a piece of wire bent into a hook, lift out the tappet slides and rollers and keep them in the correct order of removal.

6 Remove the camshaft drive chain and sprocket as described previously and remove the camshaft thrust plate, located behind the sprocket.

7 The camshaft can now be withdrawn from the front of the engine. Take care not to damage the camshaft bearings as the shaft passes through them. **Note:** The tappet guides can be removed if required by undoing the retaining bolts from the side of the block (photo) and pulling out the guides using a slide hammer.

14 Pistons and connecting rods - removal

1 The pistons and connecting rods can be removed with the engine still in the vehicle or with the engine on the bench.

2 With the cylinder head and sump removed undo the big-end retaining nuts.

3 The connecting rods and pistons are lifted out from the top of the cylinder block.

4 Remove the big-end caps one at a time,

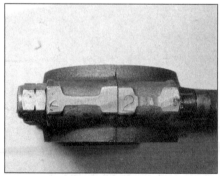

14.5 Identification marks on connecting rod and bearing cap

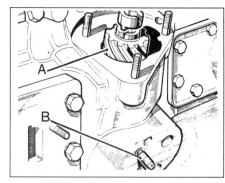

Fig. 1.11. Distributor adaptor plate and coupling

A Distributor bolts
B Distributor adaptor
C Joint washer
D Cork washer
E Distributor
F Adaptor nuts
G Top driveshaft, early engines
H Driveshaft coupling, later engines
J Vertical drivegear housing

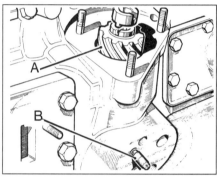

Fig. 1.12. Distributor drivegear and securing screw

A Drivegear   B Grubscrew

 HAYNES HiNT *Also ensure that the shell bearings are kept with their correct connecting rods and caps unless they are to be renewed.*

taking care to keep them in the right order and the correct way round.

5 It is a good idea to mark the side face of each rod and cap with identification marks using a centre punch and light hammer, unless the caps are already marked (photo). Use a single dot for No. 1 connecting rod, two dots for No. 2 and so on. This will ensure there is no mix-up on reassembly, as it is very important that the caps are refitted to the connecting rods from which they were removed.

6 If the big-end caps are difficult to remove they may be gently tapped with a soft-faced mallet.

7 To remove the shell bearings, press the bearing opposite the groove in both the connecting rod, and the connecting rod caps and the bearings will slide out easily.

8 Withdraw the pistons and connecting rods upwards and ensure they are kept in the correct order for replacement in the same bore.

15 Flywheel, flywheel housing and rear crankshaft oil seal - removal

1 These components can be removed with the engine still in the vehicle if preferred, but first the transmission must be removed (see Chapter 6), and also the sump.
2 Bend back the locking tabs, remove the eight securing bolts and lift off the flywheel.
3 Remove the bolts securing the flywheel housing to the rear of the cylinder block and lift off the housing. Note that there is an O-ring type seal fitted in the housing aperture (photos).
4 Remove the two retaining bolts and tap out the rear main bearing cap using a soft alloy drift.
5 Using a socket, undo the bolts retaining the upper half of the seal retainer to the rear of the cylinder block. Prise the retainer rearwards until it clears the dowels and then lift it off.
6 Remove the coil spring from around the rear main bearing oil seal and pull the seal off the crankshaft.

16 Crankshaft and main bearings - removal

1 To remove the crankshaft and bearings, the engine must be lifted from the vehicle and placed on a bench.
2 Drain the engine oil and remove the timing gears, flywheel and housing, sump, connecting rod bearings, and the oil pump, as described in the previous Sections.
3 Mark the main bearing caps and cylinder block faces to ensure the caps are replaced the correct way round.
4 Undo and remove the bolts retaining the three bearing caps to the cylinder block.
5 Remove the main bearing caps and the bottom half of each bearing shell, taking care to keep the bearing shells in the right caps.
6 When removing the centre bearing cap, note the bottom semicircular halves of the thrust washers, one half lying on either side of the main bearing. Lay them with the centre bearing along the correct side.
7 Slightly rotate the crankshaft to free the upper halves of the bearing shells and

15.3a Flywheel housing prior to removal

thrust washers which can be lifted away and placed over the correct bearing cap when the crankshaft has been lifted out.
8 Remove the crankshaft by lifting it away from the crankcase.
9 Lift away the bearing shells.

17 Examination and renovation - general

With the engine stripped down and all parts thoroughly cleaned, it is now time to examine everything for wear. The following items should be checked and where necessary renewed or renovated as described in the following Sections.

18 Oil pump - examination and renovation

1 Remove the oil pump as described in Section 11. Undo the four securing bolts and detach the cover plate and driveshaft housing (photo).
2 Lift out the two gears and unscrew the relief valve from the pump housing. Withdraw the valve spring, plunger and steel ball.
3 Clean all the components in petrol and blow dry with an airline, if available.
4 Refit the gears and measure the clearance between the top of the gears and the pump housing face using a steel rule and a feeler gauge, (photo). For the clearance dimensions refer to the Specifications given at the beginning of this Chapter.

15.3b Location of flywheel housing oil seal

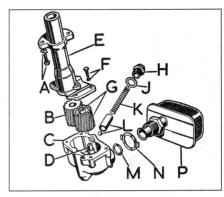
Fig. 1.13. Exploded view of oil pump

A Bolt, oil pump to cylinder block
B Pump drivegear
C Pump body
D Idler gear spindle
E Pump cover and shaft housing
F Bolt, cover to body
G Idler gear and bush assembly
H Threaded plug
J Washer
K Spring
L Relief valve ball and plunger
M Sealing ring
N Lockwasher
P Oil filter

5 Using the feeler gauges, check the clearance between the gears and the pump body (photo), and also the backlash between the gears themselves. Again refer to the specifications for the correct dimensions.

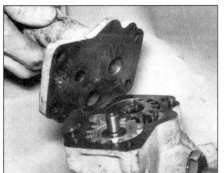
18.1 Removing oil pump cover plate

18.4 Checking the pump gear endfloat

18.5 Checking the clearance between the oil pump gears and the body

6 If the gear endfloat, clearance, or backlash dimensions are not within those given in the specifications, the best policy is to replace the complete pump assembly with a new or reconditioned unit. Although it is possible to renew the gear bushes, they require reaming and drilling and this is a specialist job.

7 Check the relief valve ball for grooving or wear and if evident, renew it. Examine the ball seating inside the pump body for similar signs of wear. The seat can be lapped using a steel ball soldered to a length of tube, and using very fine grinding paste, but if any doubt exists the most sensible decision is to renew the complete pump.

8 Reassemble the pump noting that the drive gear fits into the pump body with the plain section of the bore uppermost.

19 Crankcase ventilation system

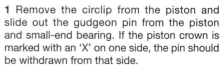

On earlier Land Rover engines, crankcase ventilation is achieved by a breather filter on the rocker cover and an additional one on the oil filter tube, (see Fig. 1.14).

Later models are fitted with a closed-circuit ventilation system, comprising a hose, connecting the rocker cover breather directly into the aircleaner, and a second hose leading from the oil filler tube into the carburettor body via a non-return valve.

The hoses should be periodically checked for perishing or damage and the clips checked for security. The breather filters should be cleaned at the intervals given in the Routine Maintenance section at the front of this Manual.

20 Crankshaft and main bearings - examination and renovation

1 Remove the crankshaft rear oil seal and discard it.

2 Examine the bearing surfaces of the crankshaft for scratches or scoring and, using a micrometer, check each journal and crankpin for out of round. Where this is found to be in excess of 0.001 in (0.0254 mm) the crankshaft

Fig. 1.14. Crankcase ventilation breathers

will have to be reground and undersize bearings fitted.

3 The crankshaft can be reground to a maximum of 0.040 in (1.016 mm) undersize, but your Leyland dealer will decide how much is required and supply the matching undersize main and big-end shell bearings.

4 Crankshaft endfloat, with main bearing caps fully tightened, should be between 0.002 and 0.006 in (0.05 and 0.15 mm). The endfloat is controlled by the thrust flanges on the centre main bearing shells.

5 If the gearbox input shaft spigot bush needs renewal, extract it by tapping a thread in it. The new bush requires no lubrication.

21 Cylinder block and crankcase - examination and renovation

1 The cylinder bores must be examined for taper, ovality, scoring and scratches. Start by carefully examining the top of the cylinder bores. If they are at all worn a very slight ridge will be found on the thrust side. This marks the top of the piston ring travel. The owner will have a good indication of the bore wear prior to dismantling the engine, or removing the cylinder head.

> **HAYNES HiNT** *Excessive oil consumption accompanied by blue smoke from the exhaust is a sure sign of worn cylinder bores and piston rings.*

2 Measure the bore diameter just under the ridge with a micrometer and compare it with the diameter at the bottom of the bore, which is not subject to wear. If the difference between the two measurements is more than 0.008 in (0.2032 mm), then it will be necessary to fit special pistons and rings or have the cylinders rebored and fit oversize pistons.

3 If the bores are slightly worn but not so badly worn as to justify reboring them, then special oil control rings and pistons can be fitted which will restore compression and stop the engine burning oil. Several different types are available and the manufacturer's instructions concerning their fitting must be followed closely.

4 If the cylinders have already been bored out to the maximum of + 0.040 in (1.016 mm), it is possible to have cylinder liners fitted. This is obviously a specialist job and should be entrusted to your Leyland dealer.

5 If new pistons are being fitted and the bores have not been rebored, it is essential to slightly roughen the hard glaze on the sides of the bores with fine glass paper so the new piston rings will have a chance to bed in properly.

6 Examine the crankcase for cracks and leaking core plugs. To renew a core plug, drill a hole in its centre and tap a thread in it. Screw in a bolt and using a distance piece, tighten the bolt and extract the core plug. When installing the new plug, smear its outer edge with gasket cement.

7 Probe oil galleries and waterways with a piece of wire to make sure that they are quite clear.

22 Piston/connecting rod assemblies - examination and renovation

1 Remove the circlip from the piston and slide out the gudgeon pin from the piston and small-end bearing. If the piston crown is marked with an 'X' on one side, the pin should be withdrawn from that side.

2 If the gudgeon pin is tight in the piston immerse the piston in hot water and heat it to approximately 55°C (131°F). The gudgeon pin should then slide out quite easily.

3 To remove the piston rings, slide them carefully over the top of the piston taking care not to scratch the aluminium alloy of the piston. Never slide them off the bottom of the piston skirt. It is very easy to break piston rings if they are pulled off roughly so this operation should be done with extreme caution. It is helpful to use an old 0.020 inch feeler gauge to facilitate their removal.

4 Lift one end of the piston ring to be removed, out of its groove and insert the end of the feeler gauge under it.

5 Turn the feeler gauge slowly round the piston and as the ring comes out of its groove it rests on the land above. It can then be eased off the piston with the feeler gauge stopping it from slipping into any empty grooves, if it is any but the top piston ring that is being removed.

6 Piston ring wear can be checked by first removing the rings from the pistons as described previously. Then place the rings in the cylinder bores from the top, pushing them down about 1.5 inches (38.1 mm) with the head of a piston (from which the rings have been removed) so that they rest square in the cylinder. Then measure the gap at the ends of the ring with a feeler gauge. If it exceeds the limits specified at the beginning of this Chapter then they will need renewal.

7 The grooves in which the rings locate in the piston can also become enlarged in use. The clearance between ring and piston, in the

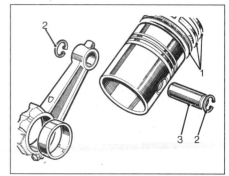

Fig. 1.15. Piston and connecting rod assembly

1 Piston rings   2 Circlip   3 Gudgeon pin

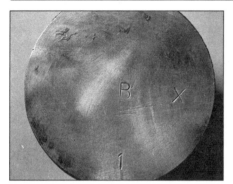

22.11a Piston identification marks

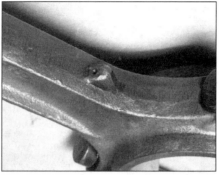

22.11b Oil hole in the side of a connecting rod

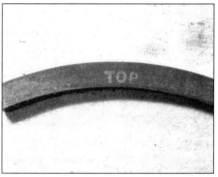

22.12 'TOP' identification of compression ring

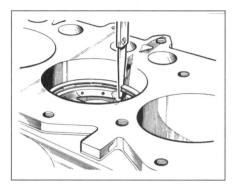

Fig. 1.16. Checking a piston ring in a bore

groove should not exceed the limits specified at the beginning of this Chapter.

8 Check that the fit of the gudgeon pin in the connecting rod small end bush is within the limits given in the Specifications at the beginning of this Chapter.

9 If new small-end bushes are required, the job should be entrusted to a specialist as the new bushes have to be reamed to fit the gudgeon pins.

10 When refitting the piston to the con-rod, note that the 'X' on the piston crown faces towards the front of the engine and the oil spray hole in the side of the connecting rod faces towards the camshaft (photos).

11 The two compression rings must be fitted with the 'T' or 'TOP' uppermost on the piston (photo). The scraper ring may be fitted either way up.

12 Refitting the gudgeon pin is a reversal of the removal procedure, but ensure that the connecting rod is the correct way round.

23 Camshaft and tappets - examination and renovation

1 Examine the camshaft bearing surfaces, cam lobes and gearteeth for wear or scoring. Renew the shaft if evident.

2 If the camshaft bearings require renewal the cylinder block should be taken to your local Leyland dealer or engineering works who will

have the special tools for fitting the bearings and reaming them.

3 Check the tappet rollers for pitting or scoring and the tappet slides for excessive wear and renew them if necessary.

24 Timing gears and chain - examination and renovation

1 Examine the teeth on the camshaft, crankshaft and tensioner sprockets. If they are worn or hooked in appearance they must be renewed.

2 Check the tensioner piston and cylinder for wear, also check the sprocket bush and ratchet bush. Renew the components where necessary.

3 Inspect the rubber strip on the chain damper attached to the cylinder block, and if badly grooved, renew it.

4 Examine the timing chain. If it has been in operation for a considerable time or if when held horizontally (link plates facing downwards) it takes on a deeply bowed appearance, renew it.

25 Cylinder head - decarbonising, valve grinding, renovation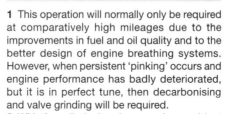

1 This operation will normally only be required at comparatively high mileages due to the improvements in fuel and oil quality and to the better design of engine breathing systems. However, when persistent 'pinking' occurs and engine performance has badly deteriorated, but it is in perfect tune, then decarbonising and valve grinding will be required.

2 With the cylinder head removed, use a blunt scraper to remove all trace of carbon and deposits from the combustion spaces and ports. Scrape the cylinder head free from scale or old pieces of gasket or jointing compound. Clean the cylinder head by washing it in paraffin and take particular care to pull a piece of rag through the ports and cylinder head bolt holes. Any grit remaining in these recesses may well drop onto the gasket or cylinder block mating surface as the cylinder

head is lowered into position and could lead to a gasket leak after reassembly is complete.

3 If the engine is in the vehicle, clean the tops of the pistons and the upper edges of the cylinder bores. It is essential that great care is taken to ensure that no carbon gets into the cylinder bores as this could scratch the cylinder walls or cause damage to the piston and rings. To ensure this does not happen, first turn the crankshaft so that two of the pistons are at the top of their bores. Stuff rag into the other two bores or seal them off with paper and masking tape.

> **HAYNES HiNT** *The waterways should also be covered with small pieces of masking tape to prevent particles of carbon entering the cooling system and damaging the water pump.*

4 Press a little grease into the gap between the cylinder walls and the two pistons which are to be worked on. With a blunt scraper carefully scrape away the carbon from the piston crown, taking great care not to scratch the aluminium. Also scrape away the carbon from the surrounding lip of the cylinder wall. When all the carbon has been removed, scrape away the grease which will now be contaminated with carbon particles, taking care not to press any into the bores. To assist prevention of carbon build-up the piston crown can be polished with a metal polish. Remove the rag or masking tape from the other two cylinders and turn the crankshaft so that the two pistons which were at the bottom are now at the top. Place rag or masking tape in the cylinders which have been decarbonised and proceed as just described.

5 Examine the heads of the valves for pitting and burning, especially the heads of the exhaust valves. The valve seatings should be examined at the same time. If the pitting on valve and seat is very slight the marks can be removed by grinding the seats and valves together with coarse, and then fine, valve grinding paste.

6 Where bad pitting has occurred to the valve seats it will be necessary to recut them and fit new valves.

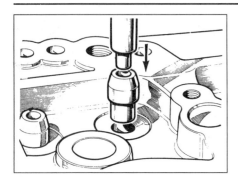

Fig. 1.17. Driving in a new valve guide

7 Valve grinding is carried out as follows: Smear a trace of coarse carborundum paste on the seat face and apply a suction grinder tool to the valve head. With a semi-rotary motion, grind the valve head to its seat, lifting the valve occasionally to redistribute the grinding paste. When a dull matt even surface finish is produced on both the valve seat and the valve, wipe off the paste and repeat the process with fine carborundum paste, lifting and turning the valve to redistribute the paste as before. A light spring placed under the valve head will greatly ease this operation. When a smooth unbroken ring of light grey matt finish is produced, on both valve and valve seat faces, the grinding operation is completed.

8 Clean away every trace of grinding paste and if available, use an airline to blow out the ports and valve guides.

9 Insert the valves into their respective guides and check that the amount of wear

does not exceed the dimensions given in the Specifications.

10 If the clearance is excessive the guides can be removed by driving them out using a suitable sized stepped drift, (see Fig, 1.17) from the combustion chamber side of the cylinder head.

11 Special drifts are available from the manufacturers for this job, and it is recommended that they are used, when refitting, to avoid damaging the new guides.

12 If the original valve springs have been in use for more than 20,000 miles (32,000 kms), they should be renewed together with new valve stem oil seals (the latter are included in the de-coke set).

26 Rockers and rocker shaft - examination and renovation

1 Thoroughly clean the rocker shaft and then check the shaft for straightness by rolling it on a flat surface. It is most unlikely that it will deviate from normal, but, if it does, then a judicious attempt may be made to straighten it. If this is not successful purchase a new shaft. The surface of the shaft must be free from any worn ridges caused by the rocker arms. If any wear is present renew the shaft.

2 Check the rocker arms for wear of the bushes, for wear at the rocker arm face which bears on the valve stem, and for wear of the adjusting ball ended screws. Wear in the rocker arm bush can be checked by gripping the rocker arm tip and holding the rocker

arm in place on the shaft, noting if there is any lateral rocker arm shake. If the shake is present, and the arm is very loose on the shaft a new rocker arm must be fitted.

3 Check the pushrods for straightness by rolling them on the bench. Renew any that are bent.

27 Flywheel - examination and renovation

1 Examine the clutch driven plate mating surface of the flywheel. If this is scored or shows signs of many small cracks, then it should either be renewed or refaced (see Specifications).

2 Examine the teeth of the flywheel starter ring gear. If they are chipped or worn, the ring must be renewed. To do this, split the ring with a cold chisel.

3 Heat the new ring to 392°F (200°C) in an electric oven and then quickly fit it to the flywheel so that the chamfered side of the teeth is towards the engine side of the flywheel.

4 Allow the ring to cool naturally without quenching.

28 Engine reassembly - general

To ensure maximum life with minimum trouble from a rebuilt engine, not only must everything be correctly assembled, but everything must be spotlessly clean, all the oilways must be clear, locking washers and spring washers must always be fitted where indicated and all bearing and other working surfaces must be thoroughly lubricated during assembly.

Before assembly begins renew any bolts or studs, the threads of which are in any way damaged, and whenever possible use new spring washers.

Gather together a torque wrench, oil can and clean rag, also a set of engine gaskets, crankshaft front and rear oil seals and a new oil filter element.

29 Crankshaft oil seal and main bearings - refitting

1 Clean the backs of the bearing shells and the bearing recesses in both the crankcase and the caps.

2 Make sure that the centre thrust washers are located in the crankcase and then fit the remaining shells (photo).

3 Oil the bearings liberally.

4 It will be found easier to fit the rear oil seal before refitting the crankshaft. First loop the oil seal coil spring around the rear oil seal journal on the crankshaft. Open the split in the seal just enough to pass it over the crankshaft journal with the recess in the seal facing forwards.

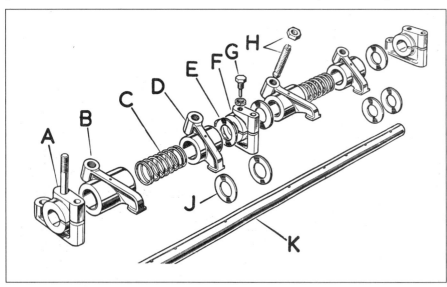

Fig. 1.18. Rocker gear components

A Rocker brackets. Front, centre and rear brackets carry studs for top cover fixings
B Exhaust valve rockers (4 off)
C Rocker shaft springs (4 off)
D Inlet valve rockers (4 off)
E Spacing washers (6 off)
F Intermediate rocker bracket (2 off)

G Locating screw for rocker shaft (2 off on early models)
H Tappet screws adjacent to larger fixing holes in brackets
J Spacing washers for diesel models. Not applicable for petrol models
K Valve rocker shaft (2 off on early models)

29.2a Location of centre main bearing thrust washers and upper shell bearing

29.2b Fitting a shell bearing to one of the main bearing caps

29.2c Location of the rear, upper main bearing shell

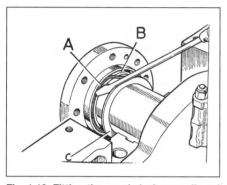

Fig. 1.19. Fitting the crankshaft rear oil seal

A Coil spring   B Seal

5 With the spring ends hooked together, carefully push the spring into the seal recess using a small screwdriver (Fig. 1.19).

6 Make sure the join in the spring is positioned 90° away from the split in the seal.

7 Smear a trace of sealing compound on the inner recess of the upper half (cylinder block side) of the seal retainer and bolt into place.

8 With the split in the seal facing vertically towards the top of the engine, lower the crankshaft into position. Make sure that the seal fits snugly into the upper seal retainer without distortion (photo).

9 Fit the 'T' seals onto either side of the rear main bearing cap and bolt the lower seal retainer onto the cap (Fig. 1.20).

10 Smear a trace of sealing compound on

the inner recess of the lower seal retainer and fit the rear main bearing cap and shell onto the cylinder. Great care must be taken to ensure that the 'T' seals are not pushed out of place and the rear oil seal does not get distorted (photo). Fit the bearing cap bolts but do not tighten at this stage.

11 Fit the front and centre main bearing caps, not forgetting to fit the thrust washers on either side of the centre cap.

12 Tighten all the bearing cap bolts to the specified torque and check that the crankshaft rotates smoothly without any tight spots (photo).

13 Check the crankshaft endfloat using a dial gauge or feeler blade (photo). Refer to the Specifications for the permissible limit.

29.8 Crankshaft installed in the engine block

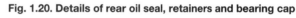
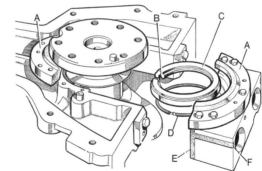

Fig. 1.20. Details of rear oil seal, retainers and bearing cap

A Retainer halves
B Split line of seal to be towards top of engine when fitted
C Split oil seal
D Garter spring, hook and eye to be midway between split and hinge of oil seal when fitted
E 'T' seal
F These ends should protrude 1/32 in (0.8 mm)

29.10 Fitting the rear main bearing cap using a feeler gauge to avoid damaging the 'T' seal

29.12 Tightening the main bearing cap bolts

29.13 Checking the crankshaft endfloat using feeler gauges

30.4 inserting a piston into the cylinder block

30 Piston/connecting rod - refitting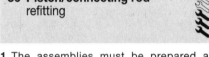

1 The assemblies must be prepared as described in Sections 21 and 22.
2 Apply engine oil liberally to the cylinder bores and to the piston rings.
3 Fit a piston ring compressor to No. 1 piston and then insert the connecting rod into the cylinder bore nearest the front of the block. Check that the 'X' mark on the piston crown faces the front of the engine.
4 With the piston skirt having entered the cylinder bore and the compressor resting squarely against the block, place the wooden handle of a hammer on the centre of the piston crown and then tap the head of the handle sharply to drive the piston assembly into the bore (photo).
5 With the crankpin at its lowest point, carefully pull the connecting rod downward and connect it to the crankshaft. Make sure that the big-end bearing shell has not become displaced.
6 install the big-end bearing cap complete with the bearing shell, making sure that the

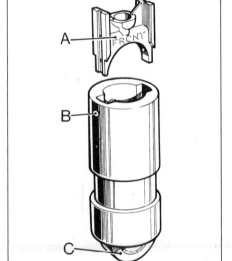

Fig. 1.21. Tappet assembly
A Slide   B Guide   C Roller

30.7 Tightening the big-end bearing nuts

matching marks on the rod and cap are in alignment and are on the correct side of the engine. This will be automatic, provided the piston and connecting rod have been correctly assembled and the mark on the piston crown is correctly positioned.
7 Screw on the big-end nuts and tighten to the specified torque (photo).
8 Repeat the foregoing operations on the remaining three piston assemblies.

31 Camshaft and tappets - refitting

1 Lubricate the camshaft bearings with engine oil and carefully install the camshaft from the front of the engine (photo).
2 Fit the camshaft thrust plate and check

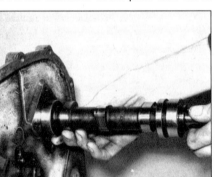

31.1 Sliding the camshaft into the block

31.3a Inserting a tappet roller into the block ...

that the camshaft endfloat is within 0.0025 in to 0.0055 in (0.06 to 0.14 mm). If the endfloat exceeds this limit a new thrust plate must be fitted (photo).
3 Oil the tappet rollers and fit them into the guides followed by the tappet slides. Make sure that the rollers and slides are correctly seated. Note that the tappet slides are marked 'FRONT' and this side must face towards the front of the engine. The chamfered side of the rollers also faces the front of the engine (photos).

32 Timing components - refitting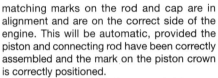

1 First rotate the crankshaft until the TDC mark on the flywheel is aligned with the pointer or, on engines with the timing pointer on the front cover, rotate the crankshaft until the keyway is in a vertical position (Fig. 1.9)
2 Refit the camshaft sprocket making sure that the alignment marks described in Section 12 are lined up.
3 Loop the timing chain over the crankshaft and camshaft sprockets taking care that neither sprocket moves from its set position. Make sure that the slack in the chain is on the tensioner sprocket side (photo).
4 Re-check that with the chain correctly fitted, all timing marks described in Section 12 are lined up.
5 Assemble the chain tensioner complete with sprocket. Lift up the ratchet arm and

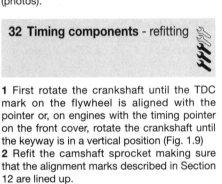

31.2 Camshaft thrust plate in position

31.3b ... followed by a tappet slide

32.3 Refitting the camshaft timing chain

32.6 Timing chain tensioner installed

32.8 Refitting the camshaft sprocket securing bolt

32.10 Installing the crankshaft pulley and securing bolt

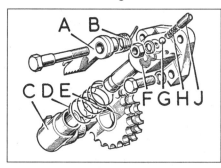

Fig. 1.22. Chain tensioner components

A Ratchet
B Ratchet spring
C Cylinder
D Chain tensioner
   spring
E Idler wheel
F Piston
G Non-return ball
   valve
H Spring for ball
   valve
J Spring retainer plug

compress the piston into the cylinder as far as it will go. Refit the tensioner onto the engine making sure that the dowels are correctly located in the piston housing and the spigot fits into the slot on the front of the engine.
6 Refit the ratchet arm, spring and securing bolt and release the cylinder allowing the sprocket to take up the timing chain slack. Refit the other retaining bolt and nut and tighten all three (photo).
7 Fit the timing chain vibration damper and adjust it so there is a clearance of 0.010 in (0.25 mm) between the rubber strip and the chain.

8 Carry out a last check to make sure all the timing positions and marks are still correctly aligned and then tighten the camshaft securing bolt and bend over the locking tab (photo).
9 Remove the timing cover oil seal and drive in a new one, using a piece of tubing as a drift. Apply engine oil to the seal lips and then install the timing cover, using a new gasket. Tighten the bolts only finger-tight at this stage.
10 Install the crankshaft pulley and tighten its securing bolt to the specified torque (photo).
11 Finally tighten the timing cover bolts.

33 Distributor and oil pump drive gear - refitting

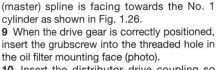

1 It is essential that the distributor drive gear engages the camshaft gear in the correct position otherwise the ignition timing will be completely out of phase.
2 Firstly, the crankshaft must be positioned so that the No. 1 (front) piston is at the top-dead-centre (TDC) position on the compression stroke.
3 To do this, rotate the crankshaft until with the No. 1 piston approaching TDC, both the No. 1 cylinder tappets are resting on the heel of the cam (fully down). This can be checked by lightly pressing the tappet slides with the fingers and feeling them rise and fall as the crankshaft is rotated.
4 If work is being carried out with the engine in the vehicle and the cylinder head is still attached, remove the No. 1 cylinder spark plug and with a finger pressed over the plug hole, rotate the engine until pressure is felt. This indicates that No. 1 piston is rising on the compression stroke.
5 On engines with the timing marks on the flywheel, rotate the engine in the necessary direction until the TDC mark lines up with the pointer. If using a higher octane fuel than 74-76 turn the flywheel to the 3 or 6 mark as required (see Fig. 1.24).
6 If the engine is fitted with a timing pointer on the front cover, align the notch on the pulley with the required octane tongue as shown in Fig. 1.25.
7 Position the distributor drive gear bush so

that the small hole is facing towards the oil filter mounting face at the point where the grubscrew is located (Fig. 1.12).
8 Insert the drive gear into the block (photo) and turn the gear so that when it is fully engaged with the camshaft gear, the largest (master) spline is facing towards the No. 1 cylinder as shown in Fig. 1.26.
9 When the drive gear is correctly positioned, insert the grubscrew into the threaded hole in the oil filter mounting face (photo).
10 Insert the distributor drive coupling so that when it is fully seated in the drive gear the narrow segment faces towards the right-hand side of the engine and the slot towards the No. 1 cylinder (see Fig. 1.27).
11 If the engine has been removed from the vehicle, do not refit the distributor until just prior to refitting the engine in the vehicle. This

33.8 Inserting the distributor/oil pump drivegear

33.9 Refitting the distributor drivegear securing screw

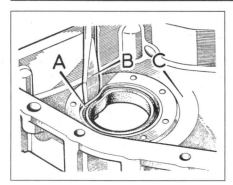

Fig. 1.23. Removing the timing cover oil seal

A Seal B Screwdriver C Inner side of cover

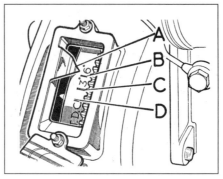

Fig. 1.24. Timing marks on flywheel (earlier engines)

A Timing pointer
B 6° mark, align when using 90-96 octane fuel
C 3° mark, align when using 80-85 octane fuel
D TDC mark, align when using 74-76 octane fuel

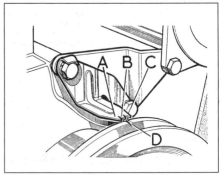

Fig. 1.25. Timing pointer on front cover

A 6° tongue, align when using 90-46 octane fuel
B 3° tongue, align when using 80-85 octane fuel
C TDC tongue, align when using 74-76 octane fuel
D Mark on crankshaft pulley, align with appropriate tongue

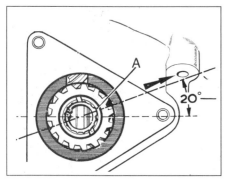

Fig. 1.26. Correct position of distributor driveshaft

A Master spline

will avoid the possibility of damaging it whilst refitting the cylinder head etc.

12 For information on refitting and adjusting the distributor refer to Chapter 4.

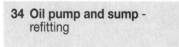

34 Oil pump and sump - refitting

1 Fit the oil pump driveshaft into the pump housing, making sure that the shaft spline engages fully with the pump gear.
2 Carefully insert the driveshaft and pump into its location in the crankcase ensuring that

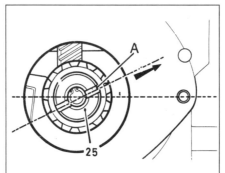

Fig. 1.27. Correct position of distributor drive coupling

A Coupling slot

the top splines on the shaft engage fully with the drive gear (photo).
3 Refit the securing bolts, tighten them and bend over the locking tabs (photo).
4 Clean the mating surfaces of the sump and the crankcase and stick the gasket in position on the sump using a light smear of grease.
5 Fit the sump to the crankcase and tighten the bolts in a diagonal sequence. Be careful not to overtighten them (photo).

35 Cylinder head - reassembly and refitting

1 Lay the cylinder head on its side, lubricate the valve stems and insert them into the guides they were removed from (photo).
2 Fit the oil seals over the valve stems ensuring the lip fits into the groove in the valve guide. **Note:** On earlier engines the oil seals fit in a groove inside the valve guides, and these must be fitted prior to inserting the valves.
3 Fit the valve spring, the retaining cap and then compress the valve spring and locate the split collets in the cut-out of the valve stem. Release the compressor. Repeat these operations on the remaining seven valves (photos).
4 When all the valves have been installed, place the cylinder head flat on the bench and using a hammer and a block of wood as an insulator, tap the end of each valve stem to settle the components.
5 Make sure that the faces of the cylinder head and the cylinder block are perfectly clean and then lay a new gasket on the cylinder block so that the word 'Front' or 'petrol' is visible from above and correctly located. Do not use any kind of jointing compound (photos).

34.2 Installing the oil pump and driveshaft

34.3 Securing the oil pump bolts with the lockwashers

34.5 Replacing the engine sump

35.1 Insert a valve into the cylinder head

35.3a Fit the valve spring ...

35.3b ... followed by the retaining cap

35.3c Compress the spring and fit the collets

35.5a Refit the head gasket with the word 'PETROL' uppermost

35.5b Correct installation of head gasket

35.6a Lowering the cylinder head into position on the block

35.6b Tightening the cylinder head bolts

35.7 Inserting a pushrod

6 Lower the cylinder head into position, insert the cylinder head bolts and tighten them to the specified torque and in the sequence shown in Fig. 1.5 (photo).

7 Insert each pushrod into the hole from which it was originally removed. Make sure that the pushrod end seats correctly on the tappet slide (photo).

8 With the rocker shaft assembly held together by means of the inverted rocker cover as described in Section 8, lower it into place making sure the spigots are correctly located in the cylinder head.

9 Make sure that rocker arms are correctly seated on the pushrods and then tighten the securing bolts evenly to the torque wrench setting given in the Specifications.

36 Valve - adjustment

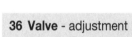

1 The valve adjustments should be made with the engine hot. The importance of correct rocker arm/valve stem clearances cannot be overstressed as they vitally affect the performance of the engine. if the clearances are set too wide, the efficiency of the engine is reduced as the valves open late and close earlier than was intended. If, on the other hand the clearances are set too close there is a danger that the stems will expand upon heating and not allow the valves to close properly which will cause burning of the valve head and seat and possible warping. If the

36.1 Removing the rocker cover

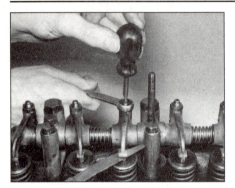

36.3 Setting the valve clearances

37.3 Refitting the oil filter

37.5 Tightening the flywheel securing bolts

engine is in the vehicle, access to the rockers is by removing the four holding down screws from the rocker cover, and then lifting the rocker cover and gasket away (photo).

2 It is important that the clearance is set when the tappet of the valve being adjusted is on the heel of the cam (ie opposite the peak). This can be ensured by carrying out the adjustments in the following order (which also avoids turning the crankshaft more than necessary):

Valves fully open	Check and adjust
Valve No. 8	*Valve No. 1*
Valve No. 6	*Valve No. 3*
Valve No. 4	*Valve No. 5*
Valve No. 7	*Valve No. 2*
Valve No. 1	*Valve No. 8*
Valve No. 3	*Valve No. 6*
Valve No. 5	*Valve No. 4*
Valve No. 2	*Valve No. 7*

The correct feeler gauge clearance between valve stem and rocker arm pad with the engine hot is 0.010 in (0.25 mm).
3 Working from the front of the engine (No. 1 valve) the correct clearance is obtained by slackening the hexagon locknut with a spanner while holding the ball pin against rotation with a screwdriver. Then pressing down with the screwdriver, insert a feeler gauge in the gap between the valve stem head and the rocker arm and adjust the ball pin until the feeler gauge will just move in and out without nipping (photo). Then still holding the ball pin in the correct position tighten the locknut.
4 When reassembling the cylinder head after a major overhaul or de-coke, the valve clearances should be set to 0.010 in (0.25 mm) with the engine cold and then re-checked after the engine has been started and warmed up to reach its normal operating temperature.

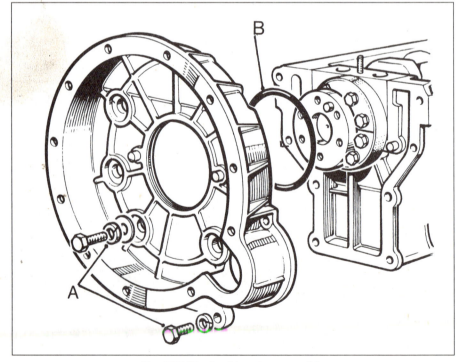

Fig. 1.28. Flywheel housing assembly

A Retaining bolts   *B Seal*

37 Ancillary components - refitting

1 This is a reversal of the removal sequence given in Section 7 of this Chapter.
2 Full details of component installation are given in the relevant Chapters of this manual but the following points should be noted.
3 Always install a new oil filter sealing ring in the cylinder block groove. Tighten the centre-bolt only to specified torque (photo).
4 When refitting the flywheel housing, the O-ring type oil seal located in a groove around the inner aperture of the housing should be renewed (see Fig. 1.28).
5 Tighten the flywheel bolts to the specified torque and bend the locking tabs over (photo).
6 Adjust the fanbelt tension as described in Chapter 2.

38 Engine - refitting

Basically the installation of the engine is the reverse procedure to the removal operation, however, mating the engine to the gearbox can be difficult unless the following method is used.
1 Make sure the clutch is centralised on the flywheel as described in Chapter 5.
2 Carefully lower the engine into the engine compartment using a suitable hoist until the flywheel housing is straight and level with the clutch housing.
3 Push the engine rearwards ensuring the gearbox input shaft enters the clutch assembly in a straight line and not at an angle.
4 If the engine begins to mate up and then stops with a couple of inches still to go, fit a spanner onto the crankshaft starter dog and turn it slowly while pushing the engine rearwards.
5 As soon as the flywheel and clutch housings touch, insert a bolt finger-tight to hold them together and then refit all the bolts and tighten them in a diagonal sequence to the specified torque.

6 Refit the engine mountings using the reverse procedure to that described in Section 5.

7 Finally, lower the hoist completely and remove the engine slings and the jack or blocks from beneath the transmission. Reconnect all the carburettor controls electrical leads fuel pipes exhaust pipe etc. checking each item against the sequence given in Section 5.

8 Do not forget to refill the cooling system and refill the engine with the recommended grade and quantity of oil.

39 Engine - adjustment after major overhaul

1 With the engine refitted to the vehicle give a final visual check to see that everything has been reconnected and that no loose rags or tools have been left within the engine compartment.

2 Turn the engine slow running screw in about 1/2 turn (to increase slow running once the engine is started) (Chapter 3). This faster slow-running will be needed due to the tightness of the new engine components.

3 Pull the choke fully out and start the engine. This may take a little longer than usual as the fuel pump and carburettor bowl will be empty and need initial priming.

4 As soon as the engine starts, push the choke in until the engine runs at a fast tickover and examine the engine for leaks. Check particularly the water hoses oil filter and fuel hose unions.

5 Allow the engine to idle until the normal operating temperature is reached.

6 Switch off the engine remove the rocker cover and re-check the valve Clearances as described in Section 36.

7 Refit the rocker cover and check the engine oil level approximately 1/2 pint (0.3 litre) will be required to fill the filter casing. Check the radiator water level and top-up if necessary. **Note:** Cover the cap with a cloth to avoid being scalded.

8 Re-start the engine and adjust the throttle stop screw to the required idling speed.

9 Where new internal components have been installed, the engine speed should be restricted for the first 500 miles (800 km) and at this mileage the engine oil should be renewed, the cylinder head bolts checked for correct torque (unscrew each bolt one 1/4 turn and then tighten to specified torque and in recommended sequence). Finally check and adjust the valve clearances.

Fault diagnosis - engine

Engine fails to start

- [ ] Discharged battery.
- [ ] Loose battery connection.
- [ ] Disconnected or broken ignition leads.
- [ ] Moisture on spark plugs, distributor or leads.
- [ ] Incorrect contact points gap, cracked distributor cap or rotor.
- [ ] Incorrect spark plug gap.
- [ ] Dirt or water in carburettor jets.
- [ ] Empty fuel tank.
- [ ] Faulty fuel pump.
- [ ] Faulty starter motor.
- [ ] Faulty carburettor choke mechanism.

Engine 'misses' at idling speed

- [ ] Incorrect spark plug gap.
- [ ] Uneven compression between cylinders.
- [ ] Faulty coil or condenser.
- [ ] Faulty contact points.
- [ ] Poor connections or condition of ignition leads.
- [ ] Dirt in carburettor jets.
- [ ] Incorrectly adjusted carburettor.
- [ ] Worn distributor cam.
- [ ] Air leak at carburettor flange gasket.
- [ ] Faulty ignition advance mechanism.
- [ ] Sticking valves.
- [ ] Incorrect valve clearance.
- [ ] Low cylinder compression.

Engine 'misses' throughout speed range

- [ ] Dirt or water in carburettor or fuel lines.
- [ ] Incorrect ignition timing.
- [ ] Contact points incorrectly gapped.
- [ ] Worn distributor.
- [ ] Faulty coil or condenser.
- [ ] Spark plug gaps incorrect.
- [ ] Weak valve spring.
- [ ] Overheating.

Engine idles erratically

- [ ] Air leak at intake manifold.
- [ ] Leaking cylinder head gasket.
- [ ] Worn timing sprockets
- [ ] Worn camshaft lobes.
- [ ] Overheating.
- [ ] Faulty fuel pump.

Engine stalls

- [ ] Incorrectly adjusted carburettor.
- [ ] Dirt or water in fuel.
- [ ] Ignition system incorrectly adjusted.
- [ ] Sticking choke mechanism.
- [ ] Faulty spark plugs or incorrectly gapped.
- [ ] Faulty coil or condenser.
- [ ] Incorrect contact points gap.
- [ ] Exhaust system clogged.
- [ ] Distributor advance inoperative.
- [ ] Air leak at intake manifold.
- [ ] Air leak at carburettor mounting flange.
- [ ] Incorrect valve clearance.
- [ ] Sticking valve.
- [ ] Overheating.
- [ ] Low compression.
- [ ] Poor electrical connections on ignition system.

Engine lacks power

- [ ] Incorrect ignition timing.
- [ ] Faulty coil or condenser.
- [ ] Worn distributor.
- [ ] Dirt in carburettor.
- [ ] Spark plugs incorrectly gapped.
- [ ] Incorrectly adjusted carburettor.
- [ ] Faulty fuel pump.
- [ ] Weak valve springs.
- [ ] Sticking valve.
- [ ] Incorrect valve timing.
- [ ] Incorrect valve adjustment.
- [ ] Blown cylinder head gasket.
- [ ] Low compression.
- [ ] Brakes dragging.
- [ ] Clutch slipping.
- [ ] Overheating.

Notes

Chapter 1B
Diesel engine

For modifications, and information applicable to later models, see Supplement at end of manual

Contents

Degrees of difficulty

Easy, suitable for novice with little experience	**Fairly easy,** suitable for beginner with some experience	**Fairly difficult,** suitable for competent DIY mechanic	**Difficult,** suitable for experienced DIY mechanic	**Very difficult,** suitable for expert DIY or professional

Specifications

Engine, general
Capacity (piston displacement)	2286 cc (139.5 cu in)
Number of cylinders	4
Bore	3.562 in (90.49 mm)
Stroke	3.5 in (88.9 mm)
Compression ratio	23 : 1
BHP at 4000 rpm	62
Maximum torque	103 lbf ft (139 Nm) at 1,750 rpm
Firing order	1 - 3 - 4 - 2

Camshaft
Journal diameter	1.842 in - 0.001 (46.70 mm - 0.025)
Clearance in bearing	0.001 to 0.002 in (0.02 to 0.05 mm)
Endfloat	0.0025 to 0.0055 in (0.06 to 0.14 mm)
Cam lift - inlet	0.262 in (6.65 mm)
Cam lift - exhaust	0.279 in (7.10 mm)

Camshaft bearings
Type	Split, steel backed, white metal lined
Internal diameter (line-reamed in position)	1.843 in + 0.0005 (46.8 mm + 0.012)

Connecting rods

Bearing fit on crankpin	0.001 to 0.0025 in (0.025 to 0.063 mm)
Bearing nip	0.002 to 0.004 in (0.05 to 0.10 mm)
Endfloat at big-end	0.007 to 0.011 in (0.20 to 0.30 mm)
Gudgeon pin bush, fit in small end	0.002 to 0.004 in (0.05 to 0.1 mm) interference
Gudgeon pin bush internal diameter - reamed in position	1.1875 + 0.0005 in (30.15 + 0.012 mm)
Fit of gudgeon pin in bush	0.0002 to 0.0008 in (0.005 to 0.02 mm) clearance

Crankshaft

Journal diameter	2.5 in - 0.001 in (63.5 mm - 0.02 mm)
Crankpin diameter	2.312 to 2.31275 in (58.725 to 58.744 mm)
Endfloat (controlled by thrust washers at centre bearing)	0.002 to 0.006 in (0.05 to 0.15 mm)

Flywheel

Number of teeth	100
Thickness	1.484 in (38 mm)
Maximum run-out	0.002 in (0.05 mm)
Maximum refacing depth	0.030 in (0.76 mm)

Gudgeon pin

Fit in piston	Zero to 0.0002 in (0.005 mm) interference
Fit in connecting rod bush	0.0002 to 0.0008 in (0.005 to 0.02 mm) clearance

Main bearings

Clearance on crankshaft journal	0.001 to 0.002 in (0.02 to 0.05 mm)
Bearing nip	0.004 to 0.006 in (0.10 to 0.15 mm)

Pistons

Type	Light alloy with swirl-inducing recess in crown
Clearance in bore measured at bottom of skirt at right angles to gudgeon pin	0.004 to 0.005 in (0.10 to 0.12 mm)
Fit of gudgeon pin in piston	Zero to 0.0002 in (0.005 mm) interference
Gudgeon pin bore	1.187 + 0.0005 in (30.14 + 0.012 mm)

Piston rings

No. 1 compression:

Type	Square friction edge-chromium plated
Gap in bore	0.014 to 0.019 in (0.40 to 0.50 mm)
Clearance in groove	0.0025 to 0.0045 in (0.06 to 0.11 mm)

Nos 2 and 3 compression:

Type	Bevelled friction edge marked 'T' on upper side
Gap in bore	0.010 to 0.015 in (0.25 to 0.40 mm)
Clearance in groove	0.0025 to 0.0045 in (0.06 to 0.11 mm)

No 4 scraper:

Early type, one piece	Slotted, square friction edge, double landed
Gap in bore	0.010 to 0.015 in (0.25 to 0.40 mm)
Clearance in groove	0.0025 to 0.0045 in (0.06 to 0.11 mm)
Later type, three piece	Expander and rails
Gap in bore	0.015 to 0.045 in (0.38 to 0.14 mm)
Clearance in groove	0.0015 to 0.0025 in (0.038 to 0.064 mm)

Rocker gear

Bush internal diameter	0.530 + 0.001 in (13.4 + 0.02 mm)
Shaft clearance in rocker bush	0.0005 to 0.0025 in (0.0127 to 0.062 mm)
Valve clearance	0.010 in (0.25 mm) hot or cold

Timing chain tensioner

Fit of bush in cylinder	0.003 to 0.005 in (0.07 to 0.12 mm) interference
Fit of bush in idler wheel	0.001 to 0.003 in (0.02 to 0.07 mm) interference
Fit of idler wheel on stub shaft	0.001 to 0.003 in (0.02 to 0.07 mm) clearance
Fit of piston in cylinder bush	0.0003 to 0.0013 in (0.008 to 0.033 mm) clearance

Thrust bearings, crankshaft

Type	Semi-circular, steel back, tin plated on friction surface
Standard size, total thickness	0.093 in - 0.002 (2.362 mm - 0.05)
Oversizes	0.0025 in (0.06 mm); 0.005 in (0.12 mm); 0.0075 in (0.18 mm); 0.010 in (0.25 mm)

Valves

Inlet valve:
   Diameter (stem) .... 0.3112 in - 0.0005 (7.9 mm - 0.013 mm)
   Face angle .... 45° - 1/4
Exhaust valve:
   Diameter (stem) .... 0.3415 - 0.0005 in (8.67 mm - 0.013)
   Face angle .... 45° - 1/4
Fit of inlet valves in guide .... 0.001 to 0.003 in (0.02 to 0.07 mm)
Fit of exhaust valves in guide .... 0.0023 to 0.0038 in (0.058 to 0.096 mm)

Valve seat

Seat angle - inlet and exhaust .... 45° - 1/4

Valve springs

Early type:
   Inner:
      Length-free .... 1.61 in (40.89 mm)
      Length under 12 lb (5.44 Kgs) load .... 1.45 in (36.9 mm)
   Outer:
      Length - free .... 1.76 in (44.9 mm)
      Length under 33 lb (15 Kgs) load .... 1.57 in (40.1 mm)
Later type:
   Inner:
      Length - free .... 1.680 in (42.67 m)
      Length under 17.7 lb (8.0 kg) load (Series II and IIA) .... 1.466 in (37.23 mm)
                                      (Series III) .... 1.587 in (40.30 mm)
   Outer:
      Length - free .... 1.822 in (46.28 mm)
      Length under 46 lb (21 kg) load .... 1.587in (40.3 mm)

Valve timing

Inlet opens .... 16° BTDC
Inlet closes .... 42° ABDC
Inlet peak .... 103° ATDC
Exhaust opens .... 51° BBDC
Exhaust closes .... 13° ATDC
Exhaust peak .... 109° BTDC

Vertical driveshaft gear

Backlash .... 0.006 to 0.010 in (0.15 to 0.25 mm)
Internal diameter of bush .... 1.00 + 0.001 in (25.4 + 0.02 mm)
Fit of gear in bush .... 0.001 to 0.003 in (0.02 to 0.07 mm) clearance

Oil pump

Type .... Skew gear
Drive .... Splined shaft from camshaft drive gear
Endfloat of gears:
   Steel gear .... 0.002 to 0.005 in (0.05 to 0.13 mm)
   Aluminium gear .... 0.003 to 0.006 in (0.07 to 0.15 mm)
Radial gear clearance .... 0.001 to 0.004 in (0.02 to 0.010 mm)
Backlash of gears .... 0.006 to 0.012 in (0.15 to 0.30 mm)
Oil pressure
   At 2000 rpm, engine warm .... 45 to 65 lbf/in² (3.16 to 4.56 kgf/cm²)
Oil pressure relief valve:
   Type .... Non-adjustable
   Spring free length .... 2.670 in (67.82 mm)
   Compressed length at 5.7 lb (2.6 kg) load .... 2.45 in (61.23 mm)

Torque wrench settings

	lbf ft	kgf m
Big-end cap nuts	25	3.5
Main bearing cap bolts	100	14
Cylinder head bolts:		
5/16 in UNF	18	2.4
1/2 in UNF	90	12.5
Rocker shaft bolts:		
5/16 in UNF	18	2.4
1/2 in UNF	90	12.5
Crankshaft pulley	200	28
Flywheel bolts	60 to 65	8.5 to 9
Camshaft sprocket bolt	30	415

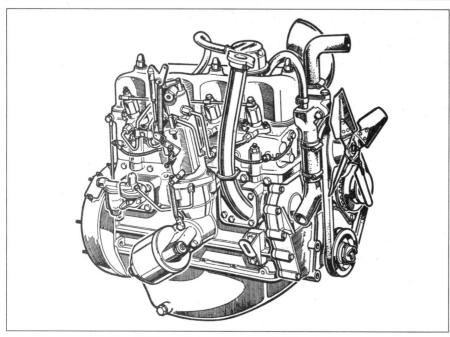

Fig. 1.1 General view of engine, right-hand side

1 General description

The Land Rover Diesel engine covered by this manual is of 4 cylinder in-line configuration utilizing pushrod operated overhead valves and having a displacement of 2286 cc (139.5 cu in).

The cylinder block is of cast iron and may be rebored to 0.040 in (1.0 mm) oversize. Further cylinder block reclamation is possible by fitting cylinder liners.

The crankshaft is supported by three renewable shell type bearings, and crankshaft endfloat is controlled by thrust washers fitted to the centre main bearing.

The camshaft is chain driven from the crankshaft and runs in four white metal lined steel bearing shells. Timing chain tension is controlled by an idler sprocket tensioner operated by the engine oil pressure. The camshaft lobes act directly on roller type

cam followers which operate the valve via a pushrod and rocker arm.

Engine lubrication is by a pressure fed oil system incorporating a camshaft driven oil pump and full flow oil filter.

2 Major operations possible with the engine in the vehicle

1 The following components can be removed from the engine for inspection or overhaul without having to lift the engine out of the vehicle.
(a) Cylinder head
(b) Oil sump
(c) Oil pump (after removing sump)
(d) Timing cover and oil seal
(e) Timing sprockets tensioner and chain
(f) Pistons and connecting rods (through top of cylinder bores after removing sump and cylinder head)
(g) Camshaft and followers

5.7 Location of starter solenoid electrical connections

5.8 Location of alternator electrical plug

(h) Flywheel housing and flywheel (after removing transmission)
(i) Crankshaft rear oil seal (after removing flywheel flywheel housing and sump)

3 Major operations only possible after removal of the engine from the vehicle

1 The Land Rover engine is very accessible; however, removal of the crankshaft, replacing the camshaft bearings, or reboring the cylinder block requires the removal of the engine from the vehicle.

4 Method of engine removal

1 Before the engine can be removed it is necessary to detach it from the clutch housing. It is not possible to remove the engine complete with transmission.

5 Engine - removal

The sequence of operations listed in this Section is not critical as the position of the person undertaking the work or the tool in his hand will determine to a certain extent the order in which the work is tackled. Obviously the engine cannot be removed until everything is disconnected from it and the following sequence will ensure that nothing is forgotten.
1 Remove the bonnet as described in Chapter 12.
2 Disconnect the battery leads, remove the battery clamp and lift out the battery.
3 Remove the air cleaner as described in Chapter 3.
4 Referring to Chapter 2, drain the cooling system and remove the grille panel and radiator.
5 Remove the front floor and gearbox tunnel cover as described in Chapter 12.
6 Undo and remove the four nuts and washers securing the exhaust pipe flange to the manifold and ease the pipe off the four studs.
7 Make a note of their positions and disconnect the electrical connections to the starter motor solenoid (photo) and the starter motor earth strap to the chassis if fitted.
8 Disconnect the two electrical connections on the rear of the dynamo, or the plug-in connector on the alternator (photo).
9 If the heater is fitted slacken the hose clips and remove the heater hoses from the rear of the engine.
10 Disconnect the electrical connection to the heater plugs from the terminal plate on the bulkhead (photo).
11 Undo and remove the two unions securing the fuel pipe from the filter and the spill return pipe to No. 4 injector.

12 Undo and remove the fuel pipes and unions on the top of the injection/distributor pump and on the side of the mechanical lift pump. Certain models are fitted with an additional filter or sedimentor, disconnect any additional fuel pipes connecting these units to the lift pumps or injection/ distributor pump as necessary.

13 Disconnect the oil pressure switch lead from the oil filter and the temperature gauge lead from the transmitter.

14 Prise open the retaining clip and remove the throttle linkage from the injection/distributor pump (photo).

15 Slacken the securing screws and withdraw the engine stop cable from its location on the injection/distributor pump.

16 If a brake servo is fitted, disconnect the butterfly control rod and remove the vacuum hose from the inlet manifold.

17 Using a suitable hoist, attach lifting slings or chains to the engine and raise the hoist until the weight of the engine is just being supported.

18 Undo and remove the upper securing nuts from both engine mounting rubbers.

19 Undo and remove the lower securing nut from the left-hand engine mounting rubber, and the two bolts securing the right-hand engine mounting bracket to the chassis.

20 Raise the hoist to give a sufficient clearance for both engine mountings to be removed, and then lower the engine to its original position.

21 Undo and remove the nuts and bolts securing the clutch housing to the flywheel housing noting the position of any brackets and cable clips that may be fitted. Move the clutch slave cylinder to one side.

22 Place a jack or block of wood beneath the front of the gearbox to support it when the engine is lifted clear.

23 Check carefully that all cables, pipes, and wires have been detached and removed from retaining clips, where fitted.

24 Pull the engine forward on the hoist sufficiently to disengage the gearbox input shaft from the engine and clutch assembly, then slowly lift the engine out of the vehicle (photo).

6 Engine dismantling - general

1 It is best to mount the engine on a dismantling stand but if one is not available, then stand the engine on a strong bench so it is at a comfortable working height. Failing this, the engine can be stripped down on the floor.

2 During the dismantling process the greatest care should be taken to keep the exposed parts free from dirt. As an aid to achieving this, it is sound advice to thoroughly clean down the outside of the engine, removing all traces of oil and congealed dirt.

3 Use paraffin or a good grease solvent. The latter will make the job much easier, after the solvent has been applied and allowed to stand

5.10 Electrical connections on heater plug terminal plate

for a time, a vigorous jet of water will wash off the solvent and all the grease and filth. If the dirt is thick and deeply embedded, work the solvent into it with a wire brush.

4 Finally wipe down the exterior of the engine with a rag and only then, when it is quite clean should the dismantling process begin. As the engine is stripped, clean each part in a bath of paraffin or petrol.

5 Never immerse parts with oilways in paraffin, ie: the crankshaft, but to clean, wipe down carefully with a petrol dampened rag.

 Oilways can be cleaned out with wire. If an air line is present all parts can be blown dry and the oilways blown through as an added precaution.

6 Re-use of old engine gaskets is false economy and can give rise to oil and water leaks, if nothing worse. To avoid the possibility of trouble after the engine has been reassembled always use new gaskets throughout.

7 Do not throw away old gaskets away as it sometimes happens that an immediate replacement cannot be found and the old gasket is then very useful as a template. Hang up the old gaskets as they are removed on a suitable hook or nail.

8 To strip the engine it is best to work from the top down. The sump provides a firm base on which the engine can be supported in an upright position. When the stage is reached

5.24 Removing the engine from the vehicle

5.14 Removing the throttle linkage from the fuel injection/distributor pump

where the sump must be removed, the engine can be turned on its side and all other work carried out with it in this position.

9 Wherever possible, refit nuts, bolts and washers fingertight from wherever they were removed. This helps avoid later loss and muddle. If they cannot be replaced then lay them out in such a fashion that it is clear from where they came.

7 Ancillary components - removal

1 With the engine removed from the vehicle and thoroughly cleaned, the externally mounted ancillary components should now be removed before dismantling begins.

2 The following is a suggested sequence of removal, detailed descriptions are to be found in the relevant Chapters of this manual.

Dynamo or alternator (Chapter 10)
Clutch assembly (Chapter 5)
Starter motor (Chapter 10)
Fuel pump (Chapter 3)
Fuel injection/distributor pump (Chapter 3)
Fuel injectors (Chapter 3)
Fan water pump and thermostat (Chapter 2)
Heater plugs (Chapter 10)

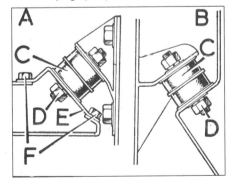

Fig. 1.2 Front engine mounting details

A Right-hand side mounting
B Left-hand side mounting
C Rubber mountings
D Lower securing nut
E Mounting bracket
F Securing bolts

8.10 Remove the oil gallery banjo union from the rear of the cylinder head

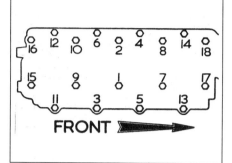

Fig. 1.3 Tightening sequence for cylinder head bolts

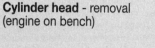
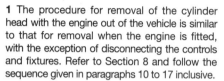

9 Cylinder head - removal (engine on bench)

1 The procedure for removal of the cylinder head with the engine out of the vehicle is similar to that for removal when the engine is fitted, with the exception of disconnecting the controls and fixtures. Refer to Section 8 and follow the sequence given in paragraphs 10 to 17 inclusive.

10 Cylinder head - dismantling

1 Undo and remove the nuts and bolts securing the inlet and exhaust manifolds to the cylinder head and lift off the two manifolds complete with gasket (photo).
2 The valves can be removed from the cylinder head by the following method. Compress each spring in turn with a valve spring compressor until the two halves of the collets can be removed. Release the compressor and remove the springs and spring retainer (photo).
3 If, when the valve spring compressor is screwed down, the valve spring retaining cap refuses to free, to expose the split collet, do not continue to screw down on the compressor as there is a likelihood of damaging it.
4 Gently tap the top of the tool directly over the cap with a soft-faced mallet. This will free the cap. To avoid the compressor jumping off the valve spring retaining cap when it is tapped, hold the compressor firmly in position with one hand.
5 Slide the rubber oil control seal off the top of each valve guide and valve and then drop out each valve through the combustion chamber.
6 It is essential that the valves are kept in their correct sequence unless they are so badly worn that they are to be renewed. Numbering from the front of the engine, exhaust valves are 1-4-5-8 and inlet valves 2-3-6-7.

8 Cylinder head - removal (engine in vehicle)

1 Remove the bonnet as described in Chapter 12.
2 Remove the air cleaner as described in Chapter 3.
3 Disconnect the battery earth terminal.
4 Withdraw the engine breather hose from its attachment on the breather cap. If a brake servo unit is fitted, disconnect the vacuum pipe and control rod.
5 Undo and remove the three dome nuts securing the rocker cover and carefully lift off the cover. Recover the rocker cover gasket.
6 Drain the cooling system as described in Chapter 2.
7 Disconnect the electrical leads to No. 4 heater plug, and the water temperature transmitter (where fitted).
8 Undo and remove the four nuts securing the exhaust pipe flange to the manifold and lift off the pipe clear of the studs.
9 If a heater is fitted slacken the hose clips and remove the hoses from the rear of the engine.
10 Undo and remove the bolt securing the oil gallery banjo union to the rear of the cylinder head (photo). Recover the two copper washers.
11 Remove the fuel injectors as described in Chapter 3.
12 Slacken the hose clips and remove the radiator top hose and the bypass hose.

13 Undo and remove the large and small bolts securing the rocker shaft and rockers to the cylinder head. Turn the rocker cover upside down and place it in position over the three long studs. Secure the cover with the domed nuts. This operation is necessary to stop the rocker assembly springing apart when it is lifted off the cylinder head. With the rocker assembly secured to the inverted rocker cover, the complete assembly may be carefully removed.
14 Lift out the pushrods and keep them in the correct order to ensure that each pushrod is refitted in its original position. Punch eight holes in a piece of cardboard, number them one to eight and place the pushrods in order through the card.
15 Undo all the cylinder head retaining bolts half a turn in the reverse order to that shown in Fig. 1.3, then remove them from the cylinder head.
16 With all the bolts removed lift the cylinder head from the block. If the head is stuck, try to rock it to break the seal. Under no circumstances try to prise it apart from the cylinder block using a screwdriver or cold chisel, as damage may be caused to the mating faces of the cylinder head and block. If it is extremely stubborn strike the head sharply with a soft faced mallet or with a metal hammer with an interposed block of wood to cushion the blow. Under no circumstances hit the head directly with a metal hammer as this may cause the casting to fracture.
17 Remove the cylinder head gasket.

11 Sump - removal

1 The sump can be removed quite easily with the engine still in the vehicle.
2 First drain the engine oil into a suitable container.
3 The Land Rover has considerable ground clearance, and it is possible to remove the sump without raising the vehicle. However, if it is decided to jack the vehicle up, ensure that it is securely supported on heavy duty axle-stands before working beneath it.
4 Unscrew and remove all the sump bolts, releasing them only one half turn at a time in a diagonal sequence to avoid distortion.
5 If the sump is stuck tight, run a blunt knife round the gasket to release it. Remove the gasket.

10.1 Remove the inlet and exhaust manifolds

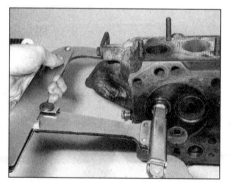

10.2 Using a valve spring compressor to release the valve spring collets and springs

12 Oil pump and oil filter - removal

1 If the oil pump is to be removed with the engine still in the vehicle, first remove the sump as described in the previous Section.

2 Remove the two securing bolts and withdraw the pump complete with drive shaft.

3 The oil filter is simply removed by unscrewing the centre bolt. As the oil filter body is withdrawn, a loss of oil trapped within it will occur so have a suitable container at the ready to drop the oil into.

4 Discard the internal filter element. The new element will be supplied complete with new sealing rings.

5 To remove the oil filter housing, first detach the oil pressure switch lead and then remove the two retaining bolts and prise the housing away from the cylinder block (photo).

6 When refitting the housing, a new gasket must be used.

13 Timing cover, gears and chain - removal

If the timing cover gears and chain are being removed with the engine in the vehicle then the following operations must first be carried out:
Drain the cooling system
Remove the radiator and fanbelt
Remove the water pump pulley and fan
Remove the dynamo/alternator adjusting arm
Separate the by-pass hose from the thermostat housing

1 Unscrew and remove the crankshaft starter dog. If the sump has been removed, place a block of wood between a crankshaft web and the internal wall of the crankcase to prevent the crankshaft rotating as the bolt is unscrewed. If the engine is in the car or the sump has not yet been removed, withdraw the starter motor and jam the flywheel starter ring gear with a large screwdriver or cold chisel. The crankshaft starter dog can then be unscrewed.

2 Withdraw the crankshaft pulley. If this is tight, use two levers placed behind the pulley at opposite points to extract it.

3 Unscrew and remove all the nuts and bolts securing the timing cover and water pump to the cylinder block, including the front sump bolts and lift off the cover and pump assembly (photo). Remove the gaskets.

4 Before the chain or tensioner is removed, the following method should be used to ensure correct engine timing during reassembly.

5 Remove the inspection plate from the flywheel housing and rotate the engine until the 'EP' mark on the flywheel is in line with the pointer (photo).

6 Using a scriber and steel rule, scratch an alignment mark on the camshaft and camshaft sprocket (photo) and a matching mark on the cylinder block adjacent to the sprocket.

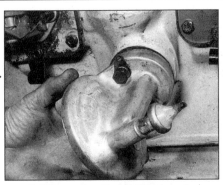
12.5 Removing the oil filter housing

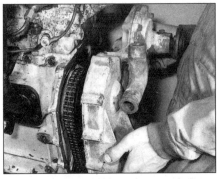
13.3 Withdraw the timing cover and water pump as a complete assembly

13.5 'EP' timing mark approaching pointer

13.6 Timing gears and chain showing alignment marks scribed across sprocket

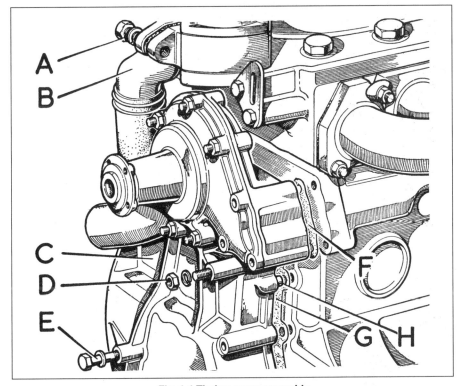

Fig. 1.4 Timing cover assembly

A Securing bolts
B By-pass pipe
C Timing cover
D Dynamo arm fixing nut
E Securing bolt
F Gasket
G Gasket
H Dowel

14.2 Lifting out the fuel injection/distributor pump drive gear

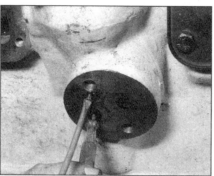

14.3a Remove the grub screw . . .

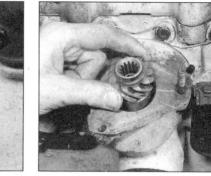

14.3b . . . and lift out the vertical drive gear

7 As an added precaution make a similar mark on the crankshaft sprocket and cylinder block.

8 Undo and remove the securing bolt and withdraw the tensioner ratchet and spring.

9 Unscrew the retaining nut and bolts, compress the tensioner by hand and lift off the complete assembly. Unbolt the vibration damper pad and remove the timing chain.

10 Bend back the lockwasher and undo and remove the camshaft sprocket securing bolt.

11 Using two flat levers or screwdriver gently ease off the camshaft and crankshaft sprockets.

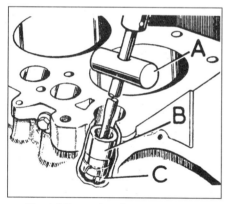

Fig. 1.5 Removing the tappet guides

A Slide hammer   B Tappet guide
C Adaptor for slide hammer

14 Camshaft and tappets - removal

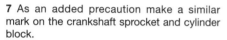

1 It is possible to remove the camshaft with the engine still in the vehicle, but first the fuel injection/distributor pump must be removed as described in Chapter 3, followed by the cylinder head, timing cover and chain as described in the previous Sections. The fuel lift pump must also be removed.

2 If the camshaft is being removed with the engine in the vehicle, lift out the fuel injection/distributor pump drive shaft from the centre of the vertical drive gear if not previously removed with the pump (photo).

3 Unscrew the small grubscrew from the oil filter housing face and lift out the fuel injection/distributor pump vertical drive gear using a pair of thin nosed pliers (photos).

4 Using a piece of wire bent into a hook lift out the light tappet slides and rollers and keep them in the correct order of removal.

5 Remove the camshaft drive chain and sprocket as described previously, and undo and remove the two bolts securing the camshaft thrust plate.

6 Lift off the thrust plate and carefully withdraw the camshaft from the front of the engine (photo). Take care not to damage the camshaft bearings as the camshaft passes through them. Note the tappet guides may be removed if required by removing the locking

wire and retaining bolts from the side of the cylinder block (photo) and then pulling out the guides using a small slide hammer, if they prove difficult to remove by hand.

15 Pistons and connecting rods - removal

1 The pistons and connecting rods can be removed with the engine still in the vehicle or with the engine on the bench.

2 With the cylinder head and sump removed undo the big-end cap retaining nuts.

3 The connecting rods and pistons are lifted out from the top of the cylinder block.

4 Remove the big-end caps one at a time, taking care to keep them in the right order and the correct way round.

> **HAYNES HINT** *Also ensure that the shell bearings are kept with their correct connecting rods and caps unless they are to be renewed.*

5 It is a good idea to mark the side face of each rod and cap with identification marks using a centre punch and light hammer, unless the caps are already marked (photo). Use a single dot for No. 1 connecting rod, two dots for No. 2 and so on. This will ensure there is no mix-up on reassembly, as it is very important

14.6a Removing the camshaft

14.6b Remove the retaining bolts . . .

14.6c . . . and lift out the tappet guides

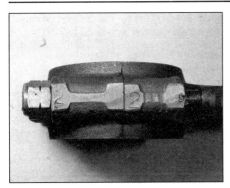

15.5 Identification marks on connecting rod and bearing cap

16.2 Remove the bolts and lift off the flywheel

thrust washers, one half lying on either side of the main bearing. Lay them with the centre bearing along the correct side.

6 Slightly rotate the crankshaft to free the upper halves of the bearing shells and thrust washers which can be lifted away and placed over the correct bearing cap when the crankshaft has been lifted out.

7 Remove the crankshaft by lifting away from the crankcase.

8 Lift away the bearing shells.

18 Engine components - examination for wear

1 When the engine has been stripped down and all parts properly cleaned, decisions have to be made as to what needs renewal and the following sections tell the examiner what to look for. In any border line case it is always best to decide in favour of a new part. Even if a part may be serviceable its life will have been reduced by wear and the degree of trouble needed to replace it in the future must be taken into consideration. However, these things are relative and it depends on whether a quick 'survival' job is being done or whether the vehicle as a whole is being regarded as having many thousands of miles of useful and economical life remaining.

19 Oil pump - examination and renovation

1 Bend back the lockwasher and unscrew the union nut securing the oil pick-up filter to the pump body. Lift off the pick-up filter and sealing ring.

2 Undo and remove the four bolts and lift off the cover from the oil filter body. Withdraw the two gears.

3 Unscrew the pressure relief valve retaining plug from the pump body. Take care not to lose the spring which may fly out as the plug is removed. Withdraw the sealing washer, spring, plunger, and steel ball (photo).

4 Clean all components in paraffin or petrol and dry using a lint free rag or preferably an air line.

5 Examine the pump body, gears, pressure

that the caps are refitted to the connecting rods from which they were removed.

6 If the big-end caps are difficult to remove they may be gently tapped with a soft-faced mallet.

7 To remove the shell bearings, press the bearing opposite the groove in both the connecting rod, and the connecting rod caps and the bearings will slide out easily.

8 Withdraw the pistons and connecting rods upwards and ensure they are kept in the correct order for refitment in the same bore.

16 Flywheel, flywheel housing and crankshaft rear oil seal - removal

1 If these components are to be removed with the engine still in the vehicle, first remove the transmission as described in Chapter 6, and the clutch as described in Chapter 5, followed by the sump as described previously in this Chapter, and the starter motor as described in Chapter 10. Support the weight of the engine with a hoist.

2 Place a block of wood between a crankshaft web and the cylinder block to prevent the crankshaft turning. Undo and remove the eight flywheel retaining bolts in a diagonal sequence and lift off the flywheel (photo).

3 Undo and remove the bolts securing the flywheel housing to the rear of the cylinder block and lift off the housing. Note that there is an O-ring type seal fitted in the housing aperture (photos).

4 Undo and remove the two retaining bolts and carefully tap out the rear main bearing cap using a soft alloy drift.

5 Using a socket undo and remove the bolts retaining the upper half of the seal retainer to the rear of the cylinder block. **Note:** *There is a cut-out in the crankshaft flange to provide access to the retaining bolts.* Prise the retainer rearwards until it clears the dowels and then lift off.

6 Remove the coil spring from around the rear main bearing oil seal and pull the seal off the crankshaft. Note that the seal is split at one end.

7 Unbolt the lower half of the seal retainer from the rear main bearing cap.

17 Crankshaft and main bearings - removal

1 With the engine removed from the vehicle and the timing gears, flywheel and housing, sump, connecting rod bearings and oil pump removed, the crankshaft and main bearings are removed as follows.

2 Mark the main bearing caps and cylinder block faces to ensure the caps are refitted the correct way round.

3 Undo and remove the bolts retaining the three bearing caps to the cylinder block.

4 Remove the main bearing caps and the bottom half of each bearing shell, taking care to keep the bearing shells in the right caps.

5 When removing the centre bearing cap, note the bottom semi-circular halves of the

16.3a Flywheel housing prior to removal

16.3b Location of flywheel housing oil seal

19.3 Unscrew the oil pressure relief valve retaining plug and lift out the spring

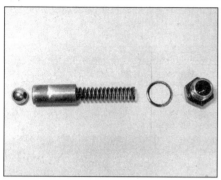

19.5 Oil pressure relief valve components

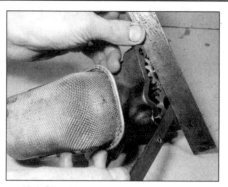

19.6 Checking oil pump gear endfloat

relief valve ball and seat (photo) for scoring pitting or obvious signs of wear or damage, and if present renew the complete pump.

6 If the pump is in satisfactory condition, refit the glass to the pump body and using feeler gauges and a steel rule, measure the endfloat of the gears (photo).

7 If the clearance obtained does not fall within the tolerance given in the Specifications, the pump must be renewed.

8 Liberally lubricate the pump drive gears and pump body and reassemble the gears with the plain portion of the drive gear uppermost.

9 Smear the jointing faces with jointing compound and refit the cover to the pump body. Secure with the retaining bolts.

10 Refit the relief valve assembly ensuring that the concave ball seat on the plunger is adjacent to the steel ball.

11 Place the pick-up filter in position on the pump and secure with the union nut and lockwasher. Position the filter so that it will be square to the sump baffle plate when fitted.

20 Crankshaft and main bearings - examination and renovation

1 Carefully examine the crankshaft main and big-end journals for scratches and scoring. Using a micrometer measure the journals for ovality and compare the figures obtained with those given in the Specifications at the beginning of this Chapter.

2 If the crankshaft journals are worn, scored

22.1 Withdraw the gudgeon pin circlips using circlip pliers

or excessively oval, a new standard size replacement crankshaft should be fitted. It is not recommended to fit a reground crankshaft and undersize bearing shells to these engines.

3 Renew the main bearing shells if any signs of scoring or worn areas are evident.

21 Cylinder block and crankcase - examination and renovation

1 The cylinder bores must be examined for taper, ovality, scoring and scratches. Start by carefully examining the top of the cylinder bores. If they are at all worn a very slight ridge will be found on the thrust side. This marks the top of the piston ring travel. The owner will have a good indication of the bore wear prior to dismantling the engine, or removing the cylinder head.

> **HAYNES HiNT** *Excessive oil consumption accompanied by blue smoke from the exhaust is a sure sign of worn cylinder bores and piston rings.*

2 Measure the bore diameter just under the ridge with micrometer and compare it with the diameter at the bottom of the bore, which is not subject to wear. If the difference between the two measurements is more than 0.008 in (0.2032 mm), then it will be necessary to have the cylinders rebored and fit oversize pistons.

3 If the bores are slightly worn but not so badly worn as to justify reboring them, then special

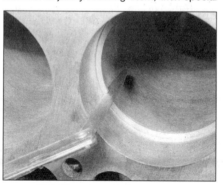

22.5 Checking piston ring gap

oil control rings and pistons can be fitted which will restore compression and stop the engine burning oil. Several different types are available and the manufacturer's instructions concerning their fitting must be followed closely.

4 If the cylinders have already been bored out to the maximum of + 0.040 in (1.016 mm), it is possible to have cylinder liners fitted. This is obviously a specialised job and should be entrusted to your Land Rover dealer.

5 If new pistons are being fitted and the bores have not been rebored, it is essential to slightly roughen the hard glaze on the sides of the bores with fine emery so the new piston rings will have a chance to bed in properly.

6 Examine the crankcase for cracks and leaking core plugs. To renew a core plug, drill a hole in its centre and tap a thread in it, Screw in a bolt and using a distance piece, tighten the bolt and extract the core plug. When fitting the new plug, smear its outer edge with gasket cement.

7 Probe oil galleries and waterways with a piece of wire to make sure that they are quite clear.

22 Piston/connecting rod assemblies - examination and renovation

1 Using a pair of circlip pliers, remove the circlips from the piston and slide out the gudgeon pin from the piston and connecting rod small end bearing (photos). If the gudgeon pin is a tight fit, immerse the piston in hot water. The gudgeon pin should then slide out quite easily.

2 To remove the piston rings, slide them carefully over the top of the piston taking care not to scratch the aluminium alloy of the piston. Never slide them off the bottom of the piston skirt. It is very easy to break piston rings if they are pulled off roughly so this operation should be done with extreme caution. It is helpful to use an old 0.020 inch feeler gauge to facilitate their removal.

3 Lift one end of the piston ring to be removed, out of its groove and insert the end of the feeler gauge under it.

4 Turn the feeler gauge slowly round the piston and as the ring comes out of its groove it rests on the land above. It can then be eased off the piston with the feeler gauge stopping it from slipping into any empty grooves, if it is any but the top piston ring that is being removed.

5 Piston ring wear can be checked by first removing the rings from the pistons as described previously. Place each ring in the cylinder bores individually from the top and push them down the bores approximately 1.5 inches (38 mm) with the head of a piston, so that they rest square in the cylinder. Then measure the gap at the ends of the rings with a feeler gauge (photo). If the gap exceeds the figures given in the Specifications the rings will need renewal.

6 The groove in which the rings locate in the piston can also become enlarged in use. If the clearance between ring and piston in the piston ring groove is outside the limits given in the Specifications, the piston and rings must be renewed.

7 Examine the connecting rods carefully, They are not subject to wear, but in extreme cases such as partial engine seizure they could be distorted. Such conditions may be visually apparant, but It doubt exists they should be changed or checked for alignment by engine reconditioning specialists. If new gudgeon pin bushes are required, this job should also be entrusted to a specialist as the new bushes have to be reamed to fit the gudgeon pins.

8 If new pistons are being fitted they will be supplied with the rings already assembled. If new rings are to be fitted to existing pistons, follow the manufacturers fitting instructions supplied with the rings.

9 Refitting the piston to the connecting rod is the reverse sequence to removal, ensuring that the point of the V-shaped recess in the piston crown is toward the oil spray hole in the side of the connecting rod (photo).

23 Camshaft and tappets - examination and renovation

1 Examine the camshaft bearing surfaces, cam lobes and gearteeth for wear or scoring. Renew the shaft if evident.

2 If the camshaft bearings require renewal the cylinder block should be taken to your local Land Rover dealer or engineering works who will have the special tools for fitting the bearings and reaming them.

3 Check the tappet rollers for pitting or scoring and the tappet sides for excessive wear and renew them if necessary.

24 Timing gears and chain - examination and renovation

1 Examine the teeth on the camshaft, crank-shaft and tensioner sprockets. If they are worn or hooked in appearance they must be renewed.

2 Check the tensioner piston and cylinder for wear, also check the sprocket bush and ratchet brush. Renew the components where necessary (photo).

3 Inspect the rubber strip on the chain damper attached to the cylinder block, and if badly grooved, renew it.

4 Examine the timing chain. If it has been in operation for a considerable time or if when held horizontally (link plates facing downwards) it takes on a deeply bowed appearance, renew it.

25 Timing cover oil seal - removal and refitting

1 With the timing cover removed from the engine as described in Section 13, drill out the rivets securing the mud shield to the timing cover and lift off the shield.

2 Drive the oil seal from the timing cover using a tube of suitable diameter or a drift.

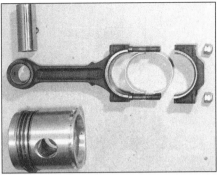

22.9 Piston and connecting rod assembly

3 Place a new oil seal in position on the timing cover and gently tap it in place using a block of wood or a suitably sized tube.

4 Refit the mud shield to the timing cover and secure it in position with the self tapping screws supplied with the oil seal.

26 Cylinder head - decarbonising. valve grinding, and renovation
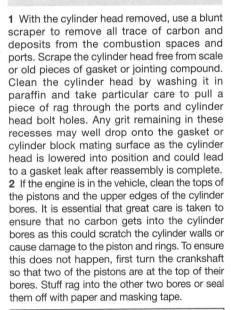

1 With the cylinder head removed, use a blunt scraper to remove all trace of carbon and deposits from the combustion spaces and ports. Scrape the cylinder head free from scale or old pieces of gasket or jointing compound. Clean the cylinder head by washing it in paraffin and take particular care to pull a piece of rag through the ports and cylinder head bolt holes. Any grit remaining in these recesses may well drop onto the gasket or cylinder block mating surface as the cylinder head is lowered into position and could lead to a gasket leak after reassembly is complete.

2 If the engine is in the vehicle, clean the tops of the pistons and the upper edges of the cylinder bores. It is essential that great care is taken to ensure that no carbon gets into the cylinder bores as this could scratch the cylinder walls or cause damage to the piston and rings. To ensure this does not happen, first turn the crankshaft so that two of the pistons are at the top of their bores. Stuff rag into the other two bores or seal them off with paper and masking tape.

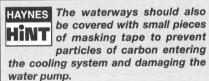
HAYNES HiNT *The waterways should also be covered with small pieces of masking tape to prevent particles of carbon entering the cooling system and damaging the water pump.*

3 Press a little grease into the gap between the cylinder walls and the two pistons which are to be worked on. With a blunt scraper carefully scrape away the carbon from the piston crown, taking great care not to scratch the aluminium. Also scrape away the carbon from the surrounding lip of the cylinder wall. When all the carbon has been removed, scrape away the grease which will now be contaminated with

24.2 Timing chain tensioner components

carbon particles, taking care not to press any into the bores. To assist prevention of carbon build-up the piston crown can be polished with a metal polish. Remove the tag or masking tape from the other two cylinders and turn the crankshaft so that the two pistons which were at the bottom are now at the top. Place rag or masking tape in the cylinders which have been decarbonised and proceed as just described.

4 Scrape off all traces of carbon and deposits from the valve head and valve stems.

5 Examine the heads of the valves for pitting and burning, especially the heads of the exhaust valves. The valve seatings should be examined at the same time. If the pitting on valve and seat is very slight the marks can be removed by grinding the seats and valves together with coarse, and then fine, valve grinding paste.

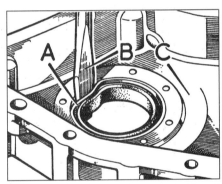

Fig. 1.6 Removing the timing cover oil seal

A Oil seal B Suitable lever C Timing cover

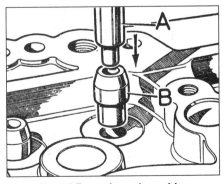

Fig. 1.7 Renewing valve guides

A Suitable stepped drift B Valve guide

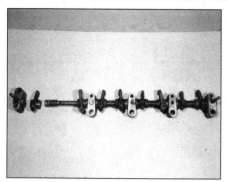
27.1 Dismantling the rocker gear

6 Where bad pitting has occurred to the valve seats it will be necessary to recut them and fit new valves.

7 Insert the valves into their respective guides and check that the amount of wear does not exceed the dimensions given in the Specifications.

8 If the clearance is excessive the guides can be removed by driving them out using a suitable sized stepped drift, from the combustion chamber side of the cylinder head.

9 Special drifts are available from the manufacturers for this job, and it is recommended that they are used, when refitting, to avoid damaging the new guides.

10 Valve grinding is carried out as follows: Smear a trace of coarse carborundum paste on the seat face and apply a suction grinder tool to the valve head. With a semi-rotary motion, grind the valve head to its seat, lifting the valve occasionally to redistribute the

grinding paste. When a dull matt even surface finish is produced on both the valve seat and the valve, wipe off the paste and repeat the process with fine carborundum paste, lifting and turning the valve to redistribute the paste as before. A light spring placed under the valve head will greatly ease this operation. When a smooth unbroken ring of light grey matt finish is produced, on both valve and valve seat faces, the grinding operation is completed.

11 Clean away every trace of grinding paste and if available, use an airline to blow out the ports and valve guides.

12 If the original valve springs have been in use for more than 20 000 miles (32 000 kms), they should be renewed together with new valve stem oil seals (the latter are included in the de-coke set).

13 Unless the vehicle has covered a very high mileage it is not normally necessary to remove the swirl chambers or pushrod tubes from the cylinder head. If this work is necessary, it should be entrusted to a Land Rover garage or engineering works.

27 Rockers and rocker shaft - examination and renovation

1 Slide the rocker posts, rocker arms, springs and spacing washers off the rocker shaft, noting their positioning and keeping them in order as they are removed (photo). Thoroughly clean all components in paraffin or petrol and dry with a lint free rag or air line.

2 Examine the rocker shaft for straightness by rolling it along a flat surface. Check the shaft for any worn ridges or scoring caused by the

rocker arms. If the shaft is worn or distorted it must be renewed.

3 Examine the rocker arms for wear of the bushes, wear of the rocker face which bears on the valve stem, and for wear of the adjusting ball ended screw. Wear of the rocker arm bush can be checked by placing the rocker on the shaft and twisting it from side to side. Renew any worn rockers.

4 Check the pushrods for straightness by rolling them on a flat surface. Renew any that are bent.

5 Ensure that the oil feed holes in the rocker posts, arms and shaft are clear and reassemble in the reverse sequence to removal.

28 Flywheel - examination and renovation

1 Examine the clutch driven plate mating surface of the flywheel. If this is scored or shows signs of many small cracks, then it should either be renewed or refaced (see Specifications).

2 Examine the teeth of the flywheel starter ring gear. If they are chipped or worn, the ring must be renewed. To do this, split the ring with a cold chisel.

3 Heat the new ring to 437°F (225°C) in an electric oven and then quickly fit it to the flywheel so that the chamfered side of the teeth is towards the engine side of the flywheel.

4 Allow the ring to cool naturally without quenching.

5 If the gearbox input shaft spigot bearing bush is worn excessively, remove it from the flywheel with a suitable soft metal drift. Soak the new bush in clean engine oil for 24 hours, then press it into the flywheel until it is flush with the clutch side of the flywheel. Ream the new bush to between 0.878 and 0.8785 in (22.30 and 22.3127 mm) on Series II and IIA models, and to between 0.8755 and 0.8757 in (22.237 and 22.242 in) on Series III models.

29 Engine reassembly - general

To ensure maximum life with minimum trouble from a rebuilt engine, not only must everything be correctly assembled, but everything must be spotlessly clean, all the oilways must be clear, locking washers and spring washers must always be fitted where indicated and all bearing and other working surfaces must be thoroughly lubricated during assembly.

Before assembly begins renew any bolts or studs, the threads of which are in any way damaged, and whenever possible use new spring washers.

Gather together a torque wrench, oil can and clean rag, also a set of engine gaskets, crankshaft front and rear oil seals and a new oil filter element.

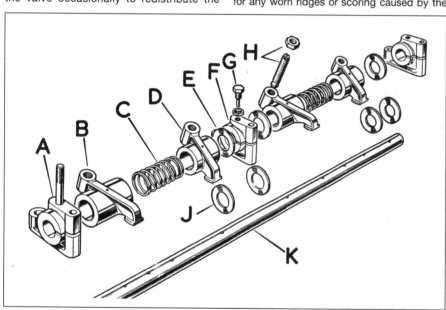

Fig. 1.8 Rocker shaft and valve gear arrangement (Sec 27)

A Rocker brackets
B Exhaust valve rocker arm
C Rocker springs
D Inlet valve rocker arm

E Spacing washer (where fitted)
F Rocker bracket
G Locating screw

H Adjusting screw and locknut
J Spacing washer
K Rocker shaft

30 Crankshaft, oil seal and main bearings - refitting

1 Wipe both sides of the main bearing shells with a petrol moistened cloth to remove the protective coating, and place the upper bearing valves in position with the bearing tongue locating in the grooves in the cylinder block. Note that the oil feed holes are offset in the rear bearing shell (photo).

2 It will be found easier to fit the rear oil seal before refitting the crankshaft. First loop the oil seal coil spring around the rear oil seal journal on the crankshaft. Open the split in the seal just enough to pass it over the crankshaft journal with the recess in the seal facing forwards (photo).

3 With the spring ends hooked together, carefully push the spring into the seal recess using a small screwdriver. Make sure that the join in the spring in positioned 90° away from the pin in the seal.

4 Smear a trace of sealing compound on the inner recess of the upper half (cylinder block side) of the seal retainer, and secure in position with the retaining bolts. Only tighten the bolts finger tight at this stage.

5 Liberally oil the previously fitted main bearing shells (photo).

6 Apply a trace of medium grease to the outside face of the oil seal, and with it positioned so that the split in the seal is facing vertically towards the top of the engine, lower

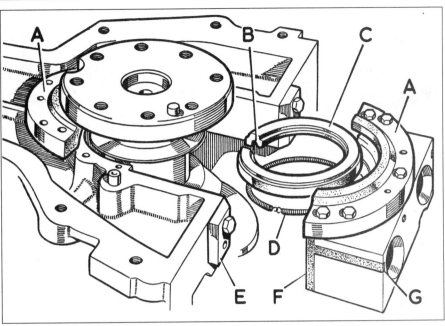

Fig. 1.9 Crankshaft rear oil seal components (Sec 30)

A Seal retainer
B Oil seal split (towards top of engine)
C Oil seal
D Oil seal spring
E Oil seal guides (where applicable)
F Cork 'T' seal
G Trim these edges when fitted to protrude 1/32 in (0.8 mm)

the crankshaft into position. Make sure that the seal fits snugly into the upper seal retainer without distortion (photo).

7 Slide the two crankshaft thrust washers into position on either side of the centre main bearing (photo), with their plated faces against the crankshaft. Using feeler gauges measure the crankshaft endfloat (photo) and compare

30.1 Position of oil feed holes in rear main bearing shell

30.2 Refitting the crankshaft rear oil seal

30.5 Liberally oil the bearing shells prior to fitting the crankshaft

30.6 Crankshaft and rear oil seal in position

30.7a Slide the thrust washers into position on the centre main bearing

30.7b Checking crankshaft endfloat

30.8 Fitting the rear main bearing cap cork seals

30.11a Fit the front and centre main bearing caps . . .

30.11b . . and tighten to the specified torque

31.5 Using a piston ring compressor to assist fitting of the piston assemblies

30.9 Avoid damaging the cork seals on the edge of the block when fitting the bearing cap

the figures obtained with those given in the Specifications. If the clearance is excessive, oversize thrust washers are available.

8 Fit the cork 'T' seals onto either side of the rear main bearing cap and bolt the lower seal retainer onto the cap, finger tight only at this stage (photo).

9 Smear a trace of sealing compound on the inner recess of the lower seal retainer and fit the rear main bearing cap and bearing shell onto the cylinder block (photo). Smear the sides of the 'T' seals with grease and use a thin feeler blade to guide them as the bearing cap is fitted. Take great care not to damage the 'T' seals and ensure that the rear oil seal does not distort as the bearing cap is pushed fully home.

31.2 Apply engine oil liberally to the crankshaft journals prior to assembling the big-end caps

31.7 Assemble the bearing cap to the connecting rod with the notches adjacent

10 Fit the bearing cap bolts but do not tighten at this stage.

11 Fit the front and centre main bearing caps and shells and tighten all the main bearing bolts to the torque figure given in the Specifications (photos). Check that the crankshaft rotates freely without any high spots. If it does appear to be binding in any one place, investigate now before proceeding.

12 Tighten the oil seal retainer bolts using a socket through the cut-out in the crankshaft flange. Make sure that the hexagon bolts are positioned so that they will not foul the flywheel housing seal.

31 Pistons and connecting rods - refitting

1 Place the big end bearing shells in position on the connecting rods and caps, with the notches on the bearing shells engaged in the groove of the rod and cap.

2 Apply engine oil liberally to the cylinder bores, piston rings and crankshaft journals (photo).

3 Position the piston rings so that their gaps are staggered around the thrust side of the piston (camshaft side of engine).

4 Insert the connecting rod and piston assembly into the top of the cylinder ensuring that the connecting rod oil hole, and the point of the V-shaped groove in the piston crown are towards the camshaft side of the engine.

5 Compress the piston rings using a piston ring compressor and tap the pistons firmly into the cylinder bores using a block of wood against the centre of the piston crown (photo).

6 With the crankshaft journal at its lowest point, continue pushing the piston down the bore until the connecting rod and bearing shell are firmly seated on the crankshaft journal.

7 Assemble the big-end bearing cap and shell onto the connecting rod, with the notches on the shells on adjacent sides (photo).

8 Refit the retaining nuts and tighten to the torque figure given in the Specifications.

9 Ensure that the correct endfloat exists between connecting rod and crankshaft (photo).

10 Repeat the foregoing operations on the remaining three piston assemblies.

31.9 Checking connecting rod endfloat

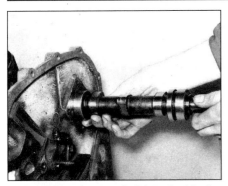

32.1 Sliding the camshaft into the block

32.4a Refit the tappet rollers with their chamfered edges facing forward . . .

32.4b . . . followed by the tappet slides

32 Camshaft and tappets - refitting

1 Lubricate the camshaft bearings with engine oil and carefully insert the camshaft from the front of the engine (photo).
2 Fit the camshaft thrust plate and temporarily fit the camshaft sprocket. Check that the camshaft endfloat is within the limits given in the Specifications. If the endfloat is outside the limits a new thrust plate must be fitted.
3 Refit the tappet guides to the cylinder block with their locating bolt holes towards the camshaft side of the engine. Secure the guides with the retaining bolts just sufficiently to hold them in position.
4 Lubricate the tappet rollers and place them in position on the guides (photo) with the larger chamfer towards the front. Fit the tappet slides with the word FRONT facing forward (photo).
5 Fully tighten the tappet guide retaining bolts and lock them in position using suitable gauge soft iron wire (photos).

33 Flywheel housing and flywheel - refitting

1 Fit a new O-ring oil seal to the recess in the flywheel housing and place the housing in position on the cylinder block. Refit the securing bolts and tighten to the torque figure given in the Specifications.

2 Refit the flywheel on the crankshaft locating it on the dowel. Refit the bolts and tighten to the correct torque (photo).

34 Timing components - refitting

1 If a new camshaft sprocket or camshaft are being fitted, refer to paragraphs 11 to 21 inclusive. If the original timing components are being refitted, proceed as follows.
2 Rotate the engine until the EP mark on the flywheel is aligned with the pointer on the flywheel housing.
3 Place the camshaft sprocket in position on the camshaft, lining up the previously made

32.5 Locking the tappet guide retaining bolts with soft iron wire

marks on the camshaft, sprocket and cylinder block as described in Section 13.
4 Slide the crankshaft sprocket onto the crankshaft and key, noting that the sprocket goes on large shoulder first. Place the timing chain in position over the two sprockets (photo). Check that the marks on the camshaft sprocket and cylinder block are still aligned with the chain pulled tight against the guide.
5 Compress the spring on the chain tensioner and place it in position over the locating dowels (photo). Refit the ratchet, spring and securing bolts and tighten the bolts to the specified torque.
6 Refit the camshaft sprocket washer, locktab and retaining bolt (photo) and tighten the bolt to the specified torque, securing with the locktab.

33.2 Tighten the flywheel retaining bolts to the specified torque

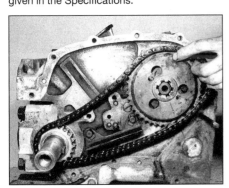

34.4 Refitting the timing chain

34.5 Timing chain tensioner installed

34.6 Refitting the camshaft sprocket securing bolt

34.9 Installing the crankshaft pulley and securing nut

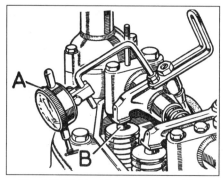

Fig. 1.10 Dial test Indicator in position

A *Dial test indicator*
B *No. 1 cylinder exhaust valve fully open*

35.2 Timing marks on flywheel aligned with pointer

7 Adjust the vibration damper to give a clearance of 0.010 in (0.25 mm) between the rubber strip and the chain.
8 Smear medium grease onto both sides of a new timing cover gasket and place it in position on the cylinder block. Apply engine oil to the lips of the timing cover oil seal and refit the cover to the engine. Fit the retaining bolts but do not fully tighten at this stage.
9 Fit the crankshaft pulley and tighten its securing bolt to the specified torque (photo).
10 Finally tighten the timing cover bolts.
11 If a new camshaft, or camshaft sprocket are to be fitted, or if for any reason the previously made timing marks have been lost, carry out the following procedure.
12 Rotate the engine until the EP mark on the flywheel is aligned with the pointer on the flywheel housing.
13 Temporarily place the camshaft sprocket on to the camshaft, but do not fit the retaining bolt at this stage.
14 Insert No.1 cylinder exhaust valve pushrod into position on its tappet slide. Support the pushrod and observe its movement as the camshaft sprocket is slowly rotated. When the pushrod has risen to its highest point (No. 1 exhaust valve fully open), suitably mark the camshaft sprocket and cylinder block relative to each other. Carry out this operation slowly and carefully as it is most important that the exact position of the exhaust valve fully open

position or the pushrod fully extended position is ascertained. If the cylinder head is in position on the engine with the pushrods and rockers fitted, greater accuracy can be achieved using a dial test indicator as shown in Fig 1.10.
15 Refit the timing chain to the crankshaft and camshaft sprockets. Pull the chain tight on the driving side running against the guide. If it is not possible to align the previously made marks on the camshaft sprocket and cylinder block by altering the position of the chain, one tooth at a time either way, then the timing procedure described above will have to be repeated after moving the camshaft sprocket to a different spline position on the camshaft.
16 Refitting the timing chain tensioner in position over the locating dowels. Refit the ratchet, spring and securing bolts and tighten the bolts to the specified torque.
17 Refit the camshaft sprocket washer, locktab and retaining bolt and tighten the bolt to the specified torque, securing with the locktab.
18 Adjust the vibration damper to give a clearance of 0.010 in (0.25 mm) between the rubber strip and the chain.
19 Smear medium grease onto both sides of a new timing cover gasket, and place it in position on the cylinder block. Apply engine oil to the lips of the timing cover oil seal and refit the cover to the engine. Fit the retaining bolts but do not fully tighten at this stage.
20 Fit the crankshaft pulley and tighten its securing bolt to the specified torque.
21 Finally tighten the timing cover bolts.

35 Fuel injection/distributor pump vertical drive gear - refitting

1 Rotate the engine in the normal direction of rotation until No. 1 cylinder approaches TDC on the compression stroke. This can be checked by pressing the fingers on No. 1 cylinder tappet slides and feeling them rise and fall as the engine is rotated. On the compression stroke both sides should be resting on the heel of the cam (fully down). If the cylinder head is in position, observe the movement of the valves, which should both be closed.
2 Continue turning until the applicable timing mark is in line with the timing pointer on the flywheel housing (photo). On early pumps set the pointer adjacent to the 16° mark on the flywheel. On later pumps fitted to engines having a 14° and 16° mark stamped on the flywheel, set the timing at 15°, that is midway between the two marks. If the flywheel is stamped with 13° and 14° marks, set the timing at 13°. Ensure that the marks approach the pointer in the direction of rotation. If the pointer is passed, turn back and start again.
3 Refer to Fig 1.11 and using a protractor, scribe a line at 20° to the horizontal on the pump mating face of the cylinder block.
4 Position the vertical drive gear bush so that the small hole is facing towards the oil filter mounting face at the point where the grub screw is located.
5 Insert the drive gear into the block (photo),

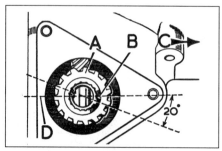

Fig.1.11 Vertical drive gear correctly positioned

A *Vertical drive gear*
B *Master spline at 20° to engine centre line*
C *Front of engine*
D *Line drawn parallel with engine centre line*

35.5 Refitting the vertical drive gear

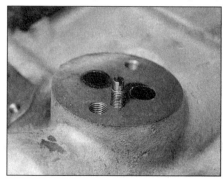

35.6 Refitting the vertical drive gear grub screw

36.2 Refitting the oil pump

36.5 Placing the sump in position on the crankcase

37.2 Place the oil seals in position over the valve stems

and turn the gear so that when it is fully engaged with the camshaft, the largest (master) spline is in line with the scribed mark.
6 When the drive gear is correctly positioned, fit the grubscrew into the threaded hole in the oil filter mating face (photo).

36 Oil pump and sump - refitting

1 Fit the oil pump driveshaft into the pump housing, making sure that the shaft spline engages fully with the pump gear.
2 Carefully insert the driveshaft and pump into its location in the crankcase, ensuring that the top splines on the shaft engage fully with the drive gear (photo).
3 Refit the securing bolts, tighten them and bend over the locking tabs.
4 Clean the mating surfaces of the sump and the crankcase and stick the gasket in position on the sump using a light smear of grease.
5 Fit the sump to the crankcase and tighten the bolts in a diagonal sequence. Be careful not to overtighten them (photo).

37 Cylinder head - reassembly and refitting

1 Lay the cylinder head on its side, lubricate the valve stems and insert them into the guides they were removed from.

2 Fit the oil seals over the valve stems ensuring the lip fits into the groove in the valve guide (photo). **Note:** *On earlier engines the oil seals fit in a groove inside the valve guides, and these must be fitted prior to inserting the valves. Where two types of oil seal are supplied, fit the type with springs to the inlet valve.*
3 Fit the valve springs, the retaining cap and then compress the valve spring and locate the split collets in the cut-out of the valve stem. Release the compressor. Repeat these operations on the remaining seven valves (photos).
4 When all the valves have been fitted, place the cylinder head flat on the bench and using a hammer and a block of wood as an insulator, tap the end of each valve stem to settle the components.
5 Lightly smear both faces of a new cylinder head gasket with jointing compound and place it in position on the cylinder block with the lettering DIESEL uppermost (photo).
6 Lower the cylinder head onto the gasket and secure with the retaining bolts. Do not fully tighten the bolts at this stage.
7 Insert each pushrod into the hole from which it was originally removed. Make sure that the pushrod end seats correctly in the tappet slide.
8 With the rocker shaft assembly held together by means of the inverted rocker cover as described in Section 8, lower it into place, making sure the spigots are correctly located in the cylinder head (photo).

9 Make sure the rocker arms are correctly seated on the pushrods, and then tighten the cylinder head and rocker shaft securing bolts evenly, in the sequence shown in Fig 1.3, to the torque wrench settings given in the Specifications (photo).

38 Valve clearances - adjustment

1 Valve adjustments may be carried out with the engine hot or cold. The importance of correct rocker arm/valve stem clearance cannot be overstressed as they vitally

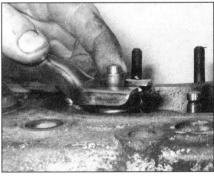

37.3 Insert the retaining collets in position on the valve stems

37.5 Head gasket in position on the cylinder block

37.8 Refitting the rocker gear

37.9 Using a torque wrench to tighten the cylinder head bolts

38.1 Removing the rocker cover and gasket

38.3 Adjusting the valve/rocker arm clearance

Basically the installation of the engine is the reverse procedure to the removal operation, however, mating the engine to the gearbox can be difficult unless the following method is used.

1 Make sure the clutch is centralised on the flywheel as described in Chapter 5.
2 Carefully lower the engine into the engine compartment using a suitable hoist until the flywheel housing is straight and level with the clutch housing.
3 Push the engine rearwards ensuring the gearbox input shaft enters the clutch assembly in a straight line and not at an angle.
4 If the engine begins to mate up and then stops with a couple of inches still to go, fit a spanner onto the crankshaft starter dog and turn it slowly while pushing the engine rearwards.
5 As soon as the flywheel and clutch housings touch, insert a bolt fingertight to hold them together, and then refit all the bolts and tighten them in a diagonal sequence.
6 Refit the engine mountings using the reverse procedure to that described in Section 5.
7 Finally, lower the hoist completely and remove the engine slings and the jack or blocks from beneath the transmission. Reconnect all the controls, electrical leads, fuel pipes, exhaust pipe, etc., checking each item against the sequence given in Section 5.
8 Do not forget to refill the cooling system, and refill the engine with the recommended grade and quantity of oil.

affect the performance of the engine. If the clearances are set too wide the efficiency of the engine is reduced as the valves open later and close earlier than intended. If, however the clearances are too tight, there is a danger that the stems will expand upon heating and not allow the valves to close properly, which causes burning of the valve head and seat, and loss of compression. If the engine is in the vehicle, access to the rockers is by removing the three domed securing nuts and lifting off the rocker cover and gasket (photo).
2 It is important that the clearance is set when the tappet of the valve being adjusted is on the heel of the cam, (ie opposite the peak). This can be ensured by carrying out the adjustments in the following order (which also avoids turning the crankshaft more than necessary):

Valves fully open	Check and adjust
Valve No. 8	Valve No. 1
Valve No. 6	Valve No. 3
Valve No. 4	Valve No. 5
Valve No. 7	Valve No. 2
Valve No. 1	Valve No. 8
Valve No. 3	Valve No. 6
Valve No. 5	Valve No. 4
Valve No. 2	Valve No. 7

The correct feeler gauge clearance between valve stem and rocker arm pad with the engine hot or cold is 0.010 in (0.25 mm).

3 Working from the front of the engine (No. 1 valve) the correct clearance is obtained by slackening the hexagon locknut with a spanner while holding the ball pin against rotation with a screwdriver. Then, still pressing down with the screwdriver, insert a feeler gauge in the gap between the valve stem head and the rocker arm and adjust the ball pin until the feeler gauge will just move in and out without nipping (photo). Then, still holding the ball pin in the correct position, tighten the locknut.
4 When reassembling the cylinder head after a major overhaul or decoke, the valve clearances should be set to 0.010 in (0.25 mm) with the engine cold and then re-checked after the engine has been started and run to allow all the parts to seat correctly.

39 Ancillary components - refitting

1 This is a reversal of the removal sequence given in Section 7 of this Chapter.
2 Always use new gaskets when refitting previously removed components and refer to the appropriate Chapter of this manual for full installation instructions for the component concerned.
3 Always use a new oil filter sealing ring when refitting the filter and tighten the securing bolt to the specified torque (photo).

1 With the engine refitted to the vehicle, give a visual check to see that everything has been reconnected and that no loose rags or tools have been left within the engine compartment.
2 Make sure that the battery is fully charged and that all coolant and lubricants are fully replenished. Prime the fuel system as described in Chapter 3.
3 The engine should start after the fuel priming operation.
4 As soon as the engine fires and runs, keep it going at a fast tickover only (no faster) and bring it up to normal working temperature.
5 As the engine warms up there will be odd smells and some smoke from parts getting hot and burning off oil deposits. The signs to look for are leaks of water or oil which will be obvious, If serious. Check also the exhaust pipe and manifold connections as these do not always find their exact gas tight position until the warmth and vibration have acted on

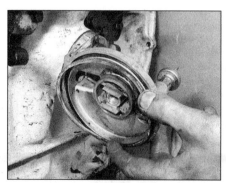

39.3a Place a new oil filter sealing ring in position . .

39.3b . . . and then refit the oil filter

them and it is almost certain that they will need tightening further. This should be done, of course, with the engine stopped.

6 When normal running temperature has been reached, adjust the engine idle speed as described in Chapter 3.

7 Stop the engine and wait a few minutes to see if any lubricant or coolant is dripping out when the engine is stationary.

8 After the engine has run for 20 minutes remove the engine top cover and recheck the tightness of the cylinder head bolts. Also check the tightness of the sump bolts. In both cases use a torque wrench.

9 Road test the vehicle to check that the vehicle engine is giving the necessary smoothness and power. Do not race the engine - if new bearings and/or pistons have been fitted it should be treated as a new engine and run in at a reduced speed for the first 1000 miles {2000 km).

Fault finding - engine

Engine will not rotate when attempting to start

- [ ] Battery discharged
- [ ] Loose battery connection
- [ ] Faulty starter motor or solenoid
- [ ] Engine earth strap broken or disconnected
- [ ] Fault in starting circuit wiring

Engine rotates but will not start

- [ ] Air in fuel system
- [ ] Heater plugs faulty
- [ ] Faulty or incorrectly adjusted fuel injection/distributor pump or injectors
- [ ] Fuel injection/distributor pump timing incorrect
- [ ] Fuel not reaching injection pump or injectors
- [ ] Low cylinder compressions

Engine will not idle

- [ ] Idling speed incorrectly set
- [ ] Fuel injectors faulty
- [ ] Incorrect valve clearance

Engine runs roughly with reduced power

- [ ] Valves incorrectly set
- [ ] Valve spring broken
- [ ] Low or uneven cylinder compressions
- [ ] Faulty or worn fuel injectors
- [ ] Fuel injection/distributor pump timing incorrect or pump out of adjustment
- [ ] Engine internal components worn

Low oil pressure

- [ ] Oil level too low
- [ ] Oil pressure warning light or gauge faulty
- [ ] External oil leakage
- [ ] Faulty oil pump or blocked filter
- [ ] Oil pressure relief valve faulty
- [ ] Engine internal components worn

Black smoke emitted from exhaust

- [ ] Faulty fuel injectors
- [ ] Fuel injection/distributor pump timing incorrect

Blue smoke emitted from exhaust

- [ ] Blocked or overfilled air cleaner
- [ ] Valve clearances incorrect
- [ ] Low or uneven cylinder compressions
- [ ] Engine burning oil due to general wear

Notes

Chapter 2
Cooling system

Contents

Degrees of difficulty

Easy, suitable for novice with little experience	**Fairly easy,** suitable for beginner with some experience	**Fairly difficult,** suitable for competent DIY mechanic	**Difficult,** suitable for experienced DIY mechanic	**Very difficult,** suitable for expert DIY or professional

Specifications

Type of system. . . . . Pressurised system, assisted by pump and fan with thermostat temperature control

Coolant
Type/specification. . . . . Antifreeze to BS 3151, 3152 or 6580

Thermostat
Type . . . . Ethyl-alcohol or wax filled
Location . . . . Front of cylinder head
Initial opening temperature:
  Ethyl-alcohol type. . . . . 161°F to 168°F (72°C to 76°C)
  Wax type. . . . . 159°F to 167°F (71°C to 75°C)
Fully open temperature . . . . 185°F (85°C)

Radiator
Type . . . . Corrugated fin
Cap opening . . . . 9 or 10 lb/in^2 (0.6 or 0.7 kg/cm^2)

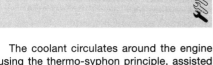

1 General description

The coolant circulates around the engine using the thermo-syphon principle, assisted by an impeller type water pump. A four-bladed cooling fan is fitted to the pump and both items are belt-driven from the crankshaft pulley.

A thermostat is located under the water outlet pipe at the front of the cylinder head. Earlier engines were fitted with an Ethyl-alcohol filled thermostat that was replaced on later models with the more efficient wax-filled type.

The cooling system functions in the following manner. Cold water from the bottom of the radiator is drawn up the lower radiator hose to the water pump which forces it through the passages in the cylinder block, cooling the cylinders and indirectly, the pistons.

The water then travels up into the cylinder head and circulates round the combustion spaces and valve seats absorbing more heat, and then, when the engine is at its correct operating temperature, travels out of the cylinder head, past the open thermostat into the upper radiator hose and so into the radiator header tank.

The water travels down the radiator where it is rapidly cooled by the in-rush of cold air through the radiator core, which is created by both the fan and the motion of the vehicle. The water, now much cooler reaches the bottom of the radiator when the cycle is repeated.

When the engine is cold the thermostat (which is a valve which opens and closes according to the temperature of the water) maintains the circulation of the same water in the engine.

Only when the correct minimum operating temperature has been reached, as shown in the Specifications, does the thermostat begin to open, allowing water to return to the radiator.

2 Cooling system - draining

With the vehicle on level ground drain the system as follows:

1 If the engine is cold, remove the filler cap from the radiator by turning it anticlockwise. If the engine is hot, turn the filler cap very slightly until the pressure in the system has had time to disperse.

HAYNES HiNT *Use a rag over the cap to protect your hand from escaping steam. If, with the engine very hot, the cap is released suddenly, the drop in pressure can cause the water to boil. With the pressure released the cap can be removed.*

2 If antifreeze is in the cooling system, drain it into a clean bowl for re-use. A wide bowl will be necessary to catch all the coolant.

3 If a heater is fitted, close the heater supply tap on the engine to avoid air-locks forming in the heater matrix.

4 Open the tap or plug located at the bottom of the radiator and allow the coolant to drain out into the bowl . Repeat the process with the tap located on the left-hand side of the cylinder block. When the water has finished running, probe the taps with a piece of short wire to dislodge any particles of rust or sediment which may be causing a blockage and preventing all the coolant from draining out.

3 Cooling system - flushing

1 With time the cooling system will gradually lose its efficiency as the radiator becomes choked with rust scale, deposits from the water and other sediment. To clean the system out, first drain it – leaving the drain taps open. Then remove the radiator cap and leave a

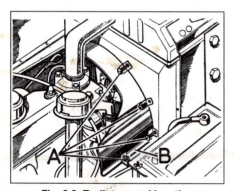

Fig. 2.3. Radiator cowl location

A Retaining screws and nuts B Cowl

Fig. 2.1. Coolant drain points

1 Cylinder block drain tap
2 Radiator drain plug /tap on some models)

hose running in the radiator cap orifice for ten to fifteen minutes.

2 In very bad cases the radiator should be reverse flushed. This can be done with the radiator in position. A hose must be arranged to feed water into the lower radiator outlet pipe. Water, under pressure, is then forced up through the radiator and out of the header tank filler orifice.

3 The hose is removed and placed in the filler orifice and the radiator washed out in the usual manner.

4 Cooling system - filling

1 Close the radiator and cylinder block drain taps.

2 Move the heater control to the hot position and fill the system slowly to ensure that air locks are minimised.

3 Do not fill the system higher than within 0.5 in (13.0 mm) of the filler cap orifice. Overfilling will merely result in wastage, which is especially to be avoided when antifreeze is in use.

4 On later models fitted with an overflow reservoir, fill the container with sufficient coolant to cover the end of the overflow pipe from the radiator.

5 Only use antifreeze mixture with an ethylene glycol base. See Section 9 for further information.

6 Replace the radiator cap and run the engine

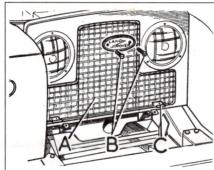

Fig. 2.4 Radiator grille attachment points

A Grille B Securing screws C Bottom clips

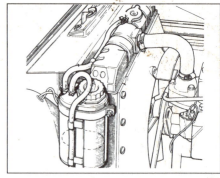

Fig. 2.2. Location of reservoir bottle on later models

at a fast idle speed for approximately half a minute and remove the filler cap slowly. Top-up as necessary and finally refit the filler cap turning it clockwise firmly to lock it in position.

5 Radiator - removal, inspection, cleaning and refitting

1 Refer to Section 2 and drain the cooling system.

2 Remove the top hose connecting the radiator to the thermostat housing.

3 Remove the earth lead from the battery.

4 Undo the screws securing the fan shroud to the radiator and lift the shroud rearwards over the fan.

5 Undo the screws retaining the Land-Rover badge to the radiator grille and lift the grille away from the vehicle.

6 Remove the bottom radiator hose.

7 Undo the nuts and bolts securing the radiator assembly to the front grille panel. Access to these are gained through the grille aperture.

8 Carefully lift the radiator out of the vehicle taking care not to damage the radiator core on the fan blades. If difficulty is experienced in clearing the fan blades, lower the radiator and remove the fan and pulley as described in Section 7 of this Chapter.

9 With the radiator away from the vehicle any leaks can be soldered or repaired with a suitable kit. Clean out the inside of the radiator by flushing as described earlier in this Chapter. When the radiator is out of the vehicle it is advantageous to turn it upside down and reverse flush. clean the exterior of the radiator by carefully using a compressed air jet or a strong jet of water to clear away any road dirt, flies, etc.

10 Inspect the radiator hoses for cracks, internal or external perishing and damage by overtightening of the securing clips. Also inspect the overflow pipe. Renew the hoses if suspect. Examine the radiator hose clips and renew them if they are rusted or distorted.

11 Refit the radiator using the reverse sequence to the removal procedure. Refill the cooling system as described in Section 4.

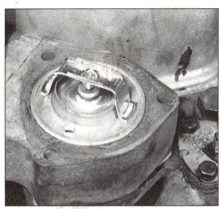

6.4 Location of thermostat

7.7 Lifting off the cooling fan

7.8 Removing the water pump

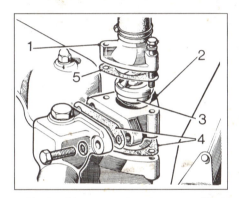

Fig. 2.5. Thermostat housing assembly

1 Water outlet pipe   4 Housing gaskets
2 Thermostat housing   5 Water outlet
3 Thermostat   gasket

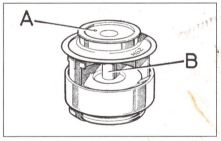

Fig. 2.6. Ethyl-alcohol type thermostat

A Bleed hole   B Operating valve

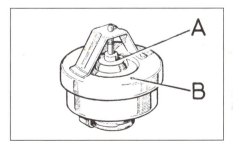

Fig. 2.7. Wax-type thermostat

A Operating valve   B Bleed hole

6 Thermostat - removal, testing, and refitting

1 The thermostat is located in the housing on the top and at the front of the cylinder head (Fig. 2.5).
2 First undo the radiator drain tap (or plug) and drain off approximately 6 pints (3.75 litres) of coolant.
3 Slacken the clips and remove the top hose from the thermostat outlet pipe and radiator.
4 Remove the three bolts and lift off the outlet pipe exposing the top of the thermostat (photo).
5 Carefully prise out the thermostat from the housing. If difficulty is experienced, remove the housing and push the thermostat out.
6 Examine the thermostat for damage and if it is stuck open, renew it. To test a thermostat, use the following procedure.
7 Suspend it by a piece of string together with a thermometer in a saucepan of cold water. Neither the thermostat nor the thermometer should touch the sides or bottom of the saucepan or a false reading could be obtained.
8 Heat the water stirring it gently with the thermometer to ensure temperature uniformity, and note when the thermostat begins to open. Note the temperature and this should be comparable with the figure given in the Specifications Section at the beginning of this Chapter.
9 Continue heating the water until the thermostat is fully open. Now let it cool down naturally and check that it closes fully. If the thermostat does not fully open or close then it must be renewed.
10 Refitting the thermostat is the reverse of the removal procedure. Always clean the mating faces thoroughly and use new gaskets.
Note: A wax-type thermostat cannot be fitted in place of the ethyl alcohol type unless a modified water outlet pipe is fitted (obtainable from your Leyland dealer).

7 Water pump - removal and refitting

1 Refer to Section 2 and drain the cooling system.
2 Refer to Section 5 and remove the radiator.
3 Refer to Section 10 and remove the fan belt.
4 Slacken the bottom hose clip and carefully detach the hose from the water pump.
5 Slacken the water bypass hose clip and carefully detach the bypass hose from the water pump.
6 If a dynamo is fitted (earlier models) remove the adjusting arm to gain access to the pump retaining bolts.
7 Undo and remove the four bolts securing the fan and hub assembly to the water pump spindle flange and lift away the fan assembly (photo).
8 Undo and remove the bolts securing the water pump body to the cylinder block. Lift away the water pump and recover the old gasket (photo) .
9 Refitting the water pump is the reverse sequence to removal, but the following additional points should be noted:
a) Make sure the mating faces of the pump body and cylinder block are clean. Always use a new gasket.
b) Refer to Section 10 and adjust the fan belt tension. If the belt is too tight, undue strain will be placed on the water pump and alternator (or dynamo) bearings. If the belt is too loose, it will slip and wear rapidly as well as giving rise to possible engine overheating and low alternator (or dynamo) output.

8 Water pump - dismantling, overhaul and reassembly

1 Before dismantling the water pump check the economics of overhaul compared with the cost of a guaranteed new unit. Then make quite sure all the spare parts required are to hand.

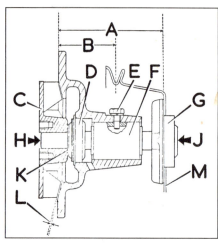

Fig. 2.8. Cross sectional view of water pump

A Dimension, 3.510 in (89.15 mm) – Series II
   and IIA, 3.523 in (89.48 mm) – Series III
B Dimension, 1.930 in (49.0 mm)
C Impeller
D Carbon ring and seal assembly
E Locating bolt
F Pump spindle and bearing assembly
G Fan hub
H Support here when fitting hub
J Support here when fitting impeller
K Carbon seal faced toward impeller
L Dimension, 0.025 in (0.63 mm)
M Fan belt pulley

2 Referring to Fig. 2.8, remove the bearing retaining bolt and with the pump body held in a soft-jawed vice, drift out the impeller, bearing and spindle assembly from the pump body and flange.

3 Cut through the seal and discard it. Support the impeller between two large blocks of wood and drive the spindle and bearing out of the impeller.

4 Examine the bearing for wear and the impeller and spindle for excessive corrosion, if either are evident, renew the components affected.

5 On later models fitted with a deflector washer, check that there is a clearance of 0.018 in (0.46 mm) between the washer and the bearing housing face.

6 Before reassembling, insert a few drops of thick oil into the location hole in the bearing.

7 Mark a line on the pump body and the bearing assembly to enable the retaining bolt holes to be lined up during reassembly.

8 Insert the spindle and bearing assembly into the pump body and fit the retaining bolt.

9 Press the pulley flange onto the spindle until the dimension 'A' in Fig. 2.8 is achieved.

10 Fit the carbon ring and seal into the bore of the pump body ensuring the carbon ring is towards the rear of the pump.

11 Press the impeller onto the spindle until there is 0.025 in (0.63 mm) clearance between the impeller and pump body (see Fig. 2.8). The clearance can be checked using feeler gauges.

12 Refit the pump to the engine as described in Section 7, ensuring that a new gasket is used between the mating surfaces.

9 Antifreeze coolant solution

1 Where temperatures are likely to drop below freezing point (0°C, 32°F) the cooling system must be adequately protected by the addition of antifreeze. It is still possible for water to freeze in the radiator with the engine running in very cold conditions, particularly if the engine cooling is being adequately dealt with by the heater radiator. The thermostat will remain closed and the coolant in the radiator will not circulate.

2 Before refilling the coolant system with antifreeze solution it is best to drain and flush the system as described in Sections 2 and 3 of this Chapter.

3 Because antifreeze has a greater searching effect than water, make sure that all hoses and joints are in good condition.

4 The table below gives the details of the antifreeze percentage to be used.

%	Complete protection	
25	–11 °C	12.2°F
30	–14°C	6.8° F
35	–19°C	–2.2°F
40	–23°C	–9.4° F
45	–29°C	–20.0° F
50	–35°C	–31.0°F

5 Mix the equal quantity of antifreeze with 4 pints (2.27 litres) of water and pour into the cooling system. Top-up with water and check the level as described in Section 4.

10 Fan belt - removal, refitting and adjustment

1 If the fan belt is worn or has stretched unduly it should be renewed. A common reason for renewal is breakage in use, so always carry a spare.

2 Even though the belt may have broken and fallen off, go through the removal routine. First loosen the dynamo or alternator securing bolts and push it towards the engine and lift off the old belt.

3 Position the new belt over the pulleys.

4 The dynamo or alternator must now be used as a tensioner, in effect, by pulling it away from the engine and locking in the required position. This can call for some sustained effort unless the pivot bolts are slackened only a little so that the dynamo or alternator is quite stiff to move. A lever between the dynamo or alternator and cylinder block will help. However, avoid applying pressure to the rear end-cover or it may break. Always tighten the front end-cover securing bolts first.

5 The movement of the belt under finger pressure of the belt, midway between the water pump and dynamo or alternator pulleys should be set to 0.5 in (13 mm). If in doubt it is better for it to be a little too slack rather than too tight. Only slipping will occur if it is too slack. If too tight, damage can be caused by excessive strain on the pulley bearing (photo).

6 When the adjustment is correct tighten the dynamo or alternator mountings fully.

10.5 Checking the fan belt tension

Fault finding – cooling system

Overheating

- [ ] Insufficient water in cooling system.
- [ ] Fan belt slipping (accompanied by a shrieking noise on rapid engine acceleration).
- [ ] Radiator core blocked or radiator grille restricted.
- [ ] Water hose collapsed, impeding flow.
- [ ] Thermostat not opening properly.
- [ ] Fuel distributor pump settings incorrect
- [ ] Exhaust system partially blocked.
- [ ] Oil level in sump too low.
- [ ] Blown cylinder head gasket (water/steam pipe under pressure).
- [ ] Engine not yet run-in.
- [ ] Brakes binding.

Underheating

- [ ] Thermostat jammed open.
- [ ] Incorrect thermostat fitted allowing premature opening of valve.
- [ ] Thermostat missing.

Loss of cooling water

- [ ] Loose clips on water hoses.
- [ ] Top, bottom, or bypass water hoses perished and leaking.
- [ ] Radiator core leaking.
- [ ] Thermostat gasket leaking.
- [ ] Radiator pressure cap spring worn or seal ineffective.
- [ ] Blown cylinder head gasket (pressure in system forcing water/steam down overflow pipe).
- [ ] Cylinder wall or head cracked.
- [ ] Core plug leaking.

Notes

Chapter 3A
Fuel exhaust and emission control system – petrol models

For modifications, and information applicable to later models, see Supplement at end of manual

Contents

Degrees of difficulty

Easy, suitable for novice with little experience	**Fairly easy,** suitable for beginner with some experience	**Fairly difficult,** suitable for competent DIY mechanic	**Difficult,** suitable for experienced DIY mechanic	**Very difficult,** suitable for expert DIY or professional

Specifications

Fuel pump	AC mechanical

Carburettor (Solex)

Choke size	28 mm
Main jet	125
Correction jet	185
Pilot jet	50
Pump jet	65
Economy jet	Blank
Air bleed jet	1.5
Starter air jet	–
Starter petrol jet	145
Economy system - petrol jet	100
Petrol level	5/8 in ± 1/8 in (16 mm ± 3 mm) below float chamber joint face

Jet sizes to be used when operating at high altitudes:

Main jet (120)	5,000 ft to 7,000 ft (1.524 m to 2.134 m)
Main jet (117.5)	7,000 ft to 9,000 ft (2.134 m to 2.740 m)
Main jet (115)	
Pilot jet (45)	9,000 ft to 12,000 ft (2.740 m to 3.655 m)
Main jet (112.5)	
Pilot jet (45)	12,000 ft to 14,000 ft (3.655 m to 4.268 m)

Carburettor (Zenith)

Choke size	27 mm
Main jet	125
Enrichment jet	150
Slow running jet (ball type)	60
Pump jet (short stroke outer hole)	65
Part throttle air bleed	3.0
Full throttle air bleed	1.5 drilled
Slow running air bleed	1.4
Spring loaded ball valve in pump circuit	105
Fast idle	1.20
Needle valve	1.75
Needle valve washer	2.00
Fuel level	1.22-1.23 in (31-32 mm)

Air cleaner oil bath

Oil type/specification . . . .   Multigrade engine oil, viscosity range SAE 10W/40 to 20W/50, to
. . . .   API SE or SF

Fuel filters . . . .   One integral with fuel pump plus in-line cartridge type on
models fitted with emission control system

Fuel tank capacity . . . .   10 Imp. gals. 12 US gals (45 litres)

Torque wrench settings

	lbf ft	kgf m
Manifold to cylinder head nuts.	17	2.3
Inlet manifold to exhaust manifold nuts	17	2.3

1 General description

Basically the fuel system comprises a fuel tank located beneath the driver's seat, (or at the rear right-hand side on station wagon models), a mechanical fuel pump driven from the camshaft and either the Zenith 36 IV or the Solex 40 PA carburettor. Air is drawn into the carburettor intake via an oil bath type filter.

Certain export models are fitted with various emission control features to comply with the air pollution laws in different countries (mainly the USA). Section 16 describes the emission control systems used.

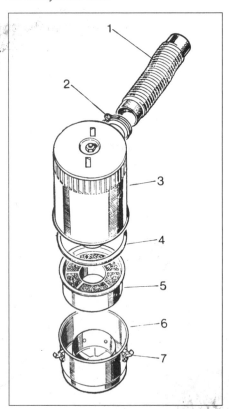

Fig. 3.1. Air cleaner assembly

1 Hose to carburettor	5 Mesh filter
2 Hose clip	6 Oil container
3 Top canister	7 Toggle clip
4 Sealing ring	

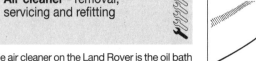

2 Air cleaner - removal, servicing and refitting

1 The air cleaner on the Land Rover is the oil bath and wire mesh type. It is essential to service it at the intervals stated in the Routine Maintenance Section at the beginning of this Manual, especially when operating in dusty conditions.
2 To service the air cleaner, it is necessary to remove the complete assembly from the vehicle (photo).
3 Slacken the clip and remove the intake hose from the top of the carburettor.
4 Undo the wingnut from the retaining strap and lift up the hinged section of the strap. Remove the complete air cleaner assembly.
5 Keep the cleaner in an upright position. Release the clips at the base and withdraw the bottom oil container section.
6 Remove the seal and lift out the wire mesh element.
7 Drain off the old oil and wash the wire mesh and container in clean petrol. Refill the bottom container with fresh engine oil until it is level with the groove (approximately 1.5 Imp. pints, 0.85 litre).
8 Refit the air cleaner to the vehicle using the reverse procedure to removal.

3 Carburettor - description

The Zenith and Solex carburettors are similar in design and operation; both being the single barrel downdraught type with mechanically operated chokes.

2.2 Air cleaner assembly

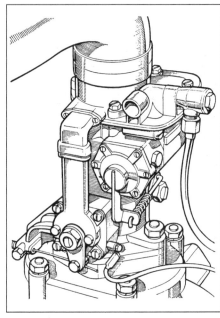

Fig. 3.2. General view of Solex carburettor

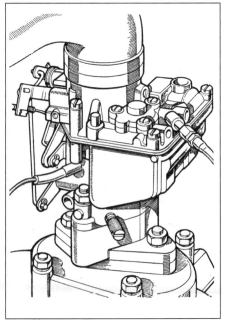

Fig. 3.3. General view of Zenith carburettor

4.3 Throttle operating rod

The main difference between the two types of carburettor is the choke, or cold starting mechanism. On the Solex model a rotating valve and duct is fitted with the option of an electrical heater element, while the Zenith has the more conventional flap valve. The accelerator pump on the Zenith is the piston type as opposed to the diaphragm operated type on the Solex.

The use of fixed diameter jets for the idling, slow running and full power modes ensure smooth running throughout the engine speed range combined with maximum economy.

The only adjustments necessary at the specified service intervals are the mixture control and slow running screw settings.

4 Carburettor - removal and refitting

1 The procedure for removing the Zenith and the Solex carburettor is virtually the same.
2 Undo the clip holding the air cleaner hose to the top of the carburettor and remove it.
3 Disconnect the choke inner and outer cables and the throttle control rod (photo).
4 Disconnect the distributor vacuum control pipe at the carburettor end.
5 Disconnect the fuel inlet pipe from the carburettor union and tape over the end to prevent dirt ingress.
6 Undo the two nuts securing the carburettor to the inlet manifold and lift it away from the engine. Push some clean rag into the manifold aperture to prevent any dirt getting in.
7 Refitting the carburettor is the reverse sequence to removal, however, it will be necessary to check the carburettor adjustments as described later in this Chapter.

5 Solex carburettor - dismantling, inspection and reassembly

1 Undo the screws securing the top cover to the carburettor body and lift off the cover complete with the cold start elbow. Do not lose the rubber seal located between the cold start elbow and duct.

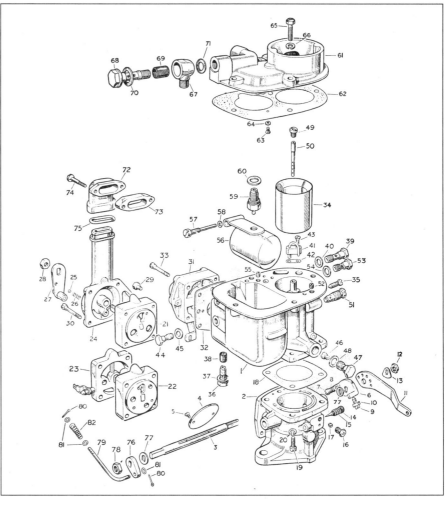

Fig. 3.4. Exploded view of Solex carburettor

1 Carburettor body	30 Special screw fixing starter body	60 Fibre washer for valve
2 Throttle chamber	31 Accelerator pump complete	61 Top cover for carburettor
3 Spindle for throttle	32 Joint washer for pump	62 Joint washer for top cover
4 Butterfly for throttle	33 Special screw securing pump	63-64 Screw - joint washer to top cover
5 Special screw securing butterfly	34 Choke tube	65-66 Screws - top cover to body
6 Plate, throttle abutment	35 Special screw securing choke tube	67 Banjo union
7 Special screw [1]	36 Non-return valve	68 Special bolt for union
8 Spring [1]	37 Fibre washer for valve	69 Filter gauze for union
9 Special screw [2]	38 Filter gauze for non-return valve	70 Fibre washer, large
10 Locknut [2]	39 Jet, accelerator pump	71 Fibre washer, small
11 Throttle lever	40 Fibre washer for jet	72 Elbow for top cover
12 Nut securing throttle lever	41 Pump injector	73 Distance piece, elbow to top cover
13 Lockwasher for nut	42 Joint washer for pump injector	74 Screw fixing elbow to top cover
14 Special screw [3]	43 Special screw securing injector	75 Rubber sealing washer, elbow to starter cover
15 Spring [3]	44 Economy jet (blank)	76 Lever for accelerator pump rod
16 Screwed union [4]	45 Joint washer for blank jet	77 Special washer for lever
17 Olive [4]	46 Main jet	78 Nut securing lever to spindle
18 Joint washer for throttle chamber	47 Main jet carrier	79 Control rod for accelerator pump
19-20 Screw and washer chamber to carburettor body	48 Fibre washer for carrier	80 Split pin [6]
21 Starter body and valve, without starter heater element	49 Correction jet	81 Plain washer [6]
22 Starter body and valve complete with starter heater element	50 Emulsion tube	82 Spring [6]
23 Heater element for starter	51 Pilot jet	
24 Cover for starter	52 Jet air bleed	[1] For slow running adjustment
25 Ball [5]	53 Starter jet, petrol	[2] For throttle stop
26 Spring [5]	54 Fibre washer for jet	[3] For mixture control
27 Lever for starter	55 Economy jet	[4] For suction pipe
28 Nut securing starter lever	56 Float	[5] For starter valve
29 Special bolt fixing starter cable	57 Spindle for float	[6] For control rod
	58 Copper washer for spindle	
	59 Needle valve completer	

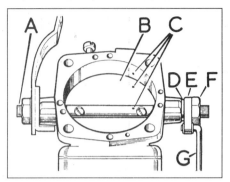

Fig. 3.5. Throttle butterfly flap and spindle

A Spindle for throttle
B Butterfly for throttle
C Markings inserted as required
D Special washer for lever   pump
E Lever for accelerator pump
F Nut fixing lever to spindle
G Control rod for accelerator

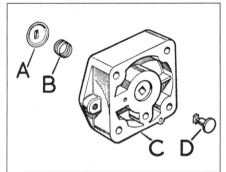

Fig. 3.6. Accelerator pump body and valve assembly

A Economy valve washer
B Economy valve spring
C Pump body
D Economy valve

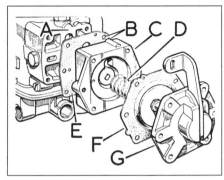

Fig. 3.7. Assembling the accelerator pump

A Carburettor body
B Location peg and hole for pump body to gasket
C Pump body
D Pump spring
E Pump body gasket body to gasket
F Pump membrane assembly
G Top pump cover

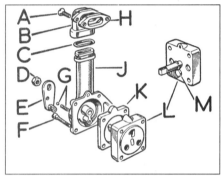

Fig. 3.8. Cold start valve and cover assembly

A Screw for elbow
B Elbow
C Rubber sealing washer
D Nut securing starter leve
E Lever for starte
F Screw securing starter body
G Ball and spring for starter valve
H Distance piece for elbow
J Starter top cover
K Heater element for starter
L Starter body
M locator

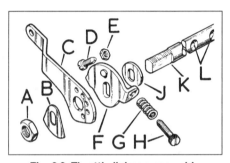

Fig. 3.9. Throttle linkage assembly

A Spindle nut
B Spindle nut tab washer
C Throttle lever
D Screw   }
E Nut   } Throttle stop
F Abutment plate
G Spring   }
H Screw   } Slow running
K Throttle spindle
L Countersunk screw holder
J Special washer

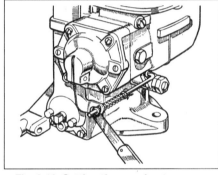

Fig. 3.10. Setting the accelerator pump clearance

2 Unscrew the needle valve assembly from the inside of the top cover.
3 Disconnect the operating rod from the accelerator pump lever, taking care not to lose the small washers and spring.
4 Undo the volume control screw, remove the four securing screws and detach the lower throttle chamber from the main carburettor body. Recover the gasket.
5 If it is intended to remove the throttle flap and control rod, carefully scratch a mark on the flap, rod and side of the venturi as shown in Fig. 3.5. to ensure correct reassembly.
6 Undo the four retaining screws and withdraw the cold start unit from the side of the throttle chamber.
7 Remove the operating lever from the cold

start unit, taking care not to lose the small steel ball and spring.
8 Remove the cold start unit from the outer cover and duct assembly and recover the rubber seal.
9 If a heating element is fitted, remove the circlip and withdraw the element from the cold start valve unit.
10 Lift the starter valve out of the valve casing.
11 To dismantle the carburettor main body assembly, first undo the securing bolt and lift out the float assembly.
12 Undo the retaining screws and remove the accelerator pump assembly from the side of the body.
13 Unscrew the air correction jet from inside the choke tube and withdraw the emulsion tube.
14 Referring to Fig. 3.4, unscrew and remove the economy jet, the pilot jet, the starter jet and the accelerator pump jet. Remove the

main jet holder and the main jet and then the non-return valve, complete with filter.
15 To dismantle the accelerator pump assembly, first undo the retaining screws and remove the outer cover.
16 Withdraw the pump membrane assembly and coil spring.
17 Twist the economy valve washer and remove the washer, spring and valve (Fig. 3.6).
18 The carburettor is now completely dismantled and all the components should be washed in clean petrol and blown dry with compressed air.
19 Check that all the jet size numbers are the same as those given in the Specifications.
20 Examine the throttle spindle bushes for wear, and, if wear is evident, the complete throttle chamber will have to be renewed.
21 Check the float for leaks and the accelerator diaphragm for splitting or perishing. Renew the components if any damage is evident.
22 Before reassembling the carburettor, obtain a new set of gaskets and seals from your Leyland dealer.
23 Reassembly is basically the reverse procedure to dismantling. Commence by

rebuilding the accelerator pump and refit it to the side of the carburettor body (Flg. 3.7). Reassemble the cold start valve into the cover as shown in Fig. 3.8 and refit to the carburettor. When refitting the throttle flap and spindle, ensure that the location marks made previously are lined up and the throttle linkage components are refitted in the correct sequence (Fig 3.9).

24 Continue to reassemble the carburettor components referring to the associated illustrations where necessary. When refitting the accelerator pump operating rod, ensure that the throttle flap is fully closed with the slow running screw slackened right off. Add washers to the end of the rod up to the nearest split pin hole until there is 0.020 in (0.5 mm) clearance between the pump operating arm and the first washer, when the split pin is inserted (see Fig. 3.10). Compress the coil spring and fit the inner split pin.

25 After refitting the carburettor to the engine, it must be adjusted as described in Section 7.

6 Zenith carburettor - dismantling, inspection and reassembly

1 As most of the important parts of the carburettor are located in the top cover it is usually not necessary to remove the carburettor from the engine for cleaning purposes.

2 Withdraw the split pins and detach the pump linkage and choke control rod (Fig. 3.12).

3 Undo and remove the four screws and spring washers that secure the top cover to the main body. Note the location of these screws as they are of different lengths.

4 Carefully lift the cover from the main body so as not to tear the gasket or bend or damage the delicate float assembly which is attached to the cover.

5 To gain access to the jets and accelerator pump, the emulsion block must be removed from the underside of the cover (Fig. 3.13).

6 Withdraw the float arm pivot pin and lift away the float assembly. Lift out the small needle valve.

7 Using a suitable size box spanner unscrew the needle valve seat and lift away together with the special washer.

8 Unscrew the two screws that secure the emulsion block to the cover. Lift the emulsion block upwards and take care to prevent the accelerator pump and spring dropping out. Recover the sealing ring.

9 The economy device is held on the top cover by three screws and spring washers which should next be removed. Lift away the cover, diaphragm and spring.

10 Unscrew the jets in the top cover and put in a safe place. The pump jet may be removed from the emulsion block after removing the plug located on the side.

11 Wash the top cover in petrol and blow out the drillings using compressed air. Inspect the economy device diaphragm for signs of

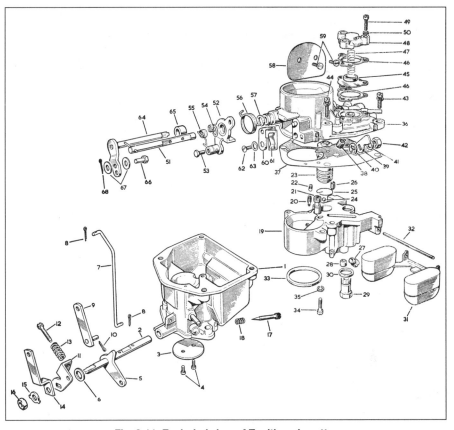

Fig. 3.11. Exploded view of Zenith carburettor

1 Carburettor main body	28 Enrichment jet	55 Spring, small[7]
2 Throttle spindle	29 Needle valve	56 Spring, large[7]
3 Butterfly for throttle	30 Special washer (2 mm)	57 Plain washer for choke spindle
4 Special screw securing butterfly	31 Float	58 Butterfly for choke
5 Floating lever on throttle spindle	32 Spindle for float	59 Special screw securing butterfly
6 Plain washer on spindle for floating lever	33 'O' ring, emulsion block to body	60 Bracket and clip for choke cable
7 Interconnecting link, throttle to choke	34 Special screw[3]	61 Clip for choke bracket
8 Split pin fixing link to levers	35 Spring washer[3]	62 Special screw[8]
9 Relay lever, throttle to accelerator pump	36 Top cover for carburettor	63 Shakeproof washer[8]
10 Split pin securing relay lever to floating lever	37 Gasket for top cover	64 Spindle and lever for accelerator pump
11 Throttle stop and fast idle lever	38 Ventilation screw (3.0 for choke)	65 Spacing washer for pump spindle
12 Special screw[1]	39 Pump lever, internal	66 Pin[9]
13 Spring[1]	40 Retaining ring for pump lever	67 Plain washer[9]
14 Throttle lever	41 Shakeproof washer[4]	68 Split pin[9]
15 Lockwasher[2]	42 Special nut[4]	
16 Special nut[2]	43 Screw and spring washer, short[5]	[1]For throttle stop
17 Volume control screw	44 Screw and spring washer, long[5]	[2]Securing throttle levers
18 Spring for control screw	45 Diaphragm for carburettor	[3]Securing emulsion block to body
19 Emulsion block	46 Gasket for diaphragm	[4]Securing pump lever
20 Pump jet	47 Spring for diaphragm	[5]Securing top cover to main body
21 Pump discharge valve	48 Cover for diaphragm	[6]Securing diaphragm cover
22 Plug for pump jet	49 Screw[6]	[7]For choke lever
23 Piston for accelerator pump	50 Spring washer[6]	[8]Securing choke bracket to top cover
24 Ball for piston	51 Spindle and pin for choke lever	[9]Securing relay lever to pump lever
25 Circlip for piston	52 Lever and swivel for choke	
26 Slow running jet	53 Screw for choke lever swivel	
27 Main jet	54 Circlip securing choke lever to top cover	

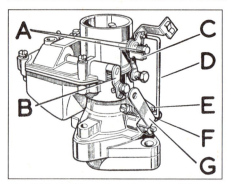

Fig. 3.12. Zenith carburettor control linkage

A Choke linkage return springs
B Accelerator pump spindle lever
C Choke operating tab
D Interconnecting link
E Throttle spindle relay lever
F Throttle spindle floating lever
G Throttle lever

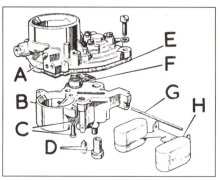

Fig. 3.13. Zenith carburettor top cover and emulsion block

A Carburettor top cover
B Emulsion block
C Emulsion block attachment screws and washers
D Needle valve and housing
E Top cover gasket
F Accelerator pump piston assembly
G Hinge pin
H Float assembly

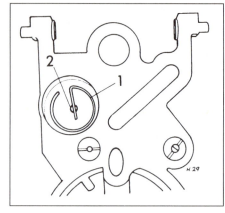

Fig. 3.14. Location of accelerator pump ball and spring clip

1 Retaining clip   2 Ball

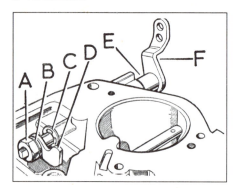

Fig. 3.15. Accelerator pump spindle assembly (Zenith)

A Securing nut
B Shakeproof washer
C Circlip
D Accelerator pump arm
E Distance piece oilite bush
F Spindle and lever for accelerator pump

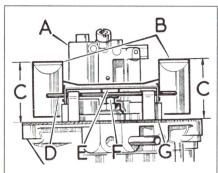

Fig. 3.16. Checking the float setting (Zenith)

A Emulsion block
B Highest points on floats
C Dimension to be 1 5/16 in (33 mm)
D Hinge pin
E Central tongue on float carrier
F Needle valve

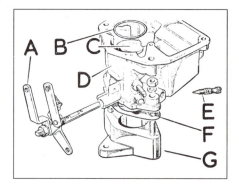

Fig. 3.17. Carburettor body and adaptor (Zenith)

A Throttle control   E Volume control screw
B '0' ring seal   F Adaptor gasket
C Venturi barrel   G Adaptor body
D Carburettor body

damage and, if evident, obtain a new one ready for reassembly.
12 Reassembly starts with the refitting of the emulsion block to the cover. Refer to Fig. 3.14. and make sure that the accelerator pump inlet ball and circlip are installed in the bottom of the cylinder. Refit the jets to the top cover.
13 Fit the new gasket to the top cover and ensure that the accelerator pump lever is correctly positioned as shown in Fig. 3.15.
14 Examine the needle valve for any signs of ridging on the bevelled face and renew both the needle and seat if in doubt.
15 Position the emulsion block on the top cover and secure with the two screws.
16 Refit the needle valve seating and special washer. Insert the needle.
17 Refit the float assembly and retain in position with the spindle. Hold the cover upside down and measure the distance from the bottom of the float to the face of the

cover gaskets. It should be 1 5/16 in (33 mm). Make any adjustments necessary by carefully bending the float arm centre tag which contacts the needle. This setting is important (Fig. 3.16).
18 Before replacing the cover onto the body, check that the sealing ring located as shown in Fig. 3.17 is in good order. A bad seal will result in fuel leaking from the float chamber. Secure the cover with the four screws and spring washers. Take care because these are of different lengths.
19 Reconnect the accelerator pump linkage noting that the pin should always be fitted to the upper hole in the pump spindle lever.
20 The choke control rod is not provided with any obvious adjustment. With the choke flap held shut there should be a 0.040 in (1 mm) gap down the side of the throttle flap. For this

a number 61 drill is useful. Bend the control rod if necessary to obtain this setting.
21 The choke flap spindle return spring must engage the first notch on the lever.

---

7 Carburettor - setting and adjustment (both types)

1 Before adjusting the carburettor controls ensure that the spark plug gaps and valve clearances are correctly set and the ignition static timing is set up as described in Chapter 4.
2 Screw the mixture control screw right in but do not overtighten. Then slacken it 1 1/2 turns.
3 Turn the slow running screw in until it just touches the stop on the carburettor body then rotate it one complete turn.
4 Operate the accelerator pedal and check that the linkage moves freely and the throttle operating rod has full travel.
5 Start the engine and allow it to run until normal working temperature is reached.

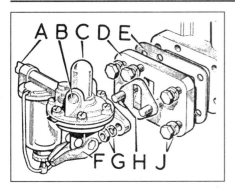

Fig. 3.18. Fuel pump and adaptor assembly

A Fuel inlet pipe
B Fuel outlet pipe
C Fuel pump
D Side cover
E Joint washer for side cover
F Hand prime lever
G Pump nuts
H Joint washer
J Bolts for side cover

6 Turn the mixture control screw in the required direction until the engine speed increases and runs smoothly. Now adjust the slow running screw until the idling speed is approximately 500 rpm. **Note:** On vehicles fitted with emission control the idling speed should be between 750 and 800 rpm (see Section 16).
7 Dab the throttle fully open and close it to check that the engine does not stall. If it does, slightly increase the idling speed.

8 Fuel pump - removal and refitting

1 Remove the air cleaner as described in Section 2 of this Chapter.
2 Undo and remove the inlet and outlet fuel pipe unions from the pump body.
3 Remove the two securing nuts and withdraw the pump and gasket. If difficulty is experienced in removing the two nuts, undo the four bolts and remove the pump complete with side cover plate and gasket (see Fig. 3.18).
4 Refitting is a reversal of this procedure but ensure that a new gasket is fitted.

9 Fuel pump - dismantling

1 Clean the outside of the pump and wipe dry using a dry non-fluffy rag.
2 Using a file make a mark on the flanges of the upper and lower body to ensure that they are correctly reassembled.
3 Unscrew the stirrup thumb screw and swing the stirrup out of the way. Hold the glass bowl to ensure that it does not drop. Lift away the sediment bowl followed by the cork seal and gauze filter. Inspect the cork gasket for signs

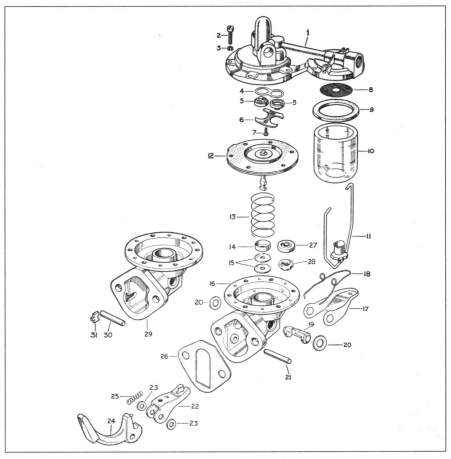

Fig. 3.19. Exploded view of fuel pump

1 Top cover	13 Diaphragm spring
2 Securing screws	14 Oil seal retainer[1]
3 Spring washer	15 Sealing washers[1]
4 Valve gasket	16 Pump body[1]
5 Valves	17 Hand priming lever
6 Retainer for valves	18 Return spring for hand lever
7 Screw for retainer	19 Hand rocker
8 Gauge filter disc	20 Cork washers
9 Lock sealing gasket	21 Rocker arm pivot pin, early type
10 Sediment bowl	22 Operating link
11 Bowl retainer	
12 Diaphragm assembly	

23 Plain washers
24 Rocker arm
25 Return spring
26 Joint washer
27 Oil seal retainer[2]
28 Oil seal[2]
29 Pump body[2]
30 Rocker arm pivot pin[2]
31 Retainer for pivot pin[2]
[1]Early type
[2]Latest type

of damage or flattening and obtain a new one ready for reassembling.
4 Undo and remove the six body securing screws and spring washers and separate the two halves.
5 Invert the upper body and undo the two valve retaining plate screws and lift away the screws, retaining plate, the two valve assemblies and the valve gasket from the upper body.
6 Note the position of the lip on the diaphragm relative to the lower body to ensure correct reassembly and remove the diaphragm by rotating through 90° in an anti-clockwise direction and lifting it away from the lower body and the link.
7 It is recommended that the lower body parts are not dismantled unless either the

seal, hand priming lever or the link assembly require attention.

10 Fuel pump - examination and reassembly

1 Check the condition of the cork sediment bowl sealing washer and if it has hardened or broken it must be renewed. The diaphragm should be checked similarly and renewed if faulty. Clean the pump thoroughly and agitate the valves in paraffin or petrol to clean them out. This will also improve the contact between the valve seat and the valve. It is unlikely that the pump body will be damaged but check for fractures and cracks.

2 To reassemble the pump proceed as follows. If the lower body has been dismantled refit the rocker arm assembly comprising the operating link, rocker arm, anti-rattle spring and washers in their relative positions in the lower body. Align the holes in the body and insert the pivot pin.

3 Refit the circlips to the grooves in each end of the pivot pin. **Note:** On later models the pivot pin is held in place by two retainers (see Fig. 3.19). After refitting the pivot pin, tap the retainers into their grooves and secure them in place by lightly peening over the ends of the grooves with a small chisel.

4 Invert the upper body and replace the gasket, valves, valve retaining plate and tighten the two plate retaining screws. The two valves are interchangeable so care must be taken to ensure they are fitted the correct way round. The inlet valve should be fitted into the offset and shallower part with its spring facing the diaphragm, whilst the outlet valve is fitted to the centre part with its spring facing away from the diaphragm.

5 Place the seal and retainer in the lower body and place the diaphragm spring over them.

6 Refit the diaphragm and pullrod assembly with the pullrod downwards and ensure the small tab on the diaphragm lines up to the previously noted position which should have been adjacent to the centre of the flange and rocker arm.

7 With the body of the pump held so that the rocker arm is facing away, press down the diaphragm, turning it a quarter of a turn to the left at the same time. This engages the slot on the pullrod with the operating lever. The small tab on the diaphragm should now be at an angle of 90° to the rocker arm and the diaphragm should be firmly located.

8 Move the rocker arm until the diaphragm is level with the body flanges and hold the arm in this position. Reassemble the two halves of the pump ensuring that the previously made marks on the flanges are adjacent to each other.

9 Insert the six screws and lockwashers and tighten them down finger tight.

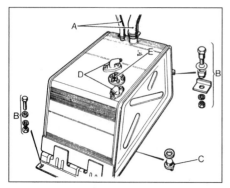

Fig. 3.21. Front mounted fuel tank

A Filler and breather hoses
B Securing bolts
C Drain plug
D Fuel supply union (one only)
E Sender unit

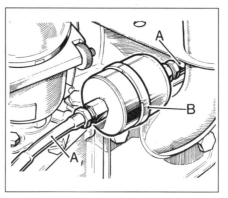

Fig. 3.20. Disposable fuel filter (models fitted with emission control)

A Inlet and outlet fuel pipes
B Securing clip

10 Move the rocker arm up and down several times to centralise the diaphragm, and then with the arm held down, tighten the screws securely in a diagonal sequence.

11 Replace the gauze filter, cork washer and sediment bowl and refit the stirrup thumbscrew to the base of the sediment bowl. Tighten lightly only to ensure a fuel tight joint as overtightening will crack the bowl.

11 Fuel filters - general

All models have a wire gauze filter in the glass bowl attached to the fuel pump. This should be removed as described in the previous Section and cleaned at the recommended service intervals (photo).

The Solex carburettor has a filter in the banjo union on the top cover (see photo) This should be removed and cleaned at periodic intervals.

On vehicles equipped with emission control (export models) a renewable fuel filter is fitted in the outlet pipe from the fuel pump. When fitting a new filter unit, ensure the end marked 'IN' is facing towards the fuel pump. If the filter is marked with an arrow this must point away from the pump.

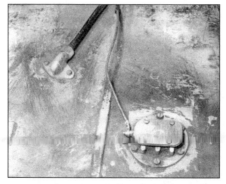

13.5 Fuel tank sender unit and outlet pipe

11.1 Removing the fuel pump filter bowl

11.2 Filter in carburettor inlet pipe union

12 Fuel gauge and sender unit

The fuel gauge and sender unit are integrated into the electrical system of the vehicle and therefore the description and all notes regarding the fuel sensor system are included in Chapter 10.

13 Fuel tank - description, removal and refitting

1 On the standard models the fuel tank is located on the right-hand side below the seat base. The station wagon models are fitted with a fuel tank at the rear right-hand side of the vehicle.

2 Always work on the fuel system in a well ventilated building or, preferably, outside. Pick a time when the tank is almost empty. Disconnect the battery earth lead before draining the petrol from the tank into a suitable container.

Front mounted tank

3 Remove the right-hand side seat cushion and fold the seat squab forward.

4 Slacken the clips and pull the filler hose and breather hose off the tank unions.

5 Remove the cover panel and disconnect the fuel supply pipe union and the sender unit wire terminal (photo).

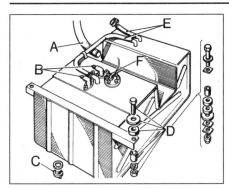

Fig. 3.22. Rear mounted fuel tank

A Filler hose
B Fuel supply union (one only)
C Drain plug
D Securing bolts
E Breather and balance pipes
F Sender unit

6 Support the weight of the tank, remove the securing bolts and carefully lower the tank and remove it from beneath the vehicle.
7 Refitting the tank is the reverse of the removal procedure. Do not forget to tighten the drain plug.

Rear mounted tank

8 Slacken the clip securing the filler hose to the tank and detach the hose.
9 Support the weight of tank, remove the securing bolts and then lower the tank just enough to give access to the pipes and leads on the top of the tank.
10 Disconnect the fuel supply pipe, breather pipe, air balance pipe and the sender unit wire terminal.
11 Lower the tank to the ground and remove it from beneath the vehicle.
12 Refit the tank using the reverse of the removal procedure. Check the drain plug is tight and before attempting to start the engine, prime the carburettor with fuel using the priming lever on the pump.

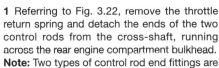

14 Accelerator linkage -
removal and refitting

1 Referring to Fig. 3.22, remove the throttle return spring and detach the ends of the two control rods from the cross-shaft, running across the rear engine compartment bulkhead.
Note: Two types of control rod end fittings are used, either the ball and socket type or the spring clip type.
2 Slacken the pinch bolt securing the operating lever to the accelerator pedal shaft and remove the lever. Undo the two bolts securing the shaft to the bulkhead and remove the pedal and shaft assembly from inside the vehicle.
3 Undo the bolts securing the cross-shaft to the rear bulkhead and remove the shaft complete with levers.
4 Examine the control rod ends for wear and

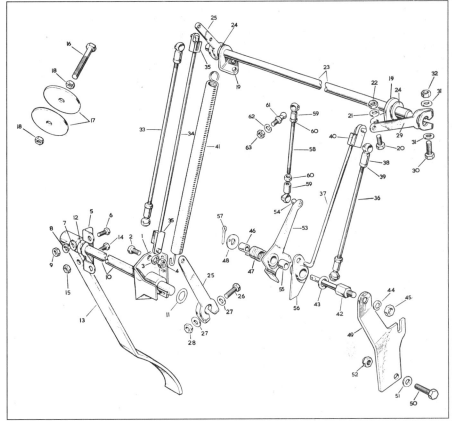

Fig. 3.23. Accelerator pedal and linkage

1 Housing for accelerator shaft and pedal stop
2 Bolt (1/4 in UNF x 1/2 in long)[1]
3 Spring washer[1]
4 Nut (1/4 in UNF)[1]
5 Bracket for accelerator pedal shaft
6 Bolt (1/4 in UNF x 5/8 in long)[2]
7 Plain washer[2]
8 Spring washer[2]
9 Nut (1/4 in UNF)[2]
10 Shaft for accelerator pedal
11 Special washer[3]
12 Plain washer[3]
13 Accelerator pedal
14 Bolt (5/16 in UNF x 7/8 in long)[4]
15 Nut (5/16 in UNF)[4]
16 Bolt (5/16 in UNF x 1 1/8 in long)[5]
17 Plain washer[5]
18 Nut (5/16 in UNF)[5]
19 Bracket for accelerator cross-shaft 'L' shaped
20 Bolt (1/4 in UNF x 5/8 in long)[6]
21 Spring washer[6]
22 Nut (1/4 in UNF)[6]
23 Cross-shaft for accelerator
24 Distance washer for lever
25 Lever for accelerator
26 Bolt (1/4 in UNF x 1 3/4 in long)[7]

27 Plain washer[7]
28 Nut (1/4 in UNF)[7]
29 Lever for cross-shaft
30 Bolt (1/4 in UNF x 1 1/4 in long)[8]
31 Plain washer[8]
32 Nut (1/4 in UNF)[8]
33 Control rod, pedal shaft to cross-shaft
34 Control rod, pedal shaft to cross-shaft
35 Linkage clip for control rod
36 Control rod, cross-shaft to engine
37 Control rod, cross-shaft to engine
38 Balljoint socket for rods
39 Locknut for socket
40 Linkage clip for control rod, cross-shaft to engine
41 Return spring for pedal
42 Spindle for carburettor bell crank
43 Plain washer[9]
44 Spring washer[9]
45 Nut (3/8 in UNF)[9]
46 Spacer for spindle
47 Torsion spring for bell crank
48 Special washer for torsion spring
49 Bracket for accelerator controls
50 Bolt (3/8 in UNF x 1 in long)[10]

51 Plain washer[10]
52 Self-locking nut (3/8 in UNF)[10]
53 Carburettor bell crank lever assembly
54 Ball end for lever
55 Bush for bell crank
56 Carburettor relay lever
57 Split pin securing levers to spindle
58 Control rod, bell crank to carburettor
59 Balljoint[11]
60 Locknut (2 BA)[11]
61 Ball end for carburettor lever
62 Spring washer[12]
63 Nut (1/4 in UNF)[12]

[1]Securing housing and pedal stop to dash
[2]Securing bracket to dash
[3]On accelerator shaft
[4]Securing pedal to shaft
[5]Pedal stop to floor
[6]Securing bracket to dash
[7]Securing levers to shaft
[8]Securing lever to cross-shaft
[9]Securing spindle
[10]Securing bracket to steering column support bracket
[11]For control rod
[12]Securing ball end to carburettor lever

the holes in the levers for ovality. If renewal is necessary, mark the position of the levers on the cross-shaft to ensure they are refitted at the correct angle.

> **HAYNES HiNT**
> *If adjustable socket type control rods are fitted mark the threads adjacent to the locknut before unscrewing the socket. This will enable the rod to be adjusted to the correct length when reassembling.*

5 Refit the pedal and linkage using the reverse procedure to removal. With the linkage correctly installed, check that the throttleflap in the carburettor is fully open when the accelerator pedal is pressed down onto the stop and fully closed when the pedal is released. Adjust the linkage as necessary.
6 Finally, run the engine until it is warm and adjust the carburettor controls as described in Section 7.

15 Exhaust system - general

The exhaust system on the 4-cylinder Land Rover comprises basically of a front pipe clamped to the exhaust manifold, an intermediate pipe section leading into the silencer and tailpipe assembly. On models prior to 1961 the front pipe was fitted with two heat shields. Some models are fitted with a heat shield around the exhaust manifold (see Fig. 3.24).

The exhaust system should be examined periodically for corrosion and, when using the vehicle in rough terrain, damage. If any defects are found, the effected section of pipe (or the silencer) should be renewed.

The task of removing the exhaust system is straightforward as the pipe sections are connected by flanged joints, which are considerably easier to dismantle than the more common sleeve connections.

If any of the flange or bracket nuts are seized, try soaking them overnight in penetrating oil. If this fails they will have to be cut off with a hacksaw or cold chisel.

15.5 A socket will be required to remove these exhaust manifold securing nuts

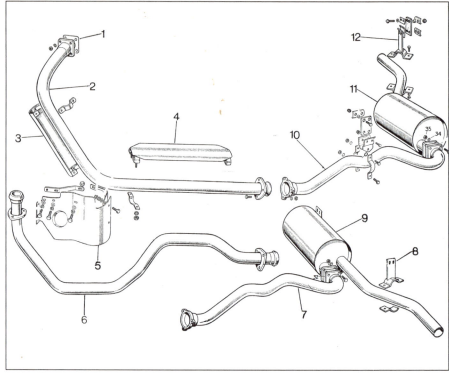

Fig. 3.24. Exhaust system components

1 Gasket	6 Front pipe (1961 onwards)	10 Intermediate pipe ('109'
2 Front pipe (prior to 1961)	7 Intermediate pipe ('88'	models)
3 Front heat shield	models)	11 Silencer (right-hand drive
4 Rear heat shield	8 Bracket	models)
5 Manifold heat shield	9 Silencer (left-hand drive	12 Support bracket
assembly	models)	

The exhaust and inlet manifolds are attached to the cylinder head by studs and nuts. Some of the lower nuts will require a socket and extension bar to remove them (photo).

On earlier models the manifold gasket is in one piece while on later models only the inlet manifold is fitted with gaskets. Always use new gaskets when refitting the manifolds.

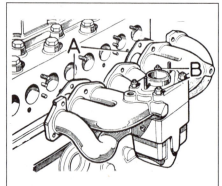

Fig. 3.25. Inlet and exhaust manifold assembly

A Gaskets, late type shown. Position gaskets with raised rings towards cylinder head
B Nuts, inlet manifold to exhaust manifold

16 Emission control systems - general

Export models of the Land Rover, (primarily for the USA) are fitted with various devices to reduce air pollution. Three separate systems can be fitted and these comprise; crankcase ventilation, fuel evaporation control and exhaust emission control. While the servicing procedures described in this Section can be carried out by the home mechanic, any alterations or major adjustments to the systems must be left to an authorised dealer to avoid contravening the pollution laws, which in certain countries are very strict.

Crankcase emission control

This system consists of a hose connected between the sealed crankcase oil filler tube and the inlet manifold via a non-return valve. A second hose connects the breather on top of the rocker cover to the air cleaner elbow (see Fig. 3.26).

When the engine is running the fumes which collect in the crankcase are drawn into the combustion chambers via the inlet manifold. These are reburnt while clean air is admitted through the breather to assist in purging.

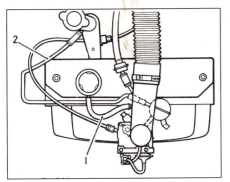

Fig. 3.26. Crankcase emission control system

1 *Hose connecting breather to air cleaner hose*
2 *Hose and valve connecting oil filler pipe and inlet manifold*

1 Every 12,000 miles (20,000 km), remove the clip securing the non-return valve cover, lift out the diaphragm and spring and clean the cover and the inside of the valve body with methylated spirits, taking care not to allow any of the methylated spirits to come into contact with the diaphragm.
2 Check the diaphragm for damage and renew if necessary. Refit the valve components and secure the cover with the spring clip.

Fuel evaporation control

The purpose of this system is to prevent fuel vapour from the petrol tank escaping into the atmosphere.

A special filler cap is fitted to prevent loss of vapour and a breather pipe leads from the main fuel tank through an expansion tank into a charcoal canister in the engine compartment. A second pipe connects the top of the charcoal canister to the air cleaner. As fuel vapour builds up in the expansion tank it is fed into the canister and absorbed by the charcoal. When the engine is running the vapour in the charcoal is drawn into the combustion chambers via the air cleaner and inlet manifold. Air is drawn into the canister through a renewable filter.

3 Every 12,000 miles (20,000 km) the filter should be renewed. The canister is located at the rear of the engine compartment on the right-hand side. Note the respective positions of the two hoses and then remove them.
4 Remove the bolts securing the canister to the bracket and lift the canister away from the vehicle.
5 Unscrew the base of the canister and withdraw the filter (see Fig. 3.28). Fit the new filter with the smooth side facing inward.

 Warning: Do not attempt to clean the inside of the canister with compressed air as this may cause the charcoal filling to self-ignite.

6 Fit a new sealing ring, screw on the base and refit the canister into the engine compartment ensuring the pipe on the side of the canister faces towards the rear of the engine compartment.

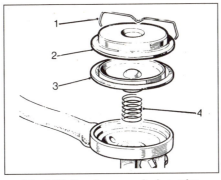

Fig. 3.27. Crankcase emission valve components

1 *Retaining clip*   3 *Diaphragm*
2 *Top cover*   4 *Coil spring*

Exhaust emission control

Exhaust emission control is achieved by modifications to the carburettor and ignition system. In the case of the carburettor, the normal jets are replaced with ones having special flow characteristics and can be identified by their cadmium plated finish. To improve combustion on the overrun, a small servo unit is connected to a throttle prop lever on the carburettor and when the inlet manifold depression is high, (on the overrun) a trigger switch connected to the manifold actuates the servo unit, which causes the throttle prop lever to open the throttle flap a small amount, thus improving the fuel/air mixture in the carburettor.

The engine idle speed on vehicles equipped with emission control has been increased to 750-800 rpm. To prevent running-on due to this high idle speed the idle by-pass drilling and progression chambers within the carburettor are cut off by a solenoid operated needle valve, whenever the ignition switch is turned off. The valve, which is located next to the mixture control screw (see Fig. 3.29) is preset and must not be adjusted.

7 The carburettor slow running adjustment is very important on vehicles equipped with emission control and should be checked every 6,000 miles (10,000 km) using the following procedure:

a) *Before adjusting the carburettor, ensure the valve clearances and ignition timing are correctly set and that the throttle linkage is free to move.*
b) *With the engine thoroughly warmed up, unlock the mixture control screw and turn it gently clockwise until it is fully in. Then screw it out for 3/4 of a turn.*
c) *Adjust the throttle stop screw to obtain an idling speed of 800 rpm. A suitable tachometer must be used to obtain this setting.*
d) *Turn the mixture control either in or out as necessary to get the highest engine idle speed, and reset the idle speed to 800 rpm using the throttle stop screw.*

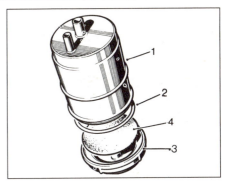

Fig. 3.28. Charcoal filter canister

1 *Main body*   3 *End cap*
2 *Sealing ring*   4 *Filter*

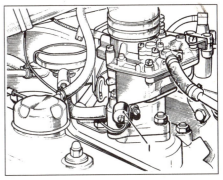

Fig. 3.29. Fuel cut-off valve

1 *Location of valve*

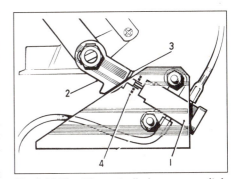

Fig. 3.30. Throttle controlled vacuum switch

1 *Vacuum switch*
2 *Throttle linkage cam*
3 *Switch plunger extended*
4 *Switch plunger retracted*

e) *Turn the mixture control screw clockwise until the idling speed drops to 750 rpm and then enrich the mixture slightly by turning the screw 1/4 turn anticlockwise. Lock the mixture control screw.*
f) *Reset the idling speed to 800 rpm using the throttle stop screw and then lock it. Remove the tachometer and switch off the engine.*

Some changes were made to the ignition system of vehicles which have emission control systems. These are, a special distributor, and a throttle controlled vacuum switch. When the throttle is closed the switch opens the vacuum line to the distributor and retards the ignition. The purpose of this is to retard the ignition when the throttle is closed at high engine speeds.

8 To adjust the switch plunger position in relation to the cam on the throttle linkage, proceed as follows:

a) First check that the throttle linkage is in the correct Idle position.

b) Push the switch plunger right down into the switch and measure the clearance between the cam and the plunger. This should be 0.030 in (0.76 mm).

c) Adjust the clearance if necessary by slackening the nuts securing the switch mounting bracket to the inlet manifold. Move the switch and bracket assembly in the required direction. When the clearance is correct tighten the bracket securing nuts.

The correct ignition timing on vehicles fitted with the exhaust emission control system is absolutely essential and the static timing method described in Chapter 4 is not accurate enough. It is strongly recommended that the vehicle is taken to a Leyland dealer, or engine tuning specialist who will have the electronic equipment necessary to do the job properly.

9 However, for the home mechanic who has a strobe lamp and tachometer, the ignition timing can be checked using the following procedure:

a) Set the engine idling speed as close as possible to 800 rpm without exceeding this speed.

b) Set the vernier adjustment nut on the side of the distributor to the fully advanced position. This is to prevent the ignition being subsequently advanced beyond the correct setting.

c) Slacken the distributor clamping bolt and rotate the distributor until the flash of the strobe light, (which must be connected to No 1 plug lead) is synchronised with the 6° A TDC timing pointer on the front engine cover and the mark on the crankshaft pulley (see Fig. 3.31).

d) Tighten the distributor clamping bolt and recheck the timing.

Fig. 3.31. Timing pointer location (strobe lamp timing}

1 Correct alignment of timing marks

Fault diagnosis - fuel system and carburation

Unsatisfactory engine performance and excessive fuel consumption are not necessarily the fault of the fuel system or carburettor. In fact they more commonly occur as a result of ignition and timing faults. Before acting on the following it is necessary to check the ignition system first. Even though a fault may lie in the fuel system it will be difficult to trace unless the ignition is correct. The faults below therefore, assume that this has been attended to first (where appropriate).

Smell of petrol when engine is stopped

☐ Leaking fuel lines or unions.
☐ Leaking fuel tank.

Smell of petrol when engine is idling

☐ Leaking fuel line unions between pump and carburettor.
☐ Overflow of fuel from float chamber due to wrong level setting, ineffective needle valve or punctured float.

Excessive fuel consumption for reasons not covered by leaks or float chamber faults

☐ Worn jets.
☐ Over-rich jet settings.
☐ Sticking mechanism.

Difficult starting, uneven running, lack of power, cutting out

☐ One or more jets blocked or restricted.
☐ Float chamber fuel level too low or needle valve sticking.
☐ Fuel pump not delivering sufficient fuel.

Chapter 3B
Fuel and exhaust systems – diesel models

For modifications, and information applicable to later models, see Supplement at end of manual

Contents

Degrees of difficulty

Easy, suitable for novice with little experience	**Fairly easy,** suitable for beginner with some experience	**Fairly difficult,** suitable for competent DIY mechanic	**Difficult,** suitable for experienced DIY mechanic	**Very difficult,** suitable for expert DIY or professional

Specifications

Air cleaner
Type . . . . AC centrifugal oil bath
Oil capacity . . . . 1.5 Imp pints (1.8 US pints, 0.85 litre)

Fuel pump
Type . . . . AC mechanical

Fuel injection/distributor pump
Type . . . . CAV mechanically governed distributor type
Injection timing (see text)
  Early models . . . . 16° BTDC
  Later models . . . . 15° BTDC (13°BTDC,1973 on)
Pump idling speed . . . . 590 ± 20 rpm
Maximum pump speed . . . . 4,200 ± 20 rpm

Fuel injectors
Type . . . . CAV Pintaux

Torque wrench settings

	lbf ft	kgf m
Fuel injector securing nuts	6 to 8	0.8 to 1.1

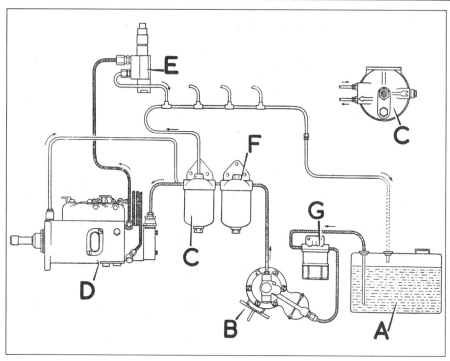

Fig. 3.1 General layout of diesel fuel system (Sec 1)

A Fuel tank
B Fuel pump
C Main filter
D Fuel injection distributor
   pump
E Fuel injector
F Additional filter (if fitted)
G Sedimentor (if fitted)

2.5 Dismantling the air cleaner assembly

2.6a Lift out the wire mesh element

1 General description

The fuel system on diesel engine Land Rovers comprises a fuel tank, mechanical fuel pump, fuel injection/distributor pump, and four fuel injectors.

Clean fuel is essential for the efficient operation of the fuel injection/distributor pump and for this reason there are a minimum of three fuel filters incorporated in the system. In addition to the fuel line filters, clean air is drawn into the intake manifold via an oil bath type air filter.

The system operates in the following manner; Fuel is drawn from the tank by a mechanical lift pump driven off the camshaft. It is then delivered via the filters to the fuel injection/distributor pump. A precisely controlled amount of fuel, depending on engine demand is supplied to the injectors where it enters the engine combustion chamber as a fine spray. Air is also drawn into the cylinders via the air filter and intake manifold to form the correct air/fuel ratio necessary for combustion.

Due to the complex nature of the fuel injection/distributor pump and the need for specialist knowledge and equipment, no attempt should be made to overhaul the fuel injection/distributor pump or injectors. If these units give trouble they should be renewed or overhauled by your Land Rover dealer or diesel injection specialists.

 Warning: It is necessary to take certain precautions when working on the fuel system components, particularly the fuel injectors Before carrying out any operations on the fuel system, refer to the precautions given in Safety first, and to any additional warning notes at the start of the relevant Sections

2 Air cleaner -
removal, servicing and refitting

1 The air cleaner on the Land Rover is the oil bath and wire mesh type. It is essential to service it at the intervals stated in the Routine Maintenance Section at the beginning of this Manual, especially when operating in dusty conditions.

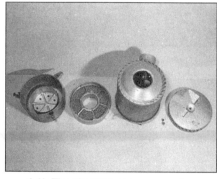

2.6b The air cleaner components

2 To service the air cleaner, it is necessary to remove the complete assembly from the vehicle.
3 Slacken the clip and remove the intake hose from the top of the inlet manifold.
4 Undo the wingnut from the retaining strap and lift up the hinged section of the strap. Remove the complete air cleaner assembly.
5 Keep the cleaner in an upright position. Release the clips at the base and withdraw the bottom oil container section (photo).
6 Remove the seal and lift out the wire mesh element (photos).
7 Drain off the old oil and wash the wire mesh and container in clean petrol. Refill the bottom container with fresh engine oil until it is level with the groove (approximately 1.5 Imp. pints, 0.85 litre) (photo).
8 Refit the air cleaner to the vehicle using the reverse procedure to removal.

2.7 Refilling the container with engine oil

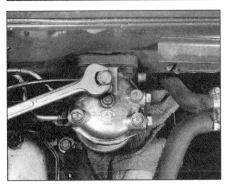

3.2 Bleeding the fuel filter

3.3 Fuel emerging from bleed pipe during priming

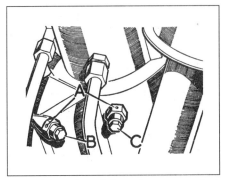

Fig. 3.2 Location of air vent screws on fuel injection distributor pump

A *Fuel orifice*
B *Air vent screw on pump body*
C *Air vent screw on control cover*

3 Fuel system - priming

1 If for any reason the vehicle has been allowed to run out of fuel or if the fuel lines, fuel injection/distributor pump, or filters have been removed, it will be necessary to remove all the air from the system before attempting to start the engine. If the filter bowl has been cleaned or any of the filters have been serviced follow paragraphs 2 to 6 inclusive. If the fuel system has been completely emptied, carry out the full priming procedure.
2 Slacken the air vent or bleed pipe union on the filter that has been serviced (photo).
3 Operate the fuel pump hand priming lever until fuel free from air bubbles emerges from the air vent or bleed pipe (photo).
4 Tighten the air vent or bleed pipe union whilst still pumping.
5 Operate the hand priming lever twice more to clear any remaining air bubbles into the bleed pipe.
6 Start the engine in the normal way and carefully check for any fuel leaks.
7 If the fuel system has been completely drained or if the engine will not start after carrying out the procedure in paragraphs 2 to 6, repeat paragraphs 2 to 6 inclusive and then proceed as follows.

8 Slacken the air vent screw on the side of the fuel injection/distributor pump (Fig. 3.2)
9 Operate the fuel pump hand priming lever until fuel free from air bubbles emerges from the air vent.
10 Tighten the air vent screw whilst pumping.
11 Slacken the air vent screw on the fuel injection/distributor pump control cover, (Fig. 3.2) and repeat paragraphs 9 and 10.
12 Start the engine in the normal way and carefully check for any fuel leaks.

4 Fuel filters - general description

The engines are fitted with three fuel filters on home market models and four filters on export models. The first is incorporated in the fuel tank and requires no maintenance. Early models have a sediment bowl and filter fitted to the fuel pump which is described in Sec-tion 12. The main fuel filter is mounted on the engine on early models and on the engine compartment bulkhead on later models. All export models incorporate an additional filter mounted on the engine compartment bulkhead adjacent to the main filter. On later models this additional filter is replaced by a sedimentor which removes large droplets of water and particles of foreign matter from the fuel, thus increasing the life of the main filter. A final filter is incorporated in the injection pump behind the inlet pipe union connection.

5.9 Main fuel filter securing bolt and pipe connections

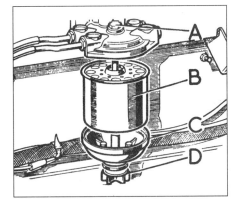

Fig. 3.3 Latest type of main fuel filter

A *Retaining bolt*
B *Filter element*
C *Filter element holder*
D *Water drain plug*

5 Main fuel filter - removal, servicing and refitting

Early type - engine mounted

1 Slacken the plug on the bottom of the filter body and drain the fuel into a suitable container.
2 Unscrew and remove the bleed back pipe from the top of the filter unit.
3 Support the filter body and unscrew and remove the centre cap securing nut on top of the filter.
4 Withdraw the filter body complete with the small sealing ring on the top of the element, and recover the large sealing ring from the underside of the filter cover.
5 Discard the element and wash the container and all components thoroughly in clean diesel fuel.
6 Inspect the sealing rings and if worn or damaged they must be renewed.
7 Place a new element in position in the container and refit using the reverse procedure to removal.
8 Prime the fuel system as described in Section 3.

Later type - bulkhead mounted

9 Support the element holder from below and unscrew and remove the retaining bolt on the top of the main filter body (photo) Withdraw the element and holder.
10 Discard the element and thoroughly wash the element holder in clean diesel fuel.
11 Inspect the sealing rings and if worn or damaged they must be renewed.
12 Place a new element in position on the main filter body with the perforated holes uppermost. Refit the element holder and secure the assembly with the retaining bolt.
13 Prime the fuel system as described in Section 3.
14 If an additional filter of the same type is fitted alongside the main filter it may be removed and serviced in the same manner. If the additional

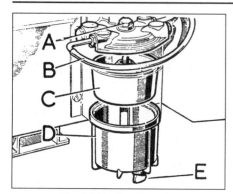

Fig. 3.4 Fuel sedimentor

A *Retaining bolt* D *Bowl*
B *Inlet pipe* E *Water drain plug*
C *Element*

filter is of the sedimentor type (Fig. 3.4), refer to Section 6 for service procedures.

6 Fuel sedimentor - removal, servicing and refitting

1 Unscrew and remove the fuel inlet pipe union and position the pipe above fuel tank level to prevent syphoning.
2 Support the sediment bowl and unscrew and remove the securing bolt on the top of the main body. Lift off the sediment bowl and element.
3 Thoroughly clean all components in clean diesel fuel.
4 Inspect the seals and renew if worn or damaged.
5 Refitting is the reversal of the removal procedure.
6 Prime the fuel system as described in Section 3.

7 Fuel injection/distributor pump filter - removal and refitting

1 Unscrew and remove the inlet pipe union from the fuel filter.
2 Unscrew and remove the large pipe connection from the fuel injection distributor pump head. Withdraw the gauze filter.

8.12 Aligning the timing marks on the flywheel with the pointer

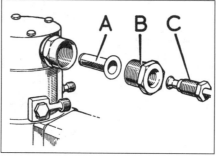

Fig. 3.5 Fuel injection distributor pump filter

A *Filter*   B *Union nut*   C *Inlet pipe*

3 Wash the filter in clean diesel fuel and if possible blow through with an air line.
4 Refit the filter in the pump head followed by the pipe connection and inlet pipe union. Before tightening the inlet pipe, operate the hand priming lever on the fuel pump until all the air is removed and clean diesel fuel emerges from the union. Fully tighten the union while operating the priming lever.

8 Fuel injection/distributor pump - removal and refitting

1 Two types of fuel injection/distributor pumps are fitted. Early pumps have internal timing marks viewed through an inspection window. Later pumps are identified by 'DPA No. 3248760' stamped on the manufacturer's label. These pumps have an external timing mark on the lower flange used in conjunction with a pointer on the engine. The removal and refitting instructions are similar and any differences will be described where necessary.
2 For efficient running of the engine accurate fuel injection/distributor pump timing is essential. Providing the procedures listed below are strictly followed no problems should be encountered. However if a new or reconditioned fuel injection/distributor pump is to be fitted, Land Rover special tool No. 605863 will be required to accurately set the injection timing. (This tool is only necessary

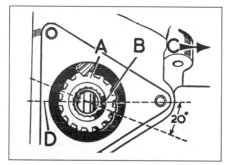

Fig. 3.7 Vertical drive gear positioning

A *Vertical drive gear*
B *Master spline at 20° to engine centre line*
C *Front of engine*
D *Line parallel with engine centre line*

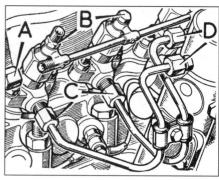

Fig. 3.6 Fuel injection distributor pump and injection fuel lines

A *Spill pipe union*
B *Injector spill pipe fixings*
C *Fuel lines to injectors*
D *Fuel lines to fuel injection distributor pump*

on later type fuel injection/ distributor pumps with external timing marks).
3 Disconnect the battery earth terminal.
4 Remove the air cleaner as described in Section 2.
5 Disconnect the engine stop inner and outer cable from its fixing on the fuel injection/ distributor pump and remove the stop spring.
6 Prise off the retaining clip and lift off the accelerator linkage rod from the bellcrank lever on the fuel injection/distributor pump upper body.
7 Slacken off the fuel inlet pipe unions at the injectors and remove all the fuel pipes from the fuel injection/distributor pump. If necessary mark their positions to aid reassembly.
8 Accurately mark the pump mounting flange in relation to the cylinder block using a scribe or a centre punch. This is most important as the fuel injection/distributor pump must be refitted in exactly the same position otherwise the injection timing will be incorrect.
9 Undo and remove the three nuts and washers securing the pump to the engine and lift off the pump.
10 To refit the fuel injection/distributor pump, remove the valve rocker cover and the inspection cover for the timing pointer on the flywheel housing.
11 Turn the engine in the normal direction of rotation until both valves on No 1 cylinder are closed and there is a clearance between the valve stems and rockers.
12 Continue turning slowly in the normal direction of rotation until the applicable timing mark is in line with the timing pointer on the flywheel housing (photo). On early fuel injection/distributor pumps set the pointer adjacent to the 16° mark on the flywheel. On later fuel injection/distributor pumps fitted to engines having a 14° and 16° mark stamped on the flywheel, set the timing at 15°, that is midway between the two marks. If the flywheel is stamped with 13° and 14° marks set the timing at 13°. Ensure that the marks approach the pointer In the normal direction of rotation. If the pointer is passed, start again.
13 Refer to Fig. 3.7 and using a protractor,

8.14 Vertical drive gear master spline set at 20° to the horizontal

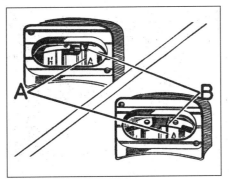

Fig. 3.8 Early type fuel injection distributor pump timing markings 8)

A *Timing mark on pump rotor*
B *Scribed mark on straight edge as applicable*

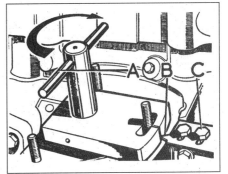

Fig. 3.9 Timing gauge in position

A *Timing gauge*
B *Timing pointer in line with mark on gauge*
C *Securing bolts*

scribe a line at 20° to the horizontal on the fuel injection/distributor pump mating face of the cylinder block.

14 Observe the fuel injection/distributor pump vertical drive gear master spline and ensure that it is in line with the scribed mark (photo).

15 If the original fuel injection/distributor pump is being used, it may now be refitted using the reverse sequence to removal. Ensure that the previously made marks on the fuel injection/distributor pump flange and cylinder block are in line before tightening the securing nuts. With the pump in position and all the fittings reconnected, refer to paragraphs 25 to 28 inclusive.

16 If a new or reconditioned fuel injection/distributor pump of the early type is being fitted remove the inspection cover from the side of the fuel injection/distributor pump and observe the driving plate through the viewing window. Rotate the spindle until the line marked 'A' on the driving plate is in line with the mark on the circlip (Fig. 3.8).

17 Place the fuel injection/distributor pump in position on the engine and engage the drive. Refit the securing nuts and washers but do not fully tighten at this stage.

18 Observe the timing marks through the viewing window and make any final corrections necessary to bring them in line, by turning the fuel injection/distributor pump body. When turning the fuel injection/distributor pump in the normal direction of rotation, hold the driving plate against the direction of rotation to take up any backlash in the gears. Now fully tighten the securing nuts.

19 Reconnect all pipes and fittings using the reverse sequence to removal, then refer to paragraphs 25 to 28 inclusive.

20 If a new or reconditioned fuel injection/distributor pump of the later type is being fitted, remove the short drive shaft from the vertical drive gear and place the timing gauge (Land Rover special tool No. 605863) in position as shown in Fig. 3.9.

21 Turn the gauge clockwise to take up any backlash in the gears and hold it in this position. The arrow on the timing pointer should now be in line with the mark on the timing gauge. If necessary slacken the bolts and reposition the pointer.

22 Remove the timing gauge and refit the drive gear, narrow portion first.

23 Position the master spline on the fuel injection/distributor pump spindle to line up with the master spline on the drive gear and place the pump in position on the engine. Align the mark on the pump flange with the pointer and refit and fully tighten the securing nuts and washers (photo).

24 Reconnect all pipes and fittings using the reverse sequence to removal.

25 With all components reconnected undo the two air vent screws on the side of the fuel injection/distributor pump body and operate the hand priming lever on the fuel pump until fuel emerges with no trace of air bubbles, then tighten the air vent screws.

26 With an assistant operating the starter switch and the engine turning on the starter motor, slacken the fuel feed pipe to one of the injectors. When fuel free from air bubbles emerges tighten the feed pipe.

27 Start the engine and check for any fuel leaks.

28 If a new or reconditioned fuel injection/distributor pump has been fitted, set the engine slow running control screw on the fuel injection/distributor pump to give the slowest possible tickover consistant with even running. The pump maximum output control screw should be set to give a maximum engine speed of 4200 rpm. This can be set by a road test: 4200 rpm being equal to 48 mph (77 kph) in third gear (Fig. 3. 10).

8.23 Fuel injection/distributor pump timing mark in line with pointer

9 Fuel injectors - testing on engine

> *Warning: Exercise extreme caution when working on the fuel injectors. Never expose the hands or any part of the body to injector spray, as working pressure can cause the fuel to penetrate the skin with possibly fatal results. You are strongly advised to have any work which involves testing the injectors under pressure carried out by a dealer or fuel injection specialist*

1 It is not recommended that any attempt be made to dismantle or repair a fuel injector as this requires specialist knowledge and equipment outside the scope of the average DIY mechanic. The best policy is to renew a faulty injector or have it reconditioned by your Land Rover dealer or diesel injection specialists.

2 The two tests described in the following paragraphs may be used when determining whether an injector is the cause of rough running and loss of power.

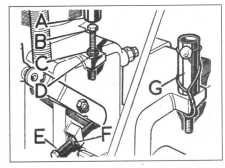

Fig. 3.10 Fuel injection/distributor pump control screws

A *Collar*
B *Maximum output control screw*
C *Locknut*
D *Screw retainer*
E *Slow running screw*
F *Locknut*
G *Screw collar lockwired after setting*

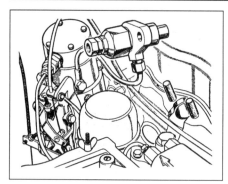

Fig. 3.11 Testing injector on engine

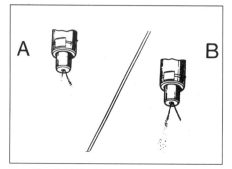

Fig. 3.12 Fuel injection spray form

A Correct   B Incorrect

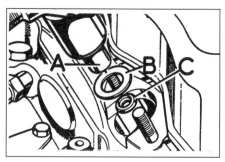

Fig. 3.13 Location of Injector sealing washer

A Injector
B Copper sealing washer
C Corrugated sealing washer

3 With the engine idling, slacken the fuel feed pipe union on each injector in turn and note any variation in engine speed. Repeat this test with the engine running at approximately 1000 rpm.

4 If the injector is operating correctly there will be a distinct reduction in engine speed accompanied by obvious roughness. If the injector is faulty there will be very little difference in engine speed when the union is slackened.

5 Having isolated the faulty injector using the this procedure, the injector nozzle spray form may be checked as described in the following paragraphs.

6 Remove the suspect injector as described in Section 10, and slacken the fuel inlet unions on the remaining injectors.

7 Reconnect the fuel inlet pipe to the previously removed injector and position it in such a way that the fuel emission may be observed (Fig.3.11).

8 Have an assistant operate the starter switch and with the engine cranking observe the spray form emitting from the end of the injector. Place rags over the engine compartment to protect it from fuel spray.
Caution: Do not allow diesel fuel under pressure from the injector to come into contact with the skin as injury may result from diesel fuel penetration.

9 Compare the observed spray form with the correct form shown in Fig. 3.12.

10 With the engine turning over at starter

speed there should be a fine spray ejected from the auxiliary hole with very little fuel emitted from the main spray hole.

11 If the ejected fuel is more in the form of a liquid rather than a spray or if excessive fuel is emitted from the main spray hole, this indicates that the injector is in need of renewal or overhaul by your Land Rover dealer or diesel injection specialist.

12 On completion of the test refit the injector and fuel pipes as described in Section 10, and if necessary prime the fuel system as described in Section 3.

10 Fuel injectors - removal and refitting

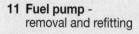

Caution: Refer to the warning note at the beginning of Section 9 before proceeding

1 Remove the air cleaner as described in Section 2.

2 Slacken the fuel pipe unions at the injection pump and remove them completely from the injectors.

3 Unscrew and remove the unions securing the spill pipe to the four injectors and lift off the pipe. Take care not to lose the copper washers under the union and spill pipe fixings.

4 Undo and remove the nuts (and bracket on early engines) securing the injectors to the cylinder head.

5 Carefully lift out the injectors from their

locations in the cylinder head and recover the two washers from each injector (photo). Ensure that none of the washers are left behind in the injector housing. **Note:** *Handle the injectors with care as there is a small needle valve protruding from the end of each injector which is easily damaged.*

6 Refitting is the reverse procedure to removal, bearing in mind the following points:

(a) *Always use new copper and steel sealing washers and fit the steel washers with the raised corrugation uppermost*

(b) *Tighten the retaining bolts to the torque figure given in the Specifications*

(c) *Prime the fuel system as described in Section 3*

11 Fuel pump - removal and refitting

1 Remove the air cleaner as described in Section 2 of this Chapter.

2 Undo and remove the inlet and outlet fuel pipe unions from the pump body (photo).

3 Remove the two securing nuts and withdraw the pump and gasket (photo). If difficulty is experienced in removing the two nuts, undo the four bolts and remove the pump complete with side cover plate and gasket.

4 Refitting is a reversal of this procedure but ensure that a new gasket is fitted. Prime the fuel system as described in Section 3.

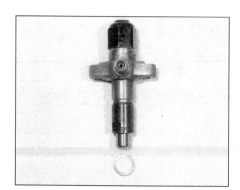

10.5 Fuel injector and sealing washers

11.2 Fuel pump and pipe fittings

11.3 Removing the fuel pump

12 Fuel pump - dismantling

The following procedure is for pumps incorporating a glass filter bowl. Later pumps are identical with the exception of the filter bowl which is omitted.

1 Clean the outside of the pump and wipe dry using a dry non-fluffy rag.

2 Using a file make a mark on the flanges of the upper and lower body to ensure that they are correctly reassembled.

3 Unscrew the stirrup thumb screw and swing the stirrup out of the way. Hold the glass bowl to ensure that it does not drop. Lift away the sediment bowl followed by the cork seal and gauze filter. Inspect the cork gasket for signs of damage or flattening and obtain a new one ready for reassembling.

4 Undo and remove the six body securing screws and spring washers and separate the two halves.

5 Invert the upper body and undo the two valve retaining plate screws and lift away the screws, retaining plate, the two valve assemblies and the valve gasket from the upper body.

6 Note the position of the lip on the diaphragm relative to the lower body to ensure correct reassembly and remove the diaphragm by rotating through 90° in an anti-clockwise direction and lifting it away from the lower body and the link.

7 It is recommended that the lower body parts are not dismantled unless either the seal, hand priming lever on the link assembly require attention.

13 Fuel pump - examination and reassembly

1 Check the condition of the cork sediment bowl sealing washer and if it has hardened or broken it must be renewed. The diaphragm should be checked similarly and renewed if faulty. Clean the pump thoroughly and agitate the valves in paraffin or petrol to clean them out. This will also improve the contact between the valve seat and the valve. It is unlikely that the pump body will be damaged but check for fractures and cracks.

2 To reassemble the pump proceed as follows. If the lower body has been dismantled refit the rocker arm assembly comprising the operating link, rocker arm, anti-rattle spring and washers in their relative positions in the lower body. Align the holes in the body and insert the pivot pin.

3 Refit the circlips to the grooves in each end of the pivot pin. On later models the pivot pin is held in place by two retainers. After refitting the pivot pin, tap the retainers into their grooves and secure them in place by lightly peening over the ends of the grooves with a small chisel.

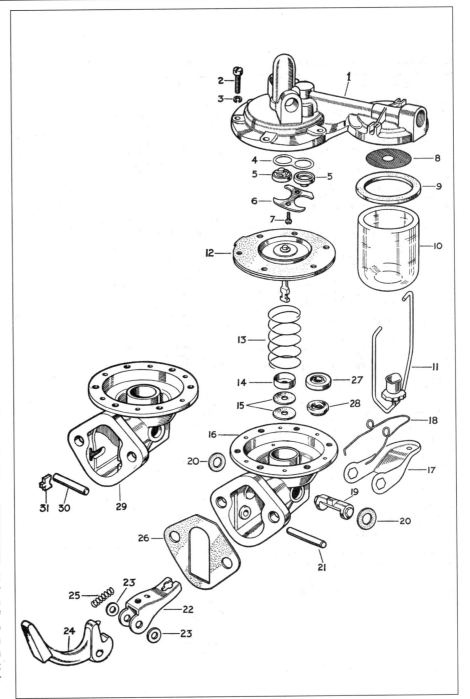

Fig. 3.14 Exploded view of fuel pump

1 Top cover
2 Securing screws
3 Spring washer
4 Valve gasket
5 Valves
6 Retainer for valves
7 Screw for retainer
8 Gauze filter disc[1]
9 Lock sealing gasket[1]
10 Sediment bowl[1]
11 Bowl retainer[1]
12 Diaphragm assembly
13 Diaphragm spring
14 Oil seal retainer[2]
15 Sealing washers[2]
16 Pump body[2]
17 Hand priming lever
18 Return spring for hand lever
19 Hand rocker
20 Cork washers
21 Rocker arm pivot pin, early type
22 Operating link
23 Plain washers
24 Rocker arm
25 Return spring
26 Joint washer
27 Oil seal retainer
28 Oil seal[3]
29 Pump body[3]
30 Rocker arm pivot pin type[3]
31 Retainer for pivot pin[3]
[1]Not fitted to late models
[2]Early type
[3]Latest type

14.5 Fuel tank sender unit and outlet pipe

4 Invert the upper body and fit the gasket, valves, valve retaining plate and tighten the two plate retaining screws. The two valves are interchangeable so care must be taken to ensure they are fitted the correct way round. The inlet valve should be fitted into the offset and shallower part with its spring facing the diaphragm, whilst the outlet valve is fitted to the centre part with its spring facing away from the diaphragm.

5 Place the seal and retainer in the lower body and place the diaphragm spring over them.

6 Refit the diaphragm and pullrod assembly with the pullrod downwards and ensure the small tab on the diaphragm lines up to the previously noted position which should have been adjacent to the centre of the flange and rocker arm.

7 With the body of the pump held so that the rocker arm is facing away, press down the diaphragm, turning it a quarter of a turn to the left at the same time. This engages the slot on the pullrod with the operating lever. The small tab on the diaphragm should now be at an angle of 90° to the rocker arm and the diaphragm should be firmly located.

8 Move the rocker arm until the diaphragm is level with the body flanges and hold the arm in this position. Reassemble the two halves of the pump ensuring that the previously made marks on the flanges are adjacent to each other.

9 Insert the six screws and lockwashers and tighten them down finger tight.

10 Move the rocker arm up and down several times to centralise the diaphragm, and then with the arm held down, tighten the screws securely in a diagonal sequence.

11 Fit the gauze filter, cork washer and sediment bowl and refit the stirrup thumbscrew to the base of the sediment bowl. Tighten lightly only to ensure a fuel tight joint, as overtightening will crack the bowl.

14 Fuel tank -
removal and refitting

1 On the standard models the fuel tank is located on the right-hand side below the seat base. The Station Wagon models are fitted with a fuel tank at the rear right-hand side of the vehicle.

2 Always work on the fuel system in a well ventilated building or, preferably, outside. Pick a time when the tank is almost empty. Disconnect the battery earth lead before draining the diesel from the tank into a suitable container.

Front mounted tank

3 Remove the right-hand side seat cushion and fold the seat squab forward.

4 Slacken the clips and pull the filler hose and breather hose off the tank unions.

5 Remove the cover panel and disconnect the fuel supply and spill return pipe unions, then disconnect the sender unit wire terminal (photo).

6 Support the weight of the tank, remove the securing bolts and carefully lower the tank and remove it from beneath the vehicle.

7 Refitting the tank is the reverse sequence to removal. Ensure the drain plug is tight before filling with fuel. Prime the fuel system as described in Section 3.

Rear mounted tank

8 Slacken the clip securing the filler hose to the tank and detach the hose.

9 Support the weight on the tank, remove the securing bolts and then lower the tank just enough to give access to the pipes and leads on the top of the tank.

10 Disconnect the fuel supply pipe, breather pipe, air balance pipe, spill return pipe, and the sender unit wire terminal.

11 Lower the tank to the ground and remove it from beneath the vehicle.

12 Refitting the tank is the reverse sequence to removal. Ensure the drain plug is tight before filling with fuel. Prime the fuel system as described in Section 3.

15 Acceleration linkage -
removal and refitting

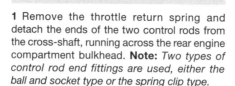

1 Remove the throttle return spring and detach the ends of the two control rods from the cross-shaft, running across the rear engine compartment bulkhead. **Note:** *Two types of control rod end fittings are used, either the ball and socket type or the spring clip type.*

2 Slacken the pinch bolt securing the operating lever to the accelerator pedal shaft and remove the lever. Undo the two bolts securing the shaft to the bulkhead and remove the pedal and shaft assembly from inside the vehicle.

3 Undo the bolts securing the cross-shaft to the rear bulkhead and remove the shaft complete with levers.

4 Examine the control rod ends for wear and the holes in the levers for ovality. If renewal is necessary, mark the position of the levers on the cross-shaft to ensure they are refitted at the correct angle. If adjustable socket type control rods are fitted mark the threads adjacent to the locknut before unscrewing the

socket. This will enable the rod to be adjusted to the correct length when reassembling.

5 Refit the pedal and linkage using the reverse procedure to removal. With the linkage correctly fitted check that the control arm on the fuel injection/distributor pump opens fully with the accelerator pedal pressed down onto the stop, and closes fully when the pedal is released. Adjust the linkage as necessary.

16 Engine stop cable -
removal and refitting

Vehicles without steering lock

1 Disconnect the inner and outer cables from their fixings on the fuel injection/distributor pump and remove the stop spring.

2 Prise out the control cable grommet on the engine compartment bulkhead.

3 Undo and remove the securing screws and lift off the steering column upper and lower shrouds.

4 Undo and remove the locknut and washer securing the stop cable to the steering column mounting bracket.

5 Push the outer cable forward and lift off the inner cable through the slot in the bracket. Withdraw the complete cable through the bulkhead and into the passenger compartment.

6 Refitting is the reverse sequence to removal. Ensure that with the cable refitted, full movement is obtained on the fuel injection/distributor pump cut-off lever.

Vehicles with steering lock

7 Disconnect the inner and outer cables from their fixings on the fuel injection/distributor pump and remove the stop spring.

8 Prise out the control cable grommet on the engine compartment bulkhead.

9 Withdraw the outer cable through the bulkhead and off the inner cable.

10 Undo and remove the securing screws and lift off the steering column upper and lower shrouds.

11 Slacken the small stop screw adjacent to the stop cable knob on the steering lock bracket sufficiently to allow the inner cable to be withdrawn. Remove the inner cable from the steering lock bracket into the passenger compartment.

12 Refit the cable using the reverse sequence to removal but do not tighten the inner cable fixing on the cut-off lever at this stage.

13 With the small stop screw refitted, pull the control knob fully out and position the cable in the engine 'stop' position.

14 Move the cut-off lever on the fuel injection/distributor pump to the 'stop' position and tighten the cable fixing.

15 Check that the cable moves into the 'start' position when the key is turned to 'II' position, and that with the key removed the cable remains engaged in the 'stop' position, when pulled out.

17 Exhaust system -
general description

The exhaust system on diesel engine Land Rovers comprises of a front pipe bolted to the exhaust manifold, and an intermediate pipe section leading into the silencer and tailpipe assembly. All three sections are connected by flange joints bolted together.

The exhaust system should be examined periodically for corrosion and, when using the vehicle over rough terrain, for damage. If any defects are found, the affected section of pipe (or the silencer) should be renewed.

The complete system is suspended from the vehicle chassis by metal brackets attached to either rubber or composite rubber/fabric mountings.

18 Exhaust front pipe -
removal and refitting

1 Undo and remove the four nuts and washers securing the front pipe to the exhaust manifold.

2 Undo and remove the nuts and bolts securing the front pipe to intermediate pipe flange joint (photo). If the nuts are corroded use liberal amounts of penetrating oil and allow to soak. In cases of extreme rust and corrosion the bolt may have to be sawn through with a hacksaw to remove.

3 Withdraw the pipe from underneath the vehicle.

4 Refitting is the reverse sequence to removal. Use a new gasket on the manifold flange joint and tighten all nuts and bolts progressively and evenly to ensure a gas tight seal.

5 Run the engine and check for leaks.

19 Exhaust intermediate pipe
and rear silencer -
removal and refitting

1 The intermediate pipe and rear silencer may be removed individually or as a complete unit if required.

Rear silencer

2 Undo and remove the nuts and bolts securing the rear silencer and intermediate pipe joint flanges. If the bolts are corroded use liberal amounts of penetrating oil and allow to soak. In extreme cases the bolts may have to be cut with a hacksaw to remove.

3 Undo and remove the bolts securing the exhaust mounting(s) to the silencer and lower the silencer to the ground.

4 Refitting is the reverse of the removal sequence.

Intermediate pipe

5 Undo and remove the nuts and bolts securing the intermediate pipe and rear silencer joint flanges and the nuts and bolts securing the intermediate pipe and front pipe pint flanges. If the bolts are corroded use liberal amounts of penetrating oil and allow to soak. In extreme cases the bolts may have to be cut with a hacksaw to remove them.

6 Undo and remove the bolts securing the exhaust mounting and remove the intermediate pipe.

7 Refitting is the reverse of the removal procedure.

Rear silencer and intermediate pipe

8 To remove the rear silencer and intermediate pipe as one piece, undo and remove the nuts and bolts securing the intermediate pipe and the front pipe joint flanges.

> **HAYNES HiNT** *If the bolts are corroded use liberal amounts of penetrating oil and allow to soak. In extreme cases the bolts may have to be cut with a hacksaw to remove them.*

9 Undo and remove the bolts securing the exhaust mountings and remove the rear silencer and intermediate pipe.

10 Refitting is the reverse of the removal procedure.

20 Exhaust mountings -
removal and refitting

1 Undo and remove the nuts and bolts

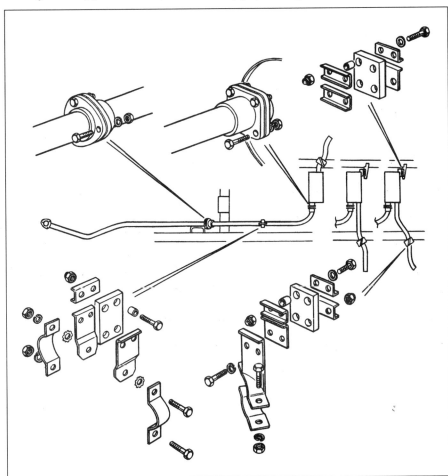

Fig. 3.15 General layout of exhaust system and mountings – long and short wheel base models

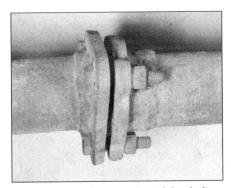

18.2 Exhaust flange and retaining bolts

20.1 Exhaust system intermediate mounting

securing the mounting to the exhaust pipe and chassis (photo).
2 Lift off the complete mounting from the vehicle.

3 Examine the rubber or composite fabric part of the mounting for tears, cracking, or distortion around the bolt holes. If worn or damaged it must be renewed.
4 Examine the strap or clamp that secures the mounting to the exhaust pipe. Ensure that it is a snug fit around the pipe with no slackness when fully tightened. If worn, corroded, or damaged it must be renewed.
5 Refitting is the reverse sequence to removal. Ensure that there is adequate clearance between the exhaust system and the body and if necessary reposition the mounting.

21 Exhaust manifold - removal and refitting

1 Slacken the securing clamp and withdraw the air cleaner convoluted hose from the inlet manifold.
2 Remove the engine breather hose from the pipe at the end of the inlet manifold.
3 Undo the securing nuts and lift off the exhaust front pipe from the exhaust manifold flange. Recover the gasket.
4 Withdraw the oil level dipstick.
5 If a brake servo is fitted, disconnect the manifold throttle control rod and the vacuum supply hose.
6 Using a socket and long extension, undo and remove the four upper and five lower securing nuts and lift off the inlet and exhaust manifolds.
7 Withdraw the manifold gasket.
8 Refitting is the reverse sequence to removal using new gaskets on the manifold face and exhaust flange joints.

Fault finding - fuel system

Difficult starting when cold

- [ ] Heater plugs or heater circuit faulty or inoperative
- [ ] Fuel injection/distribution pump timing incorrect
- [ ] Air in fuel system

Erratic slow running or stalling

- [ ] Slow running control screw out of adjustment
- [ ] Fuel injection/distributor pump timing incorrect
- [ ] Worn fuel injectors or fuel injection/distributor pump

Poor acceleration

- [ ] Fuel injection/distributor pump timing incorrect
- [ ] Accelerator linkage worn or out of adjustment
- [ ] Worn fuel injectors or fuel injection/distributor pump
- [ ] Engine worn internally

Engine issues excessive smoke on acceleration

- [ ] Fuel injection/distributor pump timing incorrect
- [ ] Worn fuel injectors or fuel injection/distributor pump
- [ ] Excessive wear on internal engine components

Engine runs roughly or erratically

- [ ] Fuel lines blocked
- [ ] Fuel filters choked
- [ ] One or more fuel injectors worn or faulty
- [ ] Fuel injection/distributor pump worn or incorrectly timed

Persistent heater plug failure

- [ ] Over advanced distributor pump

Chapter 4
Ignition system – petrol models

For modifications, and information applicable to later models, see Supplement at end of manual

Contents

Degrees of difficulty

Easy, suitable for novice with little experience	**Fairly easy,** suitable for beginner with some experience	**Fairly difficult,** suitable for competent DIY mechanic	**Difficult,** suitable for experienced DIY mechanic	**Very difficult,** suitable for expert DIY or professional

Specifications

Distributor

Contact breaker gap	0.014 - 0.016 in (0.36 - 0.40 mm)
Rotation of rotor.	Anti-clockwise
Centrifugal advance	

Crankshaft angle	**Engine rev/min**
38° to 42°	4500
30° to 34°	3500
22° to 26°	2500
12° to 16°	1200
4° to 12°	900
0° to 4°	600
No advance below	450

Vacuum advance:
Starts	89 mm (3.5 in) Hg
Finishes	635 mm (25.0 in) Hg

Static ignition timing

8.0 : 1 compression ratio	TDC using 90 octane fuel 3° ATDC using 85 octane fuel
7.0 : 1 compression ratio	6° BTDC using 90 octane fuel 3° BTDC using 83 octane fuel

Firing order. . . . . 1 - 3 - 4 - 2

Spark plugs

Type	Bosch WR 8 D+
Electrode gap.	0.8 mm

Torque wrench setting	**lbf ft**	**kgf m**
Spark plugs.	25	3.5

1 General description

In order that the engine may run correctly it is necessary for an electrical spark to ignite the fuel/air mixture in the combustion chamber at exactly the right moment in relation to engine speed and load. The high tension voltage generated by the ignition system is powerful enough to jump the spark plug gap in the combustion chambers many times a second under high compression pressure, providing that the ignition system is in good working order and that all adjustments are correct.

The ignition system comprises two individual circuits known as the low tension circuit and the high tension circuit.

The low tension circuit (sometimes known as the primary circuit) comprises the battery, lead to ignition switch, lead to the low tension or primary coil windings and the lead from the low tension coil windings to the contact breaker points and condenser in the distributor.

The high tension circuit (sometimes known as the secondary circuit) comprises the high tension or secondary coil windings, the heavily insulated ignition lead from the centre of the coil to the centre of the distributor cap, the rotor arm, the spark plug leads and the spark plugs.

The complete ignition system operation is as follows:

Low tension voltage from the battery is changed within the ignition coil to high tension voltage by the opening and closing of the contact breaker points in the low tension circuit. High tension voltage is then fed via a contact in the centre of the distributor cap to the rotor arm of the distributor. The rotor arm revolves inside the distributor cap, and each time it comes in line with one of the four segments in the cap (these being connected to the spark plug leads) the opening and closing of the contact breaker points causes the high tension voltage to build up, jump the gap from the rotor arm to the appropriate segment and so, via the spark plug lead, to the spark plug where it finally jumps the gap between the two spark plug electrodes, one being connected to the earth system.

The ignition timing is advanced and retarded automatically to ensure the spark occurs at just the right instant for the particular load at the prevailing engine speed.

The ignition advance is controlled both mechanically and by a vacuum operated system. The mechanical governor mechanism comprises two weights which move out under centrifugal force from the central distributor shaft as the engine speed rises. As they move outwards they rotate the cams relative to the distributor shaft, and so advance the spark. The weights are held in position by two light springs, and it is the tension of the springs which is largely responsible for correct mechanical advancement.

The vacuum control comprises a diaphragm, one side of which is connected via a small bore tube to the carburettor, and the other side to the contact breaker plate. Depressions in the induction manifold and carburettor, which varies with engine speed and throttle opening, causes the diaphragm to move, so moving the control breaker plate and advancing or retarding the spark. A fine degree of control is achieved by a spring in the vacuum assembly.

2 Contact breaker points - adjustment

1 To adjust the contact breaker points so that the correct gap is obtained; first, release the two clips securing the distributor cap to the distributor body, and lift away the cap. Clean the inside and outside of the cap with a dry cloth. It is unlikely that the four segments will be badly burnt or scored, but if they are the cap should be renewed. If only small deposits are on the segments they may be scraped away using a small screwdriver.
2 Push in the carbon brush, located in the top of the cap, several times to ensure that it moves freely. The brush should protrude by at least 0.25 in (6.35 mm).
3 Gently press the contact breaker points open to examine the condition of their faces. if they are rough, pitted or dirty it will be

2.5 Setting the contact breaking gap using a feeler gauge

necessary to remove them for resurfacing, or for new points to be fitted.
4 Presuming the points are satisfactory, or that they have been cleaned or renewed, measure the gap between the points by turning the engine over using the starting handle until the contact breaker arm is on the peak of one of the four cam lobes. A 0.014 - 0.016 in (0.36 - 0.41 mm) feeler gauge should now just fit between the points.
5 If the gap is either too wide or too small, slacken the screw securing the contact plate and adjust the gap by inserting a screwdriver in the notches shown in Fig. 4.1 and twist it in the appropriate direction until the gap is correct. Tighten the securing screw and re-check the gap (photo).
6 Refit the rotor arm and clip the distributor cap back into position.

3 Contact breaker points - renovation or renewal

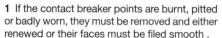

1 If the contact breaker points are burnt, pitted or badly worn, they must be removed and either renewed or their faces must be filed smooth .
2 To remove the points first detach the distributor cap and rotor arm. Unscrew the terminal nut and remove it together with the washer under its head. Remove the flanged nylon bush, the condenser lead and the low tension lead from the terminal pin. Lift off the contact breaker arm and remove the large fibre washer from the terminal pin.
3 The adjustable contact breaker plate is removed by unscrewing one screw and then withdrawing the plate.
4 To reface the points, rub the faces on a fine carborundum stone, or on fine emery paper. It is important that the faces are rubbed flat and parallel to each other so that there will be complete face to face contact when the points are closed. One of the points will be pitted and the other will have deposits on it.
5 It is necessary to completely remove the built up deposits, but unnecessary to rub the pitted point right to the stage where all the pitting has disappeared, though obviously, if this is done it will prolong the time before the operation of refacing the points has to be repeated.

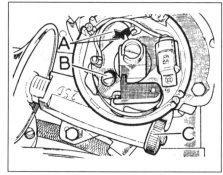

Fig. 4.1. Contact breaker adjustment

A Gap adjustment notches
B Contact securing screw
C Vernier advance adjusting nut

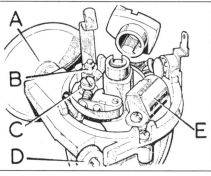

Fig. 4.2. Distributor components

A Vacuum advance unit
B Contact breaker terminal
C Securing screw
D Advance adjusting nut
E Condenser

6 If the points are badly pitted or worn they should be renewed.
7 To refit the points: first, position the adjustable contact breaker plate and secure it with its screw, spring and flat washer. Fit the fibre washer to the terminal pin and fit the contact breaker arm over it. Insert the flanged nylon bush with the condenser lead immediately under its head, and the low tension lead under that, over the terminal pin. Fit the steel washer and screw on the securing nut.
8 The points are now reassembled and the gap should be set as detailed in Section 2.

4 Condenser - testing, removal and refitting

1 The purpose of the condenser (sometimes known as a capacitor) is to ensure that when the contact breaker points open there is no sparking across them which would waste voltage and cause excessive wear.
2 The condenser is fitted in parallel with the contact breaker points. If it develops a short circuit, it will cause ignition failure, as the points will be prevented from interrupting the low tension circuit.

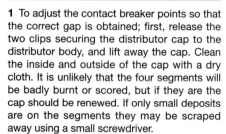

4.5 Removing the condenser lead

5.2a Lubricating the cam spindle centrifugal advance mechanism

5.2b Contact breaker base plate removal

3 If the engine becomes very difficult to start, or begins to misfire after several miles running, and the breaker points show signs of excessive burning, then the condition of the condenser must be suspect. A further test can be made by separating the points by hand with the ignition switched on. If this is accompanied by a flash it is indicative that the condenser has failed.

4 Without special test equipment, the only sure way to diagnose condenser trouble is to replace a suspected unit with a new one and note if there is any improvement.

5 To remove the condenser from the distributor, remove the distributor cap and rotor arm. Unscrew the contact breaker arm terminal nut, remove the nut, washer, and flanged nylon bush and release the condenser (photo).

6 Undo and remove the condenser securing screw and lift away the condenser.

7 Refitting the condenser is simply a reversal of the removal procedure. Take particular care that the condenser lead does not short circuit against any portion of the breaker plate.

5 Distributor - lubrication

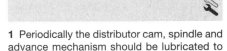

1 Periodically the distributor cam, spindle and advance mechanism should be lubricated to prevent possible seizure.

2 Remove the distributor cap and rotor arm,

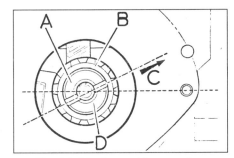

Fig. 4.3. Distributor drive coupling

A Top drive coupling
B Vertical drive gear
C No. 1 cylinder
D Narrow segment of coupling

and inject a few drops of thin oil into the top of the cam spindle (photo). Apply a few more drops onto the side of the cam and allow it to run down through the contact breaker base plate, thus lubricating the advance mechanism beneath it (photo).

3 Lightly oil the moving contact pivot point. Wipe off any excess oil and refit the rotor arm and cap.

6 Distributor - removal and refitting

1 Disconnect the HT leads from the spark plugs and the centre terminal of the coil.

2 Disconnect the LT lead from the terminal on the side of the distributor.

3 Undo the pipe from the vacuum advance control.

4 To avoid altering the timing, use a scriber to mark the position of the bolt in the slotted plate that secures the distributor to the engine block.

5 Remove the bolt and lift out the distributor from its recess. Do not slacken the securing plate pinch bolt otherwise it will be necessary to re-set the ignition as described in Section 8.

6 To refit the distributor, line up the offset lugs on the distributor shaft with the offset slot in the top of the driveshaft visible in the engine recess (see Fig. 4.3).

7 With the distributor correctly installed in the cylinder block, insert the securing bolt and tighten it, making sure that the line scribed on the distributor plate is in its original position against the bolt head.

7 Distributor - dismantling and reassembly

1 Remove the distributor from the engine as described in Section 6.

2 Referring to Fig. 4.4, unhook the vacuum advance spring from the baseplate, remove the two securing screws and lift out the complete contact breaker and baseplate assembly, sliding the LT terminal from the distributor body at the same time.

3 Remove the small circlip from the end of

the vernier adjusting nut and rotate the nut until the vacuum control assembly can be withdrawn from the distributor body; take care not to lose the small spring and ratchet.

4 Drive out the pin from the drive dog and remove the dog from the end of the shaft. Pull the shaft out from the top of the distributor complete with the advance mechanism.

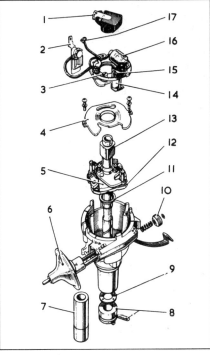

Fig. 4.4. Exploded view of distributor

1 Rotor arm
2 LT terminal
3 Fixed contact plate securing screw
4 Contact breaker baseplate
5 Centrifugal advance control weights and mechanism
6 Vacuum advance control unit
7 Bearing bush
8 Driving dog and pin
9 Thrust washer
10 Vernier adjustment nut
11 Distance collar
12 Baseplate
13 Cam
14 Contact breaker moving plate
15 Contacts
16 Condenser
17 CB earth connector

5 To dismantle the centrifugal advance mechanism, remove the two springs from the counter-weights, after noting which spring fits which post. Undo the screw from the centre of the cam. Make a careful note of the slot above the cam in relation to the drive dog (temporarily refit the dog onto the shaft) and then remove the cam and plate assembly from the shaft. Note the distance collar on the shaft.

6 Examine all the components for wear or breakage. if the distributor is in a poor condition due to high mileage, it is best to renew it.

7 If a new driveshaft bush is to be fitted, the new bush must be left to soak in engine oil for 24 hours before installation. Drill an oil hole in the new bush using the old bush as a guide to its correct location.

8 Reassemble the distributor using the reverse procedure to dismantling. Lubricate the driveshaft before refitting, and if a new bush has been fitted, ensure that the shaft rotates freely. When fitting the centrifugal

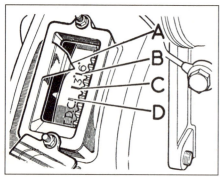

Fig. 4.5 Timing pointer on flywheel housing (earlier engine)

A Timing pointer
B 6° mark, align when using 90 - 96 octane fuel
C 3° mark, align when using 80 - 85 octane fuel
D TDC mark, align when using 74 - 76 octane fuel

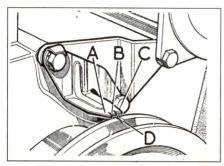

Fig. 4.6. Timing pointer on front timing chain cover (later engines)

A 6° tongue, align when using 90 - 96 octane fuel
B 3° tongue, align when using 80 - 85 octane fuel
C TDC tongue, align when using 74 - 76 octane fuel
D Mark on crankshaft pulley, align with appropriate tongue

advance springs, take care not to stretch them any more than absolutely necessary.

9 Note that one of the baseplate screws is also used to secure the earthing wire.

10 Check the contact breaker gap as described in Section 2 and refit the distributor to the engine (see Section 6).

8 Ignition timing - adjustment

1 The first procedure is to ascertain that the No. 1 piston is on its compression stroke. To do this, remove the front cylinder spark plug and with a finger held over the plug hole, have a friend turn the engine over with the starting handle, until pressure is felt on the finger.

2 On earlier engines, remove the small plate on the right-hand side of the flywheel housing and continue to rotate the engine until the appropriate TDC or octane mark on the flywheel is aligned with the pointer (see Fig. 4.5).

3 On later engines the TDC marks are on a pointer attached to the front timing cover and a notch on the crankshaft pulley. These should be lined up as shown in Fig. 4.6.

4 Remove the distributor cap and connect a test lamp between the coil LT lead to the distributor and a good earth.

5 Slacken the distributor clamp pinch bolt.

6 Switch on the ignition and turn the distributor body in the required direction until the test lamp just lights up, indicating the points have just opened.

7 Tighten the pinch bolt taking care not to alter the position of the distributor. Switch off the ignition and remove the test lamp.

8 Refit the distributor cap.

9 Coil - general

The coil is located inside the engine compartment and attached to the rear bulkhead by two screws (photo).

Periodically check that the centre HT lead is firmly in place and the two LT terminals are clean and tight.

If the coil is suspect, the best method of

9.1 Location of ignition coil

checking it is to temporarily exchange for one that is known to be good and then check if there is any improvement in engine efficiency.

10 Spark plugs and HT leads

The correct functioning of the spark plugs is vital for the proper running and efficient operation of the engine.

At regular intervals the plugs should be removed, examined, cleaned, and if worn excessively, renewed. The condition of the spark plugs can also tell much about the general condition of the engine.

If the insulator nose of the spark plug is clean and white, with no deposits, this is indicative of a weak mixture, or too hot a plug (a hot plug transfers heat away from the electrodes slowly - a cold plug transfers heat away quickly).

If the insulator nose is covered with hard black looking deposits then this is indicative that the mixture is too rich. Should the plug be black and oily then it is likely that the engine is worn, as well as the mixture being too rich.

If the insulator nose is covered with light tan to greyish brown deposits, then the mixture is correct, and it is likely that the engine is in good condition.

If there are any traces of long brown tapering stains on the outside of the white portion of the plug, then the plug will have to be renewed, as this shows that there is a faulty joint between the plug body and the insulator and compression is being allowed to leak away.

Plugs should be cleaned by a sand blasting machine, which will free them from carbon completely. The machine will also test the condition of the plugs under compression. Any plug that fails to spark at the recommended pressure should be renewed.

The spark plug gap is of considerable importance, as, if it is too large, or too small, the size of spark and its efficiency will be seriously impaired. The spark plug gap should be set as recommended in the 'Specifications' Section at the beginning of this Chapter.

1 To set it, measure the gap with a feeler gauge, and then bend open, or close, the outer plug electrode until the correct gap is obtained. The centre electrode must never be bent as this will crack the insulation and cause plug failure if nothing worse.

2 When refitting the plugs, remember to use new washers and refit the leads from the distributor cap in the correct firing order, which is 1 3 4 2 - number 1 cylinder being the one nearest the fan.

3 The plug leads require no maintenance other than being kept clean and wiped over regularly. At regular intervals, however, pull each lead off the plug In turn and remove them from the distributor cap. Water can seep down their joints giving rise to a white corrosive deposit which must be carefully removed from the end of each cable.

Fault diagnosis - ignition system

By far the majority of breakdowns and running troubles are caused by faults in the ignition system either in the low tension or high tension circuits.

There are two main symptoms indicating ignition faults. Either the engine will not start or fire, or the engine is difficult to start and misfires. If it is a regular misfire, ie. the engine is running on only two or three cylinders, the fault is almost certain to be in the secondary or high tension circuit. If the misfiring is intermittent, the fault could be in either the high or low tension circuits. If the vehicle stops suddenly, and will not start at all, it is likely that the fault is in the low tension circuit. Loss of power and overheating, apart from faulty combustion settings, are normally due to faults in the distributor or to incorrect ignition timing.

Engine fails to start

1 If the engine fails to start and the car was running normally when it was last used, first check there is fuel in the petrol tank. If the engine turns over normally on the starter motor and the battery is evidently well charged, then the fault may be in either the high or low tension ignition circuits. First check the HT circuit. **Note:** If the battery is known to be fully charged, the ignition light comes on, and the starter motor fails to turn the engine, **check the tightness of the leads on the battery terminals** and also the secureness of the earth lead at its **connection to the body**. It is quite common for the leads to have worked loose, even if they look and feel secure. If one of the battery terminal posts gets very hot when trying to work the starter motor this is a sure indication of a faulty connection to that terminal.

2 One of the more common reasons for bad starting is wet or damp spark plug leads and/or distributor. Remove the distributor cap and if condensation is visible internally dry the cap with a rag and also wipe over the leads. Replace the cap.

3 If the engine still fails to start, check that current is reaching the plugs, by disconnecting each plug lead in turn at the spark plug end, and holding the end of the cable about 3/16 inch (5 mm) away from the cylinder block. Spin the engine on the starter motor.

4 Sparking between the end of the cable and the block should be fairly strong with a strong regular blue spark. (Hold the lead with rubber to avoid electric shocks). If current is reaching the plugs, then remove them, and clean and regap them. The engine should now start.

5 If there is no spark at the plug leads take off the HT lead from the centre of the distributor cap and hold it to the block as before. Spin the engine on the starter once more. A rapid succession of blue sparks between the end of the lead and the block indicates that the coil is in order and that the distributor cap is cracked, the rotor arm faulty, or the brush in the top of the distributor cap is not making good contact with the rotor arm. Possibly the points are in bad condition. Clean and reset them as described in Sections 2 and 3 of this Chapter.

6 If there are no sparks from the end of the lead from the coil, check the connection at the coil end of the lead. If it is in order start checking the low tension circuit.

7 Use a 12v voltmeter or a 12v bulb and two lengths of wire. With the ignition switched on and the points open, test between the low tension wire to the coil lit is marked SW) and earth. No reading indicates a break in the supply from the ignition switch. Check the connections at the switch to see if any are loose. Refit them and the engine should run. A reading shows a faulty coil or condenser, or broken lead between the coil and the distributor.

8 Take the condenser wire off the points assembly terminal and with the points open test between the moving point and earth. If there now is a reading, then the fault is in the condenser. Fit a new one and the fault should be cleared.

9 With no reading from the moving point to earth, take a reading between the earth and CB terminal of the coil. A reading here shows a broken wire which will need to be renewed between the coil and distributor. No reading confirms that the coil has failed and must be renewed, after which the engine will run once more. Remember to refit the condenser wire to the points assembly terminal. For this test it is sufficient to separate the points with a piece of thin, dry, card while testing with the points open.

Engine misfires

1 If the engine misfires regularly run it at a fast idling speed. Pull off each of the plug caps in turn and listen to the note of the engine. Hold the plug cap in a dry cloth or with a rubber glove as additional protection against a shock from the HT supply.

2 No difference in engine running will be noticed when the lead from the defective circuit is removed. Removing the lead from one of the good cylinders will accentuate the misfire.

3 Remove the plug lead from the end of the defective plug and hold it about 3/16 inch (5 mm) away from the block. Re-start the engine. If the sparking is fairly strong and regular the fault must lie in the spark plug.

4 The plug may be loose, the insulation may be cracked, or the points may have burnt away giving too wide a gap for the spark to jump. Worse still, one of the points may have broken off. Either renew the plug, or clean it, reset the gap and then test it.

5 If there is no spark at the end of the plug lead, or if it is weak and intermittent, check the ignition lead from the distributor to the plug. If the insulation is damaged renew the lead. Check the connections at the distributor cap.

6 If there is still no spark, examine the distributor cap carefully for tracking. This can be recognised by a very thin black line running between two, or more, electrodes; or between an electrode and some other part of the distributor cap. These lines are paths which now conduct electricity across the cap thus letting it run to earth. The only answer is a new distributor cap.

7 Apart from the ignition timing being incorrect, other causes of misfiring have already been dealt with under the section dealing with the failure of the engine to start. To recap, these are:

a) *The coil may be faulty giving an intermittent misfire.*

b) *There may be a damaged wire or loose connection in the low tension circuit.*

c) *The condenser may be short circuiting.*

d) *There may be a mechanical fault in the distributor (broken driving spindle or contact breaker spring).*

8 If the ignition timing is too far retarded, it should be noted that the engine will tend to overheat, and there will be quite a noticeable drop in power. If the engine is overheating and the power is down, and the ignition timing is correct, then the carburettor should be checked, as it is likely that this is where the fault lies.

Notes

Chapter 5
Clutch

Contents

Degrees of difficulty

Easy, suitable for novice with little experience	Fairly easy, suitable for beginner with some experience	Fairly difficult, suitable for competent DIY mechanic	Difficult, suitable for experienced DIY mechanic	Very difficult, suitable for expert DIY or professional

Specifications

Clutch type	Borg and Beck single dry plate with coil spring or diaphragm spring pressure plate
Operation	Hydraulically actuated

Diameter
Coil spring type	9 in 1230 mm)
Diaphragm spring type	9.5 in (241 mm)

Driven plate
Lining thickness	0.330 in (8.38 mm)
Maximum permissible wear	0.120 in (3.0 mm)

Master cylinder
Type	Girling with integral or separate hydraulic fluid reservoir
Bore	0.75 in (19 mm)
Stroke	1.375 in (35 mm)

Slave cylinder
Type	Girling
Bore	0.875 in (22 mm)

Withdrawal mechanism
Flanged bush clearance on cross-shaft	0.001 to 0.003 in (0.02 to 0.07 mm)
Left-hand bush clearance on cross-shaft	0.004 to 0.006 in (0.102 to 0.14 mm)
Bush clearance on withdrawal sleeve	0.003 to 0.006 in (0.07 to 0.15 mm)

Clutch pedal unit
Pedal shaft bush clearance	0.001 to 0.003 in (0.02 to 0.07 mm)
Bash reamed bore	0.750 in (19 mm)

Torque wrench settings
	lbf ft	kgf m
Clutch cover bolts	22 to 25	3 to 3.5

Fig. 5.1. Exploded view of early and later type clutch assemblies

1 Flywheel housing
2 Stud fixing flywheel housing to bellhousing
3 Stud for inspection cover
4 Stud for starter motor
5 Sealing ring for flywheel housing
6 Inspection cover plate (early type engines)
7 Joint washer for cover plate
8 Nut for cover plate
9 Bolt   } Fixing
10 Bolt   } flywheel
11 Spring washer } housing to
12 Plain washer   } cylinder block
13 Indicator for engine timing (early type engines)
14 Drain plug for housing
15 Stowage bracket for drain plug. On later engines the plug is stowed In a blind tapping in the flywheel housing
16 Flywheel assembly
17 Dowel locating clutch cover plate
18 Bush for primary pinion
19 Special fitting bolt fixing clutch cover plate, applicable to certain models only
20 Set bolt
21 Spring washer
22 Lock tab
23 Special set bolt
24 Cover plate for coil spring type clutch
25 Pressure plate
26 Release lever
27 Strut for release lever
28 Eyebolt and nut for release lever

29 Pin for release lever
30 Antirattle spring for release lever
31 Clutch coil spring (9 off)
32 Clutch driven plate
33 Diaphragm spring type clutch
34 Clutch driven plate

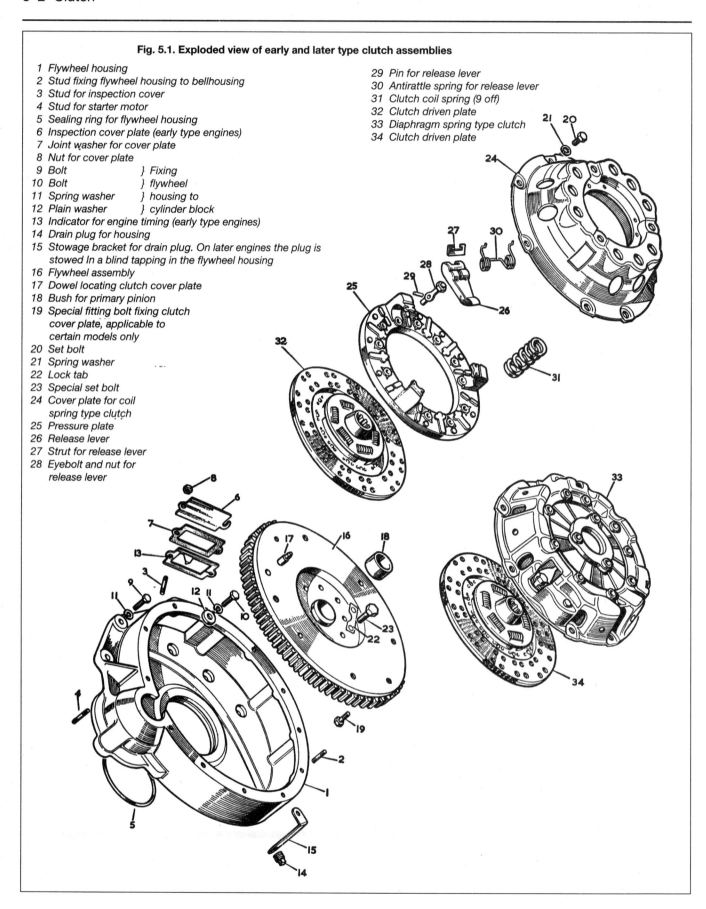

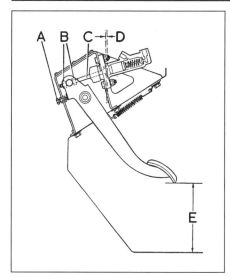

Fig. 5.2 Pedal height and master cylinder pushrod adjustments – all models

A Pedal height setting bolt
B Master cylinder pushrod locknuts
C Pushrod
D Free play 1/16 in (1.5 mm)
E Pedal height,
    early models: 6 1/4 in (158 mm),
    later models: 5 1/2 in (140 mm)

1 General description

The Series II and IIA Land Rovers are fitted with either the 9 inch (230 mm) diameter clutch or the 9.5 inch (241 mm) diameter clutch while all Series III models are fitted with 9.5 inch (241 mm) clutch. The pressure plate on the 9 inch (230 mm) unit is actuated by coil springs while the 9.5 inch (241 mm) type is fitted with a diaphragm actuating spring.

The clutch is hydraulically operated by a master cylinder connected to the clutch pedal. A single hydraulic pipe from the master cylinder supplies hydraulic fluid to a slave cylinder attached to the clutch bellhousing.

When the clutch pedal is depressed hydraulic fluid under pressure is supplied to the slave cylinder from the master cylinder. This causes a piston in the slave cylinder to travel down its bore thus moving an adjustable linkage directly coupled to the clutch release arm. The release arm moves the clutch release sleeve and bearing forward against the thrust plate forks (coil spring type) or against the centre of the diaphragm (diaphragm ring type). The pressure plate spring tension is thus progressively released allowing the clutch driven plate, splined to the gearbox input shaft, to disengage. In this condition no drive is transmitted to the gearbox. When the clutch pedal is released slowly the pressure plate progressively clamps the driven plate to the flywheel face thus transmitting engine power to the gearbox.

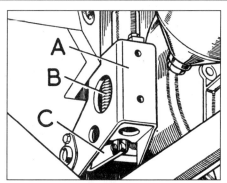

Fig. 5.3 Identification of early type clutch mechanism

A Support bracket encloses slave cylinder
B Operating lever return spring
C Straight operating lever

2 Clutch - adjustment

To ensure adequate working clearances are maintained in the clutch operating linkages and to take up any excess free movement that may develop as wear takes place on the clutch friction linings, three adjustments are provided on early models and two on later versions. These are on early models, clutch pedal height adjustment, master cylinder free play adjustment and operating linkage free play adjustment. On later versions the clutch operating linkage is self adjusting and only the clutch pedal height and master cylinder free play require attention.

Should it be felt that clutch adjustment is necessary the following procedure should be adopted to ensure that adequate clearances are maintained through the entire system.

Clutch pedal height adjustment

1 Refer to Fig 5.2 and measure the distance between the bottom of the clutch pedal and the floor. If adjustment is necessary, open the bonnet and slacken the pedal stop bolt locknut located on the pedal bracket back plate.

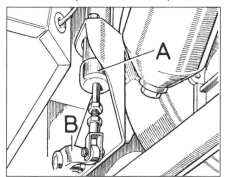

Fig. 5.4 Identification of later type clutch mechanism

A Exploded slave cylinder
B Cranked operating rod

2 Turn the bolt in or out until the correct pedal height is achieved: then tighten the locknut.

Master cylinder free play adjustment

3 Gently depress the clutch pedal until the first resistance is felt. This is the master cylinder pushrod to piston clearance and should be approximately 5/16 in (8 mm) at the pedal pad.
4 If the clearance is incorrect, undo and remove the six screws securing the top cover to the clutch pedal bracket.
5 Slacken the two locknuts and rotate the pushrod until the correct clearance exists.
6 Tighten the locknuts and refit the top cover.

Operating linkage free play adjustment

Three types of operating linkages are used on models covered by this manual and it is necessary to determine the type fitted to your vehicle before any adjustment is carried out. Series III versions have a slave cylinder and operating linkage mounted on the lower left-hand side of the clutch housing. This unit is self-adjusting and therefore no further adjustment to the clutch system is necessary. Series II and IIA units are identified as follows. Early models have a fully enclosed slave cylinder, an operating linkage return spring and a straight operating rod (Fig 5.3). Later models have an exposed slave cylinder and a cranked operating rod. A return spring is not fitted (Fig 5.4). Adjustment of both types is described as follows.

Early models

7 Remove the floor assembly as described in Chapter 12.
8 Gently depress the clutch pedal. A total free movement of approximately 1 1/2 in (38 mm) at the pedal pad should exist before firm resistance is felt. This free movement is felt in two stages, light movement of approximately 5/16 in (8 mm) to take up the master cylinder free play and a further heavier movement of approximately 1 3/16 in (30 mm) which takes up the operating linkage free play.

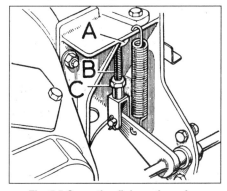

Fig. 5.5 Operating linkage free play adjustment – early models

A Slave cylinder B Pushrod C Locknut

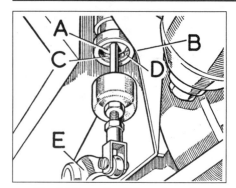

Fig. 5.6 Operating linkage free play adjustment – later models

A Piston
B Exploded slave cylinder
C Clearance: 1/8 in (3 mm)
D Circlip
E Cranked operating rod

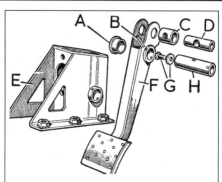

Fig. 5.7 Clutch pedal components

A Pedal bush   E Pedal bracket
B Locating pin   F Clutch pedal
C Trunnion distance   G Oil plug and
   piece   washer
D Pedal trunnion   H Pedal shaft

5.1 Combined clutch and brake reservoir (early models)

9 If the second heavier movement is incorrect, slacken the locknut on the slave cylinder push rod and rotate the pushrod until the correct free movement exists.
10 Tighten the locknut and refit the floor assembly as described in Chapter 12.

Later models

11 Remove the floor assembly as described in Chapter 12.
12 Fully depress the clutch pedal and retain it with a suitable length of wood placed between the seat and the pedal or alternatively have an assistant hold it down for you.
13 Withdraw the rubber dust cover from the end of the slave cylinder and measure the clearance between the bottom of the piston and the circlip (Fig 5.6). A clearance of approximately 1/8 in (3 mm) should exist.
14 If the clearance is incorrect slacken the lower locknut and rotate the pushrod until the correct clearance is obtained. Tighten the locknut and refit the rubber dust cover on the slave cylinder.
15 Refit the floor assembly as described in Chapter 12.

3 Clutch hydraulic system - bleeding

On Series II and IIA models access to the slave cylinder bleed screw is gained by removing a circular rubber grommet on the right-hand side of the interior transmission tunnel. On Series III models the grommet is located on the left-hand side of the transmission tunnel.

1 Obtain a clean glass jar, a length of rubber/plastic tubing which fits tightly over the bleed nipple and a tin of the correct type of hydraulic fluid.
2 Check that the master cylinder reservoir is full, if not fill it and also fill the bottom two inches of the jar with hydraulic fluid.
3 Remove the rubber dust cap from the bleed nipple and with a suitable spanner open the bleed nipple approximately 3/4 of a turn.

4 Place one end of the tube over the nipple and insert the other end in the jar, so that the tube orifice is below the level of the fluid.
5 Depress the clutch pedal and hold it down at the end of its stroke. Close the bleed screw and allow the pedal to return to its normal position.
6 Continue this series of operations until clean hydraulic fluid, without any traces of air bubbles emerges from the end of the tubing. Be sure that the reservoir is checked frequently to ensure that the hydraulic fluid does not drop too far, thus letting air into the system.
7 When no further air bubbles appear tighten the bleed nipple during a downstroke.
8 Refit the rubber dust cap to the bleed nipple and the rubber grommet to the transmission tunnel.

4 Clutch pedal - removal and refitting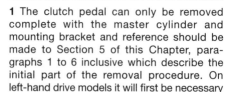

1 The clutch pedal can only be removed complete with the master cylinder and mounting bracket and reference should be made to Section 5 of this Chapter, paragraphs 1 to 6 inclusive which describe the initial part of the removal procedure. On left-hand drive models it will first be necessary to remove the left-hand front wing.
2 To remove the clutch pedal from the mounting bracket, undo and remove the six screws securing the cover plate and gasket to the pedal bracket and lift off the cover plate.
3 Undo and remove the nut on the end of the master cylinder pushrod and push the rod into the master cylinder until it is clear of the pedal trunion.
4 Using a small punch tap out the pin from the end of the pedal shaft.
5 Tap out the pedal shaft from the pedal bracket and lift away the pedal.
6 Examine the pedal shaft and bushes for wear. If the bushes require renewal a special tool is required to ream them to the correct

inside diameter. It is advisable to entrust this operation to your local Land Rover garage or motor engineering specialist. If however you have access to a set of expandable reamers, the correct dimensions and tolerances are given in the Specifications at the beginning of this Chapter.
7 Reassembly is the reverse of the removal sequence bearing in mind the following points:
(a) *Before reassembling the pedal and shaft, remove the oil filler plug from the end of the pedal shaft and fill the shaft with clean engine oil. Refit the plug.*
(b) *Refer to Section 5 of this Chapter and refit the pedal and master cylinder assembly to the vehicle*
(c) *Bleed the hydraulic system as described in Section 3*
(d) *Adjust the clutch linkage as described in Section 2*

5 Clutch master cylinder - removal and refitting

1 Two types of master cylinder are fitted to the Land Rover. The earlier type has a separate reservoir clamped to the master cylinder bracket (photo), while the later type has an integral reservoir. The internal components of each type of cylinder are the same. On vehicles fitted with left-hand drive it is necessary to remove the left-hand front wing as described in Chapter 12 and the pedal bracket assembly as described below. On right-hand drive models the master cylinder may be removed separately.

Left-hand drive models

2 If a separate reservoir is fitted undo the brake and clutch outlet pipe unions and allow the fluid to drain into a suitable container. Tape over the unions to prevent dirt ingress.
3 Undo and remove the nut retaining the reservoir clamp to the mounting bracket and lift off the reservoir and clamp (Series II and IIA only). Take care not to spill any hydraulic fluid on the vehicle paintwork as it will act as a paint stripper.
4 Undo and remove the clutch outlet pipe union from the master cylinder body (also the inlet pipe if a separate reservoir is fitted).

5 From inside the vehicle undo and remove the six bolts securing the pedal bracket assembly to the bulkhead. Note the position of the bolt carrying the pedal return spring mounting tag and lift off the spring.

6 From inside the engine compartment ease out the master cylinder, mounting bracket and pedal assembly complete.

7 Undo and remove the six screws securing the top cover and gasket to the mounting bracket. Lift off the cover and recover the gasket.

8 Unscrew the lower nut from the master cylinder pushrod and lift off the nut and flat washer.

9 Undo and remove the two nuts and bolts securing the master cylinder to the mounting bracket and withdraw the cylinder rearwards from the bracket.

Right-hand drive models

10 If a separate reservoir is fitted undo the brake and clutch outlet pipe unions and allow the fluid to drain into a suitable container. Tape over the unions to prevent dirt ingress.

11 Undo and remove the nut retaining the reservoir clamp to the mounting bracket and lift off the reservoir and clamp (Series II and IIA only). Take care not to spill any hydraulic fluid on the vehicle paintwork as it will act as a paint stripper.

12 Undo and remove the clutch outlet pipe union from the master cylinder body (also the inlet pipe if a separate reservoir is fitted).

13 Undo and remove the six screws securing the top cover to the master cylinder mounting bracket. Lift off the cover and recover the gasket.

14 Unscrew the lower nut from the master cylinder pushrod and lift off the nut and flat washer.

15 Undo and remove the two nuts and bolts securing the master cylinder to the mounting bracket and withdraw the cylinder rearwards from the bracket.

All models

16 Refitting the master cylinder is the reverse of the removal sequence bearing in mind the following points.

(a) Bleed the hydraulic system as described in Section 3

(b) Adjust the clutch linkages as described in Section 2

(c) Bleed the brake hydraulic system where necessary as described in Chapter 9

6 Clutch master cylinder - dismantling, examination and reassembly

1 Before dismantling the master cylinder, spread a clean sheet of paper on the workbench and lay each component out in the order of removal from the cylinder.

2 Pull the rubber bolt off the end of the

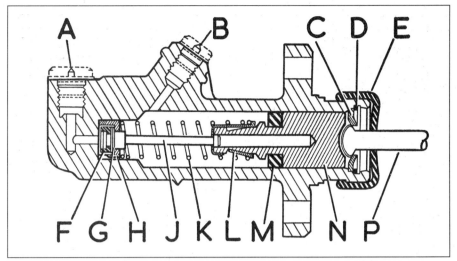

Fig. 5.8 Cross section of clutch master cylinder – separate reservoir type

A Fluid inlet port	F Valve seal	L Spring retainer
B Fluid outlet port	G Spring washer	M Piston seal
C Spring washer	H Valve spacer	N Piston
D Circlip	J Valve stem	P Pushrod
E Dust cover	K Return spring	

cylinder and remove the circlip from inside the cylinder. The pushrod and retaining washer can now be withdrawn.

3 Tap the cylinder body gently on a wooden surface until the piston emerges from the end of the cylinder. Withdraw the complete piston, spring and valve assembly.

4 To remove the piston from the spring and valve assembly, prise up the locking tag on the spring retainer until it is clear of the piston shoulder and pull off the spring and retainer from the piston.

5 Make a note of the correct way the seal is fitted to the piston and then ease it off using the fingers only.

6 Disengage the valve stem from the spring retainer by compressing the spring and positioning the stem so that it can pass through the larger hole in the retainer.

7 Slide the valve spacer and spring washer off the stem and remove the seal from the valve assembly.

8 Thoroughly wash all parts with hydraulic fluid or methylated spirit and wipe dry.

9 Carefully examine all parts, especially the piston cups, for signs of distortion, swelling, splitting or other wear and check the piston and cylinder for wear or scoring. Renew any

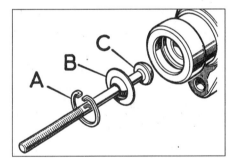

Fig. 5.9 Master cylinder pushrod assembly

A Circlip   B Spring washer   C Pushrod

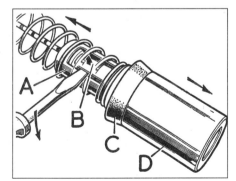

Fig. 5.10 Releasing the master cylinder return spring from the piston

A Spring retainer   C Rubber seal
B Locking tag   D Piston

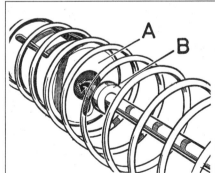

Fig. 5.11 Location of valve stem in spring retainer

A Retainer   B Valve stem

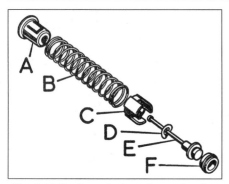

Fig. 5.12 Master cylinder valve and spring components

A Spring retainer   D Spring washer
B Spring   E Valve stem
C Valve spacer   F Valve seal

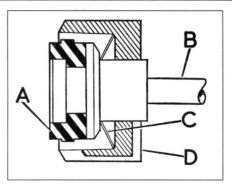

Fig. 5.13 Correct assembly of master cylinder valve

A Valve seal   C Spring washer
B Stem   D Spacer

7.5 Location of clutch slave cylinder (Series III models)

parts that are suspect. It is recommended, that, whenever a master cylinder is dismantled, new rubber seals are always fitted.

10 When reassembling the components to the master cylinder all components to be fitted must be lubricated with clean hydraulic fluid.

11 Fit a new seal onto the valve head and slide the spring washer and valve spacer onto the valve stem.

12 Refit the piston return spring centrally on the spacer, insert the retainer into the spring and depress it until the valve stem engages in the keyhole of the retainer.

13 Ensure that the spring is central on the spacer before fitting a new piston seal onto the piston.

14 Insert the reduced end of the piston into the retainer until the leaf engages under the shoulder of the plunger, and press home the leaf.

15 Check that the master cylinder bore is clean and smear with clean hydraulic fluid. With the piston suitably wetted with hydraulic fluid, carefully insert the assembly into the bore, valve end first. Ease the lips of the piston seal carefully into the bore.

16 Refit the pushrod and the circlip into the groove in the cylinder bore. Smear the sealing areas of the dust cover with a little rubber grease and pack the cover with the rubber grease so as to act as a dust trap. Fit the cover to the master cylinder body. The master cylinder is now ready for refitting to the vehicle.

7 Clutch slave cylinder - removal and refitting

1 Wipe the top of the clutch master cylinder and unscrew the cap. Fill the cylinder to the top with the correct type of hydraulic fluid. Place a piece of polythene sheet over the top to prevent hydraulic fluid syphoning out when the slave cylinder is removed. Refit the cap.

Series II and IIA

2 Remove the front floor assembly as described in Chapter 12.

3 Undo the hydraulic fluid pipe union from the slave cylinder and tape over the end to prevent dirt ingress.

4 Undo and remove the two nuts and bolts securing the slave cylinder to the mounting bracket and withdraw the slave cylinder from the bracket and pushrod.

Series III

5 Access to the slave cylinder is gained from beneath the clutch bellhousing (photo). if it is necessary to jack the vehicle up make sure it is firmly supported on heavy duty axle-stands.

6 Disconnect the bleed pipe and fluid pipe from the slave cylinder and tape over the ends to prevent dirt ingress.

7 Release the plastic clip from the clutch release lever and slide it back along the slave cylinder pushrod.

8 Undo and remove the two securing bolts and lift the slave cylinder away from the clutch housing.

All models

9 Refitting both types of slave cylinder is the reverse procedure to removal. In the case of Series II and IIA units make sure the pushrod is correctly located in the cylinder piston and that the system is adjusted as described in Section 2.

10 Bleed the hydraulic system as described in Section 3.

8 Slave cylinder - dismantling, examination and assembly

1 Clean the exterior of the slave cylinder using a dry non-fluffy rag.

2 Carefully ease back the dust cover from the body and lift away.

3 Using a pair of circlip pliers, remove the piston retaining circlip (if fitted).

4 Gently tap the open end of the slave cylinder on a wooden surface to extract the piston and spring.

5 Inspect the inside of the cylinder for score marks caused by impurities in the hydraulic fluid. If any are found a new slave cylinder will be necessary.

6 If the cylinder is sound, thoroughly clean it out with fresh hydraulic fluid.

7 Remove the old seal and smear the new one with hydraulic fluid before fitting it to the piston. Note that the raised lip of the seal must face towards the smaller end of the piston.

8 Smear some hydraulic fluid on the cylinder bore and refit the spring, (wider end first) and then the piston, taking care not to damage the seal.

9 Push the seal down the bore with the piston and retain the piston assembly in the bore with the circlip (if fitted).

10 Smear the sealing areas of the new dust cover with hydraulic fluid or rubber grease and refit to the slave cylinder.

9 Clutch - removal and refitting

1 To remove the clutch assembly only, it is not necessary to remove the seat base and lift the gearbox out of the vehicle. Refer to Chapter 6 and proceed with the gearbox removal operations with the exception of seat base removal.

2 With the gearbox supported on a trolley jack, move it rearwards approximately 5 inches (127 mm): this will give sufficient clearance to enable the clutch cover and driven plate to be removed.

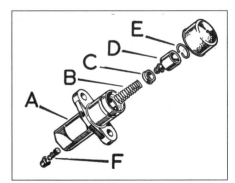

Fig. 5.14 Exploded view of slave cylinder – all models

A Cylinder body   D Piston
B Spring   E Circlip (where fitted)
C Piston seal   F Bleed nipple

9.5 Removing the clutch plate and cover (coil spring type)

9.10a Clutch driven plate exactly in line with the input shaft bush

9.10b Using an aligning tool to centralise the clutch driven plate

3 With a scriber or file, mark the relative position of the clutch cover and flywheel to ensure correct refitting if the original parts are to be re-used.

4 Undo and remove the bolts securing the clutch cover to the rear face of the flywheel. Unscrew the bolts diagonally half a turn at a time to prevent distortion of the cover flange.

5 With the bolts removed carefully lift the cover off its locating dowels on the flywheel. Be prepared to catch the driven plate which will slide down as the cover is removed (photo).

6 Do not allow oil or grease to come into contact with the clutch friction linings or the pressure plate and flywheel faces. It is advisable to handle the parts with clean hands and to wipe down the pressure plate and flywheel faces with a clean dry rag before inspection or refitting commences.

7 To refit the clutch assembly place the driven piate with the words 'Flywheel side' against the flywheel and the larger end of the central hub towards the gearbox.

8 Holding the driven plate in position refit the clutch cover loosely on the dowels. Refit the securing bolts and tighten them finger tight so that the clutch driven plate is gripped but can still be moved. **Note:** *If a new clutch cover assembly is being fitted it will be coated with a thin film of grease which must be removed with methylated spirit or paraffin before fitting.*

9 The clutch driven plate must now be centralised so that when the engine and gearbox are mated, the gearbox input shaft splines will pass through the splines in the centre of the hub.

10 Centralise the clutch disc by using an old gearbox input shaft inserted through the splines on the driven plate and into the input shaft bearing in the flywheel. Alternatively use a long bar (socket extension bar) and a mirror and move the driven plate until it appears exactly in line with the input shaft bearing in the flywheel (photo). if difficulty is experienced a special centralisation tool, part number 605022 is available from your Land Rover dealer.

11 Progressively tighten the clutch cover bolts in a diagonal sequence to the torque figure given in the Specifications at the beginning of this Chapter.

12 Apply a trace of medium grease to the splines on the gearbox input shaft and refit the gearbox as described in Chapter 6.

13 Adjust the clutch linkages as described in Section 2.

10 Clutch - inspection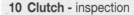

1 Examine the clutch disc friction lining for wear, loose or broken springs and rivets. The linings must be proud of the rivets and light in appearance, with the material structure visible. If it is dark in appearance, further investigation is necessary as it is a sign of oil contamination caused by oil leaking past the crankshaft rear seal.

2 Check the machined faces of the flywheel and pressure plate for signs of grooving. If evident new parts should be fitted. Inspect the pressure plate for hair line cracks usually caused by overheating, and if evident a new unit must be fitted.

3 Place the driven plate on the input shaft of the gearbox and check that it is free to slide up and down the splines without signs of binding.

4 Check the release bearing for smoothness of operation. There should be no harshness

or slackness in it. It should spin freely with no sign of roughness from the bearing.

5 Should either the release bearing, driven plate or clutch cover assembly require renewal practical experience has shown that whenever possible all three units should be renewed together. Renewal of indivdual clutch components separately can sometimes cause judder, squeal, and a general roughness of the clutch as new components do not easily bed into old ones. However cost is the major consideration and it is left to the owner's discretion as to which course of action he chooses.

11 Clutch release bearing - removal and refitting

1 To remove the release bearing on all models, it is necessary to first remove the gearbox from the vehicle as described in Chapter 6.

Series II and IIA

2 With the gearbox removed from the vehicle, withdraw the split pin and flat washer from the pin securing the connecting tube to the withdrawal unit cross-shaft. Tap out the pin and remove the connecting tube. Undo and remove the securing nuts and withdraw the clutch release assembly from the bellhousing studs. Recover the gasket.

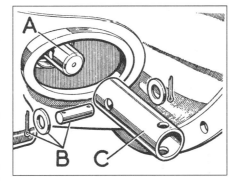

Fig. 5.15 Cross-shaft connecting tube – Series II and IIA

A *Clutch withdrawal unit*
B *Connecting tube retaining fixings*
C *Connecting tube*

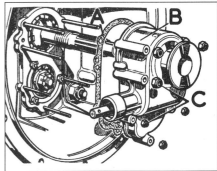

Fig. 5.16 Clutch release mechanism – Series II and IIA

A *Gasket*   B *Housing*   C *Retaining nuts*

11.7 inserting the clutch withdrawal sleeve into the housing (Series II and IIA)

11.8 Correct location of thrust bearing and cross-shaft in the housing (Series II and IIA)

11.9 Refitting the clutch release assembly into the bellhousing (Series II and IIA)

3 Undo the screws from the cover plate on the side of the housing, and drift out the cross-shaft from right to left. The operating

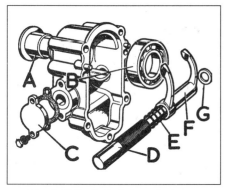

Fig. 5.17 Exploded view of release components Series II and IIA (Sec 11)

A Clutch withdrawal sleeve
B Release bearing
C Cross-shaft cover plate
D Cross-shaft
E Spring
F Operating fork
G Thrust washer

fork, thrust washer and spring can now be removed from the housing.

4 Support the housing on wooden blocks and, using a suitable sized piece of tubing, drift the withdrawal sleeve from the bearing.

5 Remove the oil seal from the right-hand side of the housing and examine the cross-shaft bushes and withdrawal sleeve bush for wear. Renew as necessary. **Note:** *These bushes have to be reamed when renewed and this task should be entrusted to your Land Rover dealer or an engineering company.*

6 The cross-shaft oil seal and thrust bearing should be renewed as a matter of course unless the latter is in perfect condition. When refitting the cross-shaft oil seal, ensure the knife-edge of the seal faces in towards the housing.

7 Refit the withdrawal sleeve into the housing and drift the thrust bearing onto the sleeve shoulder using a large piece of tubing (photo).

8 Place the release fork, spring and spacer into the housing in the order shown in Fig. 5.18. Ensure the withdrawal sleeve is protruding from the housing 7/16 in (11 mm), by placing a steel bar of this diameter between the sleeve and housing and with the hole in the

cross-shaft in line with the sleeve (Fig. 5.19) driven in the cross-shaft through the housing and release fork assembly (photo).

9 Refit the cross-shaft cover plate and gasket and, after checking the release assembly for correct operation, refit it to the clutch bellhousing using a new gasket (photo).

Series III

10 The clutch release mechanism on the later models is a much simpler design than the earlier type.

11 With the gearbox out of the vehicle, remove the retaining clip and withdraw the thrust bearing and sleeve from the release fork.

12 Inspect the thrust bearing for wear and, unless in perfect condition, it should be driven off the sleeve, using a suitable sized piece of tubing and wooden support blocks or a vice.

13 Press on the new bearing using a vice and packing pieces. Note that the domed side of the bearing faces towards the engine.

14 Apply some high melting point grease to the contact surfaces of the release lever and pivot point.

15 Refit the bearing and carrier, using the reverse sequence to the removal procedure.

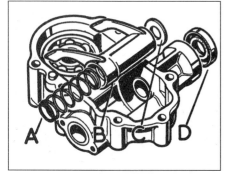

Fig . 5.18 Refitting release fork components – Series II and IIA (Sec 11)

A Spring   C Thrust washer
B Fork   D Oil seal

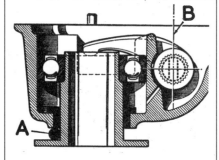

Fig. 5.19 Correct installation of release fork – Series II and IIA (Sec 11)

A Sleeve held out by 7/16 in (11 mm) diameter bar
B Hole in cross-shaft must be in line with sleeve

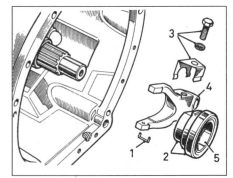

Fig . 5.20 Clutch release mechanism – Series III (Sec 11)

1 Retaining clip
2 Release bearing and sleeve
3 Release fork securing clip and fixings
4 Release fork
5 Release bearing

Fault finding - clutch

Clutch pedal appears spongy accompanied by harsh engagement of gears

☐ Air in hydraulic system
☐ Leaks in fluid pipe or unions
☐ Bulging in flexible hose
☐ Faulty master cylinder

Excessive clutch pedal travel

☐ Clutch linkages out of adjustment
☐ War in linkages and bearings
☐ Faulty master cylinder

Hydraulic system will not maintain pressure (vehicle creeps forward with pedal fully depressed)

☐ Faulty seals in master and/or slave cylinder
☐ Leaking hydraulic pipe, hose or union

Clutch will not fully disengage

☐ Driven plate sticking on input shaft
☐ Driven plate sticking to flywheel due to oil contamination
☐ Broken pressure plate springs

Clutch slip (engine speed increases with no increase in road speed)

☐ Clutch driven plate badly worn
☐ Pressure plate faulty
☐ Oil or grease contamination of friction linings
☐ Insufficient free play on release linkages

Clutch judder

☐ Oil or grease contamination of friction materials
☐ Worn or loose engine or gearbox mountings
☐ Excess run-out of flywheel
☐ Excess wear of clutch assembly
☐ Faulty release mechanism

Squeal or rumble when depressing clutch pedal

☐ Worn or faulty release bearing
☐ Worn or broken pressure plate springs (diaphragm type)

Notes

Chapter 6
Gearbox

For modifications, and information applicable to later models, see Supplement at end of manual

Contents

Degrees of difficulty

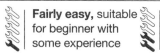

Easy, suitable for novice with little experience	**Fairly easy,** suitable for beginner with some experience	**Fairly difficult,** suitable for competent DIY mechanic	**Difficult,** suitable for experienced DIY mechanic	**Very difficult,** suitable for expert DIY or professional

Specifications

Main gearbox

Type:
Series II and IIA.	Four speed and reverse with synchromesh on 3rd and 4th gears only
Series III	Four speed and reverse with synchromesh on all forward gears
Lubricant type/specification.	Hypoid gear oil, viscosity SAE 90EP, to API GL4
Oil capacity.	2 1/2 pints (1.5 litres)
Oil level plug.	Left-hand side of casing

Gear ratios:
	Up to gearbox suffix 'B'	From gearbox suffix 'C' onwards
Top	1: 1	1: 1
Third	1.377: 1	1.50: 1
Second.	2.043: 1	2.22: 1
First	2.996: 1	3.60: 1
Reverse.	2.547: 1	3.02 : 1

Transfer gearbox

Type	Two speed (high or low ratio)
Lubricant type/specification.	Hypoid gear oil, viscosity SAE 90EP, to API GL4
Oil capacity.	4 1/2 pints (2.5 litres)

Gear ratios:
	Up to gearbox suffix 'B'	From gearbox suffix 'C' onwards
High	1.148: 1	1.148: 1
Low	2.888: 1	2.350: 1

Overall gear ratios

	Main gearbox	Transfer box	
		High ratio	Low ratio
Up to gearbox suffix 'B'	Top	5.396	13.578
	Third	7.435	18.707
	Second	11.026	27.742
	First	16.171	40.688
	Reverse	13.745	34.585
From gearbox suffix 'C' onwards.	Top	5.40 : 1	11.28 : 1
	Third	8.15 : 1	17.06 : 1
	Second	11.98 : 1	25.04 : 1
	First	19.42 : 1	40.61 : 1
	Reverse	16.30 : 1	34.07 : 1
Optional helical gear transfer box	Top	7.19 : 1	15.4 : 1
	Third	10.8 : 1	23.1 : 1
	Second	15.96 : 1	34.1 : 1
	First	25.9 : 1	55.3 : 1
	Reverse	21.7 : 1	46.4 : 1

Speedometer drive

Ratio	2.2:1
Location	Rear of transfer box

Transmission brake

Type . . . . Drum, on transfer box output shaft

Main gearbox dimensions

Reverse gear bush:
  Reamed bore . . . . 0.8125 in + 0.001 in (20.637 mm + 0.0254 mm)
Mainshaft bush:
  Fit in gears . . . . 0.0025 in to 0.0035 in (0.0635 mm to 0.0889 mm)
  Fit on shaft . . . . Zero to 0.001 in (zero to 0.0254 mm)
  Endfloat . . . . 0.001 in to 0.008 in (0.0254 mm to 0.20 mm)
2nd and 3rd speed gears:
  Endfloat on distance sleeve . . . . 0.004 in to 0.007 in (0.10 mm to 0.18 mm)
Synchronising clutch load . . . . 15 lb to 20 lb (6.5 kg to 9 kg)
2nd gear stop:
  Adjustment . . . . 0.002 in (0.05 mm) clearance
Reverse gear stop:
  Adjustment . . . . 0.002 in (0.05 mm) clearance

Transfer gearbox dimensions

Dog clutch selector shaft bush:
  Reamed bore . . . . 1.148 in – 0.001 in (29.17 mm – 0.025 mm)
Output shaft front and rear bearings:
  Endfloat . . . . Zero
  Preload . . . . 2 lb to 4 lb (0.28 kg to 0.55 kg)
High speed gear:
  Endfloat . . . . 0.004 in to 0.008 in (0.10 mm to 0.20 mm) (after adjusting output shaft endfloat)
Intermediate gear:
  Endfloat . . . . 0.004 in to 0.008 in (0.10 mm to 0.20 mm)
Note: *The dimensions of the optional helical gear transfer box are as above with the following exceptions:*
Low speed gear:
  Endfloat . . . . 0.002 in to 0.009 in (0.05 mm to 0.23 mm)
High speed gear:
  Endfloat . . . . 0.005 in to 0.022 in (0.12 mm to 0.57 mm)

Front output shaft housing dimensions

Transfer selector shaft, spring:
  Free length . . . . 7.156 in (181.76 mm)
  Length in position . . . . 3.875 in (98.43 mm)
  Load in position . . . . 24 lb (10.89 kg)
Dog clutch selector springs:
  Free length . . . . 2.75 in (69.8 mm)
  Solid length . . . . 0.64 in (16.2 mm)
  Maximum load . . . . 13 lb (5.9 kg)

Torque wrench settings

	lbf ft	kgf m
Output drive flange nut.	85	11.75
Layshaft bolt (Series III)	50	6.9
Layshaft nut (Series II and IIA)	75	10.0

1 General description

The transmission unit on the Land Rover provides four forward speeds and one reverse in either high or low ratio gearing, thus giving a total selection of eight forward and two reverse speeds. When the low ratio gearing is selected, four wheel drive is automatically engaged while the high ratio can be used in either two or four wheel drive as required.

Basically the transmission assembly is comprised of three units. First there is the main four speed gearbox with synchromesh on third and fourth gears (Series III models have synchromesh on all four gears). Attached to the rear of the main gearbox is the two speed (high or low) transfer box. On earlier models the high ratio gear wheels have helical cut teeth, while the low ratio gears have straight-cut teeth. On the later models all the gear wheels in the transfer box are of the helical type. The third part of the transmission is the four wheel drive selector unit attached to the front of the transfer box. This comprises the front wheel driveshaft and housing and a dog clutch and selector mechanism .

When viewed as a complete assembly, the transmission may appear to be a rather complex mechanism. However, providing the three basic units are dealt with separately as described, the DIY mechanic with a well equipped workshop, and a reasonable engineering knowledge, should not experience any major problems in overhauling part, or all of the transmission assembly.

2 Transmission - removal and refitting

1 Because the gearbox can only be removed from inside the vehicle through the passenger doorway it is essential that a wheeled hoist with an extended lifting arm is available. This will enable the transmission assembly to be lifted from its mountings and then manoeuvred through the doorway.
2 Begin by removing the front floor panels and transmission cover panels as described in Chapter 1.
3 It is necessary to remove the complete seat base. Commence by lifting out the seat cushions and then release the seat squab retaining straps from the support rail.

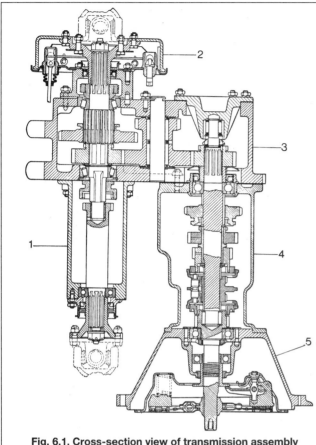

Fig. 6.1. Cross-section view of transmission assembly

1 Output shaft housing	3 Transfer box	5 Bellhousing
2 Transmission brake	4 Main gearbox	

Fig. 6.2. Exploded view of gearbox and transfer box internal components

1 Primary pinion and constant gear
2 Shield for primary pinion
3 Ball bearing for primary pinion
4-5 Nut and washer for bearing
6-8 Fixings for bearing
9 Layshaft
10 Mainshaft
11 Peg for 2nd gear thrust washer
12 Peg for mainshaft distance sleeve
13 Thrust washer for 2nd speed gear
14 1st speed layshaft gear
15 1st speed mainshaft gear
16 2nd speed layshaft and mainshaft gear
17 Split ring for 2nd speed layshaft gear (early gearboxes)
18 3rd speed layshaft and mainshaft gear
19 Distance sleeve for mainshaft
20 Thrust washer for 3rd speed mainshaft gear
21 Spring ring fixing 2nd and 3rd mainshaft gears
22 Sleeve for layshaft
23 Bearing for layshaft, front
24-26 Fixings for bearing to layshaft
27 Bearing plate assembly for layshaft
28 Stud for bearing cap
29 Distance piece for layshaft
30 Retaining plate for layshaft front bearing
31-32 Fixings for cap and bearing
33 Bearing for layshaft rear
34 Synchronising clutch
35 Detent spring for clutch
36 Roller bearing for mainshaft
37 Ball bearing for mainshaft
38 Housing for mainshaft bearing, rear
39 Peg, housing to casing
40 Circlip, bearing to housing
41 Circlip, housing to casing

42 Oil seal for rear of mainshaft
43 Oil thrower for mainshaft
44 Distance piece, rear of mainshaft
45 Mainshaft gear for transfer box
46-47 Nut and washer for gear
48 Shaft for reverse gear
49 Reverse wheel assembly
50 Bush for reverse wheel
51 Gear, intermediate
52 Roller bearing for intermediate gear
53 Thrust washer for intermediate gear
54 Shim for intermediate gear
55 Shaft for intermediate gear
56 Sealing ring for intermediate gear
57 Retaining plate for shaft
58-59 Nut and washer for plate
60 Low gear wheel
61 High gear wheel
62 Output shaft, rear drive
63 Thrust washer for high gear wheel
64 Circlip fixing washer to shaft
65 Bearing for output shaft, front
66 Circlip fixing bearing to case
67 Bearing for output shaft, rear
68 Oil seal for output shaft
69 Speedometer worm complete
70 Flange for output shaft, rear drive
71 Mudshield for flange
72 Fitting bolt for brake drum
73 Retaining flange for brake drum bolts
74 Fitting bolt for propeller shaft
75 Circlip retaining bolts and flange
76-78 Fixings for flange
79 Speedometer pinion
80 Retaining plate for pinion
81 Screw fixing plate to housing
82 Sleeve for pinion
83 Sealing ring for sleeve
84 Joint washer for sleeve
85 Oil seal for pinion

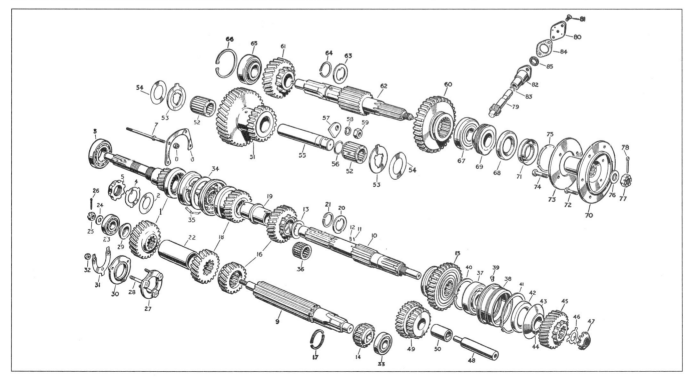

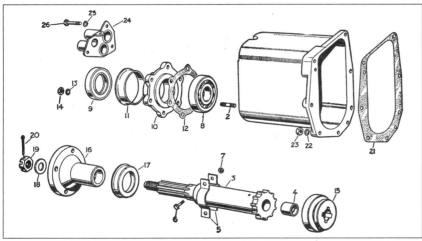

Fig. 6.3. Output shaft and housing assembly

1	Output shaft housing assembly	12	Joint washer for retainer
2	Stud for oil seal retainer	13-14	Nut and washer for retainer
3	Front output shaft assembly	15	Locking dog, four wheel drive
4	Bush for shaft	16	Flange for transfer shaft
5	Oil thrower for output shaft	17	Mudshield for flange
6-7	Nut and bolt for oil thrower	18-20	Nut for flange
8	Bearing for front output shaft	21	Joint washer for transfer housing
9	Oil seal for shaft	22-23	Nuts for housing
10	Retainer for oil seal	24	Dust cover plate for selector shafts
11	Mudshield for retainer	25-26	Bolt for dust cover

4 Working underneath the vehicle, undo the two nuts securing the handbrake lever assembly to the chassis. Note: On early

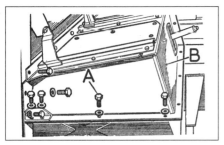

Fig. 6.4. Seat base attachment bolts

A Securing bolts   B Seat base

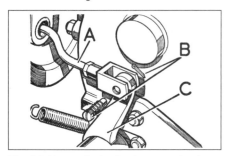

Fig. 6.5. Transmission brake operating lever

A Brake rod   C Operating lever
B Split pin and clevis pin

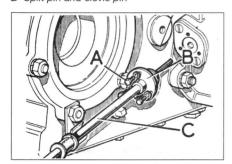

Fig. 6.6. Speedometer cable

A Securing bolts   C Cable assembly
B Retaining plate

models fitted with the short horizontal brake lever this operation is not necessary as it is possible to lift the seat base over the lever.
5 Undo and remove all the bolts securing the seat base to the floor structure (see Fig. 6.4).
6 With an assistant, lift the complete seat base out of the vehicle. If the earlier type handbrake lever is fitted, move the seat assembly forward first to enable the lever to pass through the aperture in the front of the seat base.
7 Drain the transfer box and gearbox oil into a suitable container (refer to the Maintenance Section at the front of this manual for the location of the two drain plugs).
8 Disconnect the rear propeller shaft from the transmission brake drum studs and the front propeller shaft from the output flange (refer to Chapter 7 if necessary). If a winch is fitted, the driveshaft for this must also be removed.
9 Remove the split pin and unscrew the threaded clevis pin and spring from the transmission brake operating lever (see Fig. 6.6).
10 Undo the securing nut, unhook the return spring and lift away the transmission brake operating lever assembly (see Fig. 6.5). Note: On left-hand drive models it is necessary to remove the brake lever cross-shaft.
11 Undo the two retaining screws and withdraw the speedometer cable from the rear of the transfer box (see Fig. 6.6).
12 Remove the two bolts from each of the transmission assembly mountings (see Fig. 6.7). On some models it may be necessary

to remove the front exhaust pipe which passes over the left-hand mounting.
13 If a tie-rod is fitted between the chassis and the gearbox, remove the two front bracket securing bolts and push the tie-rod clear of the chassis (see Fig. 6.8).
14 On earlier models, remove the clevis pin from the clutch operating shaft, undo the three nuts securing the clutch slave cylinder bracket to the bellhousing and lift away the slave cylinder bracket and cross-shaft assembly. Tie the assembly out of the way taking care not to strain the flexible hydraulic pipe.
15 On later models undo the two retaining bolts and withdraw the slave cylinder from the side of the bellhousing. Avoid any excessive bending of the hydraulic inlet pipe.
16 Remove the earthing strap between the gearbox and chassis, if fitted.
17 Jack up the rear of the engine just enough to fit a 1 in (25 mm) wooden block between the flywheel housing and the chassis crossmember and then lower the jack.
18 Place a suitable sling around the transmission assembly and raise the hoist sufficiently to support the weight.
19 Undo and remove the remaining nine nuts and washers securing the bellhousing to the rear of the engine.
20 Withdraw the transmission rearwards until the input shaft is clear of the clutch assembly and then carefully lift the complete transmission assembly out of the vehicle (photos).

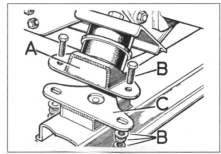

Fig. 6.7. Transmission assembly

A Upper mounting plate   C Chassis plate
B Securing bolt and nut

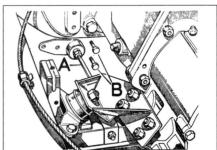

Fig. 6.8. Transmission tie-rod (if fitted)

A Tie-rod assembly   B Securing bolts

21 Refitting is basically the reverse of the removal procedure. However, if the clutch cover has been removed, ensure the driven plate is centralised as described in Chapter 5, before attempting to refit the transmission.
22 After refitting, check and top-up the gearbox and transfer box oil levels and check the clutch adjustment as described in Chapter 5.

3 Transmission – separation into major assemblies

1 Before the four speed gearbox or transfer box assembly can be dismantled for inspection and repair, it is necessary to separate the three major transmission units from each other, ie; the transfer box must first be removed from the gearbox and then the front output shaft (four wheel drive) housing from the transfer box.
2 Before commencing work, clean off all dirt and grease from the transmission casing using paraffin or a water soluble grease solvent.
3 Remove the large split-pinned nut securing the brake drum and output flange and remove the drum and flange assembly from the splined shaft.
4 Remove the four nuts and washers and remove the complete brake anchor plate and shoe assembly (see Fig. 6.9).
5 To separate the transfer box from the gearbox, first undo the bolts securing the transfer gearlever bracket to the bellhousing and remove the complete lever and bracket assembly. Take care not to lose the spacers or the small spring on the lever ball (see Fig. 6.10).
6 Undo the ten screws and remove the inspection plate from the bottom of the transfer box.
7 Remove the nuts and prise off the mainshaft rear bearing housing (see Fig. 6.11). **Note:** If the optional power take-off drive unit is fitted it must be removed.
8 Remove the nut and retaining plate that secures the grooved end of the intermediate shaft to the transfer box casing.
9 Support the intermediate gear cluster with one hand and extract the intermediate shaft using a sprocket puller. If a puller is not available, the intermediate shaft can be

2.20a Withdrawing the transmission from the engine

extracted using a tyre lever and a suitable piece of bar as a fulcrum.
10 Remove the intermediate gear cluster and any associated shims and thrust washers.
11 Referring to Fig. 6.12, remove the nuts and washers securing the transfer box to the gearbox and separate the two components.
12 Undo the plug from the top of the transfer box and remove the selector shaft spring and plunger.
13 Remove the cover plate from the top of the transfer box and unscrew the pinch bolt from the transfer selector fork (see Fig. 6.13).
14 Undo the nuts securing the output shaft housing to the transfer box and remove the

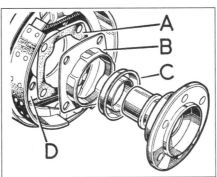
Fig. 6.9. Transmission brake components

A Joint washer for oil catcher
B Oil catcher
C Mud shield for flange
D Brake anchor plate

2.20b Complete transmission assembly removed from vehicle

housing complete with output shaft and selector mechanism. Retrieve the four wheel drive locking dog which is now released.
15 Lift out the selector fork from inside the transfer box.
16 The transmission assembly is now separated into its three major component parts. To dismantle each unit, refer to the following Sections.

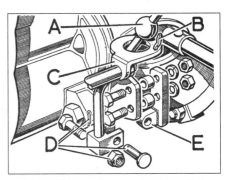
Fig. 6.10. Transfer gear lever bracket

A Transfer gear lever
B Spring, lever ball to gearbox link
C Link, for lever
D Alternative fixings, lever to bellhousing
E Bracket lever to bellhousing

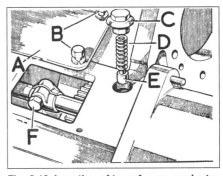
Fig. 6.13. Location of transfer gear selector and detent spring

A Top cover, transfer box
B Bolts, top cover
C Plug for plunger
D Spring for plunger
E Plunger, transfer selector shaft
F Pinch bolt securing selector fork

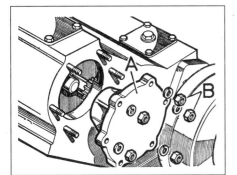
Fig. 6.11. Mainshaft rear bearing housing

A Bearing housing *B Securing nuts*

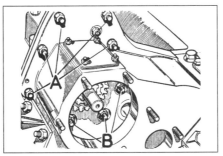
Fig. 6.12. Location of transfer box attachment bolts

A External securing nut
B Internal securing nuts

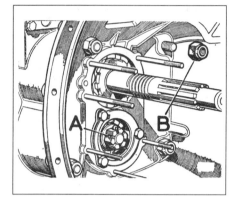

Fig. 6.14. Bellhousing attachment points

A Layshaft securing nut (earlier type)
B Bellhousing securing nuts

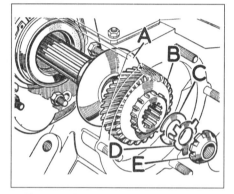

Fig. 6.17. Transfer gear on rear end of mainshaft

A Oil thrower   D Lockwasher
B Mainshaft gear   E Special nut
C Shim washer

4 Main gearbox – dismantling

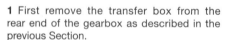

1 First remove the transfer box from the rear end of the gearbox as described in the previous Section.
2 Remove the clutch release assembly from inside the bellhousing as described in Chap-ter 5.
3 Undo the two rear nuts and two front bolts and remove the gearchange lever and bracket from the gearbox.
4 From inside the bellhousing, remove the split pin and undo the large nut from the end of the layshaft (Fig. 6.14). On later models nut is replaced by a bolt and large washer which must be removed.

HAYNES HiNT *To prevent the layshaft rotating while the nut (or bolt) is removed, select top gear and grip the main output shaft at the rear of the gearbox.*

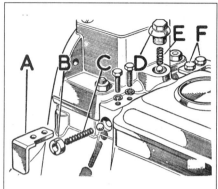

Fig. 6.15. Location of top cover detent balls and springs

A Retainer plate
B Rubber sealing grommet
C Spring reverse selector shaft
D Plug
E Spring, 1st-2nd selector shaft
F Bolts, 3rd-4th selector spring

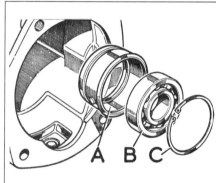

Fig. 6.18. Removing the mainshaft rear bearing

A Bearing housing   C Circlip
B Bearing

5 Unscrew the four retaining nuts and carefully remove the bellhousing, complete with primary shaft from the gearbox casing.
6 Referring to Fig. 6.15, remove the two retaining plates and the centre plug from the rear of the top cover and lift out the three **selector springs.**
7 Unscrew the securing nuts and remove the top cover. Retrieve the three selector balls from the top cover.
8 The type of selector forks and the method of removal is different on the earlier gearbox, fitted with synchromesh on third and fourth **gears only, compared with the later all-synchromesh unit.**
9 On the earlier type, select first gear and remove the reverse gear elector shaft and fork by lifting it up and turning it approximately a quarter of a turn to the left (see Fig. 6.16). Lift out the interlocking plunger.
10 Next, push the first/second selector shaft fully forward (second gear position) and lift it out. Remove the second interlocking plunger.

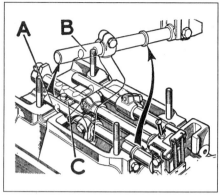

Fig. 6.16. Removing the reverse gear selector shaft (Series II and IIA)

A Reverse gear selector shaft in position
B Method of removal
C Interlocking plunger

11 Push the third/fourth selector shaft fully rearward (third gear position) and lift it out.
12 If working on the later all-synchromesh gearbox, first select third gear and lift out the third/fourth gear selector, turning it as necessary to clear the casing. Remove the interlocking plunger.
13 Withdraw the first/second selector shaft followed by the reverse selector shaft, and lift out the second interlocking plunger.
14 The next task is to remove the layshaft. First slide off the large constant speed gear from the front of the layshaft and withdraw the synchromesh clutch unit from the mainshaft.
15 Manoeuvre the layshaft forward and downwards to clear the mainshaft and withdraw it from the gearbox.
16 Turning to the rear end of the mainshaft, bend up the lock tab and remove the large castle nut using special tool No. 600300. If this tool is not available, use an alloy drift and a light hammer, but take care not to burr over the edges of the nut.
17 Withdraw the lockwasher, shim, mainshaft gear and oil thrower from the end of the mainshaft (see Fig. 6.17).
18 Using a soft-faced mallet drive the mainshaft out from the rear of the gearbox.
19 To remove the reverse gear assembly, gently warm the gear casing with a gas blowtorch and drive out the reverse gear shaft from inside the casing.
20 The mainshaft rear oil seal can be prised out of the rear bearing housing.
21 Check the mainshaft rear bearing for wear. If it is decided to renew it, remove the circlip retaining the bearing housing to the casing, and, using a suitable drift, drive the housing and bearing assembly forward into the casing until it is free (see Fig. 6.18).
22 Remove the inner circlip from the bearing housing and press out the bearing.
23 The gearbox is now stripped out and the individual gears and synchromesh components can be dismantled and examined for wear as described in the following Sections.

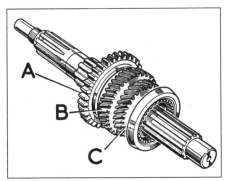

Fig. 6.19. Mainshaft assembly (Series II and IIA)

A 1st speed gear   C 3rd speed gear
B 2nd speed gear

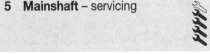

5 Mainshaft – servicing

1 Examine the gear teeth for excessive wear or chipping. If, even with the clutch correctly adjusted, the gears crashed when changing gear, the synchromesh units will require attention. Do not forget that the Series II and IIA models only have synchromesh on third and fourth gears.
2 The mainshaft fitted to the Series III models has synchromesh on all four gears and is different from the earlier type, so the servicing procedures are described under separate headings.

Series II and IIA mainshaft

3 First withdraw the first speed gear from the rear end of the mainshaft (see Fig. 6.19).
4 Prise out the spring ring located in front of the third speed gear and withdraw the thrust washer, third speed gear, distance sleeve and second speed gear (see Fig. 6.20).
5 To remove the second speed thrust washer, it is necessary to remove the locating peg which is a press fit in the mainshaft (see Fig. 6.21).
6 Examine the shaft and gears for wear and renew if necessary. Check the synchromesh

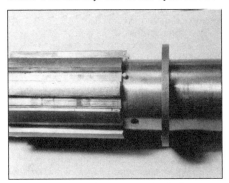

5.8 Fitting the inner mainshaft thrust washer

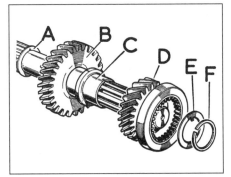

Fig. 6.20. Removing the mainshaft gears (front end)

A Thrust washer, 2nd speed gear
B 2nd speed gear
C Distance sleeve
D 3rd speed gear
E Thrust washer, 3rd speed gear
F Spring ring

unit and if worn, a complete new assembly must be obtained. If the mainshaft sleeve has worn it should be replaced by the new type which has a groove cut in the centre flange.
7 During reassembly of the mainshaft, smear all components with gear oil,
8 If the inner thrust washer was removed, slide it onto the shaft ensuring it is correctly located on the peg (photo).
9 Before fitting the larger sleeve locating peg, temporarily refit the sleeve onto the shaft and refit the outer spacer and spring ring.
10 Now check the endfloat of the sleeve, which should be between 0.001 to 0.008 in (0.03 to 0.20 mm). Adjustment can be made by fitting different thrust washers which are available in a range of thicknesses.
11 If the endfloat is correct, remove the sleeve and fit the second gear onto the end of the sleeve with the larger slot. Fit a new locating peg in the shaft and slide on the sleeve and gear with the dog coupling facing towards the rear end of the shaft (photo).
12 Holding the sleeve hard against the inner thrust washer, check that the endfloat of the second speed gear is within 0.004 to 0.007 in (0.10 to 0.18 mm). (See Fig. 6.22).
13 Slide the third speed gear onto the sleeve

5.11 Fitting the 2nd gear and sleeve onto the mainshaft, (note the sleeve locating peg)

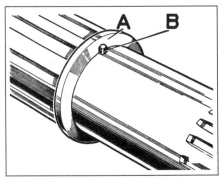

Fig. 6.21. 2nd gear thrust washer

A Thrust washer   B Peg for sleeve

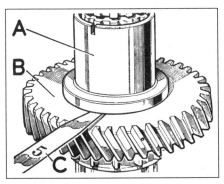

Fig. 6.22. Checking the 2nd gear end-float

A Sleeve   B 2nd gear   C Feeler gauge

followed by the thrust washer and, holding the thrust washer hard against the sleeve, check that the third gear endfloat is within the same tolerance given for the second gear. **Note:** If the clearance is insufficient, a new sleeve must be fitted. Excessive clearance can be reduced by carefully rubbing down the appropriate end face of the sleeve using a sheet of emery cloth on a facing plate or thick piece of glass.
14 When the clearances are correct, fit a new spring ring in front of the third gear thrust washer.

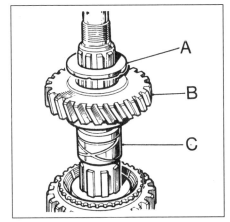

Fig. 6.23. Mainshaft rear end assembly (Series III)

A Thrust washer   B 1st gear   C Bush

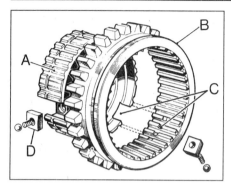

Fig. 6.24. 1st/2nd gear synchromesh unit (Series I I I)

A Inner hub
B Outer gear assembly
C Locating grooves
D Sliding blocks (3 off)

15 Fit the first speed gear onto the rear end of the shaft ensuring it engages with the second gear dog.

16 The mainshaft is now ready to be refitted Into the gearbox casing (see Section 9).

Series III mainshaft

17 From the rear end of the mainshaft, lift off the thrust washer and withdraw the first speed gear and bush (see Fig. 6.23).

18 Withdraw the rear synchro cone and lift off the complete first/second speed synchro unit followed by the front synchro cone.

19 Remove the second and third speed gears from the front of the mainshaft using the procedure described in paragraphs 4 and 5 in this Section.

20 Examine the shaft and gears for wear and renew if necessary. Check the third/fourth gear synchromesh clutch unit and if worn, a complete new assembly must be obtained.

21 The first/second gear synchromesh is a fairly complex unit containing a number of balls and springs that tend to fly out when the inner hub is removed, therefore, unless it is obviously badly worn it should be left well alone.

22 If it must be dismantled, ensure the workbench is clear and spread some clean paper over it.

23 Cover the synchro unit with a piece of clean cloth and push out the inner hub; remove the cloth and retrieve the three springs, balls and sliding blocks.

24 Check the components for wear and renew where necessary. The springs should be renewed as a matter of course.

25 To reassemble the synchro unit, first refit the inner hub into the outer gear unit with the detent spring holes aligned with the ball retaining grooves in the outer gear unit. Note that the longer splines on the inner hub must be entered into the outer unit from the gear teeth side (see Fig. 6.24).

26 If the inner hub is a tight fit, withdraw it and rotate it 120° in either direction until an easy sliding fit is obtained.

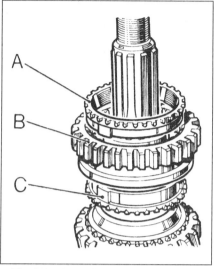

Fig. 6.25. Assembling the 1st/2nd gear synchromesh unit onto the mainshaft (Series III)

A Rear Synchro cone
B 1st/2nd gear synchromesh unit
C Front synchro cone

27 Position the sliding blocks on the inner hub with the radiused face outwards and fit the springs through the blocks and into the holes in the inner hub.

28 Position the balls on the ends of the springs and push them down as far as possible by hand. At this stage the help of a friend will be advantageous .

29 With the balls held down, push the inner hub fully home into the outer gear unit until the balls are correctly located in the retaining grooves.

30 To reassemble the mainshaft, first refit the second and third speed gears to the front end of the mainshaft as described in paragraphs 8 to 14 in this Section.

31 Hold the mainshaft in a soft-jawed vice with the rear end uppermost and slide a synchro cone down the shaft onto the second speed gear.

32 Fit the first/second gear synchromesh unit to the shaft with the gear uppermost and position the second synchro cone on the inner synchro hub (Fig. 6.25).

33 Refit the first gear bush with the oil groove facing towards the rear of the shaft. Temporarily refit the thrust washer and check that the clearance between the end of the bush and the thrust washer is within 0.002 to 0.007 in (0.05 to 0.18 mm). Adjustment is made by grinding down or renewing the bush.

34 When the clearance is correct, remove the thrust washer and fit the first speed gear followed by the thrust washer with the stepped side facing to the rear end of the shaft.

35 The mainshaft assembly is now ready to be installed into the gearbox casing. Note that the third/ fourth synchromesh clutch unit is assembled on the mainshaft after it is refitted in the casing.

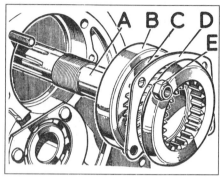

Fig. 6.26. Removing the input shaft (Series II and IIA)

A Primary pinion
B Bearing for pinion
C Shield for pinion
D Retaining plate for pinion
E Nuts retaining plate

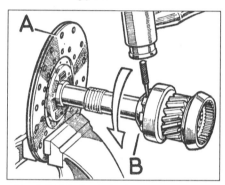

Fig. 6.27. Method of gripping input shaft while removing nut

A Old clutch plate   B Drifting off the nut

6 Input shaft – servicing

Series II and IIA

1 Remove the four nuts securing the input shaft bearing retaining plate to the gearbox side of the bellhousing. Carefully warm the bellhousing using a gas blowlamp and then drive out the input shaft and bearing using a soft-faced mallet (see Fig. 6.26).

2 Grip the input shaft in a soft-jawed vice using an old clutch plate as shown in Fig. 6.27 and remove the **left-hand** threaded nut from the input shaft using an alloy drift.

3 Press the bearing and shield from the shaft.

4 Examine the bearing for wear and renew it if necessary. If the input shaft pinion gear is chipped or worn, a complete new input shaft assembly must be obtained.

5 To reassemble, first fit the shield onto the shaft with the dished side towards the pinion gear.

6 Press the bearing onto the shaft and refit the lockwasher and special **left-hand** threaded nut. Tighten the nut using an alloy drift and bend over the lockwasher.

6.7 Input shaft bearing retaining plate

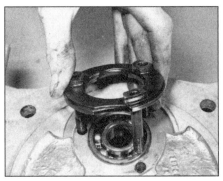

7.4 Layshaft bearing retaining plate

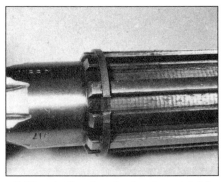

7.8 Layshaft spring ring (earlier models)

7 Drive the shaft and bearing back into the bellhousing and refit the bearing retaining plate (photo).

Series III

8 The input shaft servicing procedure for the Series III models is the same as that described for the Series II and IIA with an exception, the special nut and lockwasher are replaced by a circlip and distance washer which must be removed before the bearing can be pressed off the input shaft (see Fig. 6.28).

7 Gearbox layshaft and bearings – servicing

1 With the exception of the large constant speed gear on the front of the layshaft, the gears on the Series III models are integral with the shaft and if they are worn or chipped, the complete layshaft assembly must be renewed.
2 On the Series II and IIA models the gears are renewable and the third and fourth gears can be withdrawn from the shaft together with the sleeve.
3 Using a suitable puller, withdraw the bearing

and first gear from the rear end of the shaft.
4 On both types of gearbox, examine the front and rear bearings for wear and renew if necessary. The front bearing can be pressed out from the bellhousing after first removing the bearing retainer plates (photo).
5 The rear bearing outer race can be removed by first warming the gearbox casing around the race, then driving it out through the two access holes provided. Alternatively, allow the heated race to shrink onto a close-fitting mandrel and withdraw it.
6 To reassemble the earlier type layshaft, first refit the first gear onto the shaft with the chamfered side of the teeth facing towards the front of the shaft.
7 Press the rear bearing onto the shaft until it fits tightly against the first gear.
8 On earlier Series II models, fit the spring ring into the groove on the rear end of the shaft (photo). Note that on later models the ring is replaced by a shoulder (see Fig. 6.29).
9 Fit the second gear with the recessed side facing towards the rear end of the shaft.
10 Fit the third gear onto the shaft with the thicker shoulder facing towards the front of the shaft. Refit the sleeve.
11 Temporarily refit the conical distance piece and constant gear and insert the shaft

into the bellhousing bearing, ensuring that the constant speed gear is correctly meshed with the input pinion (see Fig. 6.30).
12 Secure the shaft with the washer and castle nut and check the gears do not have any endfloat on the shaft. If endfloat is present a new sleeve should be fitted and the shaft re-checked.
13 When the tolerances are correct, remove the layshaft assembly from the bellhousing.

8 Reverse pinion and gear casing – servicing

1 To remove the reverse idler gear, gently warm the gearbox casing and then drive out the reverse gear shaft from inside the casing.
2 Lift out the reverse gear assembly.
3 Examine the gear teeth for excessive wear or chipping and renew the gear assembly if necessary. If the bush in the gear assembly is worn it can be pressed out and a new one fitted. However, the bush must be reamed to .8125 in + or – .001 in (20.637 mm + or – .25 mm) diameter and this task is best left to an engineering firm.
4 When refitting the reverse gear into the

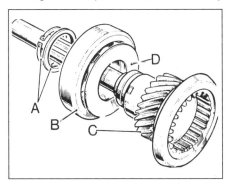

Fig. 6.28. Input shaft and bearing (Series III)

A Circlip and washer
B Bearing
C Pinion gear
D Oil shield

Fig. 6.29. Rear end of layshaft (Series II and IIA)

A Bearing
B Chamfered teeth on Ist speed gear
C Integral shoulder (or split ring on early shafts) for 2nd speed gear location

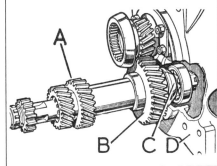

Fig, 6.30. Checking the layshaft endfloat

A Layshaft
B Constant gear
C Conical distance piece
D Bellhousing

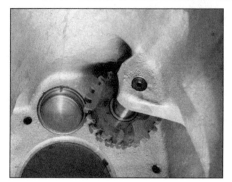

8.4 Correct installation of reverse idler gear

9.3 Transfer gear installed on rear end of mainshaft

9.5 Installing the 3rd/4th gear synchro unit

casing, make sure the smaller gear (or boss, Series III) is to the rear of the gearbox (photo).
5 Holding the reverse gear in position carefully drive in the shaft. Note that on later models the spring pin in the end of the shaft must align with the slot in the rear face of the gearbox casing.

9 Gearbox – reassembly

1 To avoid damaging the rear mainshaft oil seal, fit the oil thrower in the seal.
2 Make sure the rear thrust washer (if fitted) is positioned on the mainshaft and then insert the shaft through the front of the gearbox. Carefully drive it through the rear bearing using a soft-faced mallet.
3 Refit the transfer gear, shim washer, lockwasher and special nut. Tighten the nut and secure with the lockwasher (photo).
4 Lubricate the rear bearing of the layshaft and install the layshaft through the front of the gearbox, ensuring the rear bearing is correctly located in the outer race.
5 Now fit the first/second gear synchromesh clutch assembly, ensuring that the recessed end of the inner hub faces towards the rear of the mainshaft (photo).
6 Fit the roller bearing onto the front end of the mainshaft (photo).
7 Install the constant speed gear onto the front end of the layshaft, followed by the conical distance piece (chamfered side towards the front of the shaft).
8 Fit a new gasket to the front face of the gearbox, lubricate the front mainshaft roller bearing and carefully lower the bellhousing into position ensuring the input shaft pinion fits correctly over the mainshaft roller bearing and that the layshaft enters the front bearing. Gently tap the bellhousing with a soft-faced mallet until it is flush with the gearbox front face (photo).
9 Tighten the four bellhousing securing nuts. Refit the layshaft washer and castle nut and tighten to the specified torque before fitting a new split pin. On later models the castle nut is replaced by a bolt and this must be tightened to the specified torque.

9.6 Refitting the front mainshaft bearing

10 Check that the mainshaft and layshaft rotate freely with minimum endfloat.
11 Refit the clutch release bearing assembly referring to Chapter 5 if necessary.
12 The basic gearbox components are now installed and the selector rods and forks can be refitted using the procedures described in the following Section.

9.8 Reassembling the bellhousing to the gearbox

10 Gearbox selector forks – reassembly

1 The methods of reassembling the Series II and IIA and Series III selector forks are different and are therefore described under the following separate headings.

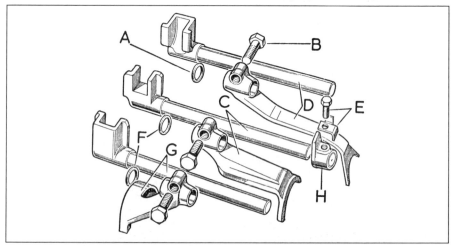

Fig. 6.31. Selector shafts and forks (Series II and IIA)

A Seal, reverse gear selector shaft
B Bolt for selector fork
C 1st-2nd gear selector shaft and fork
D Reverse gear selector shaft and fork

E Bolt for 1st-2nd stop
F Seal, forward selector shafts
G 3rd-4th gear selector shaft and fork
H Stop, 1st-2nd gear selector shaft

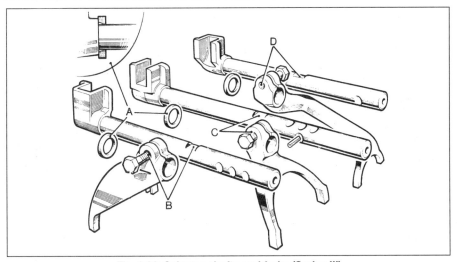

Fig. 6.32. Selector shafts and forks (Series III)

A Seals and fitting detail
B 3rd/4th gear selector shaft and fork
C 1st/2gear selector shaft and fork
D Reverse gear selector shaft and fork

10.6a Correct installation of selector shafts and forks (Series II and IIA)

Series II and IIA

2 Using a long blunt screwdriver, push the inner hub of the synchromesh unit fully rearward into the third gear position.

3 Carefully fit the third/ fourth gear selector shaft and fork making sure that the seal on the shaft is correctly located in the front gearbox casing groove.

4 Push the synchromesh inner hub forward to the neutral position and then move the second gear fully rearwards. Fit the first/second gear selector shaft and fork ensuring that the seal is correctly seated.

5 Move the first/second gear selector shaft fully rearward and push the reverse idler gear fully forward. Fit the reverse gear selector shaft by inserting the fork into the gearbox with the shaft turned approximately 90° to the left and then manoeuvre the shaft and fork down to the correct position.

6 Push all the selector shafts into the neutral position and fit the interlocking plungers (photos).

7 Check that all the selector forks are correctly engaged and then fit the top cover (photo).

8 Refit the balls and springs into each hole in either side of the top cover noting that the reverse selector spring is slightly thicker. Fit the seals and spring retaining plates (photos).

9 Refit the top cover spring and ball and retaining plug (photo).

10 Check the operation of the three selector shafts and, rotating the input shaft by hand, ensure that all gears (including reverse) are obtainable.

11 Select second gear and, using a feeler gauge through the inspection cover, adjust the second gear stop bolt to obtain a .002 in (0.05 mm) clearance between the bolt head and the stop on the selector shaft (photo). Tighten the locknut.

10.6b Interlocking plungers installed

10.7 Refitting the top gearbox cover

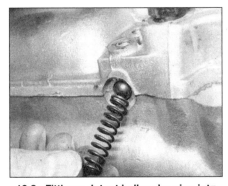

10.8a Fitting a detent ball and spring into the side of the top cover ...

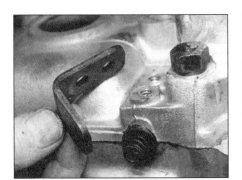

10.8b ... followed by a seal and retaining plate

10.9 Installing the detent ball and spring in the top of the cover

10.11 Checking the second gear stop bolt clearance (Series II and IIA only)

10.13 Gearlever and bracket assembly

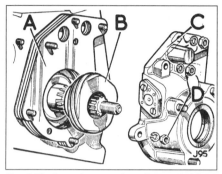

Fig. 6.33. Speedometer housing and shims

A Shims C Housing
B Worm gear   D Securing nuts

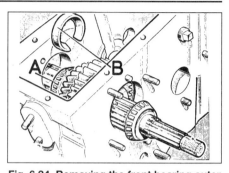

Fig. 6.34. Removing the front bearing outer race

A Front inner bearing
B Tubular packing piece

12 After the transfer box has been refitted to the main gearbox the reverse gear stop bolt must be adjusted, as described in Section 12.

13 Refit the gearchange lever and bracket assembly (photo) and adjust the reverse hinge stop screw so that the hinge prevents accidental selection of the reverse gear, but when the lever is pushed firmly over to the reverse position the hinge rides smoothly up the lever.

Series III

14 If new seals are fitted to the selector shaft ensure that the larger diameter seal is fitted on the reverse selector shaft and all seals are positioned with the larger inside diameter facing towards the front of the shaft.

15 First fit the reverse selector shaft and fork ensuring that the seal is correctly located in the gearbox casing groove.

16 Next fit the first/second selector shaft and fork.

17 Push the third/fourth gear synchro hub unit fully rearward, into the third gear position and fit the third/ fourth gear selector shaft by inserting the fork into the gearbox with the shaft turned approximately 90° to the left and then turning and lowering the shaft and fork to its correct position.

18 Push all the selector shafts to the neutral position and fit the interlocking plungers.

19 Refit the top cover and check the operation of the gears and carry out the reverse gear adjustments as described in paragraphs 7 to 10 and 12 and 13 in this Section. Note that

there is no second gear stop bolt on the Series I I I gearbox.

20 The gearbox and selector mechanism are now completely reassembled.

11 Transfer box – dismantling and inspection

1 Remove the transfer box from the gearbox and the output shaft and housing from the transfer box as described in Section 3.

2 The main task on the transfer box is the removal of the output shaft assembly. Begin by removing the securing nuts and washers and withdrawing the speedometer drive housing. Retrieve the shims and worm gear (see Fig. 6.33).

3 There are two types of transfer box used on the Land Rover, the earlier type is fitted with a combination of helical and spur gears, while the later type has all helical gearing. As the method of dismantling and reassembling differ, the instructions are given under separate headings.

Helical and spur gear type

4 To remove the output shaft, first remove the circlip retaining the front bearing in the transfer box casing.

5 Using a soft-faced mallet, drive the output shaft rearwards to free the rear bearing outer race from the casing.

6 Refit the flange nut onto the threaded end

of the output shaft to avoid damage and then drive the shaft forward as far as possible. To free the front bearing completely from the casing, the output shaft must now be slid back to the rear and a suitable sized tubular packing piece inserted between the outer race and the shaft (see Fig. 6.34).

7 With the packing piece in position continue to drive the shaft forward until the front bearing outer race is freed from the casing.

8 Using a mild steel wedge or chisel inserted between the helical gear and the front bearing inner race, drive the bearing off the output shaft.

9 Remove the circlip and thrust washer from the front of the output shaft. Withdraw the shaft and remove the gears through the bottom of the casing.

10 The rear bearing inner race can now be pressed off the output shaft, or driven off using a mild steel chisel.

11 The transfer box is now completely dismantled and all components should be examined for wear and the gear teeth for chipping. Renew where necessary. Note that the larger low speed gear wheel is meant to be a loose fit on the shaft, allowing it to tilt in operation and grip the splines.

12 Earlier transfer boxes are fitted with a bush for the selector shaft which is a press fit in the casing. If the bush is renewed it must be reamed out to 1.148 in (29.17 mm).

All-helical gear type

Note: This type of box can be identified by a selector shaft adjusting bolt on the front of the output shaft housing (see Fig. 6.35).

13 To remove the output shaft assembly, first remove the circlip retaining the front bearing outer race.

14 Place two pieces of 0.625 in (16 mm) mild steel bar between the near face of the larger (low speed) gear wheel and the inside of the transfer box.

15 Hold the bars in position and using a soft-faced mallet, drive the output shaft rearwards until the low speed gear wheel just touches the bars.

16 Insert a mild steel chisel between the smaller (high speed) gear bush and the front bearing and lever the bearing outward through the casing approximately 0.25 in (6 mm) (see Fig. 6.36).

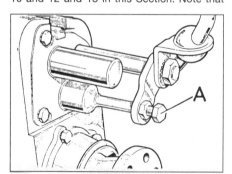

Fig. 6.35. Identification of all-helical transfer box

A Adjustable selector shaft stop bolt

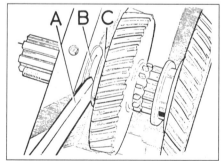

Fig. 6.36. Levering out the front bearing

A Mild steel chisel C Bush
B Front bearing

17 Separate the change speed inner hub from the high speed gear wheel and rotate the output shaft until the peg is visible on the shaft.

18 Locate the slot in the thrust washer and using a thin bladed knife or feeler gauge, move the thrust washer rearwards over the peg (see Fig. 6.37).

19 Again position the steel bars between the low speed gear wheel and the casing and, using a soft-faced mallet, drive the output shaft rearwards until it can be withdrawn, complete with the thrust washer and roller bearing, from the casing.

20 Remove the gear assembly and front bearing from the casing.

21 Press the rear bearing from the shaft and retrieve the thrust washer. If it requires renewal, carefully drift the front bearing outer race from the casing.

22 Examine all the components for wear, especially the roller bearing and splined sections of the output shaft. Renew all components that show signs of excessive wear. Check that the locating pegs in the shaft are not burred over.

23 If the selector shaft bush is renewed it must be reamed out to 1.148 in (29.17 mm) after refitting.

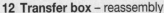

12 Transfer box – reassembly

Helical and spur gear type

1 Before refitting the output shaft in the transfer casing, temporarily assemble the high speed gear wheel onto the shaft, followed by the thrust washer and circlip. Using a set of feeler gauges, check that the clearance between the gear and the shaft is within .006 to .008 in (0.15 to 0.20 mm). If the clearance is excessive, fit a new thrust washer and circlip (see Fig. 6.38).

2 When the correct clearance has been obtained remove the circlip, thrust washer and gear wheel and press the inner roller bearing onto the rear end of the shaft.

3 Hold the gear assembly in the transfer casing and insert the shaft through the rear

12.5b ... and secure with the circlip

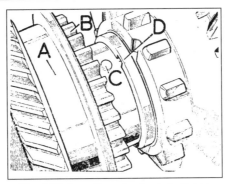
Fig. 6.37. Location of output shaft peg

A Outer member for transfer change speed
B Inner member for transfer wheel gear wheel
C Peg for output shaft
D Thrust washer for high gear wheel

Note: The space shown between the change speed outer member and the high gear wheel has been exaggerated for clarity.

aperture and guide it through the gears (photo).

4 Fit the thrust washer and circlip onto the output shaft (photo).

5 Refit the front bearing outer race into the casing and secure with the circlip (photos).

6 Carefully drift the rear inner roller bearing onto the shaft and then refit the outer race (photo) and tap it lightly in until all the output shaft endfloat is removed but it still rotates freely (photo).

12. 4 Fitting the thrust washer and circlip to the input shaft

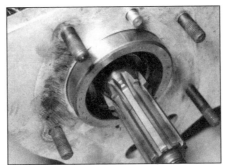
12.6a The rear bearing outer race prior to tapping home

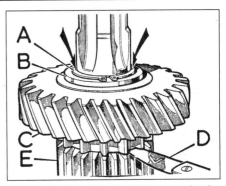
Fig. 6.38. Checking the high gear wheel endfloat

A Circlip D Feeler gauges
B Thrust washer   E Output shaft
C High gear wheel

12.3 Installing the input shaft into the transfer box

12.5a Refit the front bearing outer race ...

12.6b After installation check that the input shaft rotates freely

12.9 Speedometer worm gear in position

12.10 Speedometer housing oil seal removed

12.12 Refitting the transfer box to the gearbox

7 The output shaft bearing preload should be checked using the following method:

a) *Refit the speedometer housing without the shims and tighten the nuts finger tight.*

b) *Wind a piece of nylon cord or a similar type of cord around the selector groove in the low gear wheel and attach a spring balance to the end.*

c) *The bearing pre-load is correct when a pull of 2 to 4 lb (0.9 to 1.8 kg) is required to rotate the shaft. To achieve this figure tighten the speedometer housing nuts progressively and evenly.*

d) *When the pre-load is correct, measure the gap between the speedometer housing and the transfer box using feeler gauges, ensuring the gap is even all the*

12.13 Tightening the internal transfer box securing nuts

way round. The measurement obtained is equal to the total thickness of shims required.

8 Remove the cord and spring balance.

9 Fit the pre-determined number of shims over the speedometer housing studs and slide on the speedometer worm drive (photo).

10 Before refitting the speedometer housing, examine the oil seal and, if necessary, drive it out and fit a new one (photo).

11 Before installing the intermediate gears and shaft, the transfer box must be reassembled onto the rear end of the gearbox. If the output shaft housing has been removed for overhaul, it should be refitted on the transfer box as described in Section 14.

12 Fit a new gasket to the rear face of the gearbox and offer up the transfer box, locating it on the studs and dowel (photo).

13 Screw on the outer retaining nuts and the nuts located inside the transfer box. Tighten them using a ring spanner (photo).

14 Apply a thin film of grease on the two intermediate shaft thrust washers and stick them in place inside the transfer casing (photo).

15 Carefully examine the roller bearings for pitting or scoring before fitting them into the intermediate gear assembly (photo). Renew if necessary.

16 Examine the intermediate shaft for areas of excessive wear (see photo) and renew if necessary.

17 Hold the intermediate gear assembly inside the transfer casing and slide the shaft through the casing, bearings and thrust washers (photos).

18 Using a set of feeler gauges, check that the intermediate gear endfloat is within 0.004 to 0.008 in (0.10 to 0.20 mm). If the endfloat is excessive (see Fig. 6.39) fit a thicker thrust washer which is available in steps of 0.010 in (0.25 mm). **Note:** When fitting the thrust washers, ensure that the bronze faces are towards the intermediate gear assembly.

19 When the endfloat is correct, fit the

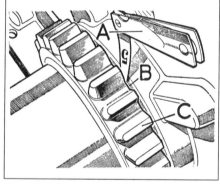

Fig, 6.39. Checking the intermediate gear endfloat

A Feeler gauge   C Intermediate gear
B Thrust washer

12.15 Installing the intermediate gear roller bearings

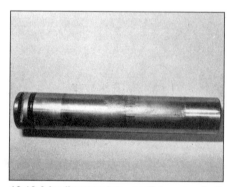

12.16 A badly worn intermediate gear shaft

12.14 Intermediate gear thrust washer

12.17a Hold the intermediate gear in position ...

12.17b ... and slide the shaft in

12.20 Mainshaft rear bearing assembly

12 21 Refitting the rear bearing housing

12.22 Refitting the speedometer drive pinion

12.23a Location of reverse gear stop bolt

retaining plate in the slot in the end of the intermediate shaft and over the adjacent stud and secure with a washer and nut.

20 Examine the gearbox mainshaft rear bearing for wear before installing it in the rear bearing housing and retaining it with the circlip (photo). Renew if necessary.

21 Fit a new gasket over the studs around the rear bearing aperture on the transfer box and then refit the bearing housing, ensuring the gearbox mainshaft is correctly located in the bearing before tightening the securing nuts (photo).

22 Fit the speedometer drive pinion assembly

12.23b Checking the reverse stop clearance

into the side of the speedometer drive housing (photo), ensuring that the oil seals are in good condition.

23 Remove the inspection cover from the top at the rear of the gearbox and select reverse gear. Slacken the locknut on the reverse gear stop bolt and adjust it to obtain a clearance of 0.002 in (0.05 mm) between the end of the reverse gear selector shaft and the stop bolt (photos). Tighten the locknut.

24 Refit the transmission brake anchor plate and shoe assembly, followed by the drum and output shaft flange. For further details of the transmission brake refer to Chapter 9.

25 Refit the transfer box bottom cover plate and tighten the securing screws.

26 Before refitting the transmission assembly into the vehicle make sure that the transfer box and gearbox drain plugs are fully tightened. The transmission oil levels can be filled prior to refitting, but must be re-checked after the transmission is installed in the vehicle.

All-helical gear type

27 Before refitting the output shaft in the transfer casing, temporarily fit the steel thrust washer and rear bearing onto the rear end of the shaft.

28 Now slide the low gear wheel and bush onto the shaft and holding it firmly against the

thrust washer, check that the low gear wheel endfloat is within 0.002 to 0.009 in (0.05 to 0.22 mm) (see Fig. 6.40).

29 Remove the low gear wheel from the shaft and refit the centre bush. Fit the change speed inner member, the thrust washer and the high speed gear wheel complete with bush.

30 Holding the high speed gear wheel bush in firm contact with the thrust washer, check that the high speed gear wheel endfloat is

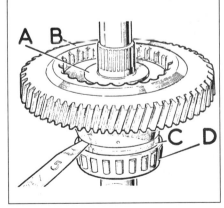

Fig. 6.40. Checking the low gear wheel endfloat

A Bush   C Thrust washer
B Low gear wheel   D Rear bearing

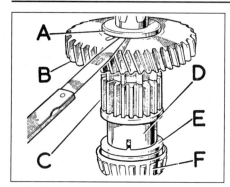

Fig. 6.41. Checking the high gear wheel endfloat, (all helical type)

A Bush for high gear wheel
B High gear wheel
C Change speed inner member
D Bush for low gear wheel
E Steel thrust washer
F Rear bearing for output shaft

within 0.005 to 0.022 in (0.12 to 0.55 mm) (see Fig. 6.41).

31 Insufficient endfloat on either gear wheel should be rectified by fitting a new bush. If the endfloat is excessive the respective bush should be reduced in length by carefully rubbing down the end on a piece of fine emery cloth stretched across a face plate.

32 When the endfloat clearances are correct, remove all the components from the output shaft with the exception of the steel thrust washer and the rear, inner roller bearing.

33 Referring to Fig. 6.42, fit the bush in the low speed gear with the flange on the internal teeth side of the gear, followed by the change speed inner and outer hubs. Note that the recessed side of the inner hub must be facing the bush.

34 Place the high gear wheel minus its bush against the low gear assembly with the dog teeth abutting the change speed hub, and hold the complete gear assembly in position inside the transfer casing.

35 Insert the output shaft through the rear of the casing and on through the gear assembly ensuring the low speed gear wheel bush is correctly located on the peg in the shaft.

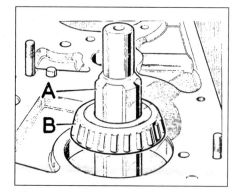

Fig. 6.44. Refitting the front inner bearing

A Shaft   B Roller bearing

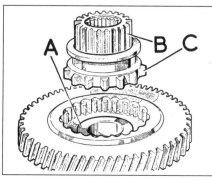

Fig. 6.42. Assembling the inner hub to the low gear

A Bush   B Inner hub   C Outer hub

36 Slide the thrust washer over the front of the shaft and through the centre of the high speed gear, ensuring that the washer passes over the peg and is correctly located in the change speed hub recess. Fit the bush through the high speed gear wheel ensuring that it is also located on the peg (see Fig. 6.43)

37 Fit the flange nut onto the threaded end of the output shaft to protect the thread and turn the casing on its side so that the threaded end is resting on the bench. Carefully drift the front inner roller bearing onto the shaft, taking care not to separate the gears and hub assembly (Fig. 6.44).

38 Now tap the front outer race into the casing and retain with a circlip. Gently drive the output shaft forward until the bearing is hard against the circlip.

39 Fit the rear bearing into the casing and lightly tap it in until all the output shaft endfloat is just taken up.

40 For instructions on setting the output shaft pre-load and the remaining transfer box reassembly procedures, refer back to paragraphs 7 to 26 in this Section. Note that on the all-helical transfer boxes the intermediate gear assembly comprises a cluster of three gears.

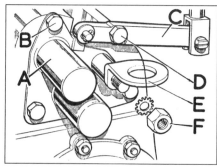

Fig. 6.45. Front view of output shaft housing

A Dust cover, selector shafts
B Cover fixings
C Selector lever, four wheel drive
D Lever fixings
E Link, transfer gear lever
F Link fixings

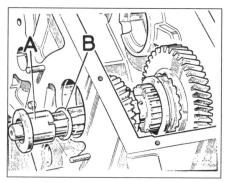

Fig. 6.43. Refitting the high gear thrust washer and bush

A Bush   B Thrust washer

13 Front output shaft housing – dismantling and inspection

1 First remove the complete output shaft housing from the transfer box as described in Section 3.

2 Remove the nut and washer and withdraw the transfer gear lever support bracket from the end of the selector shaft.

3 Undo the pivot bolt and remove the four wheel drive control lever and locking pin.

4 Undo the three securing bolts and withdraw the metal dust cover from the ends of the selector shafts (Fig. 6.45).

5 Carefully withdraw the complete selector shaft assemblies and locking dog from the housing. **Note:** It is highly unlikely that any wear will have occurred to the selector shaft assemblies and unless any of the components are broken it is strongly recommended that no attempt be made to dismantle the selector shafts.

6 If the shafts are dismantled, carefully lay out the components on a clean sheet of paper in the order of removal and refer to Figs. 6.46 and 6.47 for correct reassembly.

7 To remove the front output shaft from the housing, undo the castle nut and withdraw the flange from the end of the shaft.

8 Undo the securing nuts and remove the oil

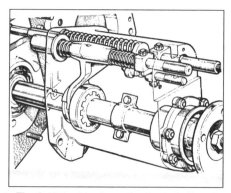

Fig. 6.46. Inside view of output shaft and elector shafts

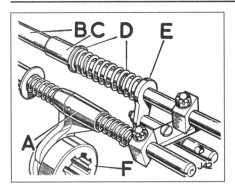

Fig. 6.47. Selector shaft assemblies

A Selector shaft, four wheel drive
B Selector shaft, transfer gear
C Distance tube
D Locating bush and spring for selector fork
E Gearchange pivot shaft assembly
F Locking dog, four wheel drive

seal housing and gasket from the front of the output shaft housing.

9 Withdraw the output shaft from the housing and, if worn and requiring renewal, drive out the front bearing.

10 Examine all the components for wear and renew where necessary. If the bush located inside the rear end of the front output shaft is renewed it must be reamed after installation to .8755 + or − .0005 in (22.2 mm + or − 0.013 mm) diameter.

11 If the dog teeth on the output shaft are worn, the complete shaft assembly must be renewed. Refer to Fig. 6.48 for the correct location of the oil thrower.

14.2 Output shaft installed in housing

14.6 Location of oil seals in output shaft housing

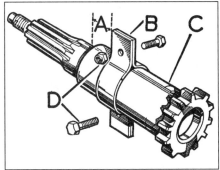

Fig. 6.48. Four-wheel drive output shaft

A 1 in ± 1/32 in (25.4 mm ± 0.75 mm)
B Oil thrower
C Front output shaft
D Securing nut and bolt

14 Front output shaft housing – reassembly

1 Commence by refitting the front bearing into the output shaft housing (photo).

2 Insert the output shaft into the housing and carefully drive it through the front bearing until it is fully home (photo).

3 Fit a new gasket to the front end of the housing and install the seal retainer assembly (photo). **Note:** If the seal is renewed it must be fitted with the lipped side facing the output shaft housing.

4 Refit the output shaft flange and tighten the nut. Secure the nut with a new split pin (photo).

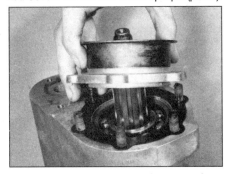

14.3 Installing the seal retainer onto the front of the housing

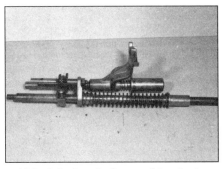

14.6a Selector shaft assembly prior to installation

14.1 Refitting the bearing into the front of the output shaft housing

5 Check that the selector shaft and locking pin O ring seal are correctly located in the end of the housing (photo).

6 With the selector shafts correctly assembled, fit the four wheel drive locking dog into the selector fork and carefully insert the complete assembly into the housing, ensuring that the ends of the shafts slide through the holes in the front of the housing and that the locking dog is correctly engaged on the output shaft gear (photos).

7 Fit the four wheel drive locking pin through the hole in the front face of the housing, making sure it passes through the hole in the pivot shaft inside the housing (photo).

8 Fit a new gasket to the front face of the transfer box.

9 Position the transfer gear selector fork in the transfer box and install the output shaft

14.4 Refitting the output shaft flange

14.6b Installing the selector shafts into the housing

14.6c Correct location of output shaft locking dog

14.7 Installation of four-wheel drive locking pin

14.9a Refitting the output shaft housing to the transfer box

14.9b Refitting the detent spring and plug

14.15 Transfer gear lever and top bracket

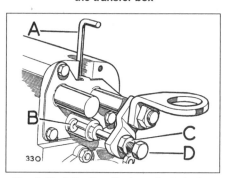

Fig. 6.49. Adjusting the transfer selector shaft stop bolt (later models only)

A *Four wheel drive locking pin*
B *Pivot shaft* C *Locknut* D *Adjuster bolt*

housing onto the transfer box making sure the selector shaft passes through the fork (photo). Refit and tighten the housing nuts.

10 Refit the pinch bolt through the selector fork and the groove in the shaft and tighten.

11 Install the plunger and spring in the top of the transfer box and retain it with the threaded plug (photo).

12 Check that the selector fork is correctly located on the transfer gear hub and then refit the transfer box inspection cover.

13 Refit the four wheel drive selector lever and arm to the front of the housing and secure the locking pin to the arm using a new split pin.

14 Refit the selector shaft dust cover.

15 Refit the transfer gear lever bracket to the end of the selector shaft (photo) .

16 On later models fitted with a transfer stop bolt, engage four wheel drive low ratio and adjust the stop bolt so that the locking pin is an easy sliding fit through the housing and pivot shaft (see Fig. 6.49). Tighten the locknut.

17 When the transfer box and output shaft housing have been installed on the main gearbox, refit the transfer gear lever bottom bracket to the bellhousing.

18 Rotate the gearbox input shaft by hand and check the operation of the four wheel drive and high and low gear selection before refitting the complete transmission into the vehicle as described in Section 2.

Fault finding - gearbox

Ineffective synchromesh
☐ Worn baulk rings or synchro hubs.

Jumps out of one or more gears (on drive or over-run)
☐ Weak detent spring, worn selector forks, worn gears or worn synchro sleeves.

Noisy, rough, whining and vibration
☐ Worn bearings and/or thrust washers (initially) resulting in extended wear generally due to play and backlash

Noisy and difficult engagement of gears
☐ Clutch fault.

Transfer box is excessively noisy
☐ Insufficient oil in box.
☐ Excessive endfloat of intermediate gear, or worn bearings.

Jumps out of high transfer gear
☐ Rubber boot on transfer gear lever fitted incorrectly. Weak or broken selector detent spring.
☐ Either of the above reasons, or excessive endfloat of the intermediate gear in transfer box.

Difficulty in engaging four-wheel drive
☐ Locking pin seized in casing, broken selector shaft spring or selector shafts sticking in the casing.

Difficulty in disengaging four-wheel drive
☐ Spring on selector lever, (yellow knob) broken or missing.
☐ Selector shafts sticking in casing or broken selector shaft spring.
☐ Different type tyres fitted on the front and rear wheels or excessively worn tyres.

Note: *It is sometimes difficult to decide whether it is worthwhile removing and dismantling the gearbox for a fault which may be nothing more than a minor irritant. Gearboxes which howl, or where the synchromesh can be 'beaten' by a quick gear change, may continue to perform for a long time in this stage. A worn gearbox usually needs a complete rebuild to eliminate noise because the various gears, if re-aligned on new bearings will continue to howl when different wearing surfaces are presented to each other.*

The decision to overhaul therefore, must be considered with regard to time and money available, relative to the degree of noise or malfunction that the driver can tolerate.

Chapter 7
Propeller shaft

For modifications, and information applicable to later models, see Supplement at end of manual

Contents

Degrees of difficulty

Easy, suitable for novice with little experience ⚒	Fairly easy, suitable for beginner with some experience ⚒	Fairly difficult, suitable for competent DIY mechanic ⚒	Difficult, suitable for experienced DIY mechanic ⚒	Very difficult, suitable for expert DIY or professional ⚒

Specifications

Type . . . . Tubular shaft with Hardy Spicer joint at each end

Shaft diameter . . . . 2 in (50.8 mm)

Shaft length
38 in model (front) . . . . 23.812 in (604.8 mm)
88 in model (rear) . . . . 21.812 in (554 mm)
109 in model (front) . . . . 23.812 in (604.8 mm)
109 in model (rear) . . . . 42.812 in (1,087 mm)

Universal joints
Lubricant type/specification . . . . Multi-purpose lithium based grease, to NLG1-2

1 General description

The drive from the transmission assembly to the front and rear axles is transmitted by two tubular propeller shafts fitted with a universal joint at each end. The universal joints cater for the varying angle between the axle and transmission, caused by road spring deflection, while any fore-or-aft variation is taken care of by means of a splined sleeve in each shaft.

Although of different lengths, the front and rear propeller shafts are virtually identical in construction with the exception of the position of the spline sleeve which is on the transmission end of the rear shaft and the axle end of the front shaft.

2 Propeller shaft - removal and refitting ⚒

1 The method of removing either the front or rear propeller shaft is the same. Any differences in procedure will be mentioned where necessary.

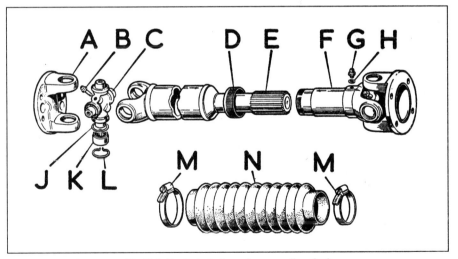

Fig. 7.1. Exploded view of a propeller shaft

A Flanged yoke
B Grease nipple for universal joint
C Journal for bearings
D Dust cap
E Splined shaft
F Splined sleeve
G Grease nipple for splined pint
H Washer for nipple
J Seal for journal bearing
K Needle roller bearing assembly
L Circlip retaining bearing
M Clips fixing rubber grommet
N Rubber grommet for sliding joint

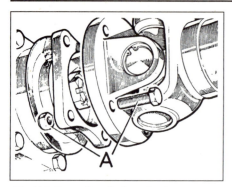

Fig. 7.2. Propeller shaft and axle coupling flanges

A Securing nut and bolt - 4 off

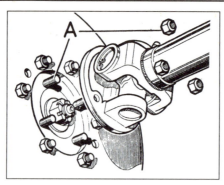

Fig. 7.3. Rear propeller shaft and transmission brake coupling flanges

A Studs and securing nuts

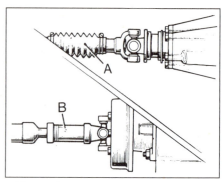

Fig. 7.4. Location of splined sleeves on front and rear propeller shafts

A Front propeller shaft sleeve
B Rear propeller shaft sleeve

2 Depending on the shaft to be removed, jack-up the appropriate end of the vehicle until the wheels are just clear of the ground. Place heavy duty axle stands beneath the chassis.

3 Scribe a line across the side of the axle coupling flange and the propeller shaft flange, remove the four nuts and bolts and lower the end of the shaft to the ground (see Fig. 7.2).

4 If the rear propeller shaft is being removed, undo the four nuts securing the shaft flange to the brake drum. Pull the shaft rearwards to clear the studs and remove the complete shaft assembly from beneath the vehicle (see Fig. 7.3).

5 In the case of the front propeller shaft,

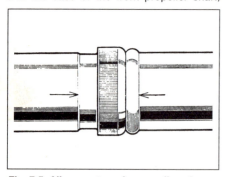

Fig. 7.5. Alignment marks on spline sleeve and shaft

remove the four nuts and bolts securing the rear end of the shaft to the front output shaft flange on the transfer box and remove the shaft assembly from the vehicle.

6 Refitting the propeller shafts is the reverse sequence to removal. Note that the splined sleeve on the front shaft must be towards the front axle while the sleeve on the rear shaft must be adjacent to the transmission brake (see Fig. 7.4).

3 Universal joints - inspection and repair

1 Wear in the needle roller bearings is characterised by vibration in the transmission, 'clonks' on taking up the drive and in extreme cases of lack of lubrication, metallic squeaking, and ultimately grating and shrieking sounds as the bearings break up.

2 To test the universal joints for wear prior to removing the propeller shaft(s) from the vehicle, apply the handbrake and engage four-wheel drive in the low ratio. Working under the vehicle, grip the shaft to be tested and try and rotate it. Wear is indicated by movement between the shaft yoke and the coupling flange. Check both universal joints using this method.

3 To check the splined sleeve on the front of both shafts, attempt to push the shaft from side-to-side and note any excessive movement between the sleeve and the shaft.

4 If the universal joint is worn, a repair kit comprised of a new spider, bearings and seals should be purchased prior to removing the affected shaft.

4 Universal joints and sleeve - dismantling and inspection

1 If a protective rubber boot is fitted over the sleeve section, slacken the hose clips and slide the boot rearwards.

2 Check that the alignment marks are visible on the sleeve and shaft, (see Fig. 7.5). If no marks can be found, scribe a line along the sleeve and shaft to ensure the splined shaft and sleeve are reassembled in the original position to maintain the balanced setting.

3 Unscrew the dust cap and withdraw the front universal joint and sleeve assembly from the splined end of the shaft (Fig. 7.6).

4 Clean away all traces of dirt and grease from the circlips located on the ends of the spiders, and remove the circlips by pressing their open ends together with a pair of circlip pliers and lever them out with a screwdriver.

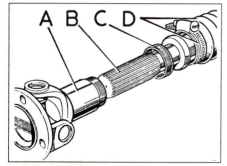

Fig. 7.6. Withdrawing the front univeral joint and sleeve (front shaft)

A Sleeve   C Dust cap
B Splined shaft   D Hose and clips

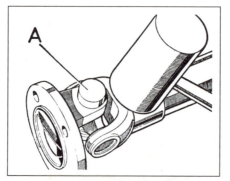

Fig. 7.7. Removing the universal joint bearings

A Bearing cup

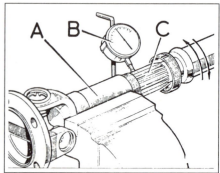

Fig. 7.8. Check the sleeve splines for wear

A Sleeve   C Splined end of shaft
B Dial test indicator

HAYNES HiNT *If they are difficult to remove, tap the bearing face resting on top of the spider with a mallet which will ease the press pressure on the circlip.*

5 Hold the joint housing in one hand and remove the bearing caps and needle rollers by tapping the yoke at each bearing with a soft-faced mallet (see Fig. 7.7). As soon as the bearings start to emerge they can be drawn out with the fingers. If the bearing cup refuses to move, then place a thin bar against the inside of the bearing and tap it gently until the cup starts to emerge.

6 With the bearings removed it is relatively easy to extract the spiders from their yokes. If the bearings and spider journals are thought to be badly worn this can easily be ascertained visually with the universal joints dismantled.

7 Temporarily fit the splined end of the shaft into the sleeve, and then grip the sleeve in a soft-jawed vice and ascertain the amount of spline wear by turning the shaft in either direction. The maximum permissible movement is 0.004 in (0.10 mm) and this can be checked using a dial test indicator as shown in Fig. 7.8.

5 Universal joints - reassembly

1 Clean out the yokes and trunnions and fit new oil seals to the spider journals.

2 Place the spider on the propeller shaft yoke and assemble the needle rollers into the bearing cups retaining them with some thick grease.

3 Fill each bearing cup about 1/2 full with multi-purpose lithium based grease. Also fill the grease holes on the spider with grease taking care that all air bubbles are eliminated.

4 Refit the bearing cups on the spider and tap the bearings home so that they lie squarely in position.

5 Lock the cups in position with new circlips. Check the spider movement and if it is tight try tapping the yokes with a mallet. If this does not do the trick then something is amiss requiring investigation.

6 If the grease nipple was removed, screw it back into the spider.

7 Smear the splines on the end of the shaft with grease. Carefully match up the alignment mark and slide the shaft into the sleeve. Tighten the dust cap.

Note: Do not pack grease into the sleeve prior to fitting the shaft as it may prevent the shaft being pushed fully home.

8 If the front propeller shaft is being serviced, pull the rubber boot over the sleeve and tighten the hose clips.

9 Refit the shaft to the vehicle as described in Section 2 and lubricate the bearings using a grease gun applied to the universal joint and sleeve nipples.

 HAYNES HiNT *If the sleeve is fitted with a plug instead of a grease nipple, replace it with a nipple to enable lubrication of the sleeve splines.*

Fault finding - propeller shaft

Vibration

- ☐ Wear in sliding sleeve splines.
- ☐ Worn universal joint bearings.
- ☐ Propeller shaft out of balance.
- ☐ Distorted propeller shaft.

Knock or 'clunk' when taking up drive

- ☐ Worn universal joint bearings.
- ☐ Worn rear axle drive pinion splines.
- ☐ Loose rear drive flange bolts.
- ☐ Excessive backlash in rear axle gears.

Notes

Chapter 8
Front and rear axles

For modifications, and information applicable to later models, see Supplement at end of manual

Contents

Degrees of difficulty

Easy, suitable for novice with little experience	**Fairly easy,** suitable for beginner with some experience	**Fairly difficult,** suitable for competent DIY mechanic	**Difficult,** suitable for experienced DIY mechanic	**Very difficult,** suitable for expert DIY or professional

Specifications

Axle type
Front . . . . Rover (spiral bevel)
Rear:
    Series II and IIA. . . . . Rover or ENV (spiral bevel)
    Series III . . . . Rover (spiral bevel) or Salisbury (hypoid)

Ratio . . . . 4.7 : 1

Axle lubrication
Lubricant type/specification. . . . . Hypoid gear oil, viscosity SAE 90EP to API GL4
Rover . . . . 3 Imp. pints (3.5 US pints, 1.75 litres)
ENV . . . . 2.6 Imp. pints (3.1 US pints, 1.4 litres)
Salisbury . . . . 4.5 Imp. pints (5.5 US pints, 2.5 litres)

Front and rear hub lubrication
Lubricant type/specification. . . . . Multi-purpose lithium-based grease, to NLG1-2

Hub endfloat
ENV and early Rover . . . . 0.004 to 0.006 in (0.10 to 0.15 mm)
Salisbury and later Rover . . . . 0.002 to 0.004 in (0.05 to 0.10 mm)

Swivel pin housing
Lubricant type/specification. . . . . Hypoid gear oil, viscosity SAE 90EP, to API GL4
Oil capacity. . . . . 1 Imp pint (1.2 US pints - 1.4 litres)

Swivel pin settings
Coil spring type . . . . Resistance of 14 lb to 16 lb (6.3 kg to 7.3 kg) at steering lever eye
Railko bush type . . . . Resistance of 12 lb to 14 lb (5.4 kg to 6.3 kg) at steering lever eye
Clearance between stub and halfshaft yoke lugs and swivel pin end faces. . 0.050 in (1.27 mm)
Cone spring:
    Number of working coils. 3
    Free length . . . . 1.150 ± 0.010 in (29.2 ± 0.25 mm)
    Length in position . . . . 0.687 in (17.4 mm)
    Rate . . . . 660 lb/in^2 (7.5 kg/m^2)
    Fit of retaining collar on shaft. . . . . 0.001 in (0.025 mm) interference (selective assembly)

Torque wrench settings

	lbf ft	kgf m
Hub flange bolts:		
ENV and early Rover	28	3.9
Salisbury and later Rover	30 to 38	4.2 to 5.2

Torque wrench settings (cont.)

	lbf ft	kgf m
Hub securing nut (front):		
Early Rover	10 to 15	1.4 to 5.2
Later Rover	15 to 20	2.0 to 2.7
Hub securing nut (rear)*	10 to 15	1.4 to 2.0
Pinion flange nut (for oil seal renewal):		
Rover	85	11.7
ENV	100 to 120	14.0 to 16.0
Salisbury	see text	
Steering balljoint nuts	30	4.0

* Rover type axle only

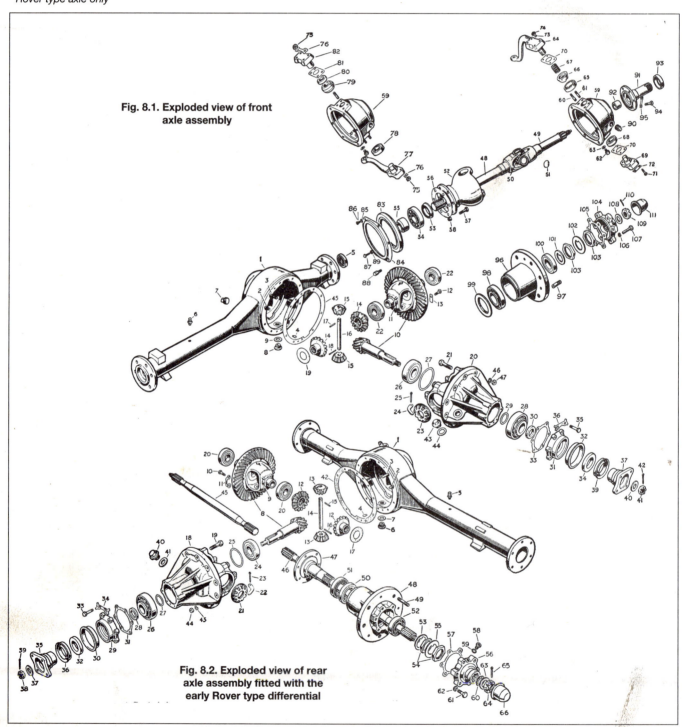

Fig. 8.1. Exploded view of front axle assembly

Fig. 8.2. Exploded view of rear axle assembly fitted with the early Rover type differential

Key to Fig. 8.1. Exploded view of front axle assembly

1 Axle casing complete
2-3 Fixings, bevel pinion housing to axle casing
4 Dowel, locating housing
5 Oil seal, in casing
6 Breather
7 Oil filler plug
8-9 Drain plug and joint washer
10 Crownwheel and bevel pinion
11 Differential casing
12 Set bolt
13 Locker (double type)
14 Differential wheel
15 Differential pinion
16 Spindle for pinion
17 Plain pin[1]
18 Split pin[1]
19 Thrust washer
20 Bevel pinion housing
21 Special bolt, fixing bearing cap
22 Taper roller bearing for differential
23-24 Bearing adjustment
25 Split pin, fixing lock tab
26 Bearing for bevel pinion, pinion end
27 Shim, bearing adjustment, pinion end
28 Bearing for bevel pinion, flange end

29 Shim, bearing adjustment, flange end
30 Washer for pinion bearing
31 Retainer for oil seal
32 Mudshield for retainer
33 Joint washer for oil seal retainer
34 Oil seal for pinion
35-36 Fixings, oil seal retainer
37 Driving flange
39 Mudshield for driving flange
40-42 Fixings for flange
43-44 Oil filler plug and joint washer
45 Joint washer, differential to axle casing
46-47 Fixings, differential to axle casing
48 Halfshaft
49 Stub shaft
50 Journal assembly
51 Circlip for journal
52 Housing for swivel pin bearing
53 Distance piece for bearing
54 Bearing for halfshaft
55 Retaining collar for bearing
56 Joint washer for housing
57-58 Fixings, housing to front axle casing
59 Housing assembly for swivel pin[2]

60 Special stud for steering lever and bracket[2]
61 Stud for steering lever[2]
62-63 Drain plug and joint washer[2]
64 Swivel pin and steering lever[2]
65 Cone seat for swivel pin, top[2]
66 Cone bearing for swivel pin, top[2]
67 Spring for cone bearing[2]
68 Bearing for swivel pin, bottom[2]
69 Swivel pin and bracket[2]
70 Shim, for swivel pin bearing[2]
71-74 Fixings, swivel pin to swivel pin housings[2]
75-76 Fixings, swivel pins to swivel pin housings[3]
77 Swivel pin and steering lever[3]
78 Bearing for bottom swivel pin[3]
79 Bush for top swivel pin[3]
80 Thrust washer for bush[3]
81 Shim for top swivel pin[3]
82 Swivel pin and bracket[3]
83 Oil seal for swivel pin bearing housing
84 Retainer for oil seal
85-89 Fixings, retainer and lock stop plate to swivel pin housing
90 Oil filler plug for swivel pin housing
91 Stub axle assembly

92 Bush for driving shaft, early models only
93 Distance piece for inner bearing
94-95 Fixings, stub axle to swivel pin housing
96 Front hub assembly
97 Stud for roadwheel
98 Bearing for front hub, inner
99 Oil seal for inner bearing
100 Bearing for front hub
101 Keywasher[4]
102 Locker[4]
103 Special nut
104 Driving member for front hub
105 Joint washer for driving member
106-107 Fixings, driving member to front hub
108 Plain washer[5]
109 Slotted nut[5]
110 Split pin[5]
111 Hub cap, front[5]

[1]For spindle
[2]Early type
[3]Latest type
[4]Fixing front hub bearing
[5]Fixing driving member to driving shaft

Key to Fig. 8.2. Exploded view of rear axle assembly fitted with the early Rover type differential

1 Rear axle casing
2-3 Bolts securing differential
4 Dowel locating differential
5 Breather
6-7 Oil drain plug
8 Crownwheel and bevel pinion
9 Differential casing
10-11 Bolt and locking tab for crownwheel
12 Differential wheel
13 Differential pinion
14 Spindle for pinions
15-16 Pins for spindles
17 Thrust washer for differential
18 Bevel pinion housing
19 Bolt securing bearing cap
20 Roller bearings for differential
21 Serrated nut }
22 Lock tab } For bearing adjustment
23 Split pin }
24 Bearing for bevel pinion, pinion end
25 Shims for bearing adjustment, pinion end
26 Bearing for bevel pinion, flange end
27 Shims for bearing adjustment, flange end
28 Washer for bearing
29 Retainer for oil seal
30 Mudshield for retainer
31 Joint washer for retainer
32 Oil seal for pinion

33-34 Bolt and locking tab for retainer
35 Driving flange
36 Dust shield for driving flange
37-39 Washer, nut and split pin for driving flange
40-41 Oil filler plug and washer
42 Joint washer for differential
43-44 Nut and washer for differential
45 Axle shaft, right-hand
46 Axle shaft left-hand
47 Rear hub bearing sleeve
48 Rear hub assembly
49 Stud for roadwheel
50 Hub bearing, inner
51 Oil seal for inner bearing
52 Hub bearing, outer
53-55 Nuts and lockwasher - for hub bearing
56 Driving member for rear hub
57 Joint washer for driving member
58 Filler plug for hub driving member
59 Joint washer for filler plug
60 Oil seal for rear axle shaft
61-62 Bolt and washer - driving member to rear hub
63-65 Washer, nut and split pin - axle shaft to driving member
66 Hub cap, rear

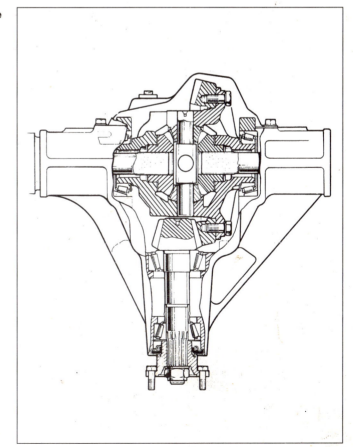

Fig. 8.3. Sectional view of Salisbury type differential

1 General description

Both the front and rear axles on the Land Rover are of a similar design, comprising a one piece steel casing housing the differential assembly and two driveshafts (halfshafts). The rear shafts are solid steel bars, the inner end of which is splined into the differential assembly while the outer end drives the rear wheel hub via a flange.

To enable the front wheels to turn from lock-to-lock while being driven, the front halfshafts incorporate a universal coupling on the outer end.

The universal couplings run inside oil-filled swivel pin housings, the bottom swivel pin is located in a tapered roller bearing while the top pin turns in a plain bush.

Both the front and rear axle assemblies are attached to the chassis via semi-elliptical leaf springs and telescopic shock absorbers.

2 Rear axle halfshafts - removal and refitting

Rover and Salisbury axles

1 The rear halfshafts are exceptionally easy to remove from the Land Rover as it is not necessary to jack the vehicle up or remove the brake drums.

2 If possible, park the vehicle on flat and level ground. Chock the front wheels to prevent the vehicle from moving. Remove the six bolts securing the halfshaft to the wheel hub. Carefully prise the flange away from the brake drum and withdraw the halfshaft from the axle (see Fig. 8.4).

3 The flange can be withdrawn from the shaft by prising off the hub cap and removing the castle nut, washer and seal (Fig. 8.5) (Rover) or Circlip (Salisbury).

ENV axle

4 Jack up the rear of the vehicle, chock the front wheels, then remove the rear wheel and brake drum, referring to Chapter 9 if necessary.

5 Disconnect the brake pipe at the brake anchor plate, remove the bolts securing the plate to the axle casing, then remove the plate assembly and bearing sleeve. Finally, withdraw the hub and halfshaft assembly,

6 The drive flange can be separated from the hub by removing the securing bolts, and from the halfshaft by prising off the hub cap and removing the circlip (Fig. 8.6).

All models

7 Refitting is a reverse of the removal procedure. In the case of the ENV axle, bleed the brakes upon completion.

3 Front and rear wheelbearings - removal

1 Jack-up the appropriate end of the vehicle and remove the relevant roadwheel and brake drum (refer to Chapter 9 if necessary).

2 If working on a rear wheel, for Rover and Salisbury axles, remove the halfshaft as described in the previous Section. For ENV axles, prise off the hub cap, remove the circlip from the halfshaft (Fig. 8.6), and unbolt the drive flange. Withdraw the flange from the hub. In the case of a front wheel, prise off the hub cap and remove the castle nut and washer. Undo the six securing bolts and prise the drive flange off the stub axle and hub (see Fig. 8.7 and photo).

3 From inside the hub, tap back the lockwasher using a hammer and screwdriver and remove the two large nuts and washers that secure the hub and bearings to the stub axle (see Fig. 8.8).

4 Hold one hand over the end of the hub to prevent the outer bearing from falling out and withdraw the hub and bearings from the stub axle.

5 Withdraw the outer roller bearing from the hub. Carefully prise out the oil seal from the rear of the hub and remove the inner roller bearing (see Fig. 8.9).

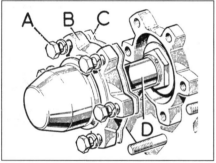

Fig. 8.4. Removing a rear halfshaft (Rover)

A Securing bolts   C Gasket
B Driving flang   D Halfshaft

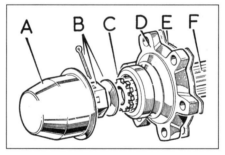

Fig. 8.5. Halfshaft flange assembly (Rover)

A Hub cap   D Flange
B Retaining nut and washer   E Gasket
C Seal   F Halfshaft

3.2 Front hub driving flange removed

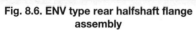

Fig. 8.6. ENV type rear halfshaft flange assembly

A Hub cap   C Circlip   E Axle halfshaft
B Oil seal 'O' rin D Driving member

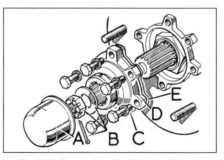

Fig. 8.7. Removing the front halfshaft driving flange

A Hub cap   D Flange
B Securing nut and washer E Gasket
C Flange bolts

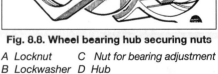

Fig. 8.8. Wheel bearing hub securing nuts

A Locknut   C Nut for bearing adjustment
B Lockwasher   D Hub

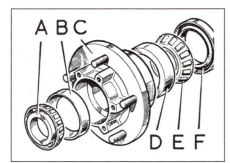

Fig. 8.9. Hub and bearings assembly

A Outer roller bearing
B Outer race for outer bearing
C Hub
D Outer race for inner bearing
E Inner roller bearing
F Oil seal

6 Examine the bearings for wear. If the outer races require renewal, support the hub on wooden blocks and drive the races out using a suitable drift.

4 Front and rear wheelbearings - refitting

1 Carefully drive the outer bearing races into the hub ensuring the smaller inside diameter of each race faces in toward the centre of the hub.
2 Refit the inner wheel bearing. Smear some sealing compound around the outside of the oil seal. Place it in the hub with the lipped side facing towards the centre of the hub and carefully tap it home, using a flat block of wood until it is flush with the rear face of the hub.
3 Pack the inside of the hub with the correct grade of grease. Pack the outer roller bearing with the same grease and fit it in the outer race.
4 Holding the outer roller bearing in position slide the hub assembly onto the stub axle.
5 Fit the inner washer and nut and tighten the nut just enough to take up the hub endfloat. Spin the hub several times to settle the bearings and check that it turns easily with no harshness. The endfloat should be as specified, but this can only be accurately checked using a dial gauge indicator.
6 When the hub is adjusted correctly, fit the lockwasher and outer nut; tighten the outer

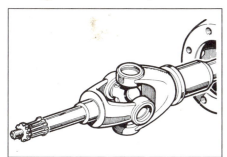

Fig. 8.10. Withdrawing the front halfshaft

nut and recheck that the hub rotates freely before securing it with the lockwasher.
7 Refit the hub driving flange (and halfshaft if working on the rear axle) and tighten the securing bolts to the specified torque.
8 In the case of the front axle hubs, refit the washer and castle nut onto the end of the driveshaft. Tighten the nut to the specified torque and secure with a new split pin.

5 Front axle halfshafts - removal and refitting

1 Jack-up the front of the vehicle and place heavy duty axle stands beneath the chassis.
2 Remove the roadwheel and brake drum and drain the oil from the swivel pin housing and the differential casing into a suitable container.
3 Remove the front hub and bearings as described in the previous Section.
4 Remove the brake anchor plate assembly as described in Chapter 9. Note that it is not necessary to disconnect the brake pipes and flexible hose but the anchor plate should be tied out of the way to avoid straining the hose.
5 The stub axle can now be drawn off the halfshaft. Remove the gasket from the swivel pin housing.
6 Carefully withdraw the complete halfshaft assembly from the axle casing (see Fig. 8.10).
7 Examine the halfshaft universal joint for wear by gripping each end of the shaft and turning them in opposite directions. Any movement in the joint indicates worn needle bearings.
8 The procedure for renewing the universal joint is the same as that described in Chapter 7 for the propeller shaft joints.
9 Check the bearing on the inner section of the halfshaft for wear. The bearing is retained in place by a steel collar which is an extremely tight fit on the shaft. if the bearing requires renewal the shaft should be taken to a Leyland dealer who will have the special tool and adaptor kit (Part No. 275870) that is essential for the removal of the collar and bearing.
10 To refit the halfshaft assembly, carefully insert the long end of the shaft through the swivel pin housing and axle casing until

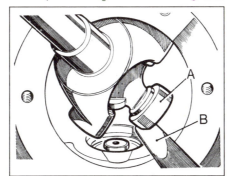

Fig. 8.11. Measuring the clearance of the front halfshaft coupling

A Coupling yoke   B Feeler gauges

the splines on the end of the shaft are fully engaged in the differential unit.
11 Rotate the shaft and with the universal joint turned at an angle, check the clearance between the joint yokes and the swivel pin face which should be at least 0.050 in (1.2 mm). If the clearance is insufficient the chamfered side of the joint yokes must be carefully filed down (see Fig. 8.11)
CAUTION: Great care must be taken not to remove too much metal from the yokes.
12 Refit the stub axle to the swivel pin housing using a new gasket.
13 Refit the brake anchor plate assembly referring to Chapter 9 if necessary .
14 Refit the hub and adjust the wheel bearing pre-load as described in Section 4.
15 Refill the swivel pin housing and axle with Hypoid gear oil viscosity SAE 90EP to the top of the filler/level plugs. Refit the plugs and tighten.
16 Refit the roadwheel remove the axle stands and lower the vehicle to the ground.

6 Front axle swivel pin housing - removal servicing and refitting

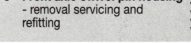

1 Jack-up the front of the vehicle and support it on axle stands.
2 Remove the roadwheel and drain the oil from the swivel pin housing and front axle into a suitable container.
3 Remove the brake drum and the wheel bearing hub as described in Section 3.
4 Remove the brake anchor plate, stub axle and halfshaft assembly as described in the previous Section.
5 Disconnect the trackrod ball joint from the swivel pin housing steering lever using the method described in Chapter 11.
6 Remove the nuts and bolts securing the swivel pin housing assembly to the axle casing flange. Note the positions of the steering lock stop and jack stop (see Fig. 8.12).

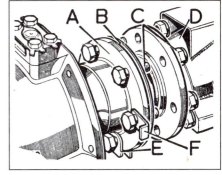

Fig. 8.12. Removing the swivel pin housing

A Swivel pin housing
B Joint washer
C Bolts, swivel pin housing to axle case
D Axle case
E Location stop for jack (RH side only)
F Lock stop plate

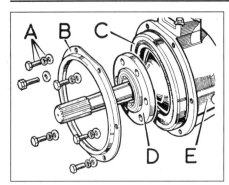

Fig. 8.13. Swivel pin housing oil seal assembly

A Bolts (6 off), oil seal retainer to swivel pin housing
B Oil seal retainer
C Oil seal
D Swivel pin bearing housing
E Swivel pin housing

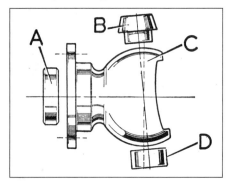

Fig. 8.16. Location of the bush and bearings

A Roller bearing for axle halfshaft
B Railko bush
C Top of housing
D Outer race for taper roller bearing

7 Withdraw the complete swivel pin housing assembly and remove the gasket.

8 Before dismantling the swivel pin housing it should be noted that the earlier type of spring-loaded bush fitted to the top swivel pin has been replaced by a Railko type bush which considerably improves steering damping and reduces any tendency to wheel wobble. A

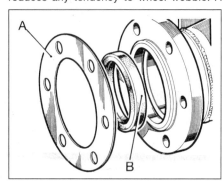

Fig. 8.17. Axle flange oil seal
A Gasket   B Oil seal

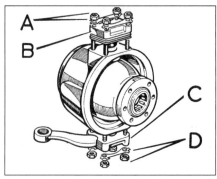

Fig. 8.14. Later type swivel pin housing

A Securing nuts (top)
B Top swivel pin assembly
C Bottom steering arm and pin assembly
D Securing nuts (bottom)

Railko bush conversion kit is available from Leylands under Part No. 532268, and if the top swivel pin assembly requires renewal it is recommended that this kit is obtained before commencing work.

9 To dismantle the housing first remove the six bolts from the inner side of the housing, remove the retaining ring and prise out the oil seal from the housing (see Fig. 8.13).

10 Remove the four bolts securing the top swivel pin assembly to the housing and lift it out of the housing complete with any shims and in the case of the earlier type, the cone spring.

11 Remove the four bolts securing the bottom swivel pin assembly to the housing and lift it out of the housing complete with any shims. **Note:** On earlier models the steering arm is attached to the top of the swivel pin housing while on later models it is located on the bottom of the housing (see Fig. 8.14).

12 Withdraw the inner bearing housing assembly and remove the bottom roller bearing (see Fig. 8.15).

13 Examine the roller bearing and bottom swivel pin for wear and renew if necessary. The outer bearing race can be driven from the bearing housing using a suitably sized drift.

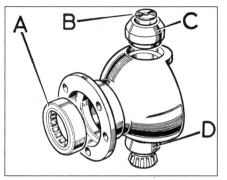

Fig. 8.18. Refitting the bearings into the housing

A Roller bearing for axle halfshaft
B Thrust washer for top swivel pin (early models)
C Railko bush for top swivel pin
D Outer race for bottom swivel pin bearing

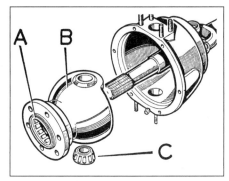

Fig. 8.15. Swivel pin bearing housing

A Roller bearing for axle halfshaft
B Bearing housing
C Taper roller bearings for bottom swivel pin

14 Check the upper swivel pin and bush (or cone) for excessive wear and renew if necessary. In the case of the earlier spring-loaded cone, this should be replaced with the Railko bush conversion kit mentioned earlier in this Section.

15 Inspect the roller bearing inside the bearing housing for wear and if it requires renewal drive it out from the inside of the housing using a suitably sized drift (see Fig. 8.16).

16 Remove the oil seal located in the end of the axle casing. Smear jointing compound around the outside of the new seal and fit it into the casing with the lipped side inwards (Fig. 8.17). Carefully tap it home until it is flush with the recessed end of the axle casing.

17 Begin reassembly by fitting the tapered roller bearing into the bearing housing. Note that if the bearing outer race was removed it must be refitted with the narrower inside diameter facing upwards.

18 Lubricate the top swivel pin bush with gear oil and press it into the top of the bearing housing followed by the thrust washer if fitted (see Fig. 8.18).

19 If the earlier type cone bearing is being renewed ensure it is refitted in the bearing housing with the oil hole in the position shown in Fig. 8.19.

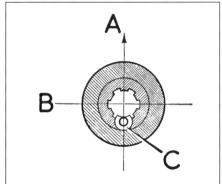

Fig. 8.19. Correct location of earlier cone type bush

A Front of vehicle   C Oil hole
B Front axle centre line

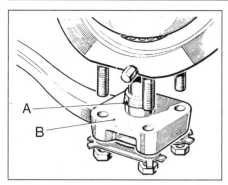

Fig. 8.20. Lower swivel pin and steering arm (later models)

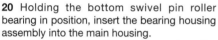

A 'O' ring   B Steering arm

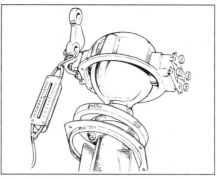

Fig. 8.21. Checking the bearing resistance

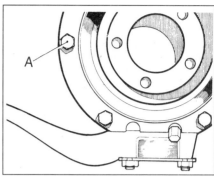

Fig. 8.22. Location of stop bolt 'A'

20 Holding the bottom swivel pin roller bearing in position, insert the bearing housing assembly into the main housing.

21 Smear some sealing compound on the face of the bottom swivel pin assembly, refit any shims that were removed and insert the pin through the housing and into the taper roller bearing. Secure the swivel pin plate with the four nuts, but do not bend over the locking tabs at this stage.

22 Note that on later models with the steering arm fitted to the bottom swivel pin plate, there is an O ring type oil seal on the pin and there are no shims (see Fig. 8.20).

23 If the cone type bearing for the top swivel pin is being used fit the thrust spring into the bearing.

24 Insert the top swivel pin assembly through the housing and into the top bush (or cone). Secure with the four nuts but do not bend over the locking tabs at this stage.

Note: On later models any shims that were beneath the top swivel pin plate must be refitted prior to the pin.

25 Check that the outer housing turns smoothly on the inner bearing assembly. If it feels excessively tight add another shim between the swivel pin plate and the housing, tighten the nuts and recheck it.

26 Should the outer housing turn far too easily and feels slack, remove one of the shims.

27 As a final check hold the flange of the inner bearing housing in a soft-jawed vice, attach a spring balance to the end of the steering arm and check that a pull of 14 to 16 lb (6.3 to 7.3 kg) is required to turn the outer swivel pin housing. Add or remove shims as necessary to obtain the correct amount of resistance (see Fig. 8.21).

28 When the swivel pins are correctly adjusted bend the locking tabs over the securing nuts.

29 Pack a new swivel pin housing oil seal with grease, fit it to the rear of the housing and secure it in place with the retainer and six bolts and washers. Note that the steering lock stop bolt must be fitted on the forward edge of the housing flange (see Fig. 8.22) .

30 Check that the seal is a tight fit across the complete face of the inner bearing housing when the outer housing is turned from lock-to-lock. Slacken the retainer bolts and reset the seal if necessary.

31 Smear both sides of a new gasket with grease and position on the axle casing flange.

32 Offer up the swivel pin housing assembly to the axle flange, fit the bolts and secure with the locknuts. Ensure the jack stop and steering stop plates are correctly positioned (see Fig. 8.12).

33 Refit the trackrod balljoint(s) to the steering arm, tighten the nuts to a torque wrench setting of 30 lbf ft (4 kgf m) and secure with a split pin.

34 Turn the housing onto full lock and adjust the steering lock stop bolt to obtain

a clearance of 1/2 in (12.5 mm) between the bolt head and the stop plate (see Fig. 8.23). Tighten the locknut.

35 Refit the halfshaft, stub axle and brake anchor plate as described in Section 5.

36 Refit the hub and bearings as described in Section 3.

37 Refill the swivel pin housing and axle with Hypoid gear oil viscosity SAE 90EP (photo).

38 Refit the roadwheel and lower the vehicle to the ground. Before road testing check the steering at full lock to ensure the front wheels do not touch the chassis. If necessary re-adjust the steering lock stop bolt.

7 Differential pinion oil seal - renewal

1 Failure of the front or rear pinion oil seal will be indicated by oil thrown around the differential casing and in extreme cases, oil dripping out of the pinion housing.

2 The procedure for renewing both front and rear differential pinion oil seals is the same on the Rover type axles. The Salisbury and ENV type rear axles differ slightly and details are given where necessary.

3 Disconnect the front or rear propeller shaft as appropriate from the axle flange as described in Chapter 7.

4 Get an assistant to apply the footbrake to lock the rear wheels. On Salisbury axles, carefully mark the relationship between the pinion shaft, pinion flange and flange nut. (It is important that the nut is eventually refitted the same number of turns to its precise previous position.) Where applicable, remove the split pin from the flange castle nut; undo the nut using a socket wrench.

CAUTION: If the vehicle has been jacked up, take great care not to dislodge it from the axle stands when applying the foot brake.

5 Remove the flange from the pinion shaft.

6 Except on early Rover axles, the seal can now be prised out of the end of the pinion housing (see Fig. 8.25).

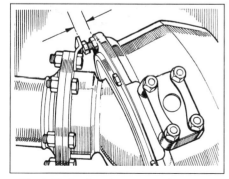

Fig. 8.23. Setting the steering lock stop bolt (dimension between arrows must be 1/2 in (12.5 mm)

6.37 Front axle filler plug

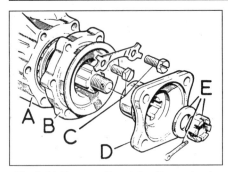

Fig. 8.24. Remove the pinion flange (early Rover type axle)

A Bevel pinion housing
B Oil seal retainer
C Fixings, oil seal retainer
D Driving flange for bevel pinion
E Nut and washer for bevel pinion driving flange

7 In the case of early Rover axles, remove the bolts securing the oil seal retainer to the pinion housing and remove the oil seal retainer and gasket (Fig. 8.24).
8 Drive the oil seal out of the retainer (see Fig. 8.26).
9 Except on early Rover axles, smear the outside diameter of the seal with jointing compound and carefully tap the seal into the pinion housing with the lipped side facing in towards the axle.
10 On ENV and later Rover axles, refit the pinion flange and securing nut and, with the footbrake firmly applied, tighten the nut to the specified torque. On Salisbury axles, refit the pinion flange, nut and washer, making sure that the marks made on dismantling are correctly aligned. On no account must the nut be excessively tightened.
11 If working on the early Rover type axle, gently warm the seal retainer, smear the outside of the seal with jointing compound, and fit it into the retainer with the lipped side facing the bolt holes.
12 Smear both sides of a new gasket with jointing compound and refit the seal retainer to the end of the pinion housing ensuring that the oilways in the housing gasket and retainer are aligned.
13 Tighten the retainer securing bolts and bend over the locking tabs.

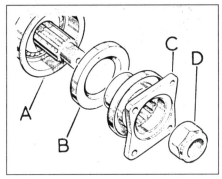

Fig. 8.25. Pinion flange and seal (ENV type axle)

A Pinion housing   C Flange
B Seal   D Securing nut

14 Refit the pinion flange, washer and, with the rear wheels locked by means of the foot brake, tighten the nut to the specified torque wrench setting. Secure the nut with a split pin.
15 Finally, refit the propeller shaft, check the axle oil level and lower the vehicle to the ground.

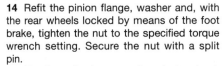
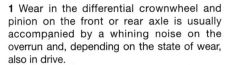

8 Differential assemblies - removal and refitting

1 Wear in the differential crownwheel and pinion on the front or rear axle is usually accompanied by a whining noise on the overrun and, depending on the state of wear, also in drive.
2 As the condition of the differential gears deteriorate, the noise will increase to a deep growl, and although it may be possible to carry on for many thousands of miles with the axle in this condition, there is always the possibility of the differential breaking up at any time.
3 The task of overhauling the differential assembly is a highly skilled job that requires a considerable number of special tools, and because of the high cost of new gears and bearings and the time involved, it is not really an economical proposition.
4 The best course of action for the D-I-Y

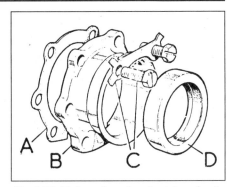

Fig. 8.26. Pinion oil seal and retainer (early Rover type axle)

A Gasket   C Bolts and locking tabs
B Retainer   D Oil seal

mechanic is to replace the complete differential assembly with a new or reconditioned unit obtainable from a Leyland dealer.
5 All models are fitted with Rover type differentials to the front axle (Fig. 8.27), although early and late versions differ slightly in design. The rear differential may be of ENV, Rover or Salisbury design (see Specifications).

Rover and ENV type differential

6 The method of removing and refitting either the front or rear differential assembly is basically the same. Commence by jacking up the front or rear of the vehicle as appropriate, place axle stands beneath the chassis and drain the oil from the axle.
7 Withdraw both halfshafts until the inner splines are clear of the differential. Refer to Section 2 for instructions on removing the rear shafts and Section 5 for the front shafts.
8 Disconnect the relevant propeller shaft from the axle as described in Chapter 7.
9 Remove the nuts and washers securing the pinion shaft housing to the axle casing (see Fig. 8.30).
10 Support the pinion housing with both hands and carefully withdraw the complete housing and differential assembly from the axle casing. Remove the gasket.
11 Refitting the differential assembly is the reverse sequence of the removal procedure. Use a new gasket between the pinion housing

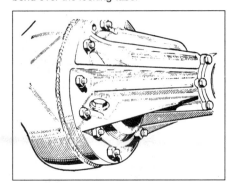

Fig. 8.27. Rover type differential

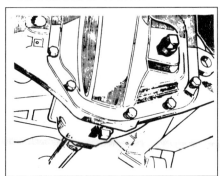

Fig. 8.28. Salisbury type differential

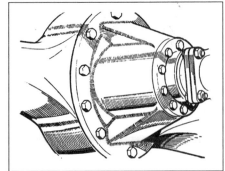

Fig. 8.29. ENV type differential

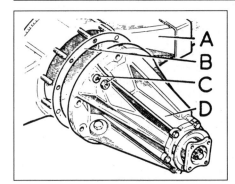

Fig. 8.30. Removing the pinion housing and differential assembly (Rover)

A Axle casing   C Securing nuts and washers
B Gasket   D Pinion housing

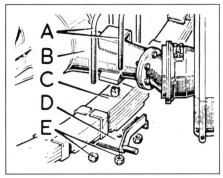

Fig. 8.31. Axle 'U' bolts and clamp

A 'U' bolts   D Bottom clamp
B Axle casing   E Securing nuts
C Road spring

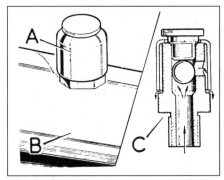

Fig. 8.32. Axle case breather valve

A Breather   C Flow through breather
B Axle case

and axle case and do not forget to refill the axle with EP 90 gear oil.

Salisbury type differential

12 The Salisbury differential fitted to the rear axle of some Series III models differs considerably from the Rover and ENV types. To remove the differential assembly, the complete axle casing must be removed from the vehicle and then, after the rear cover and bearing caps are removed, a special spreader tool must be used which literally stretches the casing apart to enable the differential assembly to be levered out.

13 Due to the damage that could be caused by incorrect use of the spreader tool, (presuming one could be obtained) it is strongly recommended that the vehicle is taken to a Land Rover dealer or transmission specialist should the differential require attention.

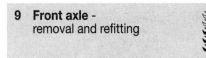

9 Front axle - removal and refitting

1 Slacken the front wheel nuts, jack-up the front of the vehicle and support it on stands.
2 Remove both front wheels.
3 Disconnect the front propeller shaft from the front axle as described in Chapter 7.
4 Remove the front flexible brake hoses from the pipe unions and securing brackets on each side of the chassis (refer to Chapter 9 if necessary). Plug the ends of the brake pipes to avoid losing all the fluid.
5 Refer to Chapter 11 and disconnect the steering drag-link ball joint from the relay lever.

6 Disconnect the lower ends of the shock absorbers from the road spring bottom plates.
7 Undo the nuts and remove the four U bolts securing the axle casing to the front spring (see Fig. 8.31). Note which way round the bottom plates are fitted.
8 Support the weight of the axle on a trolley jack, remove the front shackle pins from both road springs (Chapter 11) and lower them to the ground.
9 Lower the jack and withdraw the complete axle assembly from beneath the vehicle.
10 installation is the reversal of the removal procedure, but before refitting the axle, check that the axle case breather valve is clear (see Fig. 8.32).
11 Before the spring shackle pins and locknuts are fully tightened, lower the vehicle to the ground and move it backwards and forwards to settle the springs and then tighten the shackle pins.
12 Refill the axle to the correct level with gear oil and bleed the brakes as described in Chapter 9.

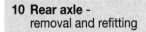

10 Rear axle - removal and refitting

1 Slacken the rear wheel nuts, jack-up the rear of the vehicle and support it on stands. Remove both rear wheels.
2 Disconnect the propeller shaft from the rear axle as described in Chapter 7.
3 Disconnect the rear flexible brake hose from the pipe union and the chassis bracket, (refer to Chapter 9 if necessary). Plug the end of the flexible pipe to prevent all the fluid escaping.

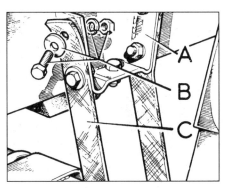

Fig. 8.33. Axle check strap

A Chassis   B Securing bolts   C Check strap

4 Support the axle assembly on a trolley jack and remove the nuts and bolts securing one end of each check strap (see Fig. 8.33).
5 Remove the two rear shock absorbers as described in Chapter 11.
6 Undo the nuts and remove the four U bolts securing the rear axle casing to the road springs.
7 Make sure the axle is supported by the trolley jack and then remove the rear shackle pins from both road springs (Chapter 11) and lower them to the ground.
8 Lower the jack and withdraw the complete axle assembly from beneath the vehicle.
9 Refitting is the reversal of the removal procedure, but before the rear shackle pins are fully tightened, the vehicle should be lowered to the ground and pushed backwards and forwards to settle the springs before finally tightening the shackle pins.
10 Refill the axle with the correct grade of gear oil, and bleed the brakes as described in Chapter 9.

Fault finding - front and rear axles

Vibration

☐ Worn halfshaft bearings.
☐ Loose drive flange bolts.
☐ Out of balance propeller shaft.
☐ Wheels require balancing.
☐ Worn swivel pins/bearings.
☐ Universal joints on front halfshafts worn.

Noise

☐ Insufficient lubricant.
☐ Worn gears and differential components generally.

'Clunk' on acceleration or deceleration

☐ Incorrect crownwheel and pinion mesh.
☐ Excessive backlash due to wear in crownwheel and pinion teeth.
☐ Worn halfshaft or differential side gear splines.
☐ Loose drive flange bolts.
☐ Worn drive pinion flange splines.

Oil leakage

☐ Faulty pinion or halfshaft oil seals.
☐ May be caused by blocked axle housing breather.

Chapter 9
Braking system

For modifications, and information applicable to later models, see Supplement at end of manual

Contents

Degrees of difficulty

| Easy, suitable for novice with little experience | 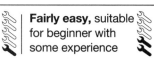 | Fairly easy, suitable for beginner with some experience | | Fairly difficult, suitable for competent DIY mechanic | | Difficult, suitable for experienced DIY mechanic | | Very difficult, suitable for expert DIY or professional | |

Specifications

Type	Hydraulically operated drum brakes. Mechanically operated transmission brake

Hydraulic fluid

Type/specification. . . . . Hydraulic fluid to FMVSS 116 DOT 3

10 in diameter type (SWB models)

Lining:
  Length . . . . 8 ½ in (215 mm) – 8.7 in (221 mm) Series III
  Width . . . . 1 ½ in (38 mm)
  Thickness . . . . ³⁄₁₆ in (4.75 mm)
Drum regrinding limit . . . . + 0.030 in (+ 0.75 mm) oversize

11 in diameter type (LWB model)

Lining (front):
  Length . . . . 10.45 in (265 mm)
  Width . . . . 2 ¼ in (57 mm)
  Thickness . . . . ³⁄₁₆ in (4.75 mm)
Lining (rear):
  Length . . . . 8.6 in (218 mm) – 10.42 in (265 mm) Series III
  Width . . . . 2 ¼ in (57 mm)
  Thickness . . . . ³⁄₁₆ in (4.75 mm)
Drum regrinding limit . . . . As for 10 in drums

Transmission brake

Lining:
  Length . . . . 8.64 in (219 mm) – 8.25 in (210 mm) Series III
  Width . . . . 1 ¾ in (44.5 mm)
  Thickness . . . . ³⁄₁₆ in (4.75 mm)
Drum diameter . . . . 9 in (228.6 mm)
Drum regrinding limit . . . . As for 10 in drums

Master cylinder

Type (SWB models) . . . . Girling CV
  Bore . . . . ¾ in (19 mm)
  Stroke . . . . 1 ½ in (38 mm)
Type (LWB models). . . . . Girling CV or CB
  Bore . . . . 1 in (25 mm)
  Stroke . . . . 1 ½ in (38 mm)
Pushrod free movement . . . . ¹⁄₁₆ in (1.5 mm)

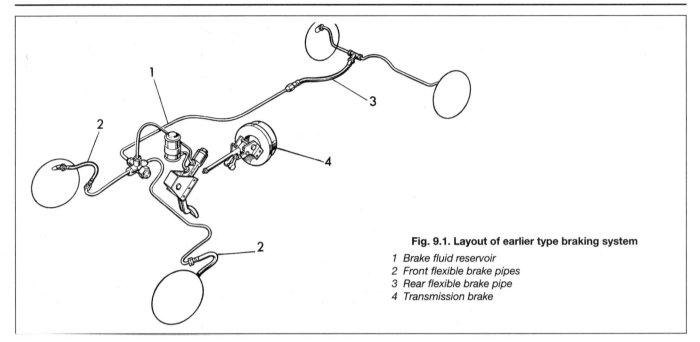

Fig. 9.1. Layout of earlier type braking system

1 Brake fluid reservoir
2 Front flexible brake pipes
3 Rear flexible brake pipe
4 Transmission brake

1 General description

The braking system on the 2 1/4 litre Land Rovers is comprised of drum brakes on the front and rear wheels operated by an hydraulic master cylinder connected to the brake pedal. The handbrake lever is mechanically linked to a drum brake mounted on the rear of the gearbox. Application of the lever locks the rear propeller shaft and if four-wheel drive is selected, also the front propeller shaft.

The short wheel based (SWB) models are fitted with 10 in (254 mm) diameter drums on the front and rear wheels, while the long wheel based (LWB) models are equipped with 11 in (279 mm) diameter drums.

The Series IIA and III models have the option of a dual braking system with servo assistance.

2 Front and rear brakes - adjustment

1 At the service intervals detailed in the Routine Maintenance Section at the beginning of the Manual, it will be necessary to adjust the brakes to compensate for lining wear.
2 The SWB models are fitted with a single hexagon adjustment bolt at the back of each brake anchor plate (see photo) while

2.2 Front wheel brake adjuster (SWB models)

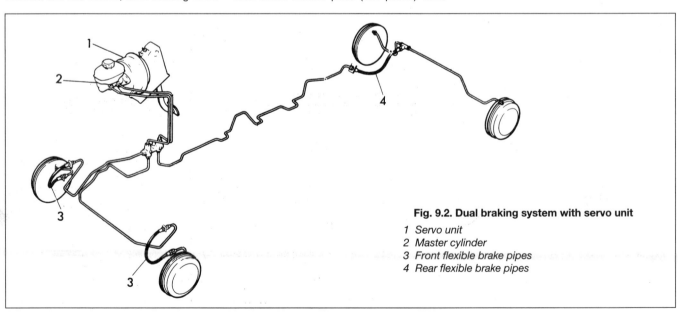

Fig. 9.2. Dual braking system with servo unit

1 Servo unit
2 Master cylinder
3 Front flexible brake pipes
4 Rear flexible brake pipes

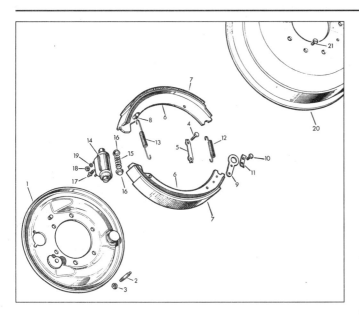

Fig. 9.3. Exploded view of the 10 in diameter brakes fitted to all SWB models (front and rear)

1 Brake anchor plate assembly
2 Shoe, steady post
3 Locknut for steady post
4 Set bolt (3/8 x 1 in long), securing front anchor plate to axle case
5 Locker, securing front anchor plate to axle case
6 Brake shoe assembly, front and rear
7 Linings complete with rivets, for brake shoe
8 Spring post for brake shoe
9 Anchor for brake shoe
10 Special set screw, securing anchor
11 Locking plate for bolt
12 Pull off spring for brake shoe
13 Pull-off spring for leading shoe
14 Wheel cylinder assembly
15 Spring for piston, front
16 Washer for spring, front
17 Bleed screw
18 Special nut securing wheel cylinder
19 Spring washer, securing wheel cylinder
20 Brake drum
21 Set screw, securing brake drum

Fig. 9.4. Exploded view of the front brake fitted to all LWB models

1 Brake anchor plate
2 Steady post for brake shoe
3 Bush for steady post
4 Special nut securing steady post
5 Brake shoe assembly
6 Lining complete with rivets, for brake shoe
7 Pull-offspring for brake shoe
8 Wheel cylinder assembly - 2 off
9 Spring (5/8 in diameter), for piston
10 Air excluder, for piston
11 Sealing ring for cylinder
12 Bleed screw
13 Spring washer, securing wheel cylinder
14 Special nut, securing wheel cylinder
15 Connecting pipe for wheel cylinder
16 Brake drum

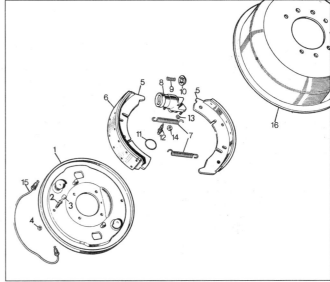
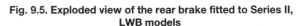

Fig. 9.5. Exploded view of the rear brake fitted to Series II, LWB models

1 Brake anchor plate
2 Steady post for brake shoe
3 Bush for steady post
4 Special nut for steady post
5 Brake shoe assembly
6 Lining complete with rivets, for brake shoe
7 Spring, adjuster end, for brake shoe
8 Spring, wheel cylinder end, for brake shoe
9 Adjuster housing
10 Spring washer, securing adjuster housing
11 Special set bolt securing adjuster housing
12 Plunger, LH
13 Plunger, RH
14 Cone for adjuster
15 Wheel cylinder assembly
16 Spring
17 Air excluder
18 Bleed screw
19 Brake shoe abutment plate
20 Retainer for brake shoe abutment plate
21 Screw, securing retainer and abutment plate
22 Shakeproof washer, securing retainer and abutment plate
23 Dust cover plate for brake wheel cylinder
24 Spring washer, securing wheel cylinder
25 Self-locking nut, securing wheel cylinder
26 Brake drum

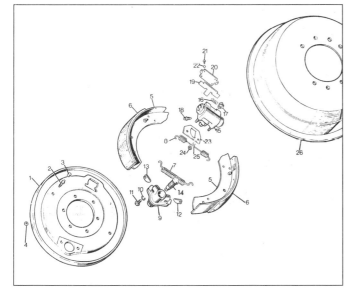

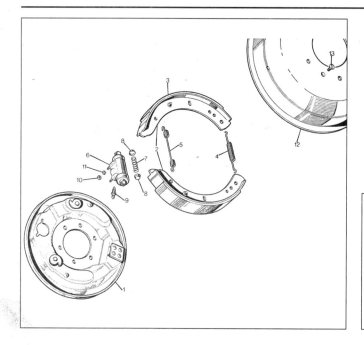

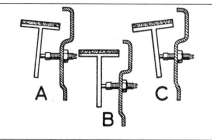

Fig. 9.6. Exploded view of the rear brake fitted to Series IIA and III, LWB models

1 Brake anchor plate
2 Brake shoe assembly
3 Lining complete with rivets, for brake shoe
4 Spring, abutment end, for brake shoe
5 Spring, wheel cylinder end, for brake shoe
6 Wheel cylinder assembly
7 Spring for piston
8 Washer for spring
9 Screw
10 Special nut securing wheel cylinder
11 Spring washer, securing wheel cylinder
12 Brake drum
13 Set screw, securing brake drum

Fig. 9.7. Adjustment of brake shoe steady post

A Incorrect
B Correct
C Incorrect

the LWB models are equipped with two hexagon adjusters on each anchor plate. **Note:** On some earlier LWB models a single square-headed adjuster is fitted on the rear brakes.

3 The method of adjusting the brakes on all models is basically the same. Jack-up each wheel in turn until the tyre is just clear of the ground and support the vehicle on axle stands. It is not necessary to remove the wheels.

4 From the rear of the anchor plate, check that the wheel turns freely (slacken the adjuster(s) if necessary) and then turn the adjuster(s) clockwise until the brake shoes are in firm contact with the drum.

5 Slacken the adjuster(s) anti-clockwise just enough to enable the wheel to rotate freely.

6 Lower the vehicle to the ground and repeat the operation on the other three wheels.

7 For handbrake adjustment refer to Section 4.

3 Brake drums and shoes - removal, inspection and refitting

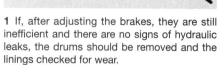

1 If, after adjusting the brakes, they are still inefficient and there are no signs of hydraulic leaks, the drums should be removed and the linings checked for wear.

2 The procedure for removing the brake drums and shoes is basically the same for all models. Commence by jacking-up the front of the vehicle, place axle stands under the chassis and remove the roadwheels.

3 Slacken off the brake adjuster(s) as described in Section 2, remove the screws securing the drum to the hub and draw it off. If the drum tends to stick, tap the periphery with a soft-faced mallet to loosen it.

4 Examine the friction surface on the interior of the drum. Normally this should be completely smooth and bright. Remove any dust with a dry cloth and examine the surface for any score marks or blemishes. Very light hairline scores running around the surface are not serious but indicate that the shoes may be wearing out or heavy grit and dirt have got into the drum at some time. If there are signs of deep scoring the drum needs reconditioning or renewal.

5 The brake linings should be renewed if they are so worn that the rivet heads are flush with the surface of the lining. If bonded linings are fitted they must be renewed when the material has worn down to 1/32 inch at its thinnest point.

> **HAYNES HiNT** *If the shoes are being removed to give access to the wheel cylinders then cover the linings with masking tape to prevent any possibility of their becoming contaminated with grease.*

6 Using a screwdriver scratch a mark alongside the holes in each shoe through which the return springs are hooked. This will avoid any confusion when the springs are refitted.

7 Slacken the adjuster(s) right back.

8 On the SWB models remove the anchor plate securing the trailing shoe to the pivot post (see Fig. 9.3).

9 Using a screwdriver or a pair of grips, carefully lever the bottom ends of the shoes away from the anchor post. If working on the LWB model, lever the trailing end of each shoe from the plain end of each wheel cylinder (see Fig. 9.4).

10 Release the other end of each shoe and remove them complete with springs.

11 Place a rubber band round each wheel cylinder piston to prevent their coming out, causing loss of brake fluid and the necessity of bleeding the braking system.

12 Thoroughly clean all traces of dust from the shoes backplates and brake drums with a dry paint brush and compressed air if available. Do not breathe in any dust as it will be of asbestos nature. Brake dust can cause squeal and judder and it is therefore important to clean out the brakes thoroughly.

13 Check that the pistons are free in their cylinders and that the rubber dust covers are undamaged and in position and that there are no hydraulic fluid leaks.

14 Prior to reassembly smear a trace of white brake grease to all sliding surfaces. It is vital that no grease or oil comes into contact with the brake drums or the brake linings.

15 Refitting is a straight forward reversal of the removal procedure but note the following points:

a) Ensure that the return springs are located in the correct holes in the shoes.

b) Check that the snail type adjusting cam(s) are correctly located against the post on the shoe.

c) After refitting the drums, adjust the brakes as described in Section 2.

d) If brake shoe steady posts are fitted and have been disturbed, these should be adjusted to the position shown in Fig. 9.7.

16 After reassembling the front brakes carry out the same procedure on the rear brakes. It will be noticed that there are differences in design between the slave cylinders fitted to the SWB and LWB models, but providing reference is made to the exploded diagrams in this Chapter, no major problems should be encountered.

4.5 Handbrake lever vertical adjuster rod

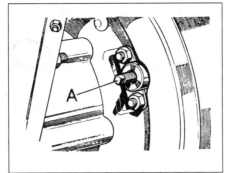

Fig. 9.8. Transmission brake adjuster 'A'

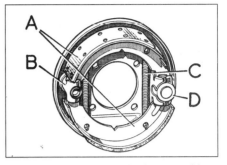

Fig. 9.9. Transmission brake assembly

A Brake shoes   C Brake shoe return springs
B Adjuster unit   D Expander unit

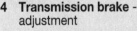

4 Transmission brake - adjustment

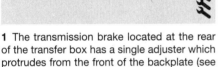

1 The transmission brake located at the rear of the transfer box has a single adjuster which protrudes from the front of the backplate (see Fig. 9.8).

2 Access can be gained to the brake adjuster either by removing the centre seat box panel or from beneath the vehicle. If working beneath the vehicle, place chocks on either side of two wheels, as the handbrake must be in the off position while adjusting the brake.

3 Rotate the adjuster clockwise until the brake shoes are in firm contact with the drum. **Note:** The adjuster is not very accessible and a proper square-jawed brake adjusting spanner should be used to avoid burring over the head of the adjuster.

4 Unscrew the adjuster just enough to release the brake (approximately two clicks) and then apply and release the handbrake lever to centralise the shoes.

5 Adjust the two locknuts on the handbrake lever vertical adjuster rod so that the lever has two clicks free movement on the ratchet before the brake is applied (photo).

5 Transmission brake drum and shoes - removal, inspection and refitting

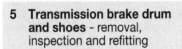

1 Access to the transmission brake is gained from beneath the vehicle. Ensure that the wheels are firmly chocked before commencing work.

2 Remove the six nuts securing the brake drum to the output shaft flange and withdraw the drum rearwards over the propeller shaft. If the drum is difficult to remove, slacken the brake adjuster several turns.

3 Using a screwdriver mark the holes in the shoes through which the return springs are hooked to ensure correct reassembly.

4 Lever the end of each shoe out of the adjuster unit and then slide the other ends out of the expander unit (Fig. 9.9). Remove the shoes and return springs.

5 Examine the drum and linings for wear as

described in Section 3 and renew if necessary.

6 Check that the plungers in the adjuster unit move freely. If they are stiff or seized, unscrew the two securing nuts from the front of the backplate and remove the complete unit (see Fig. 9 10)

7 Unscrew the adjuster cone and tap out the two plungers Clean all the components in petrol and allow to dry before reassembly using grease.

8 Do not forget to bend the locking tabs over the adjuster retaining nuts when refitting.

9 Check the brake shoe expander unit for correct operation.

10 If it is necessary to remove the expander unit from the backplate first remove the clevis pin securing the expander rod fork to the handbrake linkage.

11 Unhook the return spring and remove the rubber dust cover from the front of the backplate.

12 On later models remove the spring clip securing the expander unit to the backplate (see Fig. 9.12).

13 Withdraw the complete expander unit from the backplate.

14 Remove the spring clip and tap out the plungers and rollers from the expander unit. Note that on earlier models steel balls are used in place of rollers and the plungers are retained by split pins.

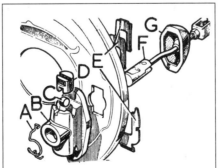

Fig. 9.12. Transmission brake expander assembly

A Spring clip   E Fixings for expander unit
B Housing   F Operating rod
C Roller   G Rubber dust excluder
D Plunger

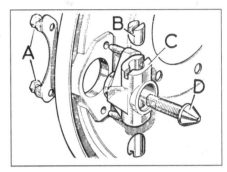

Fig. 9.10. Transmission brake adjuster assembly

A Securing nuts   C Housing
B Plungers   D Adjuster cone

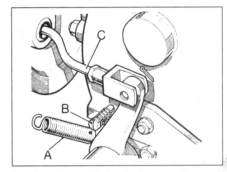

Fig. 9.11. Transmission brake operating rod

A Return spring   C Operating rod
D Clevis pin

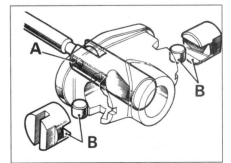

Fig. 9.13. Correct assembly of expander rod and plungers

A Expander rod   B Plunger and rollers

Fig. 9.14. Expander unit retaining plates (later models)

A Expander housing   C Locking plate
B Packing piece   D Retaining spring

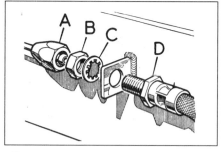

Fig. 9.17. Flexible brake hose connection

A Pipe from master cylinder
B Locknut
C Shakeproof washer
D Flexible brake pipe

15 Clean the components in petrol and grease them before reassembling.

16 Reassembling of the brake adjuster unit, expander unit and brake shoes is basically the reverse procedure to removal. Refer to Figs. 9.13 and 9.14 for the correct reassembly of the expander unit and (on later models) the securing clips.

Note: *If difficulty is experienced in removing or refitting any of the transmission brake components, it may be necessary to remove the propeller shaft as described in Chapter 7. Then undo the large castle nut and withdraw the output shaft flange complete with drum (see Fig. 9.15).*

17 After reassembly adjust the transmission brake as described in Section 4.

6 Handbrake lever - removal and refining

1 The handbrake lever can be removed from beneath the vehicle. Ensure the wheels are firmly chocked before commencing work.

2 Remove the clevis pin securing the operating rod to the relay lever.

3 Remove the nut securing the relay lever to the chassis and withdraw the lever (Fig. 9.16). Disconnect the return spring.

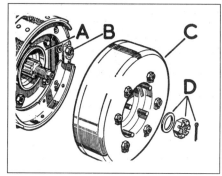

Fig. 9.15. Transmission brake drum and output drive flange removed

A Brake anchor plate
B Anchor plate securing nuts
C Brake drum and flange
D Securing nut

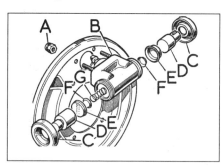

Fig. 9.18. Wheel cylinder components (SWB models)

A Fixings for wheel cylinder
B Wheel cylinder
C Dust cove   E Seal
D Piston   F Support for seal
                     G Spring

4 Remove the two nuts and washers securing the handbrake lever assembly to the chassis bracket.

5 Carefully withdraw the complete handbrake assembly through the aperture in the front of the seat box.

6 Refit the handbrake using the reversal of the removal procedure. If necessary adjust the locknuts on the vertical operating rod as described in Section 4.

7 Wheel cylinders (SWB models) - removal inspection and refitting

1 The procedure for overhauling either the front or rear wheel cylinders on the SWB models is basically the same.

2 Jack-up the vehicle, support it on stands and remove the roadwheel .

3 Remove the brake drum and shoes as described in Section 3.

4 Before continuing, examine the rubber boots on each end of the wheel cylinder for fluid leakage then get someone to gently press the footbrake and check that the pistons push the shoes outwards and return fully. Do not push

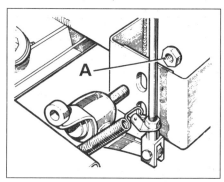

Fig. 9.16. Handbrake relay lever

A Securing nut

the pedal too far down as the piston may be ejected from the cylinder and it will become necessary to bleed the system after refitting it.

5 Disconnect the brake pipe from the rear side of the wheel cylinder. Note that the front brakes are fitted with a flexible pipe and this must first be disconnected from the pipe union on the side of the chassis member (see Fig. 9.17).

6 Plug the ends of the hydraulic pipes to reduce fluid loss.

7 Remove the two retaining nuts and withdraw the complete wheel cylinder from the backplate.

8 Withdraw the rubber boots, pistons, seals and spring from the wheel cylinder making a careful note of the assembly order (Fig. 9.18).

9 Inspect the surfaces of the pistons and cylinder bores. If any scoring or bright wear areas are evident renew the complete assembly.

10 If the components are in good condition discard the rubber seals and obtain new ones in the form of a repair kit.

11 Install the new seals using the fingers only to manipulate them into position. Dip the pistons into clean hydraulic fluid before installing them and then fit the dust excluders.

12 Installation is a reversal of removal, but make sure that the locating boss on the cylinder body is engaged correctly in the hole in the backplate.

13 Refit the brake shoes and drum and bleed the system as described in Section 18.

14 Refit the roadwheel, adjust the brakes and lower the vehicle to the ground.

7.3 Brake shoes and wheel cylinder (SWB models)

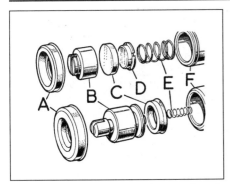

Fig. 9.19. The two types of piston and seals fitted in the front wheel cylinders of the LWB models

A Dust cover
B Piston
C Seal for piston
D Support for seal
E Spring
F Wheel cylinder

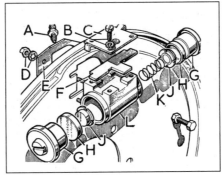

Fig. 9.20. Wheel cylinder assembly fitted to the rear brakes of LWB models

A Bleed nipple
B Screws for retainer
C Retainer for abutment plate
D Nuts for dust cover
E Dust cover
F Abutment plate for shoes
G Piston
H Seal for piston
J Support for seal
K Spring
L Wheel cylinder

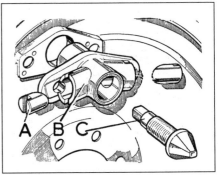

Fig. 9.21. Rear wheel brake adjuster (Series II LWB)

A Plunger
B Adjuster housing
C Adjuster cone

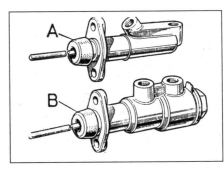

Fig. 9.22. Two types of master cylinder fitted to earlier models

A 'CV' type   B 'CB' type

8 Wheel cylinders (LWB models) - removal inspection and refitting

1 The front brakes of the LWB model are fitted with two single piston wheel cylinders while the rear brakes have a single twin piston wheel cylinder. The overhaul procedure for both types of cylinder is basically the same but any differences will be detailed where necessary.

2 Remove the brake drum and shoes as described in Section 3.

3 Check the wheel cylinder(s) for leaks or faulty operation as described in Section 7, paragraph 4.

4 Disconnect the brake pipe from the rear wheel cylinder. In the case of the front wheels remove the crossfeed pipe from each wheel cylinder and then disconnect the flexible hose from the chassis union first, before unscrewing the other end from the wheel cylinder.

5 Plug the ends of the hydraulic pipes to reduce fluid loss.

6 Remove the securing nuts and withdraw the wheel cylinder(s) from the backplate.

7 Referring to Fig. 9.19 (front cylinder) or Fig. 9.20 (rear cylinder) as appropriate remove the pistons, seals and spring from the wheel cylinder. Note that the rear cylinder fitted to the Series IIA model is exactly the same as that fitted to the SWB model (see Section 7, Fig. 9.18).

8 Examine the pistons and cylinders for wear and then fit new seals as described in Section 7, paragraphs 9 to 11 inclusive.

9 Refit the wheel cylinder(s) using the reversal of the removal procedure. Check the operation of the brake adjuster and if necessary remove clean and lubricate the plungers and threaded adjuster cone (see Fig. 9.21).

10 Refit the brake shoes and drum and bleed the system as described in Section 18.

11 Refit the roadwheel, adjust the brakes and lower the vehicle to the ground.

9 Master cylinder - removal and refitting

1 Three different types of master cylinder have been fitted to the Land Rover. The Series II and IIA models are equipped with either the centre valve (CV) type or the compression barrel (CB) type (see Fig. 9.22).

2 Series III models are fitted with either the CV type, or on later models the dual system type (see Fig. 9.23). The latter type is fitted in conjunction with a servo unit.

CB type master cylinder

3 With a suitable container in readiness remove the brake and clutch pipe unions from the combined fluid reservoir and allow the fluid to drain into the container.

4 Remove the single securing nut and lift the reservoir off the bracket.

5 Disconnect the two hydraulic pipes from the master cylinder.

6 From inside the vehicle remove the brake pedal return spring and unscrew the bolts securing the pedal bracket to the bulkhead (see Fig. 9.24).

7 Withdraw the bracket and master cylinder

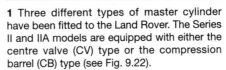

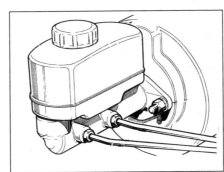

Fig. 9.23. Later type of dual master cylinder

from the engine compartment manoeuvring it as necessary to enable the pedal to pass through the bulkhead aperture.

8 Remove the top cover and gasket from the bracket.

9 Remove the nut and washer securing the master cylinder pushrod to the brake pedal trunnion. Remove the two nuts and bolts securing the cylinder to the bracket and withdraw the complete cylinder (see Fig. 9.25).

10 Refit the master cylinder and bracket using the reversal of the removal procedure. Adjust the pushrod nuts to obtain 1/16 in (1.5 mm) free-play on the pushrod (see Fig. 9.26).

11 Refit the fluid reservoir and bleed the brakes as described in Section 18.

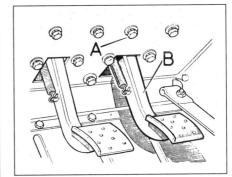

Fig. 9.24. Brake pedal attachment bolts

A Securing bolts   B Brake pedal

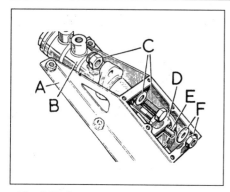

Fig. 9.25. Removing the CB type master cylinder

A Brake pedal bracket D Brake pedal trunnion
B Master cylinder   E Pushrod
C Securing nuts   F Pushrod securing nuts

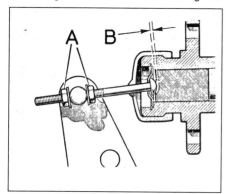

Fig. 9.26. Master cylinder pushrod adjustment

A Adjusting nuts
B Free play - 1/16 in (1.5 mm)

CV type master cylinder (without servo unit)

12 Drain and remove the fluid reservoir as described in paragraph 3 of this Section.
13 Disconnect the two hydraulic pipes from the master cylinder.
14 Remove the top cover and gasket from the brake pedal bracket.
15 Undo the master cylinder pushrod nut and the two flange nuts and withdraw the cylinder rearwards from the bracket.
16 Refit the master cylinder using the reverse procedure. Adjust the pushrod nuts as shown in Fig. 9.26.
17 Refit the fluid reservoir and bleed the brakes.

CV type and dual master cylinder (with servo unit)

18 Disconnect the hydraulic pipe(s) from the master cylinder.
19 Remove the two securing nuts and washers and withdraw the complete master cylinder and reservoir assembly from the servo unit.
20 Refit using the reverse procedure and bleed the brakes as described in Section 18.

10 Master cylinder - overhaul

CB type master cylinder

1 With the master cylinder on the bench, remove the nut from the pushrod and prise off the rubber cover from the end of the cylinder.
2 Remove the circlip from inside the end of the cylinder and withdraw the pushrod and retaining washer.
3 Gently tap the cylinder on a wooden block until the piston emerges from the cylinder. Withdraw the piston and spring (Fig. 9.28).
4 Turning to the other end of the cylinder, unscrew the end cap and remove the recuperating seal assembly (Fig. 9.29).
5 Examine the piston and cylinder bore surfaces for scoring or bright wear areas. Where these are evident renew the complete master cylinder.
6 If the components are in good order discard the seals and obtain new ones, preferably in the form of a repair kit.
7 Lubricate the new seals and the cylinder barrel with brake fluid and fit the seal into the piston groove with the larger outside diameter of the seal facing away from the pushrod end of the piston (see Fig. 9.30).
8 Insert the piston into the cylinder taking care not to pinch the seal. Refit the pushrod retaining washer and circlip.
9 Fit the washer and seal into the other end of the cylinder making sure that the flat face of the seal faces the piston (see Fig. 9.31).
10 Insert the spring into the centre bore of the piston and refit the seal support gasket and end cap and tighten the cap.
11 Smear some rubber grease inside the rubber cover and fit it over the pushrod and cylinder.
12 Refit the master cylinder to the vehicle as described in Section 9.

CV type master cylinder

13 The CV type master cylinder is exactly the same as the clutch master cylinder and the overhaul procedure and illustrations given in Chapter 5 should be used when servicing this type of master cylinder.

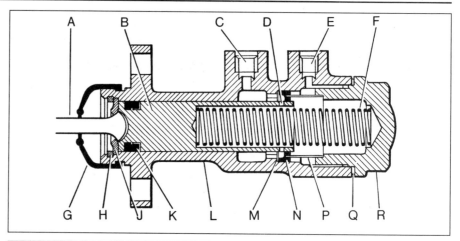

Fig. 9.27. Sectional view of CB type master cylinder

A Pushrod   J Retaining washer
B Piston   K End seal
C Inlet from reservoir   L Cylinder
D Inlet ports   M Shim
E Outlet to wheel   N Recuperating seal
  cylinders   P Seal support
F Piston spring   Q Gasket
G Dust cover   R End cap
H Circlip

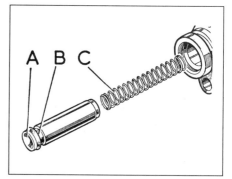

Fig. 9.28. Removing the piston and spring from master cylinder (CB type)

A Seal   B Piston   C Spring

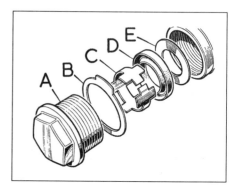

Fig. 9.29. End cap assembly (CB type)

A End cap   D Recuperating seal
B Gasket for end cap   E Shim
C Support for seal

Dual type master cylinder

14 Undo and remove the two screws holding the reservoir to the cylinder body. Lift away the reservoir. Using a suitable sized Allen key or wrench unscrew the tipping valve nut and lift away the seal. Using a suitable diameter rod push the primary plunger down the bore this operation enabling the tipping valve to be withdrawn (see Fig. 9.32).

15 Using a compressed air jet carefully applied to the rear outlet pipe connection blow out all the master cylinder internal components. Alternatively shake out the parts. Take care that adequate precautions are taken to ensure all parts are caught as they emerge.

16 Separate the primary and secondary plungers from the intermediate spring. Use the fingers to remove the gland seal from the primary plunger.

17 The secondary plunger assembly should be separated by lifting the thimble leaf over the shouldered end of the plunger. Using the fingers, remove the seal from the secondary plunger.

18 Depress the secondary spring allowing the valve stem to slide through the keyhole in the thimble thus releasing the tension in the spring.

19 Detach the valve spacer taking care of the spring washer which will be found located under the valve head.

20 Examine the bore of the cylinder carefully for scores ridges or excessive wear. If the bore is found to be completely smooth with only negligible wear, new seals can be fitted. If however there is any doubt about the condition of the bore, fit a new cylinder.

21 Thoroughly clean all parts in either fresh hydraulic fluid or methylated spirits. Ensure that the bypass ports are clear.

22 All components should be assembled wet by dipping in clean brake fluid. Using fingers only fit new seals to the primary and secondary plungers ensuring that they are the correct way round. Place the dished washer with the dome against the underside of the valve seat. Hold it in position with the valve spacers ensuring that the legs face towards the valve seal.

23 Refit the plunger return spring centrally on the spacer, insert the thimble into the spring and depress until the valve stem engages in the keyhole of the thimble.

24 Insert the reduced end of the plunger into the thimble until the thimble engages under the shoulder of the plunger and press home the thimble leaf. Refit the intermediate spring between the primary and secondary plungers.

25 Check that the master cylinder bore is clean and smear with clean brake fluid. With the complete assembly suitably lubricated with brake fluid carefully insert the assembly into the bore. Ease the lips of the plunger seals carefully into the bore. Push the assembly fully home.

26 Refit the tipping valve assembly and seal into the cylinder and tighten the securing nut. Refit the fluid reservoir and tighten the two retaining screws.

27 The master cylinder can now be refitted to the vehicle as described in Section 9.

11 Servo unit - description

The vacuum servo unit is fitted into the brake hydraulic circuit in series with the master cylinder to provide assistance to the driver when the brake pedal is depressed. This reduces the effort required by the driver to operate the brakes under all braking conditions. The unit operates by vacuum obtained from the induction manifold and comprises basically a booster diaphragm control rod, slave cylinder and non-return valve.

The servo unit and hydraulic master cylinder are connected together so that the servo unit piston rod acts as the master cylinder pushrod. The driver's braking effort is transmitted through another pushrod to the servo unit piston and its built-in control system. The servo unit piston does not fit tightly into the cylinder but has a strong diaphragm to keep its edges in contact with the cylinder wall so assuring an air-tight seal between the two parts. The forward chamber is held under vacuum conditions created in the inlet manifold of the engine and during periods when the brake pedal is not in use, the

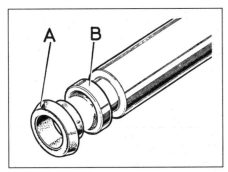

Fig. 9.30. Correct location of piston seal
A Seal   B Piston

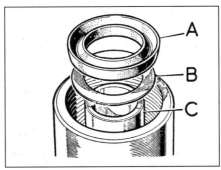

Fig. 9.31. Correct location of recuperating seal
A Seal   B Shim   C Piston

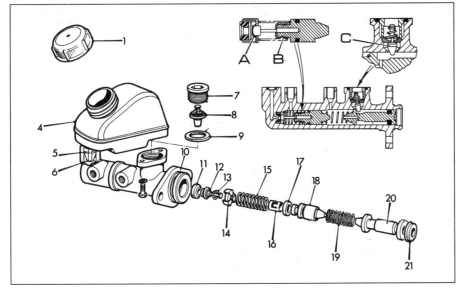

Fig. 9.32. Dual master cylinder components

1 Filler cap	10 Cylinder body	16 Spring retainer
4 Reservoir - dual	11 Valve seal	17 Seal
5 Circlip - internal	12 Valve stem	18 Secondary plunger
6 Seal	13 Spring washer - curved	19 Intermediate spring (black)
7 Securing nut	14 Valve spacer	20 Primary plunger
8 Tipping valve	15 Secondary spring	21 Gland seal
9 Face seal		

A Correct assembly of spring washer in centre valve
B Leaf of spring retainer
C As the brakes are applied the primary plunger moves down the cylinder and allows the tipping valve (C) to close the primary supply port. The assembly shows the unit in the off position

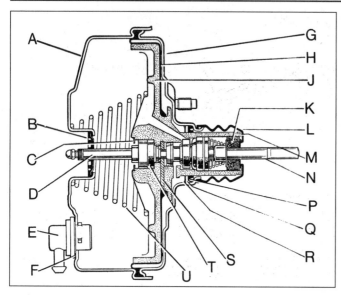

-Fig. 9.33. Sectional view of servo unit

A Front shell
B Seal and plate assembly
C Retainer sprag washer
D Hydraulic pushrod
E Non-return valve
F 'O' ring
G Rear shell
H Diaphragm
J Diaphragm plate
K Filter

L Dust cover
M End Cap
N Valve operating rod assembly
P Seal
Q Bearing
R Retainer
S Valve retaining plate
T Reaction disc
U Diaphragm return spring

controls open a passage to the rear chamber, so placing it under vacuum conditions as well. When the brake pedal is depressed the vacuum passage to the rear chamber is cut off and the chamber opened to atmospheric pressure. The consequent rush of air pushes the servo piston forward in the vacuum chamber and operates the main pushrod to the master cylinder.

The controls are designed so that assistance is given under all conditions and when the brakes are not required, vacuum in the rear chamber is established when the brake pedal is released. All air from the atmosphere entering the rear chamber is passed through a small air filter.

Under normal operation conditions the vacuum servo unit is very reliable and does not require overhaul except at very high mileage. In this case it is necessary to obtain a service exchange unit rather than attempt to repair the original unit.

12 Servo unit - removal and refitting

1 Refer to Section 9 and remove the master cylinder from the servo unit.
2 Slacken the clip and disconnect the vacuum hose from the servo unit non-return valve.
3 Remove the screws securing the switch plate to the top of the pedal box and lift off the switch and plate (see Fig. 9.34).
4 Prise out the rubber plugs either side of the pedal box. Remove the split pin and withdraw the clevis pin securing the servo rod to the brake pedal.
5 Remove the four nuts and washers securing the servo unit to the pedal box and lift away the complete servo unit.
6 Refitting the servo unit is the reverse sequence to removal. It will be necessary

to bleed the brakes as described in Section 18.

13 Servo unit non-return valve - removal and refitting

1 The servo unit should not be completely dismantled, so if it develops an internal fault it should be renewed. Even if the unit is dismantled there would probably be extreme difficulty in obtaining spare parts. The only two service operations that may be carried out are renewing the non-return valve (this Section) and the air filter (Section 14).
2 To renew the non-return valve first detach the vacuum hose from the valve union.
3 Note the angle of the valve union and then insert a wide blade screwdriver between the valve and grommet. Pull on the valve whilst

Fig. 9.34. Removing the servo unit

1 Servo unit
2 Vacuum pipe

3 Brake switch
4 Rubber plugs

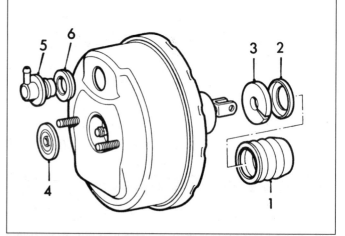

Fig. 9.35. Servo unit components

1 Rubber dust cover
2 Retainer
3 Filter

4 Grommet
5 Non-return valve
6 Grommet

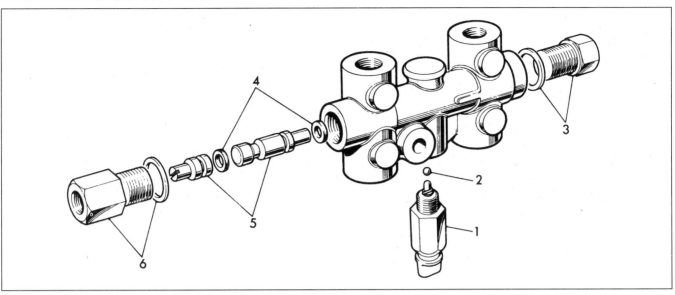

Fig. 9.36. Brake failure valve (dual braking system)

1 Switch   2 Switch ball   3 End plug and gasket   4 Seals   5 Pistons   6 End union and gasket

twisting the screwdriver to release it from the body.

4 Recover the grommet.

5 Refitting the grommet and valve is the reverse sequence to removal. Lubricate the ribs of the valve with a little rubber grease.

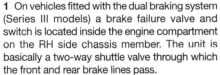

14 Servo unit filter -
removal and refitting

1 Carefully pull back the dust cover and then ease the filter retainer from the servo neck.

2 Using a small screwdriver ease out the filter. Cut it in half and lift away.

3 Cut a new filter diagonally to the centre hole, fit it over the pushrod and carefully ease it into the housing.

4 Refit the filter retainer and dust cover.

15 Brake failure valve (dual braking system only) -
removal, inspection and refitting

1 On vehicles fitted with the dual braking system (Series III models) a brake failure valve and switch is located inside the engine compartment on the RH side chassis member. The unit is basically a two-way shuttle valve through which the front and rear brake lines pass.

2 In the event of a leakage in either the front or rear braking system, the faulty system is cut off but hydraulic braking pressure is maintained in the remaining system. At the same time the switch on the valve is actuated by the movement of the piston and the brake warning light on the instrument panel will illuminate.

3 To test the valve switch remove the wire

from the switch terminal and earth it against the valve body with the ignition switched on. The brake warning lamp will illuminate.

4 To remove the valve unit, disconnect the five hydraulic pipe unions, detach the switch wire and remove the single retaining bolt. Lift the unit away from the chassis member.

5 Referring to Fig. 9.36 remove the switch and ball and the two end plugs. Using a soft drift carefully push out the two-part piston.

6 Examine the piston and valve bore for signs of scoring and if evident renew the affected component.

7 Dip some new seals in brake fluid and fit them to the piston using the fingers only.

8 Fit the pistons back into the valve bore ensuring they are the correct way round.

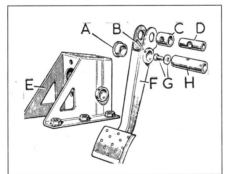

Fig. 9.37. Brake pedal assembly

A Bush for pedal
B Pin for pedal shaft
C Distance piece
D Trunnion for pedal
E Bracket for brake pedal
F Brake pedal
G Oil plug and washer
H Shaft for pedal

9 Refit the ball and switch ensuring the ball is located in the piston groove.

10 Screw on the end cap and union and tighten them. Refit the valve unit to the vehicle using the reverse procedure to removal.

11 Bleed the brake system as described in Section 18.

12 The valve must now be reset. First apply the brake pedal hard and the warning light should go out and stay out even when the brake pedal is released.

13 Should the light not go out the pressure in the system is unbalanced and the valve or the switch should be checked for correct operation.

14 If the brake failure warning light is off, check that the bulb is in order. Press the test-push and the light should glow.

15 Apply pressure to the brake pedal. The warning light will remain off if the hydraulic system is functioning satisfactorily and will come on to indicate hydraulic failure in one side of the system.

16 Brake pedal -
removal and refitting

1 Referring to Section 9, paragraphs 3 to 9 inclusive, remove the complete brake pedal and bracket.

2 Using a suitable punch, drive out the pin securing the pedal shaft to the bracket. Remove the shaft and withdraw the pedal complete with bushes and trunnion (see Fig. 9.37).

3 Examine the bushes and shaft for wear and renew if necessary. Note that new bushes must be reamed to 0.750 in (15.875 mm) before fitting.

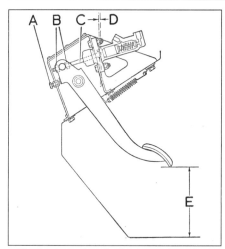

Fig. 9.38. Setting the brake pedal height

A Pedal stop
B Locknuts for master cylinder pushrod
C Master cylinder pushrod
D 1/16 in (1.5 mm)
E Pedal height 6 1/4 in (158 mm)

4 Grease the pedal shaft and bushes and refit using the reverse procedure to removal.
5 Bleed the brake system and adjust the pedal height and pushrod free-play to the dimensions shown in Fig. 9.38.

17 Hydraulic pipes and hoses - general

1 Carefully examine all brake pipes/hoses, pipe hose connections and unions periodically.
2 First examine for signs of leakage where the pipe unions occur. Then examine the flexible hoses for signs of chafing and fraying and of course, leakage. This is only a preliminary part of the flexible hose inspection, as exterior condition does not necessarily indicate the interior condition which will be considered later.
3 The steel pipes must be examined carefully and methodically. They must be cleaned off and examined for any signs of dents, corrosion or other damage and corrosion should be scraped off and if the depth of pitting is significant, the pipes will need renewal. This is particularly likely in those areas underneath the vehicle body where the pipes are exposed and unprotected.
4 If any section of pipe is to be taken off, first wipe and then remove the fluid reservoir cap and place a piece of polythene over the reservoir neck. Refit the cap, this will stop syphoning during subsequent operations .
5 Rigid pipe removal is usually quite straightforward. The unions at each end are undone, the pipe and union pulled out and the centre sections of the pipe removed from the body clips. Where the pipes are exposed to the full force of road and weather they can sometimes be very tight. As one can only use an open ended spanner and the unions are not large, burring of the flats is not uncommon when attempting to undo them. For this reason a self-locking grip wrench (mole) is often the only way to remove a stubborn union.
6 To remove a flexible hose, wipe the unions and bracket free from dust and undo the union nut from the metal pipe end.
7 Detach the hose from the bracket be it either a clip or locknut.
8 The flexible hose may now be unscrewed from its attachment.
9 With the flexible hose removed, examine the internal bore. If it is blown through first, it should be possible to see through it. Any specks of rubber which come out or signs of restriction in the bore mean that the rubber lining is breaking up and the pipe must be renewed.
10 Rigid pipes which need renewing can usually be purchased at any garage where they have the pipe unions and special tools to make them up. All they need to know is the total length of the pipe, the type of flare at each end with the union and the length and thread of the union.
11 Refitment of the pipe is a straightforward reversal of the removal procedure. If the rigid pipes have been made up it is best to get all the sets (bends) in them before trying to install them. Also, if there are any acute bends, ask your supplier to put these in for you on a special tube bender otherwise you may kink the pipe and thereby decrease the bore area and fluid flow.
12 With the pipes refitted remove the polythene from the reservoir cap and bleed the system as described in Section 18.

18 Bleeding the hydraulic system

Whenever the brake hydraulic system has been overhauled, partially renewed or the level in the reservoir becomes too low, air will have entered the system necessitating bleeding. During the operation the level of hydraulic fluid in the reservoir should not be allowed to fall below half full, otherwise air will be drawn into the system again.
1 Obtain a clean and dry glass jar plastic tubing at least 15 inches (40 cm) long and of suitable diameter to fit tightly over the bleed screw and a supply of hydraulic fluid.
2 Fill the master cylinder reservoir and the bottom inch of the jar with hydraulic fluid.

> **HAYNES HINT** *Take extreme care that no fluid is allowed to come into contact with the paintwork as it acts as a solvent and will damage the finish.*

3 **Single master cylinder type system:** Start bleeding at the front bleed screw which is furthest from the master cylinder and finish at the rear brake nearest to the master cylinder. The correct sequence is as follows: Front left, front right, rear left and rear right.
4 **Tandem master cylinder type system:** Bleed the system supplied by the secondary master cylinder chamber first. Commence bleeding at the front bleed screw and then bleed the diagonally opposite rear brake. The correct sequence is as follows: Front right, rear left, front left, and rear right.
5 **All models:** Having decided the procedure open the first bleed screw about three quarters of a turn. Place one end of the bleed tube over the bleed nipple and submerge the other end of the tube in the fluid in the jar. **Note:** The end of the tube must remain submerged throughout the bleeding operation.
6 An assistant should now pump the brake pedal by first depressing it one full stroke followed by three short but rapid strokes and allowing the pedal to return of its own accord. Check the fluid level in the reservoir. Carefully watch the flow of fluid into the glass jar and. when air bubbles cease to emerge with the fluid during the next down stroke, tighten the bleed screw. Remove the plastic bleed tube and tighten the bleed screw. Do not overtighten. Refit the rubber dust cap supplied. Top up the fluid in the reservoir.
7 Continue bleeding the hydraulic system until all four units have been bled.
8 Sometimes it may be found that the bleed operation for one or more cylinders is taking a considerable time. The cause is probably air being drawn past the bleed screw threads when the screw is loose. To counteract this condition, it is recommended that at the end of each downward stroke the bleed screw be tightened to stop air being drawn past the threads.
9 If after the bleed operation has been completed the brake pedal operation still feels spongy, this is an indication that there is still air in the system or that the master cylinder is faulty.
10 Brake failure valve (dual line system only). Should it be noticed that during the bleed operation and with the ignition switched on the warning light glows, the bleed operation must be continued until all traces of air are removed. Ascertain which wheel caused the light to glow and then attach a tube to the bleed screw at the opposite end of the vehicle and open the bleed screw. Slowly depress the brake pedal and when the light goes out, release the pedal and tighten the bleed screw.
11 Check and top up the reservoir fluid level with fresh hydraulic fluid. Never re-use old brake fluid. Finally check the drum brake adjustment.

Fault finding - braking system

Before diagnosing faults from the following chart, check that any braking irregularities are not caused by:

1 Uneven and incorrect tyre pressures.
2 Incorrect 'mix' of radial and cross-ply tyres.
3 Wear in the steering mechanism.

4 Defects in the suspension and dampers.
5 Misalignment of the body frame.

Pedal travels a long way before the brakes operate

☐ Brake shoes set too far from the drums.

Stopping ability poor even though pedal pressure is firm

☐ Linings and/or drums badly worn or scored
☐ Failure of one circuit dual hydraulic system
☐ One or more wheel hydraulic cylinders seized, resulting in some brake shoes not pressing against the drums
☐ Brake linings contaminated with oil
☐ Wrong type of linings fitted (too hard)
☐ Brake shoes wrongly assembled
☐ Servo unit not functioning (if fitted)

Vehicle veers to one side when the brakes are applied

☐ Brake linings on one side are contaminated with oil
☐ Hydraulic wheel cylinder(s) on one side partially or fully seized
☐ A mixture of lining materials fitted between sides
☐ Unequal wear between sides caused by partially seized wheel cylinders

Pedal feels spongy when the brakes are applied

☐ Air is present in the hydraulic system

Pedal feels springy when the brakes are applied

☐ Brake linings not bedded into the drums (after fitting new ones)
☐ Master cylinder or brake backplate mounting bolts loose
☐ Severe wear in brake drums causing distortion when brakes are applied

Pedal travels right down with little or no resistance and brakes are virtually non-operative

With dual braking systems this would be extraordinary as both systems would have to fail at the same time

☐ Leak in hydraulic systems resulting in lack of pressure for operating wheel cylinders
☐ If no signs of leakage are apparent all the master cylinder internal seals are failing to sustain pressure

Binding, juddering, overheating

☐ One or a combination of causes given in the foregoing sections

Notes

Chapter 10A
Electrical system – petrol models

For modifications, and information applicable to later models, see Supplement at end of manual

Contents

Degrees of difficulty

Easy, suitable for novice with little experience 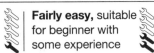	Fairly easy, suitable for beginner with some experience	Fairly difficult, suitable for competent DIY mechanic	Difficult, suitable for experienced DIY mechanic	Very difficult, suitable for expert DIY or professional

Specifications

System type . . . . 12v, positive earth, (negative earth on vehicles from suffix D onwards)

Battery rating . . . . 58 amp/hour

Dynamo

	Series II	Series IIA
Type	Lucas C39	Lucas C40/1
Output	19 amps	22 amps
Cut-in speed.	1450 rpm	1350 rpm
Field resistance	6 ohms	5.9 ohms
Number of brushes.	2	2
Brush length (new)	0.718 inch (18.24 mm)	0.718 inch (18.24 mm)
Minimum brush length	0.28 inch (7.11 mm)	0.28 inch (7.11 mm)
Brush spring pressure (new)	30 oz (850 g)	30 oz (850 g)

Alternator

Type	Lucas 11AC	Lucas 16ACR
Output	45 amps	34 amps
Voltage	12v	12v
Field resistance	3.8 ohms	4.33 ohms
Minimum brush length	0.2 in (5 mm)	0.2 in (5 mm)
Maximum continuous speed	12,500 rpm	12,500 rpm

Starter motor

Make/type	Lucas M418G
Brush spring tension	850 to 1134 g (30 to 40 oz)
Brush minimum length	0.312 in (8.0 mm)
Shaft endfloat	Zero

Fuses

Quantity	Two
Amperage.	35
Protecting:	
A1–A2	Interior lamps, fog lamps, etc, as applicable
A3–A4	Windscreen wiper, fuel tank level unit and stop lights

Bulbs and units

Headlamps with bulbs:	
LHStg Italy	Lucas 410, 12v, 45/40w, Duplo clear
LHStg France	Lucas 411, 12v, 45/40w, Duplo yellow
Headlamps with sealed beam units:	
RHStg	Lucas 54521872 60/45w
LHStg Europe except France and Italy	Lucas 54523079 60/50w
LHStg except Europe.	Lucas 54522231 50/40w
Sidelamps.	Lucas 207,12v, 6w
Stop, tail lamps	Lucas 380, 12v, 21/6w
Flasher lamps.	Lucas 382, 12v, 21w
Rear number plate lamp.	Lucas 989, 12v, 6w
Instrument panel lights.	Lucas 987, 12v, 2.2w MES
Warning lights.	Lucas 987, 12v, 2.2w MES
Warning light, brakes	Lucas 281,12v, 2w
Warning light, flashers	Magnatex GBP 12v, 2.2w
Interior light	Lucas 382, 12v, 21w

Torque wrench setting

	lbf in	kgf m
Alternator through bolts	45 - 50	0.518 - 0.576

1 General description

The electrical system on all Land Rovers is 12 volt. Generally speaking the Series II and IIA models have a positive earth system, while the later Series III models have a negative earth system. However, before fitting a radio or tape player or wiring up a similar device, a careful check must be made to check which battery terminal is connected to earth.

The basic units of the electrical system comprise a lead acid type battery, a dynamo or alternator belt driven from the crankshaft pulley, a starter motor of the inertia engaged drive type and the necessary voltage regulating and cut-out equipment.

Although repair procedures and methods are fully described in this Chapter, in view of the long life of the major electrical components, it is recommended that when a fault does develop, consideration should be given to exchanging the unit for a factory reconditioned assembly rather than renew individual components of a well worn unit.

2 Battery – removal and refitting

1 The battery is located at the front, right hand side of the engine compartment.
2 Disconnect the earth lead from the battery terminal post and then the live lead similarly. The leads are held by either a clamp, which necessitates slackening the clamp bolt and nut, or by a screw driven through an all enclosing shroud.

3 Remove the battery clamp and carefully lift the battery out of its compartment. Hold the battery vertical to ensure that none of the electrolyte is spilled.
4 Refit the battery using the reverse procedure to that of removal. Before refitting the terminals clean off any corrosion and smear them with petroleum jelly (vaseline). Always refit the earth lead last.

3 Battery – maintenance and inspection

1 Normal weekly battery maintenance consists of checking the electrolyte level of each cell to ensure that the separators are covered by 1/4 inch of electrolyte. If the level has fallen, top up the battery using distilled water only. Do not overfill. If a battery is overfilled or any electrolyte spilled, immediately wipe away the excess as electrolyte attacks and corrodes any metal it comes into contact with very rapidly.
2 As well as keeping the terminals clean and covered with petroleum jelly, the top of the battery, and especially the top of the cells, should be kept clean and dry. This helps prevent corrosion and ensures that the battery does not become partially discharged by leakage through dampness and dirt.
3 Once every three months, remove the battery and inspect the battery securing bolts, the battery clamp plate, tray and battery leads for corrosion (white fluffy deposits on the metal which are brittle to touch). If any corrosion is found, clean off the deposits with ammonia and paint over the clean metal with an anti-rust/anti-acid paint.
4 At the same time inspect the battery case

for cracks. If a crack is found, clean and plug it with one of the proprietary compounds marketed by firms for this purpose. If leakage through the crack has been excessive, then it will be necessary to refill the appropriate cell with fresh electrolyte as detailed later. Cracks are frequently caused to the top of battery cases by pouring in distilled water in the middle of winter AFTER instead of BEFORE a run. This gives the water no chance to mix with the electrolyte and so the former freezes and splits the battery case.
5 If topping up the battery becomes excessive and the case has been inspected for cracks that could cause leakage, but none are found, the battery is being overcharged and the voltage regulator will have to be checked and reset.
6 With the battery on the bench at the three monthly interval check, measure its specific gravity with a hydrometer to determine the state of charge and condition of the electrolyte. There should be very little variation between the different cells and if a variation in excess of .025 is present it will be due to either:

a) Loss of electrolyte from the battery at some time caused by spillage or a leak, resulting in a drop in the specific gravity of the electrolyte when the deficiency was replaced with distilled water instead of fresh electrolyte.

b) An internal short circuit caused by buckling of the plates or a similar malady pointing to the likelihood of total battery failure in the near future.

7 The specific gravity of the electrolyte for fully charged conditions at various electrolyte temperatures, is listed in Table A. The specific gravity of a fully discharged battery at different temperatures of the electrolyte is given in Table B.

TABLE A
Specific gravity - battery fully charged
1.268 at 100°F or 38°C electrolyte temperature
1.272 at 90°F or 32°C electrolyte temperature
1.276 at 80°F or 27°C electrolyte temperature
1.280 at 70°F or 21°C electrolyte temperature
1.284 at 60°F or 16°C electrolyte temperature
1.288 at 50°F or 10°C electrolyte temperature
1.292 at 40°F or 4°C electrolyte temperature
1.296 at 30°F or -1.5°C electrolyte temperature

TABLE B
Specific gravity - battery fully discharged
1.098 at 100°F or 38°C electrolyte temperature
1.102 at 90°F or 32°C electrolyte temperature
1.106 at 80°F or 27°C electrolyte temperature
1.110 at 70°F or 21°C electrolyte temperature
1.114 at 60°F or 16°C electrolyte temperature
1.118 at 50°F or 10°C electrolyte temperature
1.122 at 40°F or 4°C electrolyte temperature
1.126 at 30°F or -1.5°C electrolyte temperature

4 Battery electrolyte replenishment

1 If the battery is in a fully charged state and one of the cells maintains a specific gravity reading which is .025 or more lower than the others, and a check of each cell has been made with a voltage meter to check for short circuits (a four to seven second test should give a steady reading of between 1.2 to 1.8 volts), then it is likely that electrolyte has been lost from the cell with the low reading at some time.

2 Top the cell up with a solution of 1 part sulphuric acid to 2.5 parts water. If the cell is already fully topped up draw some electrolyte out of it with an hydrometer.

⚠ *Warning: When mixing the sulphuric acid and water NEVER ADD WATER TO SULPHURIC ACID – always pour the acid slowly onto the water in a glass container. IF WATER IS ADDED TO SULPHURIC ACID IT WILL EXPLODE.*

3 Continue to top up the cell with the freshly made electrolyte and then recharge the battery and check the hydrometer readings.

5 Battery charging

1 In winter time when heavy demand is placed upon the battery, such as when starting from cold, and much of the electrical equipment is continually in use, it is a good idea occasionally to have the battery fully charged from an external source at the rate of 3.5 to 4 amps.

2 Continue to charge the battery at this rate until no further rise in specific gravity is noted over a four hour period.

3 Alternatively, a trickle charger, charging at the rate of 1.5 amps can be safely used overnight.

4 Specially rapid 'boost' charges which are claimed to restore the power of the battery in 1 to 2 hours are not recommended as they can cause serious damage to the battery plates through overheating.

5 While charging the battery note that the temperature of the electrolyte should never exceed 100°F.

6 Alternator - general description and maintenance

1 The Series II and IIA Land Rovers were usually fitted with a dynamo as standard equipment, but had the option of the Lucas 11 AC alternator. The Series III models are equipped with the Lucas 16ACR alternator as a standard fitment.

2 The type 16ACR alternator incorporates its own built-in regulator and is shown in exploded form in Fig. 10.1.

3 Maintenance consists of occasionally wiping away any dirt or oil which may have collected around the apertures in the slip ring end bracket and moulded cover.

4 Check the fan belt tension every 5,000 miles (8,000 km) and adjust as described in Chapter 2 by loosening the mounting bolts. Pull the alternator body away from the engine block, do not use a lever as it will distort the alternator casing.

5 No lubrication is required as the bearings are grease sealed for life.

6 Take extreme care when making circuit connections to a vehicle fitted with an alternator and observe the following:

When making connections to the alternator from a battery always match correct polarity.

Before using electric-arc welding equipment to repair any part of the vehicle, disconnect the connector from the alternator and disconnect the positive battery terminal.

Never start the car with a battery charger connected.

Always disconnect both battery leads before using a mains charger.

If boosting from another battery, always connect in parallel using heavy cable.

It is not recommended that testing of an alternator should be undertaken at home due to the testing equipment required and the possibility of damage occurring during testing. It is best left to automotive electrical specialists.

7 Alternator - removal and refitting

1 Loosen the alternator mounting bracket bolts and strap, push the unit towards the engine block sufficiently to enable the fan belt to be slipped off the alternator pulley.

2 Remove the cable connectors from the alternator and withdraw the mounting bracket bolts. Lift away the alternator.

3 Refitting is a reversal of removal procedure but ensure that the connections are correctly made and that the fan belt is adjusted as described in Chapter 2.

8 Alternator - servicing (type 16ACR)

1 Servicing other than renewal of the brushes is not recommended. The major components should normally last the life of the unit and in the event of failure a factory exchange replacement should be obtained.

2 To renew the brushes, refer to Fig. 10.1, remove the two cover screws and withdraw the moulded cover.

3 Unsolder the three stator connections to the rectifier assembly noting carefully the order of connection.

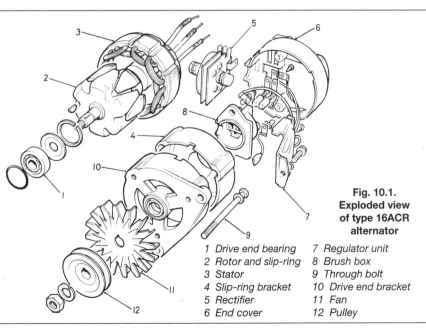

Fig. 10.1. Exploded view of type 16ACR alternator

1 Drive end bearing	7 Regulator unit
2 Rotor and slip-ring	8 Brush box
3 Stator	9 Through bolt
4 Slip-ring bracket	10 Drive end bracket
5 Rectifier	11 Fan
6 End cover	12 Pulley

4 Withdraw the two brush moulding securing screws, slacken the nut on the rectifier assembly bolt.

5 Remove the regulator securing screw and (if fitted) the suppressor cable at the rectifier.

6 Withdraw the brush moulding and rectifier assembly complete with short linking cable.

7 Inspect the brushes which should protrude 2 inch (5 mm) beyond the box moulding when in a free position. Renew if worn to, or below this amount, and do not lose the leaf spring fitted at the side of the inner brush.

8 Should a brush stick, then clean it with petrol or lightly rub with a smooth file.

9 The surfaces of the slip rings should be clean and smooth. If necessary, clean with a petrol moistened cloth. If there is evidence of burning, use very fine glass paper to clean (not emery).

9 Alternator - servicing (type 11AC)

1 As in the case of the type 16 ACR alternator servicing should be restricted to the inspection or renewal of the brushes.

2 After removing the fan and pulley nut, the through bolts may be removed. Mark the position of the end covers relative to the stator and withdraw the drive end cover and rotor together. The brushes may be checked for length and the slip rings cleaned up with fine glass paper.

10 Dynamo - routine maintenance

1 Routine maintenance consists of checking the tension of the fan belt, and lubricating the dynamo rear bearing once every 5,000 miles.

2 The fan belt should be tight enough to ensure no slip between the belt and the dynamo pulley. If a shrieking noise comes from the engine when the unit is accelerated rapidly, it is likely that it is the fan belt slipping. On the other hand, the belt must not be too taut or the bearings will wear rapidly and cause dynamo failure or bearing seizure.

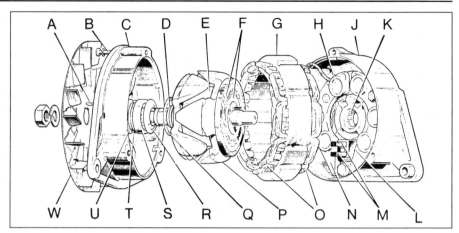

Fig. 10.2. Exploded view of type 11 AC alternator

A Woodruf key
B Through bolt (3)
C Drive end bracket
D Jump ring shroud
E Rotor (field) winding
F Slip rings
G Stator lamination
H Silicon diodes (6)
J Slip-ring end bracket
K Needle roller bearing
L Brush box
M Brushes (2)
N Diode heat sink (2)
O Stator winding
P Rotor
Q Circlip
R Bearing retaining plate
S Ball bearing, drive end
T 'O' ring
U 'O' ring retaining washer
W Fan

Ideally 1/2 inch of total free movement should be available at the fan belt, midway between the fan and the dynamo pulley.

3 To adjust the fan belt tension, slightly slacken the three dynamo retaining bolts, and swing the dynamo on the lower two bolts outwards to increase the tension, and inwards to lower it.

4 It is best to leave the bolts fairly tight so that considerable effort has to be used to move the dynamo, otherwise it is difficult to get the correct setting. If the dynamo is being moved outwards to increase the tension and the bolts have only been slackened a little, a long spanner acting as a lever placed behind the dynamo with the lower end resting against the block, works very well in moving the dynamo outwards. Retighten the dynamo bolts and check that the dynamo pulley is correctly aligned with the fan belt.

5 Lubrication on the dynamo consists of inserting three drops of SAE 30 engine oil in the small oil hole in the centre of the commutator end bracket. This lubricates the rear bearing. The front bearing is pre-packed with grease and requires no attention. See Fig. 10.3.

11 Dynamo - testing in position

1 If, with the engine running, no charge comes from the dynamo or the charge is very low, first check that the fan belt is in place and is not slipping. Then check that the leads from the control box to the dynamo are firmly attached and that one has not come loose from its terminal.

2 The lead from the D terminal on the dynamo should be connected to the D terminal on the control box, and similarly the F terminals on the dynamo and control box should also be connected together. Check that this is so and that the leads have not been incorrectly fitted.

3 Make sure none of the electrical equipment

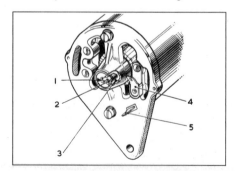

Fig. 10.3. End view of dynamo

1 Lubrication hole
2 Felt ring
3 Bearing bush
4 Terminal connector
5 Terminal connector

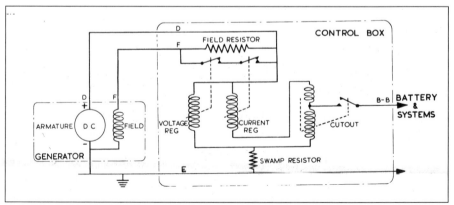

Fig. 10.4. Wiring diagram for dynamo charging system

(such as the lights or radio) is on, and then pull the leads off the dynamo terminals marked D and F. Join the dynamo terminals together with a short length of wire.

4 Attach to the centre of this length of wire the negative clips of a 0 - 20 volts voltmeter and run the other clip to earth on the dynamo yoke. Start the engine and allow it to idle at approximately 750 rpm. At this speed the dynamo should give a reading of about 15 volts on the voltmeter. There is no point in raising the engine speed above a fast idle as the reading will then be inaccurate.

5 If no reading is recorded, then check the brushes and brush connections. If a very low reading of approximately 1 volt is observed, then the field winding may be suspect.

6 If a reading of between 4 to 6 volts is recorded, it is likely that the armature winding is at fault.

7 If the voltmeter shows a good reading, then with the temporary link still in position, connect both leads from the control box to D and F on the dynamo ID to D and F to F). Release the lead from the D terminal at the control box end and clip one lead from the voltmeter to the end of the cable, and the other lead to a good earth. With the engine running at the same speed as previously, an identical voltage to that recorded at the dynamo should be noted on the voltmeter. If no voltage is recorded, then there is a break in the wire. If the voltage is the same as recorded at the dynamo, then check the F lead in similar fashion. If both readings are the same as at the dynamo, then it will be necessary to test the control box.

8 Fig. 1 0.4 shows the system circuit in diagrammatic form.

12 Dynamo -
removal and refitting

1 Slacken the two dynamo retaining bolts, and the nut on the sliding link and move the dynamo in towards the engine so that the fan belt can be removed (photo).

2 Disconnect the two leads from the dynamo terminals.

3 Remove the nut from the sliding link bolt and remove the two upper bolts. The dynamo Is then free to be lifted away from the engine.

4 Refitting is a reversal of the above

12.1 Dynamo top securing bracket

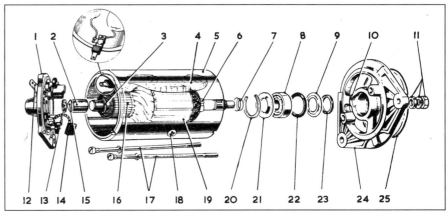

Fig. 10.5. Exploded view of dynamo

1 Commutator end bracket	10 Extractor notch	18 Pole shoe screw
2 Bearing bush	11 Nut and washers	19 Armature
3 Fibre washer	12 Terminal D	20 Circlip
4 Field winding	13 Felt ring	21 Bearing retaining plate
5 Yoke	14 Carbon brush	22 Pressure ring
6 Armature shaft	15 Felt ring retainer	23 Felt ring
7 Retaining cup	16 Commutator	24 Drive end bracket
8 Drive end bearing	17 Through bolts	25 Pulley
9 Pressure ring plate		

procedure. Do not finally tighten the retaining bolts and the nut of the sliding link until the fan belt has been tensioned.

13 Dynamo -
dismantling and inspection

1 Mount the dynamo in a vice and unscrew and remove the two through bolts from the commutator end bracket (1) (Fig. 10.5)

2 Mark the commutator end bracket and the dynamo casing so the end bracket can be refitted in its original position. Pull the end bracket off the armature shaft. **Note:** Some versions of the dynamo may have a raised pip on the end bracket which locates in a recess on the edge of the casing. If so, marking the end bracket and casing is not necessary. A pip may also be found on the drive end bracket at the opposite end of the casing.

3 Lift the two brush springs and draw the brushes out of the brush holders.

4 Measure the brushes and, if worn down to 0.28 in (7.1 mm) or less, undo the screws holding the brush leads to the end bracket. Take off the brushes complete with leads.

5 If no locating pip can be found, mark the drive end bracket and the dynamo casing so that the drive end bracket can be replaced in its original position. Then pull the drive end bracket complete with armature out of the casing.

6 Check the condition of the ball bearing in the drive end plate by firmly holding the plate and noting if there is visible side movement of the armature shaft in relation to the end plate. If play is present, the armature assembly must be separated from the end plate. If the bearing

is sound there is no need to carry out the work described in the following two paragraphs.

7 Hold the armature in one hand (mount it carefully in a vice if preferred) and undo the nut holding the pulley and fan in place. Pull off the pulley and fan.

8 Next remove the Woodruff key from its slot in the armature shaft and also the bearing locating ring.

9 Place the drive end bracket across the open jaws of a vice with the armature downwards and gently tap the armature shaft from the bearing in the end plate with the aid of a suitable drift. Support the armature so that it does not fall to the ground.

10 Carefully inspect the armature and check it for open or short circuited windings. It a good indication of an open circuited armature when the commutator segments are burnt. If the armature has short circuited the commutator segments will be very badly burnt, and the over-heated armature windings badly discoloured. If open or short circuits are suspected substitute the suspect armature with a new one.

11 Check the resistance of the field coils. To do this, connect an ohmmeter between the field terminal and the yoke and note the reading on the ohmmeter which should be about 6 ohms. If the ohmmeter reading is infinity this indicates an open circuit in the field winding. If the ohmmeter reading is below 5 ohms this indicates that one of the field coils is faulty and must be renewed.

12 Field coil renewal involves the use of a wheel operated screwdriver, soldering iron, caulking and riveting and this operation is considered to be beyond the scope of most owners. Therefore, if the field coils are at fault either purchase a rebuilt dynamo, or take the casing to a Leyland dealer or electrical

engineering works for new field coils to be fitted.

13 Next check the condition of the commutator (arrowed). If it is dirty and blackened, as shown, clean it with a petrol dampened rag. If the commutator is in good condition the surface will be smooth and quite free from pits or burnt areas, and the insulated segments clearly defined.

14 If, after the commutator has been cleaned, pits and burnt spots are still present, wrap a strip of glass paper round the commutator taking great care to move the commutator 1/4 of a turn every ten rubs till it is thoroughly clean.

15 In extreme cases of wear the commutator can be mounted in a lathe and with the lathe turning at high speed, a very fine cut may be taken off the commutator. Then polish the commutator with glass paper. If the commutator has worn so that the insulators between the segments are level with the top of the segments, then undercut the insulators to a depth of 1/32 in (0.8 mm). This applies to fabricated commutators only, Do NOT undercut moulded commutators. (See Fig. 10.6). The best tool to use for this purpose is half a hacksaw blade ground to the thickness of the insulator, and with the handle end of the blade covered in insulating tape to make it comfortable to hold.

16 Check the bush bearing in the commutator end bracket for wear, by noting if the armature spindle rocks when placed in it. If worn, it must be renewed.

17 The bush bearing can be removed by a suitable extractor or by screwing a 5/8 in (15.87 mm) tap four or five times into the bush. The tap complete with bush is then pulled out of the end bracket.

18 Note: The bush bearing is made of a porous bronze material which needs to be saturated in engine oil before use. Oil can be forced through it, before installation, by blocking one end with a thumb, filling it with oil and squeezing it through the material by forcing a finger in at the other end. Otherwise, soak it in oil for several hours, If the oil is hot it will saturate the material more quickly.

19 Carefully fit the new bush into the end plate, pressing it in until the end of the bearing is flush with the inner side of the end plate. If available, press the bush in with a smooth shouldered mandrel the same diameter as the armature shaft.

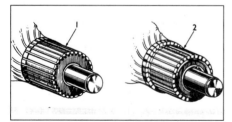

Fig. 10.6. Different types of dynamo commutators

1 Moulded type   2 Fabricated type

14 Dynamo - repair and reassembly

1 To renew the ball bearing fitted to the drive end bracket, drill out the rivets which hold the bearing retainer plate to the end bracket and lift off the plate (see Fig. 10.7) . On later models the bearing is held by a circlip which is quite simply removed to release the bearing from the end plate.

2 Press out the bearing from the end bracket and remove the corrugated and felt washers from the bearing housing.

3 Thoroughly clean the bearing housing and the new bearing, and pack with high melting point grease.

4 Place the felt washer and corrugated washer, in that order, in the end bracket bearing housing. On later models when the bearing is retained by a circlip there is a felt ring, retaining washer and pressure ring to be assembled in the housing before the bearing.

5 Then fit the new bearing.

6 Gently tap the bearing into place with the aid of a suitable drift.

7 Refit the bearing plate and fit three new rivets (or fit the collar and circlip) .

8 Open up the rivets with the aid of a suitable punch.

9 Finally peen over the open end of the rivets with the aid of a ball pein hammer.

10 Refit the drive end bracket to the armature shaft. Do not try and force the bracket on but, with the aid of a suitable socket abutting the bearing, tap the bearing on gently, so pulling the end bracket down with it.

11 Slide the spacer up the shaft and refit the Woodruff key.

12 Refit the fan and pulley and then fit the spring washer and nut and tighten the latter. The drive bracket end of the dynamo is now fully assembled .

13 If the brushes are a little worn and are to be used again then ensure that they are placed in the same holders from which they were removed. When refitting brushes, either new or old, check that they move freely in their holders.

> *If either brush sticks, clean with a petrol moistened rag and if still stiff, lightly polish the sides of the brush with a very fine file until the brush moves quite freely in its holder.*

14 Tighten the two retaining screws and washers which hold the wire leads to the brushes in place.

15 It is far easier to slip the end piece with brushes over the commutator if the brushes are raised in their holders, and held in this position by the pressure of the springs resting against their flanks.

16 Refit the armature to the casing and then the commutator end plate, and screw up the two through bolts.

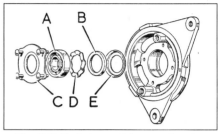

Fig. 10.7. Early type of dynamo bearing retainer

A Bearing   *D Corrugated washer*
B Felt washer   *E Retaining washer*
C Bearing retaining plate

17 Finally, hook the ends of the two springs off the flanks of the brushes and onto their heads so that the brushes are forced down into contact with the armature.

15 Starter motor - general description

The starter motor is mounted on the right-hand lower side of the engine backplate and is held in position by two bolts which also clamp the bellhousing flange. The motor is of the four field coil, four pole piece type and utilizes four spring loaded commutator brushes. Two of these brushes are earthed, and the other two are insulated and attached to the field coil ends.

Starter motor - testing in engine

1 If the starter motor fails to operate then check the condition of the battery by turning on the headlamps. If they glow brightly for several seconds and then gradually dim, the battery is in an uncharged condition.

2 If the headlamps glow brightly and it is obvious that the battery is in good condition then check the tightness of the battery wiring connections (and in particular the earth lead from the battery terminal to its connection on the body frame). Check the tightness of the connections at the relay switch and at the starter motor. Check the wiring with a voltmeter for breaks or shorts.

3 If the wiring is in order then check that the starter motor switch is operating, To do this press the rubber button in the centre of the relay switch under the bonnet (later models only). If it is working the starter motor will be heard to 'click' as it tries to rotate. Alternatively check it with a voltmeter.

4 If the battery is fully charged, the wiring in order, and the switch working and the starter motor fails to operate then it will have to be removed from the vehicle for examination. Before this is done, however, ensure that the starter pinion has not jammed in mesh with the flywheel. Check this by turning the square end of the armature shaft with a spanner. This will free the pinion if it is stuck in engagement with the flywheel teeth.

16 Starter motor - removal and refitting

1 First remove the bonnet as described in Chapter 1 and disconnect both battery terminals.

2 Unscrew the securing bolts and remove the heat shield from the exhaust/inlet manifold.

3 Remove the three nuts retaining the front exhaust pipe to the manifold and carefully move the pipe to one side. If necessary remove the clamp securing the lower end of the pipe.

4 Disconnect the electrical lead from the starter motor.

5 Unscrew and remove the two nuts that hold the starter motor to the engine backplate and the flywheel housing flange.

6 Lift the starter motor out of the engine compartment.

7 Refitting is a straightforward reversal of the removal procedure.

17 Starter motor - dismantling and reassembly

1 With the starter motor on the bench, loosen the screw on the cover band and slip the cover band off. With a piece of wire bent into the shape of a hook, lift back each of the brush springs in turn and check the movement of the brushes in their holders by pulling on the flexible connectors. If the brushes are so worn that their faces do not rest against the commutator, or if the ends of the brush leads are exposed on their working face, they must be renewed.

2 If any of the brushes tend to stick in their holders, then wash them with a petrol moistened cloth and, if necessary, lightly polish the sides of the brush with a very fine file, until the brushes move quite freely in their holders.

3 If the surface of the commutator is dirty or blackened, clean it with a petrol dampened rag. Secure the starter motor in a vice and

check it by connecting a heavy gauge cable between the starter motor terminal and a 12 volt battery.

4 Connect the cable from the other battery terminal to earth in the starter motor body. If the motor turns at high speed it is in good order.

5 If the starter motor still fails to function or if it is wished to renew the brushes, then it is necessary to further dismantle the motor.

6 Lift the brush springs with the wire hook and lift all four brushes out of their holders one at a time.

7 Remove the terminal nuts and washers from the terminal post on the commutator end bracket.

8 Unscrew the two through bolts which hold the end plates together and pull off the commutator end bracket. Also remove the driving end bracket which will come away complete with the armature.

9 At this stage if the brushes are to be renewed, their flexible connectors must be unsoldered and the connectors of new brushes soldered in their place. Check that the new brushes move freely in their holders as detailed above. If cleaning the commutator with petrol fails to remove all the burnt areas and spots, then wrap a piece of glass paper round the commutator and rotate the armature.

10 If the commutator is very badly worn, remove the drive gear as detailed in the following Section. Then mount the armature in a lathe and, with the lathe turning at high speed, take a very fine cut out of the commutator and finish the surface by polishing with glass paper. **Do not undercut the mica insulators between the commutator segments.**

11 With the starter motor dismantled, test the four field coils for an open circuit. Connect a 12-volt battery with a 12 volt bulb in one of the leads between the field terminal post and the tapping point of the field coils to which the brushes are connected. An open circuit is proved by the bulb not lighting.

12 If the bulb lights, it does not necessarily mean that the field coils are in order, as there is a possibility that one of the coils will be earthing to the starter yoke or pole shoes.

To check this, remove the lead from the brush connector and place it against a clean portion of the starter yoke. If the bulb lights, the field coils are earthing. Renewal of the field coils calls for the use of a wheel operated screwdriver, a soldering iron, caulking and riveting operations and is beyond the scope of the majority of owners. The starter yoke should be taken to a reputable electrical engineering works for new field coils to be fitted. Alternatively, purchase an exchange Lucas starter motor.

13 If the armature is damaged this will be evident after visual inspection. Look for signs of burning, discoloration, and for conductors that have lifted away from the commutator. Reassembly is a straightforward reversal of the dismantling procedure.

18 Starter motor drive - servicing

1 On earlier models the starter motor drive gear is secured on the shaft by a special nut and split pin.

2 Using a pair of pliers, remove the split pin and undo the nut.

3 Slide off the spring, thrust washer, screwed sleeve and pinion, second thrust washer, and smaller spring and sleeve (see Fig. 10.8).

4 On later types of starter motor the drive gear is retained on the shaft by a spring clip.

5 To remove the clip it is necessary to compress the spring using a special spring compressor obtainable either from a Leyland dealer or Accessory shop. If a spring compressor is not available it is possible to do the job using a vice and a piece of tubing.

6 After removing the spring clip, withdraw the drive gear components and lay them out in the correct order of removal.

7 Clean the components in petrol and examine them for wear. If there are any doubts regarding their condition it is best to renew the complete drive assembly.

8 Refit the drive assembly to the starter shaft using the reversal of the removal procedure.

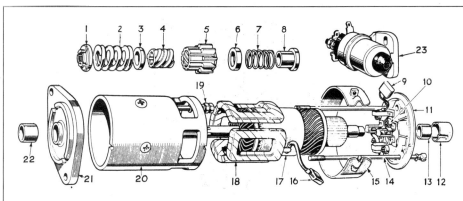

1 Starter drive nut	12 Cover
2 Starter drive spring	13 Bush
	14 Bolt
3 Thrust washer	15 Brush cover
4 Screwed sleeve	16 Brush
5 Pinion	17 Field coil connection
6 Thrust washer	
7 Spring	18 Field coil
8 Collar	19 Terminal
9 Brush	20 Yoke
10 Brush spring	21 Drive end cover
11 Commutator end bracket	22 Bush
	23 Starter solenoid

Fig.10.8. Exploded view of starter motor

19 Starter motor solenoid - description

1 Earlier Land Rovers were not fitted with a starter solenoid, the starting circuit being closed by the contacts of the push-type starter switch.

2 Later models have a solenoid in the starter circuit located in the engine compartment. Operation of older solenoids can be checked by pressing the rubber cover on the end of the solenoid thus manually over-riding the starter switch circuit.

3 If it is suspected that the solenoid is faulty, the best method is to substitute it for a new one. It is not possible to repair the solenoid.

20 Voltage control box (dynamo only) - general description

The control box is positioned on the engine compartment bulkhead and is comprised of three units; two separate vibrating armature type single contact regulators and a cut-out relay. One of the regulators is sensitive to changes in current and the other to changes in voltage.

Adjustment can only be made with a special tool which resembles a screwdriver, with a multi-toothed blade. This can be obtained through Lucas agents.

The regulators control the output from the dynamo depending on the state of the battery and the demands of the electrical equipment, and ensures that the battery is not overcharged. The cut-out is really an automatic switch and connects the dynamo to the battery when the dynamo is turning fast enough to produce a charge. Similarly, it disconnects the battery from the dynamo when the engine is idling or stationary so that the battery does not discharge through the dynamo.

21 Cut-out and regulator contacts - maintenance

1 Every 12,000 miles check the cut-out and regulator contacts. If they are dirty, rough or burnt place a piece of fine glass paper **(do not use emery paper or carborundum paper)** between the cut-out contacts, close them manually and draw the glass paper through several times.

2 Clean the regulator contacts in exactly the same way, but use emery or carborundum paper and not glass paper. Carefully clean both sets of contacts from all traces of dust with a rag moistened in methylated spirits.

22 Current regulator - adjustment

1 The regulator requires very little attention during its service life, and should there be any reason to suspect its correct functioning, tests of all circuits should be made to ensure that they are not the reason for the trouble.

2 These checks include the tension of the fan belt, to make sure that it is not slipping and so providing only a very low charge rate. The battery should be carefully checked for possible low charge rate due to a faulty cell, or corroded battery connections.

3 The leads from the generator may have been crossed during refitting, and if this is the case then the regulator points will have stuck together as soon as the dynamo starts to charge. Check for loose or broken leads from the dynamo to the regulator.

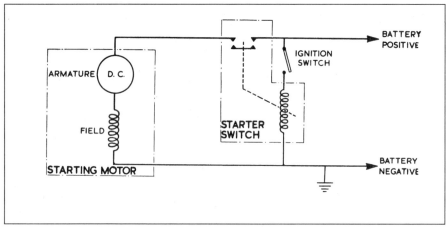

Fig. 10.9. Starter motor diagram (solenoid switch)

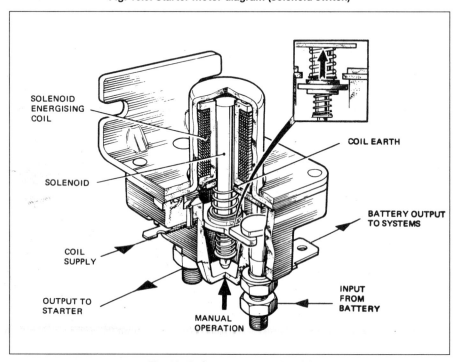

Fig. 10.10. Starter motor solenoid

Later solenoids do not have a manual operation feature

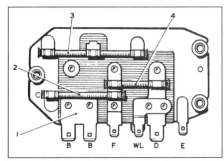

Fig. 10.11. Underside of electrical control box

1 Terminal plate B-B
3 Swamp resistor
2 Field parallel resistor (when fitted)
4 Field series resistor

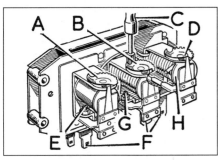

Fig. 10.12. Current voltage regulator

A Adjustment cam of voltage regulator
B Adjustment cam of current regulator
C Special setting tool
D Adjustment cam of cut-out relay
E Adjustable contact of voltage regulator
F 'Lucar' connection terminals
G Adjustable contact of current regulator
H Core face of cut-out relay

4 If, after a thorough check, it is considered advisable to test the regulator, this should only be carried out by an electrician who is well acquainted with the correct method, proceed by reference to Fig. 10.11.

5 Pull off the Lucar connections from the two adjacent control box terminals 'B'. To start the engine it will now be necessary to join together the ignition and battery leads with a suitable wire.

6 Connect a 0.-30 volt voltmeter between terminal 'D' on the control box and terminal 'WL', Start the engine and run it at 2000 rpm. The reading on the voltmeter should be steady and lie between the limits detailed in the Specifications.

7 If the reading is unsteady this may be due to dirty contacts. If the reading is outside the specified limits stop the engine and adjust the voltage regulator in the following manner.

8 Take off the control box cover and start and run the engine at 2000 rpm. Using the correct tool turn the voltage adjustment cam anticlockwise to raise the setting and clockwise to lower it. To check that the setting is correct, stop the engine, and then start it and run it at 2000 rpm noting the reading. Refit the connections to the 'WL' and 'D' terminals.

9 The output from the current regulator should equal the maximum output from the dynamo which is 19 amps (22 amps model C40-I). To test this it is necessary to bypass the cut-out by holding the contacts together.

10 Remove the cover from the control box and with a bulldog clip hold the cut-out contacts together (see Fig. 10.12).

11 Pull off the wires from the adjacent terminals 'B' and connect a 0.40 moving coil ammeter to one of the terminals and to the leads.

12 All the other load connections including the ignition must be made to the battery.

13 Turn on all the lights and other electrical accessories and run the engine at 2000 rpm. The ammeter should give a steady reading between 19 and 25 amps. If the needle flickers it is likely that the points are dirty. If the reading is

too low turn the special Lucas tool clockwise to raise the setting and anticlockwise to lower it.

23 Cut-out - adjustment

1 Check the voltage required to operate the cut-out by connecting a voltmeter between the control box terminals 'D' and 'WL'. Remove the control box cover, start the engine and gradually increase its speed until the cut-outs close. This should occur when the reading is between 12.6 to 13.4 volts.

2 If the reading is outside these limits turn the cut-out adjusting cam, (Fig. 10.12) by means of the adjusting tool a fraction at a time clockwise to raise the voltage and anticlockwise to lower it.

3 To adjust the drop off voltage bend the fixed contact blade carefully. The adjustment to the cut-out should be completed within 30 seconds of starting the engine otherwise heat build-up from the shunt coil will affect the readings.

4 If the cut-out fails to work, clean the contacts, and, if there is still no response, renew the cut-out and regulator unit,

5 Air gap settings of the control box are accurately set during manufacture and should not be altered.

24 Fuses

1 Earlier models are equipped with a fuse box located on the engine compartment bulkhead. Two fuses are used; fuse no. A3-A4 protects the wiper, fuel tank unit and stop light circuits while fuse no. A1-A2 protects the interior and auxiliary lighting circuits.

2 Two spare fuses are carried in the fuse box and only 35 amp cartridge fuses should be used when renewing.

3 The fuse box on later models is attached on the underside of the steering column nacelle and contains four fuses (see Fig. 10.14).

4 Fuse no. 7-8 protects the fuel gauge, water gauge and stop light circuits, fuse no. 5-6 protects the direction indicator and wiper circuits while fuse no. 1-2 protects the lighting circuits (fuse no. 3-4 is a spare circuit),

5 If a fuse blows always replace it with a 35 amp fuse. If the trouble persists, refer to the appropriate wiring diagram and check the affected circuit for earthing faults.

25 Flasher circuit - fault tracing and rectification

1 The flasher unit is located behind the instrument panel. To gain access to it, withdraw the instrument panel as described in Section 37. Pull off the electrical leads,

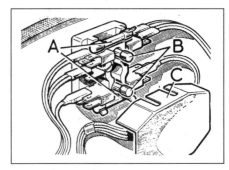

Fig. 10.13. Fuse box (earlier models)

A Fuses   B Spare fuses   C Cover

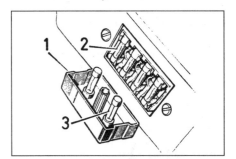

Fig. 10.14. Fuse box (later type)

1 Cover   2 Fuses   3 Spare fuses

undo the securing screw (earlier models) and remove the flasher unit.

The flasher unit is a sealed component and cannot be repaired.

2 If the flasher unit fails to operate, or works very slowly or very rapidly, check out the flasher indicator circuit as detailed below, before assuming there is a fault in the unit itself.

3 Examine the direction indicator bulbs front and rear for broken filaments.

4 If the external flashers are working but the internal flasher warning light has ceased to function, check the filament of the warning bulb and renew if necessary.

5 With the aid of the wiring diagram check all the flasher circuit connections if a flasher bulb is sound but does not work.

6 In the event of total direction indicator failure, check the appropriate fuse.

7 If all other items check out then the flasher unit itself is faulty and must be renewed.

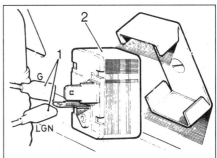

Fig. 10.15. Flasher unit (later type)

1 Wiring connectors   2 Flasher unit

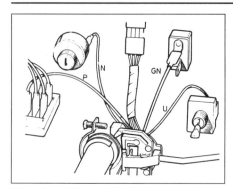

Fig. 10.16. Wiring connections on the later type flasher/dipswitch

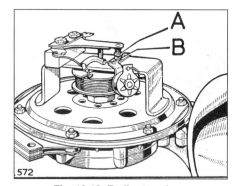

Fig. 10.18. Earlier type horn

A Adjustable contact   B Locknut

26 Flasher switch - removal and refitting

1 First withdraw the instrument panel as described in Section 37.
2 Disconnect the lead from the flasher unit and the main harness at the rear of the instrument panel.
3 Withdraw the flasher switch leads through the grommet in the side of the instrument box and release the retaining clips on the steering column.
4 Remove the securing bolt from the flasher switch bracket and withdraw the switch and bracket from the steering column (see Fig. 10.17).

28.2 Removing the horn button

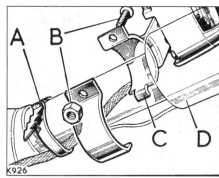

Fig. 10.17. Flasher switch attachment clamp (earlier type shown)

A Wiring clip   C Flasher switch
B Clamp bolt   D Steering column

Fig. 10.19. Later type horn

Note: On later models the flasher switch also operates the horn and headlight dip facility. The removal procedure is basically the same but it is necessary to remove both halves of the switch shroud from the steering column.
5 The flasher switch cannot be repaired and if faulty must be renewed.

27 Horn - adjustment

1 The horn is located behind the radiator grille. Remove the grille as described in Chapter 2.
2 Disconnect the electrical leads from the snap connectors (or horn terminals), remove

29.1 Headlamp with rim removed

the securing bolts and lift out the horn.
3 To adjust the earlier type Lucas horn, first remove the securing clip and lift off the domed cover.
4 Clean the contact points and adjust them until they are almost touching, then turn the adjusting screw one half a turn to increase the gap (see Fig. 10.18).
5 Check the operation of the horn and, if unsatisfactory, a new one should be fitted.
6 To adjust the horn on Series IIA models remove the domed cover and turn the adjustment screw a small amount either way until a good note is obtained. To avoid blowing the fuse the horn should be connected directly to the battery.
7 The latest type horns have no adjustment and the only check necessary is to ensure the wiring connectors are clean and tight.
8 Refit the horn using the reversal of the removal procedure.

28 Horn button - removal and refitting

1 Series II and IIA models are fitted with a horn push button in the centre of the steering wheel.
2 To remove the button, carefully prise out the centre section of the steering wheel using a thin-bladed screwdriver (photo).
3 Check the button for correct operation and clean the contacts.
4 Refit the horn assembly using the reverse procedure to removal.

29 Headlamps mounted in grille panel - removal and refitting

1 Remove the screw from the bottom of the headlamp rim and carefully prise off the rim and rubber dust cover (photo).
2 Press the headlamp unit inwards and rotate it anticlockwise to release it from the spring-loaded adjustment screws.
3 Turn the bulb holder anticlockwise to release it and remove the bulb.

29.4a Removing headlamp assembly

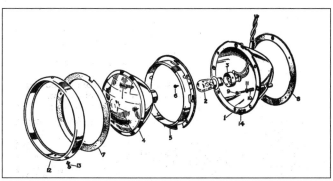

Fig. 10.20. Headlamp assembly (earlier models)

1 Body for headlamp
2 Bulb
3 Adaptor for bulb
4 Light unit
5 Rim complete for light unit
6 Special screw for light unit rim
7 Rubber gasket for headlamp rim
8 Gasket
9 Special screw. Light unit adjustment
10 Spring. Light unit adjustment
11 Cup washer. Light unit adjustment
12 Rim for headlamp
13 Screw. Retaining rim
14 Spire nut. Retaining rim

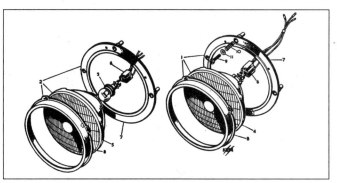

Fig. 10.21. Headlamp assemblies fitted to later models

1 Headlamp complete, sealed beam
2 Headlamp complete
3 Bulb
4 Light unit, sealed beam
5 Light unit
6 Adaptor and leads for headlamp
7 Rim for light unit
8 Rim for headlamp

9 Screw. For light unit adjustment and fitting headlamp to front grille
10 Spring. For light unit adjustment and fitting headlamp to front grille
11 Fibre washer. For light unit adjustment and fitting headlamp to front grille

4 If the headlamp is the sealed beam type, remove the three screws securing the rim to the headlamp shell, support the light unit and pull off the electrical plug from the rear of the unit (see photos).

5 Refit the headlamp assembly using the reverse procedure to removal.

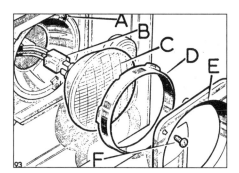

Fig. 10.22. Removing the sealed beam unit

A Screws for rim
B Connector, electrical leads
C Light unit
D Rim for headlamp
E Bezel
F Screws for bezel

30 Headlamps (wing mounted) - removal and refitting

1 Referring to Fig. 10.22, remove the four screws securing the headlamp bezel to the wing.
2 Slacken the three screws securing the chrome rim, turn it enough to clear the screw heads and lift off.
3 Withdraw the light unit and disconnect the electrical plug (or bulb holder) .
4 Renew the bulb or light unit as applicable and refit the headlamp assembly using the reversal of the removal procedure.

31 Headlamp beam - adjustment

1 The headlights may be adjusted for both vertical and horizontal beam position by the screws located as shown in Fig. 10.23 and photo.
2 They should be set so that on full or high beam, the beams are set slightly below

parallel with a level road surface. Do not forget that the beam position is affected by how the vehicle is normally loaded for night driving and set the beams loaded to this condition. Before adjustment is commenced check that the tyre pressures are correct.

3 Although this adjustment can be approximately set at home using a vertical wall it is recommended that this be left to the local garage who will have the necessary optical equipment to do the job more accurately.

32 Front and rear sidelights - removal and refitting

1 The method of removing the front and rear side, flasher and stop lamps is the same on all vehicles.
2 Remove the two retaining screws and ease the lens out of the rubber moulding (photo).
3 Renew the bulb if necessary and refit the lens into the moulding ensuring the beaded lip fits snugly around the base of the lens.
4 Refit the two retaining screws taking care not to overtighten them.

29.4b Electrical plug at rear of sealed beam unit

31.1 Headlamp vertical adjusting screw (earlier models)

32.2 Removing a rear light lens

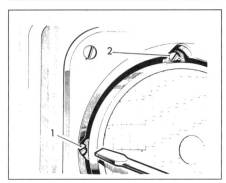

Fig. 10.23. Headlamp adjustment screws (later models)

1 Horizontal adjustment screw
2 Vertical adjustment screw

33 Windscreen wiper motor (early type) - removal and refitting

1 The Series II Land Rovers were fitted with a single wiper arm driven directly from a motor located below the windscreen (photo).
2 To remove the motor, slacken the nut on the wiper arm spindle, give it a sharp tap to release the collets and withdraw the complete arm and blade (photo).
3 Undo the securing nuts and remove the wiper arm stop and rubber mounting block from the front of the windscreen.
4 Withdraw the motor from inside the cab and retrieve the brass spindle bushes.

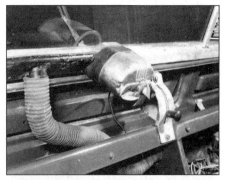

33.1 Location of earlier type wiper motor

33.2 Removing the wiper blade and arm (earlier models)

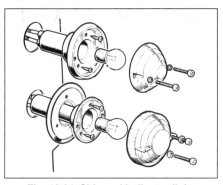

Fig. 10.24. Side and indicator light assemblies

5 Refit the motor using the reversal of the removal procedure. Before refitting the wiper arm and blade set the motor to the parked position and refit the arm accordingly.

34 Windscreen wiper motor (early type) - servicing

1 If the movement of the wiper arm is erratic or stops altogether, remove the motor as described previously and lubricate the spindle bushes with thin oil.
2 With the motor withdrawn from the screen but the wires still connected, switch on the ignition and motor, and check that the spindle moves backwards and forwards quite freely.

If, on refitting the motor, arm and blade, the performance is still unsatisfactory, the fault probably lies in the armature windings and it is best to obtain a replacement motor.

35 Windscreen wiper motor end linkage (twin wipers) - removal and refitting

1 Later versions of the Land Rover are fitted with a wiper motor located in the glove compartment behind a cover plate which drives the two wiper arms via a cable and two wheel boxes (see Fig. 10.25).
2 To remove the motor, first disconnect the battery earth terminal and remove the dash cover plate, secured by four screws (Fig. 10.26).
3 Unscrew the nut securing the drive cable outer tube to the motor.
4 On earlier versions remove the four bolts securing the motor mounting plate to the side of the glove box.

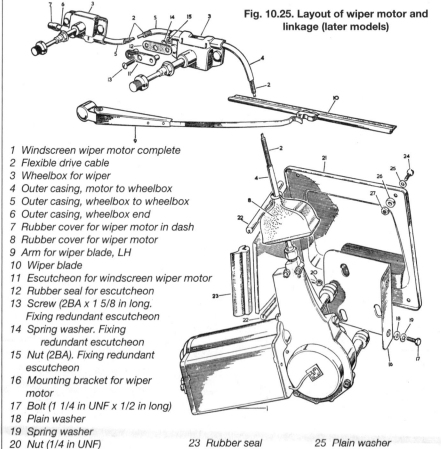

Fig. 10.25. Layout of wiper motor and linkage (later models)

1 Windscreen wiper motor complete
2 Flexible drive cable
3 Wheelbox for wiper
4 Outer casing, motor to wheelbox
5 Outer casing, wheelbox to wheelbox
6 Outer casing, wheelbox end
7 Rubber cover for wiper motor in dash
8 Rubber cover for wiper motor
9 Arm for wiper blade, LH
10 Wiper blade
11 Escutcheon for windscreen wiper motor
12 Rubber seal for escutcheon
13 Screw (2BA x 1 5/8 in long. Fixing redundant escutcheon
14 Spring washer. Fixing redundant escutcheon
15 Nut (2BA). Fixing redundant escutcheon
16 Mounting bracket for wiper motor
17 Bolt (1 1/4 in UNF x 1/2 in long)
18 Plain washer
19 Spring washer
20 Nut (1/4 in UNF)
21 Cover plate for wiper motor
22 Rubber finisher
23 Rubber seal
24 Screw (2BA x 1/2 in long)
25 Plain washer
26 Distance washer
27 Nut (2BA)

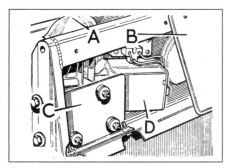

Fig. 10.26. Location of wiper motor (later models)

A *Rubber cover for wiper*
B *Cover for glove box aperture*
C *Mounting bracket for wipe*
D *Wiper motor*

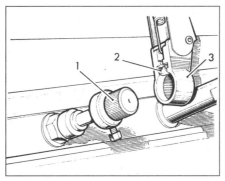

Fig. 10.27. Wiper arm attachment point (later models)

1 *Splined adaptor* 3 *Wiper arm*
2 *Spring clip*

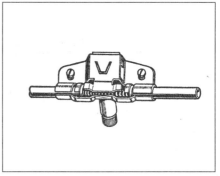

Fig. 10.28. Correct assembly of wiper drive box

Fig. 10.29. Exploded view of wiper motor

1 *Drive box*	12 *End cover*
2 *Jet and bush assembly*	13 *Brushes*
	14 *Armature*
3 *Nut*	15 *Circlip*
4 *Rigid tubing - right-hand side*	16 *Washer*
	17 *Final drive wheel*
5 *Wiper arm*	18 *Cable rack*
6 *Blade*	19 *Rigid tubing- left-hand side*
7 *Wiper arm*	
8 *Field coil assembly*	20 *Spacer*
	21 *Connecting rod*
9 *Brush gear*	22 *Circlip*
10 *Tension spring & retainers*	23 *Parking switch contact*
11 *Brush gear retainer*	24 *Rigid tubing - centre section*

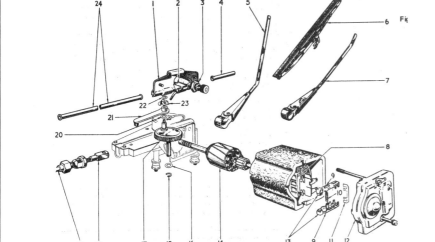

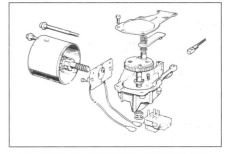

Fig. 10.30. Exploded view of latest type wiper motor

5 Prise off each wiper arm from the drive spindles and then withdraw the motor complete with the inner drive cable.

6 On later models the motor is secured by two bolts in the glove box and a nut plate on the engine compartment bulkhead. After removing these, withdraw the motor and inner cable as described previously.

7 The two wiper arm drive boxes can be removed by first unscrewing the six screws securing the windscreen lower panel and lifting off the panel.

8 Remove the wiper arms and then slacken the lockscrew and pull off the splined adaptors from the spindles (see Fig. 10.27).

9 Remove the rubber grommet (or escutcheon plate) from the spindles and undo the spindle locknuts.

10 Remove the motor and inner cable as described previously.

11 The drive boxes can now be withdrawn from inside the cab complete with the cable tubes.

12 Undo the two securing screws and remove the cover plate from each drive box. Check the gears and cable for wear and renew if necessary.

13 Lubricate the spindles, gears and the inside of the cable tubes with grease.

14 Reassemble the tubes onto the drive boxes and secure with the cover plate. Make sure the flared ends of the tubes are correctly positioned as shown in Fig. 10.28.

15 Refit the drive boxes and motor using the reverse procedure to that of removal. Grease the inner drive cable before sliding it through the outer tubes.

16 After reconnecting the battery terminal and motor electrical leads, switch the motor on and then off so that the spindles stop in the parked position and then refit the wiper arms and blades in the parked position.

36 Windscreen wiper motor (later type) - overhaul

1 Mark the domed cover in relation to the flat gearbox lid, undo the four screws holding the gearbox lid in place and lift off the lid and domed cover.

2 Pull off the small circlip and remove the limit switch wiper. The connecting rod and cable

rack (18) can now be lifted off. Take particular note of the spacer located between the final drive wheel and the connecting rod.

3 Undo and remove the two through bolts from the commutator end cover. Pull off the end cover.

4 Lift out the brush gear retainer and then remove the brush gear. Clean the commutator and brush gear and, if worn, fit new brushes. The resistance between adjacent commutator segments should be 0.34 to 0.41 ohm.

5 Carefully examine the internal wiring for signs of chafing, breaks or chafing which would lead to a short circuit. Insulate or renew any damaged wiring.

6 Measure the value of the field resistance which should be between 12.8 and 14 ohms. If a lower reading than this is obtained it is likely that there is a short circuit and a new field coil should be fitted.

7 Renew the gearbox gear if the teeth are damaged, chipped or worn.

8 Reassembly is a straightforward reversal of the dismantling sequence, but ensure the following items are lubricated:

a) *Immerse the self-aligning armature bearing in engine oil for 24 hours before assembly.*

b) *Oil the armature bearings with engine oil.*

c) *Soak the felt lubricator in the gearbox with engine oil.*

d) *Grease generously the wormwheel bearings, crosshead, guide channel, connecting rod, crank pin, worm, cable rack and wheelboxes and the final gear shaft.*

Note: Some Series IIA, and all Series III Land Rovers are fitted with a later type wiper motor. The method of overhauling this motor is virtually identical to the one described in this Section, and providing reference is made to Fig. 10.30, no problems should be encountered.

37 Instrument panel - removal and refitting

1 Disconnect the battery earth terminal and remove the instrument panel retaining screws.

2 Withdraw the instrument panel far enough to gain access to the rear of the panel (photo). **Note: On Series III models it may be necessary to remove the steering wheel to provide sufficient clearance.**

3 Disconnect the drive cable from the rear of the speedometer.

4 Prise out all the illumination and warning light bulb holders from the rear of the panel and the speedometer housing.

5 Disconnect the inspection lamp socket leads.

6 Disconnect the wiring leads from the lighting switch and the fuel mixture warning light (if fitted).

7 Disconnect all the wires from the dynamo warning light (earlier models) and the instrument panel gauges. Make a careful note of the location of each wire and if necessary identify it with paint or coloured tape as it is removed.

8 On later models, disconnect the Lucar connectors from the rear of the panel as

37.1 Withdrawing the instrument panel

necessary and slacken the knurled nut securing the earth leads.

9 Disconnect the wires from the wiper switch, ignition switch and voltage stabiliser where fitted.

10 Make a careful check that all the leads have been disconnected and then lift the panel away complete with instruments.

11 The instruments can be removed from the panel by releasing the retaining clips or brackets. The switches and warning lights are secured either by circlips or threaded bezels.

12 Refit the instruments and panel assembly using the reverse procedure to that of removal.

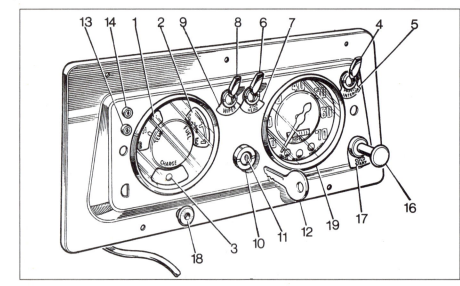

Fig. 10.31. Instrument panel assembly (Series II and early IIA type)

1 Water temperature gauge
2 Fuel gauge
3 Charging light (red)
4 Switch for panel and interior lights
5 Nameplate for switch, 'Panel/Interior'
6 Switch for lamps
7 Nameplate for switch, 'Side/Head '
8 Switch for wiper motor
9 Nameplate for switch, 'Wiper'
10 Switch for ignition and starter
11 Barrel lock for ignition switch
12 Ignition key
13 Socket for inspection lamp (black)
14 Socket for inspection lamp (red)
16 Cold start control
17 Nameplate for control, 'Cold Start'
18 Grommet
19 Speedometer and warning lights

Fig. 10.32. Rear views of instrument panel (Series III models)

1 Panel securing screws
2 Inspection lamp socket
3 Illumination and warning lamps
4 Speedometer cable
5 Earth terminal nuts
6 'Lucar' connectors

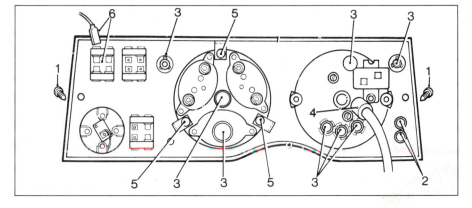

38 Fuel gauge sender unit - removal and refitting

1 The fuel gauge sender unit is located on the top of the fuel tank and is basically a float operated variable resistor that controls the amount of current to the fuel gauge. If the fuel gauge appears to give a faulty reading it is probably due to the float arm sticking or the resistor coil breaking down.

2 To remove the unit, first disconnect the battery earth terminal and lift off the right-hand seat cushion and remove the tank cover panel. **Note:** In the case of a rear mounted tank remove the inspection cover from the rear floor section.

3 Mark the position of the sender unit in relation to the top of the tank and disconnect the electrical lead and earth lead.

4 Remove the retaining screws and lift out the sender unit complete with float.

5 Check that the float moves freely without sticking. If the resistor coil is suspect the complete unit must be renewed as it cannot be repaired.

6 Refit the unit in the tank using a new gasket smeared with a fuel resistant jointing compound such as 'Osotite'.

39 Temperature gauge sender unit - removal and refitting

1 The temperature gauge sender unit is located on the front left-hand side of the engine adjacent to the thermostat housing (photo). It is basically a bi-metal resistor that increases the current to the gauge as it is progressively heated by the coolant.

2 Drain the coolant as described in Chapter 2, slacken the domed nut and remove the feed wire.

3 Remove the three securing bolts and lift out the sender unit.

4 The unit cannot be repaired and if faulty must be renewed. When refitting the sender unit always use a new gasket. **Note:** On some later models the sender unit is the plug type that screws into an adaptor plug beneath the thermostat housing.

5 Do not forget to refill the radiator after refitting the sender unit. Run the engine and check for coolant leaks.

Fault diagnosis - electrical system

Starter motor fails to turn engine

No electricity at starter motor

Battery discharged.
Battery defective internally.
Battery terminal leads loose or earth lead not securely attached to body.
Loose or broken connections in starter motor circuit.
Starter motor switch or solenoid faulty.

Electricity at starter motor: faulty motor

Starter motor pinion jammed in mesh with flywheel gear ring.
Starter brushes badly worn, sticking, or brush wire loose.
Commutator dirty, worn or burnt.
Starter motor armature faulty.
Field coils earthed.

Starter motor turns engine very slowly

Electrical defects

Battery in discharged condition.
Starter brushes badly worn, sticking, or brush wires loose.
Loose wires in starter motor circuit.

Starter motor operates without turning engine

Dirt or oil on drive gear

Starter motor pinion sticking on the screwed sleeve.
Pinion or flywheel gear teeth broken or worn.

Electrical defect

Battery almost completely discharged.

Starter motor noisy or excessively rough engagement

Lack of attention or mechanical damage

Pinion or flywheel gear teeth broken or worn.
Starter drive main spring broken.
Starter motor retaining bolts loose.

Battery will not hold charge for more than a few days

Wear or damage

Battery defective internally.
Electrolyte level too low or electrolyte too weak due to leakage.
Plate separators no longer fully effective.
Battery plates severely sulphated.

Insufficient current flow to keep battery charge

Battery plates severely sulphated.
Fan belt slipping.
Battery terminal connections loose or corroded.
Alternator (or dynamo) regulator unit not working correctly.
Short in lighting circuit causing continual battery drain.
Generator regulator unit not working correctly.

Ignition light fails to go out, battery runs flat in a few days

Generator not charging

Fan belt loose and slipping or broken.
Brushes worn, sticking, broken or dirty.
Brush springs weak or broken.
Slip rings dirty, greasy, worn or burnt.
Alternator stator coils burnt, open or shorted.

Horn

Horn operates all the time

Horn push either earthed or stuck down.
Horn cable to horn push earthed.

Horn fails to operate

Blown fuse.
Cable or cable connection loose, broken or disconnected.
Horn has an internal fault.

Horn emits intermittent or unsatisfactory noise

Cable connections loose or horn needs adjusting.

Fault diagnosis - electrical system

Lights

Lights do not come on

- [ ] If engine not running, battery discharged.
- [ ] Light bulb filament burnt out or bulbs broken.
- [ ] Wire connections loose, disconnected or broken.
- [ ] Light switch shorting or otherwise faulty.

Lights come on but fade out

- [ ] If engine not running, battery discharged.
- [ ] Light bulb filament burnt out or bulb or sealed beam units broken.
- [ ] Wire connections loose, disconnected or broken.
- [ ] Light switch shorting or otherwise faulty.

Lights give very poor illumination

- [ ] Lamp glasses dirty.
- [ ] Lamps badly out of adjustment.

Lights work erratically - flashing on and off, especially over bumps

- [ ] Battery terminal or earth connection loose.
- [ ] Lights not earthing properly.
- [ ] Contacts in light switch faulty.

Wipers

Wiper motor fails to work

- [ ] Blown fuse.
- [ ] Wire connections loose, disconnected or broken.
- [ ] Brushes badly worn.
- [ ] Armature worn or faulty.
- [ ] Field coils faulty.

Wiper motor works very slowly and takes excessive current

- [ ] Commutator dirty, greasy or burnt.
- [ ] Armature bearings dirty or unaligned.
- [ ] Armature badly worn or faulty.

Wiper motor works slowly and takes little current

- [ ] Brushes badly worn.
- [ ] Commutator dirty, greasy or burnt.
- [ ] Armature badly worn or faulty.

Wiper motor works but wiper blades remain static

- [ ] Wiper motor gearbox parts badly worn.

Series II petrol models, positive earth

1 Battery, 12 volt
2 Horn
3 Horn push button
4 Inspection light sockets
5 Panel illumination
6 Panel illumination
7 Tail light
8 Number plate illumination
9 Tail light
10 Side light
11 Side light
12 Starter switch
13 Starter
14 Panel light switch
15 Ammeter
16 Ignition and lighting switch
17 Headlight dipswitch
18 Voltage control box
19 Fuse box
20 Fuel gauge
21 Screen wiper. plug and socket
22 Stop light switch
23 Main beam warning light
24 Dynamo
25 Mixture warning light
26 Ignition coil
27 Charging warning light
28 Oil pressure warning light
29 Mixture switch
30 Distributor
31 Fuel gauge, petrol tank
32 Stop light
33 Stop light
34 Headlight, main
35 Headlight, main
36 Headlight, dip
37 Headlight, dip
38 Oil pressure switch
39 Thermostat
40 Snap connectors
41 Earth connections via terminals and
   fixing bolts
42 Junction box terminals

Key to cable colours

B Black   U Blue
G Green   W White
N Brown   Y Yellow
P Purple   RN Red with Brown, etc.
R Red

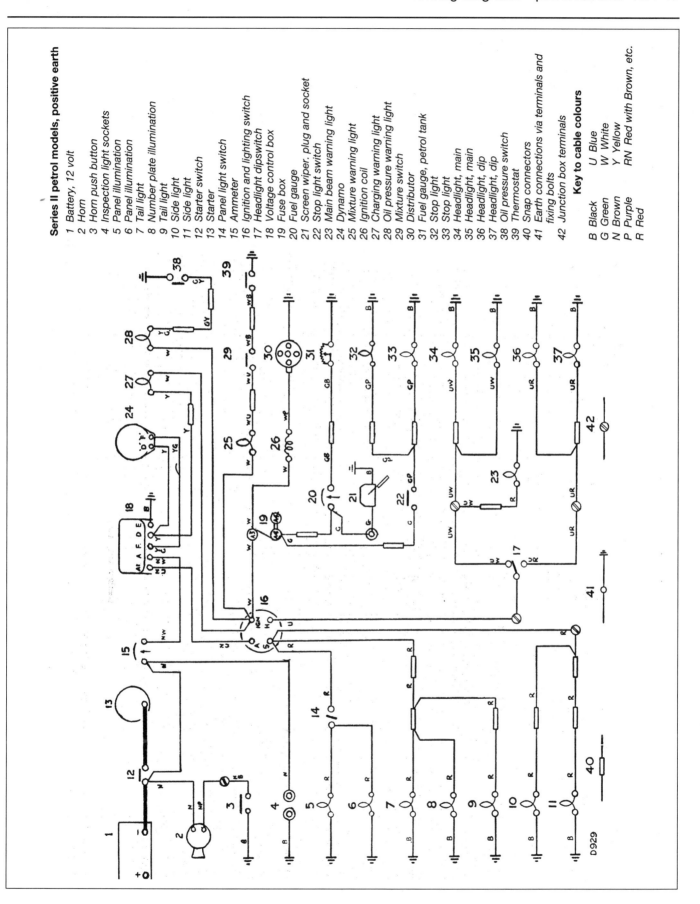

D929

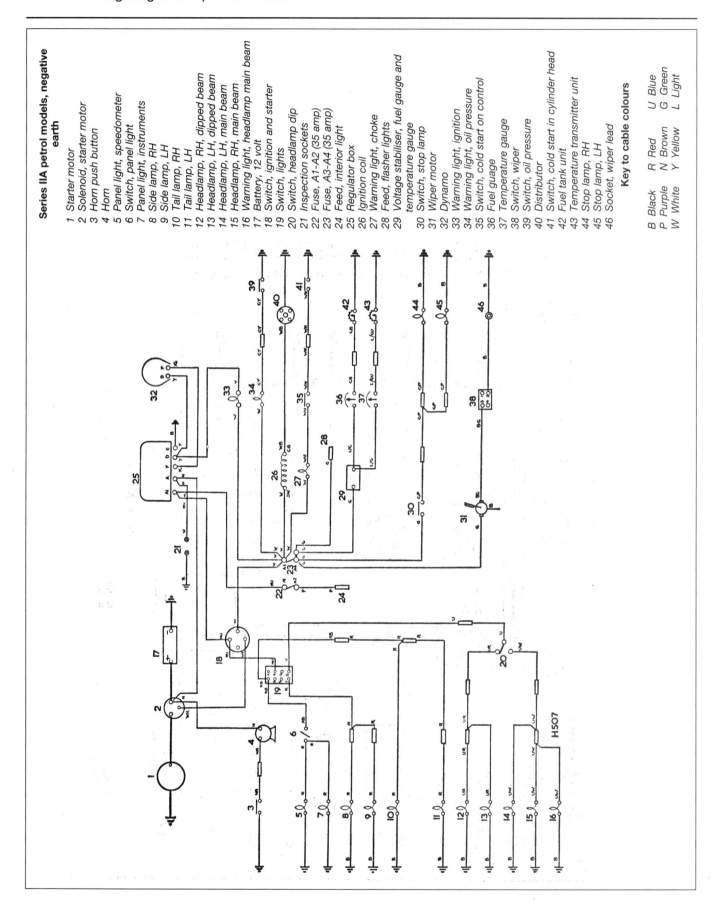

Series IIA petrol models, negative earth

1 Starter motor
2 Solenoid, starter motor
3 Horn push button
4 Horn
5 Panel light, speedometer
6 Switch, panel light
7 Panel light, instruments
8 Side lamp, RH
9 Side lamp, LH
10 Tail lamp, RH
11 Tail lamp, LH
12 Headlamp, RH, dipped beam
13 Headlamp, LH, dipped beam
14 Headlamp, LH, main beam
15 Headlamp, RH, main beam
16 Warning light, headlamp main beam
17 Battery, 12 volt
18 Switch, ignition and starter
19 Switch, lights
20 Switch, headlamp dip
21 Inspection sockets
22 Fuse, A1-A2 (35 amp)
23 Fuse, A3-A4 (35 amp)
24 Feed, interior light
25 Regulator box
26 Ignition coil
27 Warning light, choke
28 Feed, flasher lights
29 Voltage stabiliser, fuel gauge and temperature gauge
30 Switch, stop lamp
31 Wiper motor
32 Dynamo
33 Warning light, ignition
34 Warning light, oil pressure
35 Switch, cold start on control
36 Fuel guage
37 Temperature gauge
38 Switch, wiper
39 Switch, oil pressure
40 Distributor
41 Switch, cold start in cylinder head
42 Fuel tank unit
43 Temperature transmitter unit
44 Stop lamp, RH
45 Stop lamp, LH
46 Socket, wiper lead

Key to cable colours

B Black   R Red   U Blue
P Purple   N Brown G Green
W White   Y Yellow L Light

Series IIA petrol models, positive earth

1 Battery, 12 volt
2 Horn
3 Horn push button
4 Inspection light sockets
5 Panel illumination
6 Panel illumination
7 Tail light
8 Number plate illumination
9 Tail light
10 Side light
11 Side light
12 Starter switch
13 Starter
14 Panel light switch
15 Ammeter
16 Ignition and lighting switch
17 Headlight dipswitch
18 Voltage control box
19 Fuse box
20 To interior lights
21 Fuel gauge
22 Screen wiper, plug and socket
23 Stop light switch
24 Main beam warning light
25 Dynamo
26 Ignition coil
27 Mixture switch
28 Mixture warning light
29 Charging warning light
30 Oil pressure warning light
31 Oil pressure switch
32 Distributor
33 Mixture thermostat switch
34 Carburettor heater element, optional equipment
35 Gauge, fuel tank
36 Stop light
37 Stop light
38 Headlight, main
39 Headlight, main
40 Headlight, dip
41 Headlight, dip
42 Snap connectors
43 Earth connections via terminals and fixing bolts
44 Earth connections via cables

Key to cable colours

B Black   U Blue
G Green   W White
N Brown   Y Yellow
P Purple   RN Red with Brown etc
R Red

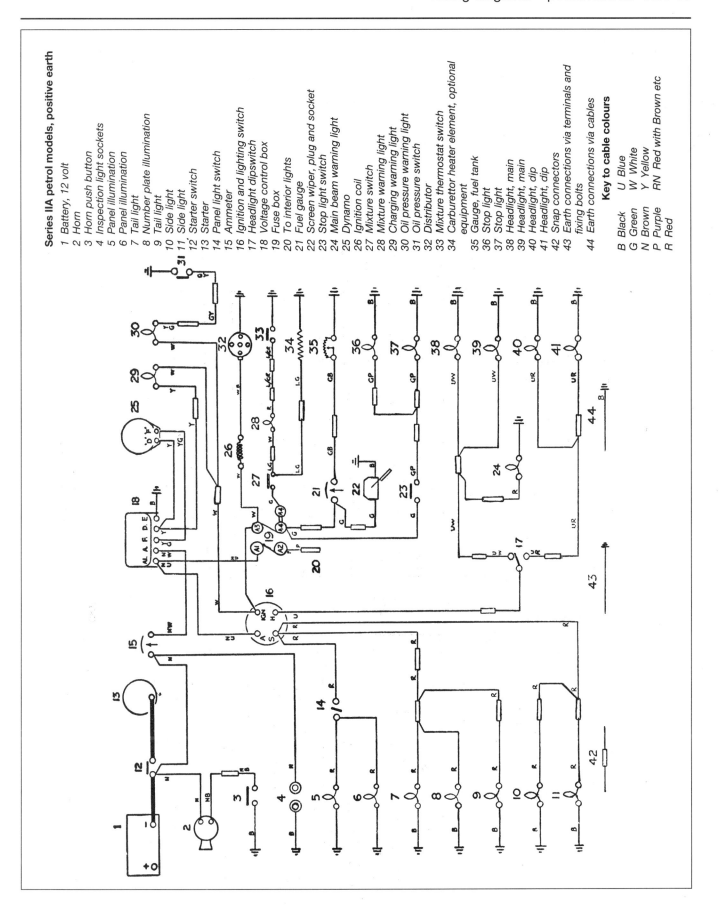

Series IIA petrol models with headlamps in the front wings (negative earth)

1 Starter motor
2 Solenoid, starter motor
3 Horn push button
4 Horn
5 Panel light speedometer
6 Switch, panel light
7 Panel light, instruments
8 Side lamp, RH
9 Side lamp, LH
10 Tail lamp, RH
11 Tail lamp, LH
12 Headlamp, RH, dipped beam
13 Headlamp, LH, dipped beam
14 Headlamp, LH, main beam
15 Headlamp, RH, main beam
16 Warning light, headlamp main beam
17 Battery, 12 volt
18 Switch, ignition and starter
19 Switch, lights
20 Switch, headlamp dip
21 Inspection sockets
22 Fuse, A1-A2 (35 amp)
23 Fuse, A3-A4 (35 amp)
24 Feed, interior light
25 Regulator box
26 Ignition coil
27 Warning light, choke
28 Voltage stabiliser, fuel gauge and temperature gauge
29 Switch, stop lamp
30 Switch, wiper
31 Flasher indicator unit
32 Switch and warning light, flashers
33 Dynamo
34 Warning light, ignition
35 Warning light, oil pressure
36 Switch, cold start on control
37 Fuel gauge
38 Temperature gauge
39 Wiper motor
40 Switch, oil pressure
41 Distributor
42 Switch, cold start in cylinder head
43 Fuel tank unit
44 Temperature transmitter unit
45 Stop lamp, RH
46 Stop lamp, LH
47 Socket, wiper lead
48 Front flasher, RH
49 Rear flasher, RH
50 Rear flasher, LH
51 Front flasher, LH

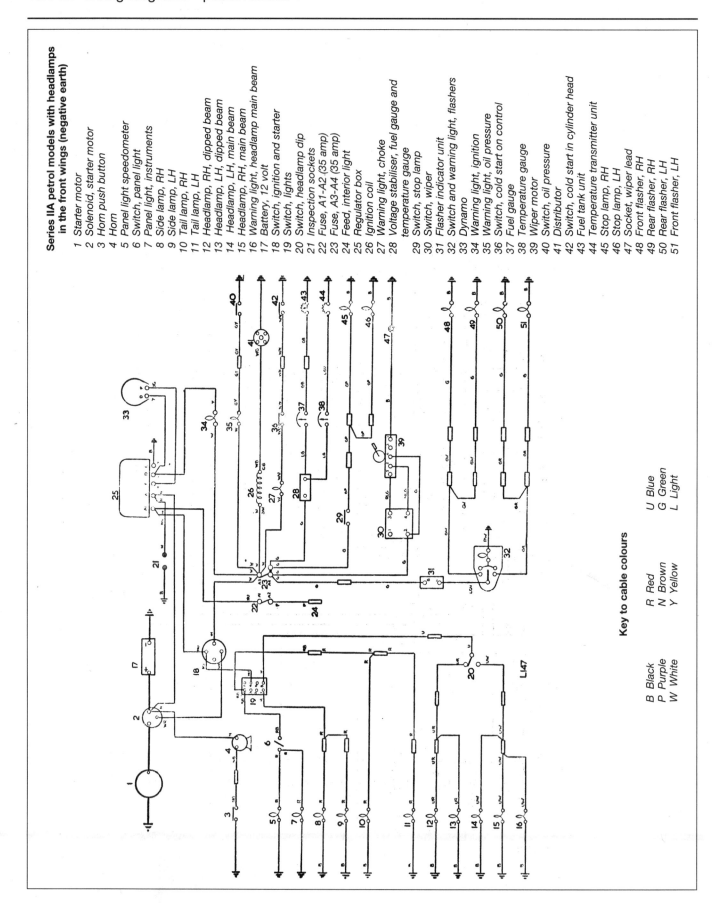

Key to cable colours

B Black	R Red	U Blue
P Purple	N Brown	G Green
W White	Y Yellow	L Light

Series III petrol models, negative earth

1 Starter motor
2 Solenoid, starter motor
3 Switch for horns
4 Horn
5 Inspection sockets
6 Instrument panel illumination
7 Instrument panel illumination
8 Switch, panel lights
9 Tail lamp, LH
10 Tail lamp, RH
11 Side lamp, LH
12 Side lamp, RH
13 Headlamp, LH dipped beam
14 Headlamp, RH dipped beam
15 Warning light, headlamp main beam
16 Headlamp, LH main beam
17 Headlamp, RH main beam
18 Direction indicator lamp, rear RH
19 Direction indicator lamp, front RH
20 Direction indicator lamp, front LH
21 Direction indicator lamp, rear LH
22 Battery
23 Switch, ignition and starter
24 Switch, lights
25 Switch, headlamp flash and dip
26 Warning light, indicator RH
27 Warning light, indicator LH
28 Fuses, 1 to 8, 35 amp
29 Indicator unit, flasher
30 Switch, direction indicators
31 Alternator, Lucas 16 ACR
32 Warning light, ignition
33 Ignition coil
34 Warning light, oil pressure
35 Warning light, choke
36 Voltage stabiliser, fuel guage and water temperature gauge
37 Switch, stop lamp
38 Switch, windscreen wiper
39 Dual fuel pump, 6 cylinder models only
40 Switch, cold start warning light
41 Fuel gauge
42 Water temperature gauge
43 Screenwiper motor
44 Distributor
45 Switch, oil pressure
46 Switch, cold start thermostat
47 Fuel tank unit
48 Water temperature transmitter unit
49 Stop lamp, LH
50 Stop lamp, RH
51 Screenwasher motor (when fitted)

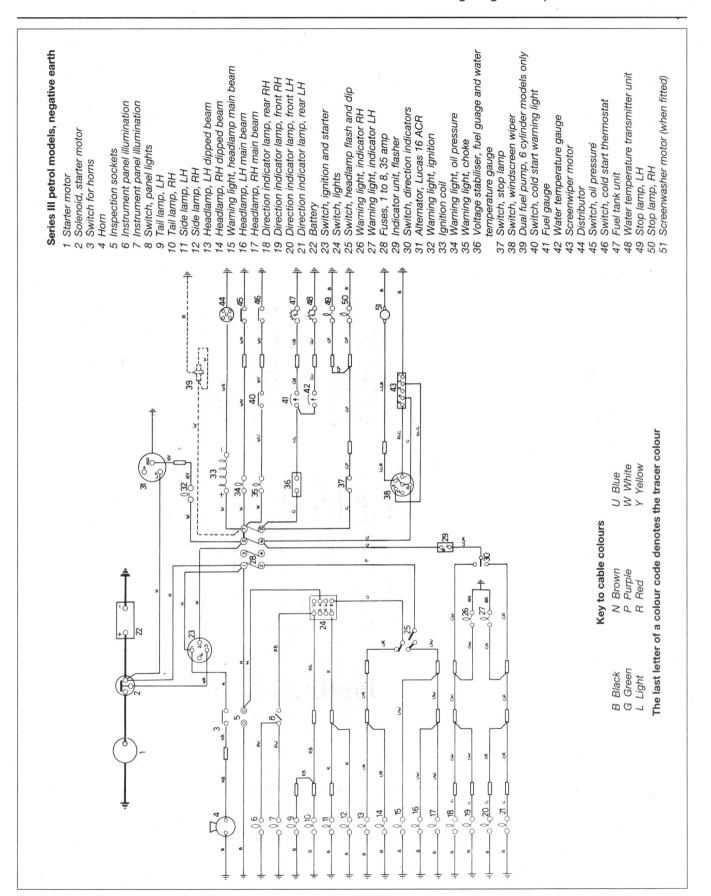

Key to cable colours

B Black	N Brown	U Blue
G Green	P Purple	W White
L Light	R Red	Y Yellow

The last letter of a colour code denotes the tracer colour

Series III petrol models, negative earth with foglamps and rear fog lamps

1 Starter solenoid
2 Solenoid, starter motor
3 Switch for horns
4 Horns
5 Inspection sockets
6 Instrument panel illumination
7 Instrument panel illumination
8 Switch, panel lights
9 Tail lamp, LH
10 Tail lamp, RH
11 Sidelamp, LH
12 Sidelamp, RH
13 Headlamp, LH dipped beam
14 Headlamp, RH dipped beam
15 Warning light, headlamp main beam
16 Headlamp, LH main beam
17 Headlamp, RH main beam
18 Direction indicator lamp, rear RH
19 Direction indicator lamp, front RH
20 Direction indicator lamp, front LH
21 Direction indicator lamp, rear LH
22 Battery
23 Switch, ignition and starter
24 Switch, lights
25 Switch, headlamp flash and dip
26 Warning light, indicator RH
27 Warning light, indicator LH
28 Fuses 1 to 8, 35 amp
29 Indicator unit, flasher
30 Switch, direction indicators
31 Alternator, Lucas 16 ACR
32 Warning light, ignition
33 Ignition coil
34 Warning light, oil pressure
35 Warning light, choke
36 Voltage stabilizer, fuel gauge and water temperature gauge
37 Switch, stop-lamp
38 Rear foglamps switch and warning light
39 Switch, windscreen wiper
40 Switch, choke
41 Switch, choke
42 Distributor
43 Fuel pump (6-cylinder models only)
44 Fuel gauge
45 Water temperature gauge
46 Screen wiper motor
47 Fuel tank unit
48 Water temperature transmitter
49 Stoplamp, LH
50 Stoplamp, RH
51 Rear foglamp, RH
52 Rear foglamp, LH
53 Front foglamp switch
54 Foglamp change over relay
55 Front foglamp, LH
56 Front foglamp, RH

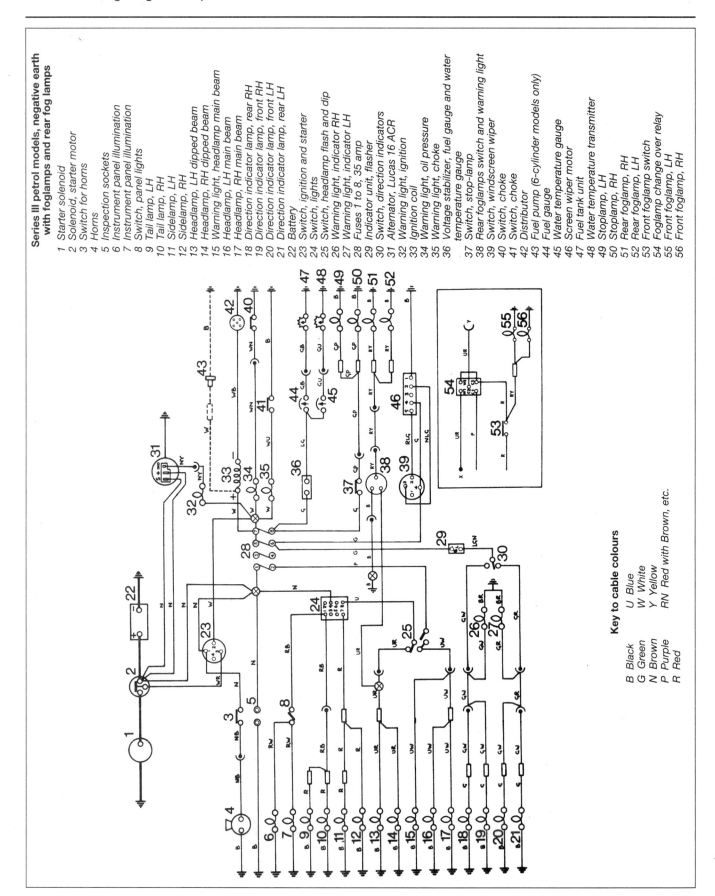

Key to cable colours

B Black	U Blue
G Green	W White
N Brown	Y Yellow
P Purple	RN Red with Brown, etc.
R Red	

Chapter 10B
Electrical system – diesel models

For modifications, and information applicable to later models, see Supplement at end of manual

Contents

Degrees of difficulty

Easy, suitable for novice with little experience 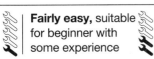 | **Fairly easy,** suitable for beginner with some experience | **Fairly difficult,** suitable for competent DIY mechanic | **Difficult,** suitable for experienced DIY mechanic | **Very difficult,** suitable for expert DIY or professional

Specifications

System type . . . . 12 volt, positive earth, (negative earth on vehicles from suffix 'D' onwards)

Battery . . . . Two 6 volt, 120 amp/hour or single 12 volt, 95 amp/hour

Dynamo
Type	Lucas C40/1
Output	22 amps
Cut-in speed	1350 rpm
Field resistance	5.9 ohms
Number of brushes	2
Brush length (new)	0.718 in (18.24 mm)
Minimum brush length	0.28 in (7.11 mm)
Brush spring pressure (new)	30 oz (850 g)

Current voltage regulator
Type	Lucas RB310 (RB340 on vehicles from suffix 'D' onwards)

Alternator

	Series II and IIA – Lucas IIAC	Series III – Lucas 16ACR
Type		
Output	43 amps	34 amps
Voltage	12 V	12 V
Field resistance	3.8 ohms	4.3 ohms
Minimum brush length	0.2 in (5 mm)	0.2 in (5 mm)
Maximum continuous speed	12 500 rpm	12 500 rpm

Starter motor

Type	Lucas M45G
Brush spring tension	30 to 40 oz (850 to 1134 g)
Brush minimum length	0.56 in (14.3 mm) – series II and IIA; 0.312 in (8.0 mm) – series III
Shaft endfloat	Zero

Fuses

Quantity:	
Series II and IIA	2
Series III	4
Amperage	35 amps

Bulbs and units

Headlamps with bulbs:	
Right-hand drive models	Lucas 414, 12V, 50/40W
Left-hand drive models, except Europe	Lucas 415, 12V, 50/40W
Left-hand drive models, Europe except France (early models)	Lucas 370
Left-hand drive models, Europe except France (late models)	Lucas 410, 12V, 45/40W
Left-hand drive models, France	Lucas 411, 12V, 45/40W
Headlamps with sealed beams (up to vehicle suffix 'A'):	
Right-hand drive models	Lucas 553921
Left-hand drive models, except Europe	Lucas 555447
Left-hand drive models, Europe except France (early type)	Lucas 553940
Left-hand drive models, Europe except France (late models)	Lucas 556452
Left-hand drive models, France only	Lucas 553948
Headlamps with sealed beams (from vehicles suffix 'B' onwards):	
Right-hand drive models	Lucas 54521872
Left-hand drive models, except Europe	Lucas 54522231
Left-hand drive models, Europe except Austria	Lucas 54522683
Left-hand drive models, Austria only	Lucas 54520883
Replacement headlamp unit (North America only)	Lucas 54522231
Sidelamps	Lucas 207, 12V, 6W
Stop, tail lamps	Lucas 380, 12V, 21/6W
Flasher lamps	Lucas 382, 12V, 21W
Rear number plate lamp	Lucas 989, 12V, 6W
Instrument panel lights	Lucas 987, 12V, 2.2W
Warning lights	Lucas 987, 12V, 2.2W
Warning light, heater plugs	Lucas 982, 6V, 1.8W
Interior light	Lucas 382, 12V, 21W

Heater plugs

Type	Coil element 1 to 7 volts, 38 to 42 amps
Make	KLG GF 210/T or Champion AG 45

Stop lamp switch

Type:	
Early models	Hydraulic in brake circuit
Later models	Mechanical on pedal or servo bracket

Torque wrench settings

	lbf ft	Nm
Alternator pulley nut	25 to 30	35 to 42
Dynamo pulley nut	25 to 30	35 to 42
Heater plugs	25	35
Solenoid to starter motor nuts	4.5	6.2
Starter motor through bolts	8	11

1 General description

The electrical system on all diesel engined Land Rovers is 12 volt of either positive or negative earth configuration. Series II and IIA models utilise two 6 volt batteries connected in series, whilst Series III models are equipped with a single 12 volt battery.

The basic units of the electrical system comprise of the battery, a dynamo or alternator (belt driven from the crankshaft pulley), a starter motor of the pre-engaged type and the necessary voltage regulating and cut-out equipment.

The battery provides a steady amount of current for the starting, lighting and other electrical circuits and provides a reserve of electricity when the current consumed by the electrical equipment exceeds that being produced by the dynamo or alternator.

The dynamo or alternator are controlled by a regulator which ensures a high output if the battery is in a low state of charge or if the demand from the electrical equipment is high, and a low output if the battery is fully charged and there is little demand from the electrical equipment.

When fitting electrical accessories to vehicles with a negative earth system, it is important, if they contain diodes or transistors, that they are connected correctly otherwise serious damage may result to the components concerned. Items such as radios, tape players, etc., should all be checked for correct polarity.

On vehicles fitted with alternators, it is important that the battery is disconnected before removing the alternator output lead as this is live at all times. Also if chassis repairs are to be carried out using electric arc welding equipment, the alternator must be disconnected otherwise it may be severely damaged. Whenever the battery has to be disconnected it must always be reconnected with the negative terminal earthed. *Do not disconnect the battery with the engine running.* If 'jumper cables' are used to start the vehicle, they must be connected correctly positive to positive and negative to negative.

2 Battery – removal and refitting

1 On Series III models the battery is located at the front right-hand side of the engine compartment. On Series II and IIA models having two 6 volt batteries connected in series, one battery is located at the front right-hand side of the engine compartment and the other is fitted under the left-hand front seat.

2 Disconnect the earth lead from the battery terminal post and then disconnect the live lead. The leads are held by either a clamp, which necessitates slackening the clamp bolt and nut, or by a screw driven through an all enclosing shroud. On Series II and IIA models repeat this procedure for the second battery.

3 Remove the battery clamp and carefully lift the battery out of its compartment. Hold the battery vertical to ensure that none of the electrolyte is spilled.

4 Refit the battery using the reverse procedure to removal. Before refitting the terminals, clean off any corrosion and smear the terminals with petroleum jelly (Vaseline). Never use grease.

3 Battery – maintenance and inspection

1 Normal weekly battery maintenance consists of checking the electrolyte level of each cell to ensure that the separators are covered by 1/4 in of electrolyte. If the level has fallen, top up the battery using distilled water only. Do not overfill. If a battery is over-filled or any electrolyte spilled, immediately wipe away the

3.1 Topping-up the battery using distilled water

excess as electrolyte attacks and corrodes very rapidly any metal it comes into contact with.

2 As well as keeping the terminals clean and covered with petroleum jelly, the top of the battery, and especially the top of the cells, should be kept clean and dry. This helps prevent corrosion and ensures that the battery does not become partially discharged by leakage through dampness and dirt.

3 Once every three months, remove the battery and inspect the battery securing bolts, the battery clamp plate, tray and battery leads for corrosion (white fluffy deposits on the metal which are brittle to touch). If any corrosion is found, clean off the deposits with ammonia and paint over the clean metal with an anti-rust/anti-acid paint.

4 With the battery on the bench at the three monthly interval check, measure its specific gravity with a hydrometer to determine the state of charge and condition of the electrolyte. There should be very little variation between the different cells and if a variation in excess of .025 is present, it will be due to either:

a Loss of electrolyte from the battery at some time caused by spillage or a leak, resulting in a drop in the specific gravity of the electrolyte when the deficiency was replaced with distilled water instead of fresh electrolyte

b An internal short circuit caused by buckling of the plates or a similar malady pointing to the likelihood of total battery failure in the near future

5 The specific gravity of the electrolyte for fully charged conditions at various electrolyte temperatures is listed in Table A. The specific gravity of a fully discharged battery at different temperatures of the electrolyte is given in Table B.

TABLE A
Specific gravity – battery fully charged
1.268 at 100°F or 38°C electrolyte temperature
1.272 at 90°F or 32°C electrolyte temperature
1.276 at 80°F or 27°C electrolyte temperature
1.280 at 70°F or 21°C electrolyte temperature
1.284 at 60°F or 16°C electrolyte temperature
1.288 at 50°F or 10°C electrolyte temperature
1.292 at 40°F or 4°C electrolyte temperature
1.296 at 30°F or – 1.5°C electrolyte temperature

TABLE B
Specific gravity – battery fully discharged
1.098 at 100°F or 38°C electrolyte temperature
1.102 at 90°F or 32°C electrolyte temperature
1.106 at 80 °F or 27°C electrolyte temperature
1.110 at 70°F or 21°C electrolyte temperature
1.114 at 60°F or 16°C electrolyte temperature
1.118 at 50°F or 10°C electrolyte temperature
1.122 at 40°F or 4°C electrolyte temperature
1.126 at 30°F or – 1.5°C electrolyte temperature

4 Battery – charging

1 In winter time when heavy demand is placed upon the battery, such as when starting from cold, and much of the electrical equipment is continually in use, it is a good idea occasionally to have the battery fully charged from an external source at the rate of 3.5 to 4 amps.

2 Continue to charge the battery at this rate until no further rise in specific gravity is noted over a four hour period.

3 Alternatively, a trickle charger, charging at the rate of 1.5 amps can be safely used overnight.

4 Specially rapid 'boost' charges which are claimed to restore the power of the battery in 1 to 2 hours are not recommended as they can cause serious damage to the battery plates through overheating.

5 Whilst charging the battery, note that the temperature of the electrolyte should never exceed 100°F (38°C).

6 Always remove the filler cap or cover during charging unless otherwise stated on the battery.

5 Alternator – general description and maintenance

1 The Series II and IIA Land Rovers were usually fitted with a dynamo as standard equipment, but had the option of the Lucas 11AC alternator. The Series III models are equipped with the Lucas 16ACR alternator as a standard fitment.

2 The type 16ACR alternator incorporates its own built-in regulator and is shown in exploded form in Fig. 10.1.

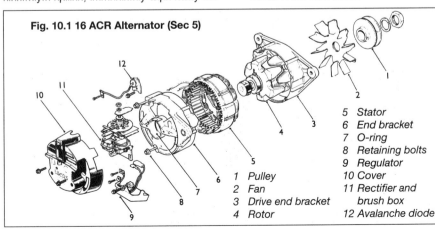

Fig. 10.1 16 ACR Alternator (Sec 5)

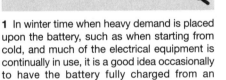

1 Pulley
2 Fan
3 Drive end bracket
4 Rotor
5 Stator
6 End bracket
7 O-ring
8 Retaining bolts
9 Regulator
10 Cover
11 Rectifier and brush box
12 Avalanche diode

3 Maintenance consists of occasionally wiping away any dirt or oil which may have collected around the apertures in the slip ring end bracket and moulded cover.

4 Check the fan belt tension every 5000 miles (8000 km) and adjust as described in Chapter 2 by loosening the mounting bolts. Pull the alternator body away from the engine block; do not use a lever as it will distort the alternator casing.

5 No lubrication is required as the bearings are grease sealed for life.

6 Take extreme care when making circuit connections to a vehicle fitted with an alternator and observe the following:

a *When making connections to the alternator from a battery, always match correct polarity*

b *Before using electric-arc welding equipment to repair any part of the vehicle, disconnect the connector from the alternator and disconnect the positive battery terminal*

c *Never start the car with a battery charger connected*

d *Always disconnect both battery leads before using a mains charger*

e *If boosting from another battery, always connect in parallel using heavy cable*

f *Never disconnect the battery with the engine running*

It is not recommended that testing of an alternator should be undertaken at home due to the testing equipment required and the possibility of damage occurring during testing. It is best left to automotive electrical specialists.

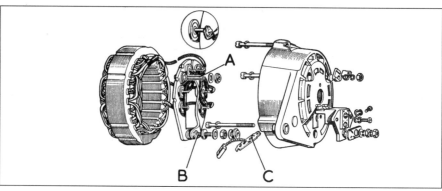

Fig. 10.2 Slip ring end of the 11AC alternator (Sec 5)

A *Warning light terminal*   B *Output terminal*   C *Terminal block securing tongue*

6 Alternator - removal and refitting

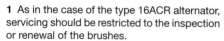

1 Loosen the alternator mounting bracket bolts and strap, push the unit towards the engine block sufficiently to enable the fan belt to be slipped off the alternator pulley.

2 Remove the cable connections from the alternator and withdraw the mounting bracket bolts. Lift away the alternator.

3 Refitting is a reversal of removal procedure but ensure that the connections are correctly made and that the fan belt is adjusted as described in Chapter 2.

7 Alternator – servicing (type 11 AC)

1 As in the case of the type 16ACR alternator, servicing should be restricted to the inspection or renewal of the brushes.

2 After removing the fan and pulley nut, the through-bolts may be removed. Mark the position of the end covers relative to the stator and withdraw the drive end cover and rotor together. The brushes may be checked for length and the slip rings cleaned up with fine glass paper.

3 To renew the brushes, undo and remove

the nut and spring washer, the large Lucar terminal and the plastic strip from the output terminal.

4 Undo and remove the two securing screws and withdraw the brush box. Note that there are two small washers between the brush box and end bracket.

5 Close up the retaining tongue at the root of each terminal blade and withdraw the brush, spring and terminal assemblies from the brush box.

6 With the brushes removed from the brush box, measure their length. If they are worn below 0.2 in (5 mm) they must be renewed.

7 Reassembly of the alternator is the reverse of the dismantling procedure.

8 Alternator – servicing (type 16ACR)

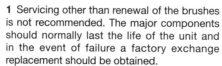

1 Servicing other than renewal of the brushes is not recommended. The major components should normally last the life of the unit and in the event of failure a factory exchange replacement should be obtained.

2 To renew the brushes, refer to Fig. 10.1, remove the two cover screws and withdraw the moulded cover.

3 Unsolder the three stator connections to the rectifier assembly noting carefully the order of connection.

4 Withdraw the two brush moulding securing screws. Slacken the nut on the rectifier assembly bolt.

5 Remove the regulator securing screw and (if fitted) the suppressor cable at the rectifier.

6 Withdraw the brush moulding and rectifier assembly complete with short linking cable.

7 Inspect the brushes which should protrude 0.2 in (5 mm) beyond the box moulding when in a free position. Renew if worn to or below this amount and do not lose the leaf spring fitted at the side of the inner brush.

8 Should a brush stick, then clean it with petrol or lightly rub with a smooth file.

9 The surfaces of the slip rings should be clean and smooth. If necessary, clean with a petrol moistened cloth. If there is evidence of burning, use very fine glass paper to clean (not emery).

9 Dynamo – routine maintenance

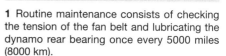

1 Routine maintenance consists of checking the tension of the fan belt and lubricating the dynamo rear bearing once every 5000 miles (8000 km).

2 The fan belt should be tight enough to ensure no slip between the belt and the dynamo pulley. If a shrieking noise comes from the engine when the unit is accelerated rapidly, it is likely that it is the fan belt slipping. On the other hand, the belt must not be too taut or the bearings will wear rapidly and cause dynamo failure or bearing seizure. Ideally 1/2 in (12.5 mm) of total free movement should be available at the fan belt, midway between the fan and the dynamo pulley.

3 To adjust the fan belt tension, slightly slacken the three dynamo retaining bolts and swing the dynamo on the lower two bolts outwards to increase the tension or inwards to lower it.

4 It is best to leave the bolts fairly tight so that considerable effort has to be used to move the dynamo, otherwise it is difficult to get the correct setting. If the dynamo is being moved outwards to increase the tension and the bolts have only been slackened a little, a long spanner acting as a lever placed behind the dynamo with the lower end resting against the block, works very well in moving the dynamo outwards. Retighten the dynamo bolts and check that the dynamo pulley is correctly aligned with the fan belt.

5 Lubrication on the dynamo consists of inserting three drops of engine oil in the small oil hole in the centre of the commutator end bracket. This lubricates the rear bearing. The front bearing is pre-packed with grease and requires no attention.

10 Dynamo – testing in position

1 If the ignition warning light fails to go out with the engine running or if it is suspected that the dynamo output may be low, first check that the fan belt is in place and is not slipping. Then check that the leads from the control box to the dynamo are firmly attached and that one has not come loose from its terminal.

2 The lead from the D terminal on the dynamo should be connected to the D terminal on the control box and similarly, the F terminals on the dynamo and control box should also be connected together. Check that this is so and that the leads have not been incorrectly fitted.

3 Make sure none of the electrical equipment (such as the lights or radio) is on and then pull the leads off the dynamo terminals marked D and F. Join the dynamo terminals together with a short length of wire.

4 Attach to the centre of this length of wire the negative clips of a 0-20 volts voltmeter and run the other clip to earth on the dynamo yoke. Start the engine and allow it to idle at approximately 1000 rpm. At this speed the dynamo should give a reading of about 15 volts on the voltmeter. There is no point in raising the engine speed above a fast idle as the reading will then be inaccurate.

5 If no reading is recorded, then check the brushes and brush connections. Ensure that the dynamo is correctly polarised as described in Section 11. If a very low reading of approximately 1 volt is observed, then the field windings may be suspect.

6 If a reading of between 4 to 6 volts is recorded, it is likely that the armature winding is at fault.

7 If the voltmeter shows a good reading, then with the temporary link still in position, connect both leads from the control box to D and F on the dynamo (D to D and F to F). Release the lead from the D terminal at the control box end, clip one lead from the voltmeter to the end of the cable and the other lead to a good earth. With the engine running at the same speed as previously, an identical voltage to that recorded at the dynamo should be noted on the voltmeter. If no voltage is recorded, then there is a break in the wire. If the voltage is the same as recorded at the dynamo, then check the F lead in similar fashion. If both readings are the same as at the dynamo, then it will be necessary to test the control box.

11 Dynamo – polarisation

1 Dynamos may be used on either positive or negative earth systems, without modification, providing they are correctly polarised. If a new or exchange dynamo is being fitted it must be polarised to suit the particular earthing configuration of the vehicle.

2 To polarise a dynamo for use on positive earth vehicles, connect a lead (i.e. a jumper lead) between the battery positive terminal and the dynamo casing. Connect another lead to the battery negative terminal and flick its free end against the F (small) terminal on the dynamo several times. In the interests of safety, do not do this in the vicinity of the battery.

3 To polarise a dynamo for negative earth

12.1 Dynamo and top adjusting arm

operation, connect the earthing lead between the negative terminal on the battery and the dynamo casing. Connect another lead to the battery positive and flick its free end against the F terminal as described in the previous paragraph. When two 6 volt batteries are fitted, connect the earth lead to a suitable part of the engine as the battery earth terminal is located beneath the left-hand front seat.

12 Dynamo – removal and refitting

1 Slacken the two dynamo retaining bolts and the nut on the sliding link and move the dynamo in towards the engine so that the fan belt can be removed (photo).

2 Disconnect the two leads from the dynamo terminals.

3 Remove the nut from the sliding link bolt and remove the two upper bolts. The dynamo is then free to be lifted away from the engine.

4 Refitting is a reversal of the above

procedure. Do not finally tighten the retaining bolts and the nut of the sliding link until the fan belt has been tensioned.

13 Dynamo – dismantling and inspection

1 Mount the dynamo in a vice and unscrew and remove the two throughbolts from the commutator end bracket.

2 Mark the commutator end bracket and the dynamo casing so that the end bracket can be refitted in its original position. Pull the end bracket off the armature shaft. Note that some versions of the dynamo may have a raised pip on the end bracket which locates in a recess on the edge of the casing. If so, marking the end bracket and casing is not necessary. A pip may also be found on the drive end bracket at the opposite end of the casing.

3 Lift the two bush springs and draw the brushes out of the brush holders.

4 Measure the brushes and, if worn down to 0.28 in (7.1 mm) or less, undo the screws that hold the brush leads to the end bracket. Take off the brushes complete with leads.

5 If no locating pip can be found, mark the drive end bracket and the dynamo casing so that the drive end bracket can be refitted in its original position. Then pull the drive end bracket complete with armature out of the casing.

6 Check the condition of the ball-bearing in the drive end plate by firmly holding the plate and noting if there is visible side movement of the armature shaft in relation to the end plate. If play is present, the armature assembly must be separated from the end plate. If the bearing is sound, there is no need to carry out the work described in the following two paragraphs.

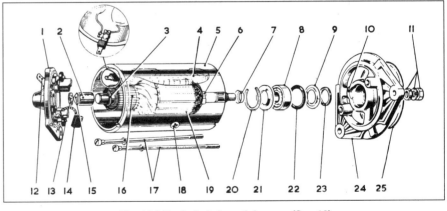

Fig. 10.3 Exploded view of dynamo (Sec 13)

1 Commutator end bracket	10 Extractor notch	18 Pole shoe screw
2 Bearing bush	11 Nut and washers	19 Armature
3 Fibre washer	12 Terminal D	20 Circlip
4 Field winding	13 Felt ring	21 Bearing retaining plate
5 Yoke	14 Carbon brush	22 Pressure ring
6 Armature shaft	15 Felt ring retainer	23 Felt ring
7 Retaining cup	16 Commutator	24 Drive end bracket
8 Drive end bearing	17 Through bolts	25 Pulley
9 Pressure ring plate		

Fig. 10.4 Differential types of dynamo commutators (Sec 13)

1 Moulded type   2 Fabricated type

7 Hold the armature in one hand (mount it carefully in a vice if preferred) and undo the nut that holds the pulley and fan in place. Pull off the pulley and fan.

8 Next remove the Woodruff key from its slot in the armature shaft, also the bearing locating ring.

9 Place the drive end bracket across the open jaws of a vice with the armature downwards and gently tap the armature shaft from the bearing in the end plate with the aid of a suitable drift. Support the armature so that it does not fall to the ground.

10 Carefully inspect the armature and check it for open or short circuited windings. It is a good indication of an open circuited armature when the commutator segments are burnt. If the armature has short circuited, the commutator segments will be very badly burnt and the over-heated armature windings badly discoloured. If open or short circuits are suspected, substitute the suspect armature with a new one.

11 Check the resistance of the field coils. To do this, connect an ohmmeter between the field terminal and the yoke and note the reading on the ohmmeter which should be about 6 ohms. If the ohmmeter reading is infinity, this indicates an open circuit in the field winding. If the ohmmeter reading is below 5 ohms, this indicates that one of the field coils is faulty and must be renewed.

12 Field coil renewal involves the use of a wheel operated screwdriver, a soldering iron, caulking and riveting. This operation is considered to be beyond the scope of most owners. Therefore, if the field coils are at fault, either purchase a rebuilt dynamo or take the casing to a Land Rover dealer or electrical engineering works for new field coils to be fitted.

13 Next check the condition of the commutator. If it is dirty and blackened, then clean it with a petrol dampened rag. If the commutator is in good condition the surface will be smooth and quite free from pits or burnt areas and the insulated segments clearly defined.

14 If, after the commutator has been cleaned, pits and burnt spots are still present, wrap a strip of glass paper round the commutator taking great care to move the commutator 1/4 of a turn every ten rubs till it is thoroughly clean.

15 In extreme cases of wear, the commutator can be mounted in a lathe. With the lathe turning at high speed, a very fine cut may be taken off the commutator. Finally, polish

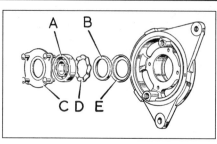

Fig. 10.5 Early type dynamo bearing retainer (Sec 13)

A Bearing   D Corrugated washer
B Felt washer   E Retaining washer
C Bearing retaining plate

the commutator with glass paper. If the commutator has worn so that the insulators between the segments are level with the top of the segments, then undercut the insulators to a depth of 1/32 in (0.8 mm). This applies to fabricated commutators only. Do not undercut moulded commutators. The best tool to use for this purpose is half a hacksaw blade ground to the thickness of the insulator and with the handle end of the blade covered in insulating tape to make it comfortable to hold.

16 Check the bush bearing in the commutator end bracket for wear by noting if the armature spindle rocks when placed in it. If worn, it must be renewed.

17 The bush bearing can be removed by a suitable extractor or by screwing a 5/8 in (15.87 mm) tap four or five times into the bush. The tap complete with bush is then pulled out of the end bracket.

18 **Note:** *The bush bearing is made of a porous bronze material which needs to be saturated in engine oil for several hours before use. If the oil is hot it will saturate the material more quickly.*

19 Carefully fit the new bush into the end plate, pressing it in until the end of the bearing is flush with the inner side of the end plate. If available, press the bush in with a smooth shouldered mandrel the same diameter as the armature shaft.

14 Dynamo – repair and reassembly

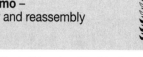

1 To renew the ball-bearing fitted to the drive end bracket, drill out the rivets that hold the bearing retainer plate to the end bracket and lift off the plate. On later models, the bearing is held by a circlip which is quite simply removed to release the bearing from the end plate.

2 Press out the bearing from the end bracket and remove the corrugated and felt washers from the bearing housing.

3 Thoroughly clean the bearing housing and the new bearing and pack with high melting point grease.

4 Place the felt washer and corrugated washer, in that order, in the end bracket bearing housing. On later models when the bearing is retained by a circlip, there is a felt

ring, retaining washer and pressure ring to be fitted in the housing before the bearing.

5 Fit the new bearing.

6 Gently tap the bearing into place with the aid of a suitable drift.

7 Refit the bearing plate and fit three new rivets (or fit the collar and circlip).

8 Open up the rivets with the aid of a suitable punch.

9 Finally peen over the open end of the rivets with the aid of a ball pein hammer.

10 Refit the drive end bracket to the armature shaft. Do not try and force the bracket on, but with the aid of a suitable socket abutting the bearing, tap the bearing on gently, so pulling the end bracket down with it.

11 Slide the spacer up the shaft and refit the Woodruff key.

12 Refit the fan and pulley, fit the spring washer and nut and tighten the latter. The drive end bracket end of the dynamo is now fully assembled.

13 If the brushes are a little worn and are to be used again, then ensure that they are placed in the same holders from which they were removed. When refitting brushes, either new or old, check that they move freely in their holders. If either brush sticks, clean with a petrol moistened rag and if still stiff, lightly polish the sides of the brush with a very fine file until the brush moves quite freely in its holder.

14 Tighten the two retaining screws and washers that hold the wire leads to the brushes in place.

15 It is far easier to slip the end piece with brushes over the commutator if the brushes are raised in their holders, and held in this position by the pressure of the springs resting against their flanks.

16 Refit the armature to the casing and then the commutator end plate. Screw up the two through-bolts.

17 Finally, hook the ends of the two springs off the flanks of the brushes and onto their heads so that the brushes are forced down into contact with the armature.

15 Current voltage regulator (dynamo only) – general description

Two types of current voltage regulator are fitted to Land Rovers covered by this manual. Early models are fitted with the Lucas RB310/37472 unit, whilst later models utilize the Lucas RB340/37387 type. The units are identified by their type numbers moulded into the plastic cover.

The current voltage regulator is positioned on the engine compartment bulkhead and is comprised of three units; two separate vibrating armature type single contact regulators and a cut-out relay. One of the regulators is sensitive to changes in current and the other to changes in voltage.

The regulators control the output from the dynamo depending on the state of the battery and the demands of the electrical equipment and ensure that the battery is not overcharged. The cut-out is an automatic switch that connects the dynamo to the battery when the dynamo is turning fast enough to produce a charge. Similarly it disconnects the battery from the dynamo when the engine is idling or stationary so that the battery does not discharge through the dynamo.

16 Current voltage regulator – adjustment

1 Before disturbing any settings in the current voltage regulator, ensure that the rest of the charging circuit is in good order. Check that the fan belt is correctly adjusted as described in Chapter 2. Inspect all wiring and if suspect, check for continuity. The dynamo must be functioning correctly and the battery should be in good condition.

2 To carry out tests and adjustments on the current voltage regulator, a good quality moving coil voltmeter of 0-20 volt range and moving coil ammeter of 0-40 amp range will be required. Also if working on the RB340 regulator, Lucas special tool no 54381742, which is a screwdriver with a small gear wheel on one end, will be required. This tool is available from Lucas agents.

Voltage regulator

3 Remove the leads from the current voltage regulator 'B' terminal and join them together using a short length of wire.
4 Connect one lead of the voltmeter to the 'D' terminal and the other lead to a good earthing point.
5 Start the engine and whilst observing the voltmeter, increase the engine speed until a dynamo speed of approximately 3000 rpm has been reached.
6 The voltmeter reading should have progressively risen to a maximum value and then flicked back to a slightly lower reading

and remained steady. This steady reading is the regulating voltage and should be within the range shown in the table below:

Ambient temperature	Voltage setting RB 310	RB340
50°F (10°C)	15.1 to 15.7	14.9 to 15.5
68°F (20°C)	14.9 to 15.5	14.7 to 15.3
86°F (30°C)	14 7 to 15.3	14.5 to 15.1
104°F (40°C)	14.5 to 15.1	14.3 to 14.9

7 An unsteady reading may be due to dirty contacts. If necessary, clean the contact points with fine glass paper and check again. If a steady reading occurs outside the specified limits, adjust the voltage regulator as follows: Carefully remove the regulator cover.
RB310 type – Slacken the locknut on the voltage regulator and turn the adjusting screw clockwise to increase the voltage or anti-clockwise to decrease it. Turn the screw only a fraction at a time and tighten the locknut, then recheck the voltage readings.
RB340 type – Insert the special tool in the voltage regulator cam and turn it just a fraction. Clockwise increases the voltage, anti-clockwise decreases it. Recheck the voltage readings.
8 Repeat this procedure as necessary until the correct readings are obtained, then refit the cover and remake the original electrical connections.

Current regulator

9 Carefully remove the regulator cover. Refer to Fig. 10.8 and short out the voltage regulator contacts using a crocodile clip attached to the voltage regulator fixed contact bracket and frame. This will allow the dynamo to produce its maximum output even if the battery is in a fully charged condition.
10 Remove the leads from the current voltage regulator 'B' terminal and connect them together using a short length of wire. Connect one lead from the ammeter to the 'B' terminal on the current voltage regulator and the other ammeter lead to the link connecting the two previously removed leads.

11 Switch on the headlights, windscreen wipers and any other electrical accessories fitted to provide an electrical load.
12 Start the engine and increase to a dynamo speed of approximately 4500 rpm. Observe the reading on the ammeter which should be steady at 22 amps.
13 An unsteady reading may be due to dirty contacts. If necessary, clean the contact points with fine glass paper and check again. If the reading is too high or too low, adjust the current regulator as follows: Stop the engine. On RB310 types, slacken the locknut and turn the adjusting screw clockwise to increase the current or anti-clockwise to decrease it. On RB340 types, insert the special tool in the cam and turn it clockwise to increase the current and vice versa.
14 Start the engine and recheck the current readings. Repeat this procedure as necessary until the correct readings (± 1 amp) are obtained, then refit the cover and remake the original electrical connections.

Cut-in voltage

15 Connect the voltmeter between the regulator 'D terminal and a good earthing point on the chassis.
16 Switch on an electrical load as described in paragraph 11.
17 Start the engine and observe the voltmeter whilst increasing the engine speed slowly.
18 Closure of the cut-in contacts, indicated by a slight drop in the voltmeter reading, should occur between 12.7 and 13.3 volts. If the cut-in occurs outside these limits, adjust the cut-in regulator as follows: Carefully remove the regulator cover. On RB310 types, slacken the locknut and turn the adjusting screw clockwise to increase the setting and anti-clockwise to decrease it. On RB340 types, insert the special tool in the cam and turn it clockwise to increase the setting and vice versa.
19 Recheck the cut-in voltage and repeat the

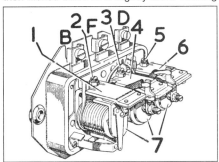

Fig. 10.6 RB 310 current voltage regulator (Sec 16)

1 Cut-out
2 Cut-out adjusting screw
3 Current adjusting screw
4 Current regulator
5 Voltage adjusting screw
6 Voltage regulator
7 Armature
B Terminal
F Terminal
D Terminal

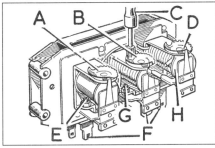

Fig. 10.7 RB 340 Current voltage regulator (Sec 16)

A Voltage adjusting cam
B Current adjusting cam
C Setting tool
D Cut-out adjusting cam
E Voltage adjustable contact
F Terminals
G Current adjustable contact
H Relay core face

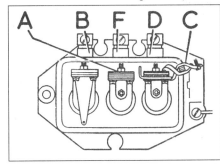

Fig. 10.8 Short circuiting voltage regulator contacts (Sec 16)

A Current adjusting screw
B Terminal
C Clip-short-circuiting
D Terminal
F Terminal

above procedure until the correct readings are obtained, then remove the voltmeter and refit the cover.

Drop-off voltage

20 Disconnect the leads from the current voltage regulator 'B' terminal.

21 Connect the voltmeter between the regulator 'B' terminal and a good earthing point on the chassis.

22 Start the engine and increase the speed to approximately quarter throttle opening, then slowly decelerate to idle and observe the voltmeter readings.

23 Opening of the contacts, indicated by the reading falling to zero, should occur between 9.5 and 11.0 volts. If the drop-off occurs outside these limits, adjust the drop-off voltage as follows:

24 Stop the engine and carefully remove the regulator cover.

25 The drop-off voltage is adjusted by carefully bending the fixed contact breaker. Reducing the contact gap will increase the drop-off voltage, increasing the gap will reduce the voltage. **Note:** *Before making the adjustment always disconnect the battery earth lead to prevent the battery discharging through the dynamo if the contact points are accidentally closed.*

26 Recheck the drop-off voltage and repeat the above procedure until the correct readings are obtained, then refit the cover and remake the original electrical connections.

17 Starter motor – general description

A pre-engaged type starter motor of Lucas manufacture is fitted to all diesel engined Land Rovers. The motor is of the four-pole, four-brush type, the brushgear being fully insulated and comprising of square shaped brushes actuated by coil springs onto the commutator face. Activation of the motor and drive pinion is by a solenoid bolted to the starter drive end bracket.

The solenoid comprises a soft iron plunger, starter switch contacts, main closing winding (series winding) and a hold on (short winding). When the starter switch is operated, both the coils are energised in parallel but the closing winding is shorted out by the starter switch contacts when they are closed.

The drive pinion is operated by a lever pivoting on an adjustable fulcrum pin threaded into the starter motor end bracket. The engagement position of the drive pinion is therefore adjustable by altering the position of the fulcrum pin.

18 Starter motor – testing on engine

1 If the starter motor fails to operate, check the condition of the battery by turning on the headlamps. If they glow brightly for several

seconds and then gradually dim, the battery is in an uncharged condition.

2 If the headlights continue to glow brightly and it is obvious that the battery is in good condition, check the tightness of the battery wiring connections (and in particular the earth lead from the battery terminal to its connection on the body frame). If a terminal on the battery becomes hot when an attempt is made to work the starter, this is a sure sign of a poor connection. To rectify, remove the terminal, clean the mating faces thoroughly and reconnect. Check the connections on the rear of the starter solenoid. Check the wiring with a meter or test lamp for breaks or shorts.

3 Test the continuity of the solenoid windings by connecting a test lamp circuit, comprising a 12 volt battery and low wattage test bulb, between the 'STA' terminal and the solenoid body. If the two windings are in order, the lamp will light. Next connect the test lamp between the solenoid main terminals. Energise the solenoid by applying a 12 volt supply between the unmarked Lucar terminal and the solenoid body. The solenoid should be heard to operate and the test bulb seen to light. This indicates full closure of the solenoid contacts.

4 If the battery is fully charged, the wiring in order, the starter switch working and the starter motor still fails to operate, it will have to be removed from the car for examination. Before this is done, ensure that the starter motor pinion has not jammed in mesh with the flywheel by engaging a gear and rocking the vehicle to and fro. This should free the pinion if it is stuck in mesh with the flywheel teeth.

19 Starter motor – removal and refitting

1 Disconnect the battery earth terminal.

2 Disconnect the electrical leads from the starter motor solenoid, noting their positions.

3 Undo and remove the nuts and bolts that secure the starter motor to the engine rear mounting plate and bellhousing.

4 Withdraw the starter motor from the engine.

5 Refitting is the reverse sequence to removal.

20 Starter motor – dismantling, servicing and reassembly

1 Two types of Lucas M45G starter motors are fitted to diesel engined Land Rovers. Their operating principles are the same but there are slight differences in the design of the two units. These differences will be described where necessary.

2 With the starter motor on the bench, unscrew and remove the nut that secures the solenoid link wire or tag to the terminal on the starter motor body. Lift off the link.

3 Mark the relative positions of the solenoid and drive end bracket, then undo and remove the two securing nuts (bolts on early models) and spring washers.

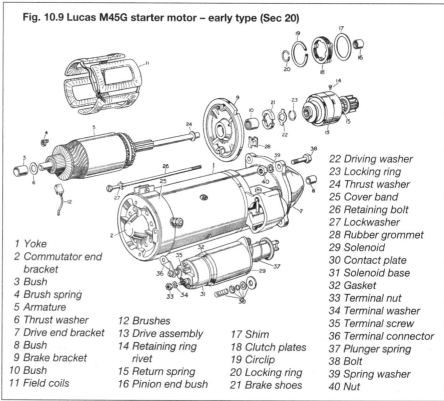

Fig. 10.9 Lucas M45G starter motor – early type (Sec 20)

1 Yoke
2 Commutator end bracket
3 Bush
4 Brush spring
5 Armature
6 Thrust washer
7 Drive end bracket
8 Bush
9 Brake bracket
10 Bush
11 Field coils
12 Brushes
13 Drive assembly
14 Retaining ring rivet
15 Return spring
16 Pinion end bush
17 Shim
18 Clutch plates
19 Circlip
20 Locking ring
21 Brake shoes
22 Driving washer
23 Locking ring
24 Thrust washer
25 Cover band
26 Retaining bolt
27 Lockwasher
28 Rubber grommet
29 Solenoid
30 Contact plate
31 Solenoid base
32 Gasket
33 Terminal nut
34 Terminal washer
35 Terminal screw
36 Terminal connector
37 Plunger spring
38 Bolt
39 Spring washer
40 Nut

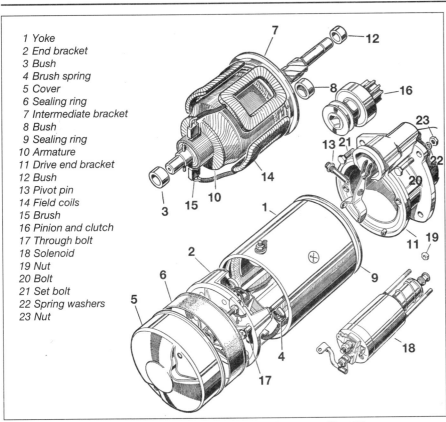

1 Yoke
2 End bracket
3 Bush
4 Brush spring
5 Cover
6 Sealing ring
7 Intermediate bracket
8 Bush
9 Sealing ring
10 Armature
11 Drive end bracket
12 Bush
13 Pivot pin
14 Field coils
15 Brush
16 Pinion and clutch
17 Through bolt
18 Solenoid
19 Nut
20 Bolt
21 Set bolt
22 Spring washers
23 Nut

Fig. 10.10 Lucas M46G starter motor – later type (Sec 20)

4 Withdraw the solenoid rearwards and disengage the solenoid plunger from the operating lever. Remove the solenoid from the starter motor.

5 Remove the rubber sealing grommet from the slot in the drive end bracket.

6 On later models, undo and remove the two nuts and rubber seals and lift off the commutator end cover and cover band. On early models, slacken the clamp screw and slide the cover band off the rear of the starter motor.

7 Using a hook shaped length of wire, lift off the brush springs and withdraw the brushes from their holders.

8 Unscrew and withdraw the two long through-bolts that secure the commutator end bracket and lift off the end bracket from the starter body and armature.

9 Remove the drive end bracket complete with armature from the starter body.

10 Slacken the locknut and undo and remove the eccentric engagement lever pivot pin from the end bracket.

11 Withdraw the armature and intermediate bracket from the drive end bracket and lift off the engagement lever.

12 Push back the lock ring cover on the end of the armature shaft and prise off the lock ring.

13 Withdraw the drive assembly and intermediate bracket from the armature shaft. Note any shims that may be fitted behind the intermediate bracket.

14 On later models, remove the brake ring, steel and tufnol washers from the commutator end bracket.

15 With the starter motor dismantled, check that the brushes move freely in their holders. If necessary, they may be cleaned with a petrol moistened cloth or by very light rubbing with a smooth file. Measure the length of the brushes, if they are worn to less than 0.562 (14.3 mm) on early types and 0.312 (8 mm) on later types, they must be renewed.

16 The brush wires are soldered or crimped to terminal tags and must be unsoldered to remove. New brush wires may then be resoldered onto the tags.

17 Clean the commutator with a petrol moistened rag and if necessary wrap a piece of glass paper around the commutator and rotate the armature to remove any burnt areas or high spots.

18 If the commutator is very badly worn, mount the armature in a lathe and with the lathe turning at high speed, take a very fine cut out of the commutator. Finish the surface by polishing with glass paper. Do not undercut the insulator between the commutator segments.

19 Check that the roller clutch rotates freely in one direction and locks up in the other. If this is not the case, the clutch must be renewed.

20 The field coil continuity may be tested as follows: Connect a 12 volt battery with a 12 volt bulb in one of the leads between the field terminal post and the tapping point of the field coils to which the brushes are connected. An open circuit is proved by the bulb not lighting.

21 If the bulb lights, it does not necessarily mean that the field coils are in order, as there is a possibility that one of the coils will be earthed to the starter yoke or pole shoes. To check this, remove the lead from the brush connector and place it against a clean portion of the starter yoke. If the bulb lights, the field coils are earthing. Renewal of the field coils calls for the use of a wheel operated screwdriver, a soldering iron, caulking and riveting operations, and is beyond the scope of the majority of owners. The starter yoke should be taken to a reputable electrical engineering works for new field coils to be fitted. Alternatively, purchase an exchange Lucas starter motor.

22 If the armature is damaged, this will be evident on inspection. Look for signs of burning, discoloration and for conductors that have lifted away from the commutator.

23 If a bearing is worn, allowing excessive play of the armature shaft, the bearing bush must be renewed. Drift out the old bush with a piece of suitable diameter rod, preferably with a shoulder on it to stop the bush collapsing.

24 Soak a new bush in engine oil for 24 hours or, if time does not permit, heat in an oil bath at 100°C (212°F) for two hours prior to fitting.

25 As new bushes must not be reamed after fitting, it must be pressed into position using a small mandrel of the same internal diameter as the bush and with a shoulder on it. Place the bush on the mandrel and press into position using a bench vice.

26 Using a test lamp and battery, test the continuity of the coil winding between terminal 'STA' and a good earth point on the solenoid body. If the lamp fails to light, the solenoid should be renewed.

27 To test the solenoid contacts for correct opening and closing, connect a 12 volt battery and a 60 watt test lamp between the main unmarked Lucar terminal and the 'STA' terminal. The lamp should not light.

28 Energize the solenoid with a separate 12 volt supply connected to the small unmarked Lucar terminal and a good earth on the solenoid body.

29 As the coil is energized the solenoid should be heard to operate and the test lamp should light with full brilliance.

30 No attempt should be made to repair a faulty solenoid. If it is faulty it must be renewed as a complete unit.

31 To reassemble the starter motor is the reverse sequence of dismantling. The following additional points should be noted:

a *When refitting the solenoid plunger to the engagement lever, turn the eccentric pin until the engagement lever is in its lowest and most forward position*

b *With the starter motor reassembled, reset the drive pinion engagement position as described in Section 21*

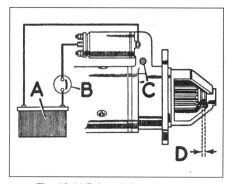

Fig. 10.11 Drive pinion clearance adjustment (Sec 21)

A Battery
B Switch
C Pivot pin
D Clearance – 0.005 to 0.015 in
   (0.12 to 0.40 mm)

21 Drive pinion clearance (starter motor) – adjustment

1 Connect one lead from a 12 volt battery to the small unmarked terminal on the starter solenoid.
2 Using a switch in the circuit, connect the other battery terminal lead to one of the solenoid fixing studs.
3 With the switch closed, the drive pinion will move forward to the engaged position. Measure the distance between the end of the pinion and the lock ring cover on the end of the armature shaft.
4 A clearance of between 0.005 and 0.015 in (0.12 to 0.40 mm) should exist with the drive pinion pushed gently back to take up any free play in the operating linkage.
5 If the clearance is incorrect, slacken the locknut and rotate the engagement arm fulcrum one way or the other until the correct clearance is obtained. Note that the adjustment arc is 180° and the arrow marked on the head of the fulcrum pin must be within 90° of either side of the cast arrow on the end casing.
6 When the clearance is correct, tighten the locknut.

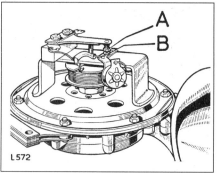
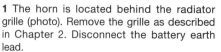

Fig. 10.12 Horn adjustment Series II models (Sec 22)

A Adjustable locknut   B Locknut

22 Horn – removal, refitting and adjustment

1 The horn is located behind the radiator grille (photo). Remove the grille as described in Chapter 2. Disconnect the battery earth lead.
2 Disconnect the electrical leads from the snap connectors (or horn terminals), remove the securing bolts and lift out the horn.
3 To adjust the earlier type Lucas horn, first remove the securing clip **and lift off the domed cover.**
4 Clean the contact points and adjust them until they are almost touching, then turn the adjusting screw one-half a turn to increase the gap.
5 Check the operation of the horn and, if unsatisfactory, a new one should be fitted.
6 To adjust the horn on Series IIA models, remove the domed cover and turn the adjustment screw a small amount either way until a good note is obtained. To avoid blowing the fuse, the horn should be connected directly to the battery
7 The latest type horns have no adjustment and the only check necessary is to ensure the wiring connectors are clean and tight.
8 Refit the horn using the reversal of the removal procedure.

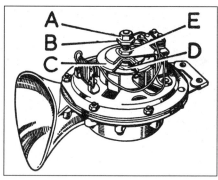
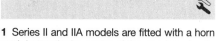

Fig. 10.13 Horn adjustment Series IIA models (Sec 22)

A Locknut   D Magnet core
B Adjusting nut   E Armature locknut
C Armature

23 Horn button – removal and refitting

1 Series II and IIA models are fitted with a horn push button in the centre of the steering wheel.
2 To remove the button, carefully prise out the centre section of the steering wheel using a thin bladed screwdriver (photo). Disconnect the battery earth lead.
3 Check the button for correct operation and clean the contacts.
4 Refit the horn assembly using the reverse sequence to removal.
5 Series III models have a horn push incorporated in the direction indicator/headlight switch. This multi function switch is a sealed unit and cannot be repaired. If a fault develops in the switch a new assembly must be obtained. Removal and refitting instructions are described in Section 34.

24 Headlamps (mounted in grille panel) – removal and refitting

1 Remove the screw from the bottom of the headlamp rim and carefully prise off the rim and rubber dust cover (photo).
2 Press the headlamp unit inwards and

22.1 Location of horn behind radiator grille

23.2 Removing the horn button (early models)

24.1 Headlamp with rim removed

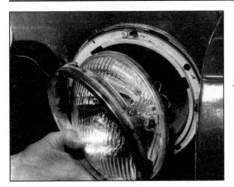

24.4a Removing headlamp assembly

24.4b Electrical plug at rear of sealed beam unit

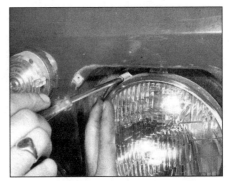

25.2 Removing the headlamp rim

rotate it anti-clockwise to release it from the spring-loaded adjustment screws,

3 Turn the bulb holder anti-clockwise to release it and remove the bulb.

4 If the headlamp is the sealed beam type, remove the three screws that secure the rim to the headlamp shell, support the light unit and pull off the electrical plug from the rear of the unit (see photos).

5 Refit the headlamp assembly using the reverse procedure to removal.

25 Headlamps (wing mounted) – removal and refitting

1 Remove the four screws that secure the headlamp bezel to the wing.

2 Slacken the three screws that secure the chrome rim, turn the headlamp enough to clear the screw heads and lift off (photo).

3 Withdraw the light unit and disconnect the electrical plug (or bulb holder) (photo).

4 Renew the bulb or light unit as applicable and refit the headlamp assembly using the reversal of the removal procedure.

25.3 Electrical connection at rear of headlamp (later models)

26.1 Adjusting the headlamp aim

26 Headlight aim – adjustment

1 The headlights may be adjusted for both vertical and horizontal beam position by the screws located as shown (photo).

2 They should be set so that on full or high beam, the beams are set slightly below parallel with a level road surface. Do not forget that the beam position is affected by how the vehicle is normally loaded for night driving. Set the beams with the vehicle loaded to this condition. Before adjustment is commenced, check that the tyre pressures are correct.

3 Although this adjustment can be approximately set at home using a vertical wall,

it is recommended that this be left to the local garage who will have the necessary optical equipment to do the job more accurately.

27 Front and rear sidelights – removal and refitting

1 The method of removing the front and rear side, flasher and stop lamps is the same on all vehicles.

2 Remove the two retaining screws and ease the lens out of the rubber moulding (photo).

3 Renew the bulb if necessary (photo) and refit the lens into the moulding ensuring the beaded lip fits snugly around the base of the lens.

4 Refit the two retaining screws taking care not to overtighten them.

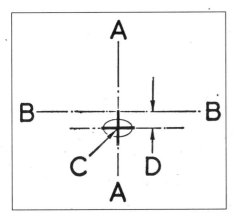

Fig. 10.14 Wall markings for headlamp aim adjustment (Sec 26)

AA Headlamp vertical centre line
BB Headlamp horizontal centre line measured from floor
C   Centre of concentrated light area
D   2 in ± 1 in (50mm ± 25mm)

27.2 Removing a sidelight lens

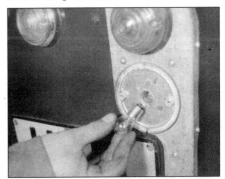

27.3 Refitting a sidelight bulb

28.1 Location of earlier type wiper motor

28.2 Removing the wiper blade and arm (earlier models)

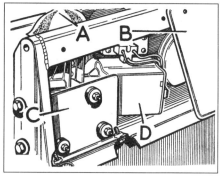

Fig. 10.15 Location of wiper motor in glove box – Series IIA and III (Sec 30)

A Rubber cover   C Mounting bracket
B Glove box cover   D Wiper motor

28 Windscreen wiper motor (early type) – removal and refitting

1 The Series II Land Rovers were fitted with a single wiper arm driven directly from a motor located below the windscreen (photo).
2 To remove the motor, slacken the nut on the wiper arm spindle, give it a sharp tap to release the collets and withdraw the complete arm and blade (photo).
3 Undo the securing nuts and remove the wiper arm stop and rubber mounting block from the front of the windscreen.
4 Withdraw the motor from inside the cab and retrieve the brass spindle bushes.
5 Refit the motor using the reversal of the removal procedure. Before refitting the wiper arm and blade, set the motor to the parked position and refit the arm accordingly.

29 Windscreen wiper motor (early type) – servicing

1 If the movement of the wiper arm is erratic or stops altogether, remove the motor as described previously and lubricate the spindle bushes with thin oil.
2 With the motor withdrawn from the screen but the wires still connected, switch on the motor and check that the spindle moves backwards and forwards quite freely.
3 If, on refitting the motor, arm and blade, the performance is still unsatisfactory, the fault probably lies in the armature windings and it is best to obtain a replacement motor.

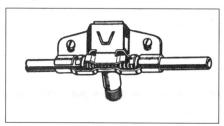

Fig. 10.16 Correct positioning of cable tubes in wheelbox (Sec 30)

30 Windscreen wiper motor and linkage (twin wiper) – removal and refitting

1 Later versions of the Land Rover are fitted with a wiper motor (located in the glove compartment behind a cover plate) which drives the two wiper arms via a cable and two wheel boxes.
2 To remove the motor, first disconnect the battery earth terminal
3 Unscrew the nut that secures the drive cable outer tube to the motor.
4 On earlier versions, remove the four bolts that secure the motor mounting plate to the side of the glove box.
5 Prise off each wiper arm from the drive spindles and then withdraw the motor complete with the inner drive cable.
6 On later models, the motor is secured by two bolts in the glove box and a nut plate on the engine compartment bulkhead. After removing these, withdraw the motor and inner cable as described previously.
7 The two wiper arm drive boxes can be removed by first unscrewing the six screws that secure the windscreen lower panel and lifting off the panel.
8 Remove the wiper arms and then slacken the lockscrew and pull off the splined adaptors from the spindles (photo).
9 Remove the rubber grommet (or escutcheon plate) from the spindles and undo the spindle locknuts.

30.8 Removing the later type wiper blade arm

10 Remove the motor and inner cable as described previously.
11 The drive boxes can now be withdrawn from inside the cab complete with the cable tubes.
12 Undo the two securing screws and remove the cover plate from each drive box. Check the gears and cable for wear and renew if necessary.
13 Lubricate the spindles, gears and the inside of the cable tubes with grease.
14 Reassemble the tubes onto the drive boxes and secure with the cover plate. Make sure the flared ends of the tubes are correctly positioned.
15 Refit the drive boxes and motor using the reverse procedure to that of removal. Grease the inner drive cable before sliding it through the outer tubes.
16 After reconnecting the battery terminal and motor electrical leads, switch the motor on and then off so that the spindles stop in the parked position and then refit the wiper arms and blades in the parked position.

31 Windscreen wiper motor (later type) – overhaul

1 Mark the domed cover in relation to the flat gearbox lid, undo the four screws that hold the gearbox lid in place and lift off the lid and domed cover.
2 Pull off the small circlip and remove the limit switch wiper. The connecting rod and cable rack can now be lifted off. Take particular note of the spacer located between the final drive wheel and the connecting rod.
3 Undo and remove the two through-bolts from the commutator and cover. Pull off the end cover.
4 Lift out the brush gear retainer and then remove the brush gear. Clean the commutator and brush gear and, if worn, fit new brushes. The resistance between adjacent commutator segments should be 0.34 to 0.41 ohm.
5 Carefully examine the internal wiring for signs of chafing, breaks or chafing which would lead to a short circuit. Insulate or renew any damaged wiring.

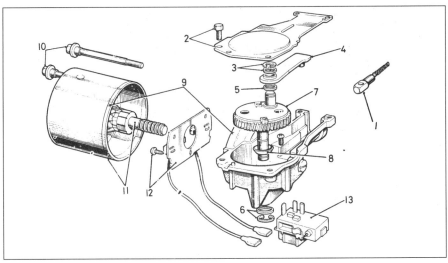

Fig. 10.17 Exploded view of wiper motor – Series III (Sec 31)

1 Drive cable	6 Circlip and washer	10 Retaining bolts
2 Cover and securing bolt	7 Drive gear	11 Yoke and armature
3 Circlip and washer	8 Dished washer	12 Brush gear
4 Connecting rod	9 Yoke and gearbox	13 Limit switch
5 Washer		

32.3 Location of the fuse box on later models

6 Measure the value of the field resistance which should be between 12.8 and 14 ohms. If a lower reading than this is obtained it is likely that there is a short circuit and a new field coil should be fitted.

7 Renew the gearbox gear if the teeth are damaged, chipped or worn,

8 Reassembly is a straightforward reversal of the dismantling sequence, but ensure the following items are lubricated:

a Immerse the self-aligning armature bearing in engine oil for 24 hours before assembly

b Oil the armature bearings with engine oil

c Soak the felt lubricator in the gearbox with engine oil

d Grease generously the wormwheel bearings, crosshead, guide channel, connecting rod, crankpin, worm, cable rack and wheelboxes and the final gear shaft

Note that some Series IIA, and all Series III Land Rovers are fitted with a later type wiper motor. The method of overhauling this motor is virtually identical to the one described in this Section, and providing reference is made to Fig. 10.17, no problems should be encountered.

32 Fuses

1 Earlier models are equipped with a fuse box located on the engine compartment bulkhead. Two fuses are used; fuse no A3-A4 protects the wiper, fuel tank unit and stop light circuits whilst fuse no A1-A2 protects the interior and auxiliary lighting circuits.

2 Two spare fuses are carried in the fuse box

and only 35 amp cartridge fuses should be used when renewing.

3 The fuse box on later models is attached on the underside of the steering column nacelle and contains four fuses (photo).

4 Fuse no 7-8 protects the fuel gauge, water gauge and stop light circuits, fuse no 5-6 protects the direction indicator and wiper circuits whilst fuse no 1-2 protects the lighting circuits (fuse no 3-4 is a spare circuit).

5 If a fuse blows always replace it with a 35 amp fuse. If the trouble persists, refer to the appropriate wiring diagram and check the affected circuits for earthing faults.

33 Flasher circuit – fault tracing and rectification

1 The flasher unit is located behind the instrument panel. To gain access to it, withdraw the instrument panel as described in Section 35. Pull off the electrical leads, undo the securing screw (earlier models) and remove the flasher unit. The flasher unit is a sealed component and cannot be repaired.

2 If the flasher unit fails to operate, or works very slowly or very rapidly, check out the flasher indicator circuit as detailed below before assuming there is a fault in the unit itself.

3 Examine the direction indicator bulbs front and rear for broken filaments.

4 If the external flashers are working but the internal flasher warning light has ceased to function, check the filament of the warning bulb and renew if necessary.

5 If a flasher bulb is sound but does not work check all the flasher circuit connections with the aid of the wiring diagram.

6 In the event of total direction indicator failure, check the appropriate fuse.

7 If all other items check out then the flasher unit itself is faulty and must be renewed.

34 Flasher switch – removal and refitting

1 Disconnect the battery earth terminal.

2 Withdraw the instrument panel as described in Section 35.

Early models

3 Disconnect the leads from the main wiring harness and flasher unit at the rear of the instrument panel.

4 Withdraw the flasher switch leads through the grommet in the side of the instrument box and release the retaining clips on the steering column.

5 Undo and remove the securing screw and nut and remove the switch and bracket from the steering column.

Later models

6 Undo and remove the securing screws and lift off the steering column top and bottom shrouds.

7 Disconnect the flasher switch wiring block

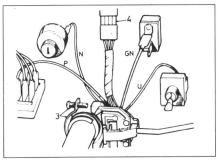

Fig. 10.18 Combined flasher switch, headlight switch and horn switch connections – Series IIA and 111 (Sec 34)

3 Bracket	N Brown
4 Switch harness block	SN Black and brown
P Purple	U Blue

35.2 Withdrawing the instrument panel (early models)

37.4 Location of the temperature gauge sender unit on later Series III models

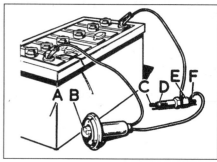

Fig. 10.19 Pedal bracket mounted stop light switch (Sec 38)

A Pedal, stop adjuster   D Switch
B End stop   E Protection plate
C Mounting bracket

connector from the main harness at the rear of the instrument panel.

8 Disconnect the headlight dip lead from the fuse box, the lead to the panel light switch and the lead to the voltage stabiliser. Disconnect the single Lucar connector from the main harness to the starter switch.

9 Undo and remove the screws that secure the switch to the steering column and lift off the switch.

10 Refitting is the reverse sequence to removal.

35 Instrument panel – removal and refitting

1 Disconnect the battery earth terminal and remove the instrument panel retaining screws.

2 Withdraw the instrument panel far enough to gain access to the rear of the panel (photo). **Note** that on Series III models it may be necessary to remove the steering wheel to provide sufficient clearance.

3 Disconnect the drive cable from the rear of the speedometer.

4 Prise out all the illumination and warning light bulb holders from the rear of the panel and the speedometer housing.

5 Disconnect the inspection lamp socket leads.

6 Disconnect the wiring leads from the lighting switch and the fuel mixture warning light (if fitted).

7 Disconnect all the wires from the dynamo warning light (earlier models) and the instrument panel gauges. Make a careful note of the location of each wire and if necessary, identify it with paint or coloured tape as it is removed.

8 On later models, disconnect the Lucar connections from the rear of the panel as necessary and slacken the knurled nut that secures the earth leads.

9 Disconnect the wires from the wiper switch, starter switch and voltage stabilisers, where fitted.

10 Make a careful check that all the leads have been disconnected and then lift the panel away complete with instruments.

11 The instruments can be removed from

the panel by releasing the retaining clips or brackets. The switches and warning lights are secured either by circlips or threaded bezels.

12 Refit the instruments and panel assembly using the reverse procedure to that of removal.

36 Fuel gauge sender unit - removal and refitting

1 The fuel gauge sender unit is located on the top of the fuel tank and is basically a float operated variable resistor that controls the amount of current to the fuel gauge. If the fuel gauge appears to give a faulty reading it is probably due to the float arm sticking or the resistor coil breaking down.

2 To remove the unit, first disconnect the battery earth terminal, then lift off the right-hand seat cushion and remove the tank cover panel. In the case of a rear mounted tank, remove the inspection cover from the rear floor section.

3 Mark the position of the sender unit in relation to the top of the tank and disconnect the electrical lead and earth lead.

4 Remove the retaining screws and lift out the sender unit complete with float.

5 Check that the float moves freely without sticking. If the resistor coil is suspect, the complete unit must be renewed as it cannot be repaired.

6 Refit the unit in the tank using a new gasket smeared with a fuel resistant jointing compound.

37 Temperature gauge sender unit – removal and refitting

1 The temperature gauge sender unit is located on the front left-hand side of the engine adjacent to the thermostat housing. It is basically a bi-metal resistor that increases the current to the gauges as it is progressively heated by the coolant.

2 Drain the coolant as described in Chapter 2, slacken the domed nut and remove the feed wire.

3 Remove the three securing bolts and lift out the sender unit.

4 The unit cannot be repaired and if faulty, must be renewed. When refitting the sender unit always use a new gasket. **Note:** *On some later models, the sender unit is the plug type that screws into an adaptor plug beneath the thermostat housing.*

5 Do not forget to refill the radiator after refitting the sender unit. Run the engine and check for coolant leaks.

38 Stop light switch – removal and refitting

1 Three types of stop light switch are fitted to Land Rover vehicles. Early models have a pressure actuated switch fitted in the brake hydraulic circuit, whilst later models have mechanical switches mounted on the brake pedal bracket or servo mounting bracket.

Hydraulic type

2 The switch is located on the brake pipe 5-way connector at the front right-hand chassis member.

3 Disconnect the leads and unscrew and remove the switch.

4 Refitting is the reverse of the removal procedure. Fit the new switch quickly to avoid brake fluid loss. If necessary, bleed the brakes as described in Chapter 9.

Mechanical type

5 On non-servo models, the switch is located on the brake pedal bracket in the passenger compartment. On vehicles equipped with a servo, the switch is mounted on the servo mounting bracket in the engine compartment.

6 On non-servo models, undo and remove the bolts and lift off the switch protection plate.

7 Remove the electrical leads from the switch.

8 On non-servo models, depress the brake pedal, remove the end stop and locknut from the switch and unscrew it from the mounting bracket. On vehicles equipped with a servo,

40.2 Removing a heater plug from the cylinder head

slacken the locknut and unscrew and remove the switch.

9 Refitting is the reverse sequence to removal, bearing in mind the following points:

a On non-servo models, set the brake pedal adjuster to give a dimension of 6.25 in (158 mm) between the bottom edge of the pedal pad and the floor. If necessary, reset the master cylinder pushrod clearance as described in Chapter 9 Section 14

b On vehicles fitted with a servo, adjust the switch to operate the stoplights at 0.75 to 1.0 in (19 to 25 mm) of pedal movement

39 Starter switch – removal and refitting

Note: *The starter/heater switch appears in the wiring diagram on page 149 (item 20). The switch is shown as having four connections – there are in fact five, of which only the four shown are actually used. This makes it even more important that the position of each lead is noted before disconnection.*

1 Disconnect the battery earth connection.

Early models

2 Make a note of their positions and disconnect the leads from the rear of the switch.

3 Unscrew and remove the large nut from the facia side of the panel and withdraw the switch.

4 Refitting is the reverse sequence to removal.

Later models

5 Unscrew and remove the two instrument panel securing screws and draw the panel forward.

6 Make a note of their positions and disconnect the leads from the rear of the switch.

7 Depress the barrel lock plunger via the small hole in the body of the switch and lift out the barrel.

8 Unscrew and remove the chrome locking ring and lift out the switch from the rear of the panel.

Models with combined starter switch/steering lock

9 Undo and remove the screws that secure the steering column lever shroud and lift off the shroud.

10 Remove the lower facia panel as described in Chapter 12.

11 Make a note of their positions and disconnect the leads from the rear of the switch.

12 Unscrew and remove the two small screws that secure the starter switch to the steering column lock assembly and withdraw the switch.

13 Refitting is the reverse sequence to removal.

40 Heater plugs – removal, testing and refitting

1 Disconnect the electrical leads from the plug, taking care to avoid distortion of the central rod. On early models, use two spanners at each terminal to prevent the insulating rod or central tube twisting.

2 Unscrew and remove the heater plug from the cylinder head (photo).

3 Scrape off any carbon from the base of the plug and element. Do not use ordinary spark plug sandblasting equipment.

4 Examine the element for signs of fracture and the seating for scoring. If these conditions are evident, renew the plug.

5 To test the heater plug internal circuit for continuity, connect the plug and a 12 volt side lamp bulb in circuit to a 12 volt battery as shown in Fig. 10.20.

6 If the bulb fails to light, there is an open circuit in the heater plug and it must be renewed.

7 Refitting the plugs is the reverse sequence to removal. Tighten the plug to the torque figure given in the Specifications.

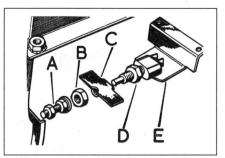

Fig. 10.20 Testing heater plugs (Sec 40)

A 12 volt battery
B 12 volt bulb
C Element
D Seating
E Insulation
F Terminal nuts

41 Speedometer cable – removal and refitting

1 Undo and remove the instrument panel securing screws and withdraw the panel forward.

2 Unscrew the knurled nut or on later models, depress the clip and remove the outer cable from the speedometer.

3 If the inner cable only is to be removed, it can now be withdrawn from the outer cable.

4 If the complete inner and outer cable is to be removed, unfasten the securing clips from the engine, flywheel housing, chassis and transfer gearbox.

5 Disconnect the cable from the main gearbox and withdraw it from inside the vehicle.

6 Refitting is the reverse sequence to removal.

42 Radios and tape players – fitting (general)

A radio or tape player is an expensive item to buy and will only give its best performance if fitted properly. If you do not wish to do the fitting yourself there are many in-vehicle entertainment specialists who can do the fitting for you.

Make sure the unit purchased is of the same polarity as the Land Rover and ensure that units with adjustable polarity are correctly set before commencing the fitting operation.

It is difficult to give specific information with regard to fitting, as final positioning of the radio/tape player, speakers and aerial is entirely a matter of personal preference.

Fault Finding commences overleaf

Fault diagnosis – electrical system

Starter motor fails to turn engine

- [ ] Battery discharged
- [ ] Battery defective internally
- [ ] Battery terminal leads loose or earth lead not securely attached to body
- [ ] Loose or broken connections in starter motor circuit
- [ ] Starter motor switch or solenoid faulty
- [ ] Starter motor pinion jammed in mesh with flywheel gear ring
- [ ] Starter brushes badly worn, or brush wire loose
- [ ] Commutator dirty, worn or burnt
- [ ] Starter motor armature faulty
- [ ] Field coils earthed

Starter motor turns engine very slowly

- [ ] Battery in discharged condition
- [ ] Starter brushes badly worn, sticking, or brush wires loose
- [ ] Loose wires in starter motor circuit

Starter motor operates without turning engine

- [ ] Pinion or flywheel gear teeth broken or worn
- [ ] Battery almost completely discharged

Starter motor noisy or excessively rough engagement

- [ ] Pinion or flywheel gear teeth broken or worn
- [ ] Starter motor retaining bolts loose

Battery will not hold charge for more than a few days

- [ ] Battery defective internally
- [ ] Electrolyte level too low or electrolyte too weak due to leakage
- [ ] Plate separators no longer fully effective
- [ ] Battery plates severely sulphated
- [ ] Fan belt slipping
- [ ] Battery terminal connections loose or corroded
- [ ] Alternator (or dynamo) regulator unit not working correctly
- [ ] Short in lighting circuit causing continual battery drain

No charge light fails to go out, battery runs flat in a few days

- [ ] Fan belt loose and slipping or broken
- [ ] Brushes worn, sticking, broken or dirty
- [ ] Brush springs weak or broken
- [ ] Slip rings dirty, greasy, worn or burnt
- [ ] Alternator stator coils burnt, open, or shorted

Horn operates all the time

- [ ] Horn push either earthed or stuck down
- [ ] Horn cable to horn push earthed

Horn fails to operate

- [ ] Blown fuse
- [ ] Cable or cable connection loose, broken or disconnected
- [ ] Horn has an internal fault

Horn emits intermittent or unsatisfactory noise

- [ ] Cable connections loose or horn needs adjusting

Lights do not come on

- [ ] If engine not running, battery discharged
- [ ] Light bulb filament burnt out or bulbs broken
- [ ] Wire connections loose, disconnected or broken
- [ ] Light switch shorting or otherwise faulty

Lights come on but fade out

- [ ] If engine not running battery discharged

Lights work erratically – flashing on and off, especially over bumps

- [ ] Battery terminal or earth connection loose
- [ ] Lights not earthing properly
- [ ] Contacts in light switch faulty

Wiper motor fails to work

- [ ] Blown fuse
- [ ] Wire connections loose, disconnected or broken
- [ ] Brushes badly worn
- [ ] Armature worn or faulty
- [ ] Field coils faulty

Wiper motor works very slowly and takes excessive current

- [ ] Commutator dirty, greasy or burnt
- [ ] Armature bearings dirty or unaligned
- [ ] Armature badly worn or faulty

Wiper motor works slowly and takes little current

- [ ] Brushes badly worn
- [ ] Commutator dirty, greasy or burnt
- [ ] Armature badly worn or faulty

Wiper motor works but wiper blades remain static

- [ ] Wiper motor gearbox parts badly worn

Wiring Diagrams commence overleaf

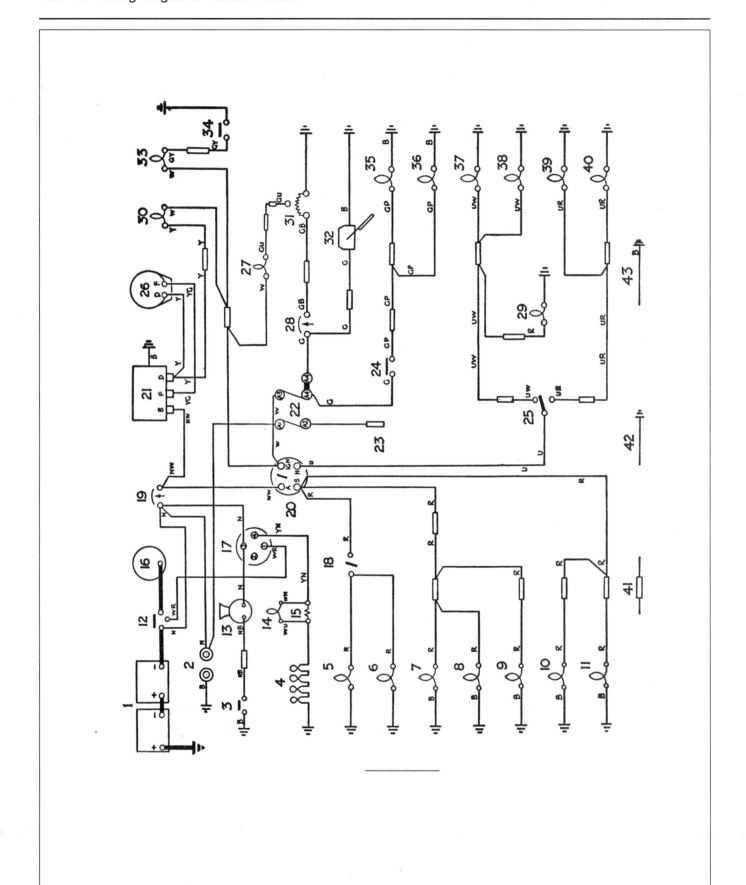

Wiring diagram Series II and IIA diesel models, positive earth

1 Batteries, two, 6 volt positive earth
2 Inspection socket
3 Horn push button
4 Heater plugs
5 Panel light
6 Panel light
7 Tail light
8 Number plate light
9 Tail light
10 Side light
11 Side light
12 Switch, starter
13 Horn
14 Warning light, heater plug
15 Resistor for heater plug

16 Starter motor
17 Switch, heater plug
18 Switch, panel light
19 Ammeter
20 Switch, electrical services and lighting
21 Current-voltage regulator
22 Fuse box
23 To interior lights
24 Switch, stop light
25 Switch, headlamp dip
26 Dynamo
27 Warning light, fuel level
28 Fuel gauge
29 Warning light, headlamp main beam
30 Warning light, charging

31 Gauge unit, fuel tank
32 Wiper motor
33 Warning light, oil pressure
34 Switch, oil pressure warning light
35 Stop light
36 Stop light
37 Headlamp, main beam
38 Headlamp, main beam
39 Headlamp, dip beam
40 Headlamp, dip beam
41 Snap connectors
42 Earth connections via terminals or fixing **bolts**
43 Earth connections via cables

Cable colour code

B Black   G Green   L Light   N Brown   O Orange   P Purple   R Red   S Slate   U Blue   W White   Y Yellow

The last letter of a colour code denotes the tracer colour. RN is Red with Brown, and so on.

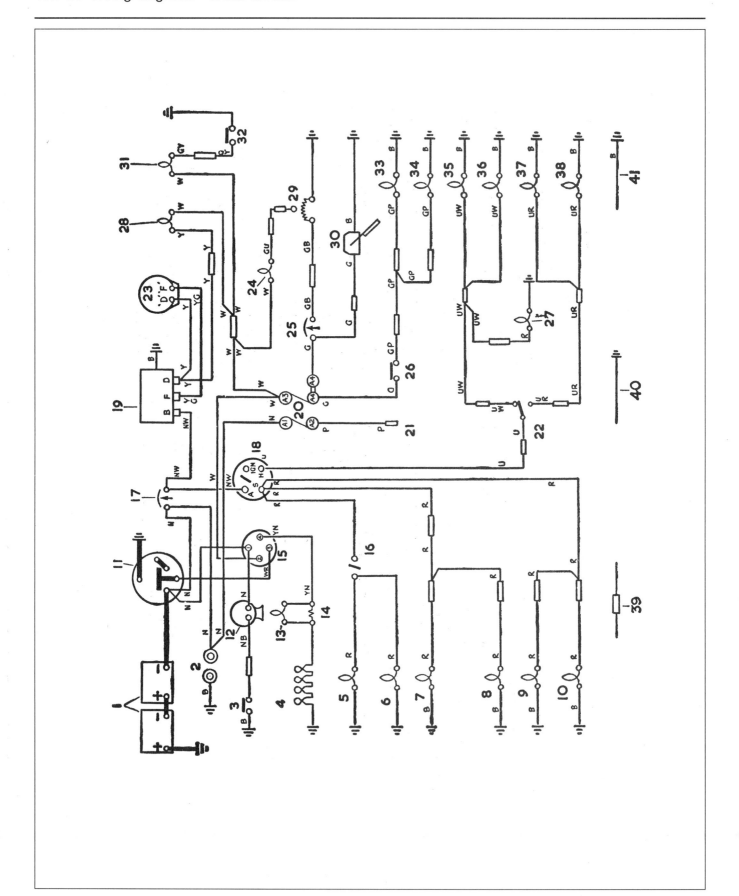

Wiring diagram Series IIA diesel models with combined electrical services, starter and heater plug switch, positive earth

1 Batteries, two, 6 volt positive earth
2 Inspection socket
3 Horn push
4 Heater plugs
5 Panel light
6 Panel light
7 Tail and number plate light
8 Tail and number plate light
9 Side light
10 Sidelight
11 Starter motor
12 Horn
13 Warning light, heater plug
14 Resistance for heater plug

15 Electrical services, starter and heater plug switch
16 Switch, panel light
17 Ammeter
18 Lighting switch
19 Current-voltage regulator
20 Fuse box
21 To interior lights
22 Switch, headlamp dip
23 Dynamo
24 Warning light, fuel level
25 Fuel gauge
26 Switch, stop light
27 Warning light, headlamp main beam
28 Warning light, charging

29 Gauge unit, fuel tank
30 Windscreen wiper motor
31 Warning light, oil pressure
32 Switch, oil pressure warning light
33 Stop light
34 Stop light
35 Headlamp, main beam
36 Headlamp, main beam
37 Headlamp, dip beam
38 Headlamp, dip beam
39 Snap connectors
40 Earth connections via terminals or fixing bolts
41 Earth connections via cables

Cable colour code

B Black   G Green   L Light   N Brown   O Orange   P Purple   R Red   S Slate   U Blue   W White   Y Yellow

The last letter of the colour code denotes the tracer colour. RN is Red with Brown, and so on.

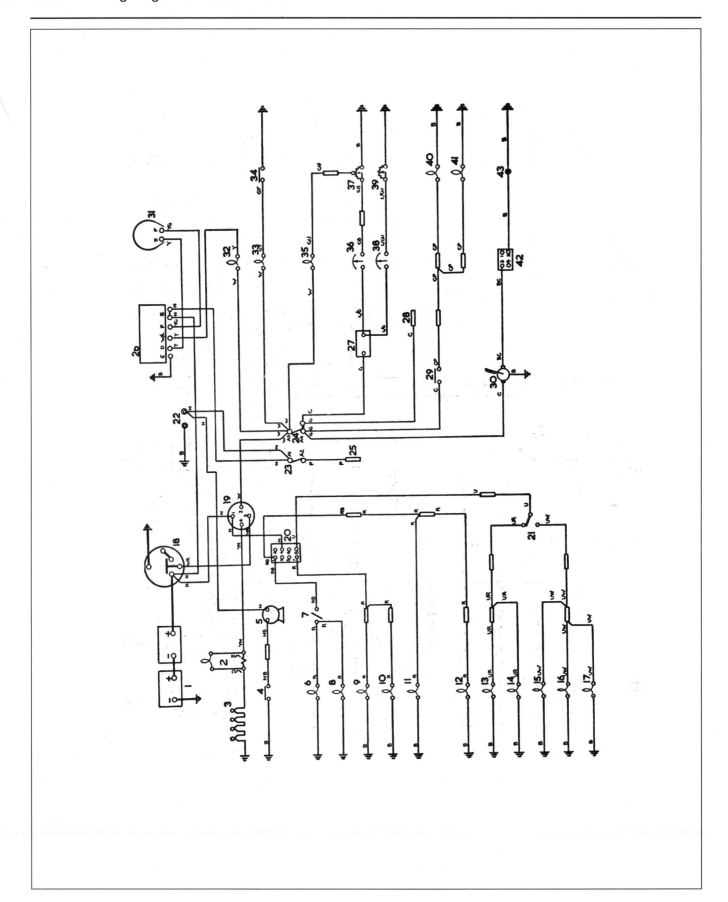

Wiring diagram Series IIA diesel models, negative earth

1 Batteries, two 6 volt
2 Warning light and resistor, heater plugs
3 Heater plugs
4 Horn push
5 Horn
6 Panel light, speedometer
7 Switch, panel light
8 Panel light, instrument
9 Side light RH
10 Side light LH
11 Tail light RH
12 Tail light LH
13 Headlamp, RH, dipped beam
14 Headlamp, LH, dipped beam
15 Headlamp, LH, main beam

16 Headlamp, RH, main beam
17 Warning light, headlamp main beam
18 Starter motor
19 Switch, starter-heater plugs
20 Switch, lights
21 Switch, headlamp dip
22 Inspection sockets
23 Fuse, A1-A2 (35 amp)
24 Fuse, A3-A4 (35 amp)
25 Feed, interior light
26 Current voltage regulator
27 Voltage stabiliser, fuel gauge and water **temperature gauge**
28 Feed, flasher lights
29 Switch, stop lights

30 Wiper motor
31 Dynamo
32 Warning light, dynamo
33 Warning light, oil pressure
34 Switch, oil pressure
35 Warning light, fuel level
36 Fuel gauge
37 Fuel tank unit
38 Temperature gauge
39 Temperature transmitter unit
40 Stop lights RH
41 Stop lights LH
42 Switch, wiper motor
43 Socket, wiper lead

Cable colour code

B Black   G Green   L Light   N Brown   P Purple   R Red   U Blue   W White   Y Yellow

The last letter of the colour code denotes the tracer colour. RN is Red with Brown, and so on.

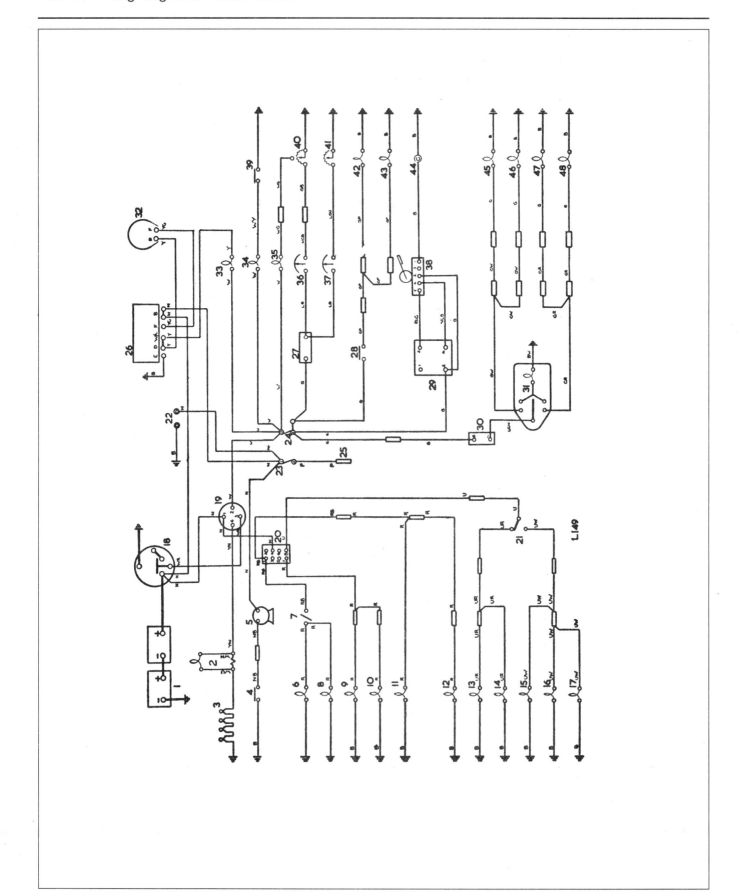

Wiring diagram Series IIA diesel models with headlamps in front wings, negative earth

1 Batteries, two 6 volt
2 Warning light and resistor, heater plugs
3 Heater plugs
4 Horn push
5 Horn
6 Panel light, speedometer
7 Switch, panel light
8 Panel light, instruments
9 Side light RH
10 Side light, LH
11 Tail light, RH
12 Tail light, LH
13 Headlamp, RH, dipped beam
14 Headlamp LH, dipped beam
15 Headlamp, LH, main beam
16 Headlamp, RH, main beam
17 Warning light, headlamp main beam

18 Starter motor
19 Switch, starter-heater plugs
20 Switch, lights
21 Switch, headlamp dip
22 Inspection sockets
23 Fuse, A1-A2 (35 amp)
24 Fuse, A3-A4 (35 amp)
25 Feed, interior light
26 Current voltage regulator
27 Voltage stabiliser, fuel gauge and water **temperature gauge**
28 Switch, stop light
29 Switch, wiper motor
30 Indicator unit, flasher
31 Switch end warning light, flasher
32 Dynamo

33 Warning light, dynamo
34 Warning light, oil pressure
35 Warning light, fuel level
36 Fuel gauge
37 Temperature gauge
38 Wiper motor
39 Switch, oil pressure
40 Fuel tank unit
41 Temperature transmitter unit
42 Stop light RH
43 Stop light LH
44 Socket, wiper lead
45 Front flasher, RH
46 Rear flasher, RH
47 Rear flasher, LH
48 Front flasher, LH

Cable colour code

B Black   G Green   L Light   N Brown   P Purple   R Red   U Blue   W White   Y Yellow

The last letter of the colour code denotes the tracer colour. RN is Red with Brown, and so on.

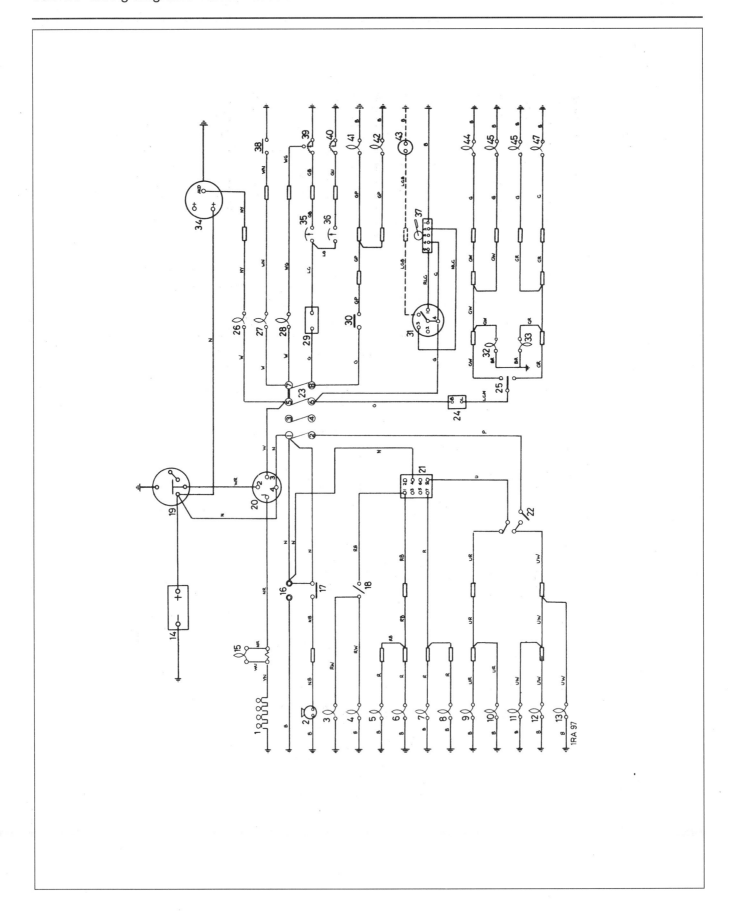

Wiring diagram, Series III diesel models, negative earth

1 Heater plugs
2 Horn
3 Instrument panel light
4 Instrument panel light
5 Tail light, LH
6 Tail light, RH
7 Side light, RH
8 Side light, LH
9 Headlamp, RH dipped beam
10 Headlamp, LH dipped beam
11 Headlamp, LH main beam
12 Headlamp, RH main beam
13 Warning light, headlamp main beam
14 Battery
15 Warning light and resistor, heater plugs
16 Inspection sockets
17 Switch, horn

18 Switch, panel light
19 Solenoid, starter motor
20 Switch, starter-heater plugs
21 Switch, lights
22 Switch, headlamp dip and flash
23 Fuses, 1 to 8, 35 amp
24 Indicator unit flasher
25 Switch, indicators
26 Warning light, alternator
27 Warning light, oil pressure
28 Warning light, low fuel level
29 Voltage stabiliser unit, fuel gauge and
   water temperature gauge
30 Switch, stop lamps
31 Switch, windscreen wiper
32 Warning light, RH indicator
33 Warning light, LH indicator

34 Alternator 16 ACR
35 Fuel gauge
36 water temperature gauge
37 Wiper motor
38 Switch, oil pressure
39 Fuel tank unit
40 Transmitter, water temperature
41 Stop light, LH
42 Stop light, RH
43 Windscreen washer motor (when fitted)
44 Indicator, front RH
45 Indicator, rear RH
46 Indicator, rear LH
47 Indicator. front LH

Cable colour code

L Light

N Brown   P Purple   R Red   U Blue   W White   Y Yellow   **The last letter**   of a colour   code denotes

B Black
G Green

the tracer colour. RN is Red with Brown, and so on.

Notes

Chapter 11
Suspension and steering

For modifications, and information applicable to later models, see Supplement at end of manual

Contents

Degrees of difficulty

Easy, suitable for novice with little experience	**Fairly easy,** suitable for beginner with some experience 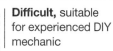	**Fairly difficult,** suitable for competent DIY mechanic	**Difficult,** suitable for experienced DIY mechanic	**Very difficult,** suitable for expert DIY or professional

Specifications

Steering

Type	Re-circulating ball
Ratio:	
Straight ahead	15.6: 1
Full	23.8:1
Number of steering wheel turns lock-to-lock	3.3

Lubricant type/specification

Steering relay and steering box	Hypoid gear oil, viscosity SAE 90EP, to API GL4
All balljoints	Multi-purpose lithium-based grease, to NLGI -2

Front wheel alignment

Wheel camber	1 1/2°
Wheel castor	3°
Swivel pin inclination	7°
Toe-in	1.2 to 2.4 mm

Front spring dimensions

Length	36.25 in (920.7 mm)
Width	2.5 in (63.5 mm)
Number of leaves:	
SWB models	9
LWB models	11

Rear spring dimensions

Length	48 in (1219 mm)
Width	2.5 in (63.5 mm)
Number of leaves:	
SWB models	11
LWB models	10

Shock absorber .... Telescopic type, front and rear

Tyre sizes

SWB models..	6.00 x 16, 6.50 x 16, 7.00 x 16, 7.10 x 16 and 7.50 x 16
LWB models..	7.50 x 16

Tyre pressures (front and rear) .... Consult handbook

Torque wrench settings

	lbf ft	kgf m
Steering wheel nut	40	5.4
Balljoint nuts.	30	4
Brackets to steering box bolts	50 to 60	7 to 8.5
Steering box brackets to chassis bolts	15	2
Drop arm securing nut	60 to 80	8.5 to 11
Relay lever pinchbolt	55	7.6

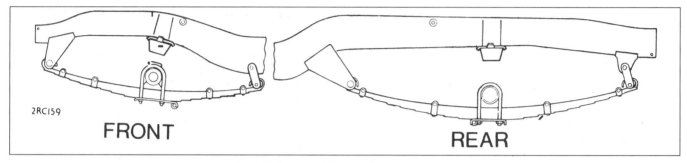

Fig. 11.1. Layout of front and rear suspension

1 General description

The suspension on the Land Rover is ruggedly simple and comprises semi-elliptical leaf springs fitted to the front and rear axle. The ends of each spring are attached to the chassis brackets via metal-clad rubber bushes. Shackle plates on each spring allow it to flex under load. Spring rebound is controlled by telescopic shock absorbers fitted between the axles and chassis. The ends of the shock absorbers are located in rubber bushes.

The steering gear is the recirculating ball type and the steering shaft lower end rotates in two ball races within the gear housing and a bush (or bearing) at the steering column end. Steering movement is transmitted from the gear housing drop arm to the trackrod via a spring-loaded relay unit and drag link.

All the steering ball joints are packed with grease during manufacture and sealed by means of a rubber boot secured with spring clips.

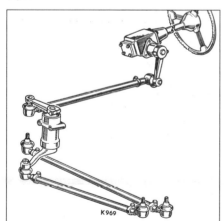

Fig. 11.2. Layout of steering gear

2 Front and rear springs - removal and refitting

1 The procedure for removing either the front or rear springs is basically the same and any differences will be detailed where necessary. It should be noted that the front and rear springs on the driver's side are not interchangeable with those on the passenger side, the driver's side springs having a greater free camber.
2 The process of ordering a new spring will be easier if the part number on the underside of the spring can be quoted (see Fig. 11.3).
3 If only the main or second leaf has broken, these can be obtained from a Leyland dealer as separate items, however, if any of the other leaves have broken a complete new spring must be obtained.
4 To remove either a front or rear spring, first jack-up the appropriate end of the vehicle and place heavy duty axle stands beneath the chassis.
5 Remove both wheels and support the weight of the axle on a jack.
6 Undo the nuts from the four axle 'U' bolts and remove the bottom spring retaining plate. **Note:** On some models the shock absorber is attached to the bottom plate but there is no need to disconnect it, simply extend the shock absorber until the plate is free, (see Fig. 11.4).
7 Make sure the axle is firmly supported and then remove the self locking nuts from the shackle pins at each end of the spring.
8 Remove both shackle pins noting that the rear pin is threaded into the inner shackle plate (photo).
9 Withdraw the road spring from beneath the vehicle.
10 To dismantle the springs, remove the bolts from the spring retaining clip and remove the clips. Remove the centre securing bolt and separate the spring leaves.
11 Examine the spring leaves for cracks

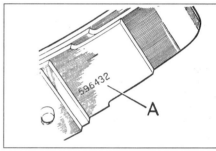

Fig. 11.3. Part No. on underside of roadspring "A"

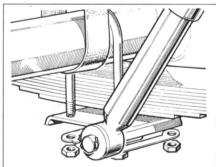

Fig. 11.4. Removing the bottom spring clamping plate

2.8 Rear spring shackle assembly

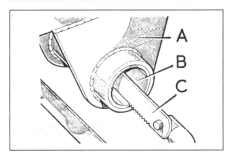

Fig. 11.5. Cutting through the outer casing of a spring shackle bush

A Chassis bracket   B Bush   C Hacksaw

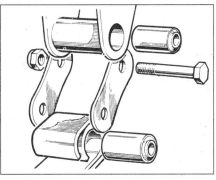

Fig. 11.6. Spring shackle plates and bushes

3.2 Front shock absorber assembly

and the bushes for wear and renew where necessary. The bushes can be driven out of the spring eyes using a suitably sized drift or piece of tubing. Remove the shackle plates from the rear spring hanger and check the top shackle bush for wear. Renew the bush if worn.

12 If while driving the bush out it breaks up leaving the outer casing jammed in the chassis bracket, it can be removed by carefully sawing through it with a hacksaw (Fig. 11.5). Take great care not to cut into the chassis bracket. If any of the shackle bolts are worn they should be renewed.

13 Smear the spring leaves and bushes with graphite grease before reassembly, Refit the shackle plates and spring to the vehicle using the reverse procedure to removal, but do not tighten any of the shackle pin nuts at this stage.

14 After the springs are correctly installed, refit the wheels and lower the vehicle to the ground. Rock the vehicle from side-to-side to settle the springs and then fully tighten all the shackle pin lock nuts.

3 Shock absorbers - removal and refitting

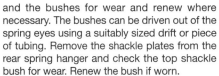

1 The front and rear shock absorbers are identical and the method of attachment is also similar, although there are minor differences

on certain models which will be described where necessary.

2 Jack-up the appropriate end of the vehicle and support it on axle stands. Remove the roadwheel (photo).

3 Remove the nut and bolt securing the top of the shock absorber to the chassis (Fig. 11.7).

4 Referring to Fig. 11.8 remove the split pin and washer securing the bottom end of the shock absorber to the spring plate. Note that on some models the end of the shock absorber terminates in a threaded stud which passes through a bracket welded to the axle. If working on the latter type, remove the securing nut and retrieve the steel and rubber washers.

5 Withdraw the ends of the shock absorber from the mounting brackets and retrieve the washers and rubber bushes.

6 Inspect the shock absorber for signs of hydraulic fluid leakage which, if evident, indicates that the unit must be renewed.

7 Clean the exterior and wipe dry with a non-fluffy rag.

8 Inspect the shaft for signs of corrosion or distortion and the body for damage.

9 Check the action by expanding and contracting to ascertain if equal resistance is felt on both strokes. If the resistance is very uneven the unit should be fully expanded and contracted at least eight times. If this does not cure the problem the unit must be renewed.

10 Check the rubber bushes and washers for signs of deterioration and obtain new if evident.

11 Refit the shock absorber using the reverse procedure to removal.

4 Steering wheel - removal and refitting

Earlier type

1 Set the front wheels in the straight ahead position and mark the position of the steering wheel in relation to the column.

2 Disconnect the battery earth terminal, prise out the horn button from the centre of the wheel and disconnect the horn lead from the snap connector at the dash panel.

3 Remove the nut and bolt securing the wheel to the column and withdraw the wheel from the splined shaft (See Fig. 11.9).

4 Refit the steering wheel using the reversal of the removal procedure ensuring the alignment marks are matched up.

Later type

5 Set the front wheels in the straight ahead position and mark the position of the steering wheel in relation to the column.

6 Prise out the cover from the centre of the steering. If the horn push is located in the

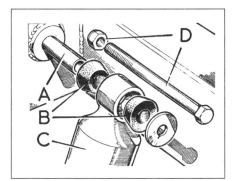

Fig. 11.7. Shock absorber top attachment point

A Chassis   C Shock absorber
B Rubber bushes   D Securing bolt

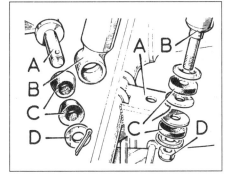

Fig. 11.8. Shock absorber lower attachment points (showing alternative method)

A Chassis   C Rubber bushes
B Shock absorber   D Securing nut (or washer)

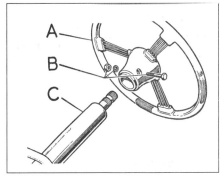

Fig. 11.9. Removing the steering wheel (earlier models)

A Wheel   C Steering column
B Securing bolt

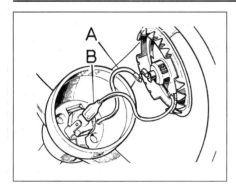

Fig. 11.10. Disconnecting the horn leads (later models)

A Connection to horn button
B Connection to steering column

centre cover, disconnect the battery and remove the horn leads (see Fig. 11.10).

7 Bend back the locking washer tab and remove the centre retaining nut. Withdraw the wheel from the splined shaft (Fig. 11.11).

8 Refit the steering wheel using the reversal of the removal procedure. Ensure the alignment marks are matched up and then tighten the retaining nut to the specified torque and bend over the locking tab.

5 Steering trackrod and drag link balljoints - removal and refitting

1 Excessive play in the steering usually indicates that one or more of the balljoints have worn. To

5.2 Front steering arm ball joints

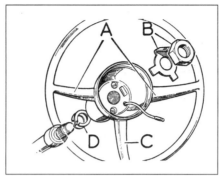

Fig. 11.11. Removing the later type steering wheel

A Spokes facing sideways
B Nut and washer for steering wheel
C Spoke facing rearward
D Special spring washer

check them, get an assistant to turn the steering wheel from side-to-side. From beneath the vehicle visually check for movement between the balljoints and the steering arms and relay lever. If wear is evident the ball joints should be renewed as soon as possible.

2 Place chocks behind the rear wheels, jack up the front of the vehicle, support it on axle stands and remove the appropriate road wheel (photo).

3 Remove the split pin and undo the castle nut securing the ball joint to the steering arm. Using an universal balljoint separator or Leyland tool No. 600590, extract the tapered shaft of the balljoint from the steering arm or relay lever (see Fig. 11 .12).

4 Carefully note how much of the threaded portion of the balljoint is protruding from the trackrod (or drag link) and mark it with some paint. Slacken the clamp and unscrew the balljoint. Note that the balljoints on one end of the trackrod and drag link have left-hand threads.

5 If the balljoint is worn it must be renewed. However, if it is in good condition, it can be lubricated by removing the rubber boot, pressing the ball down into the housing against the spring and forcing grease into the housing. Fill a new boot with grease and refit it using new spring retaining rings (see Fig. 11.13).

6 Screw the balljoint into the end of the trackrod (or drag link) up to the paint mark

made previously on the threads. If fitting a new balljoint use the mark on the old one as a guide. Check that the distance between the balljoint centres is 30.812 to 30.937 in (782.62 to 785.79 mm) on the drag link and 45.56 to 45.68 in (1157 to 1160 mm) on the trackrod. Screw the balljoint in or out as appropriate until this figure is achieved.

7 Before tightening the clamp, refit the balljoint to the steering arm, tighten the nut to the specified torque and secure with a new split pin. Then tighten the clamps.

8 Refit the wheels and lower the vehicle to the ground. As a final check take the vehicle to a Leyland dealer who will have the necessary optical alignment equipment to check that the front wheel toe-in is set correctly.

6 Steering column lock and ignition/starter switch (series III models) - removal and refitting

1 Disconnect the battery and remove the choke control cable from the carburettor (refer to Chapter 3 if necessary).

2 Undo the securing screws and lift off the steering column top shroud followed by the bottom shroud. If necessary remove the steering wheel as described in Section 4.

3 Carefully centre punch each shear bolt securing the lock assembly to the column. Drill a suitable sized hole and remove both shear bolts using an 'easy-out' extractor (see Fig. 11.14).

4 Make a note of the positions of the wiring connection on the ignition switch and then remove them.

5 Withdraw the steering lock/ignition switch assembly complete with the choke control.

6 The ignition switch can be removed by undoing the two small retaining screws and withdrawing it from the housing. It is not a repairable item and if faulty must be renewed.

7 Refit the lock and switch assembly using the reversal of the removal procedure. New shear bolts must obviously be used and these have to be tightened until the heads shear off.

8 After refitting, check that the steering column is unlocked when the ignition key is set to the 'services' position and locked when the key is withdrawn.

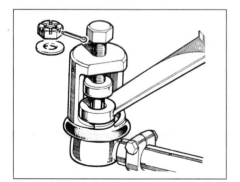

Fig. 11.12. Removing a balljoint

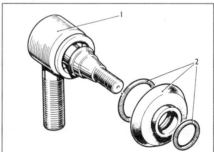

Fig. 11.13. Balljoint and seal assembly

1 Balljoint   2 Seal and retaining springs

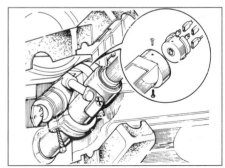

Fig. 11.14. Steering lock and ignition/ starter switch (Series III models only)

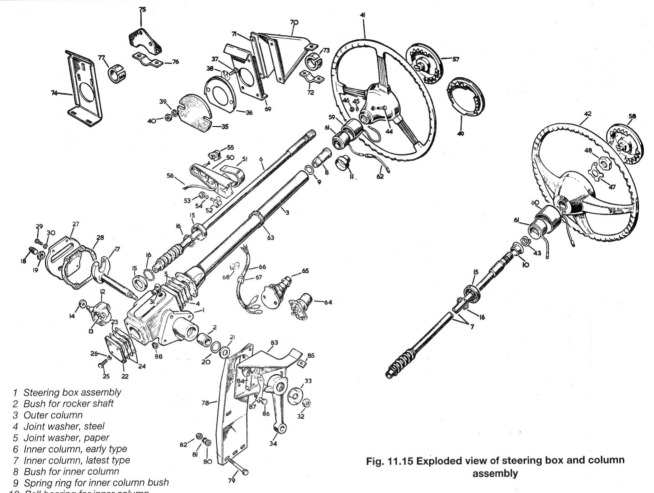

Fig. 11.15 Exploded view of steering box and column assembly

1 Steering box assembly
2 Bush for rocker shaft
3 Outer column
4 Joint washer, steel
5 Joint washer, paper
6 Inner column, early type
7 Inner column, latest type
8 Bush for inner column
9 Spring ring for inner column bush
10 Ball bearing for inner column
11 Dust shield for inner column
12 Main nut assembly
13 Steel ball (3/8 in) for main nut
14 Roller for main nut
15 Adjustable ball race
16 Steel balls (.280 in) for adjustable race
17 Rocker shaft
18 Adjuster screw for rocker shaft
19 Locknut for adjuster screw
20 Oil seal for rocker shaft
21 Washer for rocker shaft oil seal
22 End plate
23 Joint washer, steel
24 Joint washer, paper
25 Bolt (5/16 in UNC x 29/32 in long)[1]
26 Spring washer[1]
27 Side cover plate
28 Joint washer for side cover plate
29 Bolt (5/16 in UNC x 1/16 in long)[2]
30 Spring washer[2]
31 Oil filler plug
32 Special nut
33 Lock washer – Fixing
34 Steering drop arm
35 Rubber seal for steering column
36 Cover for steering column seal
37 Screw (2 BA x 3/4 in long)[3]
38 Special washer[3]
39 Spring washer[3]
40 Nut (2 BA)[3]

41 Steering wheel, early type
42 Steering wheel, latest type
43 Special spring washer on inner column for wheel
44 Bolt (5/16 in UNF x 2 in long)[4]
45 Plain washer[4]
46 Nut (5/16 in (UNF)[4]
47 Tag washer[4]
48 Special nut[4]
49 Steering wheel centre cover, early type
50 Horn push bracket
51 Clip for horn push bracket
52 Yoke assembly for horn push bracket
53 Nut (1/4 in BSF)
54 Shakeproof washer[5]
55 Horn push[5]
56 Lead, horn push to junction box
57 Horn push and centre cover for steering wheel, early type
58 Horn push and centre cover for steering wheel, latest type
59 Dust cover and horn contact, early type
60 Dust cover and horn contact, latest type
61 Slip ring complete for horn contact
62 Lead, slip ring to junction box
63 Cable cleat on steering column
64 Dip switch, early type
65 Dip switch, latest type
66 Lead, dip switch to junction box
67 Grommet for lead in toe box floor
68 Clip fixing dip switch lead to floor
69 Support bracket on dash

70 Support bracket for steering column
71 Packing piece for steering column support bracket
72 Clip for steering column
73 Rubber strip for clip
74 Support bracket on dash
75 Clamp, upper, for steering column
76 Clamp, lower, for steering column
77 Rubber strip for clamp
78 Support bracket, steering box to chassis
79 Bolt (5/16 in UNF x 3 3/4 in long)[6]
80 Plain washer, thin[6]
81 Spring washer[6]
82 Nut (5/16 in UNF)[6]
83 Stiffener bracket for steering box
84 Bolt plate[7]
85 Shim washer[7]
86 Set bolt (3/8 in UNC x 7/8 in long)[7]
87 Locking plate[7]
88 Self-locking nut (5/16 in UNF)[7]

[1]Securing end plate
[2]Securing side cover plate
[3]Securing cover and seal to dash
[4]Securing early type steering wheel, securing latest type steering wheel
[5]Securing horn push bracket
[6]Securing brackets to chassis frame
[7]Securing stiffner bracket to front face of toe box, securing steering box to chassis support bracket

Fig. 11.16. Steering column clamp (earlier models may vary slightly)

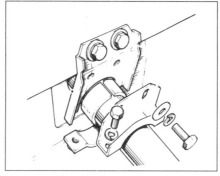

Fig. 11.17. Removing the steering box drop arm

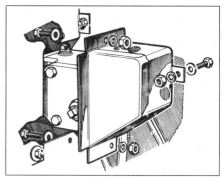

Fig. 11.18. Steering box cover

7 Steering gear assembly - removal and refitting

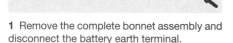

1 Remove the complete bonnet assembly and disconnect the battery earth terminal.
2 Refer to Chapter 3 and remove the air cleaner assembly.
3 Remove the steering wheel as described in Section 4 of this Chapter and the flasher/ combination switch as described in Chapter 10.
4 On Series III models, remove the ignition switch/steering column lock as described in the previous Section.
Note: On Series III models without a steering column lock, remove the ignition switch assembly by unscrewing the lock ring.
5 Referring to Fig. 11.16, remove the complete lower column support bracket assembly from the engine compartment bulkhead.
6 Remove the drop arm securing nut and washer and using Leyland special tool No. 600000, pull the arm from the steering box and move the arm and longitudinal steering tube out of the way (Fig. 11.17).
7 If working on a vehicle with left-hand steering, disconnect the throttle linkage from the steering box support bracket.
8 Slacken the nuts of the front roadwheel on the steering box side of the vehicle.
9 Chock the rear wheels, jack-up the front

of the vehicle and support it on axle stands. Remove the roadwheel.
10 Remove the nuts and bolts securing the steering gear cover box and lift away the box (see Fig. 11.18).
11 Remove all the bolts securing the steering box support brackets to the bulkhead, wing valance and chassis member (see Fig. 11.19).
12 Withdraw the steering box and column assembly complete with support brackets from beneath the front wing.
13 Refitting the steering column is basically the reverse sequence to removal, but the following points should be noted:

a) Prior to installing the steering box refit the stiffener and support brackets and tighten to the specified torque wrench setting.
b) Before tightening the bolts securing the steering box brackets to the bulkhead, wing and chassis, adjust the steering column position to obtain a snug fit in the upper support bracket and then tighten the column retaining clamp bolts. Finally, tighten the steering box bracket bolts to the specified torque wrench setting.
c) When refitting the drop arm to the steering box, set the front wheels in the straight ahead position and the steering wheel in the intermediate position and push the arm onto the splines. Tighten the securing nut to the specified torque wrench setting

Note: On later models the steering box shaft

and drop arm have alignment marks, and the forward mark on the drop arm must line up with the mark cut in the end of the shaft.

8 Steering column and gearbox - overhaul

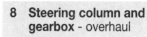

1 With the steering box and column assembly on the bench, remove the side cover plate and drain the oil into a suitable container.
2 Lift out the roller from the main nut assembly and withdraw the rocker shaft (see Fig. 11.20).
3 Hold the outer steering column in a soft-jawed vice and remove the four bolts securing the end of the column to the steering box.
4 Using a soft-faced mallet, gently tap the inner column at the steering wheel end until the steering box is free of the column. Withdraw the box and inner column complete and retrieve the steel balls from the upper race if freed from the box (see Fig. 11.21).
5 Rotate the inner column until the main nut is midway along the worm shaft. Gently tap the box away from the inner column just enough to drive out the upper ball race, (presuming it has not already come out). Retrieve the steel balls.
6 Turn the worm shaft through the main nut assembly and remove the shaft, nut and any loose bearings.
7 Undo the four retaining bolts and remove

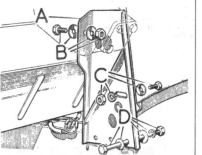

Fig. 11.19. Steering box bracket

A Support bracket   C Wing bolts
B Bulkhead bolts   D Chassis bolts

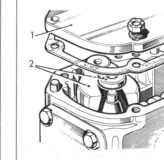

Fig. 11.20. Removing the steering box cover plate

1 Cover   2 Roller and rocker shaft

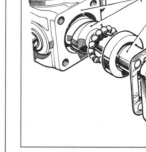

Fig. 11.21. Withdrawing the outer column assembly

1 Steering box and worm shaft
2 Inner column   3 Securing bolt

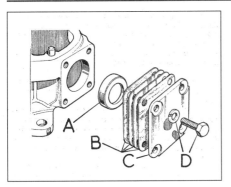

Fig. 11.22. Removing the lower end plate

A Bearing   C Cover
B Shims   D Securing bolt

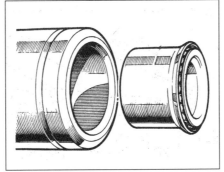

Fig. 11.23. Steering column top bearing
(bush on earlier models)

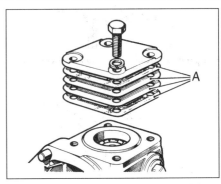

Fig. 11.24. End cover and shims "A"

the end cover, shims and lower bearing (see Fig. 11.22).

8 Tap the main nut assembly on a piece of wood until all the twelve ball bearings drop out of the recirculating tube.

9 Examine the rocker shaft and bush for wear and if necessary remove the washer and oil seal, press the bush out of the steering box and fit a new one. A new oil seal should be fitted as a matter of course.

10 Check the upper column ball race for wear (bush on earlier models and renew if necessary (see Fig. 11.23).

11 Examine the inner track on the main nut and the worm shaft for signs of pitting or scaling and renew where necessary. Check the upper and lower bail bearings and races for similar signs of wear.

12 If the worm shaft, main nut and bearings are all worn the most sensible solution is to obtain a replacement steering box assembly from a Leyland dealer.

13 Commence reassembly by retaining the ten steel balls in the upper race with grease and sliding the race over the steering wheel end of the inner column until it abuts the worm shaft.

14 Place a new gasket on the outer column flange and slide it over the inner column.

15 Locate the steel balls in the main nut with plenty of grease. Hold the nut in position inside the box and carefully wind the worm shaft through it. Ensure that none of the steel balls fall out of the main nut or upper bearing.

16 Secure the outer column to the box with the four washers and bolts.

17 Place the ten balls in the lower race using grease, and fit the race over the end of the inner column and into the box.

18 Fit a new gasket on each side of the shims and refit the shims and end cover. Tighten the four end cover securing bolts and check the inner column for freedom of rotation. It should rotate freely with no endfloat, and this condition can be achieved by removing or refitting the end cover shims as necessary (see Fig. 11.24).

19 Insert the rocker shaft into the box followed by the roller. Place a new gasket on the steering box aperture and refit the side cover ensuring the roller is correctly located in the groove on the underside of the cover. Tighten the retaining bolts.

20 Refit the steering box assembly to the vehicle as described in Section 7 and fill it with Hypoid gear oil, viscosity SAE 90EP.

9 Steering relay unit - removal and refitting

1 Remove the ' Land Rover' name plate and lift off the radiator grille.

2 Working through the grille panel aperture

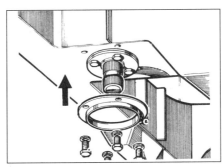

Fig. 11.26. Lower steering relay securing flange

and from beneath the vehicle. remove the pinch-bolts and prise off the upper and lower relay lever (Fig. 11.25).

3 Remove the two bolts securing the top of the relay unit to the grille panel.

4 From beneath the vehicle, remove the four bolts securing the relay unit flange plate (Fig. 11.26).

5 Remove any equipment located directly above the relay unit, then, using a brass drift, drive the unit upwards to free it from the chassis. If the unit refuses to move, apply some penetrating oil between the base of the unit and the chassis.

6 Refit the relay unit using the reverse procedure to that of removal. Ensure that the upper and lower relay levers are refitted at an angle of 90° to each other as shown in Fig. 11.27. Note that the flat boss on the upper side of the unit must face away from the radiator.

10 Steering relay unit - overhaul

1 The relay unit contains a large spring under compression and before any attempt is made to dismantle the unit a Leyland spring compression tool (Part No. 600536) should be obtained. It may be possible to compress the spring using a made-up tool or with the help of an assistant but the task may prove to be rather difficult.

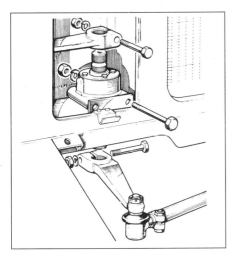

Fig. 11.25. Upper and lower steering relay levers

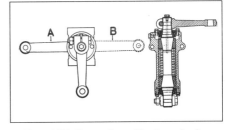

Fig. 11.27. Correct positioning of relay levers

A Lower lever, LH steering
B Lower lever, RH steering

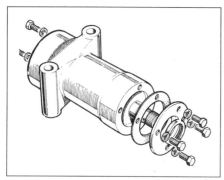

Fig. 11.28. Steering relay bottom retaining plate

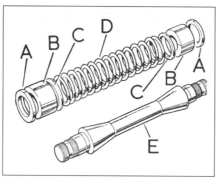

Fig. 11.29. Steering relay spring and shaft assembly

A Thrust washer   D Spring
B Split bush   E Relay shaft
C Washer for spring

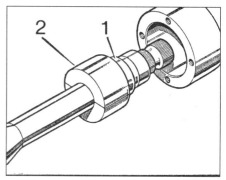

Fig. 11.30. Inserting the steering relay shaft

1 Shaft   2 Split bush

2 To dismantle the relay unit, first remove the oil filler and breather plugs from the top of the unit, (or bottom on later types) and drain out the oil.

3 Remove the four bolts from the bottom of the unit and lift off the retaining plate, oil seal and gasket (see Fig. 11.28).

CAUTION: As stated previously the relay unit contains a large spring under compression which will fly out when the shaft is driven out. To avoid injury or damage cover the bottom end of the unit with a heavy piece of cloth and tie it to the unit with string.

4 Mount the unit in a vice and with the cloth covering the bottom end, drive the shaft out from the top end of the unit.

5 Remove the piece of cloth and retrieve the spring, shaft, bushes and washers (see Fig. 11.29).

6 Remove the securing nuts and lift off the top retaining plate, oil seal and gasket.

7 The relay unit is now dismantled and the component can be examined for wear. Note

that the free length of the spring should be 7.25 in (184 mm).

8 Examine the split bushes and shaft for signs of wear and renew if necessary.

9 Fit new oil seals into the top and bottom retaining plates, smearing a little jointing compound around the outside diameter of each seal.

10 To assemble, fit the two halves of e split bush on the top cone section of the shaft and insert the shaft and bush into the bottom end of the housing (Fig. 11.30).

11 Secure the housing and shaft in a vice with the bottom end upwards and a 3/4 in (19 mm) block of wood under the end of the shaft.

12 Drop one of the washers down over the shaft and screw two of the retainer bolts into the housing diametrically opposite each other.

13 Side the spring over the shaft and into the housing and place the second washer on top of the spring.

14 Using tool No. 600536 compress the spring until it is possible to turn the tool and lock the slots over the heads of the two bolts. Take care that the spring does not fly out (see Fig. 11 .31).

15 Fit the other split bush onto the cone section of the protruding shaft and secure in place with a 2 in (50 mm) hose clip.

16 Turn the tool sufficiently to release it from the bolt heads and withdraw it from between the spring and split bush. Remove the two bolts .

17 Remove the housing from the vice and

gently tap the shaft into the housing until the bush is half way in. Remove the hose clip and continue to tap the shaft in until the bushes are correctly located in the housing.

18 Fit the thrust washer, oil seal retainer and gasket to the bottom end of the housing and secure with the four bolts.

19 Fill the housing with EP 90 oil, injecting it through one of the bolt holes in the top of the housing or the plug on the side, if fitted.

20 Refit the top thrust washer, gasket and oil seal and retainer and tighten the four securing bolts.

21 Hold the housing in the vice and temporarily refit the upper relay lever. Using a spring balance attached to the end of the lever, check that the pull required to turn the lever is not less than 12 lb (5.4 kg) and not more than 16 lb (7.3 kg).

22 If the resistance to movement is less than specified a new spring should be fitted. If an excessive pull is required to move the lever the oil seal retainers should be removed and the bushes pushed inwards to enable oil to be injected directly onto the cone sections of the shaft.

23 Refit the relay to the vehicle using the procedure described in Section 9.

11 Steering gearbox - adjustment

1 Jack-up the vehicle until the front wheels are just clear of the ground and set the steering to the straight ahead position.

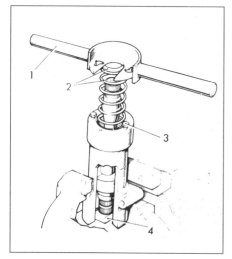

Fig. 11.31. Using the special tool to compress the spring into the housing

1 Special tool (Leyland No. 600536)
2 Spring and washer
3 Retainer bolts in position
4 Block of wood

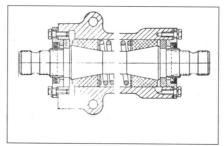

Fig. 11.32. Cross-sectional view of assembled steering relay unit

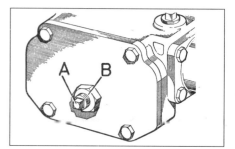

Fig. 11.33. Steering gearbox adjuster

A Adjuster   B Locknut

2 Slacken the adjuster screw and locknut located on the side of the steering gearbox and screw in the adjuster using the hand only until it stops.

3 Tighten the locknut ensuring the adjuster does not move, and then lower the vehicle to the ground.

4 If the steering is still excessively slack after adjustment, check the balljoints for wear as described in Section 5. If these appear in good condition, then it is possible that the steering gearbox requires overhauling (Section 8).

12 Steering geometry - checking and adjustment

1 Unless the front suspension has been damaged, the castor angle, camber angle and swivel pin inclination angles will not alter, provided of course, that the suspension balljoints are not worn excessively.

2 The toe-in of the front wheels is a setting which may be reset if new components are fitted - for example, after fitting new tie-rod balljoints it will be necessary to reset the toe-in.

3 Indications of incorrect wheel alignment (toe-in) are uneven tyre wear on the front wheels and erratic steering particularly when turning. To check toe-in accurately needs optical alignment equipment, so this is one job that must be left to the local Leyland garage. Ensure that they examine the linkage to ascertain the cause of any deviation from the original setting.

13 Longitudinal steering arm – removal and refitting

1 Remove the bonnet as described in Chap-ter 12.

2 Unscrew the fixings and lift off the radiator grille.

3 Refer to Chapter 3 if necessary and remove the air cleaner (right-hand drive models only).

4 From the aperture in the front panel, undo and remove the nut, bolt and spring washer that secure the upper relay lever to the relay unit. Using a screwdriver or flat bar, prise off the lever (photo).

5 At the other end of the longitudinal steering arm withdraw the split-pin and unscrew and remove the castellated nut that secures the

balljoint to the steering box drop arm. Remove the balljoint from the drop arm using the method described in Section 5, paragraph 4.

6 Manoeuvre the longitudinal steering arm through the aperture in the front panel and lift it clear of the vehicle.

7 If necessary, the balljoints may be removed using the method described in Section 5.

8 Refitting is the reverse of the removal sequence bearing in mind the following points:

  (a) *Tighten the castellated nut that secures the balljoint to the steering box drop arm to the torque setting given in the Specifications and secure with a new split-pin*

  (b) *Before refitting the relay lever ensure that the steering box is in the intermediate position (turn the steering wheel from lock to lock then stop half way). Check that with the front wheels in the straight-ahead position, the lower relay lever points directly forward. If necessary, adjust the drag link as described in Section 5. With these checks complete, refit the upper relay lever as shown in Fig. 11.35. If necessary, adjust the length of the longitudinal steering arm by turning one way or the other.*

  (c) *Ensure that sufficient clearance exists between the longitudinal steering arm and the brake pipe that runs alongside it on the chassis section. If necessary, bend the brake pipe slightly to clear the arm.*

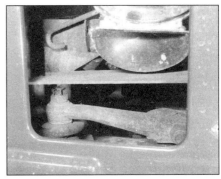

13.4 The steering relay lever is located behind the grille panel

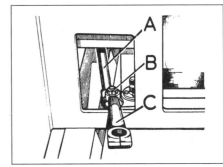

Fig. 11.34. Removing the longitudinal steering arm

A Longditudinal arm
B Balljoint castellated nut
C Upper relay lever

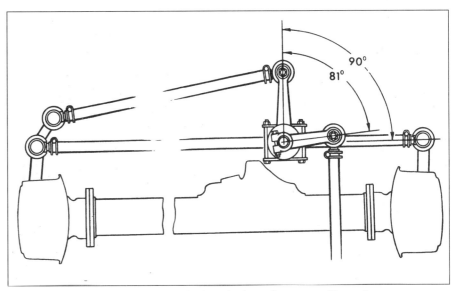

Fig. 11.35. Correct positioning of relay unit upper and lower levers

FAULT FINDING OVERLEAF

Fault finding - suspension and steering

Before diagnosing faults from the following chart check the irregularities are not caused by:
1 Binding brakes
2 Incorrect 'mix' of radial and crossply tyres
3 Incorrect tyre pressure
4 Misalignment of the chassis

Steering wheel can be moved considerably before any sign of movement is apparent at the roadwheels

☐ Wear in steering linkage, gear and column bearings.

Vehicle difficult to steer in a straight line - 'wanders'

☐ As above.
☐ Wheel alignment incorrect (shown by uneven front tyre wear).
☐ Front wheel bearings loose.
☐ Worn suspension unit swivel pins.

Excessive pitching and rolling on corners and during braking

☐ Defective damper and/or broken spring.

Steering stiff and heavy

☐ Incorrect wheel alignment (uneven or excessive tyre wear).
☐ Wear or seizure in steering linkage joints.
☐ Wear or seizure in spring shackles.
☐ Excessive wear in steering gear unit.

Wheel wobble and vibration

☐ Roadwheels out of balance.
☐ Roadwheels buckled.
☐ Wheel alignment incorrect.
☐ Wear in steering and suspension linkages.

Chapter 12
Chassis and bodywork

Contents

Degrees of difficulty

Easy, suitable for novice with little experience	Fairly easy, suitable for beginner with some experience	Fairly difficult, suitable for competent DIY mechanic	Difficult, suitable for experienced DIY mechanic	Very difficult, suitable for expert DIY or professional

1 General description

The backbone of the Land Rover is the box section chassis shown in Fig. 12.1. It is comprised of two longitudinal box section members joined by crossmembers to form a ladder type fabrication that is extremely strong and rigid.

The rear body and front sections are bolted directly onto the chassis and the extremities of the body are supported by outriggers welded to the two longitudinal sections.

The SWB model has an overall chassis length of 134.6 in (3420 mm) and a wheelbase length of 88 in (2235 mm). The LWB model has an overall chassis length of 166.9 in (4240 mm) and a wheelbase length of 109 in (2770 mm). It is for this reason that the two models are frequently referred to as '88' and the '109' model respectively.

With the exception of the radiator panel, dash panel, door frames and tail board frame which are steel, the body panels on the Land Rover are made of a magnesium-aluminium alloy known as 'Birmabright'.

This alloy is stronger than pure aluminium and will not rust or corrode under normal conditions. All the steel cappings and corner brackets are manufactured from galvanised steel.

2 Maintenance - body and chassis

1 Because most of the bodywork on the Land Rover is constructed from an aluminium alloy, rust is not a great problem. However, if the vehicle is being used in wet, muddy conditions, the worst of the dirt should be washed off at least once a month using a hosepipe and brush. The hidden portions of the body, such as the wheel arches, the chassis and the engine compartment are equally important, though obviously not requiring such frequent attention as the immediately visible paintwork.

2 Once a year or every 12,000 miles it is sound advice to visit your local main agent and have the underside of the body steam cleaned. All traces of dirt and oil will be removed and the underside can then be inspected carefully for rust, damaged hydraulic pipes, frayed electrical wiring and other faults.

3 At the same time the engine compartment should be cleaned in the same manner. If steam cleaning facilities are not available then brush a suitable similar cleanser over the whole engine and engine compartment with a stiff paintbrush, working it well in where there is an accumulation of oil and dirt. Do not paint the ignition system but protect it with oily rags when the cleanser is washed off. As the cleanser is washed away it will take with it all traces of oil and dirt, leaving the engine looking clean and bright.

3 Maintenance - upholstery and carpets

1 Mats and carpets should be brushed or vacuum cleaned regularly to keep them free of grit. If they are badly stained remove them from the car for scrubbing or sponging and make

quite sure they are dry before replacement. Seats and interior trim panels can be kept clean by a wipe over with a damp cloth. If they do become stained (which can be more apparent on light coloured upholstery) use a little liquid detergent and a soft nail brush to scour the grime out of the grain of the material. Do not forget to keep the head lining clean in the same way as the upholstery. When using liquid cleaners inside the vehicle do not over-wet the surfaces being cleaned. Excessive damp could get into the seams and padded interior causing stains, offensive odours or even rot, If the inside of the vehicle gets wet accidentally it is worthwhile taking some trouble to dry it out properly, particularly where carpets are involved. **Do not** leave oil or electrical heaters inside the car for this purpose.

4 Minor body repairs

Repair of minor scratches in the vehicle's bodywork

If the scratch is very superficial, and does not penetrate to the metal of the bodywork, repair is very simple. Lightly rub the area of the scratch with a paintwork renovator or a very fine cutting paste to remove loose paint from the scratch and to clear the surrounding bodywork of wax polish. Rinse the area with clean water.

Apply touch-up paint to the scratch using a thin paint brush, continue to apply thin layers of paint until the surface of the paint in the scratch is level with the surrounding paintwork. Allow the new paint at least two weeks to harden; then blend it into the surrounding paintwork by rubbing the paintwork in the scratch area with a paintwork renovator or a very fine cutting paste. Finally apply wax polish.

Where the scratch has penetrated right through to the metal of the bodywork, a different repair technique is required. Remove any loose paint, etc from the bottom of the scratch with a penknife. Using a rubber or nylon applicator, fill the scratch with bodystopper paste. If required, this paste can be mixed with cellulose thinners to provide a very thin paste which is ideal for filling narrow scratches. Before the stopper-paste in the scratch hardens, wrap a piece of smooth cotton rag around the top of a finger. Dip the finger in cellulose thinners and then quickly sweep it across the surface of the stopper-paste in the scratch; this will ensure that the surface of the stopper-paste is slightly hollowed. The scratch can now be painted over as described earlier in this section.

5 Body repairs

Repair of dents in the vehicle's bodywork

The alloy body panels on the Land Rover are easier to work on than steel and minor dents or creases can be beaten out fairly easily. However, if the damaged area is quite large, prolonged hammering will cause the metal to harden and to avoid the possibility of cracking, it must be softened or 'annealed'. This can be done quite easily with a gas blowlamp but great care is required to avoid actually melting the metal. The blowlamp must always be kept moving in a circular pattern whilst being held a respectable distance from the metal,

One method of checking when the alloy is hot enough is to rub down the surface to be annealed and then apply a thin film of oil over it. The blowlamp should be played over the rear side of the oiled surface until the oil evaporates and the surface is dry. Turn off the blowlamp and allow the metal to cool naturally, the treated areas will now be soft and it will be possible to work it with a hammer or mallet. After panel beating, the damaged section should be rubbed down and painted as described later in this Section.

When deep denting of the vehicle's bodywork has taken place, the first task is to pull the dent out until the affected bodywork almost attains its original shape. There is little point in trying to restore the original shape completely, as the metal in the damaged area will have stretched on impact and cannot be reshaped to its original contour. It is better to bring the level of the dent up to a point which is about 1/8 in (3 mm) below the level of the surrounding bodywork. In cases where the dent is very shallow anyway, it is not worth trying to pull it out at all.

If the underside of the dent is accessible,

it can be hammered out gently from behind using the method described earlier.

Should the dent be in a section of the bodywork which has a double skin or some other factor making it inaccessible from behind, a different technique is called for. Drill several small holes through the metal inside the dent area. particularly in the deeper sections. Then screw long self-tapping screws into the holes just sufficiently for them to gain a good purchase in the metal. Now the dent can be pulled out by pulling on the protruding heads of the screws with a pair of pliers

The next stage of the repair is the removal of the paint from the damaged area and from an inch or so of the surrounding 'sound' bodywork.

Note: *On no account should coarse abrasives be used on aluminium panels in order to remove paint. The use of a wire brush or abrasive on a power drill for example, will cause deep scoring of the metal and in extreme cases penetrate the thickness of the relatively soft aluminium alloy.*

Removal of paint is best achieved by applying paint remover to the area, allowing it to act on the paintwork for the specified time and then removing the softened paint with a wood or nylon scraper. This method may have to be repeated in order to remove all traces of paint.

> **HAYNES HiNT** *A good method of removing small stubborn traces of paint is to rub the area with a nylon scouring pad soaked in thinners or paint remover.*
>
> *Note: If it is necessary to use this method, always wear rubber gloves to protect the hands from burns from the paint remover. It is also advisable to wear protection over the eyes as any paint remover that gets into the eye will cause severe inflammation or worse.*

Finally, remove all traces of paint and remover by washing the area down with plenty of clean fresh water.

To complete the preparations for filling, score the surface of the bare metal with a screwdriver or the tang of a file, or alternatively, drill small holes in the affected area. This will provide a really good 'key' for the filler paste.

To complete the repair, see the Section on filling and respraying.

Repair of holes or gashes in the vehicle's bodywork

Remove all paint from the affected area and from an inch or so of the surrounding 'sound' bodywork, using the method described in the previous Section. With the paint removed you will be able to gauge the severity of the damage and therefore decide whether to replace the whole panel (if this is possible) or to repair the affected area. It is often quicker and more satisfactory to fit a new panel than to attempt to repair large areas of damage.

Remove all fittings from the affected area

except those which will act as a guide to the original shape of the damaged bodywork (eg. headlamp shells etc). Then, using tin snips or a hacksaw blade, remove all loose metal and other metal badly affected by damage. Hammer the edges of the hole inwards in order to create a slight depression for the filler paste.

Before filling can take place it will be necessary to block the hole in some way. This can be achieved by the use of aluminium or plastic mesh, or aluminium tape.

Aluminium or plastic mesh is probably the best material to use for a large hole. Cut a piece to the approximate size and shape of the hole to be filled, then position it in the hole so that its edges are below the level of the surrounding bodywork. It can be retained in position by several blobs of filler paste around its periphery.

Aluminium tape should be used for small or very narrow holes. Pull a piece off the roll and trim it to the approximate size and shape required, then pull off the backing paper (if used) and stick the tape over the hole; it can be overlapped if the thickness of one piece is insufficient. Burnish down the edges of the tape with the handle of a screwdriver or similar, to ensure that the tape is securely attached to the metal underneath.

Bodywork repairs – filling and respraying

Before using this Section, see the Section on dent, scratch, hole and gash repairs.

Many types of bodyfiller are available, but generally speaking those proprietary kits which contain a tin of filler paste and a tube of resin hardener are best for this type of repair. A wide, flexible plastic or nylon applicator will be found invaluable for imparting a smooth and well contoured finish to the surface of the filler.

Mix up a little filler on a clean piece of card or board. Use the hardener sparingly (follow the maker's instructions on the packet) otherwise the filler will set very rapidly.

Using the applicator, apply the filler paste to the prepared area: draw the applicator across the surface of the filler to achieve the correct contour and to level the filler surfaces. As soon as a contour that approximates the correct one is achieved, stop working the paste, if you carry on too long the paste will become sticky and begin to 'pick-up' on the applicator. Continue to add thin layers of filler paste at twenty-minute intervals until the level of the filler is just 'proud' of the surrounding bodywork.

Once the filler has hardened, excess can be removed using a metal plane or file. From then on, progressively finer grades of abrasive paper should be used, starting with a 40 grade production paper and finishing with 400 grade 'wet or dry' paper. Always wrap the abrasive paper around a flat rubber, cork, or wooden block, otherwise the surface of the filler will not be completely flat. During the smoothing of the filler surface, the 'wet-or-dry' paper should be periodically rinsed in water. This will ensure that a very smooth finish is imparted to the filler at the final stage.

At this stage, the 'dent' should be surrounded by a ring of bare metal, which in turn should be encircled by the finely 'feathered' edge of the good paintwork. Rinse the repair area with clean water, until all the dust produced by the rubbing-down operation is gone.

Spray the whole repair area with a light coat of grey primer, this will show up any imperfections in the surface of the filler. If at all possible, it is recommended that an etch-primer is used on untreated alloy surfaces, otherwise the primer may not be keyed sufficiently and may subsequently flake off. Repair imperfections with fresh filler paste or bodystopper and once more, smooth the

surface with abrasive paper. If bodystopper is used, it can be mixed with cellulose thinners to form a really thin paste which is ideal for filling small holes. Repeat the spray and repair procedure until you are satisfied that the surface of the filler, and the feathered edge of the paintwork are perfect. Clean the repair area with clean water and allow it to dry fully.

The repair area is now ready for spraying. Paint spraying must be carried out in a warm, dry, windless and dust free atmosphere. This condition can be created artificially if you have access to a large indoor working area, but if you are forced to work in the open, you will have to pick your day very carefully. If you are working

indoors, dousing the floor in the work area with water will 'lay' the dust which would otherwise be in the atmosphere. If the repair is confined to one body panel, mask off the surrounding panels; this will help to minimise the effects of a slight mis-match in paint colours. Bodywork fittings will also need to be masked off. Use genuine masking tape and several thicknesses of newspaper for the masking operation.

Before commencing to spray, agitate the aerosol can thoroughly, then spray a test area (an old tin, or similar) until the technique is mastered. Cover the repair area with a thick coat of primer; the thickness should be built up using several thin layers of paint rather one thick

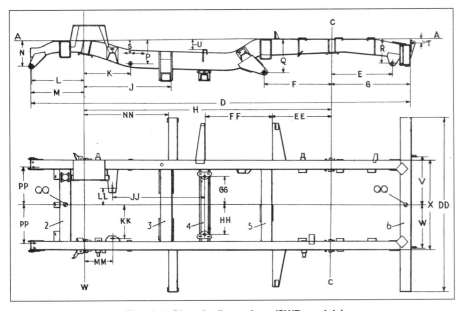

Fig. 12.1. Chassis dimensions (SWB models)

AA Datum line
CC Centre line of rear axle
D 3420mm (134.6in)
DD 1536 mm (60.5 in)
E 539.7 mm (21.25 in)
EE 539.7 mm (21.25 in)
F 610 mm (24.0 in)
FF 610 mm (24.0 in)
G 713.2 mm (28.08 in)
GG 257 ± 0.8 mm (10.12 ± 0.030 in)
H 2235 mm (88.0 in)
HH 254 ± 0.8 mm (10.00 ± 0.030 in)
J 793.7 mm (31.25 in)
JJ 835 ± 0.8 mm (32.87 ± 0.030 in)
K 422.3 mm (16.625 in)
KK 289.7 mm (11.40 in)
L 457 mm (18.0 in)

LL 166.7 mm (6.56 in)
M 472.2 mm (18.58 in)
MM 250.8 ± 1.5 mm (9.875 ± 0.060 in)
N 229 mm (9.0 in)
NN 768.3 mm (30.25 in)
P 212.7 mm (8.37 in)
PP 331.78 ± 0.5 mm (13.062 ± 0.020 in)
Q 290.5 mm (11.44 in)
QQ 9.52 mm (0.375 in) diameter holes
R 198.4 mm (7.81 in)
S 120.6 mm (4.75 in)
T 29.3 mm (1.15 in)
U 82.5 mm (3.25 in)
V 432 mm (17.0 in)
W 387.3 mm (15.25 in)
WW Centre line of front axle
X 787 mm (31.0 in)

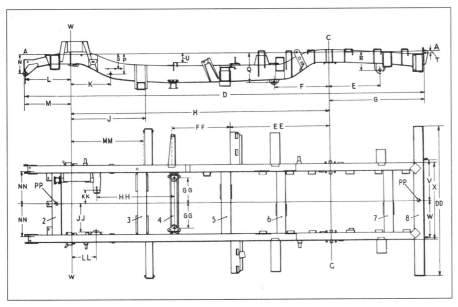

Fig. 12.2 Chassis dimensions (LWB models)

AA Datum line
CC Centre line of rear axle
D 4240 mm (166.9 in)
DD 1536 mm (60.5 in)
E 539.7 mm (21.25 in)
EE 1070 mm (42.12 in)
F 610 mm (24.0 in)
FF 641 mm (25.2 in)
G 1000 mm (39.375 in)
GG 257 ± 0.8 mm (10.125 ± 0.030 in)
H 2770 mm (109 in)
HH 835 ± 0.8 mm (32.87 ± 0.030 in)
J 793.7 mm (31.25 in)
JJ 289.71 mm (11.406 in) 2 3/4 litre
JJ 290.51 mm (11.437 in) 2.6 litre
K 422.3 mm (16.625 in)
KK 166.7 mm (6.56 in)

L 457 mm (18.0 in)
LL 250.7 mm (9.87 in) 2 1/4 litre
M 472.2 mm (18.58 in)
MM 763 mm (30 in)
N 229 mm (9.0 in)
NN 331.8 ± 0.5 mm (13.06 ± 0.062 in)
P 212.7 mm (8.37 in)
PP 9.52 mm (0.375 in) diameter holes
Q 296.8 mm (11.68 in)
R 204.7 mm (8.06 in)
S 120.6 mm (4.75 in)
T 29.3 mm (1.15 in)
U 82.5 mm (3.25 in)
V 432 mm (17.0 in)
W 387.3 mm (15.25 in)
WW Centre line of front axle
X 787 mm (31.0 in)

one. Using 400 grade 'wet or dry' paper, rub down the surface of the primer until it is really smooth. Whilst doing this the work area should be thoroughly doused with water, and the 'wet or-dry' paper periodically rinsed in water. Allow to dry before spraying on more paint.

Spray on the top coat, again building up the thickness by using several thin layers of paint. Start spraying in the centre of the repair area and then, using a circular motion, work outwards until the whole repair area and about 2 in of the surrounding original paintwork is covered. Remove all masking material 10 to 15 minutes after spraying on the final coat of paint.

Allow the new paint at least 2 weeks to harden fully; then, using a paintwork renovator or a very fine cutting paste, blend the edges of the new paint into the existing paintwork. Finally, apply wax polish.

6 Major chassis and body repairs

1 Major chassis and body repair work cannot successfully be undertaken by the average owner. Work of this nature should be entrusted to a competent body repair specialist who should have the necessary jigs, welding and hydraulic straightening equipment as well as skilled panel beaters to ensure that a proper job is done.
2 If the damage is severe it is vital that on completion of repair the chassis is in correct alignment. Less severe damage may also have twisted or distorted the chassis although this may not be visible immediately. It is therefore always best on completion of repair to check for twist and squareness to ensure that all is correct.
3 If distortion of the chassis is suspected, the chassis dimensions can be checked by reference to Fig. 12.1 or 12.2 as appropriate.

7 Maintenance - hinges and locks

1 Oil the hinges of the bonnet, tailgate and doors with a drop or two of light oil periodically. A good time is after the car has been washed.
2 Oil the bonnet release catch pivot pin and the safety catch pivot pin periodically.
3 Do not over lubricate door latches and strikers. Normally a little oil on the catch alone is sufficient.

8 Doors - tracing rattles and their rectification

1 Check first that the door is not loose at the hinges and that the latch is holding the door firmly in position. Check also that the door lines up with the aperture in the body.
2 If the hinges are loose or the door is out of alignment it will be necessary to rest the hinge positions as described in Section 12.

3 If the latch is holding the door properly it should hold the door tightly when fully latched and the door should line up with the body. If it is out of alignment it needs adjustment as described in Section 14. If loose, some part of the lock mechanism must be worn out and requiring renewal.

9 Front wing - removal and refitting

1 Remove the bonnet as described in Chapter 1.
2 Disconnect the battery earth terminal and then disconnect the sidelight and headlamp harness at the snap connectors in the engine compartment .

3 Remove the securing bolts and lift out the mudshield from under the wing. If working on the driver's side wing, remove the steering box mudshield (see Fig. 12.3).
4 Using a socket wrench, remove the bolts securing the wing to the scuttle pillar.
5 Remove the bolts securing the wing and stay to the sill panel.
6 Remove the bolts securing the rear end of the wing to the upper mounting bracket.
7 Remove the bolt securing the wing to the steering column support plate (refer to Chapter 11, if necessary).
8 Finally, remove the bolts securing the wing to the grille panel.
9 With an assistant, lift the complete wing assembly away from the vehicle.
10 Refit the wing using the reversal of the removal procedure.

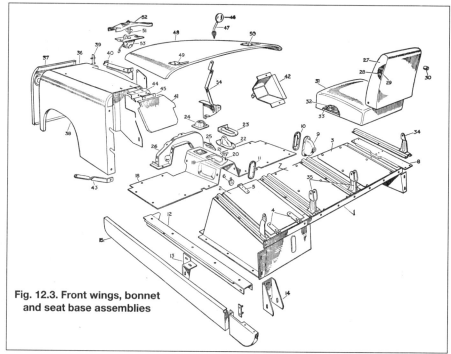

Fig. 12.3. Front wings, bonnet and seat base assemblies

1 Seat base and floor assembly
2 Tool locker lid
3 Fuel tank cover panel
4 Lid hinge
5 Locker lid hasp
6 Locker lid turnbuckle
7 Centre cover panel
8 Extension panel, at seat base ends
9 Handbrake rubber cover
10 Retainer for rubber cover
11 Handbrake slot cover plate
12 Sill channel LH front
13 Sill channel securing bracket
14 Sill channel mounting bracket, to rear body
15 Front sill panel
16 Rear sill panel
17 Fixing plate for sill panels
18 Front floor complete

19 Inspection cover, for front floor
20 Stud plate for inspection cover wing nut
21 Wing nut, securing inspection cover
22 Transfer gear lever seal
23 Transfer lever seal retainer
24 Gear lever rubber seal
25 Operating rod cover plate
26 Gearbox cover complete
27 Seat squab
28 Squab spring case
29 Squab frame
30 Buffer, for seat back rest on bracket
31 Seat cushion
32 Cushion spring case
33 Cushion frame
34 Cushion support, outer
35 Seat support, centre
36 Front wing

37 Front panel and registration plate
38 Front wing outer panel
39 Securing plate, wings to grille panel
40 Wing valance bottom panel
41 Mudshield, front wing
42 Steering unit cover box
43 Front wing stay
44 Bracket, for rear of wing
45 Securing plate - brackets to dash
46 Mirror
47 Arm for mirror
48 Bonnet top panel
49-50 Bonnet hinges
51 Bonnet catch striker pin
52 Bonnet striker bracket
53 Bonnet control
54 Bonnet prop rod

10 Windscreen assembly - removal and refitting

1 Remove the cab or hardtop as described in Section 17. If a hood is fitted, release the front support stays and disconnect the drain channels from the top of the windscreen.

2 On earlier models, disconnect the wiper lead plug from the socket on the dash panel.
3 Slacken the nuts at each bottom corner of the windscreen.
4 Remove the windscreen pivot bolts and with the help of an assistant lift away the complete windscreen assembly.
5 Refit the windscreen using the reverse procedure to that of removal.

11 Windscreen glass - removal

1 Remove the windscreen wiper blade(s) as described in Chapter 10.
2 On earlier models, disconnect the wiper motor earth wire and remove the wiper motor from the screen. Refer to Chapter 10 if necessary.
3 Remove the screws from around the perimeter of the windscreen and prise off the glass retainers. Remove the glass.
CAUTION: If the glass has been shattered, take great care when removing any remaining chips of glass from the windscreen frame.
4 Before refitting a new glass apply a 1/2 in (12 mm) wide sealing strip around the outside of both sides of the glass. Refit the glass retainers and refit the glass using the reversal of the removal procedure.

12 Side doors - removal, refitting and adjustment

1 Disconnect the door check rod (photo).
2 Get an assistant to take the weight of the door and remove the four nuts and bolts securing the two hinges to the door. Lift the door away from the vehicle.
3 Refit the door using the reverse procedure.
4 Before attempting to adjust the door, refer to Fig. 12.5 and remove the hinge bolt cone, and spring and check them for wear. Obtain new ones if necessary.
5 Refit the hinge bolt, ensuring it is well lubricated and then adjust the hinge by tightening or slackening the bottom retaining nut. When the best setting is obtained, bend over the lockwasher.

13 Side door windows - removal and refitting

Sliding window

1 Push the sliding window to one side to gain access to the top glass channel retaining screws.

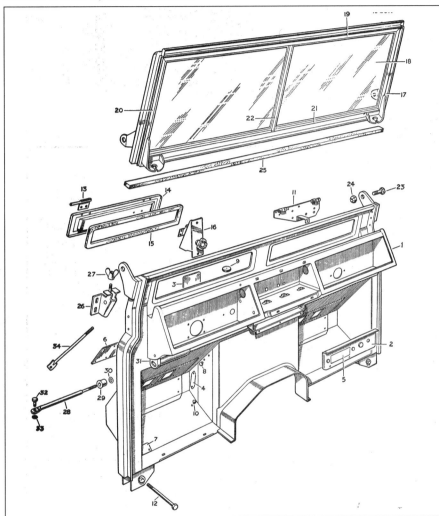

Fig. 12.4. Dash panel and windscreen an assemblies

1 Dash complete
2 Panel for controls
3 Cover panel for steering cut out
4 Cover plate for accelerator pedal hole
5 Cover panel for governor cut-out in – Petrol models
6 Cover plate for pedal holes
7 Cover plate for dipswitch hole
8 Rubber plug, redundant accelerator holes
9 Rubber grommet for demister holes
10 Rubber plug, redundant accelerator stop holes

11 Mounting plate for pump
12 Tie bolt
13 Ventilator hinge
14 Ventilator lid for dash
15 Sealing rubber for ventilator lids
16 Ventilator control mechanism complete
17 Windscreen complete assembly
18 Glass for windscreen
19 Retainer for windscreen glass, top
20 Retainer for windscreen glass, side
21 Retainer for windscreen glass, bottom

22 Cover for centre strip
23-24 Bolt for windscreen to dash
25 Rubber sealing strip for windscreen
26 Fastener for windscreen, RH
27 Wing nut for fastener
28 Check strap rod
29 Check strap buffer
30 Fixings - buffer to rod
31 Check strap mounting bracket
32-33 Pin - check strap rod to front door
34 Tie rod

12.1 Door check rod assembly

1 Tailboard assembly
2 Tailboard top capping
3 Tailboard tread plate
4 Tailboard sealing rubber, bottom
5 Tailboard hinge, RH
6 Tailboard hinge, LH
7 Tailboard chain hook
8 Tailboard locking plate
9 Front door assembly
10 Door top capping
11 Hinge complete, upper
12 Hinge complete, lower
13-17 Fixings for door hinge
18 Door lock mounting plate
19 Door lock
20 Washer, handle to cover
21 Handle
22 Door handle bracket
23 Captive plate, door lock mounting to door
24 Seal for door, front upper
25 Seal for door, front lower, dash
26 Seal for door, rear lower
27 Seal for door, bottom sill
28 Support bracket at door striker
29 Door lock striking plate
30 Side screen assembly
31 Front fixed window
32 Window retainer
33 Rear sliding window
34 Sealing rubber for front edge of sliding window
35 Sealing rubber channel
36 Buffer for sliding window, at top
37-38 Filler strip for windows
39 Top channel
40 Bottom channel
41 Rear channel
42 Sidescreen sealing strip

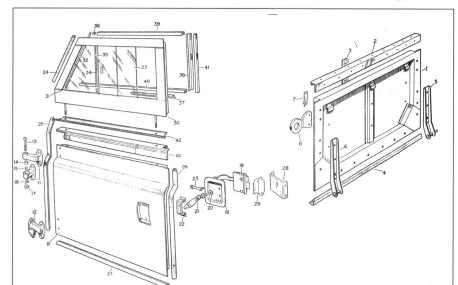

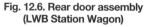

Fig. 12.5. Front side door and tailboard assemblies

**Fig. 12.6. Rear door assembly
(LWB Station Wagon)**

1 Rear side door assembly, LH
2 Mounting plate for door lock
3 Door handle complete, LH
4 Bracket for door handle, outer mounting
5 Door lock complete, LH
6 Sealing washer, handle to cover
7 Locking catch, LH
8 Door hinge, upper LH
9 Door hinge, lower LH
10 Fixed window for sidescreen
11 Retainer for sidescreen, fixed window
12 Filler, top and bottom, for side screen
13 Filler, rear, for sidescreen
14 Sliding window with knob for sidescreen
15 Sliding light channel, rear
16 Sliding light channel, top and bottom
17 Buffer for sidescreen sliding window at top
18 Sealing rubber for sliding glass
19 Retainer for sliding glass sealing rubber
20 Sliding window catch
21 Rod for check strap, LH
22 Buffer for check strap, short
23 Door check bracket, LH, for rear side door
24 Clevis pin
25 Striking plate for rear side door locks
26 Nut plate
27 Waist moulding, rear side door, LH
28 Seal retainer for rear side door, LH top
29 Rubber seal for retainer
30 Door sealing rubber for upper vertical 'D' post
31 Door sealing rubber for lower vertical 'D' post, LH
32 Door sealing rubber for sloping 'D' post
33 Door sealing rubber at rear side sills, bottom
34 Door sealing rubber at 'C' post
35 Door sealing rubber at 'B' post, lower LH
36 Door sealing rubber at B' post, upper
37 Filler piece for 'B' post seal
38 Frame for front and rear side doors, LH

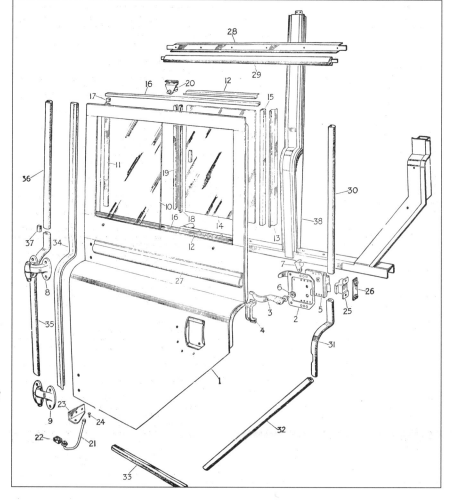

2 Remove the screws and lift out the top channel and sliding window. Remove the bottom channel if necessary.

3 Fit some new sealing strips to the window frame, and refit the glass using the reverse procedure to that of removal.

Fixed window

4 First remove the sliding window as described previously.

5 Remove the screw securing the front retainer, lift away the retainer and ease the glass out of the frame.

6 Fit some new sealing strips to the window frame and refit the glass using the reverse procedure to that of removal.

14 Door locks - removal, refitting and adjustment

1 Remove the door trim (later models only).

2 Remove the four securing nuts from the door lock (see photo) and remove the complete door lock and handle assembly.

3 The door locks cannot be repaired, and if damaged or broken a new lock assembly should be fitted.

4 Refit the door lock using the reversal of the removal procedure.

5 If the door rattles or will not shut correctly, slacken the two screws securing the striker plate to the door panel.

6 The striker should be positioned so that door draught excluders are just slightly compressed when the door is fully shut.

15 Rear tailgate - removal and refitting

1 Withdraw the tailgate securing keys and lower the tailgate.

2 Unhook both the tailgate support chains.

3 Remove the split pin and washer (or clip) from the right-hand hinge pin and with the help of an assistant slide the tailgate off the hinges.

4 Refit the rubber sealing strip if necessary and refit the tailgate using the reverse procedure to that of removal.

16 Dash panel - removal and refitting

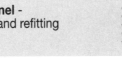

1 Disconnect the battery earth terminal.

2 Remove the bonnet as described in Chapter 1.

3 Remove the front wings as described in Section 9 of this Chapter.

4 Remove the windscreen assembly (see Section 10).

5 Remove the front doors as described in Section 12.

6 Remove the front floor panels and transmission cover panel as described in Chapter 1.

7 Remove the split pin and nut securing the longitudinal arm to the steering box drop arm and, using Leyland tool No. 600590, remove the balljoint from the drop arm (refer to Chapter 11 if necessary).

8 Disconnect the starter motor lead from the switch terminal.

9 Disconnect the high and low tension wires from the coil, and remove the oil pressure warning light lead from the switch on the side of the oil filter.

10 Disconnect the temperature gauge wire from the sender unit on top of the cylinder head.

11 Undo and remove the fluid outlet pipes from the clutch and brake master cylinders (refer to Chapter 9 if necessary).

12 Disconnect the clutch flexible hose from the bracket and rigid pipe on the dash panel.

13 Disconnect the throttle linkage and choke cable from the carburettor (see Chapter 3).

14 If a heater is fitted, drain the cooling system and remove the complete heater assembly (see Section 20).

15 Disconnect the leads from the rear of the dynamo (or alternator).

16 Disconnect the speedometer cable from the transfer box and release the cable from the clips securing it to the transfer box, chassis and flywheel housing (see Chapter 6).

17 Disconnect the horn and headlamp wires from the junction box on the dash panel.

18 Make a careful note of the position of each wire and then disconnect the main wiring harness snap connectors.

19 Remove the bolts securing the steering box support bracket to the dash panel.

20 Referring to Fig. 12.4, remove the two tie bolts, washers and nuts securing the dash panel to the chassis. Remove the nuts and bolts securing the sill panels to the dash panel.

21 Make a careful check that all electrical leads, brake pipes etc. are disconnected from the dash panel and then lift the complete panel assembly out of the vehicle.

22 Refit the dash panel using the reversal of the removal procedure. Refit the longitudinal arm to the drop arm with the front wheels in the straight ahead position. The brake and clutch systems will have to be bled as described in Chapters 5 and 9 respectively.

17 Cab assembly - removal and refitting

1 Remove the nuts and bolts retaining the front of the cab to the windscreen frame.

2 Remove the bolts securing the cab to the front mounting bracket (photo) .

3 Remove the nuts and bolts securing the cab to the centre mounting brackets.

4 Remove the nuts retaining the cab to the rear hood sockets (photo).

5 Remove the nuts and bolts securing the rear mounting brackets to the body and lift off the complete cab assembly.

6 If required, remove the rear upper door section by undoing the nuts and bolts securing the stays to the side panel. Remove the split pins and withdraw the hinge pins. The door can now be lifted away from the rear of the cab.

7 Refer to Fig. 12.7 and 12.8 and renew any of the windows, window rubbers or sealing strips that have deteriorated.

8 Refit the cab assembly using the reverse procedure to that of removal .

14.2 Door lock assembly

17.2 Cab retaining bracket (forward)

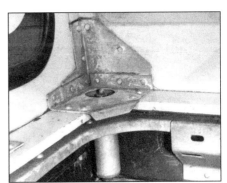

17. 4 Cab retaining bracket (rear)

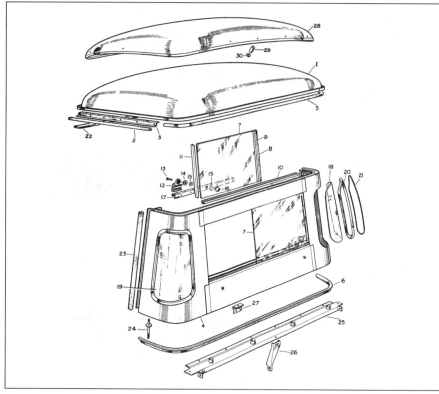

Fig. 12.7. Driver's cab and tropical roof assembly

1 Cab roof
2 Seating rubber, door top
3 Retainer for seal
4 Cab rear panel assembly
5 Rubber seal, roof to back panel, top
6 Rubber seal back panel to rear body
7 Sliding back light
8 Sealing rubber for back light
9 Channel for rubber
10 Channel top and bottom } For back
11 Channel, sides   } light
12 Back light catch
13-16 Fixings for catches
17 Runner for sliding back light catch
18 Cab quarter light, RH
19 Cab quarter light, LH
20 Weather strip   } For quarter
21 Sealing strip   } light
22 Sealing rubber, windscreen to roof
23 Sealing rubber, door side
24 Mounting stud
25 Mounting rail for cab
26 Mounting rail support bracket
27 Cab mounting distance piece
28 Cab tropical roof panel
29 Distance piece   } Securing tropical roof
30 Rubber   } panel to cab roof

Fig. 12.8. Estate wagon and rear door assembly

1 Cab roof assembly
2 Rubber seal for roof, rear
3 Seal retainer for roof, rear
4 Side panel assembly, LH
5 Mounting bracket front
6 Nut plate - securing mounting bracket to body
7 Support bracket at tailboard
8 Drain channel complete for side windows
9 Glass for side window, sliding
10 Sealing rubber for sliding light
11 Channel for sliding light rubber
12 Channel for sliding light, top
13 Channel for sliding light, sides
14 Packing strip for top channel
15 Catch for sliding glass, front
16 Washer for catch
17 Screw fixing front catch
18 Tapped plate for catch
19 Runner for sliding catch
20 Glass for rear end window
21 Retainer for rear end glass upper LH
23 Retainer for rear end glass lower LH
24 Rubber seal for rear lid, side
25 Rubber sealing strip, lower edge to body
26 Capping for front door rear seal, LH
27 Stud plate - fixing cappings to side panel
28 Seal for front door, upper, side
29 Rubber seal at door pillar top and bottom
30 Rubber seal, roof to side
31 Seal retainer for door top, LH
32 Sealing rubber for door top
33 Sealing rubber, windscreen to roof
34 Rear lid assembly
35 Lock complete for rear lid
36 Bolt end for lock
37 Guide for rear lid lock
38 Nut plate

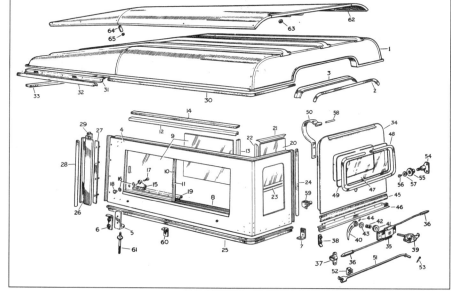

39 Handle for rear lid, outer, locking
40 Handle for rear lid, inner
41 Boss   }
42 Coil spring   }
43 Cup for coil spring } Fixing handle
44 Locking pin   }
45 Rubber seal for rear lid, bottom
46 Retainer for bottom seal
47 Glass for rear lid
48 Weather strip for back light
49 Seal strip for weather strip
50 Hinge leaf for rear lid
51 Stay for rear lid, RH
52 Spring clip for rear lid stay

53 Split pin securing rear lid stay to support
54 Mounting bracket for stay support
55 Locking nut for mounting bracket
56 Screw   }
57 Plain washer } Retaining locking nut
58 Pin for rear lid hinge
59 Socket for rear lid lock bolt LH
60 Support bracket, centre, body side
61 Mounting stud - securing hard top to body
62 Tropical roof panel
63 Rubber washer - securing panel to roof at end of stiffener
64 Distance piece   } Securing roof to
65 Rubber washer   } panel at sides

1 Side and wheelarch complete RH
2 Side and wheelarch complete LH
3 Rear floor complete

4 Rear floor cross-member and pads
5 Rear floor cross-member mounting pad
6 Rear body front panel

7 Body front panel capping
8 Body top side capping
9 Corner strengthening angle
10 Hood socket complete, rear corner
11 Corner bracket and tailboard cotter
12 Rear protection angle
13 Rear mounting angle
14 Protecting strip at rear of floor
15 Cover panel for rear lamps
16 Spare wheel clamp
17 Clamp reinforcement bracket
18 Spare wheel clamp tie bar
19 Wing nut, fixing spare wheel clamp
20 Spare wheel rubbing strip
21 Tailboard sealing rubber
22 Tailboard rubber buffer
23 Tailboard chain bracket
24 Pin, securing tailboard chain to
    bracket
25 Tailboard chain
26 Sleeve for chain
27 Hood strap staple
28 Starting handle and jack handle clip
29 Rear wing stay, front
30 Rear wing stay, rear
31 Fuel filler cowl
32 Fuel filler cover plate
33 'Land-Rover' name plate
34 Registration plate

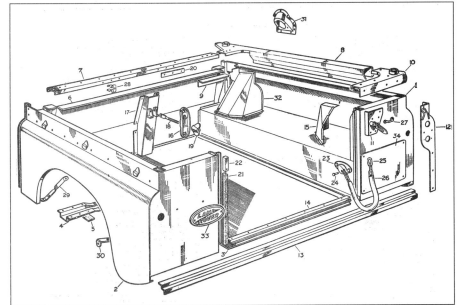

Fig. 12.9. Rear body assembly (SWB models)

**Fig. 12.10. Rear body assembly
(LWB models)**

1 Side and wheelarch complete RH
2 Side and wheelarch complete LH
3 Rear floor complete
4 Rear floor cross-member and pads
5 Rear floor cross-member mounting pad
6 Rear body front panel
7 Rear body front panel capping
8 Body top side capping
9 Corner strengthening angle
10 Hood socket complete, rear corner
11 Rear protection angle
12 Corner bracket and tailboard cotter
13 Protecting strip at rear of floor
14 Rear mounting angle
15 Rear lamp cover panel
16 Spare wheel mounting strengthening
    member
17 Nut plate
18 Spare wheel housing
19 Spare wheel clamp tie bar
20 Spare wheel clamp
21 Wing, nut securing spare wheel clamp
22 Cover plate
23 Tailboard sealing rubber
24 Tailboard rubber buffer
25 Tailboard chain bracket
26 Tailboard chain
27 Clevis pin, securing chain to bracket
28 Sleeve for chain
29 Wheelarch box locker lid
30 Locker lid hinge
31 Locker lid hasp

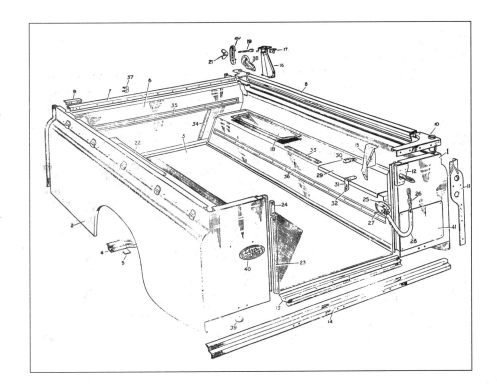

32 Locker lid turnbuckle
33 Tread plate, wheelarch box top
34 Tread plate, vertical, front panel
35 Tread plate, horizontal, front panel
36 Tread plate for rear floor and wheelarch
    box sides

37 Starting handle and jack handle clip
38 Fuel filler cover plate
39 Rubber grommet wheelarch, locker
    access hole
40 'Land-Rover' nameplate
41 Registration plate

18 Rear body section - removal and refitting

1 Remove the hood and sticks, or hard top, if fitted (see Section 17).
2 Remove the spare wheel and any other items of equipment that is stowed in the rear body.
3 On SWB models remove the seat cushions, on LWB models tilt the seat squabs forward.
4 Disconnect the fuel filler and breather hoses, referring to Chapter 3 if necessary.
5 Remove the bolts securing the rear body section to the seat base assembly.
6 Remove the bolts retaining the sill channel mounting brackets to the seat base and rear body.
7 Undo the nuts and bolts securing the rear sill panel to the body.
8 On SWB models only, remove the wing stays from the chassis members.
9 Undo the nuts and bolts securing the body to the rear crossmember mounting brackets.
10 Disconnect the wiring harness to the rear side and stop lights.
11 With the help of some assistants, lift the complete rear body section from the chassis.
12 Refit the rear body section using the reverse procedure to that of removal.

19 Heater system - general description

1 An interior heating system is available as an optional extra on all Land Rover models.
2 The earlier Smiths heater comprises a radiator/fan unit located below the instrument panel, (see photo) from which two flexible hoses lead up to demister ducts, one below each windscreen section. Engine coolant circulates around the heater matrix via inlet and outlet hoses and flaps on the heater unit enable the hot air flow to pass into the passenger compartment or be directed through the windscreen demist ducts.
3 A rheostat switch adjacent to the heater unit switches on the motor and controls its speed.
4 Later models have a more sophisticated system comprising a heater box and blower

19.2 Early type heater unit

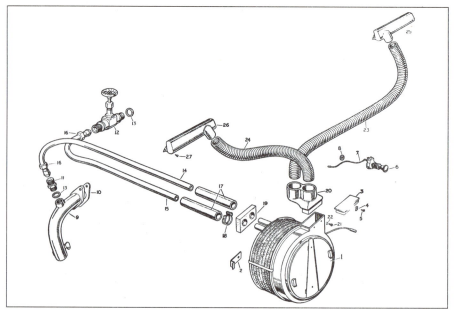

Fig. 12.11. Heater components (early models)

1 Heater	11 Reducing union for pipe	19 Rubber seal for pipes
2 Bracket for heater	12 Valve for water supply	20 Junction box for demister
3 Blanking cap	13 Joint washer for valve and	tubes
4 Spire nut	union	21-22 Screws: junction box to
5 Acme bolt	14 Water outlet pipe	heater
6 Switch for heater	15 Water inlet pipe	23 Tube for demister RH
7 Feed wire for heater	16 Union nut for heater pipe to	24 Tube demister
8 Grommet for heater leads	valve and union	25 Nozzle for demister RH
9 Inlet pipe for water pump	17 Hose for water pipes	26 Nozzle for demister, LH
10 Joint washer for pipe	18 Clip for hose	27 Drive screw fixing nozzle

motor in the engine compartment, a water control valve and cable operated flaps that enable the hot air to be directed onto the screen or through foot level vents.
5 The water valve and flaps are controlled by two sliding knobs on the right of the instrument panel. The blower motor is controlled by an on/off switch on the front of the instrument panel.

20 Heater assembly (early type) - removal and refitting

1 To avoid air locks, first shut off the heater tap on top of the cylinder block and then drain the cooling system as described in Chapter 2.
2 From behind the heater unit, slacken the two hose clips and pull off the hoses from the heater inlet/outlet pipes.
3 Remove the two securing screws and lift off the demister hose junction box from the top of the heater unit (see Fig 12.11).
4 Disconnect the heater motor feed wire at the snap connector.
5 Remove the three brackets securing the heater unit to the dash panel.
6 Lift out the heater unit from the vehicle.
7 The heater matrix can be flushed out by connecting a hosepipe to the inlet pipe on the heater unit (the left-hand pipe when looking at

the front of the heater). Continue flushing until clear water emerges from the outlet pipe.
8 The heater motor is not repairable and if faulty should be renewed.
9 Refit the heater unit using the reverse procedure to that of removal. After refilling the cooling system run the engine and check the inlet and outlet hose connections for leaks.

21 Heater assembly (later type) - removal and refitting

1 From inside the cab, remove the screws securing the trim strip below the instrument

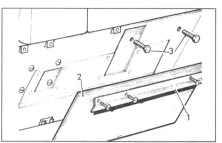

Fig. 12.12. Lower facia panel removed (later models)

1 Trim strip   3 Heater box securing bolts
2 Facia panel

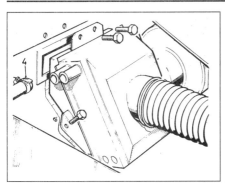

Fig. 12.13. Removing heater box assembly (later models)

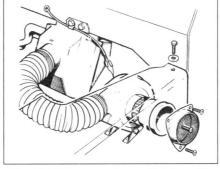

Fig. 12.14. Heater motor and intake grille (later models)

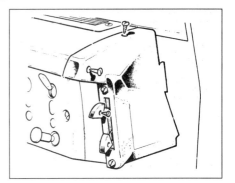

Fig. 12.15. Heater control knobs and end panel (later models)

panel and remove the strip. Lift the facia trim panel out of the bottom retaining clips and undo the two heater box lower retaining bolts (Fig. 12.12).

2 Drain the cooling system as described in Chapter 2 and from inside the engine compartment, remove the two hoses from the heater box.

3 Remove the four bolts securing the heater box to the dash panel, slacken the clip and pull off the large air inlet hose and lift out the heater box assembly from the engine compartment, (Fig. 12.13).

4 To remove the blower motor, first remove the battery earth terminal and then disconnect the two motor feed wires at the snap connectors.

5 From behind the facia trim panel removed previously, undo the four blower motor retaining screws.

6 Remove the top securing bolt from the rear of the wing panel and manoeuvre the motor assembly out from under the wing lifting the wing panel up slightly to provide the necessary clearance.

7 The heater box matrix can be flushed out using the method described in Section 18.

8 The blower motor is not a repairable item, and if faulty should be renewed.

9 Refit the motor and heater box assembly using the reverse procedure to that of removal. If difficulty is experienced in refitting the air inlet seal over the motor inlet aperture, remove the inlet grille from the side of the wing and refit the seal through the hole in the wing (Fig. 12.14).

10 After refilling the radiator check the heater box hose connections for leaks while running the engine.

22 Heater controls (later type) - removal and refitting
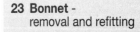

1 Remove the retaining screws and pull off the two heater control knobs.

2 Undo the two screws securing the control lever assembly to the end panel.

3 Remove the securing screws and withdraw the end panel and heater control lever assembly. To remove the control lever assembly from the vehicle slacken the clamps and grub screws securing the inner and outer control cables and withdraw the cables from the lever assembly (Figs. 12.15 and 12.16).

4 To adjust the cables, refit them to the lever assembly, and set the temperature control lever to the fully up position. Open the bonnet and check that the lever on the water control valve is fully closed. If it is not, slacken the locknut and screw on the water valve lever, push the lever to the closed position and tighten the cable retaining screw and locknut (Fig. 12.17).

5 Set the air flow lever fully up and looking through the air outlet grilles in the lower facia panel, (remove the grilles if necessary) check that the flaps are in the closed position. Adjust

the inner cable, if required, by means of the grub screw on the control lever assembly.

6 Refit the heater control levers using the reversal of the removal procedure.

23 Bonnet - removal and refitting

1 Remove the spare wheel, if bonnet mounted.

2 Withdraw the split-pin and flat washer or the circlip and washer that secure the bonnet stay lower fixing to the inside of the front wing panel.

3 On early models, remove the split-pin and flat washer from each bonnet hinge, lift the bonnet and slide it sideways and off the hinges.

4 On later models, open the bonnet fully and lift it off the hinges. Recover the two plastic hinge bushes (photo).

5 Refitting is the reverse sequence to removal.

24 Front floor - removal and refitting

1 Unscrew and remove the knob and locknut from the transfer gear lever and four-wheel drive gear lever.

2 Undo and remove the securing screws

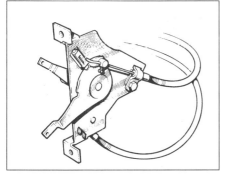

Fig. 12.16. Heater control lever assembly (later models)

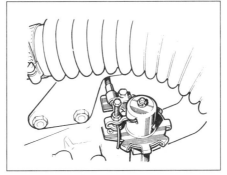

Fig. 12.17. Location of water control valve (later models)

23.4 Later type bonnet hinge

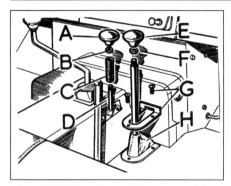

Fig.12.18. Transfer, and four wheel drive levers

A *Four-wheel drive lever knob*
B *Locknut*
C *Spring*
D *Ferrule*
E *Transfer gear lever knob*
F *Locknut*
G *Securing screws*
H *Dust cover*

and lift off the transfer lever rubber boot and retaining plate.

3 Remove the two screws and lift off the four-wheel drive positioning plate and release spring.

4 Undo and remove the securing screws and lift off both halves of the front floor the gearbox tunnel cover and the gearbox tunnel front panel.

5 Refitting is the reverse sequence to removal.

25 Front seat base - removal and refitting

1 Remove the front floor as described in Section 24.

2 Lift off the seat cushions and withdraw the seat base top panels.

3 Undo and remove the securing screws and lift off the handbrake draught excluder and retaining plate.

4 Remove the seat belt anchor brackets if fitted.

5 Undo and remove the screws bolts and nuts that secure the seat base to the body.

6 Release the passenger door check stay and open the door fully.

7 Manoeuvre the seat base over the handbrake lever and withdraw it from the vehicle through the passenger door opening.

8 Refitting is the reverse of the removal sequence.

26 Lower facia panel (Series III models) - removal and refitting

1 Undo and remove the retaining screws and lift off the steering column upper and lower shrouds.

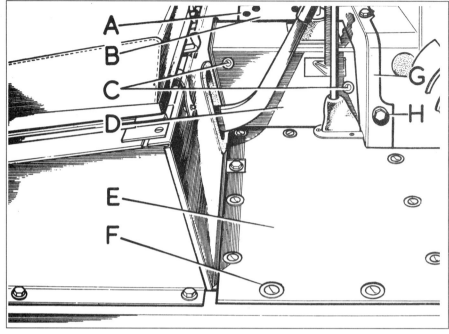

Fig. 12.19. Front floor

A *Retaining screws*
B *Floor panel*
C *Retaining screws*
D *Gearbox tunnel cover*
E *Floor panel*
F *Retaining screws*
G *Front panel*
H *Retaining screws*

2 Undo and remove the retaining screws and withdraw the heater control panel from the driver's end of the facia. Disconnect the control cables and remove the panel.

3 Undo and remove the fixings and withdraw the instrument panel forward until it is just clear of the dash panel.

4 Remove the two demister hoses from each end of the facia.

5 Withdraw the finisher strip from the top edge of the lower facia.

6 If auxiliary instruments are fitted to the centre of the lower panel disconnect and remove them where necessary.

7 Undo and remove the securing screws and lift off the end cover from the passenger's end of the facia panel.

8 Remove the parcel tray.

9 Undo and remove the remaining securing screws and withdraw the lower facia from the vehicle.

10 Refitting is the reverse sequence to removal.

27 Facia top rail (Series III models) - removal and refitting

1 Undo and remove the screws that secure the heater control panel on the driver's side and move the panel to one side.

2 Undo and remove the screws that secure the passenger's side end cover and lift off the cover.

3 Undo and remove the two nuts and bolts

that secure the rear of the facia top rail to the mounting plate.

4 Remove the screws and withdraw the two demister outlets.

5 Undo and remove the remaining screws that secure the front of the facia top rail and withdraw the rail from the vehicle.

6 Refitting is the reverse sequence to removal.

28 Facia support panel (Series III models) - removal and refitting

1 Disconnect the battery lead terminal.

2 Remove the facia top rail as described in Section 27.

3 Remove the Instrument panel as described in Chapter 10, Section 37.

4 Withdraw the two heater hoses from the demister nozzles.

5 Remove the instrument housing.

6 Undo and remove the fixings that secure the ventilator control levers to the flaps and the controls to the support panel. Withdraw the controls.

7 If an auxiliary instrument panel is fitted, disconnect the instruments and remove the panel.

8 Undo and remove the screws that secure the support panel to the dash and withdraw the facia support panel from the vehicle.

9 Refitting is the reverse sequence to removal.

Chapter 13 Supplement:
Revisions and information on later models

Contents

Degrees of difficulty

Easy, suitable for novice with little experience 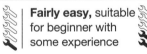	**Fairly easy,** suitable for beginner with some experience	**Fairly difficult,** suitable for competent DIY mechanic	**Difficult,** suitable for experienced DIY mechanic	**Very difficult,** suitable for expert DIY or professional

1 Introduction

This supplement contains information which is additional to, or a revision of, material in the first twelve Chapters of this manual.

The Sections of this supplement follow the same order as the Chapters to which they relate. The Specifications are all grouped together for convenience, but they follow Chapter order.

It is recommended that before any particular operation is undertaken, reference be made to the appropriate Section(s) of this supplement.

In this way, any change to procedure or components can be noted before referring to the main Chapters.

The following Specifications are supplementary to, or revisions of, those at the beginning of the preceding Chapters.

2 Specifications

Petrol engine

Connecting rods
Big-end bearing running clearance . . . .   0.0007 to 0.0025 in (0.019 to 0.063 mm)

Crankshaft
Type . . . .   Five main bearing
Main bearing running clearance. . . . .   0.0008 to 0.0022 in (0.020 to 0.055 mm)
All other dimensions are as given for the later type three bearing crankshaft

Flywheel
Minimum pressure face thickness . . . .   1.375 in (34.72 mm)

Petrol engine (continued)

Valve timing

Cast crankshaft (engine serial No 36100001A)	Timing as given for three bearing crankshaft
Forged crankshaft (engine serial No 99100001A):	
Inlet opens	16° BTDC
Inlet closes	42° ABDC
Inlet peak	103° ATDC
Exhaust opens	51° BBDC
Exhaust closes	13° ATDC
Exhaust peak*	109° BTDC

Where No 1 exhaust cam peak is 7° to the right of the camshaft keyway centre line viewed from the keyway end

Torque wrench settings	lbf ft	kgf m
Main bearing cap bolts:		
Engine serial No 36100001A	85	11.5
Engine serial No 99100001A	100	14
Connecting rod cap nuts:		
Engine serial No 36100001A	25	3.5
Engine serial No 99100001A	32.5	4.5
Flywheel bolts.	100	14

Diesel engine

Connecting rods

Big-end bearing running clearance	0.0007 to 0.0025 in (0.018 to 0.063 mm)

Crankshaft

Type	Five main bearing	
Main bearing running clearance.	0.0008 to 0.0022 in (0.020 to 0.055 mm)	
Regrind sizes:	**Journal diameter**	**Crankpin diameter**
0.010 in (0.25 mm) undersize	2.4895 to 2.4900 in	2.3020 to 2.3027 in
	(63.233 to 63.246 mm)	(58.471 to 58.490 mm)
0.020 in (0.50 mm) undersize	2.4795 to 2.4800 in	2.2920 to 2.2928 in
	(62.979 to 62.992 mm)	(58.217 to 58.236 mm)

Flywheel

Thickness (minimum)	1.455 in (36.957 mm)
Run-out	0.002 in (0.05 mm)

Torque wrench setting	lbf ft	kgf m
Flywheel bolts.	100	14

Ignition system - petrol models

Distributor

Type	Ducellier
Rotation	Anti-clockwise at rotor end
Vacuum advance:	
Starts	4 in (102 mm) Hg
Finishes.	12° at 18 in (457 mm) Hg
Dwell:	
Angle	57°
Variation	± 2° 30'
No centrifugal advance below	900 rpm
Contact breaker gap	0.017 in (0.43 mm)

Ignition timing - Series IIA

7.0 : 1 compression ratio:	
83 octane fuel.	3° BTDC
76 octane fuel.	TDC
8.0 : 1 compression ratio:	
85 octane fuel.	3° BTDC
90 octane fuel.	6° BTDC

Ignition timing - Series III

7.0 : 1 compression ratio:	
75 octane fuel.	TDC
83 octane fuel.	3° BTDC
90 octane fuel.	6° BTDC
8.0 : 1 compression ratio:	
85 octane fuel.	3° ATDC
90 octane fuel.	TDC

Gearbox - Series III vehicles, 1978 on

Main gearbox

Type	Four-speed and reverse with synchromesh on all forward gears	

Gear ratios:

Top	1 : 1	
Third	1.50 : 1	
Second	2.22 : 1	
First	3.68 : 1	

Reverse:

Suffix 'A' type	3.887 : 1	
Suffix 'B' type	4.021 : 1	

Transfer gearbox

	High	**Low**
Gear ratios:.	High	Low
Helical and spur gear type	1.15 : 1	2.35 : 1
All helical type.	1.53 : 1	3.27 : 1

Overall gear ratios

	High	**Low**
With helical and spur gear transfer:		
Top	5.4 : 1	11.1 : 1
Third	8.05 : 1	16.5 : 1
Second	12.0 : 1	24.6 : 1
First	19.88 : 1	40.7 : 1
Reverse:		
Suffix 'A' main gearbox.	20.47 : 1	42.87 : 1
Suffix 'B' main gearbox	21.6 : 1	44.31 : 1
With all helical transfer:		
Top	7.19 : 1	15.4 : 1
Third	10.81 : 1	23.1 : 1
Second	15.96 : 1	34.1 : 1
First	26.46 : 1	56.56 : 1
Reverse:		
Suffix 'A' main gearbox.	27.87 : 1	59.76 : 1
Suffix 'B' main gearbox	28.91 : 1	61.78 : 1

Overdrive (optional)

Type	Fairey, fully synchromesh
Ratio	0.782 : 1
Lubricant	Hypoid gear oil, viscosity SAE 90EP

Torque wrench setting	**lbf ft**	**kgf m**
Layshaft bolt (apply Loctite 601)	50	7

Propeller shaft

Length

Series III 109 in model (rear).	41.062 in (1042.9 mm)

Front and rear axles - 1980 on

Refer to Section 10 of this Chapter for full information on axle modifications and rationalisation

Hub endfloat

Front hubs (with oil catcher).	0.002 to 0.004 in (0.05 to 0.10 mm)
Rear hubs (with or without oil catcher)	0.004 to 0.006 in (0.10 to 0.15 mm)

Hub oil seal recess

Front and rear.	0.19 to 0.21 in (4.8 to 5.3 mm) from hub rear frame

Free wheeling hubs (optional)

Type	Fairey

Hub lubrication:

Pre intermediate front axle shaft oil seal	Axle oil
Post intermediate front axle shaft oil seal	Extreme pressure lithium-based grease

Torque wrench settings	**lbf ft**	**kgf m**
Hub oil catcher retaining bolts (apply Loctite 270).	30 to 38	4.2 to 5.2
Hub driving member retaining bolts.	30 to 38	4.2 to 5.2
Wheel nuts	75 to 85	10.3 to 11.7

Braking system

Refer to Section 11 of this Chapter for full information on brake system modifications and rationalisation

Electrical system - Series III petrol vehicles, 1978 on

Starter motor

Type	Lucas 2M 100
Brush spring tension	36 oz (1020 9)
Brush minimum length	0.375 in (9.5 mm)
Commutator minimum thickness	0.140 in (3.5 mm)
Armature maximum endfloat	0.010 in (0.25 mm)
Light running current	40 amp at 6000 rpm (approx.)
Torque at 1000 rpm	7.3 lbf ft (1.02 kgf m) with 300 amp
Lock torque	14.4 lbf ft (2.02 kgf m) with 463 amp

Wiper motor

Type	Lucas 14W single speed
Brush spring tension	5.3 to 8 oz (150 to 250 g)
Brush minimum length	0.190 in (4.8 mm)
Armature endfloat	0.002 to 0.010 in (0.051 to 0.254 mm)
Armature winding resistance	0.23 to 0.35 ohm at 60°F (16°C)
Current at 13.5V	1.4 amp (max.) with light running rack disconnected

Battery

Rating	55 amp hour

Bulbs and units

Sidelamps.	Lucas 207, 12V, 5W
Stop, tail lamps	Lucas 308, 12V, 21/5W
Rear number plate lamps.	Lucas 233, 12V, 4W
Warning light, brakes	Lucas 280, 12V, 1.5W
Warning light, flashers	Lucas 281, 12V, 2W

Torque wrench settings	lbf ft	kgf m
Alternator shaft nut.	25 to 30	3.5 to 4.2
Starter motor through-bolts	8	1.1
Wiper blade drive adaptor bolts.	2.5	0.34

Suspension and steering - Series III vehicles, 1978 on

Refer to Section 13 of this Chapter for information on tyre sizes and pressures

Torque wrench settings	lbf ft	kgf m
Suspension shackle nuts and bolts	60 to 70	8.3 to 9.7
Front and rear leaf spring U-bolts	58	8

3 Vehicle identification numbers - 1979 on

Petrol engine number prefixes

1 From November 1979, all engine numbers will have a three digit prefix denoting the particular engine specification. These prefixes are as follows:

Prefix	Vehicle type	Compression ratio
901	2286cc petrol	8 : 1
902	2286cc petrol	8 : 1
904	2286cc petrol	7 : 1

The 902 prefix was introduced upon completion of the 901 range. An S prefix before the engine number indicates a service replacement item.

Diesel engine number

1 The new 5 main bearing engine serial numbers begin from 36600001A and can also be identified by their terracotta red cylinder block.

Vehicle identification number (VIN)/chassis number

2 From October 1979, all vehicles have a vehicle identification numbering system which replaces the previous chassis number. The identification plate and the position of the number on the chassis are shown in Figs. 13.1 and 13.2 respectively.

3 The following table relates to 2286cc petrol models for the UK market and shows the VIN replacement for the old chassis number prefix:

Vehicle type	Old prefix	VIN prefix
88 in Regular	901	LBAAH IAA
88 in Half ton	951	LBBAHIAA
88 in Station wagon	921	LBABHIAA
109 in Station wagon	931	LBCMHIAA
109 in Long	911	LBCAHIAA
109 in One ton	246	LBDAHIAA

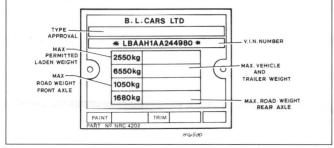

Fig. 13.1 Vehicle identification plate

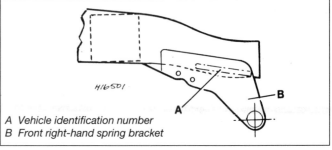

A Vehicle identification number
B Front right-hand spring bracket

Fig. 13.2 Location of vehicle identification plate

4 Petrol engine

Cylinder head

1 From engine No 36400704, the new five bearing engine is fitted with an 'Elring' type cylinder head gasket. This gasket has a non-metallic base and is latex coated; it can be identified by its material composition and grey colour.

Exhaust valves

2 From engine Nos 36100266 (8 : 1 compression ratio) and 36401012 (7 : 1 compression ratio), 'Tufrided' exhaust valves are fitted as standard. These valves can be used as replacements for the earlier type.

Piston rings

3 From engine Nos 36111177 (8 : 1 compression ratio) and 36405395 (7 : 1 compression ratio), new piston rings have been introduced. Fig. 13.3 shows the new ring set which comprises two compression rings and an oil control ring. Note that the compression rings must be fitted with the marks 'T' or 'Top' facing the piston crown. These rings are fully interchangeable with the earlier type.

Timing chain tensioner

4 From engine No 99100001 A, the timing chain tensioner has been changed from the type shown in Fig. 1.22 of Chapter 1A to the type shown in Fig. 13.4.
5 This tensioner will give a slightly greater loading on the timing chain. The removal and refitting procedures given in Chapter 1A are unaffected.

Five bearing crankshaft

Engine identification

6 The new five main bearing 2286cc petrol engine can be identified by the colour of its cylinder block which is painted red. Engine identification number prefixes are as follows:

Prefix	Compression ratio
36100001A	8 : 1
36400001A	7 : 1
99100001A	8 : 1
99200001A	7 : 1

Crankshaft rear oil seal - renewal

7 Refer to Chapter 1A and remove the engine, leaving the gearbox attached to the vehicle. Refer to Chapter 5 and detach the clutch from the engine. Refer to Chapter 1A and remove the flywheel. Alternative methods of gaining access to the oil seal which do not involve engine removal are given in the aforementioned Chapters.
8 With the flywheel housing removed, discard both the housing O-ring and oil seal. Thoroughly clean the ring and seal housings and protect the flywheel housing from further contamination.

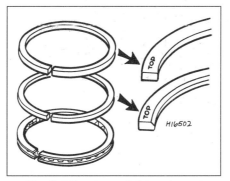

Fig. 13.3 New type of piston ring set

9 Examine the crankshaft journal for any damage which could destroy the seal lip. A guide which fits over the journal, thereby decreasing the likelihood of damage to the new seal during fitting, is available as a special tool from BL dealers. If it is not possible to obtain this tool, then ensure that the journal faces are completely smooth and the corner between them slightly radiused with no sharp edges. Smear the journal periphery with molybdenum disulphide grease. Alternatively, fit the guide and grease its periphery, having first checked for damage.
10 Before fitting the new oil seal into the flywheel housing, check that the outside periphery of the seal is clean and the seal location in the housing is free from burrs. Avoid touching the seal lip.
11 Place the flywheel housing on a flat work surface and carefully press the seal into it, the lip side leading. Keep the seal square to its housing and fit it so that its face is flush with, or a maximum of 0.020 in (0.50 mm) below, the housing face, see Fig. 13.6. If necessary, place a piece of wood across the seal and use a hammer to tap the seal home.
12 Press the new O-ring into its flywheel

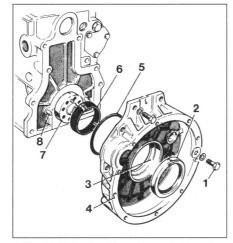

Fig. 13.5 Flywheel housing and oil seals

1 Retaining bolt	6 Oil seal guide
2 Oil seal	(special tool)
3 Seal housing	7 Crankshaft
4 Flywheel housing	journal
5 O-ring	8 Dowel

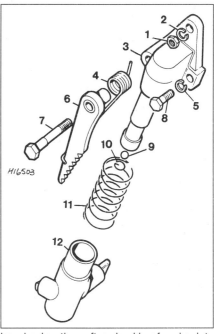

Fig. 13.4 Later type timing chain tensioner

1 Nut	7 Pivot bolt
2 Spring washer	8 Bolt
3 Body (piston	9 Ball
assembly)	10 Retainer
4 Ratchet spring	11 Tensioner
5 Spring washer	spring
6 Ratchet	12 Cylinder

cleanliness. Clean the housing and cylinder block mating surfaces.
13 Align the holes in the housing mating face with the dowels protruding from the cylinder block and carefully push the flywheel housing into position, taking care to observe that the seal lip passes smoothly over the crankshaft journal or its guide.
14 Using a soft-faced hammer, carefully

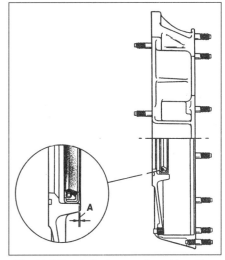

Fig. 13.6 Crankshaft rear oil seal location

A Maximum recess = 0.020 inch (0.50 mm)

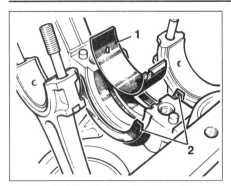

Fig. 13.7 Crankshaft thrust washers

1 Centre main bearing shell
2 Thrust washers

tap around the flywheel housing to seat it against the cylinder block. Fit the housing retaining bolts and washers, finger tight, whilst renewing any flattened spring washers. If necessary, remove the seal guide. Fully tighten the housing retaining bolts, working in a diagonal sequence and tightening a little at a time to avoid distortion.

15 After having refitted the flywheel and clutch, smear the splines of the primary shaft and clutch centre with molybdenum disulphide grease. Refer to the Specifications of this Chapter for revised torque settings.

Crankshaft - removal, examination and refitting

16 To remove the crankshaft, refer to the appropriate Sections of Chapter 1A and carry out the following tasks:

Engine removal
Sump removal
Oil pump and filter removal
Timing cover, gears and chain removal
Clutch removal (Chapter 5)
Flywheel and flywheel housing removal
Pistons and connecting rods removal
Crankshaft and main bearing removal (five bearings instead of three)

17 Note any differences in specification before commencing the procedure for crankshaft and main bearing examination and renovation given in Chapter 1A.

18 Check crankshaft endfloat by first locating the main bearing halves in the engine block and lubricating them with engine oil. Fit a thrust washer each side of the centre main bearing as shown in Fig. 13.7. The unplated side of each washer must face towards the bearing shell.

19 Position the crankshaft in the cylinder block. Set up a dial test indicator as shown in Fig. 13.8 and measure the crankshaft endfloat which should be 0.002 to 0.006 in (0.05 to 0.15 mm).

20 If crankshaft endfloat is incorrect then change the thrust washers to bring it within limits. Thrust washers are available in the following oversizes:

0.0025 in (0.06 mm)
0.0050 in (0.12 mm)
0.0075 in (0.18 mm)
0.010 in (0.25 mm)

To ensure the crankshaft remains centralised, variation of thrust washer thickness each side of the main bearing must not exceed 0.003 in (0.08 mm).

21 With endfloat correct, refit the crankshaft by first locating the bearing halves in their respective caps and then fitting the caps (1 to 4) over the crankshaft. Before fitting the cap retaining bolts note the following warning:

22 Warning: On engine Nos 36100001A and 99100001A it is essential that new bolts and washers are fitted. The bolts fitted to engine No 99100001A have plain washers whereas those fitted to engine No 36100001A have spring washers. Neither bolts nor washers are interchangeable.

23 Fit the retaining bolts through caps 1 to 4 and tighten, finger tight. Clean any old cork seal material from No 5 main bearing cap.

24 Prepare the two new cork T-seals for fitting between No 5 cap and the cylinder block by

first chamfering their inner edge as shown in Fig. 13.10. Soak the seals in engine oil and fit them in the bearing cap.

25 BL supply guides which bolt to the cylinder block and prevent the seals from tearing on the block edge as the cap is fitted. If these guides are readily available, then ensure they are fitted parallel to the block edge. Photo 29.10 of Chapter 1A shows how a feeler gauge can be used to prevent tearing of each seal in the absence of guides.

26 Press No 5 cap fully home and fit its retaining bolts and washers, finger tight. Starting at the centre main bearing, evenly tighten the cap bolts to the specified torque loading.

27 It is necessary to allow for shrinkage of the cork T-seals after fitting. Ideally, fitting of the sump should be delayed for twelve hours and the seal ends then trimmed. If delay is not possible, trim the seal ends so that each one protrudes 0.03 in (0.8 mm) above the block face. The best way to do this is to place a close fitting washer of the correct thickness over each seal end and then trim off any surplus with a razor blade. Dab sealing compound over each seal end.

28 Reverse the dismantling procedure given in paragraph 16 whilst noting the following points:

29 Each connecting rod bolt has an eccentric head which locates in slots in the connecting rod. Check each bolt head is correctly located before tightening the cap nut to the specified torque loading.

30 Refer to the information contained in this Section for crankshaft rear oil seal renewal (it is advisable to renew this seal as a matter of course), fitting of the flywheel housing and fitting of the flywheel.

Flywheel - removal, examination and refitting

31 The flywheel fitted to the five bearing crankshaft differs from the earlier type in that it has a separate reinforcing plate which

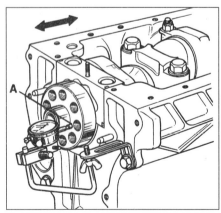

Fig. 13.8 Measuring crankshaft endfloat (Sec 4)

A Dial test indicator contact point
It is not necessary to refit the bearing caps before measuring endfloat

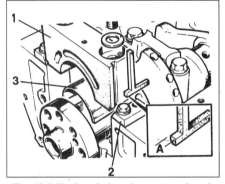

Fig. 13.9 No 5 main bearing cap and cork seals

1 No 5 main bearing cap
2 Seal guide (special tool)
3 Bearing shell
A Seal chamfer width = 0.016 in to 0.031 in (0.40 mm to 0.80 mm)

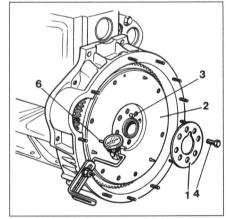

Fig. 13.10 Flywheel run-out measurement

1 Reinforcing plate
2 Flywheel
3 Dowel
4 Retaining bolt
6 Dial test indicator contact point

will become detached after removal of the flywheel retaining bolts. Otherwise, removal is as stated in Chapter 1A.

32 In addition to the examination and renovation procedure given in Chapter 1, check the flywheel for run-out as follows.

33 Clean the flywheel and crankshaft mating faces, removing any burrs which can cause flywheel run-out. Check the dowel is placed correctly in the flywheel and crankshaft flange.

34 Fit the flywheel, reinforcing plate and retaining bolts. Tighten the bolts to the specified torque loading. Refer to Fig. 13.10 and attach a dial test indicator to the cylinder block so that its pointer rests on the flywheel at a point 4.5 in (114 mm) from the flywheel centre. Rotate the flywheel and check that run-out does not exceed 0.002 in (0.05 mm). If no cause for excessive run-out can be found then renew the flywheel.

5 Diesel engine

General

1 This Chapter deals with changes to the engine not previously dealt with. The most obvious being the introduction of a five main bearing crankshaft. Detailed changes are given in the text, but the main changes between the three and five bearing engines are as follows:

Cylinder block - redesigned crankcase to accommodate the five bearing crankshaft. New seal arrangement of rear bearing

Crankshaft - redesigned to include five bearings . Main bearing journals and crankpin dimensions remain as for three bearing engine

Flywheel - modified to fit redesigned crankshaft flange

Flywheel housing - redesigned to accommodate new rear main bearing seal

Crankshaft pulley - changed

Starter dog - changed

Note: *When a five main bearing engine is fitted as a replacement for a three main bearing engine, then a new flywheel housing and seal must also be fitted.*

Cylinder head

2 From the introduction of engine number 36603030 a new Elring gasket, identified by its grey colour and non-metallic base and latex covering, is used.

3 New cylinder head bolt washers have been introduced, utilising existing bolts. The Elring gasket may be used on three main bearing engines, provided the new washers are also used. Torque setting and tightening sequence are unchanged, and the fitting of the new gasket and washers means the cylinder head bolts need no longer be check tightened after the 1000 mile interval (but should still be retorqued with the engine warm).

Camshaft and tappets

4 Later camshafts have metric threads on the sprocket retaining bolt. These camshafts are interchangeable with the older imperial threaded type, but a new metric retaining bolt and washer must be used.

5 When refitting tappet guides, these are now retained by self-locking bolts, and no longer require wire locking.

Pistons

6 New piston and piston ring pack is available and it should be noted that, although the piston rings are available separately, they are not suitable for use with the older type of pistons and should therefore only be fitted to the new type pistons.

Timing chain tensioner

7 Later engines are fitted with a new timing chain tensioner, to give a slightly greater loading on the chain (see Fig. 13.4). The servicing procedures given in Chapter 1B are unaffected.

Five bearing crankshaft
Engine identification

8 The new five bearing 2286cc diesel engine cylinder blocks are coloured terracotta red and run from engine number 36600001A.

Crankshaft rear oil seal - renewal

9 Referring to Chapter 1B, remove the engine - leaving the gearbox in the vehicle. Remove the clutch, as described in Chapter 5, and then remove the flywheel, again referring to Chapter 1B.

10 With the flywheel housing removed, discard both the housing O-ring seal and the oil seal. Clean both the ring and seal housing.

11 Examine the crankshaft journal for any damage which could destroy the seal lip. A special guide is available from the manufacturers which decreases the likelihood of damage to the seal during fitting. If this guide is not obtainable from your local dealer or agent, then ensure that the journal faces are completely smooth and the corner between them slightly radiused. Smear the outside of the journal with molybdenum disulphide grease. Alternatively, if the guide is available, check the journal for damage before fitting and grease the outside of it.

12 Check the new seal for cleanliness and that the seal location in the housing is free from burrs. Avoid touching the seal lip.

13 With the flywheel housing on a firm, flat surface, carefully press the seal into it, with the lip side leading. Keep the seal square to its housing and ensure its final position is flush with, or a maximum of 0.02 in (0.50 mm) below the housing face. If necessary, place a piece of wood across the seal and gently tap it home using a hammer.

14 Check the new O-ring for absolute cleanliness and then press it into its flywheel housing location.

15 Aligning the holes in the housing mating

face with the protruding dowels on the cylinder block, carefully push the flywheel housing into position, taking care that the seal lip passes smoothly over the crankshaft journal, or its guide.

16 Carefully, using a soft-faced hammer, tap the flywheel housing around its edges to seat it fully against the cylinder block. Fit the retaining bolts and washers, using new spring washers. Remove the seal guide if used, then fully tighten the bolts, working diametrically and tightening progressively to avoid distortion.

17 Refit the clutch and flywheel, referring to the revised torque settings in the Specifications in this Chapter, then smear the splines and clutch centre with molybdenum disulphide grease. Refit the engine, as described in Chapter 1B.

Crankshaft - removal, examination and refitting

18 It is possible to regrind the 5 main bearing crankshaft (but not the 3 main bearing crankshaft). If this is considered necessary, reference should be made to the Specifications in this Chapter for regrind tolerances.

19 The procedure for removal of the crankshaft is given in Chapter 1B.

20 Reference should also be made to the Specifications both in Chapter 1B and in this Supplement.

21 The crankshaft endfloat is checked by first fitting the bearing shells in the cylinder block, lubricating them with engine oil.

22 Fit a thrust washer to each side of the centre main bearing, the unplated sides facing toward the bearing shell.

23 Place the crankshaft in the cylinder block, then set up a dial test indicator as shown in Fig. 13.8 and measure the crankshaft endfloat (see Specifications at beginning of Chapter 1B).

24 Endfloat can also be measured with feeler gauges, as described in Chapter 1B, Section 30.

25 The crankshaft endfloat can be brought into limit by the fitting of various thrust washers available in different thicknesses. To ensure the crankshaft remains centralised, variation between thrust washers each side of the main bearing must not exceed 0.003 in (0.08 mm).

26 Once the correct endfloat is achieved, fit the bearing shells on their respective caps and fit them over the crankshaft (bearing caps 1 to 4 only).

 Warning: New bolts and plain washers should be used to refit the bearing caps. The old type bolts and spring washers are not interchangeable.

27 Fit the retaining bolts to caps 1 to 4 and tighten finger tight.

28 Clean any old cork seal material from number 5 bearing cap, and prepare two new cork T-seals for fitting by chamfering their inner edge, as shown in Fig. 13.9.

29 Soak the seals in clean engine oil, then fit them to the bearing cap.
30 If they are available, use the special guides which bolt to the cylinder block before fitting the cap to prevent the seals tearing. Alternatively careful use of feeler gauge blades or similar thin material can be used to guide the cap and seals home.
31 Press number 5 main bearing fully down and fit the retaining bolts and washers, finger tight.
32 Starting from the centre main bearing, evenly tighten the cap bolts. See the Specification in Chapter 1 for torque settings.
33 It is necessary to allow for shrinkage of the cork T-seals after fitting. Ideally, fitting of the sump should be delayed for twelve hours and the seal ends then trimmed. If delay is not possible, trim the seal ends so that each one protrudes 0.03 in (0.8 mm) above the block face. The best way to do this is to place a close fitting washer of the correct thickness over each seal end and then trim off any surplus with a razor blade. Dab sealing compound over each seal end.
34 Reassembly of the remaining parts is a reversal of the dismantling procedure, but note the following points:
35 The connecting rod bolts have an eccentric head which locates in slots in the connecting rod. Check these are seated properly before tightening the cap nuts.
36 Refer to the information contained in this Section for crankshaft rear oil seal renewal, fitting of the flywheel housing and flywheel.

Flywheel - removal, examination and refitting

37 The flywheel fitted to the five main bearing crankshaft differs from the earlier type by having a separate reinforcing plate which will become detached after removal of the flywheel retaining bolts. Otherwise, removal is as stated in Chapter 1B.
38 After examining or renovating the flywheel (see Chapter 1B) check the flywheel for run-out as follows:
39 Clean the flywheel and crankshaft mating surfaces, removing any burrs, which could

affect run-out. Check the dowel is located correctly in the flywheel and crankshaft flange.
40 Fit the flywheel, reinforcing plate and retaining bolts. Tighten the bolts to the specified torque (see Specifications, this Chapter). Refer to Fig. 13.10 and attach a dial test indicator to the cylinder block, so that its pointer rests on the flywheel at a point 4.5 in (114 mm) from the centre of the flywheel. Rotate the flywheel and check the run-out does not exceed the figure given in the Specifications.
41 If the run-out is excessive, and no cause can be found, the flywheel may be refaced provided it is not reduced beyond the minimum thickness given in the Specifications.

---

6 Fuel system - petrol models

Zenith tamperproof carburettor - idle adjustment

1 The idle adjustment screw of this carburettor is rendered 'tamperproof' by means of a locking ring surrounded by a protective shield. With the shield removed a special tool is needed to loosen the locking ring before the screw can be turned. The object of fitting both shield and ring is to discourage (and to detect) adjustment by unqualified or unskilled operators.

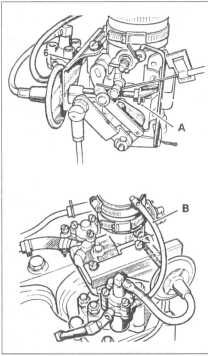

2 Before removing the shield, satisfy yourself that you are not breaking any local or national anti-pollution laws by so doing. If the vehicle is under warranty, be aware that you may be in breach of warranty conditions. Fit a new shield on completion where required by law.
3 Fig. 13.11 shows the special tool in use. Any attempt to carry out adjustment without this tool will result in damage to the screw, backing ring or carburettor. If the tool cannot easily be obtained then one will have to be manufactured from a length of steel tube of the appropriate bore and outside diameters.
4 It may be necessary to destroy the shield in order to remove it, do this very carefully. Ensure the special tool is a good fit in the locking ring and the screwdriver which passes through the tool is a good fit in the screw. On completion of adjustment, hold the screw whilst retightening the ring.

Carburettor throttle prop - adjustment (emission control system)

5 Commence adjustment of the throttle prop system by first running the vehicle for a minimum distance of 3 miles (5 km) to ensure that the engine reaches its normal working temperature.
6 It is now necessary to obtain an accurate tachometer and use it to determine that the engine is idling at 750 to 800 rpm.
7 Refer to Fig. 13.12 and loosen the locknuts which secure the vacuum unit adjusting rod to the carburettor bracket. Move the accelerator linkage so that engine speed rises to 2000 rpm, at the same time disconnecting the atmospheric bleed pipe from the air cleaner elbow and blocking the pipe end. Doing this retains the vacuum supply from the trigger valve, thereby ensuring that the throttle butterfly remains propped.
8 Now release the accelerator linkage, allowing engine speed to fall to the accelerator propped position. Turn the vacuum unit rod locknuts by equal amounts until engine speed reaches 1200 to 1250 rpm. Tighten the locknuts and reconnect the pipe to the air cleaner elbow, whereby the engine should

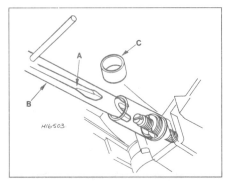

Fig. 13.11 Adjusting idle on the Zenith tamperproof carburettor (Sec 5)

A Screwdriver   C Shield
B Special tool

Fig. 13.12 Adjusting the carburettor throttle prop (emission control system) (Sec 5)

A Vacuum unit adjusting rod locknuts
B Atmospheric bleed pipe

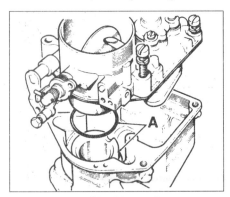

Fig. 13.13 Checking carburettor top-to-base assembly seating (Sec 5)

A Venturi 0-ring and location

return to its normal idling speed. Stop the engine and disconnect the tachometer.

9 Note that the above procedure is similar for all countries, but the setting speeds given are for UK and European vehicles only. Do not attempt to adjust the vacuum control valve, it is preset.

Fault diagnosis - carburettor

10 Where the vehicle is operating in high ambient temperatures and an excessive rich mixture condition is experienced at idle which will not respond to normal mixture adjustment, then suspect incorrect seating of the carburettor top-to-base assembly around the venturi O-ring, see Fig. 13.13.

11 If the fitting of a new O-ring fails to effect a cure, then BL recommend carburettor replacement. Note that heavy fuel consumption may accompany the above fault.

---

7 Fuel system - diesel models

Fuel injector/distributor pump - removal and refitting

Note: *This is for later type pumps with external timing marks. The procedure described in paragraphs 7 to 11 for resetting the timing pointer requires the use of special tool No MS 67 B which probably will not be available to the home mechanic. Therefore,* **do not** *disturb the timing pointer.*

1 Remove the pump, as described in Chapter 3B.

Refitting and timing

2 Remove the engine rocker cover.

3 Gain access to the pointer and timing marks on the engine flywheel (refer to the photos in Chapter 3B).

4 Turn the engine in its normal direction of rotation until both valves on number one cylinder are closed and the piston is ascending on its compression stroke.

5 Keep turning the engine until the 13° mark on the flywheel lines up exactly with the pointer when viewed from directly above. If the engine is turned too far then the operation must be repeated as it is important this position is reached with the engine turning in its normal direction of rotation.

6 The master spline on the drivegear should now be facing 20° away from the centre line of the engine, viewed from the front. If the special timing gauge is not available, continue from paragraph 12.

7 Set timing gauge (tool No MS 67 B) to 22° and lock it in this position.

8 Now invert the timing gauge and insert it into the pump housing on the engine, ensuring it engages with the injection pump drive splines.

9 Slide the body of the tool down the centre shaft engaging it in the injection pump

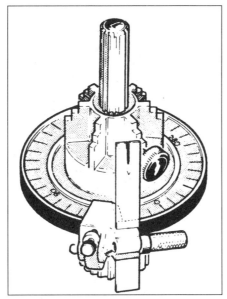

Fig. 13.14 Timing gauge MS67B

drivegear hub. Tighten the knurled retaining screw.

10 Turn the tool gently in a clockwise direction to take up any backlash or wear in gears. Hold it in this position.

11 Slacken the retaining bolts and adjust the timing pointer to align with the pointer on the timing gauge. Tighten the bolts in this position, then remove the timing gauge.

12 Rotate the driving gear on the pump to line up the master spline with that on the engine drive spline, and offer up the pump to the engine, checking that the timing mark on the pump body lines up with the timing pointer.

13 Tighten the sump retaining nuts.

14 Referring to Chapter 3B, carry out the procedures listed to complete refitting of the pump, and prime the system. **Note:** *By timing the pump in this way, with the timing pointer altered to take up backlash, it ensures the pump is timed to its optimum. Provided the engine is generally in good condition, carrying out this timing method can significantly improve performance, but this job should be left to a fully equipped dealer.*

Inlet manifold butterfly valve adjustment

15 Correct adjustment of the inlet manifold butterfly valve is important for two reasons. Firstly, if the butterfly valve does not open slightly in advance of the accelerator linkage then instances of excessive black smoke from the exhaust can occur, and secondly, if the butterfly valve does not close slightly in advance of the accelerator linkage, then ineffective brake servo action can result. The correct procedure for butterfly valve adjustment is as follows:

16 Remove the air inlet hose from the inlet manifold and check the butterfly valve is fully closed when the accelerator linkage is in the idle position. If it is not, adjustment is made

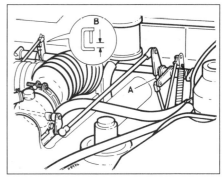

Fig. 13.15 Inlet manifold butterfly valve adjustment

A Pinch-bolt
B Forked shaft 'lost motion' gap

at the pinch-bolt which secures the butterfly valve linkage to the accelerator cross-shaft.

17 Where adjustment is required on earlier rod-operated pump linkage, make sure the gap between the front and rear arms of the forked shaft, which actuates the injection/distributor pump linkage, provides a 'lost motion' period when the accelerator cross-shaft rotates but the pump linkage does not.

18 This 'lost motion' period on vehicles with the later cable-operated pump linkage is obtained by adjusting the cable lever to allow a small amount of movement in the accelerator cross-shaft before the cable begins to operate the injection/distributor pump.

---

8 Ignition system - petrol models

Ignition timing and fuel octane rating

1 Where it is necessary to run a vehicle on fuel which has a lower octane rating than that normally used, then avoid the risk of engine damage by ensuring that the ignition system is adapted as shown in the Specifications.

Ignition timing - 1980 on

2 In order to make reading of the ignition timing easier, vehicles from 1980 have a single timing pointer fixed to the front timing cover and a scale of five notches on the crankshaft pulley, see Fig. 13.16.

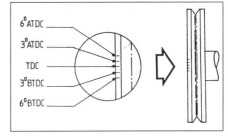

Fig. 13.16 Ignition timing marks - 1980 on (Sec 5)

Ducellier distributor

3 The Ducellier distributor supersedes the Lucas 45D4 type with which it is fully interchangeable.

Contact breaker points - renewal

4 Gain access to the points assembly by unclipping the distributor cup and then pulling the rotor arm from position. Remove the fixed contact after having released its securing screw.

5 Disconnect the suppressor lead from the connector block attached to the side of the distributor body. Disconnect the lead which runs from the connector block to the HT coil at the coil terminal.

6 Remove the moving contact retaining clip and the insulating washer. Lift the moving

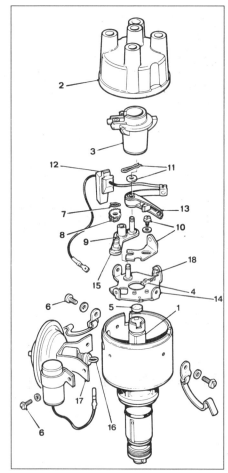

Fig. 13.17 The Ducellier distributor (Sec 6)

1 Cam	11 Clip and
2 Cap	insulating washer
3 Rotor arm	12 Connector block
4 Pressure pad	13 Moving contact
5 Felt pad	14 Baseplate
6 Screws	15 Pivot plate
7 Clip	16 Vacuum operated
8 Serrated cam	link
9 D-post	17 Vacuum unit
10 Fixed contact	18 Spring guide
and screw	

contact from its pivot, together with the connector block.

7 Fit the new points assembly by reversing the removal procedure, whilst taking care to fit the leaf spring plastic guide and the insulating washer correctly. Tighten the fixed contact securing screw finger tight.

8 Carry out a similar procedure to that given in Chapter 4 for contact breaker points adjustment, setting the breaker gap to that specified.

Distributor - overhaul

9 Using a similar procedure to that given in Chapter 4, remove the distributor from the vehicle.

10 Unclip the distributor cap. Pull away the rotor arm and dust cover and remove the felt pad from the rotor.

11 Disconnect the suppressor lead from the connector block. Remove the two screws and washers which retain the vacuum unit and suppressor and separate the suppressor from the distributor.

12 Detach the spring clip from the eccentric D-post. Mark the position of the serrated cam in relation to the spring seat of the vacuum operated link. Detach the cam and link from the D-post and separate the vacuum unit from the distributor.

13 Remove the fixed contact, after having released its securing screw and washer. Remove the moving contact retaining clip and the insulating washer. Lift the moving contact from its pivot, together with the connector block.

14 Mark the position of the baseplate in relation to the distributor body. Remove the plate retaining screws (those which also retain the cap clips), hold the pressure pad clear of the shaft and pull the plate from its position. Separate the baseplate and moving contact pivot plate.

15 Commence examination by checking the distributor shaft for excessive side-play which will obviously affect the breaker gap, causing it to fluctuate as the shaft turns. Excessive side-play will necessitate distributor renewal, although it may be possible for a competent engineer to insert bushes between the shaft and distributor body to take up any play. Renewal of the complete distributor is also recommended if the cam advance mechanism is damaged or worn.

16 Note that the distributor drive dog is designed so that it is loosely retained on the shaft, the float allowing for any misalignment. Do not mistake this float for excessive wear.

17 All other distributor components must be renewed if found to be damaged or excessively worn. Do not neglect to check the distributor cover for signs of tracking or cracks, clean the cover before doing this. Check and clean all electrical contacts, making sure the pick-up brush in the cap is not seized in its holder.

18 Reassembly is a reversal of the removal procedure, whilst noting the following points. Lubricate any pivot points and the

pressure pad by lightly smearing them with a multi-purpose grease.

19 Realign any alignment marks made before component removal. If in doubt as to correct component location, refer to Fig. 13.17. Locate the moving contact spring in its guide.

20 On completion of reassembly, lubricate the felt pad of the rotor with a few drops of light machine oil. Lightly grease the rotor cam. Set the contact breaker gap, see paragraph 8, and refit the distributor to the vehicle.

Dwell angle adjustment

21 Setting the contact breaker gap by using feeler gauges must be regarded as a basic adjustment only. For optimum engine performance, the dwell angle must be checked. Dwell angle is the number of degrees through which the distributor cam turns during the period between the instance of closure and opening of the contact breaker points.

22 Checking dwell angle not only gives a more accurate setting of the contact breaker gap but also evens out any variations in the gap which could be caused by wear between the distributor shaft and body, or difference in height of any of the cam peaks.

23 Check the angle with a dwell meter, connected in accordance with the manufacturer's instructions. Note the specified dwell angle. Proceed by running the engine until it reaches normal operating temperature. Detach the pipe from the vacuum unit and allow the engine to idle. Check the dwell angle.

24 If the angle is incorrect, then stop the engine and adjust the points gap. Increase the gap if the angle is too large and reduce the gap if the angle is too small. The dwell angle should always be adjusted before checking ignition timing.

Dwell variation and vacuum advance adjustment

25 If either of these adjustments is suspected of being incorrect (see Specifications) then refer the problem to your BL dealer who will have the necessary special tools and expertise at his disposal to effect accurate adjustment or to recommend component replacement.

Lucas sliding contact distributor

Contact breaker points - renewal

26 BL recommend that the contact breaker points fitted to this type of distributor are renewed every 25 000 miles (40 000 km), regardless of condition.

27 With the distributor cap and rotor arm removed, release the contact assembly retaining screw and lift the assembly clear of the baseplate. Detach the electrical connector from the spring. Before proceeding further, read the instructions on lubrication later in this Section.

28 Before fitting a new contact assembly, wipe the points with a petrol-soaked rag to remove their protective coating whilst observing the necessary fire precautions. Fit

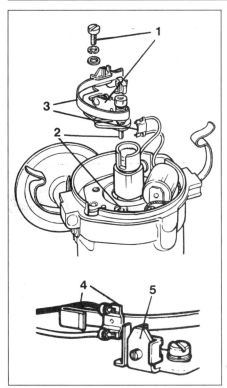

Fig. 13.18 Fitting the Lucas sliding contact assembly (Sec 6)

1 Contact breaker assembly and screw
2 Peg and baseplate location
3 Electrical connector
4 Connector fitment
5 Leaf spring location

the electrical connector to the spring; black lead uppermost.

29 Align the peg of the contact assembly with the hole in the baseplate (see Fig. 13.18) and carefully push the assembly into position. Note that the sliding contact actuating fork must also locate over the peg.

30 Refit the assembly securing screw and washers, finger tight. Ensure that the contact leaf spring is located correctly in the insulation shoe.

31 Carry out a similar procedure to that given in Chapter 4 for adjusting the contact breaker gap to 0.014 to 0.016 in (0.36 to 0.40 mm). With all lubrication complete, refit the rotor arm and distributor cap.

Lubrication

32 BL recommend that the following procedure is carried out every 12 000 miles (20 000 km).

33 Clean the cam and lightly smear it with a multi-purpose grease. Smear a little grease on the underside of the heel actuator, on the actuator ramps, the contact breaker heel ribs, the peg and the actuator fork, see Fig. 13.19.

34 Apply a few drops of clean engine oil to the felt pad beneath the rotor arm.

35 Every 25 000 miles (40 000 km), inject one or two drops of clean engine oil through

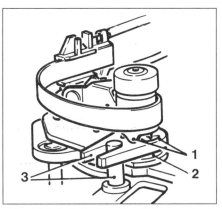

Fig. 13.19 Lubricating the sliding contact assembly (Sec 6)

1 Actuator ramps and breaker
3 Actuator fork and peg heel ribs heel ribs
2 Heel actuator underside

the aperture in the baseplate and onto the automatic advance mechanism.

36 Before refitting the distributor cap, wipe its internal and external surfaces with a clean, dry piece of nap-free cloth whilst looking for signs of corrosion or tracking.

9 Transmission

Overdrive

1 All County variants can now be fitted with a Fairey overdrive unit as an optional extra. The unit may be bought from the manufacturer and fitted by the owner, using the instructions supplied.

Routine maintenance

2 Lubrication is independent of the main and transfer gearboxes. Check the oil level weekly - filling with the recommended oil as necessary.

3 The unit should be drained and refilled with new oil after the first 500 miles (800 km) and then at 6000 mile (9000 km) intervals.

4 Also ensure the selector linkage is kept lubricated.

Running-in

5 New and rebuilt overdrive units should be run-in in the same manner as new engines, care being exercised in its use for at least the first 500 miles (800 km).

Gearbox

6 The following summary is intended to clarify the modifications introduced at each gearbox change. Where modifications involve a change of gear teeth, then this will affect the overall gear ratios, and reference should be made to the Specifications.

Suffix A (commencing gearbox No 90100001A)

7 The all synchromesh gearbox developed

for the Series III Land-Rover has an additional synchroniser unit on first and second gear, the mainshaft now being splined to accept the synchroniser inner member. The first gear is not splined to the shaft, as before, but carried in an oilite bush.

8 First, second and third gears are integral with the layshaft, the constant mesh gear remaining detachable. The layshaft is now secured by a bolt at its front end and not with a nut and split pin.

9 To improve gear retention, an offset reverse idler shaft has been fitted, and this is located radially by means of a spring pin which engages in a slot at the rear face of the main gearbox.

10 The oil scroll on the primary pinion shaft is replaced by an oil seal in the front cover.

11 A new clutch slave cylinder is attached to the bellhousing. A diaphragm type clutch is fitted. **Note:** *The transfer gearbox, transmission brake and front output shaft and housing remain unchanged.*

12 This all synchromesh gearbox may be fitted to vehicles from chassis Suffix H (Series IIA) onward, these vehicles having a large cut-out in No 3 crossmember to accommodate the new housing and clutch slave cylinder. Modification kits to bring Suffix A gearboxes to Suffix B standard are available.

Suffix B (commencing gearbox No 90338769B)

13 This incorporates an increased strength reverse geartrain and a more rigid gearbox casing in the reverse gear area. The reverse idler gear changed from 21 to 20 teeth, and the bush is replaced by a needle roller bearing.

14 A wider jaw is used on the reverse selector fork.

15 The diameter of the reverse idler shaft is increased, and the adjustable stop replaced by steel and bronze thrust washers.

16 The first/reverse outer member teeth are reduced from 31 to 30.

17 The layshaft cluster reverse gear tooth profile is changed to suit the modified reverse idler gear and outer member. **Note:** The strengthened layshaft cluster can be identified by the letter D stamped on the shaft between the gears.

Suffix C (commencing gearbox No 90435600C)

18 Introduced with a reduced number of teeth on the first gear, bringing the number of teeth on the lay cluster from 16 to 14 and on the first gear from 35 to 31.

19 This resulted in a first gear ratio change.

20 The new components are only interchangeable with earlier Suffix B gearboxes in sets.

21 When modifying Suffix A gearboxes it will be necessary to fit the modified reverse idler gear with 20 teeth and the outer member with 30 teeth, to match the reverse gear on the C layshaft cluster.

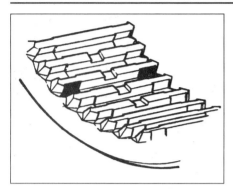

Fig. 13.20 Identifying Electro Chemical Machining (ECM) gears

Reduced inter-spline space extends to within 0.1 in (2 mm) of the spline ends

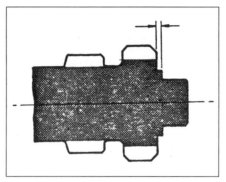

Fig. 13.21 Modified layshafts with reduced step length

Step length reduced from 0.060 in (1.5 mm) to 0.018 in (0.45 mm)

Suffix D (commencing gearbox No 90481491 D)

22 Introduced as a gearbox with improved gear retention for arduous operation. By using a process known as Electro Chemical Machining (ECM), the profile of certain splines and teeth within the gearbox have been changed.

23 This also involved dimensional changes to the 1st layshaft gear cluster, reducing a step on the shaft by 0.042 in (1.07 mm) to ensure full gearteeth engagement.

24 This new layshaft, having the same part number as its immediate predecessor, was introduced during the Suffix C gearbox Series, before the introduction of ECM gears.

25 This means that when fitting ECM gears to a Suffix C gearbox, prior to gearbox No 90420785C, a modified layshaft must be used.

26 The modified layshafts can be identified by the reduced length of the step between the rear bearing and back face of the first speed layshaft gear (Fig. 13.21).

10 Front and rear axles

Axle rationalisation and modification - 1980 on

1 In order to reduce the number of axle types, some major modifications have been made and some components made common to all axles. The result has been to reduce the number of axle types to three.

2 The following components are common to all new axles and are fully interchangeable:
Stub axles and bearing sleeves
Hub assembly

Hub driving member
Dual lip seal
Taper roller bearings
Hub nut cap
Hub cap O-ring
Locknuts and locking washers

3 The major modifications made are as follows:
New taper roller bearings (as Range Rover)
New dual lip hub seal
New intermediate front axle shaft seal
New oil catcher (except 88 in rear)

4 88 in and 109 in vehicles will have identical front axle assemblies, the 88 in being uprated to 109 in specification. Oil catchers are fitted to the hubs and both vehicles are equipped with Rover differentials and 11 in (280 mm) diameter twin leading shoe brakes.

5 The 109 in rear axle is similar to the 88 in type except for the differential being of Salisbury design, the brake drums being of 11 in (280 mm) diameter and the oil catcher being fitted. The 88 in rear axle has a Land-Rover differential and 10 in (254 mm) diameter brake drums.

Front axle hubs - servicing

6 Removal, examination and refitting of the front axle hubs is similar to that procedure given for the wheel bearings in Chapter 8. Refer to Fig. 13.22 for the fitted position of each component and note the following points:

7 Before fitting the new oil seal, check its location in the hub for any damage which could in turn damage the seal. Check the housing is clean.

8 Liberally smear (do not pack) the cavity between the seal lips with a multi-purpose grease whilst taking care not to touch the seal

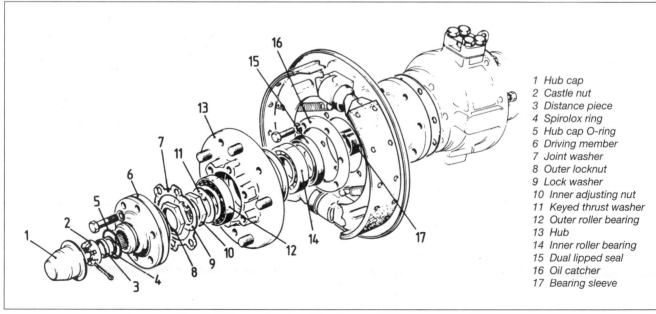

1 Hub cap
2 Castle nut
3 Distance piece
4 Spirolox ring
5 Hub cap O-ring
6 Driving member
7 Joint washer
8 Outer locknut
9 Lock washer
10 Inner adjusting nut
11 Keyed thrust washer
12 Outer roller bearing
13 Hub
14 Inner roller bearing
15 Dual lipped seal
16 Oil catcher
17 Bearing sleeve

Fig. 13.22 Front axle assembly 1980 on – 88 in and 109 in vehicles

lips. Obtain a length of metal tube (a socket is ideal) which has an overall diameter slightly less than that of the seal. Place the tube end against the four diametrically opposed pads on the seal face opposite its lipped side and use it to drift the seal home. Refer to Fig. 13.23 and recess the seal 0.19 to 0.21 in (4.8 to 5.3 mm) into the hub.

9 When fitting the bearing sleeve to the swivel housing, check the milled slot is at the bottom. Use a new joint washer and fit the backplate so that the drain hole is aligned with the milled slot, see Fig. 13.24.

10 When fitting the oil catcher to the backplate, coat its mating surface with sealing compound. Coat the threads of each retaining bolt with a locking compound, fit a serviceable spring washer to each bolt and fit and tighten the bolts to the specified torque loading. Tighten evenly and in a diagonal sequence to avoid distortion of the catcher.

11 Refer to the Specifications of Chapter 8 before checking hub endfloat. Note the torque wrench settings given for the driving member retaining bolts. Renew the hub cap O-ring if flattened or damaged.

Rear axle hubs - servicing

12 The procedure for removal, examination and refitting of the rear axle hubs is similar to that given for the wheel bearings in Chapter 8, with the additional information given in paragraphs 7 to 11 of this Section (where applicable).

13 Refer to Fig. 13.25 for the fitted position of each component. When refitting the circlip to the shaft end, check that it is not distorted and is a good fit in the shaft groove. If in doubt, renew the circlip.

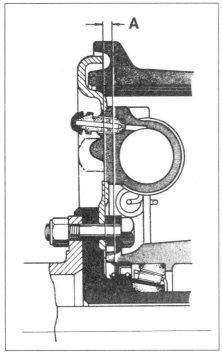

Fig. 13.23 Fitting front and rear axle hub oil seal

A = 0.19 to 0.21 in (4.8 to 5.3mm)

Differential pinion oil seal - renewal

14 Before fitting a new differential pinion oil seal to the Rover type axle, prevent the possibility of a repeat failure by carrying out the following checks:

15 Examine the old seal for signs of damage

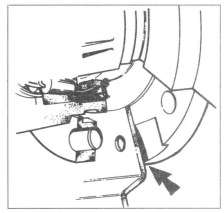

Fig. 13.24 Aligning the drain hole and milled slot (except 88 in rear hub)

or uneven wear and if necessary, renew the flange.

16 Check that the axle has not been over filled with oil, which will cause the seal to blow. Check that the axle breather is not blocked. A blocked breather will cause axle pressurisation and must be cleaned or changed.

17 Lightly grease the outer periphery of the new seal before fitting; this will prevent the possibility of its tipping after fitment. BL state that satisfactory seal location can only be obtained by use of the appropriate special tool and that any attempt to use an alternative method of fitting will result in seal damage or misalignment. Ask your BL dealer about the possibility of borrowing or hiring a tool.

Axle case remote breathers

18 Persistent oil leakage from axle seals can sometimes be attributed to high pressures within the axles. Where this is suspected it

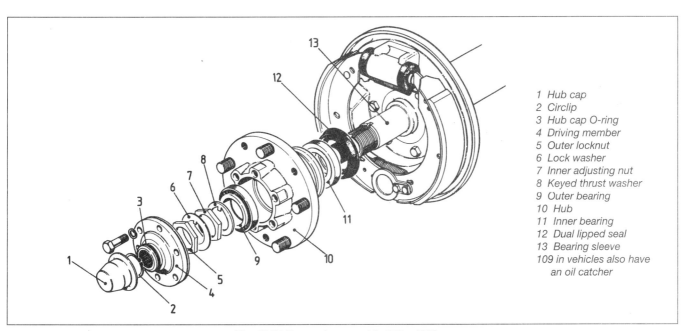

1 Hub cap
2 Circlip
3 Hub cap O-ring
4 Driving member
5 Outer locknut
6 Lock washer
7 Inner adjusting nut
8 Keyed thrust washer
9 Outer bearing
10 Hub
11 Inner bearing
12 Dual lipped seal
13 Bearing sleeve
109 in vehicles also have
     an oil catcher

Fig. 13.25 Rear axle assembly 88 in, 1980 on

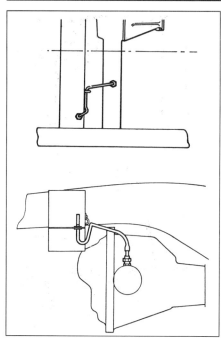

Fig. 13.26 Fitting front axle remote breathers

is possible to fit a remote breather system in place of the existing breather valves.

19 The new remote breather system is fully interchangeable with the old system and should present no problems when fitting. It is important the breather tubes are routed correctly to prevent undue bending which could cause a blockage and therefore a recurrence of axle pressurisation.

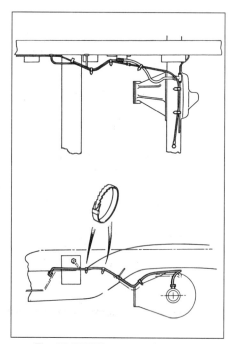

Fig. 13.27 Fitting rear axle remote breathers

Free-wheeling hubs

20 Fairey free-wheeling hubs can be fitted to all County variants. Units may be purchased from the manufacturer and fitted by the owner, following the instructions supplied.

Lubrication

21 Following the axle rationalisation programme carried out in 1980, and the fitting of the intermediate front axle oil seal, free-wheel hubs can no longer rely on oil from the axle for lubrication. Therefore each hub should be pre-lubricated with grease before fitting. Using a lithium based extreme pressure grease, remove each hub cover and apply 3 cc of grease to the splines inside the hub.

22 On pre 1980 vehicles, ensure correct hub lubrication by running the vehicle for 20 miles/32 km) in every 500 miles (800 km) with each hub set to its 4 x 4 position. Turn the hub end to select the correct position.

23 When carrying out adjustment to the wheel bearings, lightly smear the moving parts of each hub with the recommended grease.

11 Braking system

Modifications - 1980 on

1 To comply with European Legislation which requires the front wheels to lock first under all braking conditions, some major changes have been made to the braking system.

2 The 88 in now has uprated front drums, from the previous 10 inch 1254 mm) to 11 inch (280 mm) diameter.

3 When ordering replacement parts. the following changes should be borne in mind.

88 in single line system

(a) 10 inch front brake replaced by 11 inch type. Backplate as 109 in
(b) Larger diameter master cylinder, as 109 in with UNF threads
(c) Larger wheel cylinders on rear
(d) Metric pipes and fittings, except on wheel cylinders

88 in dual-line system

(a) 10 in front brake replaced by 11 in type. Backplate as 109 in
(b) Larger diameter master cylinder
(c) Larger wheel cylinders at rear
(d) Metric pipes and fittings, except on wheel cylinders
(e) Pressure differential warning actuator valve now metric

88 in dual-line system - Station Wagon EEC pressure-sensed

As standard dual-line system (above) but with new pressure-sensed pressure differential warning actuator (PDWA)

109 in single line system

Metric pipes and fittings, except on wheel cylinders. Master cylinder connection remains UNF

109 in dual-line system

(a) Larger diameter master cylinder
(b) Metric pipes and fittings, except on wheel cylinders
(c) Pressure-sensed pressure differential warning actuator
(d) System now basic fitment to all Station Wagons

12 Electrical system

Low maintenance battery - storage

1 Ideally, batteries of the low maintenance type fitted to later vehicles should be disconnected when the vehicle is not in use for long periods. Ancillary equipment, such as electric clocks and the like, can reduce a battery to a state of half charge in less than twenty weeks.

2 Any attempt to maintain battery charge by starting the vehicle at regular intervals and leaving it to run for a short time will only accelerate battery discharge. Remove the battery and store it in a cool place. The self-discharge rate of a low maintenance battery will relate directly to the storage temperature, that is the lower the temperature the less the loss.

3 If the vehicle is to be started after a long period of storage and the battery has been left connected. then it is important that the headlights are switched on for approximately thirty seconds before the battery voltage is checked, otherwise it will not be possible to obtain an accurate reading. Battery voltage should be at least 12.4 volts before starting is attempted. If possible, place the battery on a trickle charger for at least twelve hours. Any attempt at boost charging will appreciably shorten battery life.

Water temperature gauge sender unit - identification

4 When investigating water temperature problems on later models, check the colour of the insulating ring fitted beneath the spade connection of the sender unit. The colour of this ring should be beige: any other colour (black or white) will indicate that the wrong type of sender unit has been fitted.

Starter motor - servicing (Lucas 2M100 type)

5 The procedure for removing, servicing and refitting the Lucas 2M100 motor fitted to later petrol vehicles differs only in detail to that

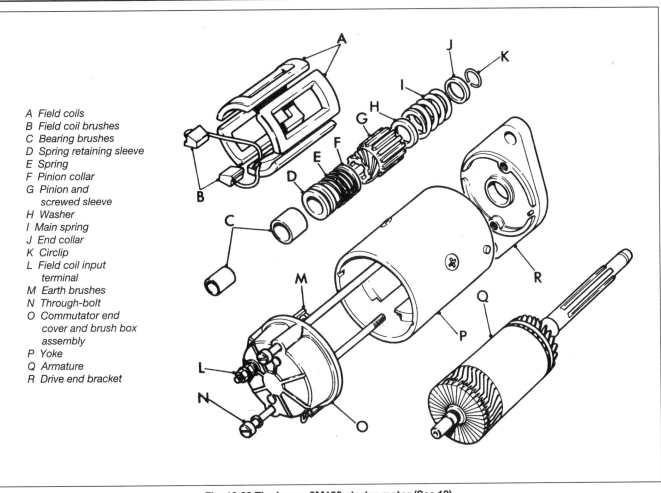

A Field coils
B Field coil brushes
C Bearing brushes
D Spring retaining sleeve
E Spring
F Pinion collar
G Pinion and
     screwed sleeve
H Washer
I Main spring
J End collar
K Circlip
L Field coil input
     terminal
M Earth brushes
N Through-bolt
O Commutator end
     cover and brush box
     assembly
P Yoke
Q Armature
R Drive end bracket

Fig. 13.28 The Lucas 2M100 starter motor (Sec 10)

given for the Lucas M418G motor in Chapter 10A. Before servicing the motor, refer to Fig. 13.28 and to the Specifications Section of this Chapter.

Stop light switch - petrol models

6 Three types of stop light are fitted to Land Rover vehicles. Refer to Chapter 10B.

13 Suspension and steering

Steering lock adjustment - warning

1 Under no circumstances should an attempt be made to improve the vehicle's turning circle by adjusting the steering lock stops on the axle. This will result in the steering rocker arm fouling the lock stops in the steering box, thereby subjecting the rocker arm to excessive loading under full lock conditions with the subsequent risk of component failure.

Steering relay levers - adjustment (Series III)

2 Fig. 13.29 shows the revised angular relationship of the upper and lower relay levers. Refer to this figure when removing and refitting the relay unit, as detailed in Chapter 11.

Body height variation

3 To check that the vehicle body height

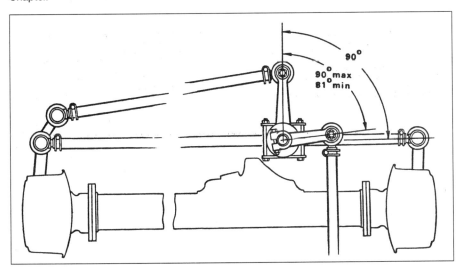

Fig. 13.29 Positioning the steering relay levers (Series III vehicles) (Sec 10)

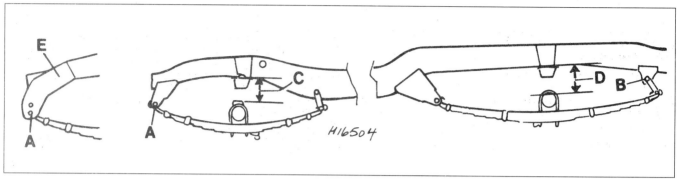

Fig. 13.30 Checking body height variation (Sec 10)

A Front body height measuring point
B Rear body height measuring point
C = 4.41 in (112 mm) – 88 in basic and heavy duty suspension
    4.80 in (122 mm) – 88 in half ton
    4.72 in (120 mm) – 109 in basic and heavy duty suspension
    6.22 in (158 mm) – 109 in extended shackle

D = 5.67 in (144 mm) – 88 in basic and heavy duty suspension
    5.59 in (142 mm) – 88 in half ton
    6.30 in (160 mm) – 109 in basic and heavy duty suspension
    8.11 in (206 mm) – 109 in extended shackle
E Detail of extended shackle

is within the acceptable limits, refer to Fig. 13.30 and measure the distance between each shackle pin centre and the ground. The vehicle must be unladen and parked on flat and level ground for any measurement to be relevant. The acceptable variation between vehicle sides in body height is 1 in (25.4 mm).

4 It has been found that apparent settling of the road springs is generally a result of 'wind up' in the shackle bushes. Reference to Fig. 13.30 will show the normal spring positioning for each vehicle type. Before attempting to remove the springs for investigation, carry out the following checks:

5 Check that the correct springs are fitted. The part number is stamped on the lower face of one of the spring leaves.

6 With the vehicle weight taken off the springs and the vehicle securely supported, remove each shackle pin and check that it is a free fit in its mating threads or rubber bush inner sleeve. If not, then clean the threads or bush sleeve to remove all corrosion and dirt.

7 Clean the ends of the inner faces of the shackle side plates so that all traces of phosphating are removed.

8 Refit the shackle pins. Upon achieving the correct spring position, tighten first the shackle pin and then its locknut to the specified torque. Recheck the pins for security and allow the springs to take the weight of the vehicle.

Tyre sizes and pressures

9 Since the writing of the main text of this Manual, BL have issued a great deal of information which relates to tyre makes and sizes. This information is being constantly updated and it is therefore recommended that should there be any doubt as to the correct tyre size for the vehicle in question, then advice should be sought from a BL dealer. Let the dealer know under which circumstances the vehicle is mainly used as this will greatly influence the choice of tyre.

10 BL state that any 88 in wheelbase vehicle fitted with 5.50 x 16 wheel rims can now be equipped with the Range Rover 205 x 16 tyres which are designed to reduce rolling resistance and therefore increase tyre life. Fitting these tyres will not affect steering lock or speedometer accuracy.

This is a guide to getting your vehicle through the MOT test. Obviously it will not be possible to examine the vehicle to the same standard as the professional MOT tester. However, working through the following checks will enable you to identify any problem areas before submitting the vehicle for the test.

It has only been possible to summarise the test requirements here, based on the regulations in force at the time of printing. Test standards are becoming increasingly stringent, although there are some exemptions for older vehicles.

An assistant will be needed to help carry out some of these checks.

The checks have been sub-divided into four categories, as follows:

1 Checks carried out **FROM THE DRIVER'S SEAT**

2 Checks carried out **WITH THE VEHICLE ON THE GROUND**

3 Checks carried out **WITH THE VEHICLE RAISED AND THE WHEELS FREE TO TURN**

4 Checks carried out on **YOUR VEHICLE'S EXHAUST EMISSION SYSTEM**

---

1 Checks carried out **FROM THE DRIVER'S SEAT**

Handbrake (parking brake)

☐ Test the operation of the handbrake. Excessive travel (too many clicks) indicates incorrect brake or cable adjustment.
☐ Check that the handbrake cannot be released by tapping the lever sideways. Check the security of the lever mountings.

☐ If the parking brake is foot-operated, check that the pedal is secure and without excessive travel, and that the release mechanism operates correctly.
☐ Where applicable, test the operation of the electronic handbrake. The brake should engage and disengage without excessive delay. If the warning light does not extinguish when the brake is disengaged, this could indicate a fault which will need further investigation.

Footbrake

☐ Depress the brake pedal and check that it does not creep down to the floor, indicating a master cylinder fault. Release the pedal, wait a few seconds, then depress it again. If the pedal travels nearly to the floor before firm resistance is felt, brake adjustment or repair is necessary. If the pedal feels spongy, there is air in the hydraulic system which must be removed by bleeding.

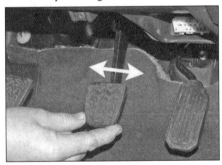

☐ Check that the brake pedal is secure and in good condition. Check also for signs of fluid leaks on the pedal, floor or carpets, which would indicate failed seals in the brake master cylinder.
☐ Check the servo unit (when applicable) by operating the brake pedal several times, then keeping the pedal depressed and starting the engine. As the engine starts, the pedal will move down slightly. If not, the vacuum hose or the servo itself may be faulty.

Steering wheel and column

☐ Examine the steering wheel for fractures or looseness of the hub, spokes or rim.
☐ Move the steering wheel from side to side and then up and down. Check that the steering wheel is not loose on the column, indicating wear or a loose retaining nut. Continue moving the steering wheel as before, but also turn it slightly from left to right.

☐ Check that the steering wheel is not loose on the column, and that there is no abnormal movement of the steering wheel, indicating wear in the column support bearings or couplings.
☐ Check that the ignition lock (where fitted) engages and disengages correctly.
☐ Steering column adjustment mechanisms (where fitted) must be able to lock the column securely in place with no play evident.

Windscreen, mirrors and sunvisor

☐ The windscreen must be free of cracks or other significant damage within the driver's field of view. (Small stone chips are acceptable.) Rear view mirrors must be secure, intact, and capable of being adjusted.

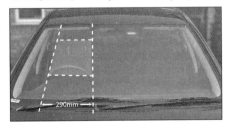

☐ The driver's sunvisor must be capable of being stored in the "up" position.

Seat belts and seats

Note: *The following checks are applicable to all seat belts, front and rear.*

☐ Examine the webbing of all the belts (including rear belts if fitted) for cuts, serious fraying or deterioration. Fasten and unfasten each belt to check the buckles. If applicable, check the retracting mechanism. Check the security of all seat belt mountings accessible from inside the vehicle, ensuring any height adjustable mountings lock securely in place.
☐ Seat belts with pre-tensioners, once activated, have a "flag" or similar showing on the seat belt stalk. This, in itself, is not a reason for test failure.
☐ The front seats themselves must be securely attached and the backrests must lock in the upright position.

Doors

☐ Both front doors must be able to be opened and closed from outside and inside, and must latch securely when closed.

Bonnet and boot/tailgate

☐ The bonnet and boot/tailgate must latch securely when closed.

2 Checks carried out WITH THE VEHICLE ON THE GROUND

Vehicle identification

☐ Number plates must be in good condition, secure and legible, with letters and numbers correctly spaced – spacing at (A) should be 33 mm and at (B) 11 mm. At the front, digits must be black on a white background and at the rear black on a yellow background. Other background designs (such as honeycomb) are not permitted.

☐ The VIN plate and/or homologation plate must be permanently displayed and legible.

Electrical equipment

☐ Switch on the ignition and check the operation of the horn.
☐ Check the windscreen washers and wipers, examining the wiper blades; renew damaged or perished blades. Also check the operation of the stop-lights.

☐ Check the operation of the sidelights and number plate lights. The lenses and reflectors must be secure, clean and undamaged.
☐ Check the operation and alignment of the headlights. The headlight reflectors must not be tarnished and the lenses must be undamaged.
☐ Switch on the ignition and check the operation of the direction indicators (including the instrument panel tell-tale) and the hazard warning lights. Operation of the sidelights and stop-lights must not affect the indicators - if it does, the cause is usually a bad earth at the rear light cluster. Indicators should flash at a rate of between 60 and 120 times per minute – faster or slower than this could indicate a fault with the flasher unit or a bad earth at one of the light units.
☐ Check the operation of the rear foglight(s), including the warning light on the instrument panel or in the switch.
☐ The warning lights must illuminate in accordance with the manufacturer's design. For most vehicles, the ABS and other warning lights should illuminate when the ignition is switched on, and (if the system is operating properly) extinguish after a few seconds. Refer to the owner's handbook.

Footbrake

☐ Examine the master cylinder, brake pipes and servo unit for leaks, loose mountings, corrosion or other damage. If ABS is fitted, this unit should also be examined for signs of leaks or corrosion.

☐ The fluid reservoir must be secure and the fluid level must be between the upper (A) and lower (B) markings.

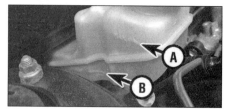

☐ Inspect both front brake flexible hoses for cracks or deterioration of the rubber. Turn the steering from lock to lock, and ensure that the hoses do not contact the wheel, tyre, or any part of the steering or suspension mechanism. With the brake pedal firmly depressed, check the hoses for bulges or leaks under pressure.

Steering and suspension

☐ Have your assistant turn the steering wheel from side to side slightly, up to the point where the steering gear just begins to transmit this movement to the roadwheels. Check for excessive free play between the steering wheel and the steering gear, indicating wear or insecurity of the steering column joints, the column-to-steering gear coupling, or the steering gear itself.
☐ Have your assistant turn the steering wheel more vigorously in each direction, so that the roadwheels just begin to turn. As this is done, examine all the steering joints, linkages, fittings and attachments. Renew any component that shows signs of wear or damage. On vehicles with power steering, check the security and condition of the steering pump, drivebelt and hoses.
☐ Check that the vehicle is standing level, and at approximately the correct ride height.

Shock absorbers

☐ Depress each corner of the vehicle in turn, then release it. The vehicle should rise and then settle in its normal position. If the vehicle continues to rise and fall, the shock absorber is defective. A shock absorber which has seized will also cause the vehicle to fail.

Exhaust system

☐ Start the engine. With your assistant holding a rag over the tailpipe, check the entire system for leaks. Repair or renew leaking sections.

3 Checks carried out
WITH THE VEHICLE RAISED AND THE WHEELS FREE TO TURN

Jack up the front and rear of the vehicle, and securely support it on axle stands. Position the stands clear of the suspension assemblies. Ensure that the wheels are clear of the ground and that the steering can be turned from lock to lock.

Steering mechanism

☐ Have your assistant turn the steering from lock to lock. Check that the steering turns smoothly, and that no part of the steering mechanism, including a wheel or tyre, fouls any brake hose or pipe or any part of the body structure.
☐ Examine the steering rack rubber gaiters for damage or insecurity of the retaining clips. If power steering is fitted, check for signs of damage or leakage of the fluid hoses, pipes or connections. Also check for excessive stiffness or binding of the steering, a missing split pin or locking device, or severe corrosion of the body structure within 30 cm of any steering component attachment point.

Front and rear suspension and wheel bearings

☐ Starting at the front right-hand side, grasp the roadwheel at the 3 o'clock and 9 o'clock positions and rock gently but firmly. Check for free play or insecurity at the wheel bearings, suspension balljoints, or suspension mount-ings, pivots and attachments.
☐ Now grasp the wheel at the 12 o'clock and 6 o'clock positions and repeat the previous inspection. Spin the wheel, and check for roughness or tightness of the front wheel bearing.

☐ If excess free play is suspected at a component pivot point, this can be confirmed by using a large screwdriver or similar tool and levering between the mounting and the component attachment. This will confirm whether the wear is in the pivot bush, its retaining bolt, or in the mounting itself (the bolt holes can often become elongated).

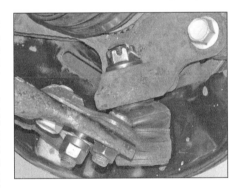

☐ Carry out all the above checks at the other front wheel, and then at both rear wheels.

Springs and shock absorbers

☐ Examine the suspension struts (when applicable) for serious fluid leakage, corrosion, or damage to the casing. Also check the security of the mounting points.
☐ If coil springs are fitted, check that the spring ends locate in their seats, and that the spring is not corroded, cracked or broken.
☐ If leaf springs are fitted, check that all leaves are intact, that the axle is securely attached to each spring, and that there is no deterioration of the spring eye mountings, bushes, and shackles.

☐ The same general checks apply to vehicles fitted with other suspension types, such as torsion bars, hydraulic displacer units, etc. Ensure that all mountings and attachments are secure, that there are no signs of excessive wear, corrosion or damage, and (on hydraulic types) that there are no fluid leaks or damaged pipes.
☐ Inspect the shock absorbers for signs of serious fluid leakage. Check for wear of the mounting bushes or attachments, or damage to the body of the unit.

Driveshafts (fwd vehicles only)

☐ Rotate each front wheel in turn and inspect the constant velocity joint gaiters for splits or damage. Also check that each driveshaft is straight and undamaged.

Braking system

☐ If possible without dismantling, check brake pad wear and disc condition. Ensure that the friction lining material has not worn excessively, (A) and that the discs are not fractured, pitted, scored or badly worn (B).

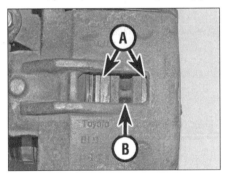

☐ Examine all the rigid brake pipes underneath the vehicle, and the flexible hose(s) at the rear. Look for corrosion, chafing or insecurity of the pipes, and for signs of bulging under pressure, chafing, splits or deterioration of the flexible hoses.
☐ Look for signs of fluid leaks at the brake calipers or on the brake backplates. Repair or renew leaking components.
☐ Slowly spin each wheel, while your assistant depresses and releases the footbrake. Ensure that each brake is operating and does not bind when the pedal is released.

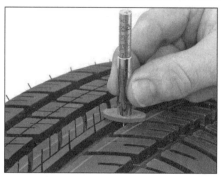

□Examine the handbrake mechanism, checking for frayed or broken cables, excessive corrosion, or wear or insecurity of the linkage. Check that the mechanism works on each relevant wheel, and releases fully, without binding.

□It is not possible to test brake efficiency without special equipment, but a road test can be carried out later to check that the vehicle pulls up in a straight line.

Fuel and exhaust systems

□ Inspect the fuel tank (including the filler cap), fuel pipes, hoses and unions. All components must be secure and free from leaks. Locking fuel caps must lock securely and the key must be provided for the MOT test.

□Examine the exhaust system over its entire length, checking for any damaged, broken or missing mountings, security of the retaining clamps and rust or corrosion.

Wheels and tyres

□Examine the sidewalls and tread area of each tyre in turn. Check for cuts, tears, lumps, bulges, separation of the tread, and exposure of the ply or cord due to wear or damage. Check that the tyre bead is correctly seated on the wheel rim, that the valve is sound and properly seated, and that the wheel is not distorted or damaged.

□Check that the tyres are of the correct size for the vehicle, that they are of the same size and type on each axle, and that the pressures are correct.

□Check the tyre tread depth. The legal minimum at the time of writing is 1.6 mm over the central three-quarters of the tread width. Abnormal tread wear may indicate incorrect front wheel alignment or wear in steering or suspension components.

□If the spare wheel is fitted externally or in a separate carrier beneath the vehicle, check that mountings are secure and free of excessive corrosion.

Body corrosion

□Check the condition of the entire vehicle structure for signs of corrosion in load-bearing areas. (These include chassis box sections, side sills, cross-members, pillars, and all suspension, steering, braking system and seat belt mountings and anchorages.) Any corrosion which has seriously reduced the thickness of a load-bearing area (or is within 30 cm of safety-related components such as steering or suspension) is likely to cause the vehicle to fail. In this case professional repairs are likely to be needed.

□Damage or corrosion which causes sharp or otherwise dangerous edges to be exposed will also cause the vehicle to fail.

Towbars

□Check the condition of mounting points (both beneath the vehicle and within boot/hatchback areas) for signs of corrosion, ensuring that all fixings are secure and not worn or damaged. There must be no excessive play in detachable tow ball arms or quick-release mechanisms.

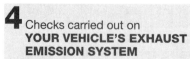

4 Checks carried out on **YOUR VEHICLE'S EXHAUST EMISSION SYSTEM**

Petrol models

□The engine should be warmed up, and running well (ignition system in good order, air filter element clean, etc).

□Before testing, run the engine at around 2500 rpm for 20 seconds. Let the engine drop to idle, and watch for smoke from the exhaust. If the idle speed is too high, or if dense blue or black smoke emerges for more than 5 seconds, the vehicle will fail. Typically, blue smoke signifies oil burning (engine wear);

black smoke means unburnt fuel (dirty air cleaner element, or other fuel system fault).

□An exhaust gas analyser for measuring carbon monoxide (CO) and hydrocarbons (HC) is now needed. If one cannot be hired or borrowed, have a local garage perform the check.

CO emissions (mixture)

□The MOT tester has access to the CO limits for all vehicles. The CO level is measured at idle speed, and at 'fast idle' (2500 to 3000 rpm). The following limits are given as a general guide:

At idle speed – Less than 0.5% CO
At 'fast idle' – Less than 0.3% CO
Lambda reading – 0.97 to 1.03

□If the CO level is too high, this may point to poor maintenance, a fuel injection system problem, faulty lambda (oxygen) sensor or catalytic converter. Try an injector cleaning treatment, and check the vehicle's ECU for fault codes.

HC emissions

□The MOT tester has access to HC limits for all vehicles. The HC level is measured at 'fast idle' (2500 to 3000 rpm). The following limits are given as a general guide:

At 'fast idle' – Less then 200 ppm

□Excessive HC emissions are typically caused by oil being burnt (worn engine), or by a blocked crankcase ventilation system ('breather'). If the engine oil is old and thin, an oil change may help. If the engine is running badly, check the vehicle's ECU for fault codes.

Diesel models

□The only emission test for diesel engines is measuring exhaust smoke density, using a calibrated smoke meter. The test involves accelerating the engine at least 3 times to its maximum unloaded speed.

Note: *On engines with a timing belt, it is VITAL that the belt is in good condition before the test is carried out.*

□With the engine warmed up, it is first purged by running at around 2500 rpm for 20 seconds. A governor check is then carried out, by slowly accelerating the engine to its maximum speed. After this, the smoke meter is connected, and the engine is accelerated quickly to maximum speed three times. If the smoke density is less than the limits given below, the vehicle will pass:

Non-turbo vehicles: 2.5m-1
Turbocharged vehicles: 3.0m-1

□If excess smoke is produced, try fitting a new air cleaner element, or using an injector cleaning treatment. If the engine is running badly, where applicable, check the vehicle's ECU for fault codes. Also check the vehicle's EGR system, where applicable. At high mileages, the injectors may require professional attention.

Whenever servicing, repair or overhaul work is carried out on the car or its components, observe the following procedures and instructions. This will assist in carrying out the operation efficiently and to a professional standard of workmanship.

Joint mating faces and gaskets

When separating components at their mating faces, never insert screwdrivers or similar implements into the joint between the faces in order to prise them apart. This can cause severe damage which results in oil leaks, coolant leaks, etc upon reassembly. Separation is usually achieved by tapping along the joint with a soft-faced hammer in order to break the seal. However, note that this method may not be suitable where dowels are used for component location.

Where a gasket is used between the mating faces of two components, a new one must be fitted on reassembly; fit it dry unless otherwise stated in the repair procedure. Make sure that the mating faces are clean and dry, with all traces of old gasket removed. When cleaning a joint face, use a tool which is unlikely to score or damage the face, and remove any burrs or nicks with an oilstone or fine file.

Make sure that tapped holes are cleaned with a pipe cleaner, and keep them free of jointing compound, if this is being used, unless specifically instructed otherwise.

Ensure that all orifices, channels or pipes are clear, and blow through them, preferably using compressed air.

Oil seals

Oil seals can be removed by levering them out with a wide flat-bladed screwdriver or similar implement. Alternatively, a number of self-tapping screws may be screwed into the seal, and these used as a purchase for pliers or some similar device in order to pull the seal free.

Whenever an oil seal is removed from its working location, either individually or as part of an assembly, it should be renewed.

The very fine sealing lip of the seal is easily damaged, and will not seal if the surface it contacts is not completely clean and free from scratches, nicks or grooves. If the original sealing surface of the component cannot be restored, and the manufacturer has not made provision for slight relocation of the seal relative to the sealing surface, the component should be renewed.

Protect the lips of the seal from any surface which may damage them in the course of fitting. Use tape or a conical sleeve where possible. Where indicated, lubricate the seal lips with oil before fitting and, on dual-lipped seals, fill the space between the lips with grease.

Unless otherwise stated, oil seals must be fitted with their sealing lips toward the lubricant to be sealed.

Use a tubular drift or block of wood of the appropriate size to install the seal and, if the seal housing is shouldered, drive the seal down to the shoulder. If the seal housing is unshouldered, the seal should be fitted with its face flush with the housing top face (unless otherwise instructed).

Screw threads and fastenings

Seized nuts, bolts and screws are quite a common occurrence where corrosion has set in, and the use of penetrating oil or releasing fluid will often overcome this problem if the offending item is soaked for a while before attempting to release it. The use of an impact driver may also provide a means of releasing such stubborn fastening devices, when used in conjunction with the appropriate screwdriver bit or socket. If none of these methods works, it may be necessary to resort to the careful application of heat, or the use of a hacksaw or nut splitter device. Before resorting to extreme methods, check that you are not dealing with a left-hand thread!

Studs are usually removed by locking two nuts together on the threaded part, and then using a spanner on the lower nut to unscrew the stud. Studs or bolts which have broken off below the surface of the component in which they are mounted can sometimes be removed using a stud extractor.

Always ensure that a blind tapped hole is completely free from oil, grease, water or other fluid before installing the bolt or stud. Failure to do this could cause the housing to crack due to the hydraulic action of the bolt or stud as it is screwed in.

For some screw fastenings, notably cylinder head bolts or nuts, torque wrench settings are no longer specified for the latter stages of tightening, "angle-tightening" being called up instead. Typically, a fairly low torque wrench setting will be applied to the bolts/nuts in the correct sequence, followed by one or more stages of tightening through specified angles.

When checking or retightening a nut or bolt to a specified torque setting, slacken the nut or bolt by a quarter of a turn, and then retighten to the specified setting. However, this should not be attempted where angular tightening has been used.

Locknuts, locktabs and washers

Any fastening which will rotate against a component or housing during tightening should always have a washer between it and the relevant component or housing.

Spring or split washers should always be renewed when they are used to lock a critical component such as a big-end bearing retaining bolt or nut. Locktabs which are folded over to retain a nut or bolt should always be renewed.

Self-locking nuts can be re-used in non-critical areas, providing resistance can be felt when the locking portion passes over the bolt or stud thread. However, it should be noted that self-locking stiffnuts tend to lose their effectiveness after long periods of use, and should then be renewed as a matter of course.

Split pins must always be replaced with new ones of the correct size for the hole.

When thread-locking compound is found on the threads of a fastener which is to be re-used, it should be cleaned off with a wire brush and solvent, and fresh compound applied on reassembly.

Special tools

Some repair procedures in this manual entail the use of special tools such as a press, two or three-legged pullers, spring compressors, etc. Wherever possible, suitable readily-available alternatives to the manufacturer's special tools are described, and are shown in use. In some instances, where no alternative is possible, it has been necessary to resort to the use of a manufacturer's tool, and this has been done for reasons of safety as well as the efficient completion of the repair operation. Unless you are highly-skilled and have a thorough understanding of the procedures described, never attempt to bypass the use of any special tool when the procedure described specifies its use. Not only is there a very great risk of personal injury, but expensive damage could be caused to the components involved.

Environmental considerations

When disposing of used engine oil, brake fluid, antifreeze, etc, give due consideration to any detrimental environmental effects. Do not, for instance, pour any of the above liquids down drains into the general sewage system, or onto the ground to soak away. Many local council refuse tips provide a facility for waste oil disposal, as do some garages. You can find your nearest disposal point by calling the Environment Agency on 08708 506 506 or by visiting www.oilbankline.org.uk.

Note: It is illegal and anti-social to dump oil down the drain. To find the location of your local oil recycling bank, call 08708 506 506 or visit www.oilbankline.org.uk.

Introduction

A selection of good tools is a fundamental requirement for anyone contemplating the maintenance and repair of a motor vehicle. For the owner who does not possess any, their purchase will prove a considerable expense, offsetting some of the savings made by doing-it-yourself. However, provided that the tools purchased meet the relevant national safety standards and are of good quality, they will last for many years and prove an extremely worthwhile investment.

To help the average owner to decide which tools are needed to carry out the various tasks detailed in this manual, we have compiled three lists of tools under the following headings: *Maintenance and minor repair*, *Repair and overhaul*, and *Special*. Newcomers to practical mechanics should start off with the *Maintenance and minor repair* tool kit, and confine themselves to the simpler jobs around the vehicle. Then, as confidence and experience grow, more difficult tasks can be undertaken, with extra tools being purchased as, and when, they are needed. In this way, a *Maintenance and minor repair* tool kit can be built up into a *Repair and overhaul* tool kit over a considerable period of time, without any major cash outlays. The experienced do-it-yourselfer will have a tool kit good enough for most repair and overhaul procedures, and will add tools from the *Special* category when it is felt that the expense is justified by the amount of use to which these tools will be put.

Maintenance and minor repair tool kit

The tools given in this list should be considered as a minimum requirement if routine maintenance, servicing and minor repair operations are to be undertaken. We recommend the purchase of combination spanners (ring one end, open-ended the other); although more expensive than open-ended ones, they do give the advantages of both types of spanner.

☐ *Combination spanners:*
Metric - 8 to 19 mm inclusive
☐ *Adjustable spanner - 35 mm jaw (approx.)*
☐ *Spark plug spanner (with rubber insert) - petrol models*
☐ *Spark plug gap adjustment tool - petrol models*
☐ *Set of feeler gauges*
☐ *Brake bleed nipple spanner*
☐ *Screwdrivers:*
Flat blade - 100 mm long x 6 mm dia
Cross blade - 100 mm long x 6 mm dia
Torx - various sizes (not all vehicles)
☐ *Combination pliers*
☐ *Hacksaw (junior)*
☐ *Tyre pump*
☐ *Tyre pressure gauge*
☐ *Oil can*
☐ *Oil filter removal tool (if applicable)*
☐ *Fine emery cloth*
☐ *Wire brush (small)*
☐ *Funnel (medium size)*
☐ *Sump drain plug key (not all vehicles)*

Repair and overhaul tool kit

These tools are virtually essential for anyone undertaking any major repairs to a motor vehicle, and are additional to those given in the *Maintenance and minor repair* list. Included in this list is a comprehensive set of sockets. Although these are expensive, they will be found invaluable as they are so versatile - particularly if various drives are included in the set. We recommend the half-inch square-drive type, as this can be used with most proprietary torque wrenches.

The tools in this list will sometimes need to be supplemented by tools from the *Special* list:

☐ *Sockets to cover range in previous list (including Torx sockets)*
☐ *Reversible ratchet drive (for use with sockets)*
☐ *Extension piece, 250 mm (for use with sockets)*
☐ *Universal joint (for use with sockets)*
☐ *Flexible handle or sliding T "breaker bar" (for use with sockets)*
☐ *Torque wrench (for use with sockets)*
☐ *Self-locking grips*
☐ *Ball pein hammer*
☐ *Soft-faced mallet (plastic or rubber)*
☐ *Screwdrivers:*
Flat blade - long & sturdy, short (chubby), and narrow (electrician's) types
Cross blade – long & sturdy, and short (chubby) types
☐ *Pliers:*
Long-nosed
Side cutters (electrician's)
Circlip (internal and external)
☐ *Cold chisel - 25 mm*
☐ *Scriber*
☐ *Scraper*
☐ *Centre-punch*
☐ *Pin punch*
☐ *Hacksaw*
☐ *Brake hose clamp*
☐ *Brake/clutch bleeding kit*
☐ *Selection of twist drills*
☐ *Steel rule/straight-edge*
☐ *Allen keys (inc. splined/Torx type)*
☐ *Selection of files*
☐ *Wire brush*
☐ *Axle stands*
☐ *Jack (strong trolley or hydraulic type)*
☐ *Light with extension lead*
☐ *Universal electrical multi-meter*

Sockets and reversible ratchet drive

Brake bleeding kit

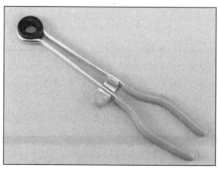

Torx key, socket and bit

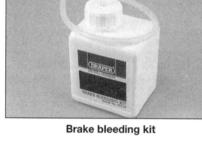

Hose clamp

Angular-tightening gauge

Special tools

The tools in this list are those which are not used regularly, are expensive to buy, or which need to be used in accordance with their manufacturers' instructions. Unless relatively difficult mechanical jobs are undertaken frequently, it will not be economic to buy many of these tools. Where this is the case, you could consider clubbing together with friends (or joining a motorists' club) to make a joint purchase, or borrowing the tools against a deposit from a local garage or tool hire specialist.

The following list contains only those tools and instruments freely available to the public, and not those special tools produced by the vehicle manufacturer specifically for its dealer network. You will find occasional references to these manufacturers' special tools in the text of this manual. Generally, an alternative method of doing the job without the vehicle manufacturers' special tool is given. However, sometimes there is no alternative to using them. Where this is the case and the relevant tool cannot be bought or borrowed, you will have to entrust the work to a dealer.

- ☐ Angular-tightening gauge
- ☐ Valve spring compressor
- ☐ Valve grinding tool
- ☐ Piston ring compressor
- ☐ Piston ring removal/installation tool
- ☐ Cylinder bore hone
- ☐ Balljoint separator
- ☐ Coil spring compressors (where applicable)
- ☐ Two/three-legged hub and bearing puller
- ☐ Impact screwdriver
- ☐ Micrometer and/or vernier calipers
- ☐ Dial gauge
- ☐ Tachometer
- ☐ Fault code reader
- ☐ Cylinder compression gauge
- ☐ Hand-operated vacuum pump and gauge
- ☐ Clutch plate alignment set
- ☐ Brake shoe steady spring cup removal tool
- ☐ Bush and bearing removal/installation set
- ☐ Stud extractors
- ☐ Tap and die set
- ☐ Lifting tackle

Buying tools

Reputable motor accessory shops and superstores often offer excellent quality tools at discount prices, so it pays to shop around.

Remember, you don't have to buy the most expensive items on the shelf, but it is always advisable to steer clear of the very cheap tools. Beware of 'bargains' offered on market stalls, on-line or at car boot sales. There are plenty of good tools around at reasonable prices, but always aim to purchase items which meet the relevant national safety standards. If in doubt, ask the proprietor or manager of the shop for advice before making a purchase.

Care and maintenance of tools

Having purchased a reasonable tool kit, it is necessary to keep the tools in a clean and serviceable condition. After use, always wipe off any dirt, grease and metal particles using a clean, dry cloth, before putting the tools away. Never leave them lying around after they have been used. A simple tool rack on the garage or workshop wall for items such as screwdrivers and pliers is a good idea. Store all normal spanners and sockets in a metal box. Any measuring instruments, gauges, meters, etc, must be carefully stored where they cannot be damaged or become rusty.

Take a little care when tools are used. Hammer heads inevitably become marked, and screwdrivers lose the keen edge on their blades from time to time. A little timely attention with emery cloth or a file will soon restore items like this to a good finish.

Working facilities

Not to be forgotten when discussing tools is the workshop itself. If anything more than routine maintenance is to be carried out, a suitable working area becomes essential.

It is appreciated that many an owner-mechanic is forced by circumstances to remove an engine or similar item without the benefit of a garage or workshop. Having done this, any repairs should always be done under the cover of a roof.

Wherever possible, any dismantling should be done on a clean, flat workbench or table at a suitable working height.

Any workbench needs a vice; one with a jaw opening of 100 mm is suitable for most jobs. As mentioned previously, some clean dry storage space is also required for tools, as well as for any lubricants, cleaning fluids, touch-up paints etc, which become necessary.

Another item which may be required, and which has a much more general usage, is an electric drill with a chuck capacity of at least 8 mm. This, together with a good range of twist drills, is virtually essential for fitting accessories.

Last, but not least, always keep a supply of old newspapers and clean, lint-free rags available, and try to keep any working area as clean as possible.

Micrometers

Dial test indicator ("dial gauge")

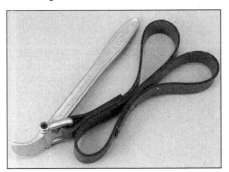

Oil filter removal tool (strap wrench type)

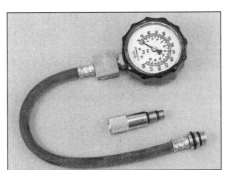

Compression tester

Bearing puller

Introduction

The vehicle owner who does his or her own maintenance according to the recommended schedules should not have to use this section of the manual very often. Modern component reliability is such that, provided those items subject to wear or deterioration are inspected or renewed at the specified intervals, sudden failure is comparatively rare. Faults do not usually just happen as a result of sudden failure, but develop over a period of time. Major mechanical failures in particular are usually preceded by characteristic symptoms over hundreds or even thousands of miles. Those components which do occasionally fail without warning are often small and easily carried in the vehicle.

With any fault finding, the first step is to decide where to begin investigations. Sometimes this is obvious, but on other occasions a little detective work will be necessary. The owner who makes half a dozen haphazard adjustments or replacements may be successful in curing a fault (or its symptoms), but he will be none the wiser if the fault recurs and he may well have spent more time and money than was necessary. A calm and logical approach will be found to be more satisfactory in the long run. Always take into account any warning signs or abnormalities that may have been noticed in the period preceding the fault – power loss, high or low gauge readings, unusual noises or smells, etc – and remember that failure of components such as fuses or spark plugs may only be pointers to some underlying fault.

The pages which follow here are intended to help in cases of failure to start or breakdown on the road. There is also a Fault Diagnosis Section at the end of each Chapter which should be consulted if the preliminary checks prove unfruitful. Whatever the fault, certain basic principles apply. These are as follows:

Verify the fault. This is simply a matter of being sure that you know what the symptoms are before starting work. This is particularly important if you are investigating a fault for someone else who may not have described it very accurately.

Don't overlook the obvious. For example, if the vehicle won't start, is there petrol in the tank? (Don't take anyone else's word on this

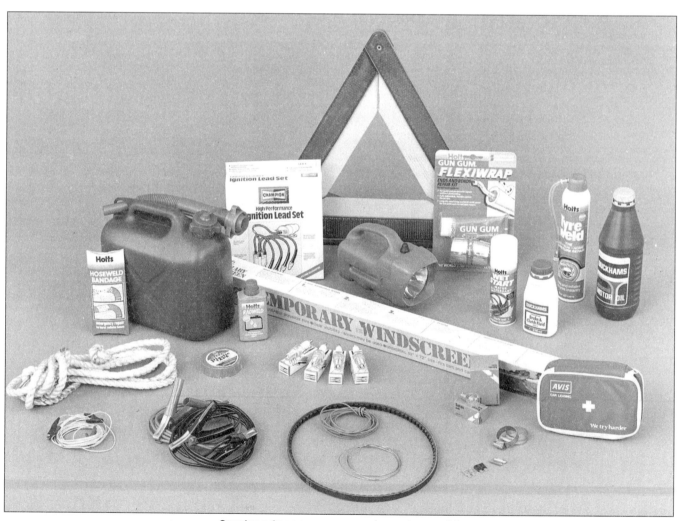

Carrying a few spares may save you a long walk!

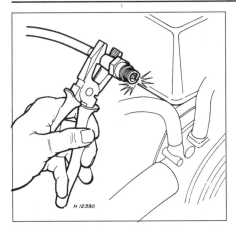

Crank petrol engine and check for spark. Note use of insulated tool to hold plug lead. Use a spare plug, not one removed from engine (fire risk)

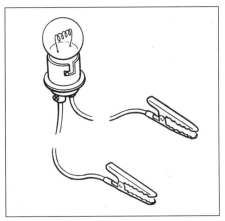

A simple test lamp is useful for checking electrical faults

Fuel emerging from the fuel filter bleed pipe during priming – diesel models

particular point, and don't trust the fuel gauge either!) If an electrical fault is indicated, look for loose or broken wires before digging out the test gear.

Cure the disease. not the symptom. Substituting a flat battery with a fully charged one will get you off the hard shoulder, but if the underlying cause is not attended to, the new battery will go the same way. Similarly, changing oil-fouled spark plugs for a new set will get you moving again, but remember that the reason for the fouling (if it wasn't simply an incorrect grade of plug) will have to be established and corrected.

Don't take anything for granted. Particularly, don't forget that a 'new' component may itself be defective (especially if it's been rattling round in the boot for months), and don't leave components out of a fault diagnosis sequence just because they are new or recently fitted. When you do finally diagnose a difficult fault, you'll probably realise that all the evidence was there from the start.

Electrical faults

Electrical faults can be more puzzling than straightforward mechanical failures, but they are no less susceptible to logical analysis if the basic principles of operation are understood. Vehicle electrical wiring exists in extremely unfavourable conditions – heat, vibration and chemical attack – and the first things to look for are loose or corroded connections and broken or chafed wires, especially where the wires pass through holes in the bodywork or are subject to vibration.

All metal-bodied vehicles in current production have one pole of the battery 'earthed', ie connected to the vehicle bodywork, and in nearly all modern vehicles it is the negative (–) terminal. The various electrical components – motors, bulb holders etc – are also connected to earth, either by means of a lead or directly by their mountings.

Electric current flows through the component and then back to the battery via the bodywork. If the component mounting is loose or corroded, or if a good path back to the battery is not available, the circuit will be incomplete and malfunction will result. The engine and/or gearbox are also earthed by means of flexible metal straps to the body or subframe; if these straps are loose or missing, starter motor, generator and ignition trouble may result.

Assuming the earth return to be satisfactory, electrical faults will be due either to component malfunction or to defects in the current supply. Individual components are dealt with in Chapter 10. If supply wires are broken or cracked internally this results in an open-circuit, and the easiest way to check for this is to bypass the suspect wire temporarily with a length of wire having a crocodile clip or suitable connector at each end. Alternatively, a 12V test lamp can be used to verify the presence of supply voltage at various points along the wire and the break can be thus isolated.

If a bare portion of a live wire touches the bodywork or other earthed metal part, the electricity will take the low-resistance path thus formed back to the battery: this is known as a short-circuit. Hopefully a short-circuit will blow a fuse, but otherwise it may cause burning of the insulation (and possibly further short-circuits) or even a fire. This is why it is inadvisable to bypass persistently blowing fuses with silver foil or wire.

Spares and tool kit

Most vehicles are supplied only with sufficient tools for wheel changing; the *Maintenance and minor repair* tool kit detailed in *Tools and working facilities*, with the addition of a hammer, is probably sufficient for those repairs that most motorists would consider attempting at the roadside. In addition a few items which can be fitted without too much trouble in the event of a breakdown should be carried. Experience

and available space will modify the list below, but the following may save having to call on professional assistance:

- [ ] *Spark plugs, clean and correctly gapped*
- [ ] *HT lead and plug cap long enough to reach the plug furthest from the distributor*
- [ ] *Distributor rotor, condenser and contact breaker points*
- [ ] *Drivebelt(s) emergency type may suffice*
- [ ] *Spare fuses*
- [ ] *Set of principal light bulbs*
- [ ] *Tin of radiator sealer and hose bandage*
- [ ] *Exhaust bandage*
- [ ] *Roll of insulating tape*
- [ ] *Length of soft iron wire*
- [ ] *Length of electrical flex*
- [ ] *Torch or inspection lamp (can double as test lamp)*
- [ ] *Battery jump leads*
- [ ] *Tow-rope*
- [ ] *Ignition waterproofing aerosol*
- [ ] *Litre of engine oil*
- [ ] *Sealed can of hydraulic fluid*
- [ ] *Emergency windscreen*
- [ ] *Worm drive clips*
- [ ] *Tube of filler paste*

If spare fuel is carried, a can designed for the purpose should be used to minimise risks of leakage and collision damage. A first aid kit and a warning triangle, whilst not at present compulsory in the UK, are obviously sensible items to carry in addition to the above.

When touring abroad it may be advisable to carry additional spares which, even if you cannot fit them yourself, could save having to wait while parts are obtained. The items below may be worth considering:

- [ ] *Throttle cable*
- [ ] *Cylinder head gasket*
- [ ] *Dynamo or alternator brushes*
- [ ] *Fuel pump repair kit*
- [ ] *Tyre valve core*

One of the motoring organisations will be able to advise on availability of fuel, etc, in foreign countries.

Engine will not start

Engine fails to turn when starter operated

- [ ] Flat battery (recharge, use jump leads or push start)
- [ ] Battery terminals loose or corroded
- [ ] Battery earth to body defective
- [ ] Engine earth strap loose or broken
- [ ] Starter motor (or solenoid) wiring loose or broken
- [ ] Ignition/starter switch faulty
- [ ] Major mechanical failure (seizure)
- [ ] Starter or solenoid internal fault (see Chapter 10)

Starter motor turns engine slowly

- [ ] Partially discharged battery (recharge, use jump leads or push start)
- [ ] Battery terminals loose or corroded
- [ ] Battery earth to body defective
- [ ] Engine earth strap loose
- [ ] Starter motor (or solenoid) wiring loose
- [ ] Starter motor internal fault (see Chapter 10)

Starter motor spins without turning engine

- [ ] Flat battery
- [ ] Starter motor pinion sticking on sleeve
- [ ] Flywheel gear teeth damaged or worn
- [ ] Starter motor mounting bolts loose

Engine turns normally but fails to start

- [ ] Damp or dirty HT leads and distributor cap (crank engine and check for spark)
- [ ] Dirty or incorrectly gapped distributor points (if applicable)
- [ ] No fuel in tank (check for delivery at carburettor)
- [ ] Excessive choke (hot engine) or insufficient choke (cold engine)
- [ ] Fouled or incorrectly gapped spark plugs (remove, clean and regap)
- [ ] Other ignition system fault (see Chapter 4)
- [ ] Other fuel system fault (see Chapter 3)
- [ ] Poor compression (see Chapter 1)
- [ ] Major mechanical failure (eg camshaft drive)

Engine fires but will not run

- [ ] Insufficient choke (cold engine)
- [ ] Air leaks at carburettor or inlet manifold
- [ ] Fuel starvation (see Chapter 3)
- [ ] Ballast resistor defective, or other ignition fault (see Chapter 4)

Engine cuts out and will not restart

Engine cuts out suddenly – ignition fault

- [ ] Loose or disconnected LT wires
- [ ] Wet HT leads or distributor cap (after traversing water splash)
- [ ] Coil or condenser failure (check for spark)
- [ ] Other ignition fault (see Chapter 4)

Engine cuts out – other causes

- [ ] Serious overheating
- [ ] Major mechanical failure (eg camshaft drive)

Engine misfires before cutting out – fuel fault

- [ ] Fuel tank empty
- [ ] Fuel pump defective or filter blocked (check for delivery)
- [ ] Fuel tank filler vent blocked (suction will be evident on releasing cap)
- [ ] Carburettor needle valve sticking
- [ ] Carburettor jets blocked (fuel contaminated)
- [ ] Other fuel system fault (see Chapter 3)

Low engine oil pressure

Gauge reads low or warning light illuminated with engine running

- [ ] Oil level low or incorrect grade
- [ ] Defective gauge or sender unit
- [ ] Wire to sender unit earthed
- [ ] Engine overheating
- [ ] Oil filter clogged or bypass valve defective
- [ ] Oil pressure relief valve defective
- [ ] Oil pick-up strainer clogged
- [ ] Oil pump worn or mountings loose
- [ ] Worn main or big-end bearings

Note: *Low oil pressure in a high-mileage engine at tickover is not necessarily a cause for concern. Sudden pressure loss at speed is far more significant. In any event, check the gauge or warning light sender before condemning the engine.*

Engine overheats

Ignition (no-charge) warning light illuminated

- [ ] Slack or broken drivebelt – retension or renew (Chapter 2)

Ignition warning light not illuminated

- [ ] Coolant loss due to internal or external leakage (see Chapter 2)
- [ ] Thermostat defective
- [ ] Low oil level
- [ ] Brakes binding
- [ ] Radiator clogged externally or internally
- [ ] Electric cooling fan not operating correctly
- [ ] Engine waterways clogged
- [ ] Ignition timing incorrect or automatic advance malfunctioning
- [ ] Mixture too weak

Note: *Do not add cold water to an overheated engine or damage may result*

Engine noises

Pre-ignition (pinking) on acceleration

- [ ] Incorrect grade of fuel
- [ ] Ignition timing incorrect
- [ ] Distributor faulty or worn
- [ ] Worn or maladjusted carburettor
- [ ] Excessive carbon build-up in engine

Whistling or wheezing noises

- [ ] Leaking vacuum hose
- [ ] Leaking carburettor or manifold gasket
- [ ] Blowing head gasket

Tapping or rattling

- [ ] Incorrect valve clearances
- [ ] Worn valve gear
- [ ] Worn timing chain or belt
- [ ] Broken piston ring (ticking noise)

Knocking or thumping

- [ ] Unintentional mechanical contact (eg fan blades)
- [ ] Worn fanbelt
- [ ] Peripheral component fault (generator, water pump, etc)
- [ ] Worn big-end bearings (regular heavy knocking, perhaps less under load)
- [ ] Worn main bearings (rumbling and knocking, perhaps worsening under load)
- [ ] Piston slap (most noticeable when cold)

Length (distance)

Inches (in)	x 25.4	= Millimetres (mm)	x 0.0394	= Inches (in)
Feet (ft)	x 0.305	= Metres (m)	x 3.281	= Feet (ft)
Miles	x 1.609	= Kilometres (km)	x 0.621	= Miles

Volume (capacity)

Cubic inches (cu in; in³)	x 16.387	= Cubic centimetres (cc; cm³)	x 0.061	= Cubic inches (cu in; in³)
Imperial pints (Imp pt)	x 0.568	= Litres (l)	x 1.76	= Imperial pints (Imp pt)
Imperial quarts (Imp qt)	x 1.137	= Litres (l)	x 0.88	= Imperial quarts (Imp qt)
Imperial quarts (Imp qt)	x 1.201	= US quarts (US qt)	x 0.833	= Imperial quarts (Imp qt)
US quarts (US qt)	x 0.946	= Litres (l)	x 1.057	= US quarts (US qt)
Imperial gallons (Imp gal)	x 4.546	= Litres (l)	x 0.22	= Imperial gallons (Imp gal)
Imperial gallons (Imp gal)	x 1.201	= US gallons (US gal)	x 0.833	= Imperial gallons (Imp gal)
US gallons (US gal)	x 3.785	= Litres (l)	x 0.264	= US gallons (US gal)

Mass (weight)

Ounces (oz)	x 28.35	= Grams (g)	x 0.035	= Ounces (oz)
Pounds (lb)	x 0.454	= Kilograms (kg)	x 2.205	= Pounds (lb)

Force

Ounces-force (ozf; oz)	x 0.278	= Newtons (N)	x 3.6	= Ounces-force (ozf; oz)
Pounds-force (lbf; lb)	x 4.448	= Newtons (N)	x 0.225	= Pounds-force (lbf; lb)
Newtons (N)	x 0.1	= Kilograms-force (kgf; kg)	x 9.81	= Newtons (N)

Pressure

Pounds-force per square inch (psi; lbf/in²; lb/in²)	x 0.070	= Kilograms-force per square centimetre (kgf/cm²; kg/cm²)	x 14.223	= Pounds-force per square inch (psi; lbf/in²; lb/in²)
Pounds-force per square inch (psi; lbf/in²; lb/in²)	x 0.068	= Atmospheres (atm)	x 14.696	= Pounds-force per square inch (psi; lbf/in²; lb/in²)
Pounds-force per square inch (psi; lbf/in²; lb/in²)	x 0.069	= Bars	x 14.5	= Pounds-force per square inch (psi; lbf/in²; lb/in²)
Pounds-force per square inch (psi; lbf/in²; lb/in²)	x 6.895	= Kilopascals (kPa)	x 0.145	= Pounds-force per square inch (psi; lbf/in²; lb/in²)
Kilopascals (kPa)	x 0.01	= Kilograms-force per square centimetre (kgf/cm²; kg/cm²)	x 98.1	= Kilopascals (kPa)
Millibar (mbar)	x 100	= Pascals (Pa)	x 0.01	= Millibar (mbar)
Millibar (mbar)	x 0.0145	= Pounds-force per square inch (psi; lbf/in²; lb/in²)	x 68.947	= Millibar (mbar)
Millibar (mbar)	x 0.75	= Millimetres of mercury (mmHg)	x 1.333	= Millibar (mbar)
Millibar (mbar)	x 0.401	= Inches of water (inH₂O)	x 2.491	= Millibar (mbar)
Millimetres of mercury (mmHg)	x 0.535	= Inches of water (inH₂O)	x 1.868	= Millimetres of mercury (mmHg)
Inches of water (inH₂O)	x 0.036	= Pounds-force per square inch (psi; lbf/in²; lb/in²)	x 27.68	= Inches of water (inH₂O)

Torque (moment of force)

Pounds-force inches (lbf in; lb in)	x 1.152	= Kilograms-force centimetre (kgf cm; kg cm)	x 0.868	= Pounds-force inches (lbf in; lb in)
Pounds-force inches (lbf in; lb in)	x 0.113	= Newton metres (Nm)	x 8.85	= Pounds-force inches (lbf in; lb in)
Pounds-force inches (lbf in; lb in)	x 0.083	= Pounds-force feet (lbf ft; lb ft)	x 12	= Pounds-force inches (lbf in; lb in)
Pounds-force feet (lbf ft; lb ft)	x 0.138	= Kilograms-force metres (kgf m; kg m)	x 7.233	= Pounds-force feet (lbf ft; lb ft)
Pounds-force feet (lbf ft; lb ft)	x 1.356	= Newton metres (Nm)	x 0.738	= Pounds-force feet (lbf ft; lb ft)
Newton metres (Nm)	x 0.102	= Kilograms-force metres (kgf m; kg m)	x 9.804	= Newton metres (Nm)

Power

Horsepower (hp)	x 745.7	= Watts (W)	x 0.0013	= Horsepower (hp)

Velocity (speed)

Miles per hour (miles/hr; mph)	x 1.609	= Kilometres per hour (km/hr; kph)	x 0.621	= Miles per hour (miles/hr; mph)

Fuel consumption*

Miles per gallon, Imperial (mpg)	x 0.354	= Kilometres per litre (km/l)	x 2.825	= Miles per gallon, Imperial (mpg)
Miles per gallon, US (mpg)	x 0.425	= Kilometres per litre (km/l)	x 2.352	= Miles per gallon, US (mpg)

Temperature

Degrees Fahrenheit = (°C x 1.8) + 32   Degrees Celsius (Degrees Centigrade; °C) = (°F - 32) x 0.56

It is common practice to convert from miles per gallon (mpg) to litres/100 kilometres (l/100km), where mpg x l/100 km = 282

A

ABS (Anti-lock brake system) A system, usually electronically controlled, that senses incipient wheel lockup during braking and relieves hydraulic pressure at wheels that are about to skid.

Air bag An inflatable bag hidden in the steering wheel (driver's side) or the dash or glovebox (passenger side). In a head-on collision, the bags inflate, preventing the driver and front passenger from being thrown forward into the steering wheel or windscreen.

Air cleaner A metal or plastic housing, containing a filter element, which removes dust and dirt from the air being drawn into the engine.

Air filter element The actual filter in an air cleaner system, usually manufactured from pleated paper and requiring renewal at regular intervals.

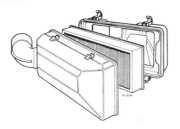

Air filter

Allen key A hexagonal wrench which fits into a recessed hexagonal hole.

Alligator clip A long-nosed spring-loaded metal clip with meshing teeth. Used to make temporary electrical connections.

Alternator A component in the electrical system which converts mechanical energy from a drivebelt into electrical energy to charge the battery and to operate the starting system, ignition system and electrical accessories.

Ampere (amp) A unit of measurement for the flow of electric current. One amp is the amount of current produced by one volt acting through a resistance of one ohm.

Anaerobic sealer A substance used to prevent bolts and screws from loosening. Anaerobic means that it does not require oxygen for activation. The Loctite brand is widely used.

Antifreeze A substance (usually ethylene glycol) mixed with water, and added to a vehicle's cooling system, to prevent freezing of the coolant in winter. Antifreeze also contains chemicals to inhibit corrosion and the formation of rust and other deposits that would tend to clog the radiator and coolant passages and reduce cooling efficiency.

Anti-seize compound A coating that reduces the risk of seizing on fasteners that are subjected to high temperatures, such as exhaust manifold bolts and nuts.

Asbestos A natural fibrous mineral with great heat resistance, commonly used in the composition of brake friction materials.

Asbestos is a health hazard and the dust created by brake systems should never be inhaled or ingested.

Axle A shaft on which a wheel revolves, or which revolves with a wheel. Also, a solid beam that connects the two wheels at one end of the vehicle. An axle which also transmits power to the wheels is known as a live axle.

Axleshaft A single rotating shaft, on either side of the differential, which delivers power from the final drive assembly to the drive wheels. Also called a driveshaft or a halfshaft.

B

Ball bearing An anti-friction bearing consisting of a hardened inner and outer race with hardened steel balls between two races.

Bearing The curved surface on a shaft or in a bore, or the part assembled into either, that permits relative motion between them with minimum wear and friction.

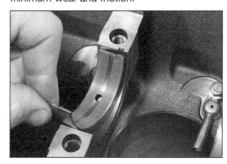

Bearing

Big-end bearing The bearing in the end of the connecting rod that's attached to the crankshaft.

Bleed nipple A valve on a brake wheel cylinder, caliper or other hydraulic component that is opened to purge the hydraulic system of air. Also called a bleed screw.

Brake bleeding Procedure for removing air from lines of a hydraulic brake system.

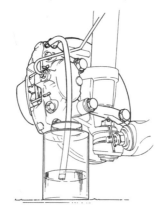

Brake bleeding

Brake disc The component of a disc brake that rotates with the wheels.

Brake drum The component of a drum brake that rotates with the wheels.

Brake linings The friction material which contacts the brake disc or drum to retard the vehicle's speed. The linings are bonded or riveted to the brake pads or shoes.

Brake pads The replaceable friction pads that pinch the brake disc when the brakes are applied. Brake pads consist of a friction material bonded or riveted to a rigid backing plate.

Brake shoe The crescent-shaped carrier to which the brake linings are mounted and which forces the lining against the rotating drum during braking.

Braking systems For more information on braking systems, consult the *Haynes Automotive Brake Manual*.

Breaker bar A long socket wrench handle providing greater leverage.

Bulkhead The insulated partition between the engine and the passenger compartment.

C

Caliper The non-rotating part of a disc-brake assembly that straddles the disc and carries the brake pads. The caliper also contains the hydraulic components that cause the pads to pinch the disc when the brakes are applied. A caliper is also a measuring tool that can be set to measure inside or outside dimensions of an object.

Camshaft A rotating shaft on which a series of cam lobes operate the valve mechanisms. The camshaft may be driven by gears, by sprockets and chain or by sprockets and a belt.

Canister A container in an evaporative emission control system; contains activated charcoal granules to trap vapours from the fuel system.

Canister

Carburettor A device which mixes fuel with air in the proper proportions to provide a desired power output from a spark ignition internal combustion engine.

Castellated Resembling the parapets along the top of a castle wall. For example, a castellated balljoint stud nut.

Castor In wheel alignment, the backward or forward tilt of the steering axis. Castor is positive when the steering axis is inclined rearward at the top.

Catalytic converter A silencer-like device in the exhaust system which converts certain pollutants in the exhaust gases into less harmful substances.

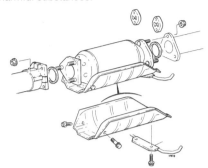

Catalytic converter

Circlip A ring-shaped clip used to prevent endwise movement of cylindrical parts and shafts. An internal circlip is installed in a groove in a housing; an external circlip fits into a groove on the outside of a cylindrical piece such as a shaft.

Clearance The amount of space between two parts. For example, between a piston and a cylinder, between a bearing and a journal, etc.

Coil spring A spiral of elastic steel found in various sizes throughout a vehicle, for example as a springing medium in the suspension and in the valve train.

Compression Reduction in volume, and increase in pressure and temperature, of a gas, caused by squeezing it into a smaller space.

Compression ratio The relationship between cylinder volume when the piston is at top dead centre and cylinder volume when the piston is at bottom dead centre.

Constant velocity (CV) joint A type of universal joint that cancels out vibrations caused by driving power being transmitted through an angle.

Core plug A disc or cup-shaped metal device inserted in a hole in a casting through which core was removed when the casting was formed. Also known as a freeze plug or expansion plug.

Crankcase The lower part of the engine block in which the crankshaft rotates.

Crankshaft The main rotating member, or shaft, running the length of the crankcase, with offset "throws" to which the connecting rods are attached.

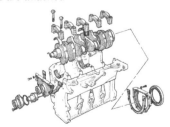

Crankshaft assembly

Crocodile clip See Alligator clip

D

Diagnostic code Code numbers obtained by accessing the diagnostic mode of an engine management computer. This code can be used to determine the area in the system where a malfunction may be located.

Disc brake A brake design incorporating a rotating disc onto which brake pads are squeezed. The resulting friction converts the energy of a moving vehicle into heat.

Double-overhead cam (DOHC) An engine that uses two overhead camshafts, usually one for the intake valves and one for the exhaust valves.

Drivebelt(s) The belt(s) used to drive accessories such as the alternator, water pump, power steering pump, air conditioning compressor, etc. off the crankshaft pulley.

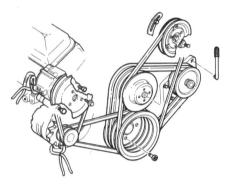

Accessory drivebelts

Driveshaft Any shaft used to transmit motion. Commonly used when referring to the axleshafts on a front wheel drive vehicle.

Drum brake A type of brake using a drum-shaped metal cylinder attached to the inner surface of the wheel. When the brake pedal is pressed, curved brake shoes with friction linings press against the inside of the drum to slow or stop the vehicle.

E

EGR valve A valve used to introduce exhaust gases into the intake air stream.

Electronic control unit (ECU) A computer which controls (for instance) ignition and fuel injection systems, or an anti-lock braking system. For more information refer to the *Haynes Automotive Electrical and Electronic Systems Manual.*

Electronic Fuel Injection (EFI) A computer controlled fuel system that distributes fuel through an injector located in each intake port of the engine.

Emergency brake A braking system, independent of the main hydraulic system, that can be used to slow or stop the vehicle if the primary brakes fail, or to hold the vehicle stationary even though the brake pedal isn't depressed. It usually consists of a hand lever that actuates either front or rear brakes mechanically through a series of cables and linkages. Also known as a handbrake or parking brake.

Endfloat The amount of lengthwise movement between two parts. As applied to a crankshaft, the distance that the crankshaft can move forward and back in the cylinder block.

Engine management system (EMS) A computer controlled system which manages the fuel injection and the ignition systems in an integrated fashion.

Exhaust manifold A part with several passages through which exhaust gases leave the engine combustion chambers and enter the exhaust pipe.

F

Fan clutch A viscous (fluid) drive coupling device which permits variable engine fan speeds in relation to engine speeds.

Feeler blade A thin strip or blade of hardened steel, ground to an exact thickness, used to check or measure clearances between parts.

Feeler blade

Firing order The order in which the engine cylinders fire, or deliver their power strokes, beginning with the number one cylinder.

Flywheel A heavy spinning wheel in which energy is absorbed and stored by means of momentum. On cars, the flywheel is attached to the crankshaft to smooth out firing impulses.

Free play The amount of travel before any action takes place. The "looseness" in a linkage, or an assembly of parts, between the initial application of force and actual movement. For example, the distance the brake pedal moves before the pistons in the master cylinder are actuated.

Fuse An electrical device which protects a circuit against accidental overload. The typical fuse contains a soft piece of metal which is calibrated to melt at a predetermined current flow (expressed as amps) and break the circuit.

Fusible link A circuit protection device consisting of a conductor surrounded by heat-resistant insulation. The conductor is smaller than the wire it protects, so it acts as the weakest link in the circuit. Unlike a blown fuse, a failed fusible link must frequently be cut from the wire for replacement.

G

Gap The distance the spark must travel in jumping from the centre electrode to the side electrode in a spark plug. Also refers to the spacing between the points in a contact breaker assembly in a conventional points-type ignition, or to the distance between the reluctor or rotor and the pickup coil in an electronic ignition.

Adjusting spark plug gap

Gasket Any thin, soft material - usually cork, cardboard, asbestos or soft metal - installed between two metal surfaces to ensure a good seal. For instance, the cylinder head gasket seals the joint between the block and the cylinder head.

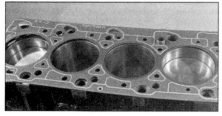

Gasket

Gauge An instrument panel display used to monitor engine conditions. A gauge with a movable pointer on a dial or a fixed scale is an analogue gauge. A gauge with a numerical readout is called a digital gauge.

H

Halfshaft A rotating shaft that transmits power from the final drive unit to a drive wheel, usually when referring to a live rear axle.

Harmonic balancer A device designed to reduce torsion or twisting vibration in the crankshaft. May be incorporated in the crankshaft pulley. Also known as a vibration damper.

Hone An abrasive tool for correcting small irregularities or differences in diameter in an engine cylinder, brake cylinder, etc.

Hydraulic tappet A tappet that utilises hydraulic pressure from the engine's lubrication system to maintain zero clearance (constant contact with both camshaft and valve stem). Automatically adjusts to variation in valve stem length. Hydraulic tappets also reduce valve noise.

I

Ignition timing The moment at which the spark plug fires, usually expressed in the number of crankshaft degrees before the piston reaches the top of its stroke.

Inlet manifold A tube or housing with passages through which flows the air-fuel mixture (carburettor vehicles and vehicles with throttle body injection) or air only (port fuel-injected vehicles) to the port openings in the cylinder head.

J

Jump start Starting the engine of a vehicle with a discharged or weak battery by attaching jump leads from the weak battery to a charged or helper battery.

L

Load Sensing Proportioning Valve (LSPV) A brake hydraulic system control valve that works like a proportioning valve, but also takes into consideration the amount of weight carried by the rear axle.

Locknut A nut used to lock an adjustment nut, or other threaded component, in place. For example, a locknut is employed to keep the adjusting nut on the rocker arm in position.

Lockwasher A form of washer designed to prevent an attaching nut from working loose.

M

MacPherson strut A type of front suspension system devised by Earle MacPherson at Ford of England. In its original form, a simple lateral link with the anti-roll bar creates the lower control arm. A long strut - an integral coil spring and shock absorber - is mounted between the body and the steering knuckle. Many modern so-called MacPherson strut systems use a conventional lower A-arm and don't rely on the anti-roll bar for location.

Multimeter An electrical test instrument with the capability to measure voltage, current and resistance.

N

NOx Oxides of Nitrogen. A common toxic pollutant emitted by petrol and diesel engines at higher temperatures.

O

Ohm The unit of electrical resistance. One volt applied to a resistance of one ohm will produce a current of one amp.

Ohmmeter An instrument for measuring electrical resistance.

O-ring A type of sealing ring made of a special rubber-like material; in use, the O-ring is compressed into a groove to provide the sealing action.

Overhead cam (ohc) engine An engine with the camshaft(s) located on top of the cylinder head(s).

Overhead valve (ohv) engine An engine with the valves located in the cylinder head, but with the camshaft located in the engine block.

Oxygen sensor A device installed in the engine exhaust manifold, which senses the oxygen content in the exhaust and converts this information into an electric current. Also called a Lambda sensor.

P

Phillips screw A type of screw head having a cross instead of a slot for a corresponding type of screwdriver.

Plastigage A thin strip of plastic thread, available in different sizes, used for measuring clearances. For example, a strip of Plastigage is laid across a bearing journal. The parts are assembled and dismantled; the width of the crushed strip indicates the clearance between journal and bearing.

Plastigage

Propeller shaft The long hollow tube with universal joints at both ends that carries power from the transmission to the differential on front-engined rear wheel drive vehicles.

Proportioning valve A hydraulic control valve which limits the amount of pressure to the rear brakes during panic stops to prevent wheel lock-up.

R

Rack-and-pinion steering A steering system with a pinion gear on the end of the steering shaft that mates with a rack (think of a geared wheel opened up and laid flat). When the steering wheel is turned, the pinion turns, moving the rack to the left or right. This movement is transmitted through the track rods to the steering arms at the wheels.

Radiator A liquid-to-air heat transfer device designed to reduce the temperature of the coolant in an internal combustion engine cooling system.

Refrigerant Any substance used as a heat transfer agent in an air-conditioning system. R-12 has been the principle refrigerant for many years; recently, however, manufacturers have begun using R-134a, a non-CFC substance that is considered less harmful to the ozone in the upper atmosphere.

Rocker arm A lever arm that rocks on a shaft or pivots on a stud. In an overhead valve engine, the rocker arm converts the upward movement of the pushrod into a downward movement to open a valve.

Rotor In a distributor, the rotating device inside the cap that connects the centre electrode and the outer terminals as it turns, distributing the high voltage from the coil secondary winding to the proper spark plug. Also, that part of an alternator which rotates inside the stator. Also, the rotating assembly of a turbocharger, including the compressor wheel, shaft and turbine wheel.

Runout The amount of wobble (in-and-out movement) of a gear or wheel as it's rotated. The amount a shaft rotates "out-of-true." The out-of-round condition of a rotating part.

S

Sealant A liquid or paste used to prevent leakage at a joint. Sometimes used in conjunction with a gasket.

Sealed beam lamp An older headlight design which integrates the reflector, lens and filaments into a hermetically-sealed one-piece unit. When a filament burns out or the lens cracks, the entire unit is simply replaced.

Serpentine drivebelt A single, long, wide accessory drivebelt that's used on some newer vehicles to drive all the accessories, instead of a series of smaller, shorter belts. Serpentine drivebelts are usually tensioned by an automatic tensioner.

Serpentine drivebelt

Shim Thin spacer, commonly used to adjust the clearance or relative positions between two parts. For example, shims inserted into or under bucket tappets control valve clearances. Clearance is adjusted by changing the thickness of the shim.

Slide hammer A special puller that screws into or hooks onto a component such as a shaft or bearing; a heavy sliding handle on the shaft bottoms against the end of the shaft to knock the component free.

Sprocket A tooth or projection on the periphery of a wheel, shaped to engage with a chain or drivebelt. Commonly used to refer to the sprocket wheel itself.

Starter inhibitor switch On vehicles with an automatic transmission, a switch that prevents starting if the vehicle is not in Neutral or Park.

Strut See MacPherson strut.

T

Tappet A cylindrical component which transmits motion from the cam to the valve stem, either directly or via a pushrod and rocker arm. Also called a cam follower.

Thermostat A heat-controlled valve that regulates the flow of coolant between the cylinder block and the radiator, so maintaining optimum engine operating temperature. A thermostat is also used in some air cleaners in which the temperature is regulated.

Thrust bearing The bearing in the clutch assembly that is moved in to the release levers by clutch pedal action to disengage the clutch. Also referred to as a release bearing.

Timing belt A toothed belt which drives the camshaft. Serious engine damage may result if it breaks in service.

Timing chain A chain which drives the camshaft.

Toe-in The amount the front wheels are closer together at the front than at the rear. On rear wheel drive vehicles, a slight amount of toe-in is usually specified to keep the front wheels running parallel on the road by offsetting other forces that tend to spread the wheels apart.

Toe-out The amount the front wheels are closer together at the rear than at the front. On front wheel drive vehicles, a slight amount of toe-out is usually specified.

Tools For full information on choosing and using tools, refer to the *Haynes Automotive Tools Manual.*

Tracer A stripe of a second colour applied to a wire insulator to distinguish that wire from another one with the same colour insulator.

Tune-up A process of accurate and careful adjustments and parts replacement to obtain the best possible engine performance.

Turbocharger A centrifugal device, driven by exhaust gases, that pressurises the intake air. Normally used to increase the power output from a given engine displacement, but can also be used primarily to reduce exhaust emissions (as on VW's "Umwelt" Diesel engine).

U

Universal joint or U-joint A double-pivoted connection for transmitting power from a driving to a driven shaft through an angle. A U-joint consists of two Y-shaped yokes and a cross-shaped member called the spider.

V

Valve A device through which the flow of liquid, gas, vacuum, or loose material in bulk may be started, stopped, or regulated by a movable part that opens, shuts, or partially obstructs one or more ports or passageways. A valve is also the movable part of such a device.

Valve clearance The clearance between the valve tip (the end of the valve stem) and the rocker arm or tappet. The valve clearance is measured when the valve is closed.

Vernier caliper A precision measuring instrument that measures inside and outside dimensions. Not quite as accurate as a micrometer, but more convenient.

Viscosity The thickness of a liquid or its resistance to flow.

Volt A unit for expressing electrical "pressure" in a circuit. One volt that will produce a current of one ampere through a resistance of one ohm.

W

Welding Various processes used to join metal items by heating the areas to be joined to a molten state and fusing them together. For more information refer to the *Haynes Automotive Welding Manual.*

Wiring diagram A drawing portraying the components and wires in a vehicle's electrical system, using standardised symbols. For more information refer to the *Haynes Automotive Electrical and Electronic Systems Manual.*

Haynes Manuals – The Complete UK Car List

Title	Book No.
ALFA ROMEO Alfasud/Sprint (74 - 88) up to F *	0292
Alfa Romeo Alfetta (73 - 87) up to E *	0531
AUDI 80, 90 & Coupe Petrol (79 - Nov 88) up to F	0605
Audi 80, 90 & Coupe Petrol (Oct 86 - 90) D to H	1491
Audi 100 & 200 Petrol (Oct 82 - 90) up to H	0907
Audi 100 & A6 Petrol & Diesel (May 91 - May 97) H to P	3504
Audi A3 Petrol & Diesel (96 - May 03) P to 03	4253
Audi A4 Petrol & Diesel (95 - 00) M to X	3575
Audi A4 Petrol & Diesel (01 - 04) X to 54	4609
AUSTIN A35 & A40 (56 - 67) up to F *	0118
Austin/MG/Rover Maestro 1.3 & 1.6 Petrol (83 - 95) up to M	0922
Austin/MG Metro (80 - May 90) up to G	0718
Austin/Rover Montego 1.3 & 1.6 Petrol (84 - 94) A to L	1066
Austin/MG/Rover Montego 2.0 Petrol (84 - 95) A to M	1067
Mini (59 - 69) up to H *	0527
Mini (69 - 01) up to X	0646
Austin/Rover 2.0 litre Diesel Engine (86 - 93) C to L	1857
Austin Healey 100/6 & 3000 (56 - 68) up to G *	0049
BEDFORD CF Petrol (69 - 87) up to E	0163
Bedford/Vauxhall Rascal & Suzuki Supercarry (86 - Oct 94) C to M	3015
BMW 316, 320 & 320i (4-cyl) (75 - Feb 83) up to Y *	0276
BMW 320, 320i, 323i & 325i (6-cyl) (Oct 77 - Sept 87) up to E	0815
BMW 3- & 5-Series Petrol (81 - 91) up to J	1948
BMW 3-Series Petrol (Apr 91 - 99) H to V	3210
BMW 3-Series Petrol (Sept 98 - 03) S to 53	4067
BMW 520i & 525e (Oct 81 - June 88) up to E	1560
BMW 525, 528 & 528i (73 - Sept 81) up to X *	0632
BMW 5-Series 6-cyl Petrol (April 96 - Aug 03) N to 03	4151
BMW 1500, 1502, 1600, 1602, 2000 & 2002 (59 - 77) up to S *	0240
CHRYSLER PT Cruiser Petrol (00 - 03) W to 53	4058
CITROËN 2CV, Ami & Dyane (67 - 90) up to H	0196
Citroën AX Petrol & Diesel (87 - 97) D to P	3014
Citroën Berlingo & Peugeot Partner Petrol & Diesel (96 - 05) P to 55	4281
Citroën BX Petrol (83 - 94) A to L	0908
Citroën C15 Van Petrol & Diesel (89 - Oct 98) F to S	3509
Citroën C3 Petrol & Diesel (02 - 05) 51 to 05	4197
Citroen C5 Petrol & Diesel (01-08) Y to 08	4745
Citroën CX Petrol (75 - 88) up to F	0528
Citroën Saxo Petrol & Diesel (96 - 04) N to 54	3506
Citroën Visa Petrol (79 - 88) up to F	0620
Citroën Xantia Petrol & Diesel (93 - 01) K to Y	3082
Citroën XM Petrol & Diesel (89 - 00) G to X	3451
Citroën Xsara Petrol & Diesel (97 - Sept 00) R to W	3751
Citroen Xsara Picasso Petrol & Diesel (00 - 02) W to 52	3944
Citroen Xsara Picasso (03-08)	4784
Citroën ZX Diesel (91 - 98) J to S	1922
Citroën ZX Petrol (91 - 98) H to S	1881
Citroën 1.7 & 1.9 litre Diesel Engine (84 - 96) A to N	1379
FIAT 126 (73 - 87) up to E *	0305
Fiat 500 (57 - 73) up to M *	0090
Fiat Bravo & Brava Petrol (95 - 00) N to W	3572
Fiat Cinquecento (93 - 98) K to R	3501
Fiat Panda (81 - 95) up to M	0793
Fiat Punto Petrol & Diesel (94 - Oct 99) L to V	3251
Fiat Punto Petrol (Oct 99 - July 03) V to 03	4066
Fiat Punto Petrol (03-07) 03 to 07	4746
Fiat Regata Petrol (84 - 88) A to F	1167
Fiat Tipo Petrol (88 - 91) E to J	1625
Fiat Uno Petrol (83 - 95) up to M	0923
Fiat X1/9 (74 - 89) up to G *	0273
FORD Anglia (59 - 68) up to G *	0001
Ford Capri II (& III) 1.6 & 2.0 (74 - 87) up to E *	0283
Ford Capri II (& III) 2.8 & 3.0 V6 (74 - 87) up to E	1309
Ford Cortina Mk I & Corsair 1500 ('62 - '66) up to D*	0214
Ford Cortina Mk III 1300 & 1600 (70 - 76) up to P *	0070
Ford Escort Mk I 1100 & 1300 (68 - 74) up to N *	0171
Ford Escort Mk I Mexico, RS 1600 & RS 2000 (70 - 74) up to N *	0139
Ford Escort Mk II Mexico, RS 1800 & RS 2000 (75 - 80) up to W *	0735
Ford Escort (75 - Aug 80) up to V *	0280
Ford Escort Petrol (Sept 80 - Sept 90) up to H	0686
Ford Escort & Orion Petrol (Sept 90 - 00) H to X	1737
Ford Escort & Orion Diesel (Sept 90 - 00) H to X	4081
Ford Fiesta (76 - Aug 83) up to Y	0334
Ford Fiesta Petrol (Aug 83 - Feb 89) A to F	1030
Ford Fiesta Petrol (Feb 89 - Oct 95) F to N	1595
Ford Fiesta Petrol & Diesel (Oct 95 - Mar 02) N to 02	3397
Ford Fiesta Petrol & Diesel (Apr 02 - 07) 02 to 57	4170
Ford Focus Petrol & Diesel (98 - 01) S to Y	3759
Ford Focus Petrol & Diesel (Oct 01 - 05) 51 to 05	4167
Ford Galaxy Petrol & Diesel (95 - Aug 00) M to W	3984
Ford Granada Petrol (Sept 77 - Feb 85) up to B *	0481
Ford Granada & Scorpio Petrol (Mar 85 - 94) B to M	1245
Ford Ka (96 - 02) P to 52	3570
Ford Mondeo Petrol (93 - Sept 00) K to X	1923
Ford Mondeo Petrol & Diesel (Oct 00 - Jul 03) X to 03	3990
Ford Mondeo Petrol & Diesel (July 03 - 07) 03 to 56	4619
Ford Mondeo Diesel (93 - 96) L to N	3465
Ford Orion Petrol (83 - Sept 90) up to H	1009
Ford Sierra 4-cyl Petrol (82 - 93) up to K	0903
Ford Sierra V6 Petrol (82 - 91) up to J	0904
Ford Transit Petrol (Mk 2) (78 - Jan 86) up to C	0719
Ford Transit Petrol (Mk 3) (Feb 86 - 89) C to G	1468
Ford Transit Diesel (Feb 86 - 99) C to T	3019
Ford Transit Diesel (00-06)	4775
Ford 1.6 & 1.8 litre Diesel Engine (84 - 96) A to N	1172
Ford 2.1, 2.3 & 2.5 litre Diesel Engine (77 - 90) up to H	1606
FREIGHT ROVER Sherpa Petrol (74 - 87) up to E	0463
HILLMAN Avenger (70 - 82) up to Y	0037
Hillman Imp (63 - 76) up to R *	0022
HONDA Civic (Feb 84 - Oct 87) A to E	1226
Honda Civic (Nov 91 - 96) J to N	3199
Honda Civic (Mar 95 - 00) M to X	4050
Honda Civic Petrol & Diesel (01 - 05) X to 55	4611
Honda CR-V Petrol & Diesel (01-06)	4747
Honda Jazz (01 - Feb 08) 51 - 57	4735
HYUNDAI Pony (85 - 94) C to M	3398
JAGUAR E Type (61 - 72) up to L *	0140
Jaguar MkI & II, 240 & 340 (55 - 69) up to H *	0098
Jaguar XJ6, XJ & Sovereign; Daimler Sovereign (68 - Oct 86) up to D	0242
Jaguar XJ6 & Sovereign (Oct 86 - Sept 94) D to M	3261
Jaguar XJ12, XJS & Sovereign; Daimler Double Six (72 - 88) up to F	0478
JEEP Cherokee Petrol (93 - 96) K to N	1943
LADA 1200, 1300, 1500 & 1600 (74 - 91) up to J	0413
Lada Samara (87 - 91) D to J	1610
LAND ROVER 90, 110 & Defender Diesel (83 - 07) up to 56	3017
Land Rover Discovery Petrol & Diesel (89 - 98) G to S	3016
Land Rover Discovery Diesel (Nov 98 - Jul 04) S to 04	4606
Land Rover Freelander Petrol & Diesel (97 - Sept 03) R to 53	3929
Land Rover Freelander Petrol & Diesel (Oct 03 - Oct 06) 53 to 56	4623
Land Rover Series IIA & III Diesel (58 - 85) up to C	0529
Land Rover Series II, IIA & III 4-cyl Petrol (58 - 85) up to C	0314
MAZDA 323 (Mar 81 - Oct 89) up to G	1608
Mazda 323 (Oct 89 - 98) G to R	3455
Mazda 626 (May 83 - Sept 87) up to E	0929
Mazda B1600, B1800 & B2000 Pick-up Petrol (72 - 88) up to F	0267
Mazda RX-7 (79 - 85) up to C *	0460
MERCEDES-BENZ 190, 190E & 190D Petrol & Diesel (83 - 93) A to L	3450
Mercedes-Benz 200D, 240D, 240TD, 300D & 300TD 123 Series Diesel (Oct 76 - 85)	1114
Mercedes-Benz 250 & 280 (68 - 72) up to L *	0346
Mercedes-Benz 250 & 280 123 Series Petrol (Oct 76 - 84) up to B *	0677
Mercedes-Benz 124 Series Petrol & Diesel (85 - Aug 93) C to K	3253
Mercedes-Benz A-Class Petrol & Diesel (98-04) S to 54	4748
Mercedes-Benz C-Class Petrol & Diesel (93 - Aug 00) L to W	3511
Mercedes-Benz C-Class (00-06)	4780
MG A (55 - 62) *	0475
MGB (62 - 80) up to W	0111
MG Midget & Austin-Healey Sprite (58 - 80) up to W *	0265
MINI Petrol (July 01 - 05) Y to 05	4273
MITSUBISHI Shogun & L200 Pick-Ups Petrol (83 - 94) up to M	1944
MORRIS Ital 1.3 (80 - 84) up to B	0705
Morris Minor 1000 (56 - 71) up to K	0024
NISSAN Almera Petrol (95 - Feb 00) N to V	4053
Nissan Almera & Tino Petrol (Feb 00 - 07) V to 56	4612
Nissan Bluebird (May 84 - Mar 86) A to C	1223
Nissan Bluebird Petrol (Mar 86 - 90) C to H	1473
Nissan Cherry (Sept 82 - 86) up to D	1031
Nissan Micra (83 - Jan 93) up to K	0931
Nissan Micra (93 - 02) K to 52	3254
Nissan Micra Petrol (03-07) 52 to 57	4734
Nissan Primera Petrol (90 - Aug 99) H to T	1851
Nissan Stanza (82 - 86) up to D	0824
Nissan Sunny Petrol (May 82 - Oct 86) up to D	0895
Nissan Sunny Petrol (Oct 86 - Mar 91) D to H	1378
Nissan Sunny Petrol (Apr 91 - 95) H to N	3219
OPEL Ascona & Manta (B Series) (Sept 75 - 88) up to F *	0316
Opel Ascona Petrol (81 - 88)	3215
Opel Astra Petrol (Oct 91 - Feb 98)	3156
Opel Corsa Petrol (83 - Mar 93)	3160
Opel Corsa Petrol (Mar 93 - 97)	3159
Opel Kadett Petrol (Nov 79 - Oct 84) up to B	0634
Opel Kadett Petrol (Oct 84 - Oct 91)	3196
Opel Omega & Senator Petrol (Nov 86 - 94)	3157
Opel Rekord Petrol (Feb 78 - Oct 86) up to D	0543
Opel Vectra Petrol (Oct 88 - Oct 95)	3158
PEUGEOT 106 Petrol & Diesel (91 - 04) J to 53	1882
Peugeot 205 Petrol (83 - 97) A to P	0932
Peugeot 206 Petrol & Diesel (98 - 01) S to X	3757
Peugeot 206 Petrol & Diesel (02 - 06) 51 to 06	4613
Peugeot 306 Petrol & Diesel (93 - 02) K to 02	3073
Peugeot 307 Petrol & Diesel (01 - 04) Y to 54	4147
Peugeot 309 Petrol (86 - 93) C to K	1266
Peugeot 405 Petrol (88 - 97) E to P	1559
Peugeot 405 Diesel (88 - 97) E to P	3198
Peugeot 406 Petrol & Diesel (96 - Mar 99) N to T	3394
Peugeot 406 Petrol & Diesel (Mar 99 - 02) T to 52	3982

* Classic reprint

* Classic reprint

All the products featured on this page are available through most motor accessory shops, cycle shops and book stores. Our policy of continuous updating and development means that titles are being constantly added to the range. For up-to-date information on our complete list of titles, please telephone: (UK) +44 1963 442030 • (USA) +1 805 498 6703 • (Sweden) +46 18 124016 • (Australia) +61 3 9763 8100

CL24.08/09

Preserving Our Motoring Heritage

< The Model J Duesenberg Derham Tourster. Only eight of these magnificent cars were ever built – this is the only example to be found outside the United States of America

Almost every car you've ever loved, loathed or desired is gathered under one roof at the Haynes Motor Museum. Over 300 immaculately presented cars and motorbikes represent every aspect of our motoring heritage, from elegant reminders of bygone days, such as the superb Model J Duesenberg to curiosities like the bug-eyed BMW Isetta. There are also many old friends and flames. Perhaps you remember the 1959 Ford Popular that you did your courting in? The magnificent 'Red Collection' is a spectacle of classic sports cars including AC, Alfa Romeo, Austin Healey, Ferrari, Lamborghini, Maserati, MG, Riley, Porsche and Triumph.

A Perfect Day Out

Each and every vehicle at the Haynes Motor Museum has played its part in the history and culture of Motoring. Today, they make a wonderful spectacle and a great day out for all the family. Bring the kids, bring Mum and Dad, but above all bring your camera to capture those golden memories for ever. You will also find an impressive array of motoring memorabilia, a comfortable 70 seat video cinema and one of the most extensive transport book shops in Britain. The Pit Stop Cafe serves everything from a cup of tea to wholesome, home-made meals or, if you prefer, you can enjoy the large picnic area nestled in the beautiful rural surroundings of Somerset.

> John Haynes O.B.E., Founder and Chairman of the museum at the wheel of a Haynes Light 12.

< Graham Hill's Lola Cosworth Formula 1 car next to a 1934 Riley Sports.

The Museum is situated on the A359 Yeovil to Frome road at Sparkford, just off the A303 in Somerset. It is about 40 miles south of Bristol, and 25 minutes drive from the M5 intersection at Taunton.
Open 9.30am - 5.30pm (10.00am - 4.00pm Winter) 7 days a week, *except Christmas Day, Boxing Day and New Years Day*
Special rates available for schools, coach parties and outings Charitable Trust No. 292048